LABOR RELATIONS

LABOR RELATIONS

Process and Outcomes

Marcus Hart Sandver

The Ohio State University

Little, Brown and Company

Boston   Toronto

Library of Congress Cataloging-in-Publication Data

Sandver, Marcus Hart
    Labor relations.

    Bibliography: p.
    Includes index.
    1. Industrial relations — United States.
2. Collective bargaining — United States.   3. Labor
laws and legislation — United States.   I. Title.
HD8072.5.S32   1987   331'.0973   86-27314
ISBN 0-316-77024-8

Library of Congress Catalog Card No. 86-27314

ISBN 0-316-77024-8

9 8 7 6 5 4 3 2 1

DON

Published simultaneously in Canada
by Little, Brown & Company (Canada) Limited

Printed in the United States of America

Credits

(continued on page 508)

To Jean, Justin, and Kimberly

Preface

Labor Relations: Process and Outcomes is a comprehensive review of the historical, legal, and institutional aspects of labor relations and collective bargaining in the United States. The topics covered in this book provide students of business and industrial relations with an interdisciplinary understanding of the field of labor relations and an introduction to some of the more important legal and contractual issues in collective bargaining.

I decided to write this book because the field of labor relations needed to be reexamined in view of recent events that have affected organized labor and management in important ways. A textbook on labor–management relations written in the late 1980s must offer reasons for the dramatic changes in labor relations and organized labor that have occurred in the past ten or so years. This cannot be done unless a systematic model of the industrial relations system is developed and then used to explain where the changes come from and how they affect the system.

My objectives in writing this text were as follows:

To make certain that the book has a contemporary, modern perspective by devoting considerable attention to those contemporary issues that are likely to be with us for some time into the future

To provide students with a sense of labor history and a perspective on the historical events that have shaped labor–management relations

To give students and instructors a sense of what it is really like to practice in the field of industrial relations by including real-world examples and cases

To provide students with a balanced and impartial discussion of management and union conflicts that precludes a pro-labor or pro-management position

A number of distinctive features characterize *Labor Relations: Process and Outcomes.*

Each chapter opens with a vignette or abstract of a recent newspaper article that illustrates how the material in the chapter relates to a contemporary issue or event.

Each chapter ends with discussion questions that allow the instructor and students to explore some of the issues covered in the chapter. The questions are a vital tool that can be used to generate class discussion and to reinforce concepts and factual information.

The chapters are well researched and extensively footnoted. The end of chapter notes can be used for more extensive research on the subject by serious students.

The text develops a model of the representation process and uses it to help students understand the factors that influence the outcome of representation elections.

The text pays great attention to the major statutes of U.S. labor law. The Railway Labor Act, the Wagner Act, the Taft-Hartley Act, and the Landrum-Griffin Act are abstracted in tabular form, and major sections of these statutes are discussed in the text itself.

The text gives an in-depth discussion of a model labor agreement. Each section of the model agreement is discussed, and the concerns of labor and management on each issue are identified. In this way, students get an appreciation for the major issues at stake when an agreement is being negotiated.

The text includes two chapters on collective bargaining; one each on the structure and process of bargaining. In these chapters, economic and behavioral theories of bargaining are related to actual strategies and techniques used in negotiations.

Appendix A offers two extensive and detailed collective-bargaining simulations based on actual situations. One simulation is based on a private-sector case and one on a public-sector case. The simulations would be appropriate for an extensive role-playing exercise.

Appendix B contains six cases that involve real-world grievance and arbitration cases. The cases could be used as role-playing exercises or as a means of generating class discussion.

To assist instructors in preparing for and teaching this course, I have developed an Instructor's Manual, which includes chapter outlines, suggested ways of approaching the end-of-chapter discussion questions, and questions that can be used for examinations. This manual can be obtained from the publisher.

Many persons contributed either directly or indirectly to the completion of *Labor Relations: Process and Outcomes.* My dear, departed mentor at the University of Colorado, George Zinke, must be thanked for instilling in me a love for the topic of labor relations at the very beginning of my academic career. Colleagues at Ohio State, especially Harry Blaine, Mike Montgomery, and David Patton, shared with me their insight and experience in this field. My good friends, William Lewis of the FMCS office in Columbus and Stuart M. Gordon of the law firm of Porter, Wright, Morris and Arthur, have likewise shared with me some of their experiences in the bargaining process and have enlightened me somewhat to the realities of the world.

I am especially indebted to reviewers of the manuscript, who contributed useful ideas that I have tried to include in my coverage of the subject. These reviewers are Richard B. Peterson of the University of Washington, Hoyt N. Wheeler of the University of South Carolina, Ellen R. Pierce of The University of North Carolina at Chapel Hill, Richard N. Block of Michigan State University, David Gray of The University of Texas at Arlington, Daniel G. Gallagher of The University of Iowa, Charles Maxey of the University of Southern California, John E. Drotning of Case Western Reserve University, and James Barnet Dworkin of Purdue University.

The production and advisory staff at Little, Brown played a key role in the development of this text. David Lipsky of Cornell University, editorial advisor for this text, was involved in this project from the very beginning through production. David's guidance was invaluable in keeping the text on the right track during its development. Alexander Greene, business editor, was a source of motivation and encouragement and a major influence on the substantive content of almost every chapter. Andrea Cava and the editorial staff did a wonderful job of transforming my prose into an artfully crafted and well-developed manuscript. I owe them a great debt.

Many students have given me assistance in the library research necessary to write this book. Among them are Olumide Ijose, Kathryn Miller, Cindy Burnell, Grace Winslow, and Gail Jones. The manuscript was typed in its entirety by Reba Lieding, whose patience and forbearance made the project a pleasant one. Finally, my family, Jean, Justin, and Kimberly, contributed their support, encouragement, and understanding at times when my energies and motivation were at their lowest levels. This project could not have been completed without the help and support of others, but I, of course, retain the ultimate responsibility for any errors or omissions contained herein.

Marcus Hart Sandver
January 1987

Contents

3 The Unionized Labor Force and Union Government   *38*

7   Labor and the Law, Part II: Statutory Control of Labor Relations   *170*

8 Representation Elections   *214*

9 The Structure of Collective Bargaining 242

10 The Process of Bargaining 266

11   The Labor Agreement   *296*

LABOR RELATIONS

ARMCO SUGGESTS IT COULD FILE FOR PROTECTION

*Warning on Possible Step Under Bankruptcy Law
Comes as Mill Is Struck*

By J. Ernest Beazley

Armco Inc. threatened to file for bankruptcy-law protection as steelworkers struck the company's main mill over a contract dispute.

The walkout by 4,187 hourly workers at Armco's Middletown, Ohio, Works jeopardized the steelmaker's campaign to rebuild its troubled operations.

The strike — the third in six weeks at a major steelmaker — underscored the deepening labor strife in the steel industry. Picket lines formed at 11 P.M. EDT Friday after Armco implemented a concessionary labor contract at Middletown, the linchpin of the company's steelmaking.

Warns Employees

R. L. Schaffnit, president of Armco's Eastern steel division, warned employees that the strike might prompt Armco to seek refuge from creditors in the bankruptcy courts.

"The loss of income and customers due to a strike could lead to the bankruptcy of Armco," he said in a letter, adding that the walkout would "inflict more harm on our company by adding to its already severe financial burden."

Other Armco officials voiced similar concerns but declined to elaborate. Since LTV Corp.'s July 17 bankruptcy-law filing, speculation about similar moves in the beleaguered steel industry has centered on Armco, the nation's No. 5 steelmaker, and No. 3 Bethlehem Steel Corp. Armco previously insisted it wasn't contemplating a filing.

Some See a Ploy

Some analysts saw the remarks as a ploy to sway the 42-year-old Armco Employees Independent Federation, the one-plant union that represents Middletown workers. "It could be a very damaging strike for Armco, but I can't see any imminent bankruptcy," said Charles Bradford, a steel analyst at Merrill Lynch Capital Markets. Union officials agreed. "They're bluffing," argued Raymond Back, the union's president.

Nonetheless, Armco said the strike could deal it a crippling blow. At June 30, the company had $236 million of cash on hand. But Armco said the strike, coupled with an $85 million pension payment due next Monday and other potential debt payments, could exhaust its cash reserves.

First Strike at Middletown

Workers walked out Friday after voting 3,592 to 247 to launch the strike — the first in the 86-year history of Middletown, Armco's headquarters until last fall. Union officers said they sought the vote because Armco's new wage-and-benefit package slashes compensation $4,000–$5,000 a year. Armco maintains the cuts will cost workers $2,600 in wages and benefits.

Armco proposed cutting workers' average base pay of $11 an hour by 50 cents, with another 25-cent reduction in incentive pay. The company also demanded suspension of cost-of-living adjustments; deletion of two holidays; cuts in vacation, Sunday and holiday premium pay; unspecified changes in medical benefits; and a two-tiered wage and benefits arrangement in which new workers and those recalled from layoff would earn less.

In return for concessions, Armco proposed a profit-sharing plan that it said could more than make up for lost wages and benefits. The company argued that the givebacks are needed if Armco is to remain competitive with other steelmakers and continue modernization of the plant, Armco's most profitable mill.

Chapter 1

Labor Relations: An Introductory Note

The preceding story from the *Wall Street Journal* describes a scenario that has been played out for almost two-hundred years in the U.S. industrial relations system: an organized group of union workers striking their employer in a dispute over wages. The dispute in the article is somewhat atypical, however, in that the dispute is over wage and benefit concessions (not increases). The employer is facing bankruptcy both if the strike lasts too long and if the employer does not receive some reductions in labor costs from the union, as other employers in this industry have received recently. The union is in a precarious position in such a dispute. The employer needs wage and benefit concessions to remain competitive and to regain profitability in a very depressed industry. The union members don't want the union to bargain away established wages and benefits, for that will reduce the average worker's standard of living. As an incentive to settlement, the employer offers to share profits with the employees if the company returns to a position of financial strength.

Almost every day the national newspapers carry a story similar to the one that begins this chapter. Many observers of the economy and of our society point to the decline of union membership since the late 1970s and forecast the demise of organized labor as a vital or strategic force in the U.S. economy. Other observers are more cautious and point out that union membership figures are cyclical and that the labor movement has rebounded from depressed levels of membership in the past. Furthermore, they add, there is some danger in drawing overly general conclusions from broad measures of union membership.

In the United States, union membership tends to be concentrated in certain industries and in certain states in which these industries are found. In industries such as manufacturing, construction, transportation, and government, in 1984 union members accounted for more than 20 percent of the labor force. In transportation, almost 40 percent of the labor force was unionized. In the service industry, however, unions accounted for a meager 7 percent of employment. In states like New York, California, Illinois, Ohio, and Michigan, union members were found in great numbers (more than 1 million members in each of these states) and they were a sizable portion of the labor force of these states as well. In other states, such as Florida, Mississippi, North Carolina, and South Carolina, union ranks were small and union members made up less than 10 percent of the labor force.

Unions have had a long and colorful history in the United States; some of this history has been accompanied by violence and bloodshed. Union power and influence has grown from being virtually insignificant at the beginning of the twentieth century to the point where the president of the United States consults with the president of the AFL–CIO before taking action on items of importance to organized labor in this country.

It may be, however, that the amount of power and influence enjoyed by organized labor in the public arena (at least in this century) has peaked and is diminishing. Union membership has been declining, by one estimate, since 1975. The nine-year, 16 percent decline in union membership between 1975 and 1984 is the longest and steepest sustained drop in union membership in this century.[1] Clearly these are times of challenge and change for the leaders of organized labor. At least one popular contender for the Democratic nomination for the U.S. presidency in 1984, Gary Hart, made it a point to distance himself from the leaders of organized labor. Research evidence is beginning to show that, at least for the uncommitted voters, the labor endorsement of Walter Mondale's presidential candidacy in 1984 may have cost Mondale more votes than it gained him.

What is the reason for this change, and what are the prospects for organized labor in the future? Some forces seem fairly obvious — the shift in employment from manufacturing to services in the U.S. economy is one that comes immediately to mind. The shift in the expansion of industry from the Northeast to the South is another. The growth in the number of white collar and female members may be another. We will discuss all these factors in more detail in Chapter 3. These, of course, are not new changes but developments that have been occurring slowly in the U.S. labor force for more than 25 years.

Legal developments also play a role in the decline of the fortunes of organized labor. Several very recent developments in National Labor Relations Board decisions have reversed long-standing precedent going back 20 years or more. Recent U.S. Supreme Court decisions allow for greater opportunities for union members to sue their organizations for failing to represent them fairly and have expanded union members' rights to resign from a union, free from restrictions or waiting periods.[2]

These legal decisions weaken the power of the labor movement, and the increasing propensity of the courts to protect individual rights at the workplace through legal protections against unjust dismissal, for example, have led some to believe that unions are not necessary for the vast majority of workers today.[3] Indeed, a *Business Week* poll conducted by Louis Harris and Associates in 1985 showed that while 73 percent of those surveyed agreed that unions improve wages and working conditions, 58 percent of those surveyed said that most employees do not need unions to get fair treatment from their employers. In this survey, 63 percent of those responding said that they would vote no if a union representation election were held at their workplaces. Interestingly, the same survey also found a deep current of discontent at the workplace, even among professional and managerial employees.[4] Finally, the survey found that women and minorities were exceptions to the general finding that employees hold negative attitudes toward unions. Employees in these groups were much more receptive than employees in other groups to the aims and goals of unions.

What does the future hold? No one can say exactly, of course, but if present trends continue, the percentage of the labor force that is unionized will continue to fall to around 13 percent of the labor force by the end of the century — about the same percentage that was unionized in 1930 (see Figure 1.1). Some experts say flatly that unions will not survive in their present form into the twenty-first century. Richard Lyles, a management consultant, predicts:

> the decline of unionism will be the most significant of many important changes buffeting the American economy between now and the turn of the century. Those unions that survive into the 21st century will become nothing more than fraternal — and perhaps social service — organizations; the term "bargaining unit" will be a forgotten reminder of a past era.[5]

Not many others are predicting such a quick demise of the labor movement, an institution in U.S. industrial society for more than 200 years. Most agree that unions are a permanent fixture in U.S. society, but one that fluctuates in power and popularity depending on the interaction of a variety of forces, some economic, some historical, some legal, and some sociological.

The Changing Environment of the Industrial Relations System

During the 1970s and 1980s the environment of the U.S. industrial relations system began undergoing a transformation. The two changes that were to have the greatest effect on both labor and management were the increase in foreign competition (especially in the steel and automobile industries), and the deregulation of certain industries (most notably airlines, over-the-road trucking, and telecommunications). Deregulation and increased foreign competition have created pressures for

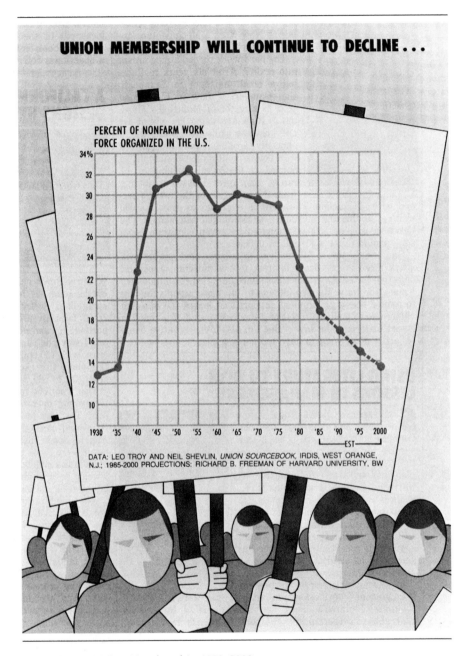

FIGURE 1-1   Union Membership 1930–2000

such developments as concession bargaining, two-tier wage systems, increased labor–management cooperation in some companies, and an intensified spirit of antiunionism in others. This change in the system has also resulted in sharp drops in membership for some unions and a general decline in the number of union members in the United States overall, a trend that has been continuing for the past ten years or so. In response, the labor movement has engaged in some serious soul-searching and reformulation. In some instances the unions have intensified organizing campaigns aimed at previously nonunion workers in order to increase membership. In some industries the unions are being encouraged to increase their participation in the internal workings of the corporation. In other industries we have seen some long and sometimes violent strikes where workers resist the attempts of management to lower wage rates or to change working conditions.

Increased Foreign Competition

In 1970, 9.2 percent of U.S. production was shipped out of the country as exports. In 1980 this figure had more than doubled to 19.6 percent; in 1982 the figure was 16.5 percent. On the other side of the balance-of-trade equation, imports were equal to 8.7 percent of total production in 1970, but climbed to 18.8 percent in 1982. In manufacturing, export trade was valued at $139.3 billion in 1984; imports, however, were valued at $222.6 billion.[6] One economist estimates that the United States lost 753,000 jobs because of a combination of the decline in exports and the increase in imports just for the years 1980–1982.[7]

There are many reasons why foreign competition has increased so dramatically in recent years. One is the fact that U.S. workers generally make higher wages than workers in other countries; these higher wage rates make U.S. goods more expensive to produce than foreign products and therefore more expensive to the consumer as well. In 1983 the average production worker's hourly compensation in U.S. manufacturing was $12.26. Labor costs in Germany were 85 percent of this figure; labor costs in Japan are less than 70 percent of this amount; and in some less developed countries costs may be as little as one-tenth of this amount.[8] This differential, in addition to the increased openness of the U.S. market to foreign producers, may be the primary force triggering the changes in the industrial relations system we are witnessing today. The increased price competitiveness of foreign producers has put tremendous pressures on U.S. producers to decrease costs and increase productivity. Wage rates are a prime target for reduction as employers increasingly feel the pinch of foreign competition.

A second factor that has enhanced the competitiveness of foreign producers in the U.S. market is the improved technological capacity of foreign producers. Our two closest competitors in manufacturing, West Germany and Japan, both spend higher percentages of domestic gross national product on research and development than does the United

States. In addition, much of U.S. research and development funds goes into military-related projects that may have little payoff for increasing the productive capacity of the nondefense industries. As a result of these technological improvements, the public perceives that the quality and reliability of some products such as Japanese electronic equipment and German automobiles exceed those for comparably priced domestic goods.

A third factor contributing to the growth of foreign competition in the U.S. market is the ease of establishing foreign operations. U.S. companies are encouraged by foreign governments to relocate operations overseas. International air travel is becoming increasingly less expensive; communication with foreign operations is becoming increasingly easier with advances in satellite communications and worldwide communications networks. The movement toward greater and greater internationalization of business operations and the expansion of foreign competition in the U.S. economy both appear inexorable.

Deregulation

The second major force producing changes in the U.S. industrial relations system is the movement toward deregulation of certain industries, most notably in the airline industry, in over-the-road trucking, and in telecommunications. Beginning with the Airline Deregulation Act of 1978, the airline industry was the first formerly regulated industry to be opened to competition. New firms were allowed to enter the industry, routes were opened up to increased interline competition, and fares were no longer regulated. Immediately new, low-cost competitors entered the market; many of them were nonunion. To stay in business the airlines were forced to cut fares to meet the competition. Some airlines were not able to survive deregulation; Braniff and Continental both went bankrupt in the wake of decontrol. Others merged to consolidate existing routes and to acquire more operating stock to expand into new areas.

The effect of decontrol in most industries is to open up the market to competition. Because they are no longer protected by regulatory controls, prices usually drop after deregulation. Inevitably, unions are pressured to reduce wages and to increase productivity. The immediate effect in the airline industry was to decrease wages, to increase flying time, and to allow the employer more flexibility in scheduling employees' hours.[9] In some instances these demands were resisted forcibly by the union; Continental pilots and flight attendants struck that airline in 1983 and did not settle their differences until late in 1985. United pilots and flight attendants struck in the summer of 1985, resisting demands for concessions. Even when concessions on wages and scheduling have been granted by the unions, employers seek more and more cost savings and productivity increases from employees to stay in business.[10] Some employees question whether it is worth granting continued concessions to an airline that may slowly go out of business anyway.

Airlines are not the only industry to be affected by deregulation. The divestiture of American Telephone & Telegraph (AT&T) of its regional operating companies makes it possible that the Communications Workers of America (CWA) will now have to bargain separately with each of the regional operating companies. Formerly the CWA negotiated one contract to cover all AT&T operating personnel nationwide; now the union may have to negotiate as many as 21 separate agreements to cover these employees. The union will almost certainly not be able to maintain the national wage scale it has maintained in the Bell System since 1974. Very recently some of the regional operating systems have created nonunion subsidiaries that will further strain labor–management relations in this industry and that will probably put a downward pressure on wages.

Employer and Union Responses to the Changes in the Environment

Increased Employer Antiunionism

Employers in the United States have historically been opposed to unions negotiating with them under the rules established under the National Labor Relations Act of 1935. Some organizations seem to be adopting aggressive antiunion philosophies; examples cited in the press are Ingersoll-Rand, which has seen the number of unionized employees drop by 50 percent between 1980 and 1984[11]; Phelps-Dodge Corporation, which won a major strike called by the Steelworkers in 1984[12]; and Litton Corporation, which was called "America's number one labor law violator" by one union leader.[13] A recent study of antiunionism among employers in New York State concludes that this is a growing trend in U.S. industry. The study found that U.S. employers spent $500 million on antiunion activities, most of this money going to union-busting consultants.[14] The report concludes that antilabor activity is more pervasive today than it has been since the years of labor–management strife in the 1920s and 1930s.[15]

The tactics that employers use in their antilabor activities include moving production from unionized to nonunionized plants, selling unionized divisions and facilities, and actually encouraging the decertification of existing unionized units.[16] The New York State Assembly task force found evidence of employer provocation of strikes and then the hiring of nonunion workers to permanently replace the strikers. Physical intimidation and force were also cited as means used to discourage workers from joining unions or supporting union activities.

An alternative form of antiunionism is manifested in some firms through the use of enlightened personnel policies and the application of behavioral science theories to the management of workers in organizations. Unions may not be openly and overtly challenged; rather unions are made unnecessary through enlightened management practice. In these firms wages and salaries are paid at a level matching or exceeding union wages in the industry; pay systems are simplified into a few job classifications or, in some cases, into an all-salaried wage system; flexibility in work assignment and job rotation is emphasized; and extensive communication and involvement with employees in workplace operations is encouraged. Verma and Kochan see the growth of the nonunion sector of the U.S. economy as one of the most significant developments in U.S. industrial relations since the 1960s.[17] In a related study, McKersie, Kochan, and Katz found that, on average, nonunion plants have higher economic performance than union plants because of lower labor costs, newer facilities, greater flexibility, and more worker participation.[18] Given these findings, it is not surprising that employers are more and more likely to seek an alternative to collective bargaining as a mechanism for regulating the workplace.

Concession Bargaining and Two-Tier Wage Systems

For those employers who maintain contact with unions and negotiate agreements, there appears to be a trend in wage moderation. In particular, employers in some industries are negotiating concession agreements: labor agreements that provide for wage and benefit reductions or freezes. A recent survey by the Bureau of National Affairs (BNA) found that 25 percent of the agreements negotiated in 1985 had provisions for either a wage freeze or a reduction.[19] The wage reductions averaged 10.4 percent for the first year of the agreement and 5.8 percent over the life of the contract. Wage concessions are a relatively new development, dating from the 1979 "give-backs" at Chrysler. In a recent survey of labor agreements, David J. B. Mitchell found some evidence of concession agreements in all but two of 41 industry groups surveyed (railroads and glass).[20] It should be pointed out that wage concession agreements appear to be on the decline somewhat; in 1983, 40 percent of all agreements contained wage freezes or wage reductions. Nevertheless, concessions are a part of bargaining today and are the chief reason why union wage increases (in percentage terms) have increased at a slower rate than wages for nonunion workers in recent years.[21] On the positive side, the moderation in union wage increases (averaging 3.1 percent for 1985) has been labeled "the most effective blow against inflation."[22]

A second recent development in bargaining is the two-tier pay system. In 1983, 3 percent of the agreements in the BNA survey contained two-tier wage systems; in 1984 the figure was 8 percent; and in 1985 it was 9 percent.[23] In two-tier wage systems newly hired workers are paid less than the established union wage scale. In some systems the difference between first-tier and second-tier employees will always remain, meaning that an employee with three years of seniority hired under the two-tier system in the second tier will never make as much salary as an employee with three years of seniority in the first tier. In other systems the tiers converge over time and eventually employees in both tiers will make the same hourly wage.

Two-tier wage systems provide labor cost relief to employers who need to hire many new employees or who perhaps have high turnover. As they leave the organization, the first-tier employees are replaced by lower paid second-tier employees, and labor cost savings will be realized by the company. This system also has advantages for the leadership of the union because current employees under two-tier systems do not have to take pay cuts — only those who are hired after the agreement is ratified will be affected by the two-tier arrangement. Thus, two-tier systems may be easier to market to union members than would a concession wage package.

Two-tier agreements can be found in most major industries although they are currently most commonly found in the aerospace industry, the retail-wholesale trade sector, and especially among the airlines. Two-tier systems are hailed as the key to modest union wage gains for the next few years and as a major force in controlling inflation in the near future.[24] There are some negative aspects to two-tier wage systems, however. Joel Popkin, a Washington economist, predicts that most two-tier systems will revert to single-tier systems because of their negative aspects, such as resentment among younger, second-tier workers who work for less money than older, first-tier workers doing exactly the same work. Some employers express concern about possible legal problems (violations of the Equal Pay Act) if a large number of newly hired second-tier workers are women being paid less salary than men doing identical work. Morale and productivity concerns are also voiced by employers who have negotiated these plans.[25] Finally, union leaders have found that two-tier systems create dissension within the union and bitterness on the part of younger workers. Richard Ramsey, executive director of the Newspaper Guild, which does have two-tier agreements with employers in Washington and New York, has commented that two-tier wage systems "tear the union apart."[26]

Nevertheless, two-tier wage systems are part of the current fabric of bargaining and are seen by employers who use them as effective in controlling labor costs. Gayle Wineriter, a special assistant to Federal Mediation and Conciliation Service Director Kay McMurray and an active mediator himself, predicts an increase in the use of two-tier agreements in the future, especially in manufacturing.[27]

Labor–Management Cooperation

The concept of labor–management cooperation is not new. Experiments in Quality of Working Life programs have been going on since the 1960s. The difference today seems to be that labor–management cooperation programs are being seen as a key to corporate survival and the protection of workers' jobs rather than as merely an attempt to improve the quality of an individual's work experience or to improve job satisfaction. The biggest emphasis on labor–management cooperative programs appears to be in the automobile industry, although such programs are also apparently growing in popularity in public service employment, especially in school districts.[28]

The most widely publicized advances to date in labor–management cooperation come from agreements negotiated between General Motors Corporation (GMC) and the United Automobile Workers Union (UAW). The UAW–GMC agreement negotiated in September 1984 has been called a "landmark in the evolution of American industrial relations."[29] The UAW–GMC agreement for 1984 provides for three strategies to improve corporate performance and competitiveness in the marketplace. First of all, it provides for labor cost savings and cost containment for the company. In contrast to most contracts negotiated in the past, the 1984 agreement provided for a very modest (2.1 percent) annual wage increase. Instead of a large "up front" cash settlement in the form of percentage increases in hourly earnings, the union agreed to a bonus payment plan that would give workers one-time cash bonuses paid out of corporate profits. An advantage of this plan is that the bonus provides workers with a payout in times of high profitability, but this payout is not translated into a permanent increase (or ratcheting) of the hourly wage rate. If profits are down in subsequent years, the bonus does not have to be maintained as would an increase in hourly wages. This type of system should reduce the need for concession bargaining in the future. In addition to the bonus system, the union also agreed that individual workers should share a part of the cost of the health insurance provided by the company. This is also a substantial saving for the company.

Second, the agreement calls for increased participation by the union in running the corporation and in expanding its markets. The 1984 agreement provides for a New Business Venture Development Group to identify new areas for GMC to expand its business activities. The venture group will be composed of representatives from both labor and management and has been called a "leap of unions into entrepreneurship."[30] To finance the venture group, GMC set aside $100 million.

The third and perhaps most innovative aspect of the 1984 UAW–GMC agreement provides for a job bank, backed by a $1 billion fund to assist workers in relocation, retraining, and readjusting to changes caused by disruptions in the industry or in the economy. In contrast to the Supplementary Unemployment Benefits Plan (SUB) already in effect at GMC, the job bank program would focus on retraining and reemploying workers rather than just providing them with money when they are laid off.

In 1985 the UAW and GMC again went to the bargaining table, this time to negotiate the Saturn agreement, which will affect about 6,000 workers at the new Saturn manufacturing facility in Spring Hill, Tennessee. The major distinguishing feature of the Saturn agreement is the degree of participation given to the union and the workers in the running of the plant. The union is given representation on the committees that administer the plant and that devise long-range strategy for the Saturn project. One of the historic innovations of the Saturn agreement is that under the contract at least 80 percent of the workers in the new plant will be shielded from layoffs. Under the agreement there will be only one job classification for production employees, and employees can be shifted from area to area in the plant as the need arises.

Under the Saturn agreement all employees will be salaried and after the first year will have their wages pegged at 80 percent of the straight-time hourly wage rate at other UAW-represented production facilities in the United States. Additional earnings will be given to workers based on corporate profitability, individual performance and productivity, and work quality. Workers will retain most of the standard UAW–GMC benefits and will have the same grievance and arbitration procedures as found in other UAW agreements.[31] UAW president Owen Bieber, who negotiated the pact for the union, stated that with the Saturn agreement the union becomes a full partner with the corporation in all decision-making and that no decision can be reached without its approval.[32] The Saturn agreement is heralded by many as the key to enhancing the U.S. auto industry's ability to meet the competition of Japanese automakers head on. Whether this turns out to be true or not, of course, remains to be seen, but the Saturn agreement does represent a dramatic step toward full labor–management cooperation and a big change in labor relations in the U.S. automobile industry.

Increased Union Efforts in Organizing Nonunion Workers

As a response to the decline in membership that unions have been experiencing over the past ten years or so, many unions are intensifying their efforts at organizing nonunion workers. Some unions to do so within 1985 are the Hotel and Restaurant Employees, the Communications Workers of America, the Service Employees International Union, the National Health Care and Hospital Workers Union, and the United Food and Commercial Workers Union. The renewed emphasis on organizing the unorganized is accompanied by changes in the tactics that some unions use in conducting organizational campaigns. For example, in 1985 the Hotel and Restaurant Employees placed ads in many national newspapers for union organizers. The ads read something like the following:

> Help wanted: Arduous work away from home. Low salary. Must like people. Willing to take abuse. Neat appearance. Late-night meetings. Car necessary. Future of organization depends on you. Apply in person.[33]

The ads generated 500 job applicants from which the union chose about 30 to work on its new organizing campaign in Boston, Chicago, Washington, DC, and Orange County, California. The new organizers were paid $300 per week and were paired with experienced organizers in each campaign. The Hotel and Restaurant Employees used this tactic of employing young, college-educated organizers in its successful campaign to organize 2,600 clerical and technical employees at Yale University in late 1984. The union's director of organizing, Vincent J. Sirabella, believes that "labor's principal deficiency to successful organizing is the lack of educated and well-trained staff members to perform this vital function."[34] Thus, recruiting, training, and mentoring new organizers is seen as the key to the union's continued success in organizing nonunion workers.

Charles McDonald, assistant director of organizing for the AFL–CIO, has identified several factors that appear to be associated with successful organizing campaigns, in particular solid financing and centralized control of the campaign. Experience seems to show that campaigns conducted from a centralized organizing office at the national union level are more successful than those orchestrated at the local level.[35] The use of young, idealistic, attractive, well-trained organizers appears to be another successful strategy in organizing. More and more unions are coming to appreciate the importance of young workers to the future growth of the labor movement. At present only 14 percent of the under-35 age group in the labor force is unionized.[36] In addition, unions are using new advanced communications techniques to get their message across to the voters.

Circulating prerecorded videotapes that workers can view in their homes or with groups of coworkers is one effective communications technique.[37] Some unions are using advertisements in national publications developed by public relations firms to get their message across to the public.[38] Other unions are developing television commercials and are using spots on cable television to increase public awareness of the role that unions play in the U.S. economy. The International Ladies Garment Workers Union (ILGWU) pioneered the use of television advertising among unions in 1975; since then the American Federation of State, County, and Municipal Employees (AFSCME), the Communications Workers of America (CWA), the United Automobile Workers (UAW), and others have developed their own television commercials. The AFL–CIO has allocated more than $6 million to its Labor Institute for Public Affairs to develop the 12-part "America Works" television series.[39]

Unions are also beginning to use and to rely on data gathered by opinion poll takers to guide their organizing campaigns. The Illinois Federation of Teachers used the Washington firm of Peter D. Hart Research Associates (a polling firm also used by Walter Mondale) to guide it in its organizing campaign conducted among teachers at the Peoria school district. The advice of the consulting firm enabled the union to tailor its campaign to the specific needs of the Peoria teachers and is credited as a major factor in helping the union win the election. Peter D. Hart and Associates now provides consulting services to the American Federation of Teachers, the United Automobile Workers, the Communication Workers of America, the Amalgamated Clothing and Textile Workers, the United Food and Commercial Workers, and others.[40]

Success in organizing campaigns, of course, depends on more than just enthusiastic organizers and slick advertising; there must be a message to communicate as well — a message that appeals to the interests and needs of the majority of employees in a work group. Unions today are concentrating on identifying issues that are important to workers and that are not being met by their employers. For workers in manufacturing, issues such as job security, advanced notification of plant closings, introduction of new technology, limitations on subcontracting, transfer rights, early retirement, and relocation allowances may be of primary interest. For younger workers the union's emphasis in organizing might emphasize personal growth, upward mobility, company-financed educational and training programs, and fairness in promotion procedures and job bidding. Campaigns tailored to units of predominantly female workers may explore comparable worth, job safety and health, employee privacy rights, employer-sponsored child care, sexual harassment, and the health hazards associated with video display terminals.[41]

The coordination of union organizing activities by the AFL–CIO appears to be a successful strategy in union organizing campaigns. The AFL–CIO's Industrial Unionism Department is currently conducting a coordinated organizing effort in the South specifically around the cities of Atlanta, Georgia; Charlotte, North Carolina; Madison, Alabama; and Tupelo and Jackson, Mississippi. In the first ten months of 1985 this campaign participated in 32 representation elections, of which it won 25.[42] Four other elections are in litigation and appeal. With a win rate of 78 percent, the coordinated effort is producing results well above the 45 percent win rate that unions achieved overall in elections in 1985. In total, 4,000 workers were potentially added to the ranks of organized labor as a result of the efforts of the AFL–CIO's organizing campaign.

In August 1985, AFL–CIO president Lane Kirkland announced the beginning of a coordinated campaign to organize the employees of Blue Cross-Blue Shield nationwide.[43] Blue Cross-Blue Shield is one of the nation's largest medical insurance carriers and represents a potential membership gain of 37,000 members for the labor federation. Very importantly, the Blue Cross-Blue Shield campaign could mark the beginning of the long-awaited push on the part of the AFL–CIO to organize office and clerical employees, potentially the largest block of unorganized workers in the nation. A union blitz to organize clerical workers in the banking industry was recently predicted at the American Institute of Banking seminar in Philadelphia by a well-known management attorney, who warned that the bankers were especially vulnerable to organizing drives and were ill equipped to deal with an intensive organizing drive, should it come.[44] Kirkland has promised increased efforts at organizing clerical employees in the near future.

In addition to sponsoring organizational campaigns aimed at workers at the workplace, the AFL–CIO has also recently inaugurated a new campaign to attract associate members. The associate member campaign has been called the most radical change in union strategy since the formation of the AFL–CIO.[45] The associate member campaign focuses on workers who do not work in unionized worksites but who want some of the services that labor unions can provide. In particular the AFL–CIO is concentrating on financial services such as credit cards and insurance and retirement accounts for associate members. Because it has so many members, the AFL–CIO can purchase these services at substantial discounts and can provide them at a very reasonable price to its associate members. The AFL–CIO can use the associate members as a base upon which to build support that may pay off in organizing campaigns in the future. The federation will also collect dues from its associate members, which may help stem the tide of financial losses the organization has been suffering from the downturn in union membership in recent years.

Summary

The pressures of foreign competition, economic downturn, and deregulation have subjected both labor and management to problems that were unknown ten years ago. In response, some organizations have embarked on campaigns of open and active opposition to unions. Some organizations and unions have negotiated concession agreements or two-tier pay systems to cut labor costs and to protect profitability. In still other organizations, the response to competitive pressures has been to increase labor–management cooperation and to encourage a sense of participation by workers in the operation of the organization. Finally, the labor movement itself has been forced to respond to the sharp drop-off in membership that unions have been experiencing in the last few years. Increased sophistication in conducting organizing campaigns, coordination of individual union efforts in organizing workers, and experiments in new types of membership relationships are all being tried to save the labor movement from a further decline in power and influence.

Discussion Questions

1. How do you feel the issue of foreign competition should be handled in the U.S. economy? What do you see as the advantages and disadvantages of strong foreign competition in our basic industries such as automobile, steel, and textile manufacturing?
2. How would you react if your employer asked you to take a 25 percent reduction in your pay to help the employer maintain operations? Which groups of employees would be most likely to accept wage cuts? Which groups less likely? Why?
3. For many people the activities of antiunion consultants are seen as immoral and unethical even when they are conducted in strict accordance with the

law. How do you feel about this? Would you go to work for an antiunion (union-busting) consulting firm if the salary was competitive with other job offers you received? Why or why not?

4. What do you see as the advantages and the disadvantages of a two-tier wage system? Would you recommend the establishment of such a system to a financially troubled employer? If you were advising a labor leader facing the layoffs of union members, would you give the same advice? Why or why not?

5. What do you see as the future of the labor movement in the United States? Do you see continued long-term decline in membership in the years ahead, or some growth in membership in the future? What factors do you take into consideration in making your prediction?

Notes

[1]Leo Troy and Neil Sheflin, *Union Sourcebook*, West Orange, NJ: Industrial Relations Data and Information Services, 1985, p. 1.

[2]Stephen Wermiel, "Justices Rule Unions Can't Fine Members Who Quit, Resume Work During Strike," *Wall Street Journal*, June 28, 1985: 5.

[3]"Beyond Unions," *Business Week*, July 8, 1985: 75.

[4]Ibid., p. 5.

[5]Paul Engel, "Labor in Retreat," *Industry Week*, July 8, 1985: 55.

[6]Lee Price, "Growing Problems for American Workers in International Trade." In Thomas Kochan, ed., *Challenges and Choices Facing American Labor*, Cambridge, MA: MIT Press, 1985, p. 126.

[7]Robert Z. Lawrence, "Is Trade Deindustrializing America? A Medium Term Perspective," *Brookings Papers on Economic Activity* I: 1983.

[8]Price, "Growing Problems for American Workers in International Trade," quoting unpublished U.S. Department of Labor figures, p. 129.

[9]"Assessment of Effects of Deregulation on Labor," *Labor Relations Reporter* 118 (1985): 50.

[10]Leslie Wayne, "Pan Am, Still Hurting, Now Tackles Unions," *New York Times*, September 23, 1984, sec. 3: 1.

[11]David Wessel, "Tough Employer: Fighting Off Unions, Ingersoll-Rand Uses Wide Range of Tactics," *Wall Street Journal*, June 13, 1985: 1.

[12]William Serrin, "The Copper Mines May Be at the Point of No Return," *New York Times*, July 29, 1984: 5.

[13]Tamar Lewin, "Litton's Angry Labor Conglomorate," *New York Times*, April 24, 1985: 1.

[14]"Anti-Unionism Found on Rise," *New York Times*, February 17, 1985: 30.

[15]"New York Report on Anti-Labor Activity," *Labor Relations Reporter* 118 (1985): 177.

[16]Wessel, "Tough Employer," p. 1.

[17]Anil Verma and Thomas Kochan, "The Growth and Nature of the Nonunion Sector Within a Firm." In Kochan, ed., *Challenges and Choices Facing American Labor*, pp. 89, 112.

[18]"New Model in Industrial Relations," *Labor Relations Reporter* 118 (1985): 26.

[19]"Summary of Current Developments," *Labor Relations Reporter* 119 (August 1985): 27.

[20]"Shift in Union Wage Patterns," *Labor Relations Reporter* 121 (January 6, 1986): 6.

[21]Steven Greenhouse, "For Wages: No Big Takeoff in Sight," *New York Times*, April 29, 1984: 26F.

[22]Peter Kilborn, "Labor Pacts Assessed as Big Blow to Inflation," *New York Times*, September 23, 1984: 13.

[23]"Summary of Developments," *Labor Relations Reporter*, 119, See also Bill Keller, "Workers Who Start and Stay at the Bottom," *New York Times*, August 19, 1984: 3E.

[24]"Shift in Union Wage Patterns," *Labor Relations Reporter* 121 (January 6, 1986): 6.

[25]"Two Tier Wage Plans," *Labor Relations Reporter* 120 (November 18, 1985): 3.

[26]Keller, "Workers Who Start and Stay at the Bottom," p. 3E.

[27]Kent Darr, "Mediator Predicts Tougher Job as Gap Between Sides Widens," *Columbus Dispatch*, January 20, 1986: 5D.

[28]"Teachers, School Boards Avoid Strikes," *Columbus Dispatch*, September 6, 1985: 3A.

[29]Quinn Mills, "A New Cooperation Sweeps Detroit," *New York Times*, October 7, 1985: p. 5.

[30]Ibid., p. 5.

[31]John Holusha, "G.M. Contract Aims to Foster Union-Management Cooperation," *New York Times*, July 28, 1985: 12.

[32]"UAW Approval of Saturn Contract," *Labor Relations Reporter* 119 (August 5, 1985): 275.

[33]James Warren, "Why Unions Are Losing Grip on Organizing," *Chicago Tribune*, June 21, 1984, sec. 2: 1, 6.

[34]"Hotel Employees' Organizing Drive," *Labor Relations Reporter* 119 (June 3, 1985): 90–91.

[35]Warren, "Why Unions Are Losing Grip on Organizing," p. 6.

[36]Steven Greenhouse, "Reshaping Labor to Woo the Young," *New York Times*, September 1, 1985, sec. 3: 1.

[37]Joann Lublin, "Laborious Task: Union Organizer Faces Harder Job than Ever in Recession-Hit South," *Wall Street Journal*, August 3, 1982: 1.

[38]Scott Hume, "Unions Test Marketing Waters," *Advertising Age*, February 27, 1984: 1.

[39]Ibid., p. 1.

[40]"Why Unions Are Losing Grip on Organizing," p. 6.

[41]"Trends in Union Organizing," *Labor Relations Reporter* 120 (December 23, 1985): 338.

[42]"Organizing Successes by AFL–CIO in South," *Labor Relations Reporter* 120 (December 2, 1985): 282.

[43]"Joint Organizing Effort at Blue Cross-Blue Shield," *Labor Relations Reporter* 119 (August 5, 1985): 339.

[44]"Union Blitz on Financial Industry," *Labor Relations Reporter* 120 (December 9, 1985): 301.

[45]Carey English, "Now It's Unions Offering Fringe Benefits to Workers," *U.S. News and World Report*, November 11, 1985: 66.

REAGAN URGES RESTRAINT

Washington Post — President Reagan, in a Detroit television interview broadcast Tuesday, said that if the United Auto Workers fails to exercise some restraint in its contract demands on the auto industry, it could "turn off the recovery, the expansion that we're having."

The president's words, in an interview with station WDIV, brought instant criticism from organized labor.

"For the president to enter into a collective-bargaining dialogue at this point is an interference clearly on the side of management," said Murray Seeger, spokesman for the AFL–CIO.

"He has never spoken out for workers when they were being asked to take lower pay and benefits. It is unseemly for him to put his nose into the tent when the two sides are only beginning to negotiate."

Labor costs have moderated markedly in the last two years. The administration would like to keep them moderate, since they are perhaps the main ingredient in the economy's inflation rate. However, the administration has previously stood aloof from private-sector negotiations.

The UAW last week opened negotiations covering 465,000 workers at General Motors Corp. and Ford Motor Co. Contracts at both will expire Sept. 14.

Chapter 2

An Overview of the Industrial Relations System

The *Columbus Dispatch* article illustrates the importance of labor negotiations to the health of our national economy. The concern that President Reagan was voicing about the effect that the General Motors–United Auto Workers negotiations would have on the 1984 economic recovery was shared by many people. This concern by the public demonstrates the fact that labor relations is not conducted in a vacuum — that the labor relations process is a part of our total social and economic system. In this chapter I will discuss some basic topical areas that make up the field of labor relations, such as labor history, labor law, labor economics, dispute resolution, and contract administration. Research and intellectual reflection about these topics are conducted by scholars in the fields of law, economics, history, sociology, psychology, political science, and business. Because the important topic areas comprising the subject of labor relations and collective bargaining are diffused in many different academic disciplines, we say that the study of this topic is *interdisciplinary.*

The study of labor relations and collective bargaining is one part of a larger field, industrial relations, defined as the study of employment relationships in an industrial economy; the central focus of this field is *employment* in all its aspects: at the levels of the individual, the firm, or society.[1] The subject areas delineated by this definition of industrial relations include the study of human resource policy at the level of society, the study of labor relations and collective bargaining at the levels of both the firm and of society, and the study of personnel management, usually studied at the level of the firm.

Historical and Conceptual Foundations

Karl Marx (1818–1883)

The beginning of the study of labor relations and collective bargaining is usually traced to Karl Marx, who saw unions as the beginning of a movement to form a socialist state. Marx believed that the process of industrialism (which was well started in Western Europe and the United States by the 1860s, when he was writing) would inevitably lead to increasing misery among members of the working class (the proletariat), and that unionism would be a natural collective protective response on the part of the working class to fight this misery. Marx believed that once workers began joining together at the workplace they would soon begin organizing on a larger and larger scale until at some point in time they could challenge the capitalist owners of the means of production (the bourgeoisie) for control of both the workplace and, eventually, society.[2] For the doctrinaire Marxist, the organization of the working class and the development of unions is a key component of social change. Unionization, however, as an end in itself was derided by the Marxists; to achieve the goal of social change the trade unions needed to be led by an enlightened intellectual. As Lenin writes:

> The history of all countries attests to the fact that, left to its own forces, the working class can only attain to trade union consciousness — that is, the conviction that it is necessary to unite in unions, wage the struggle against the bosses, attain from the government such or such labor reforms, etc. As to the socialist doctrines, they came from philosophic, historic and economic theories elaborated by certain educated representatives of the possessing classes, the intellectuals.[3]

Interest in studying unions as agents for radical social and political change has continued long after Marx and Lenin and represents a way of studying labor relations and collective bargaining even today.[4] The intellectual history of the field of industrial relations, however, generally developed in a non-Marxist perspective mainly because the predictions of Marx about the labor movement did not come true; the Marxists generally viewed unions as impotent to bring about social change in and of themselves.[5]

The Webbs (1858–1947)

A new school of thought about unions and their role in the industrial relations system developed in England, led by the husband and wife team of Sidney and Beatrice Webb. The Webbs published two encyclopedic works on the subject of trade unions and collective bargaining, *A History of Trade Unionism* in 1896, and *Industrial Democracy* in 1902. The work of the Webbs marked one of the first attempts to analyze and to scientifically study labor unions. The Webbs found that unions had not become the radical proponents of social change that Marx had predicted. Rather than working for the overthrow of the capitalist system, the Webbs found that unions were engaged mainly in activities that would improve the day-to-day working conditions for workers, such as the establishment of mutual insurance systems, legislative action, and collective bargaining with employers over wages and work rules:

> In unorganized trades the individual workman, applying for a job, accepts or refuses the terms offered by the employer without communication with his fellow-workmen, and without any other consideration than the exigencies of his own position. For the sale of his labour he makes, with the employer, a strictly individual bargain. But if a group of workmen concert together, and send representatives to conduct the bargaining on behalf of the whole body, the position is at once changed. Instead of the employer making a series of separate contracts with isolated individuals, he meets with a collective will, and settles, in a single agreement, the principles upon which, for the time being, all workmen of a particular group, or class, or grade, will be engaged.[6]

John R. Commons (1862–1945)

At about the same time that the Webbs were reading and writing about unions and collective bargaining in Great Britain, intellectual interest in the subject of trade unionism began to develop also in the United States. The leading scholar in the development of a U.S. school of thought about this subject (later dubbed the Wisconsin School) was John R. Commons, a professor of economics at the University of Wisconsin. Commons was brought to Wisconsin to teach and to head a project whose mission was to gather, catalogue, and publish documents relating to the very early history of unions in the United States.[7] In the course of this momentous project (the final product of which was the publication of an 11-volume work entitled *The Documentary History of the American Industrial Society* in 1911), Commons acquired an interest in studying labor unions as institutions and in trying to incorporate their actions into a general theory of economic activity. Commons defined an economic institution as "collective action in control of individual action."[8] He viewed unions as a countervailing power on the part of workers to the power of the corporation, also an economic institution. When representatives of economic institutions met to negotiate wages and terms of employment, this was defined as "two-sided collective action," also known as collective bargaining. In Commons's own words:

> My acquaintance with collective bargaining was begun five decades ago, in the year 1883. In that year I joined local Typographical Union No. 53 at Cleveland, Ohio, in order to get a job on the *Cleveland Herald*, owned by a corporation. Across the street was a nonunion office, the *Cleveland Leader*, where my brother had a job. . . .
>
> The two offices were alike, except in the rules that controlled the foremen and the printers. In the nonunion office the foreman was a dictator.

He had his "pets" to whom he gave steady work; and he gave to them the . . . kind of work . . . that paid better wages than other kinds of work.

But in the union office the foreman was restrained in these matters by rules agreed upon by the labor union and the owners of the newspaper. We had a rule of preference for vacancies, instead of leaving it to the foreman.

My little union of 1883 was two-sided collective action. On one side were the investors and stockholders of the *Cleveland Herald* acting collectively as owners. On the other side were the typesetters acting collectively as a labor union. . . . Where formerly it was assumed equality of individuals existed in individual bargaining, we endeavored to achieve equality of bargaining power between two organizations of individuals.[9]

Selig Perlman (1888–1959)

Commons's thoughts and theories concerning the trade union movement were further developed by his student Selig Perlman, who later also became a professor of economics at the University of Wisconsin. Perlman helped refine the institutional economics of Commons into a specialized theory of trade union function and behavior, and turned away from the grand scheme systematizing of economic behavior that had been Commons's real interest. For Perlman the real focus of attention was on the union itself, not on the whole economic system. Perlman developed a theory of union action based on two key components: (1) the economic psychology of the working class, and (2) the nature of the political and social values of society.[10] Basically, Perlman was relating union behavior to the psychological attitudes of workers and to the nature of the legal and political systems that acted to protect the interests of the employers. With Perlman's writings industrial relations emerged as a separate field of study distinct from economics.

The Ross–Dunlop Debate

In the mid-1940s the conceptual foundation of the field had matured to a point that serious theoretical debate began concerning the nature and functions of trade unions. Scholars were now testing with empirical data the basic assumptions and underpinnings of the existing theories of trade unionism. In particular, John Dunlop published a landmark empirical work in 1944 that served to show that the trade union is an economic actor in an economic system and that its behavior can be explained by an economic model of wage and employment maximization.[11] Arthur Ross, another economist, writing in 1948, reacted strongly and negatively to Dunlop's findings. Ross proposed as his central hypothesis that the union is a political agency acting in an economic environment.[12] Ross concentrated on the political power motives of union leaders in their collective bargaining activities. He replied quite directly to Dunlop's theory, that trade union wage policy can be best understood through economic analysis, by stating:

The major influences controlling union wage policy are largely the same as the major influences controlling union behavior in general. To understand them, we must understand the union itself — what kind of organism it is, how it functions, and what is the role of leadership. Where should we turn for such an understanding?

Among all the participants in economic life, the trade union is probably *least* suited to purely economic analysis. It may be that the particular form of rationality assumed in traditional economic theory can properly be assigned to the individual entrepreneur and even to the corporation, which after all is a legal individual. In any case it is not necessary to argue that point here. But a trade union is preeminently a group, a collectivity. Psychologists have been insisting for more than half a century that group behavior is fundamentally different from individual behavior. The trade union is not only a group, but an institution as well; it leads a life of its own separate and distinct from the lives of its members. Its problems are not merely those of the particular individuals it happens to represent at one point of time.[13]

The Ross–Dunlop debate was important for the field of industrial relations because it provided a rational, theoretical debate between scholars of eminent skill and training on a fundamental issue in the field: "How do unions develop and implement wage policy and how do they assert power over employers in the negotiations process?" In the course of the debate it became apparent that the positions of both Dunlop and Ross were credible and that, if anything, a synthesis was necessary to reconcile the two points of view.

The Dunlop Systems Approach

The synthesis, interestingly, came from Dunlop himself. Writing in the *Industrial and Labor Relations Review* in 1950, Dunlop proposed that to understand collective bargaining and labor–management relations an analytical framework should be used that includes the interaction of economic, technological, and social forces.[14] Dunlop expanded his own framework even more in subsequent years and incorporated some components of systems theory with it to produce his seminal work *Industrial Relations Systems*.[15] In this work Dunlop advanced a comprehensive framework for understanding the interaction of the multitude of forces that influence the nature of industrial relations systems — a framework that can be applied to virtually any industry in any country.

The Dunlop framework consists of three key elements. The first element in the system is the *actors:* workers and their organizations, managers and their organizations, and the government. The second element is the *environment:* the technological environment, the market and budgetary constraints faced by the actors, and the power relations and status of the actors in the system. The final element is the *ideology:* the body of common ideas shared by the actors that defines the role and place of each actor in the total framework. The central task of an industrial relations system for Dunlop is to explain why particular rules are established and why these rules change in response to changes that occur in one of the elements of the system. Dunlop sees the process of rulemaking and the establishment of the "web of rules" controlling the actions of the actors as central to the study of industrial relations. The rules that Dunlop is concerned with are the rules that govern the employment relationship at the workplace — rules about compensation, performance, discipline, layoff, and so forth.[16]

Dunlop's work has received some criticism in recent years, some of it quite influential in shaping the development of systematic thinking in the field. One group of authors criticizes the Dunlop system for ignoring the behavioral aspect of work relations. One author writes that "industrial relations as it is at present construed is more concerned with studying the resolution of industrial conflict than with its generation."[17] The Dunlop system looks at rules, the resolution of conflict. It does not look at where the conflict came from in the first place. Second, some authors have charged that Dunlop's model describes the interaction of organizations in the industrial relations system but ignores the role that individuals may play in the system.[18] Finally, it can be argued that the Dunlop system has too narrow a focus. By focusing solely on rulemaking, the Dunlop system does not give us anything that is objective and quantitative to study. One author goes so far as to state that "the end or purpose of employment is not rules."[19] The rulemaking process is part of the industrial relations system, but these rules do produce a product, something quantifiable and measurable such as a certain wage rate, a certain package of fringe benefits, and so forth. It is also true that the rules that are negotiated may have a profound effect on the production system and on the general efficiency and productivity of the workplace, and even on the general economy itself in the long term.[20]

A Conceptual Model of the Industrial Relations System

Sandver
Model

In this text I will follow a conceptual framework that is inspired by the Dunlop *Industrial Relations Systems* model but that is quite different from it as well. This model is illustrated in Figure 2.1. The conceptual model is an interdisciplinary one that draws upon ideas from psychology, economics, law, and sociology. In addition, the model is also multicausal, meaning that many diverse forces working together are seen as determining the nature of an industrial relations system.

Environmental Forces

The environmental context consists of those forces that are societal-level or economy-wide that are external to any particular workplace but that influence industrial relations at the workplace level. Examples of environmental forces follow.

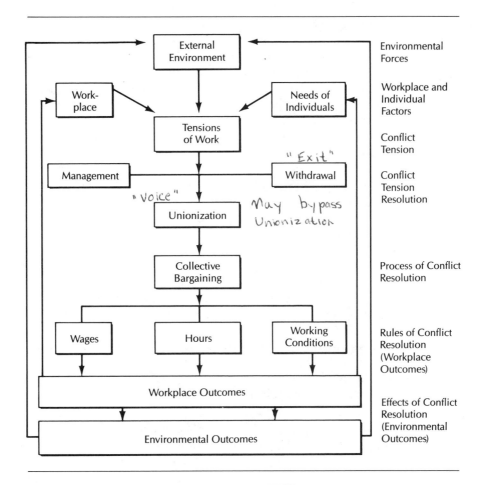

FIGURE 2-1 A Conceptual Model of the Industrial Relations System

Economic Factors. These factors are affected by the general state of the economy: inflation, unemployment, and the stage of the business cycle. For example, in times of recession and high unemployment there is a decrease in the level of demand for many products. When the level of demand for a product drops, the demand for labor to produce that product also drops. Employers may need to reduce costs or to reduce prices to remain competitive. This cost reduction may affect the labor force through layoffs or decreases in wage rates. As much as any other external force, the state of the economy and the state of the labor market have important effects on the workplace.

Technological Factors.   Technological factors are the hardware of production, such as the tools and machines used to produce a product, and the human skills such as technical, craft, and managerial skills necessary to run an organization. The technological context of the industrial relations system changes constantly as technology advances. New jobs are created by technological change; age-old skills and crafts are made obsolete by technological change as well. As Barbash observes, "virtually every major aspect of industrial relations interconnects with technology."[21]

Political and Legal Factors.   Included in this category are such factors as the nature of the laws that regulate labor–management relations, the power of the political parties, and the relative popularity of liberal versus conservative political beliefs. The political and legal environments play a crucial role in determining the nature of the workplace relationship by limiting or sanctioning the use of certain employment practices on the part of both employer and employees. The legal system in the United States today regulates whom the employer may hire and refuse to hire, the level of wages, the payment of overtime pay, the safety of the workplace, workers' rights to join unions, to strike, to picket, to boycott, and so forth. The regulation of the workplace by legislative enactment is relatively new — most would date it from 1935 with the passage of the National Labor Relations Act. As with technology, this is an aspect of the industrial relations system that is constantly changing.

Ideological Factors.   Included in this category is the general attitudinal climate in the nation regarding unions, corporations, the legitimacy of collective versus individual action, and even the ownership of private property and rights of free association.

The ideological context is also constantly evolving and changing. The process of this evolution is to some extent the product of current events that change our perspective and require us to rethink our positions on certain issues, and also to a certain extent the product of history. To understand the current ideological content we need to have some knowledge both of current events and also some knowledge of history.

The environmental context in this model corresponds to Dunlop's technical, market, power, and ideological contexts, but envisions these as being part of the industrial relations system rather than external to it. In Dunlop's system we are never really certain if the "contexts" are part of the system or external to it, a point that needs to be clearly specified.[22]

Workplace and Individual Factors

The next element in the model illustrated in Figure 2.1 are workplace and individual factors, which form the environment within which a particular pattern of relationship between an individual employer and a work group will develop.

Workplace Factors

Technology of the Workplace.   Included in this category are the general nature of what is produced (e.g., goods or services) and the nature of the production process (e.g., mass production versus craft work, office work versus factory work). Also included is the scale (size) both of the productive facility and of its work force.

One of the strongest statements concerning the effect of technology on the behavior of industrial work groups comes from the work of Joan Woodward,[23] who found that workplace relationships between supervisors and employees are related to the level of technology in a firm. Woodward found that workplace relationships are best in small-batch and craft production settings and in continuous-process settings (such as oil refineries or chemical processing facilities); workplace relations are worst in mass-production occupations such as automobile manufacturing.

Budget and Market Forces.   Included in this category are the profitability of the employer, the nature of competition in the product market, and the availability of substitutes for the good or service produced. All these factors have an effect on relationships at the workplace. An employer with a favorable market position and with a high level of profitability is likely to be more amenable to paying high wages and providing good benefits to his or her employees than is one who is losing money or who is in a very cutthroat and competitive market.

Supervision.   Included in this category are the general characteristics, actions, and attitudes of the supervisory force — its general ideology and its adherence or nonadherence to rules of conduct and procedure.

Ownership and Corporate Ideology.   Is the organization privately or publicly owned? Is it part of a large conglomerate or a free-standing independent operation? What does the ownership group think about such factors as unionization and participation of workers in management? These are all factors that help determine the ideology or philosophy of the organization.

Individual Factors

Any model of an industrial relations system must include a collection of variables that relate to the needs and characteristics of individuals in the workplace.

Economic, Safety, and Security Needs.   These needs are related to the physical well-being and security of the work force. Basic to the maintenance of the human organism, they are sometimes called physical or physiological needs.

One of the classic statements of the theory of human needs is found in Abraham Maslow's *Motivation and Personality.*[24] For Maslow, needs are arranged in a hierarchy with the physical needs at the bottom of the structure. In Maslow's theory, people are motivated by their physical needs when these needs are unsatisfied. Once satisfied, however, physical needs cease to motivate behavior, and needs at the next level in his hierarchy — security needs — now motivate behavior.

Socialization, Affiliation, and Power Needs. Several authors such as McClelland[25] and Maslow have pointed out the importance of these needs, which are thought to be learned (a product of our socialization) rather than instinctive (required to sustain life) such as our physical needs.

The social and psychological needs of individuals are "higher order" needs, meaning that they are higher on the Maslovian hierarchy, motivating behavior only after the lower level needs (physical, security) have been satisfied. Social and psychological needs are much more complicated than are physical needs, and are much more variable from person to person. While all people need food, air, and water and will direct their behavior to satisfy these needs, not everyone will modify his or her behavior to seek self-esteem or recognition.

Fairness and Equity Needs. Also learned, these needs are a product of life experiences. Human beings have a sense of equity and fairness in most exchange relationships (e.g., work, family, personal interaction) and they will adjust their behavior to achieve what they feel to be an equitable relationship between effort and reward.[26]

The sense of equity and fairness is a product of our perceptions, which vary depending on our experiences, our backgrounds, and our knowledge of the world around us. The sense of equity and fairness is an important force in determining our behavior and in determining our attitudes in work settings. If we feel that we have been treated unfairly or unjustly rewarded, we may change our behavior to correct the injustice. In addition, our attitudes and feelings about the person who is responsible for the unjust treatment may be permanently affected as well.

Values and Beliefs. This final factor associated with the behavior of individuals is what makes us truly different from each other in our behavior patterns and what accounts for much of the complexity in understanding human behavior. Our values and beliefs may be a product of our socialization process or of our personal experiences; our values will determine how attractive a certain reward may be (for example, money) for meeting one of our needs.[27] Some people value money quite highly and condition their whole lives to seek it; others are not so concerned with monetary rewards and will put forth only a minimum of effort to attain even a modest amount of it.

Conflict Tension

The interaction of the individual with the workplace may produce certain tensions. In some cases these tensions may be quite mild. For example, suppose that your job requires you to come to work at 7:00 A.M. to relieve the person who has been working on the previous shift; you have a physical need to sleep in because you were out late the night before. To the extent that the demands of the workplace conflict with your physical needs you will feel some tension in the work experience. Barbash states that the structure of industrialism causes these tensions, which result from a conflict between the demands of the workplace and the needs of workers.[28]

Barbash has compiled a lengthy list of tensions resulting from the work experience, including feelings he has labeled subordination, competitiveness, monotony and drudgery, exploitation, and economic uncertainty.[29] For example, the tension of subordination stems from the fact that in most large-scale businesses the work force is stratified into those who give orders and those who take orders. Those who are constantly following the orders given by others may feel that their needs for autonomy and freedom are being violated by the hierarchical structure of the workplace, and they may thus experience a tension from the work experience. The tension of competitiveness may develop when workers are constantly pitted against one another in competition for rewards. The tensions of monotony and drudgery develop when workers who have a need for variety and challenge are forced by the design of their jobs to do the same dull, routine work day after day. The tension of exploitation results when workers feel that they are being paid less than what they feel they are worth. The tension of economic uncertainty arises when workers never know from one day to another if they are going to be laid off or if the company they work for is going to be in business a year from now.

The major point to be learned here is that the work experience causes certain feelings to develop among individuals, feelings that may have consequences for their behavior. These feelings are affected by the external environment, the nature of the workplace, and the needs of individuals. Workers' attitudes toward their work change when there are changes in each of these three forces.[30]

Conflict Tension Resolution

Some workers may grumble or complain about tensions they experience at the workplace, tensions perhaps caused by an unpleasant interaction with a supervisor or with a coworker. Some employees may experience stress from having to scrape through the month on a paycheck that is not adequate to meet family expenses. Again, attitudes and behaviors about work may change as these tensions go unresolved. Workers who once enjoyed their jobs may now dread going to work. The satisfied employee or work group may become the disgruntled employee or work group because of the tensions of work.

Figure 2.1 identifies three possible methods by which the tensions or conflicts of work may be resolved. The first method, and perhaps the most common, is a reaction on the part of the employer (management) to resolve the conflict or tension experienced by the work force. Management-initiated methods of conflict tension resolution may take many forms depending on the source of the work tension. If employees are unhappy with wage levels, for example, the employer may resolve this tension by increasing wage rates. If employees feel disenfranchised in the workplace or feel that they have no voice in the operation of the enterprise, perhaps the company might institute some type of "workers' council" to enable them to have an input.[31] This can be a very effective way of reducing the tensions of the work experience. Programs such as job enrichment, job enlargement, job rotation, autonomous work groups, and management by objectives may all be viewed as management-initiated actions to deal with some of the tensions of the work experience.

A second type of conflict tension resolution taken by the individual worker is withdrawal. Withdrawal may take two forms, physical and psychological. Physical withdrawal from the workplace simply means to quit or turn over or to leave the employment relationship. One author has labeled this the "exit" option in dealing with workplace tension.[32] Psychological withdrawal refers to withdrawing effort, commitment, or psychological involvement from the work experience but not actually leaving the employment relationship. Another author has called this the "renegotiation of the effort bargain."[33] In some cases workers deliberately slow down and restrict output. In other cases they may abuse sick leave benefits or exhibit absenteeism and tardiness behavior patterns. In extreme cases employees turn to drugs or alcohol to resolve workplace tensions.

A third way of reducing the tensions of work may be through collective action, perhaps through unionization. The strength of this type of response will be dependent on what the tensions are, the nature of the workplace, the needs and values of the individual workers, and the nature of the environmental forces that affect the system. The unionization response is one that has been chosen by a large number of workers to ameliorate the tensions of the work experience; it is also one which has been considered and rejected by many workers as well.

Process and Rules of Conflict Resolution

In Figure 2.1 collective bargaining is emphasized as the main method used by unions in resolving or attempting to resolve the tensions experienced by members of the work group. As we shall see in later chapters, collective bargaining will begin only when a majority of the employees in a work group choose this as the appropriate response to deal with the tensions of work. Collective bargaining is a complex process and is the major activity of labor unions in dealing with workplace problems.

Collective bargaining is a process; it progresses over time and changes as the issues at the workplace change and as the needs of the work group change. The basic product of collective bargaining is the labor agreement, or the contract. In addition to setting such parameters as hours of work and compensation for them, the contract specifies when workers may or may not strike. Grievance procedures and the process for administering the labor agreement are also parts of the labor agreement.

The labor agreement is the written summary of all the issues that have been agreed to by labor and management during negotiations. While it is in effect, its provisions govern most of the interactions between labor and management at the workplace. Many commentators on the subject of collective bargaining focus exclusively on this rule-making aspect of collective negotiation.[34]

Effects of the Rules — Workplace and Environmental Outcomes

Workplace Outcomes.   It is important to emphasize, of course, that these rules have concrete effects on the workplace, including both employer and work force. Rules concerning wages will likely involve a schedule of raises and perhaps an increase in the wage bill for the employer. Rules regarding the hours of work may regulate how much overtime a particular worker may work and may require the employer to hire additional workers to meet production demands at peak periods. The regulation of working conditions may make the workplace safer or cleaner for the employee, but may also require employer to purchase new equipment or to limit the use of some equipment currently being used.

These workplace changes have an effect on the day-to-day operations and work lives of both management and workers, and are directed at resolving the tensions of the work experience. The feedback loop in Figure 2.1 illustrates this relationship.

Environmental Outcomes.   It is important to realize that the changes at the workplace will eventually have an effect on the external environment of the system. It is short-sighted to talk about the effects of collective bargaining only at the workplace because the workplace is part of a larger social and economic system.

Environmental outcomes from the bargaining process are effects that may take a long time to develop. For example, if unions are successful in negotiating favorable wage rates, what will these rates do to the cost of producing the product? How will they affect the competitiveness of the employer and the industry in the national and world economies? How will this increase in wages affect the labor force? How will it affect society if income is redistributed from employers to workers? Can collective bargaining contribute to inflation? If so, what should be the response from the government or society to deal with this problem? The same questions can be raised concerning the environmental or long-term effects from changes in hours of work or working conditions or any other subjects that are negotiated through bargaining.

Not only is the environment affected by the outcomes of bargaining; it can also affect the bargaining process in return. For example, in the inflation instance mentioned above, if bargaining is found to contribute to inflation, this finding may provoke a governmental response to control collectively bargained wage rates. The wage and price controls of the 1940s, 1950s, and 1970s are examples of such a response. If a strike has the effect of causing a threat to the national safety and welfare, this may necessitate a political response to stop the strike and to protect the citizens. If either unions or employers engage in repeated acts that threaten the well-being of society or of the economy, there will be some response from the political system to control these acts. New legislation may be necessary to restore order to the system. Perhaps a new political leader may be elected because of his or her position on issues relating to the industrial relations system.

Summary

The concept of the industrial relations system is an important one. The model in Figure 2.1 illustrates the idea that labor relations and its processes and outcomes are a product of the external environment, of the workplace, and of individuals in the workplace. Unionization is a product of a collective (work group) response to the tensions of work and can be seen as one way of ameliorating these tensions through collective bargaining. Collective bargaining is not the only means of dealing with the tensions of the work experience — there are management-level and individual-level ways of dealing with these tensions as well. Finally, in this chapter I have emphasized that labor relations and collective bargaining have effects not only on the workplace and on the individuals who work in that workplace, but also on society as a whole and on the economy as a whole.

Discussion Questions

1. Why have the predictions of Marx about the role of unions not proved true in the United States?
2. Identify the critical differences in working conditions between the *Cleveland Herald* and the *Cleveland Leader* (see Commons's quote). Where would you rather work? Why?

3. Which side would you take in the Ross–Dunlop debate? Who has the best theoretical argument? Who has the most realistic argument?
4. What do you see as the major differences between the Dunlop industrial relations systems theory and the model in Figure 2.1?
5. What do you see as the most important factor in determining the unionization of a work group — the environment, the workplace, or the characteristics of the members of the group?
6. Think about a job you have had in the past. What tensions of work did you experience? How did you resolve these tensions?
7. Reread the newspaper article that introduces this chapter. Do you agree or disagree with Murray Seeger of the AFL–CIO? Do the statements of national political figures have an effect on the negotiations process? How?

Notes

[1]Herbert G. Heneman, Jr., "Toward a General Conceptual System of Industrial Relations: How Do We Get There?" In Gerald G. Somers, ed., *Essays in Industrial Relations Theory*, Ames: Iowa State University Press, 1969, p. 4.

[2]A. N. J. Blain and John Gennard, "Industrial Relations Theory — A Critical Review," *British Journal of Industrial Relations* 8 (3) (November 1970): 389.

[3]V. I. Lenin, *What Is To Be Done?* Quoted in Selig Perlman, *A Theory of the Labor Movement*, New York: Macmillan, 1928, p. 8.

[4]See Richard Hyman, *Industrial Relations: A Marxist Introduction*, New York: Macmillan, 1975, for a modern-day Marxist approach to the subject.

[5]Philip Taft, "Commons-Perlman Theory: A Summary," *Industrial Relations Research Association Proceedings*, Madison, WI: Industrial Relations Research Association, 1950: 142.

[6]Sidney and Beatrice Webb, *Industrial Democracy*, London: Longmans, 1902, p. 173.

[7]John R. Commons, *The Economics of Collective Action*, Madison: University of Wisconsin Press, 1970, p. 1.

[8]Ibid., p. 2.

[9]Ibid., p. 25–29.

[10]Perlman, *A Theory of the Labor Movement*, Chapter 5.

[11]John T. Dunlop, *Wage Determination Under Trade Unions*, New York: Macmillan, 1944, Chapters 3, 4.

[12]Arthur M. Ross, *Trade Union Wage Policy*, Berkeley: University of California Press, 1948, p. 12.

[13]Ibid., p. 7.

[14]John T. Dunlop, "Framework for Analysis of Industrial Relations: Two Views," *Industrial and Labor Relations Review* 3 (April 1950): 384.

[15]John T. Dunlop, *Industrial Relations Systems*, New York: Henry Holt, 1958. Dunlop borrowed from the work of Talcott Parsons and N. J. Smelser as found in their *Economy and Society*, London: Routledge and Kegan Paul, 1956.

[16]Dunlop, *Industrial Relations Systems*, pp. 16, 14.

[17]C. J. Margerison, "What Do We Mean by Industrial Relations — A Behavioral Science Approach," *British Journal of Industrial Relations* 7 (2) (July 1969):273.

[18]Stephen Hill and Keith Thurley, "Sociology and Industrial Relations," *British Journal of Industrial Relations* 12 (2) (July 1974):149. See also Gerald G. Somers, "Bargaining Power and Industrial Relations Theory," in Somers, ed., *Essays in Industrial Relations Theory*, p. 44. Somers says that the "heart of industrial relations is in the worker and his interactions with other workers and management at the workplace."

[19]Heneman, "Toward a General Conceptual System of Industrial Relations," p. 15.

[20]S. J. Wood et al., "The Industrial Relations System as a Basis for Theory in Industrial Relations," *British Journal of Industrial Relations* 13 (3) (1975):300.

[21]See Jack Barbash, *The Elements of Industrial Relations* (Madison: University of Wisconsin Press, 1984) for more on this topic; quotation, p. 9.

[22]Wood et al., "The Industrial Relations System as a Basis for Theory in Industrial Relations," p. 298.

[23]Joan Woodward, *Management and Technology*, London: HMSO, 1966.

[24]A. J. Maslow, *Motivation and Personality*, New York: Harper, 1954.

[25]David C. McClelland, *The Achieving Society*, Princeton, NJ: Van Nostrand Reinhold, 1961.

[26]J. Stacy Adams, "Toward an Understanding of Inequity," *Journal of Abnormal and Social Psychology* 67 (1963):422–436.

[27]Victor H. Vroom, *Work and Motivation*, New York: Wiley, 1964.

[28]Jack Barbash, "The Elements of Industrial Relations," *British Journal of Industrial Relations* 2 (1) (1964):66–78.

[29]Jack Barbash, "The Tension of Work: Can We Reduce the Costs of Industrialism?" *Dissent*, Winter 1972:240–243.

[30]Barbash, "The Elements of Industrial Relations," pp. 35–36.

[31]See Fred K. Foulkes, *Personnel Policies in Large Nonunion Companies*, Englewood Cliffs, NJ: Prentice-Hall, 1980, for an excellent discussion of such employer-initiated programs.

[32]Albert O. Hirschman, *Exit, Voice and Loyalty*, Cambridge, MA: Harvard University Press, 1970, p. 4.

[33]Hilde Behrend, "The Effort Bargain," *Industrial and Labor Relations Review* 10 (4) (July 1957): 503–515.

[34]Allen Flanders, "Collective Bargaining: A Theoretical Analysis," *British Journal of Industrial Relations* 6 (1) (March 1968):1–26.

THE UNION MOVEMENT LOOKS IN THE MIRROR

By William Serrin

Bal Harbour, Fla. — The executive council of the AFL–CIO assembles here for a few days every winter on the Florida coast, far removed, it would seem, from the woes of the workaday world.

Last week the attention of many of the delegates at this year's meeting was firmly captured by an unusually frank study, two and a half years in the making, on the future of work and the ways in which profound changes in the work place, technical and otherwise, are affecting American unions.

Among other things, the study calls for far greater emphasis on participation in unions by their members; reaching out to non-union workers, perhaps through new categories of membership; an easing of the customary adversarial relationships with business, whenever possible; far greater emphasis on organizing, with stress on new, innovative organizing methods.

As has been the case at most of these gatherings in recent years, there was a discernible feeling of depression among union presidents and their staff assistants — although last week's pronouncements on unemployment and other difficulties confronting the working class would, to critics of labor, have a hollow ring, delivered as they were amid the glitter of an ocean-front hotel.

One immediate cause of the gloom was, of course, the fact that the federation's Presidential candidate, Walter F. Mondale, was soundly thrashed by President Reagan last year.

But for all its well-documented woes, the American labor movement appears in some respects to be surprisingly vigorous. Unions in recent weeks have won organizing victories among clerical workers at Yale University and in the Iowa state university system.

Elsewhere, unions have shown strength in attracting white-collar and other professionals, including engineers, and are finding that many women are signing up.

Unionism is reported to be strong among American orchestras, around television studios and movie lots and in the sports industry. The Hotel Employees and Restaurant Employees International Union is planning a new, spirited organizing campaign. The American Federation of State, County and Municipal Employees has taken the lead on the issue of pay equity, seeking to increase the wages of women to the level men earn in comparable jobs.

The depression here might have been further diminished by the study on work and unions, which the AFL–CIO regards as a blueprint for its activity in coming years.

American unions face enormous difficulties, as the report makes clear. Unions frequently "find themselves behind the pace of change," the study said, and added, "It is not enough merely to search for more effective ways of doing what we always have done; we must expand our notions of what it is workers can do through unions."

An immediate goal, it was agreed here, is shoring up union membership. A recent report by the Federal Bureau of Labor Statistics shows membership in unions and employees associations at 18.8 percent of the work force in 1984, down from 23.0 percent in 1980 and from a high in recent years of 24.1 percent in 1979.

Chapter 3

The Unionized Labor Force and Union Government

The industrial relations system exists within a certain environment, as was discussed in Chapter 2. One of the important elements of this environment is the labor force — the portion of the population that is either working or available and looking for work. To a large extent, the character and nature of workplace relationships are determined by the characteristics and workplace experiences of those in the labor force. As the *New York Times* article points out, leaders in the labor movement in recent years have come to realize that labor unions must adapt to the changes that are occurring in the labor force if they are to survive into the twenty-first century. The success or failure of these attempts at adaptation to these changes may be the key to the future of the labor movement in the United States.

The labor force can be described in many ways and can be categorized on many dimensions. In this chapter I first focus on several demographic and occupational characteristics of the labor force. The second section of this chapter examines that segment of the total labor force that is composed of union members, identifies several characteristics of the unionized labor force, and discusses the importance of the unionized labor force to the overall economy. The third section of this chapter describes the structure and government of labor unions in the United States and identifies the major structural characteristics of the labor movement.

The Labor Force

Definition

The term *labor force* has a very precise and technical definition when used by professionals in the field of industrial relations. The reason for this precision is that the U.S. Department of Labor is charged with the responsibility for collecting and publicizing labor force information such as the unemployment rate. The definition of what is meant by the labor force has an effect on the data that are collected and on the results that are published by the Labor Department. To assume continuity and consistency in our labor force statistics, precise and exact definitions of terms are necessary.

The labor force as defined by the U.S. Department of Labor consists of that segment of the U.S. population aged 16 years and older who are either working or actively seeking employment. The term *working* includes persons who did any work at all as paid employees during the week that includes the twelfth of the month or who worked 15 hours or more as unpaid workers in a family enterprise. Included also in this definition of *working* are workers who are temporarily absent from work because of illness, vacation, bad weather, strikes, or other personal reasons. Persons in the armed forces are included in the total number of persons in the labor force.[1]

The Unemployed

Those who are unemployed are those who did not work during the survey week but who were available for work and who actively sought work. Included in the unemployed group also are people laid off from their jobs and waiting reinstatement, or those waiting to start a new job within 30 days. Those persons classified as "not in the labor force" are those people aged 16 years and over who were in school, retired, unable to work because of physical or mental disability, unpaid home workers, or voluntarily idle, as well as those who were discouraged and who had stopped looking for work because they believed that no jobs were available for them during the survey week.[2]

Data Sources

The data for employed and unemployed persons is collected by the Census Bureau for the Bureau of Labor Statistics (BLS) every month through a household survey called the Current Population Survey (CPS). The CPS data are collected from a scientifically selected sample of about 60,000 households that are representative of the civilian population on such dimensions as age, sex, race, and earnings.[3] The basic methodology for collecting labor force statistics in the United States and the concepts behind the terms *employed* and *unemployed* have been in place since 1940.[4]

Data published by the Department of Labor's Bureau of Labor Statistics indicate that in June 1986 there were 180,503,000 persons in the United States who were noninstitutionalized and who were over the age of 16 years. Of this group, 119,644,000 persons, or 66.3 percent, were in the labor force. This percentage of the adult population in the labor force is referred to as the labor force participation rate (LFPR). Of this group, 110,869,000 persons were employed and 8,775,000 persons — 7.3 percent — were unemployed.

Labor force statistics may be divided along a number of dimensions, of course, in addition to the basic distinction between employed and unemployed. For example, the labor force may be divided between men and women. The BLS data for June 1986 indicates that there were 66,687,000 men and 52,966,000 women in the labor force. The labor force participation rate for men was 77.7 percent; for women the rate was 55.9 percent. The BLS data may also be disaggregated by race; in June 1986 there were 103,253,000 whites in the labor force (LFPR = 66.5 percent) and 12,981,000 blacks in the labor force (LFPR = 65.0 percent). Further disaggregation of labor force data can be made on the bases of age, occupation, and earnings.[5]

Labor Force Trends

It is important to spend some time studying and analyzing current labor force statistics; these data give us a picture of the state of the labor force at the present time. It is also important, however, to have some feeling for trends in labor force statistics; these trends tell us how the labor force has been changing over time and also may give us some insight into how the labor force is likely to change in the future. Through developing an understanding of the evolution of the labor force we may also gain some awareness of how the industrial relations system has been changing and how it may change in the future. Although several trends are discernible in the development of the labor force, there are four that are of critical importance in determining the present and future character of the industrial relations system: (1) the increase in the LFPR of the total population caused primarily by the increase in the LFPR of women; (2) the change in the industrial concentration of the labor force; (3) the change in the hours worked by those in the labor force; and (4) the change in the geographic concentration of the labor force.

Increase in Labor Force Participation Rate of Women

Not only are more people working in the United States than ever before, but a greater percentage of the population is working now than ever before. Especially dramatic is the change in the labor force participation rate of women. In 1948, only 32.7 percent of the civilian population of women aged 16 years and older were in the labor force; in 1986 this figure was almost 56 percent. Contrastingly, for men the percentage of civilian men aged 16 years and over who are in the labor force has dropped from 86.6 percent in 1948 to about 78 percent in 1986. Recent labor force statistics from the Labor Department show that in July 1986 the percentage of women in the labor force had increased to 44.3 percent and the percentage of men had declined to 55.7 percent. Forty years ago women comprised less than 30 percent of the labor force.[6]

The increase in the number of women in the labor force and the dramatic increase in the female LFPR over the past few years has had and will continue to have a great impact on the industrial relations system. One example of this is the attention given to the topic of comparable worth, considered by some to be "the most controversial labor issue of the '80's."[7] The comparable worth debate centers on the persistent disparity between the average earnings of men and the average earnings of women in the labor force. Proponents of the comparable worth concept point out that average wages for "women's jobs" are lower than average wages for "men's jobs" even when these jobs are of equal value as measured by the job evaluation criteria of skill, effort, responsibility, and working conditions. It is argued that discrimination has crowded women into certain jobs (such as nursing or teaching) and that this crowding has increased the supply of labor in these jobs and depressed wage rates. To remedy this depression of wage rates for "women's jobs," several large lawsuits are pending that seek damages that in some instances run into the hundreds of millions of dollars.[8] Labor unions, in many instances, have been the moving force in carrying these suits through the court system on behalf of their female members. Increased concern with compensation issues that affect women can be expected in the years ahead.

A second implication that the increase in the number of women in the labor force may have for the industrial relations system involves union power and influence. Traditionally, unions have been regarded as bastions of male dominance. Although this is changing somewhat, the unionized labor force still tends to be more dominated by males than the labor force as a whole. For example, in 1980 women constituted 42.5 percent of the total labor force, but only 30.1 percent of the membership of the AFL–CIO. In a 1980 study of union membership, it was found that differences in the education, age, location of work, and incidence of part-time work between men and women accounted for slightly over 50 percent of the differences in union membership levels for men and women.[9] The other 50 percent of the difference could not be explained by these factors and may be attributed to differences in attitudes between men and women regarding the value of union representation. While the labor movement is making some strides in increasing the participation of women in its leadership cadre, there is still much that needs to be done before women reach parity with men in their influence in the labor movement. The alienation that some women feel from the labor movement may be one of the factors responsible for the decline in the total labor force organized by unions in recent years.

Change in the Industrial Concentration of the Labor Force

Dramatic changes have occurred in the industrial concentration of the labor force over the past years (Table 3.1). In 1919 over 47 percent of the

TABLE 3-1   Industrial Concentration of the Labor Force, 1983

Year	Total Nonagricultural Labor Force	Goods	Service
1919	27,078,000	12,823,000	14,275,000
1965	60,765,000	21,926,000	38,839,000
1983	90,138,000	23,394,000	66,744,000

Source: U.S. Department of Labor, *Handbook of Labor Statistics, June 1985,* pp. 174–175.

nonagricultural labor force worked in goods-producing (mining, construction, and manufacturing) occupations, and that 53 percent worked in service-producing industries. In 1983 the figures were 26 percent of the labor force employed in goods-producing industries and 74 percent employed in service industries. Employment over the 63-year period has increased 86 percent in the goods-producing industries overall. Employment in the service industries has been up 360 percent over the same time period. Employment in the goods-producing industries has been reasonably stable since 1966, hovering around the 24 million mark. Employment in the service industries, contrastingly, has been growing rapidly over the past 20 years, growing from less than 40 million in 1965 to almost 67 million in 1983 — a growth rate of 68 percent over the 17-year period.[10]

The changes in the industrial concentration of the labor force has had and will continue to have a major impact on the industrial relations system. The goods-producing industries have traditionally been strongholds of unionism. As these industries decline or stabilize in employment, the unions that traditionally have represented these workers will decline or stagnate in membership as well. A good example is the United Steelworkers of America, which reported only 707,000 members for 1983, down from over 1 million members in 1975; as employment in the steel manufacturing industry has declined in recent years, so has the membership of the Steelworkers Union.[11] Similar examples can be seen in the mining, railway, and printing industries.

A related factor is that work in the service industries is frequently office work away from the noise, dirt, and danger of the factory. More favorable working conditions and promotional opportunities can make office work a more favorable working environment and one where workers feel less of a need for a union. This does not mean that there are no unions of office workers; the Service Employees Union is making a concerted attempt to organize office workers, particularly women, today. Nevertheless, the service sector remains largely nonunion. Finally, it may be argued that the service industries are less susceptible to the cyclical "booms and busts" in employment that have come to characterize manufacturing over the past few years and are thus more stable and secure — jobs that, again, are less likely to be unionized.

Decrease in Hours Worked

A third trend characterizing the modern labor force is the decrease in average number of hours worked by the average member of the labor force per week. Data from the Bureau of Labor Statistics show that since 1950 average weekly hours have declined over 12 percent from 39.8 hours in 1950 to 35.0 hours per week in 1983. In the retail trade industry, the average has slipped from 40.4 hours per week in 1950 to 29.8 hours per week in 1983.[12] Some of the increase has been as a result of an increase in the number of part-time workers in the labor force; today, almost 14 percent of the members of the labor force work voluntarily part-time. The part-time labor force today is about 12.5 million people, 70 percent of whom are women. Of those who worked part-time, 78 percent were employed in either finance or wholesale and retail trade. The increase in part-time workers in the labor force is not the only reason for the decline in weekly hours over the past few years, however. The shortening of the work day, and the shortening of the work year through longer vacations and the addition of more holidays (e.g., Martin Luther King Day) have also had an effect on reducing the average number of hours worked by members of the labor force as well.

The effects of the decline in hours worked may be seen in a number of areas. It may be that this decline may serve to reinforce a feeling that work is only an instrumental activity, that it is only a means to a more desirable activity such as leisure. If workers do not identify with their work or do not see it as a "central life activity," they may desire to work only enough to maintain a certain standard of living and then work no more. This instrumental attitude toward work may mean that workers are less committed to work than in years gone by. The increased demand for leisure may, however, also be an expression of demand for increased leisure from increasingly affluent two-income families. The shortening of the working day and the increase in the number of part-time workers may also have an influence on union power at the workplace. If employers are able and willing to reduce the number of hours worked per day and are willing and able to offer part-time work to those who want it, this may serve to reduce a source of tension at the workplace and a potential union organizing issue.

Change in Geographical Concentration

The data in Table 3.2 document the change in the geographical concentration of the labor force since 1939, the earliest date for which this information is available. In 1939 the states in the Northeastern and North Central regions (Regions 1, 2, 3, and 5 in Table 3.2) accounted for 65.3 percent of the total number of employed persons. In 1983, however, these Northeastern and North Central states accounted for only 47.5 percent of the total number of employed persons. Overall, the number of employed persons increased almost 200 percent from 1939 to 1983.

TABLE 3-2 U.S. Employment (nonagricultural) by Region, 1939–1983

Region	1939	1983
Region 1	(2,609,000)	(5,540,700)
Maine	212,400	420,900
New Hampshire	147,800	408,100
Vermont	74,800	205,000
Massachusetts	1,371,500	2,671,200
Rhode Island	243,000	393,200
Connecticut	558,700	1,442,300
Region 2	(5,377,900)	(10,434,100)
New York	4,130,900	7,285,300
New Jersey	1,247,000	3,148,800
Region 3	(4,514,400)	(9,275,700)
Pennsylvania	2,701,500	4,518,800
Delaware	75,900	266,100
Maryland	490,100	1,699,600
District of Columbia	333,500	595,700
Virginia	539,900	2,195,500
West Virginia	373,500	581,100
Region 4	(3,316,100)	(14,731,100)
North Carolina	622,700	2,402,200
South Carolina	310,100	1,182,400
Georgia	526,700	2,272,200
Florida	390,500	3,893,000
Kentucky	382,500	1,154,100
Tennessee	475,300	1,720,000
Alabama	405,300	1,318,400
Mississippi	203,000	788,800
Region 5	(7,454,400)	(17,341,700)
Ohio	1,783,800	4,083,800
Indiana	817,400	2,007,400
Illinois	2,294,900	4,501,100
Michigan	1,348,100[1]	3,186,300
Wisconsin	666,800	1,848,900
Minnesota	543,400	1,714,200
Region 6	(2,089,500)	(10,126,100)
Arkansas	198,000	740,000
Louisiana	410,100	1,564,100
Oklahoma	326,200	1,169,700
Texas	1,075,700	6,174,200
New Mexico	79,500	478,100
Region 7	(1,787,700)	(4,462,500)
Iowa	429,600	1,021,500
Missouri	838,600	1,917,000
Nebraska	223,600	608,500
Kansas	295,900	915,500

(continued)

TABLE 3-2   *(continued)*

Region	1939	1983
Region 8	(663,700)	(2,844,500)
North Dakota	72,100	249,400
South Dakota	85,900	233,100
Montana	108,100	269,900
Wyoming	54,300	203,400
Colorado	233,400	1,322,400
Utah	109,900	566,300
Region 9	(1,942,300)	(11,800,400)
Arizona	95,500	1,064,400
Nevada	34,800	404,900
California	1,812,000	9,928,000
Hawaii	—	403,100
Region 10	(774,000)	(3,073,200)
Idaho	84,400	316,900
Washington	431,000	1,579,400
Oregon	258,600	963,900
Alaska	—	213,000

[1]Estimated.

Source: Data for 1939 from U.S. Department of Labor, *Handbook of Labor Statistics,* *December 1980,* pp. 161–163. Data for 1983 from U.S. Department of Labor, *Handbook of Labor Statistics, June 1985,* pp. 207–209.

In the Northeastern and North Central states the overall growth was 113 percent; in the remaining states the growth was 345 percent.[13]

A similarly instructive look at geographic growth rates in the United States is to divide the nation into right-to-work and nonright-to-work states. Chapter 7 discusses in more detail that a right-to-work state is a state whose voters have outlawed the use of the union shop, in which all workers are represented by the union and all are required to pay union dues as a condition of employment. In the 20 right-to-work states in 1983 (Virginia, North Carolina, South Carolina, Georgia, Florida, Tennessee, Alabama, Mississippi, Arkansas, Louisiana, Texas, Iowa, Nebraska, Kansas, North Dakota, South Dakota, Wyoming, Utah, Arizona, and Nevada) the number of employed persons increased from 16,013,500 in 1965 to 29,517,800 in 1983 for a overall growth of 84.3 percent. In the nonright-to-work states the overall growth was 35.4 percent; for the nation as a whole the number of employed persons increased 48.3 percent during the years 1965–1983. In 1965, 26.4 percent of the number of employed persons in the United States worked in a right-to-work state; in 1983 this figure had increased to 32.9 percent.

This shift in employment from the North Central and Northeastern states to the Southern and Western states, and from the nonright-to-work states to the right-to-work states, also has important implications for our industrial relations system. The shift to the West and the South may reflect lifestyle preferences and a desire to migrate from the Snow Belt to the Sun Belt or persons migrating to seek employment opportunities. This may be an outgrowth of the increased demand for leisure time discussed above and may be part of changing preferences for work and leisure and a changing orientation toward the job as one's central life interest. In addition, the expansion in employment in the Southern and right-to-work states will have an effect on union growth as unions find it harder to win representation elections in Southern states than in non-Southern states.[14]

The Unionized Labor Force

The unionized labor force is comprised of members of the labor force who are also union members. Estimates for 1984 place U.S. labor organization membership at about 18.3 million persons, or 16.1 percent of the total labor force.[15] As can be seen from Table 3.3, total labor organization membership in the United States has been declining since 1978; the percentage of the labor force that is unionized has been dropping steadily since 1970. An alternative method of computing the percentage of the labor force that is unionized involves subtracting out

TABLE 3-3   U.S. Labor Organization Membership, 1970–1982[1] (in thousands)

		Civilian Labor Force[2]	
Year	Membership	Number	Percent Members
1970	21,248	82,771	25.7
1971	21,327	84,382	25.3
1972	21,657	87,034	24.9
1973	22,276	89,429	24.9
1974	22,809	91,949	24.8
1975	22,361	93,775	23.8
1976	22,662	96,158	23.6
1977	22,456	99,009	22.7
1978	22,757	102,251	22.3
1979	22,579	104,962	21.5
1980	22,366	106,940	20.9
1981	—	—	—
1982	19,763	110,204	17.9

[1]Includes active members reported by unions, but excludes Canadian members.
[2]Revised from "Total Labor Force" classification in Table 2 of the 1982–83 edition of the directory.
— Data not available.

Source: C. Gifford, ed., *Directory of U.S. Labor Organizations, 1982–83 Edition* (Washington, DC: BNA) and Bureau of Labor Statistics, *Handbook of Labor Statistics, December 1983* (Bulletin 2175).

those members of the labor force who are ineligible to join unions because they are supervisors, self-employed or unemployed, or in the military. Using this method of computation, the percentage of union members in the eligible work force is 27 percent. In 1984 the labor union membership in the United States was dispersed among over 50,000 local labor unions and 211 national labor organizations. Of the 211 national labor organizations, 96 were affiliated with the AFL–CIO. The membership of the AFL–CIO made up about 72 percent of total U.S. union membership.

Labor union membership in the United States is a minority of the total labor force; organized labor has always been a minority of the total labor force and probably always will be. Since 1970 the percentage of the labor force that is unionized has been declining. If present trends continue, by 1990 the percentage of the labor force that is unionized will drop to levels found in the 1930s — in the range of 10–12 percent. But even though it is a minority of the total labor force, the unionized labor force is in many instances a very powerful and influential component of that labor force. To understand this power and influence, it is instructive to consider the ways in which union membership is concentrated.

Industrial Concentration

Unionized labor is a minority of the overall labor force. In some industries, however, unionized labor comprises a majority of the labor force — in some cases, a large majority. The data in Table 3.4 show the number of workers and the percentage of the labor force on an industry-by-industry basis that were represented by unions in 1980. The largest number of unionized workers were in services (mostly in education), the second largest number in durable goods manufacturing, and the next

TABLE 3-4   Industrial Concentration of Unionized Workers, 1980

	Number	% Labor Force
All industries	22,493,000	25.7
Agriculture	55,000	3.8
Mining	314,000	35.2
Construction	1,651,000	33.1
Manufacturing (durables)	4,720,000	37.6
Manufacturing (nondurables)	2,589,000	30.7
Transportation, communications, and utilities	3,113,000	51.5
Trade	1,896,000	10.9
Finance, insurance, and real estate	250,000	4.8
Services	5,719,000	22.8
Forestry and fishing	14,000	16.1
Public administration	2,172,000	40.5

Source: C. Gifford, ed., *Directory of U.S. Labor Organizations, 1982–83 Edition* (Washington, DC: BNA), pp. 53–55. Reprinted with permission.

TABLE 3-5   Percentage of the Labor Force Unionized by Industry, 1930–1984

Year	Manuf.	Mining	Constr.	Transport.		Service	Govt.	Total Non-farm Empl.
				Total	Rail			
1984	26.0	17.7	23.5	38.7	n.a.	7.3	n.a.	19.4
1983	27.8	20.7	27.5	42.4	n.a.	7.7	34.3	20.7
1980	32.3	32.1	31.6	48.0	81.8	11.6	35.0	23.2
1977	35.5	35.1	35.7	47.6	80.3	n.a.	38.0	26.2
1975	36.0	32.0	35.4	46.6	78.6	13.9	39.5	28.9
1973	38.8	37.6	38.1	49.3	82.6	12.9	37.0	28.5
1970	38.7	35.7	39.2	44.8	n.a.	7.8	31.9	29.6
1966	37.4	35.7	41.4	50.3	n.a.	n.a.	26.0	29.6
1953	42.4	64.7	83.8	79.9	91.2	9.5	11.6	32.5
1947	40.5	83.1	87.1	67.0	75.8	9.0	12.0	32.1
1940	30.5	72.1	77.0	47.3	56.5	5.7	10.7	22.5
1939	22.8	65.4	77.3	50.9	50.3	6.0	10.8	21.2
1935	16.4	54.4	71.5	25.8	44.0	2.6	9.0	13.5
1930	7.8	21.3	64.5	22.6	39.0	2.3	8.5	12.7

Source: L. Troy and N. Sheflin, *Union Sourcebook* (West Orange, NJ: Industrial Relations Data Information Services, 1985), pp. 3–15. Reprinted with permission.

largest group in transportation. In percentage terms, the most heavily unionized industrial sectors were transportation, communications, and public utilities. The railroad industry was the most heavily unionized separate industry subdivision, with 82.8 percent of the employees in this industry represented by a union. The next most heavily unionized industrial subdivision was the Postal Service. In addition to these there are a number of industrial subdivisions in which more than half of the labor force was represented by unions in 1980; these include primary metals manufacturing, the manufacture of transportation equipment, the manufacture of paper, and the communications industry. With the exceptions of agriculture and of the finance, insurance, and real estate industries, every industry group has at least 10 percent of its labor force unionized.

It is interesting to observe the trends in the concentration of union membership over the past few years. Although the industry divisions are not exactly the same as those used in Table 3.4, the data in Table 3.5 are instructive as to the changes in union concentration over the past 54 years. Note that in most sectors, with the exception of government, the percentage of the labor force that is unionized has declined since 1950 or so. Construction has gone from an 84 percent organized labor force in 1953 to 23.5 percent today. Most of this loss has come in residential construction, which is almost totally nonunion today. The labor force in the mining industry has declined to a 17 percent union concentration rate, down from over 80 percent following World War II. In contrast, the public sector labor force is increasing in union concentration and may become the most intensively unionized industry within the next few years.

The major observation to be made from looking at Tables 3.4 and 3.5 is that union representation is concentrated in manufacturing, in transportation and communications, in education, and in public administration. Union representation is not widespread in wholesale and retail trade, in finance, insurance, real estate, and in most services. As noted in Table 3.1, these are the industries that have been expanding most rapidly over the past 20 years. Given the data in Tables 3.1 and 3.4, is there any wonder why union membership as a percentage of the total labor force has been declining?

Organizational Concentration

Table 3.6 lists all labor organizations with 100,000 members or more in 1982. This group of 45 of the 211 national unions accounted for 18,542,298 members, or 94 percent of total union membership. The top 10 labor organizations in Table 3.6 accounted for 10,728,158 members, or 54 percent of total union membership. We can see that some labor organizations are quite large indeed, with the Teamsters reporting the largest number of members (1.8 million), or almost 10 percent of total U.S. union membership.

The concentration of union membership into a few large organizations is partly the result of union industrial jurisdiction and the aggressive organization of workers by some unions in these industries. This concentration is also the result of union mergers, however. For example, in 1979–1982, 6 unions have merged just among unions in the AFL–CIO,[16] such as the Carpenters Union, the Food and Commercial Workers Union, the Service Employees Union, and the Clothing and Textile Workers Union. All these unions are among the top 20 in size already, and are growing larger as a result of merger activity. This trend in union mergers is expected to continue in the future. By the year 2000 it is possible that there will be only 30 to 40 separate national unions, all of them large. The union merger movement means that union membership will become increasingly concentrated in a smaller and smaller number of national unions that will have larger memberships, larger jurisdictions, and also larger treasuries.

Geographical Concentration

A third characteristic of the unionized labor force is its geographical concentration. The membership of U.S. unions is concentrated in certain areas of the nation. Some states have a large number of union members; others have a very small number. The industrial concentration of a state's economy and the number of union members in that state are interrelated. States with a large number of union members tend to be states with well-developed industrial and manufacturing sectors of the

TABLE 3-6 Unions Reporting 100,000 Active Members or More, Including Canadian Members, 1982[1]

Organization	Members	Organization	Members
Teamsters (IBT) (Ind.)	1,800,000	Electrical Workers (IUE)	190,786
National Education Association (NEA) (Ind.)	1,641,354	Letter Carriers (NALC)	175,000
Steelworkers (USW)	1,200,000	Graphic Communication Workers (GCIU)	165,000
Auto Workers (UAW)	1,140,370	Painters (PAT)	165,000
Food and Commercial (UFCW)	1,079,213	Firefighters (IAFF)	162,792
State, County (AFSCME)	950,000	United Electrical Workers (UE) (Ind.)	162,000
Electrical (IBEW)	883,000	Nurses (ANA) (Ind.)	160,357
Service Employees (SEIU)	700,000	Police (FOP)	160,000
Carpenters (CJA)	679,000	Iron Workers (BSOIW)	155,587
Machinists (IAM)	655,221	Bakery, Tobacco (BCTW)	152,100
Communications Workers (CWA)	650,000	Classified School (AACSE) (Ind.)	150,000
Teachers (AFT)	573,644	Mine Workers (UMW) (Ind.)	150,000
Laborers (LIUNA)	450,442	Sheet Metal Workers (SMW)	144,000
Clothing and Textile Workers (ACTWU)	400,000	Railway Clerks (BRAC)	140,000
Hotel and Restaurant (HERE)	375,000	Oil, Chemical Workers (OCAW)	125,000
Plumbers (PPF)	353,127	Bricklayers (BAC)	120,000
Operating Engineers (IUOE)	345,000	Transit Workers (ATU)	120,000
Ladies' Garment Workers (ILGWU)	276,000	Boilermakers (BBF)	117,642
Paperworkers (UPIU)	263,695	Longshoremen (ILA)	116,000
Musicians (AFM)	260,000	Transportation (UTU)	115,000
Retail (RWDSU)	250,000	Office and Professional (OPEIU)	112,793
Postal Workers (APWU)	248,000	Rubber Workers (URW)	100,175
Government Workers (AFGE)	210,000		

[1]All organizations not identified as (Ind.) are affiliated with the AFL-CIO.

Source: C. Gifford, ed., *Directory of U.S. Labor Organizations, 1984–85 Edition* (Washington, DC: BNA), p. 3.

economy. The top 10 states in total union members in 1982 are listed in Table 3.7.

With a few exceptions, union membership in the United States is largely concentrated in the North Central and Northeastern regions of the country. Union membership is definitely concentrated in a few states; in 1982 the top six states had 9,783,200 union members, half of all union members in the country. The bottom six states, by contrast, had only 1 percent of the total U.S. union membership. If we were to

TABLE 3-7   Top 10 States in Union Membership, 1982

New York	2,589,300
California	2,495,000
Illinois	1,261,300
Pennsylvania	1,229,800
Ohio	1,132,300
Michigan	1,075,500
Texas	781,600
New Jersey	612,900
Washington	516,900
Massachusetts	516,800

Source: L. Troy and N. Sheflin, *Union Sourcebook* (West Orange, NJ: Industrial Relations Data Information Services, 1985), p. 7-7.

divide the states based on their standing as right-to-work and nonright-to-work states, we would find that the 20 right-to-work states accounted for 4,165,000 union members or 18 percent of the total. These 20 states had a labor force of 29,517,800 in 1983 and accounted for about 33 percent of the nation's labor force. Only about 14 percent of the labor force in the right-to-work states were union members in 1982. In the non-right-to-work states in 1982, there were 18,710,132 union members, or about 29 percent of the labor force in these states were unionized. As we learned earlier, the labor force in the right-to-work states grew at a rate more than double that for the nonright-to-work states during the years 1965–1983. The growth of the labor force in areas and industries that are outside the area of greatest union strength may be a further cause of the decline of the percentage of the labor force that is unionized. The fact still remains, however, that for some states in the North Central

TABLE 3-8   Top 10 States in the Percentage of Unionized Labor Force, 1982

New York	35.8
Michigan	33.7
Washington	32.9
Hawaii	31.5
Alaska	30.4
West Virginia	28.9
Oregon	27.5
Illinois	27.5
Ohio	27.4
Pennsylvania	27.0

Source: L. Troy and N. Sheflin, *Union Sourcebook* (West Orange, NJ: Industrial Relations Data Information Services, 1985), p. 7-8.

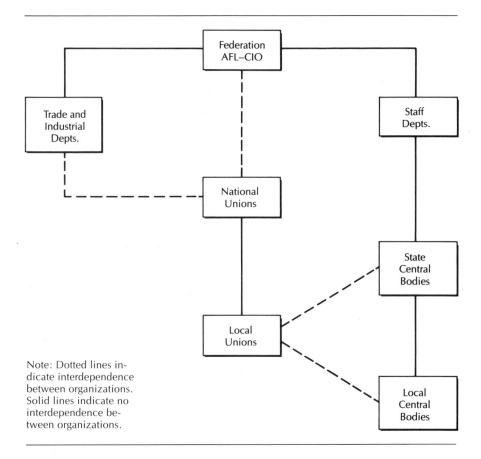

Note: Dotted lines indicate interdependence between organizations. Solid lines indicate no interdependence between organizations.

FIGURE 3-1 The Structure of Union Government

and Northeastern regions of the nation, the percentage of the labor force that is unionized is quite high — over 35 percent in New York in 1982. The contrast with a state like South Carolina, which had less than 6 percent of its labor force unionized in the same year, is quite dramatic.[17]

Union Government

The labor movement in the United States is organized into 211 national unions, over 50,000 local unions, and one dominant labor federation. The organizational structure of the labor movement in the United States may be sketched as in Figure 3.1. The major elements of this organizational model will be discussed below.

Federation

When most people think of organized labor in the United States, they first think of the AFL–CIO. The AFL–CIO itself is really not a union at all; rather, it is a federation of unions, each self-governing and autonomous. It might help to think of the AFL–CIO as the labor movement's equivalent to the United Nations. The U.N. is not a nation, but is rather a federation of autonomous, self-governing nations that have joined together for their mutual benefit. The U.N. provides many services to its members through its agencies such as UNICEF and the World Health Organization. The member nations, of course, do many things for themselves, such as defense, education, and economic regulation; but the U.N. provides them an opportunity to work together and cooperate with other countries on some issues. This is much the same type of opportunity that the AFL–CIO provides its member unions.

The federation was comprised in 1983 of 96 national unions, which enrolled 13,758,000 union members in that year. Thus the national unions affiliated with the AFL–CIO represented over 70 percent of all union members in the United States in 1983. Not all unions are members of the AFL–CIO. The two largest national unions in the United States, the Teamsters and the National Education Association, are not members. However, Table 3.6 indicates that of the 45 unions with more than 100,000 members in 1982, only five unions were not members of the AFL–CIO (the American Association of Classified School Employees, the United Electrical Workers, and the American Nurses Association, in addition to the Teamsters and the NEA).

The federation is supported by a per capita or a head tax that all national unions pay to the federation. In 1985 this per capita payment amounted to 31 cents per member per month for each national union.[18] In return for their financial support, the national unions and their affiliated local unions receive a variety of services from the federation, provided by the trade and industrial departments and by the staff departments of the federation, and by the state and local central bodies that are attached to the federation.

Trade and Industrial Departments.   In 1985 there were 8 trade and industrial departments within the federation; each is supported by a number of national unions that have a special need for the services that department may provide. The national unions pay an additional per capita tax to the federation to support the activities of the trade and industrial departments.

> Building and Construction Trades Department
> Food and Allied Services Trade Department
> Industrial Union Department
> Maritime Trades Department
> Metal Trades Department
> Professional and Employees Department
> Public Employees Department
> Union Label and Service Trades Department

Each department provides a certain type of service to its constituents. For example, the Building and Construction Trades Department (BCTD) is made up of the unions in the federation that have members who work in the construction industry. This department can provide assistance to local or national unions that are having jurisdictional disputes (disputes over whose members should be allowed to do what types of jobs on a construction project). The BCTD is active in lobbying for legislation that is of special interest to construction workers (such as the Davis-Bacon Act, which requires that prevailing area wages must be paid for all construction work supported by federal funds) and acts to coordinate union organizing campaigns in the construction industry that are targeted for certain areas of the country. The BCTD serves to coordinate the resources of the many unions that have members in the construction industry.

Staff Departments. There are 18 different staff departments in the AFL–CIO; these include political education, accounting, community services, organizing, international affairs, and research. These departments carry out the day-to-day administrative and political affairs of the organization.

One staff department of particular importance is the political education department, also called the Committee on Political Education (COPE). This department is dedicated to the support of candidates for political office who are sympathetic to the interests of organized labor. COPE provides direct financial and volunteer support to candidates for national office such as the presidency, U.S. senator, and U.S. representative. The value of COPE support for a candidate can be both positive and negative. While the financial and volunteer services that COPE can provide a candidate may help his or her campaign, identification of the candidate as a "labor candidate" may hurt his or her standing with the voters if this is perceived as control of the candidate by the interests of organized labor. The Legislation Department of the AFL–CIO handles most of the federation's lobbying activities in support of or in opposition to specific pieces of legislation in Congress. The Organization and Field Services Department of the federation handles most of the organizational activities of the federation. At the present time the Organizational and Field Services Department is the most extensive of the staff departments, and it alone receives 20 percent of the total operating budget of the federation.[19]

State and Local Central Bodies. The state and local central bodies are "minifederations" at the state and local levels and are comprised of local unions in a state or city that choose to affiliate with them. The state and local central bodies are chartered by the AFL–CIO National Office but are supported by a per capita tax paid by local unions. The services provided by these central bodies are much like the services provided by the AFL–CIO's staff departments, but at the state or local level. For example, the state central body has its own Committee on Political Education (COPE) and provides support for candidates for state office. A city central body in a locality also has a COPE fund and uses it to support candidates for local office such as mayor, city council, county commissioners, and school board members. Most of the activities of employees of the 51 state central bodies (including Puerto Rico) and the 740 city central bodies go to support or oppose political candidates or political issues that affect organized labor.

National Unions

The national unions are the most important, and most powerful, segment of the labor movement in the United States. Figure 3.1 indicates that the national unions are independent from the federation; the national unions are free to affiliate or withdraw from the federation as they please, and several of them have done this in recent years. One example is the United Auto Workers, which withdrew from the federation in 1968 because of philosophical differences between Walter Reuther and George Meany over support of the Vietnam War. The UAW reaffiliated with the AFL–CIO in 1981. Of course, as I have mentioned before, not all national unions belong to the AFL–CIO.

The national unions are self-governing, self-sustaining, and autonomous. All national unions have constitutions and hold conventions at least once very five years to elect national union officers and to attend to other official business of the organization, such as to amend their constitutions or to change their dues. Between conventions the affairs of the national unions are managed by the elected officers and staff of the organizations, just like any business enterprise. It is important to realize that labor organizations are a type of business enterprise and that while they do not have stockholders or pay dividends, they do sell a service, collect revenue, and accumulate assets. The data in Table 3.9 show the annual receipts and total assets in 1983 for the 10 largest unions — about $2.4 billion in that year. To give a rough comparison in the business world, this would represent about the same level of sales that the nation's third largest fast food chain, Wendy's, had in 1983 (McDonald's sold over $8 billion in 1983).

The leaders of the national unions are elected at the conventions of the national unions, held at least once every five years. In some cases the elections of the national union officers are controversial and hotly contested, with campaigns and issues that rival election to a major political position. The contest between Lloyd McBride and Edward Sadlowski to fill the vacant post in the Steelworkers Union left by the retirement of I. W. Abel in 1977 was such a campaign. Sadlowski lost the election, but the issues raised in the campaign received national attention. Sadlowski received campaign contributions from sympathizers outside the union to support his cause, even though the Steelworkers'

TABLE 3-9   Financial Statement of the Ten Largest National Unions, 1983

Union	1982 Members	1983 Receipts	1983 Assets
International Brotherhood of Teamsters	1,800,000	$242,948,890	$160,287,246
National Education Association	1,641,354	87,562,713	38,147,324
United Steelworkers of America	1,200,000	572,746,413	227,499,718
United Automobile Workers	1,140,370	369,165,278	610,643,703
United Food and Commercial Workers	1,079,213	128,039,117	66,473,693
American Federation of State, County and Municipal Workers	950,000	111,068,720	15,878,203
International Brotherhood of Electrical Workers	883,000	247,976,768	425,849,947
Service Employees International Union	700,000	43,100,213	18,707,422
International Brotherhood of Carpenters and Joiners	679,000	461,876,340	144,891,235
International Association of Machinists	655,221	135,135,479	158,806,645
Total	10,728,158	$2,399,619,931	$1,867,185,136

Source: C. Gifford, ed., *Directory of U.S. Labor Organizations, 1984–85 Edition* (Washington, DC: BNA), Appendix A.

constitution forbade this. Sadlowski later sued the Steelworkers Union to have this provision taken out of the union constitution. Unfortunately for him, Sadlowski lost his case before the U.S. Supreme Court in 1982.[20]

The national unions provide a variety of services to their members; very large national unions such as the Teamsters or the Food and Commercial Workers are able to provide some services that smaller unions cannot. At the very least, however, all but the very smallest national unions offer their members services in the following areas.

Bargaining and strike assistance
Grievance handling and arbitration
Research
Education
Political action
Legal assistance
Organizing
Publications and public relations
Special departments[21]

Bargaining and Strike Assistance.   The type of service that a national union can offer its members in support of their collective bargaining activities varies with the type of union. As Chapter 9 describes in more detail, unions with an industrial structure (those that represent all workers in a particular industry regardless of skill) that negotiate national contracts frequently centralize most bargaining activities with the national union officers. Some national unions provide local unions with an employee of the national union called an international representative or a district representative to conduct negotiations for the locals. In some cases the representative of the national union may serve in a consultative capacity to the locals and may advise them on bargaining strategy while not actually sitting in on negotiations. The national union may also be able to provide some research support to aid local unions in their bargaining by providing information on the financial outlook of the employer or on the results of other negotiations that have recently been conducted in this industry.

Related to the support of bargaining activities is the strike assistance that may be supplied to the local unions by the national unions, usually in the form of financial support for members while on strike. Most national unions maintain a strike fund just for this purpose and begin paying members a small weekly strike benefit (usually less than $50 per week) while they are on strike.

Grievance Handling and Arbitration.   In some national unions (most notably the Steelworkers and Autoworkers), the same district representative or international representative who assists the local union in bargaining will also provide assistance in grievance handling and arbitration. Assistance in grievance handling may take the form of advising the locals on which cases to pursue to higher levels of the grievance procedure and which cases to drop. In some cases, a representative of the national union may represent the local in grievance meetings with the employer. Frequently, a representative of the national union will represent the local in arbitration proceedings.

Research.   Most national unions of any size have research departments that may conduct research on industry trends useful for formulating negotiation strategy. The research department may gather and disseminate financial data about employers to the local unions. Research may be conducted on bargaining trends in other industries involving other unions, or on technological change and advice given to the members on how to deal with such changes.

Education.   Most national unions maintain education departments. In some unions the education director designs training programs and conducts seminars for the members on topics such as basic economics, political action, collective bargaining, labor law, occupational safety and health, and grievance handling. In other unions the education director may set up and coordinate educational programs actually taught by labor education programs offered at several large state universities around the country (e.g., the University of Wisconsin, Cornell University, Ohio State University, Rutgers University). In almost all unions the education department serves as an important link between the local and national organizations.

Political Action. Most national unions are involved in political activities of one sort or another, such as lobbying for legislation that is important to the membership. They may support candidates for office directly, or merely inform the membership about current political events that affect them as union members. In any case, the national union will be actively involved in politics and will have a position on almost any political issue.

Legal Assistance. Most national unions have an in-house legal department. A union may retain an outside legal firm to represent it as well. The legal staff handles the legal affairs of the union, which may include defending the union or its officers in court, or representing the union in negotiations or grievance cases that require some legal insight. Union attorneys play an increasingly important role in managing the affairs of the national unions. Richard Trumka, president of the United Mineworkers of America, and Robert Tobias, president of the National Treasury Employees Union, both worked as staff attorneys for the unions they now head. Arthur Goldberg was the general counsel to the Steelworkers Union prior to being appointed to the U.S. Supreme Court by President Kennedy.

Organizing. Most national unions have a department whose sole responsibility is organizing nonunion workers into their union. The organizing director coordinates the activities of field personnel (such as district representatives or international representatives) who are actually involved in the day-to-day business of organizing and participating in National Labor Relations Board representation elections. The national union supports organizing activities through the development of campaign materials, through providing trained organizers to manage the elections, and through providing financial support to fund the organizing campaigns.

Publications and Public Relations. The national unions almost always maintain publications and public relations departments to handle publicity and public affairs activities. Almost all unions publish newspapers (usually monthly) that are provided to their members. Most unions publish political or educational materials that are also provided to their members. Some unions produce television and radio advertisements that inform the public about their activities or their positions on certain issues.

Special Departments. In addition, some unions have special departments that provide services that are not provided by other unions. For example, many national unions, particularly the Teamsters and those in the building trades, have a pension and benefits department. The tradition in these unions is that the union administers the welfare and pension plan benefits for the members. Other unions may maintain a separate department of industrial engineers to advise local unions on the design and operation of wage systems based on time and motion studies. Some unions may maintain a separate department of safety and hygiene to advise members on matters of occupational safety and health or to provide educational programs on these topics.

Local Unions

The local unions constitute the most basic and elemental unit of formal union government. In 1983 there were over 50,000 separate local unions in the United States. These locals can range from very small organizations of less than 20 members to very large organizations with a membership of 10,000 or more. Some local unions are comprised of members who work for only one employer; some may include members who work for a number of employers at hundreds of different worksites. Some local unions are independent and self-sustaining and are not affiliated with a national union; most local unions, however, are affiliated with a national parent organization. In Figure 3.1 a solid line connects the national unions and the locals. Organizationally, the local unions are subordinate to the national unions and in many cases are not free to totally run their own affairs. As Chapter 7 describes, the local unions may be placed in trusteeship by the parent national union for a variety of reasons, including financial malfeasance, corruption, failing to abide by their negotiated contracts, and failing to abide by the rules and procedures established in either the national or the local union constitution.

In much the same way that the federation provides services to the national unions and that the national unions provide services to local unions, the local union provides services to its members. Most local unions provide the following kinds of services to their members.

Bargaining
Grievance handling
Political action
Social and charitable activities
Education and apprentice training

Bargaining. For unions with a craft structure (such as those in the building trades, which represent workers with a particular skill or craft), collective bargaining is usually under the control of the local unions. In the building trades, contracts are negotiated on a local-by-local basis; wage rates for workers in the same craft can vary widely from city to city. In most other unions bargaining may include some local bargaining over local issues, such as working conditions, even if the local union is covered by a national contract (such as in the automobile or steel industry). It is fair to say that some collective bargaining will be a part of virtually every local union leader's job.

In the craft unions the principal local union leader is usually called a business manager, and he or she is elected by the membership at least once every three years. The business manager is usually assisted by one or more business agents. In the craft unions the business manager and business agents are full-time, paid officials of the union and they work for the members of the local. It is common in the building trades unions for the local to operate a hiring hall, a clearinghouse in the labor market that helps connect craft workers seeking jobs and contractors needing skilled workers. The hiring hall is managed by the business manager, and local union members are the first to be referred to the job openings that are available. The hiring hall is a critical element in the control of the local labor market for skilled workers by the local unions that represent the workers.

Grievance Handling. Grievance handling is probably the most important activity for leaders of most local unions. This is especially true for locals of industrial unions that negotiate contracts at the national level. For local unions representing skilled workers, grievance handling is not such an important activity as for other workers. In the craft unions the hiring hall guarantees the workers some security. If a worker is discharged from one project he can go to the hiring hall and in a short period of time find another job. This is not true for most workers, and especially not true for unskilled or semiskilled workers. For these workers, the only job security they have is through the collectively bargained labor agreement and the grievance procedure.

In most local unions the leader of the local is called the president. Elected at least once every three years, in most local unions the president is not paid full-time to do union business. In large locals, however, the president may work for the union full-time. In most locals the president works at his or her regular job during the day and then takes care of union business at night or on weekends. In most cases, when it is necessary for the local union leader to investigate a grievance or to attend a meeting with management during working hours, he or she will go "off the clock," meaning that the union leader will not be paid by the employer for the time spent handling union business. The wages of the leader will be paid by the local union while he or she is "off the clock." Some labor agreements, however, stipulate that the employer will pay the union leader's entire salary and that time spent handling union business will be paid for by the employer.

Political Action. Local union leaders in most locals are involved in some political activity such as fund raising, voter registration drives, or serving as caucus representatives or precinct captains in some areas. Local union leaders will be active in local political races for city council or mayor or county commissions. In most cases, local union leaders work with the leaders of city central bodies to help coordinate local political activity.

Social and Charitable Activities. The local union provides social activities for its members and their families. It may support a youth or adult softball team, or a team in the bowling league. The local may sponsor monthly fish fries, barbeques, or bingo games or dances at the local union hall. In addition, the local may make contributions to local charities and will likely be an active sponsor of fundraisers for muscular dystrophy, the Heart Fund, or any of a variety of local and community charitable campaigns.

Education and Apprentice Training. The local union may provide some educational services to its members. Often these education programs are in conjunction with programs offered by the city central bodies. In the craft unions, however, the educational activities of the local union will be quite extensive. Most local craft unions provide some type of apprenticeship training for young people who would like to learn a craft or skill and who want to become union journeymen. Apprenticeship training is usually sponsored by the local union in cooperation with the local contractors (employers) association. For the union, formal apprentice training is the method whereby the union can control the number of new skilled workers entering the field in a local area. For the employer the formal apprentice program is a guarantee that new entrants to the field will be skilled, experienced, and trained in the newest methods in the industry. Access to apprentice training is also available to journeymen who want to learn new skills and new developments in the industry.

Summary

Changes in the sex composition and the industrial composition of the labor force, changes in the hours of work, and changes in the geographical concentration of the labor force have affected the industrial relations system and the labor movement.

The unionized labor force is one component of the labor force that can be described by its industrial, organizational, and geographic concentrations.

The major functional units of U.S. union government are the federation, the national union, the local union, and state and local central bodies. The functions of the local union and the national union differ in craft and in industrial unions.

Discussion Questions

[handwritten: Get women in union leadership, high turnover in service jobs.]

[handwritten margin: organize women, service sector, use women organizers.]

1. Suppose that you are the director of organizing for the AFL–CIO and that you have to devise a strategy for adapting to future changes in the labor force that would help the AFL–CIO maintain its membership. What changes do you see as being most important for the future of the labor movement?

2. The number of women in the labor force is projected to continue to increase for the next few years. What effect do you see this continued trend having on the labor movement? *[handwritten: unions may decline if don't include women]*

[handwritten margin: internal diff.]

3. Why do you feel that unions have a harder time winning representation elections in Southern states than in Northern states? Do you think this will change as the South becomes increasingly industrialized? *[handwritten: alien labor markets. Right to work laws]*

4. Within the past 20 years the construction industry has changed from a predominantly unionized industry to a predominantly nonunion industry. Why has this happened?

5. The two largest national unions in the United States do not belong to the AFL–CIO. What advantages and disadvantages can you see for a national union to affiliate with the AFL–CIO?

6. Union mergers are reducing the number of national unions and are creating a smaller number of more powerful and better financed organizations. What effect do you see from this merger movement on the internal democracy of national unions, on their bargaining power, and on their political power?

7. The AFL–CIO endorsed Walter Mondale for U.S. president in the 1984 election and spent millions of dollars on his election campaign. Many people felt that the labor endorsement was a liability, not an asset, for the Mondale campaign. What do you think? Why was this support perceived as a liability? Was this perception accurate?

Notes

[1] U.S. Department of Labor, *Handbook of Labor Statistics*, Washington, DC: U.S. Government Printing Office, December 1983, p. 1.

[2] U.S. Department of Labor, *Handbook of Labor Statistics*, p. 2.

[3] U.S. Department of Labor, *Handbook of Labor Statistics*, p. 1.

[4] U.S. Department of Commerce and U.S. Department of Labor, *Concepts and Methods Used in Labor Force Statistics Derived from the Current Population Survey*, Bureau of Labor Statistics Report 463, Washington, DC, October 1976, pp. 1–8.

[5] U.S. Department of Labor, Bureau of Labor Statistics. *Employment and Earnings*, July 1986, pp. 10–13.

[6] U.S. Department of Labor, *Handbook of Labor Statistics*, June 1985, p. 6.

[7] William French Smith, "Comparable Worth: Flirting with Disaster," *Washington Post National Weekly Edition*, February 11, 1985: 14.

[8] "Union Sues California on Sex Discrimination," *New York Times*, November 22, 1984: 21.

[9] Joseph Antos, Mark Chandler, and Wesley Mellow, "Sex Differences in Union Membership," *Industrial and Labor Relations Review* 33 (January 1980): 162–69.

[10] U.S. Department of Labor, *Handbook of Labor Statistics*, June 1985, pp. 174, 175.

[11] Courtney D. Gifford, *Directory of U.S. Labor Organizations 1984–1985* (Washington, DC: Bureau of National Affairs), p. 53.

[12] *BLS Handbook*, p. 186.

[13] U.S. Department of Labor, *Handbook of Labor Statistics*, December 1980, pp. 161–163 and *Handbook of Labor Statistics*, June 1985, pp. 207–209.

[14] Marcus H. Sandver, "South-Nonsouth Differentials in NLRB Election Outcomes," *Journal of Labor Research* 3 (1) (Winter 1982): 13–30.

[15]Leo Troy and Neil Sheflin, *Union Sourcebook*, West Orange, NJ: Industrial Relations Data Information Services, 1985, pp. 3–5.

[16]Gifford, ed., *Directory of U.S. Labor Organizations, 1982–83 Edition*, Washington, DC: BNA, p. 75.

[17]Troy and Sheflin, *Union Sourcebook*, p. 7–4.

[18]James Wallihan, *Union Government and Organization*, Washington, DC: Bureau of National Affairs, 1985, p. 155.

[19]Wallihan, *Union Government and Organization*, p. 157.

[20]*United Steelworkers of America* v. *Edward Sadlowski* 457 U.S. 102.

[21]Jack Barbash, *American Unions: Structure, Government and Politics*, New York: Random House, 1967, p. 86.

"SOLIDARITY FOREVER"

(sung to the tune of "The Battle Hymn of the Republic")

By Ralph Chaplin*

1. When the union's inspiration through
     the workers' blood shall run,
    There can be no power greater
     anywhere beneath the sun.
    Yet what force on earth is weaker than
     the feeble strength of one?
    But the union makes us strong.

Chorus: Solidarity forever!
           Solidarity forever!
           Solidarity forever!
           For the union makes us strong.

2. They have taken untold millions that
     they never toiled to earn.
    But without our brain and muscle not a
     single wheel could turn.
    We can break their haughty power, gain
     our freedom when we learn
    That the union makes us strong.

3. In our hands is placed a power greater
     than their hoarded gold,
    Greater than the might of armies
     magnified a thousand fold.
    We can bring to birth a new world from
     the ashes of the old,
    For the union makes us strong.

*Chaplin, organizer for the Industrial Workers of the World on January 17, 1915, was inspired by his experiences in the Kanawha Valley Coal Strike in 1914 and 1915.

Chapter 4

U.S. Labor History, 1789–1955

"Solidarity Forever" is a song that is still sung at union meetings today. It expresses an idea that is the dream of union leaders and union members: the dream of a solid, cohesive, enduring, powerful labor union meeting employers face to face as equals. The goal of solidarity was an elusive one in the early years of the labor movement in the United States. Organizations would form and function for a few years and then disintegrate. The search for a cohesive organizational model of unionism that was appropriate for the U.S. industrial system was really the central story of the U.S. labor movement until the last few years of the nineteenth century.

Craftsmen's Societies

At the time of the Revolutionary War, the United States was predominantly a collection of agricultural colonies with a small number of artisans, craftsmen, and merchants. The nonagricultural labor force was small, and the nation did not have an industrial wage-earning class as we know it today. In addition, there was very limited transportation and communication among cities. As a result, the market for both products and labor was mainly local.

The first evidence we have of the formation of craftsmen's societies in the colonial era was in 1724 in Philadelphia.[1] Craftsmen's societies were found in many trades during the eighteenth century, including printers, shoemakers, tailors, hatters, bricklayers, and coopers (barrelmakers).[2] The first organizations, comprised solely of wage earners whose orientation was for economic advancement and protection of their members, came in the 1790s. These journeymen's societies may be regarded as the forerunners of local unions as we know them today. Records show the existence of societies of shoemakers in Philadelphia (1792), carpenters and shoemakers in Boston (1793 and 1794), and printers and cabinetmakers in New York (1794 and 1796).[3] The cabinetmakers in New York are credited by at least one source as being "the first well-established local union in the United States," because by 1796 they had negotiated a price for their services with employers and had a 10-hour working day.[4] The rise of local journeymen's associations in the 1790s was due largely to the shortage of skilled labor (and increased bargaining power of the craftsmen), to the relative prosperity of the United States in the 1790s, and as a reaction to the formation of early employers' associations in the late 1780s.[5] The early journeymen's societies negotiated wages, union working rules that mainly protected local journeymen against the importation of journeymen from other cities, and the closed shop.[6] The early journeymen's societies did not achieve lasting success, and most of them disappeared during the economic depression that began in 1813.

The Beginnings of the U.S. Labor Movement, 1827–1837

Character of the Movement

Three main forces shaped the character of workers' organizations in the decade of the late 1820s and early 1830s: political action, economic reform, and social reform. Each of these forces was to recur at various times and in various forms in labor organizations all during the nineteenth century.

Political Action.   Beginning in Pennsylvania in 1790, in Massachusetts in 1820, and in New York in 1822, the right to vote was extended to white males in state elections. By 1824 most working men had the franchise in national elections; prior to this time, citizens were required to own property to vote. Thus, the working men's associations of the time were naturally drawn to politics and to political action.[7] The election of Andrew Jackson to the U.S presidency was made possible largely by the votes of farmers and urban working class wage earners.

Economic Factors.   Working-class grievances that had accumulated by the late 1820s were related to demands for economic reforms, for example, for the shortening of the working day to 10 hours. In the northern states in the 1830s the average working day was 11.5 hours in the winter months and 13.5 hours per day in the summer and spring, for a year-long weekly average of 73.5 hours. In the middle and southern states the average was higher at 75.5 hours per week; men, women, and children were all employed at these long hours. In the cotton industry in New England and middle Atlantic states in 1831, 58.1 percent of employees were women and 7 percent were children under 12 years. Children under the age of 16 years constituted 40 percent of the factory labor force in New England in 1832.[8] These facts gave rise to the second specific demand of members of the working class: the elimination of child labor and the institution of compulsory public education. Further grievances concerned the absence of provisions protecting workers' wages in the event that their employers went bankrupt, compulsory militia service, governmental favoritism toward banks and corporations, and imprisonment for debt.[9]

Social Reform.   The social reform movement was fundamentally different in character and direction from the forces directed at political and economic reform. This movement was led largely by intellectuals, many of them from the upper strata of society. Some early social reformers who attracted widespread working class support were Robert Dale Owen, Thomas Skidmore, and George Henry Evans.[10]

The Philadelphia Mechanics Union of Trade Associations

The three major forces of political action, economic reform, and social reform came together in the formulation of the Philadelphia Mechanics Union of Trade Associations of 1827, considered by some to be the beginning of the labor movement in the United States. This organization was formed originally through the federation of all local unions in Philadelphia in support of a strike for the 10-hour day conducted by building trades craftsmen in the construction industry in 1827. The strike was originally called by carpenters, and at one time involved 600 members of that trade. Soon painters, glaziers, bricklayers, and other trade unions joined in the movement as well.[11]

Several similar mechanics' societies or associations of local unions started in New York (1829) and in Boston (1831). In all three cities the forces for political action quickly dominated the newly formed organizations. By May 1828 the Mechanics Union of Philadelphia had formed the Workingmen's Labor Party of Philadelphia, which polled 2,400 votes in the fall of 1828 and held the balance of power in the city council.[12] In New York the Workingman's Party polled 4,000 votes out of 21,000 cast.[13] Soon after, the power of the workingmen's parties began to decline and the political movement degenerated into factionalism and divisions over which path of social reform to follow.

Local Union Activism and the Formation of City Central Bodies

The labor movement had not, however, lost its inertia or declined in numbers — just the opposite. By 1833 there were 29 organized trade union locals in New York City, 21 in Philadelphia, and 17 in Baltimore. Among the trades that were forming local unions during this period were weavers, plasterers, bricklayers, blacksmiths, cigarmakers, plumbers, tailors and tailoresses, seamstresses, printers, and carpenters. By 1836 the number of local unions in New York had grown to 52, the number in Philadelphia to 58; in some cities such as Buffalo all the crafts in the building and construction industry were unionized at this time.[14]

As the local unions of craft workers were forming in the larger cities, there began a parallel movement to form these local unions into city federations or city central bodies whose functions were to provide financial support to striking members, organize boycotts of nonunion goods, organize unorganized workers, and discourage nonunion workers from taking union members' jobs during labor disputes. Generally speaking, the city central bodies (which by 1835 were organized in Washington, D.C.; New Brunswick and Newark, New Jersey; Albany, Troy, and Schenectady, New York: and in Pittsburgh, Cincinnati, Louisville, Boston, Philadelphia, and Baltimore) did not directly support or become involved in political campaigns but primarily concerned themselves with economic matters.[15]

National Federation — The National Trades' Union

The growth of local craft unions and the formation of city labor federations soon led to a national federation of local craft unions. The National Trades' Union was founded in 1834. Its first and only president was Eli Moore, at the time the president of the New York Trades' Union and a candidate for the United States Congress, to which he was elected in 1834.[16] The National Trades' Union held conventions in 1835 and 1836 and advocated establishment of a 10-hour day by government legislation, restriction on use of female and child labor, compulsory public education, and factory legislation.[17] True to his principles, once elected to Congress Moore introduced a bill restricting the working day to 10 hours for those employees working on government projects. Although not successful in Congress, the 10-hour day was mandated for government employees by an executive order signed by President Martin Van Buren in 1840. The movement for the 10-hour day, including coordination of strike activities among government employees beginning in 1836, is regarded as the greatest accomplishment of the National Trades' Union.[18] Although the National Trades' Union survived for only a few years, it stands as a historical landmark in the development of the U.S. system of trade unionism.

The Era of Reformism, Utopianism, and National Unionism, 1837–1872

The year 1837 brought one of the worst financial and banking panics in United States history; the depression that accompanied the financial crisis lasted more than 10 years. The organizations that developed in the late 1830s and 1840s were primarily reform and utopian societies and had no lasting significance for the labor movement. In the 1850s and 1860s, however, began the development of national unions, some of which have been in continuous existence up to the present.

Associationism

The associationist movement was inspired by the writings and work of Robert Dale Owen, but it reached its fullest expression following the works of Charles Fourier, who advocated that people be organized into small, primarily agricultural phalanxes of 1,500 or so workers. Land and production equipment were to be communally owned. Individual workers would buy stock in the phalanx to get it established.

It is estimated that during the 1840s more than 40 phalanxes were started in the eastern and midwestern United States, and that many more had at least reached the serious planning stage. Virtually all the associationist communities were gone by 1850, however, victims of inadequate financing, internal friction over compensation for services, poor leadership, and lack of skill and experience among the participants.[19]

Producers' and Consumers' Cooperatives

The cooperative movement had much theoretically in common with associationism, but in practice it worked much better and had a more lasting influence on the development of the labor movement. The first record of a producers' cooperative operating in the United States was a shoemakers' cooperative operating in Philadelphia in 1836, which required simply that workers band together, raise capital by whatever means possible (usually private savings), and purchase and operate a producing facility. Producers' cooperatives were found in many industries, particularly shoemaking and foundry work, and continued to be formed by trade unionists into the 1880s. The cooperative, like the phalanx, offered an escape from the wage system and from private ownership of the enterprise. Cooperatives in most cases were self-governing, eliminating the need for supervision.

Producers' cooperatives, by and large, were not a successful alternative to the capitalist system. Few workers possessed the money required for the initial investment. When the cooperative faced hard times and when there was little or no profit to divide, the workers would be forced to sell their shares in the operation to raise money to feed themselves and their families. Eventually, the stock or shares became concentrated in the hands of one or two of the original founders.[20]

Land Reform

George Henry Evans, who was inspired by the writings and teachings of Thomas Skidmore, became the most identifiable leader of the land reform movement. Evans refined the thinking of Skidmore on the land reform issue, and abandoned Skidmore's plan for the equal division of property.[21] In its place, Evans substituted a proposal that all arable land owned by the government in the western states and territories should be opened up for homesteading. Under Evans's plan, anyone could claim ownership of a limited parcel of land without cost if that person made his or her home on that land.

Evans's plan was very popular with members of the working class. It was not radical or revolutionary like Skidmore's plan; it did not advocate taking anything away from anyone (except from the native Americans already on that land). Evans's plan acknowledged the rights of property and sought to equalize the opportunity for property ownership among all citizens. Furthermore, Evans's plan did not require establishing any type of collectivist organization; the individual would be free through his or her own effort and initiative to succeed or fail once the land was obtained.

Nonetheless, the land reform movement contributed little, if anything, to the development of trade unionism. The land reform movement was basically a political and social reform movement and thus can be considered as part of the same general social tendency that produced associationism and cooperationism. The development of the national unions began only after the working men and women began to see the futility of the social and political reforms of the 1840s and 1850s.

The Development of National Unions

Continuing in parallel to the growth of reformist and utopian organizations was the development of trade unions. Unlike the unions of the 1830s, however, the unions of the 1850s formed national organizations, some of which have continued to the present. For example, the National Typographical Union was formed in 1852, the Hat Finishers Union in 1854, the United Cigarmakers' Union in 1856, and the Iron Molders, Machinists, and Blacksmiths Union in 1859.[22]

The growth of national unions should be seen within the context of the growth of the U.S. economy during the period 1840–1860. This period is usually regarded as the era of rapid industrialization and marks the transition of the United States from a predominantly agricultural producer to a producer of both agricultural and industrial goods. Population increased rapidly from 17 million to 31 million between 1840 and 1860. The value of manufactured products increased from $483 million in 1840 to $1.8 billion in 1860.[23] Urbanization was also increasing; the percentage of the population living in cities of 8,000 or more inhabitants increased from 8.5 percent in 1840 to 16.1 percent in 1860. More than 4 million immigrants entered the United States during the period 1840–1860; more than 400,000 entered in 1854 alone.[24] Many of the new immigrants of this era were Irish, English, and German skilled craftsmen escaping social upheaval in their home countries. Many leaders of the trade unions in the 1870s and 1880s can be traced back to the immigrants arriving in the United States during the period 1840–1860.

In addition to population changes and increasing industrialism there was also a change in the transportation system and a dramatic broadening of the markets for products during the 1840–1860 era. Railway mileage in the United States had increased from 2,800 in 1840 to 30,600 in 1860.[25] Within nine years the last link in the transcontinental railroad was finished (1869). As markets widened, the movement for formation of national unions also increased. Workers could see that their interests transcended city or county or state boundaries as competition widened. Craft workers especially began to feel the need for protection against traveling itinerant workers who could undermine the trade and threaten local working conditions. Furthermore, the presence of nonunion low-wage employers anywhere in the country could threaten working conditions established by the crafts in other localities. The onset of industrialization and the widening of markets precipitated the development of craft unions on a national scale.

Reformism Revisited: The National Labor Union, 1866–1872

The National Labor Union was the first attempt to federate all labor organizations in the United States into one organization. The NLU predated both the Knights of Labor and the American Federation of Labor, the two major labor federations of the nineteenth century. Although it existed for only six years, the NLU served as an important example for all subsequently organized federations.

At the first convention of the NLU, resolutions were adopted and approved calling for establishment of national unions in all industries, organization of skilled and unskilled workers, more rigid enforcement of the apprenticeship system, compulsory arbitration of labor disputes, legal limitations of the working day to eight hours at both the national and state government levels, organization of a national labor party, support of cooperative enterprise, limitation on child and female labor, and housing reform.[26] One very important and powerful force at the founding of the NLU was the presence of members of the Eight Hour League, who followed the teachings of Ira Steward, founder of the Eight Hour movement in the United States. Legislative limitation on the length of the working day to eight hours was one of the major founding principles of the NLU. Steward's couplet regarding the eight-hour movement is often quoted:

> Whether you work by the piece or work by the day,
> Decreasing the hours increases the pay.[27]

The NLU's efforts were rewarded in 1869, when President Andrew Johnson signed a bill establishing the eight-hour day for federal employees.[28]

Subsequent NLU conventions passed resolutions calling for easy money for farmers' and producers' cooperatives, an increase in the volume of U.S. notes outstanding and a provision for their redemption in either bonds or specie (greenbacks), limitations on interest rates, limitations on profits, equal pay for men and women, reform of the national banking system, and a ban on oriental immigration.[29] At the convention in 1868 William Sylvis, president of the Molders Union, was elected president of the NLU. Sylvis immediately began active political lobbying for the NLU's program and established the first permanent lobbying committee in Washington by a labor organization.[30] In addition, Sylvis began active and serious correspondence with the International Workingmen's Association, a European federation of trade unions started by Karl Marx and a collection of British trade unions in 1864.[31] This intercourse marks the first serious consideration of an alliance by a U.S. trade union organization with a European counterpart. With the death of Sylvis in July 1869, the NLU seemed to lose its sense of direction and slowly lost power and membership. By 1872 it had disintegrated.

The Labor Movement Develops on a National Scale, 1877–1896

By the beginning of 1870 every important city in the United States had some sort of city trade assembly or central body comprised of unions formed in the four-year period 1870–1873.[32] Unions already formed showed substantial growth: the Iron Molders, Machinists, and Blacksmiths Union grew from 1,500 members in 1870 to 18,000 members in 1873. One author estimates conservatively that there were 300,000 trade unionists in the United States by 1873.[33]

The railroad industry was truly a national industry in 1869 with the completion of the transcontinental rail link. The earliest national railroad union, the Brotherhood of Locomotive Engineers, was founded in 1863, followed by the Order of Railway Conductors in 1868 and the Brotherhood of Firemen and Enginemen in 1873.[34] The panic of 1873 and its ensuing depression, however, dealt a severe blow to the railroads' economic health. It is against this background that the first strike of national importance in United States history was conducted.

The Railroad "Wars" of 1877

The year 1877 is generally regarded as the trough of the depression that followed the panic of 1873.[35] The Pennsylvania Railroad reduced wages 10 percent in 1873 and further reduced wages 10 percent on the first of June, 1877; the New York Central followed with a 10 percent cut on the first of July, 1877; and the Baltimore and Ohio reduced wages 10 percent on July 16, 1877.[36]

The Baltimore and Ohio Railroad.   Although there was some initial resistance to the reductions in June 1877, the great upheaval in the industry began on July 17 at the Baltimore and Ohio railyards in Martinsburg, West Virginia on the day following the wage cuts. On July 18, 400 federal troops from Washington and Fort McHenry, Maryland arrived at Martinsburg on a train provided by the Baltimore and Ohio Railroad to restore order and to open the rail lines. Within two days the strike had virtually paralyzed the entire Baltimore and Ohio system.[37]

Strikes were in progress as far west as Newark, Ohio, and as far east as Baltimore. In Baltimore, the Maryland National Guard was mobilized; in an ensuing gun and bayonet battle, ten protesters were killed. Rioting broke out, the depot was set afire, and federal troops again dispatched by President Rutherford Hayes were sent from the garrison in New York to stop the rioting. Peace was restored on July 23 by 700 soldiers armed with Gatling guns and field artillery. In total, 13 rioters were killed.[38] The Baltimore and Ohio railroad was not restored to full operation until August 1.

The Pennsylvania Railroad.   Meanwhile, encouraged by the news of the strikes in Martinsburg, West Virginia, workers on the Pennsylvania Railroad went on strike in Pittsburgh on July 19 to protest their wage cuts. Police and local militia were powerless to stop the strike. To protect the company's property, Governor Hartranft sent a detachment of 1,000 state militia and a battery of artillery from Philadelphia, which arrived at Pittsburgh on July 21. In the ensuing conflict and violence the militia fired into the crowd; 20 people were killed and 29 wounded, among them three small children and a woman. The crowd responded violently and began burning railroad property, including 500 freight cars, 104 locomotives, most of the shops in the railyards, the Union Depot, and the hotel.[39] Wreckage was strewn for two miles along the tracks and there was widespread looting and vandalism against the property of the Pennsylvania Railroad. Total damage was estimated at $5,000,000 and the rioting continued for another full day until the violence burned itself out.[40]

All along the Pennsylvania line freight blockades, violence, and damage to company property broke out. Strikes and blockades were in effect in Altoona, Easton, Harrisburg, Reading, Johnstown, Bethlehem, and Philadelphia, in addition to Pittsburgh. President Hayes dispatched 3,000 members of the U.S. Army to deal with the violence. In all, 10,000 troops of the Pennsylvania Militia, National Guard, and U.S. Army were used to stop the violence on the Pennsylvania road. By July 30 freight again began to be moved on the line; the trains were manned mostly by troops and strikebreakers.

The rail strikes of 1877 mark a turning point in U.S. labor history. These were the first strikes conducted on a large (multi-state) scale, although they were not planned that way and they lacked central organization or direction. It was the first time that federal troops were used to protect an employer's property against strikers. It was also the first time that the unions were joined by sympathetic citizens in what became in some cities a general strike directed at the nation's first national industry, the railroad.

In the wake of the rail strikes of 1877, the labor movement began a push for a truly strong unifying force to advance its interests. The courts and the employers responded to the events of 1877 through the use of the court injunction to halt strikes and pickets before they reached riotous proportions. The government responded to the obvious weakness of the state militias by initiating a program of building federal armories in all major cities.[41]

The Holy and Noble Order of the Knights of Labor

The Knights of Labor represents one of the most interesting and idealistic organizations in all of nineteenth-century U.S. history. Founded as a secret society of working men in 1869 by a tailor educated in the ministry named Uriah Stephens, the Knights of Labor was to become the most important labor organization of its time.[42] It was founded on a statement of principles established by Stephens and written into the initiation ritual of the organization.[43] Basically, the Knights of Labor advocated educating the public as to the legitimate aims of organized labor, encouraged political action to secure legislation favorable to working people, and favored the pursuit of mutual benefit at the workplace.[44] The platform of the Knights of Labor is summarized in Box 4.1.[45]

The beginnings of the great growth of the Knights of Labor can be traced to the ascendency of Terrence Powderly to the position of Grand Master Workman in 1878, a position held since 1869 by the original founder Uriah Stephens. Under Powderly, the secret initiation ritual was dropped and the Knights of Labor publicly embarked on a program of membership growth. With the dropping of the secret ritual the official opposition of the Roman Catholic Church to the Knights of Labor was lifted and the organization grew through the enlistment of Irish and German immigrants in the urban areas, many of whom were Roman Catholic.[46] By 1879 the Knights of Labor had over 20,000 members and more than double that number only four years later.[47] The greatest growth in membership, however, came between 1883 and 1886. Beginning in 1883 the organization conducted several large, well-publicized strikes. Although sometimes unsuccessful (as the telegraph strike of 1883 proved to be) the publicity and excitement associated with these strikes captured the spirit and imagination of all workers.

In March 1885 the Knights of Labor went on strike to protest a wage cut of 10 percent on three railroads (the Wabash; the Missouri, Kansas, and Texas; and the Missouri Pacific) owned by Jay Gould, one of the

BOX 4-1
Platform of the Knights of Labor

1. Direct representation and legislation
2. Initiative and referendum
3. Establishment of a Bureau of Labor Statistics
4. Taxation of unearned income on land
5. Abrogation of all legislation not resting equally on employers and employees
6. Laws to further health and safety and to prevent accidents and occupational diseases
7. Laws to compel corporations to pay their employees weekly
8. Abolition of the contract labor system on public works
9. Compulsory arbitration of labor disputes, disavowing the strike as a means of settlement
10. Prohibitions on the employment of children less than 15 years of age.
11. Compulsory schooling and free textbooks
12. Income and inheritance taxes
13. Prohibition on the use of convict labor
14. Retention of greenbacks (paper money) as a part of national currency
15. Monetarization of silver as legal currency
16. Government ownership of the railroads and the telegraph system
17. Merit basis for appointment and promotion in government service
18. A national cooperative industrial system
19. The eight-hour day
20. Equal rights (including equal pay for equal work) for the sexes

wealthiest and most powerful employers in the United States at the time. The strikers on the three roads numbered over 4,500 in total and included all the traditional rail crafts — engineers, firemen, brakemen, and conductors. In the face of such resistance, Gould was forced to restore wages to their previous levels.[48]

In September 1886 the Wabash reduced staffing levels to a number that virtually eliminated all Knights of Labor from employment, in violation of the agreement made in March. The Knights of Labor threatened to strike on the entire Wabash system, involving over 20,000 miles of railway, if the situation was not remedied. Gould, who at the time was having severe financial difficulties with the Wabash, agreed to the workers' demands and met with representatives of the Knights of Labor to negotiate a settlement. This meeting marked one of the first times that any labor organization had negotiated a peaceful and favorable settlement in the rail industry, as well as the first time that any Gould railroad had ever been forced to back down totally in the face of worker resistance.[49]

The second Wabash strike of 1886 dramatically increased the membership of the Order and catapulted the Knights of Labor into public prominence. In July 1885 the Knights of Labor had 104,000 members; in October 1886 the Order registered 702,824 members.[50] It is somewhat paradoxical that an organization that publicly disavowed the strike owed its greatest success to gains accomplished as a result of a strike.

Nonetheless, by 1896 the Knights of Labor was virtually defunct. This decline can be traced to three major factors. First, the Knights of Labor suffered catastrophic defeats in most strikes it conducted in 1886, defeats that some authors attribute to ineptitude in Powderly's leadership skills.[51] Second, the Knights of Labor was in direct conflict with the national unions in several industries — one of which, the Cigarmakers, forced members to make a choice between membership in a national union or in the Knights of Labor. Finally, the Knights of Labor suffered from some structural and organizational flaws. Its basic organizational unit was the mixed or industrial assembly, which lumped all workers together in the same organizational subunit regardless of skill, industry, or place of employment. Thus workers were never allowed to capitalize on the natural advantage afforded them because of their skill or concentration in an industry, but were forced to subordinate their separate interests for the good of the group as a whole. The dissipation of energies and lack of power grew even more acute as the Knights of Labor enrolled farmers, shopkeepers, and small employers into local unions designed and intended to further the legitimate and identifiable interests of the wage earner.

In the end, the combination of strike defeats, trade union opposition, structural inadequacies, heterogeneity of membership, and internal factionalism destroyed the Knights of Labor. In 1894 Powderly was defeated for reelection to its presidency. By 1896 the Knights of Labor was disbanded as an organizational entity.

The American Federation of Labor

The formation of the American Federation of Labor (AFL) in 1886 marks the birth of the only labor federation formed in the nineteenth century that continued into the twentieth. The dramatic strikes conducted by the Knights of Labor in the railroads in 1885 and 1886 illustrated the potential power of a coordinated and organized labor movement. However, the tragedy of the Haymarket bombing in May 1886 in Chicago, in which several policemen were killed while attempting to break up a Socialist workers' rally, and the negative public reaction stemming from it, showed to union leaders the danger in letting radicalism become associated with legitimate trade union activities. Finally, the organizational weakness of the Knights of Labor demonstrated the importance of finding an organizational base that could be maintained and protected.

The American Federation of Labor traces its roots back to an organization known as the Federation of Organized Trades and Labor Unions of the United States and Canada (FOTLU), founded in Pittsburgh, Pennsylvania in November 1881.[52] The FOTLU was formed as the result of the activities of the International Typographical Union, which in its 1879 convention passed a resolution calling for effort to federate the existing national unions into a common organization.[53]

The 197 representatives to the first FOTLU convention in Pittsburgh were from the national unions, from the existing city central bodies in most large cities, and from some local assemblies of the Knights of Labor.[54] In 1882 only 19 delegates were present at the second convention; in 1883 the third convention had 26 delegates, but an important event transpired with the election of 31-year-old Samuel Gompers as president.[55] Gompers was to spend the rest of his life as a trade union leader. By 1886 he and others had transformed the powerless FOTLU into the powerful and enduring American Federation of Labor.

Samuel Gompers was born into a Dutch Jewish family, and he emigrated with his family from the East Side of London to the East Side of New York City in 1863. After completing less than four years of education at a Jewish Free School in London, economic necessity forced Gompers to go to work to help support his family at the age of 10 years. Although originally apprenticed as a shoemaker, Gompers changed trades and entered a two-year apprenticeship as a cigarmaker, his father's trade.[56] Upon emigrating to the United States, Gompers became active in the Cigarmakers Union and remained active in it most of his life until his full-time association with the AFL.

After its formation in 1886 the AFL's membership grew steadily, reaching over 1 million members in 1902 and over 2 million members in 1914.[57] The years between the AFL's formation and 1897 were an especially important time in its history; it has been called the period of stabilization in U.S. trade unionism.[58] During this time economic conditions were generally favorable to the growth of labor organizations and many national unions were formed, such as the Brotherhood of Maintenance of Way Employees, the Bakers Union, the Painters Union, the Plumbers Union, and the National Association of Letter Carriers.[59] The financial panic of 1893–1896 failed to destroy or even to seriously weaken the AFL and its constituent national unions, prompting Gompers to boast of the strength and resiliency of a labor movement founded on sound business principles.

Although the period 1886–1897 may be considered one of stability in union membership and finances, serious and sometimes violent conflicts were still being waged between employers and unions. The two most notable of these were the strikes conducted at the Carnegie Steel works at Homestead, Pennsylvania in 1892 and at the Pullman Car Company in Chicago, Illinois in 1894. The Pullman strike virtually paralyzed the nation's rail system in July 1894. Federal troops were used to halt the strike and to restore railroad service to the nation. The leader of the strike and boycott, Eugene V. Debs, was imprisoned for six months for defying a federal court injunction halting the strike.

The AFL and the Knights of Labor.   The national unions were the founders of the AFL and, as we might expect, they wanted to retain the rights to govern themselves that they had enjoyed prior to the formation of the AFL. Furthermore, the formation of the AFL was accomplished largely by craft unions jealous of their jurisdiction and protective of the interests of skilled workers. Finally, the AFL was founded by experienced trade union officials — Adolph Strasser, president of the Cigarmakers Union; Samuel Gompers, president of the Cigarmakers' New York City local union; and P. J. McGuire, president of the Carpenters Union — all pragmatic, experienced men, not reformers, idealists, or dreamers. Thus, we can see three fundamental differences between the AFL and the Knights of Labor. First, the AFL was comprised of autonomous, self-governing, well-financed national unions that gave little central power to the Federation. The Knights of Labor, by contrast, was organized along geographical lines and vested all control in the hands of the national officers. Second, the AFL was comprised of craft unionists, almost all of whom were skilled. The skilled workers were naturally a cohesive group by virtue of their training and experience; furthermore, they were much more powerful in negotiations with their employers than were the unskilled workers and were thus able to win even greater economic gains. The Knights of Labor organized all workers regardless of skill or trade into their mixed assemblies. Finally, the AFL had experienced, seasoned leaders who knew from years of personal experience how best to conduct the affairs of a labor organization and who had no romantic delusions about what the job entailed. Terrence Powderly, on the other hand, was an idealist, a romantic, and a man with a religious fervor for associations of workers.[60] In the end, organizational structure, membership solidarity, and superior leadership qualities enabled the AFL to survive where the Knights of Labor had failed.

Revival and Resurgence of Left-Wing Unionism

Although they never were large, the socialist labor organizations were able to assert some influence within the labor movement. For example, at the 1893 AFL convention, a socialist-backed resolution was overwhelmingly approved that advocated "collective ownership by the people of all means of production and distribution."[61] Although through the efforts of Gompers this plank was defeated at the 1894 convention, the socialists had demonstrated their influence. Furthermore, Gompers was defeated for the presidency of the AFL at the 1894 convention by a socialist member of the United Mine Workers, John McBride. Gompers regained the presidency of the AFL in 1895 over McBride in a very close vote.

The socialists, however, never presented a united front either in national political campaigns or in internal union power plays. By 1900 the socialists who were active in the labor movement were split into a number of factions such as the Socialist Labor Party, headed by Daniel DeLeon; the Social Democratic Party, headed by Eugene V. Debs; and other successionist groups headed by Morris Hillquit and Victor Berger of Milwaukee.[62]

The Western Federation of Miners

Socialist principles were also being extolled by the leaders of at least one national union. The newly formed (1893) Western Federation of Miners (WFM) was an industrial union of "hard rock" (e.g., gold, silver, nickel, and copper) miners having almost all its members in the western mining states of Montana, Idaho, Wyoming, Colorado, Nevada, Utah, New Mexico, and Arizona. Most of its original leaders had at one time been members of the Knights of Labor,[63] but found the pacificism of Powderly unsuited to the wild and sometimes violent labor–management relations in the western mining centers. The work was dangerous and physically grueling, the miners lived in isolated communities cut off from the civilizing influence of families and friends, and the instruments of violence (dynamite, blasting powder) were tools of the trade to the miners and were in plentiful supply. It was no wonder that labor–management conflict sometimes took on the look of industrial warfare in some WFM-led strikes.

The idea for a federation of western miners was first proposed among miners jailed during the Coeur d'Alene strike of 1893 in Idaho. The founding convention of the WFM was held in Butte, Montana in May 1893, and its constitution established its jurisdiction to include all metal miners and metal mill and smelter workers. The WFM affiliated with the AFL in 1896 and for a short time (one year) joined the United Mine Workers and the United Brewery Workmen as the three industrial unions in the AFL. These other unions also traced their early formation to the Knights of Labor.[64]

The WFM in the years of its infancy conducted large-scale strikes in Cripple Creek, Colorado in 1894; Leadville, Colorado in 1896; and Coeur d'Alene, Idaho in 1899. In the 1899 Coeur d'Alene strike, led by WFM president Ed Boyle, 3,000 pounds of dynamite was used to destroy mine owners' property and federal troops were called for by Idaho Governor Steunenberg to restore law and order.[65] More than 1,200 miners were arrested once the federal troops arrived and martial law was declared in the Coeur d'Alene district. Similar violence and bloodshed were part of the WFM strikes in Telluride, Colorado in 1901 and in Cripple Creek, Colorado in 1903–1904.[66] The Telluride strike and the second Cripple Creek strike were led by WFM president Charles Moyer and Secretary-Treasurer William "Big Bill" Haywood, both colorful, charismatic figures and former miners.[67]

The Western Federation of Miners was also an avowedly political labor organization, in contrast to most unions affiliated with the AFL. In 1902 WFM leaders Moyer and Haywood joined Eugene V. Debs's Socialist Party and began actively organizing a political-industrial labor movement, something they had been trying to do since 1898.[68] Slowed by the disastrous WFM strike in Cripple Creek in 1903–1904, the movement for the formation of an active (and radical) political-industrial labor movement was not begun until late in 1904.

The Industrial Workers of the World Radical, violent

The outgrowth of the preparations begun in 1904, mostly by the leaders of the WFM, was the founding convention of the Industrial Workers of the World (IWW) held in Chicago in June 1905. The IWW was a coalition of workers in local unions dissatisfied with the conservatism of the AFL, of workers in the WFM and groups affiliated with it, and of intellectuals and socialist politicians such as Daniel DeLeon and Eugene V. Debs. It was organized along the "one big union" structure of the Knights of Labor and was committed to both economic and political goals. The economic goals were to improve the economic well-being of all members of the working class, both skilled and unskilled. The means used to reach these goals were traditional trade union tactics (e.g., strikes, pickets, boycotts) bolstered by the solidarity that comes from the industrial union structure of organizing all workers in a particular industry regardless of skill. The political goals were to be the eventual substitution of a workers' "cooperative commonwealth" (worker ownership) for private capitalism.[69] To an extent the IWW had a revolutionary philosophy; its members believed that political action and economic action were both to be part of trade union activity and that the interests of the employer and the employee were diametrically opposed.[70] Furthermore, the IWW advocated the abolition of the wage system and the overthrow of capitalism. The preamble to the IWW constitution is reprinted in Box 4.2.

Despite lofty ideals and revolutionary rhetoric, the IWW never achieved much concrete success, especially in its early years. Factional splits first among the intellectual socialists (Debs in an intellectual fight with DeLeon left the IWW in 1906) and later among the trade unionists (the WFM withdrew from the IWW in 1907) left the IWW weakened and devoid of a unifying organizational core. In 1906, Haywood and Moyers of the WFM and George Pettibone, formerly of the Knights of Labor, were indicted for the dynamite murdering in 1905 of former Governor Stuenenberg of Idaho. Although all were acquitted in the subsequent trial, the image of the leadership of the IWW was tarnished in the eyes of the public and for the average trade unionist. As a result of internal factional fighting, diminished public image, and lack of trade union support, the IWW never achieved the power and influence among members of the working class for which it had hoped.

In the end, the IWW could point to few lasting concrete gains that it had won for any of its members. The most successful IWW strike, in Lawrence, Massachusetts in 1912, was a protest against wage cuts. After a very hard-fought strike, the employer restored wages to their previous

BOX 4-2
Preamble to the IWW Constitution

The working class and the employing class have nothing in common. There can be no peace so long as hunger and want are found among millions of working people and the few, who make up the employing class, have all the good things of life.

Between these two classes a struggle must go on until the workers of the world organize as a class, take possession of the earth and the machinery of production and abolish the wage system.

We find that the centering of management of industries into fewer and fewer hands makes the trade unions unable to cope with the ever-growing power of the employing class. The trade unions foster a state of affairs which allows one set of workers to be pitted against another set of workers in the same industry, thereby helping defeat one another in wage wars. Moreover, the trade unions aid the employing class to mislead the workers into the belief that the workers have interest in common with their employers.

These conditions can be changed and the interest of the working class upheld only by an organization formed in such a way that all its members in any one industry, or in all industries if necessary, cease work whenever a strike or lockout is on in any department thereof, thus making an injury to one an injury to all.

Instead of the conservative motto, "A fair day's wage for a fair day's work," we must inscribe on our banner the revolutionary watchword, "Abolition of the wage system." It is the historic mission of the working class to do away with capitalism. The army of production must be organized, not only for the every-day struggle with capitalists, but to carry on production when capitalism shall have been overthrown. By organizing industrially we are forming the structure of the new society within the shell of the old.

Source: Paul Brissenden, *The I.W.W.* (New York: Russell and Russell, Inc., 1919), pp. 351–352.

levels. As often happened, however, within months the local organization that led the strike had withered away. The IWW actively opposed entry by the United States into World War I. As result, most of its leaders were jailed during World War I under the terms of the Espionage Act passed in 1917. The IWW ceased to be an important influence in labor–management relations in the United States after this time, although scattered groups of people claiming affiliation with the IWW still convene.[71]

Expansion and Consolidation, 1897–1920

After weathering the depression of 1897 and the attendant loss of membership, the AFL and its constituent unions began a steady period of growth right up to the end of World War I (Figure 4.1). The growth in membership of the labor movement during the entire 24-year period can be broken down into three subgroups: (1) rapid growth, 1897–1904; (2) stagnation in membership, 1904–1914; and (3) renewed rapid growth, 1914–1920.

Rapid Growth, 1897–1904

The period 1897–1904 was one of rapid growth both for the AFL and for unions as a whole; membership in all unions quadrupled from about 500,000 members in 1897 to 2 million in 1904;* membership in the AFL increased from 250,000 to 1.6 million. Between 1894 and 1904 the number of national unions affiliated with the AFL increased from 58 to 120.[72] The major growth industries for unions were coal mining, the railroads, and the construction industry. It is estimated that approximately 3.5 percent of the U.S. labor force was unionized during this period.[73]

The strikes that occurred during this period were mostly local disputes mainly over economic items and the length of the working day. The one strike of national importance conducted during the 1897–1904 period took place in the anthracite coal fields in Pennsylvania in 1902. The eight-hour day was a major trade union bargaining goal during this time and was well established in the construction, coal mining, and printing industries largely due to the activities of the unions.[74]

Stagnation in Membership, 1904–1914

The reasons for labor movement stagnation during the period 1904–1914 may be identified as emanating from three factors: (1) a conscious decision on the part of the AFL and the national unions to slow their expansion, (2) employer opposition, and (3) legal restraints on union activities.[75]

Slowed Expansion. Between the years 1904 and 1914 the number of national unions in the American Federation of Labor fell from 120 to 110 because of mergers of existing organizations.[76] Accompanying this amalgamation and consequent membership concentration was an increase in the number of union members residing in urban areas. Research evidence on the geographical distribution of trade union membership indicates that after 1904 trade union membership expanded in urban areas but contracted in rural areas.[77] Furthermore, some observers have indicated that the skilled workers in the existing unions during this era were more concerned with perfecting their control over job opportunities through a system of working rules than organizing new segments of the labor force, particularly the unskilled.[78]

---

*During this time the largest group of unions not affiliated with the AFL were those in the railroad industry.

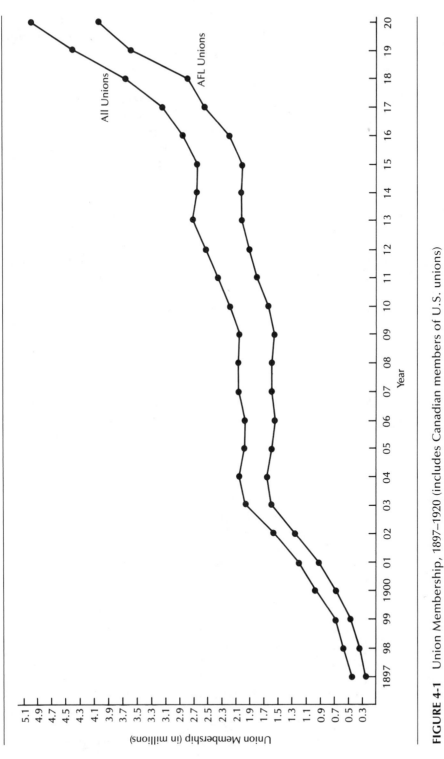

FIGURE 4-1 Union Membership, 1897–1920 (includes Canadian members of U.S. unions)

Employer Opposition.   With the stabilization and expansion of the AFL unions in the period 1897–1904 came increased union financial strength and bargaining power. For the first time in the history of U.S. labor–management relations the unions demanded and received written contractual agreements with their employers stipulating the terms and conditions of employment as well as management and union rights, and granting formal recognition to the union as the sole bargaining agent for the employees. In some cases the closed shop was also negotiated into contractual agreements, requiring that workers become union members before they could even apply for work in certain industries. The contractual agreement stabilized the bargaining relationship and gave the union a sense of security, permanency, and legitimacy in dealing with the employer.[79]

Many employers feared the growing power of unions and resented the erosion of long-established management rights by the contractual agreement. Coupled with this resentment and fear was the growing power and concentration of many industrial corporations. For example, by 1909 25.9 percent of the nation's manufacturing establishments were owned by corporations; these corporations, however, employed 75.6 percent of all wage earners in manufacturing.[80] Many organizations of employers were established specifically to help employers resist the growing power of unions, such as the Citizens Industrial Association (an offshoot of the National Association of Manufacturers), the American Anti-Boycott Association, and the National Council for Industrial Defense. In addition, "open shop" drives were organized in some cities to keep these cities union-free. Dayton, Ohio was an early example (1900) of an open shop town where unions were actively opposed by citizen and employer groups. Finally, employers in some industries simply repudiated negotiated agreements altogether and refused to abide by their terms. It should be pointed out that in many industries the unions broke the terms of agreements just as frequently as employers. Procedures had not been developed for interpreting contractual terms or for adjudicating disputes arising under the contracts. Both labor and management regarded the contract as a temporary truce or stopping point to be repudiated when conditions were more favorable to one or the other side's position.[81]

Legal Restraints.   As industries grew more concentrated and markets for goods became national, boycotts against products also sometimes assumed national market-wide proportions. In two very important decisions (the *Danbury Hatters* and the *Bucks Stove* cases, both discussed in Chapter 6), federal courts ruled that such nationwide boycotts constituted an illegal restrain of trade.[82] The ruling of the courts and the severity of the punishment, however, shocked many people in the labor movement, and many labor leaders thought twice before they engaged in boycotting activities. With one of its main tactical weapons in dealing with large employers blunted, the labor movement was weakened in its ability to bargain and to organize new members.

Renewed Rapid Growth, 1914–1920

The outbreak of war in Europe in 1914 sparked a revival and growth in unions in the United States. As the data in Figure 4.1 indicate, membership in all unions grew from about 2.5 million in 1914 to over 5 million in 1920; likewise the AFL grew from just over 2 million in 1914 to just over 4 million in 1920. This great growth can be attributed to two major forces — the revival of prosperity and the increase in production resulting from the war in Europe, and the development of favorable government policies regarding unions and collective bargaining during the years of Woodrow Wilson's presidency (1912–1920).

The Revival of Prosperity. The prosperity that accompanied the increased demand for war goods beginning in 1915 made it possible for employers once again to pay their employees higher wages. As demand increased, employers were reluctant to lose production because of strikes. In addition, the letting of government contracts on a "cost-plus" basis (that is, the government paid the contractor the full cost, including labor cost, of production plus a fair profit) made it less important for defense contractors to hold down costs to meet competition. Finally, a shortage of labor was created because the hostilities in Europe drastically reduced the supply of immigrants entering the United States and at the same time more than 5 million U.S. men were conscripted into military service.[83] Thus, labor faced an increased demand for its services, employers were reluctant to risk strikes, and wartime demand made business more profitable. It was no wonder that unions were able to win increased gains for their members and to add new members in such a favorable environment.

Favorable Political and Legal Climate. Several factors can be identified as creating a favorable political and legal climate for trade union growth during the years 1914–1920. One was the election of Woodrow Wilson as President of the United States in 1912. Wilson was consistently progressive in his attitude toward unions, and he went out of his way to garner favor with the labor movement. He made a major speech at the dedication of the new AFL headquarters in Washington, DC in 1916, proclaiming that henceforth no U.S. president would be able to ignore the labor movement. Furthermore, Wilson took the time to speak at the 1917 AFL convention in Buffalo, New York even though the nation was on the verge of going to war.[84]

Wilson also invited Samuel Gompers and other labor leaders to participate in the National Council of Defense and the War Labor Board. During the years the United States was actually in armed combat during World War I, the War Labor Board handled and arbitrated all disputes between labor and management and enforced equitable principles and policies in labor–management relations.[85] In agreeing to abide by the principles and policies of the War Labor Board, the unions gave up their right to strike, were forced to abandon restrictive work rules, and severely curtailed their rights to negotiate wage rate increases during the war.[86] In return, the employers were required to recognize the rights of employees to join and organize unions and bargain collectively. Furthermore, employers were expressly prohibited from discharging workers for trade union activities or for union membership.

In the railroad and coal mining industries, which the government operated in 1918 and 1919, the government recognized and negotiated with the unions. Never before had the U.S. government specifically given legal protection for workers' rights to join unions and to bargain collectively with their employers. Such sweeping legal protection for organizing, coupled with the uncertainty surrounding the status of injunction in labor disputes for a few years following the passage of the Clayton Act in 1914, served to revitalize the organizational activities of unions. The tremendous growth of union membership in 1917–1920 was the result.

The growth of unions in the 1914–1920 era was not uniform, however. Unions were still predominantly composed of skilled workers, and they were generally not found in industrial occupations or in mass production jobs. Furthermore, events at the end of this era, particularly in 1919, indicated that the harmonious spirit of labor–management relations that prevailed during the war years would be short lived.

The 1919 Steel Strike

The year 1919 was the year of the greatest strike activity ever recorded up to that time. In 1919 there were 3,630 labor disputes involving over 4 million workers; in 1920 (a more representative year) there were 3,411 strikes involving slightly over 1 million workers.[87] Many reasons can be cited for the high level in strike activity in 1919: prices rising much faster than wages, the pent-up militancy of a large and well-financed labor movement, and the resistance power of large profitable corporations to the unions' demands. Although there were several large strikes conducted in 1919 — the railroad shopmen's strikes and the soft coal strikes are good examples — the most widely publicized and analyzed strike of that year was the steel strike of 1919.[88]

The 1919 steel strike was a classic confrontation between a large, centralized organizing committee of 24 craft unions supported by the AFL and a large, centralized, determined group of employers called by one author "the strongest capitalist aggregation in the world."[89] The steel industry had been mostly nonunion after the 1892 Homestead strike and had been almost entirely union free since the failed strike in 1901 involving the Amalgamated Association of Iron and Steelworkers. At the AFL national convention in 1918, a committee was formed of 15 (later

24) national unions having jurisdictional claims to workers in the steel industry. The purpose of this committee was to coordinate and implement an organizing drive in the steel industry, at that time employing about 400,000 workers.[90] The organizing drive began in September 1918 in Chicago, Illinois and Gary, Indiana and was led by William Z. Foster, a former IWW activist who had successfully led an organizing campaign in the Chicago meatpacking industry a year earlier. The main grievance of the steelworkers was to eliminate the 12-hour day (a common practice in the steel industry) and the seven-day week, which a worker was required to work when he or she was rotated from the day shift to the night shift, usually every two weeks.

In the spring of 1919 the organizing campaign shifted to the Pittsburgh-Youngstown area, where the majority of steelworkers in the United States were employed. In this part of the country the union organizers met much more employer and community resistance than they had encountered in Chicago, but the organizing campaign progressed nonetheless. By June 1919 the unions claimed to represent 100,000 steelworkers, and they directed Samuel Gompers to contact E. Gary, chairman of the board of the U.S. Steel Corporation, to request the beginning of negotiations. Gary refused to meet with the unions. The unions then polled their members in the steel industry and an overwhelming majority voted to go on strike to force the companies to recognize the unions and to bargain with them.[91] The strike date was set for September 22. Throughout the process of preparing for the strike, Gompers repeatedly tried to contact Gary to avert the conflict, but Gary refused to meet or confer with the unionists.

The strike began on September 22 and 275,000 workers were reported to have been on strike the first day.[92] At its peak the strike involved over 300,000 workers, completely shutting down production in Chicago, Gary, Youngstown, Cleveland, and Wheeling. The strike was less effective in Pittsburgh, but still a majority of the steelworkers were on strike there as well.

The strike was relatively peaceful, but it involved a war of sorts in the media. The employers publicized Foster's previous IWW membership and denounced Foster as a "radical" and a "bolshevik." The public and the workers were thus alarmed that this was not simply an economic confrontation but a political and ideological one as well. In addition, the employers imported large numbers of strikebreakers in an attempt to keep the steel mills operating and to create fear of permanent job loss in the minds of the workers. Finally, the employers used private protection agencies and armed guards to intimidate the strikers and picketers and to keep open the gates to the plants. In the end the employers prevailed and on January 9, 1920 the steel strike was abandoned. From the union's point of view it had been a colossal failure. The labor movement, in a coordinated effort at the height of its power and influence, had confronted the most powerful employers in the United States in head-to-head battle, and had lost. The employers maintained a united front, successfully imported strikebreakers to keep the mills running, used the media and public opinion to their advantage, and scored a decisive victory over the unions. The nonunion status of the steel industry and the power and prestige of the employers had been maintained.

The Decline of the Labor Movement, 1920–1933

The decline in the membership of all unions and in the unions affiliated with the AFL is illustrated in Figure 4.2, which shows a sharp decline in union membership during the years 1920–1923; a period of relatively stable membership, 1924–1931; and then a further sharp drop in numbers in 1932 and 1933. The dramatic loss of membership during the 1920s was a surprise to most trade union leaders and to most experts who study the labor movement. Historical data show that unions usually grow during periods of economic prosperity, and the 1920s were generally a prosperous time with low unemployment and rising wages. The experience of unions in the 1920s illustrates that union growth (and decline) is related to a number of interrelated factors, not all of them economic. To analyze the loss of union power and prestige during the 1920s and early 1930s it is necessary to understand the forces that were operating on both business and society at the time.

Employer Opposition

Employer opposition to unions had abated somewhat during World War I. With the end of the war, and perhaps as a reaction to the 1919 strike wave, many employers began a new and vigorous campaign in opposition to unions. In some cases the antiunion campaigns were a revival of the open shop movement started in 1900.[93] In other cases, employer opposition to unionism was manifested in the form of "company unions" where the employer established an "in-house" union to represent employees as a substitute for an independent union.[94] Another form of employer opposition to unions was "welfare capitalism," where the employer centralized the personnel function in a separate department and paid as good, or better, wages and benefits than did unionized employers.[95] Particularly in the major manufacturing industries — steel, auto, rubber, glass — the employers' policies of union substitution (company unionism) and union cooptation (welfare capitalism) were major factors in the decline of union membership.

The Legal Environment

At the end of World War I the protection given unions under the War Labor Board regulations was abolished. Employers were no longer obligated to recognize unions, to bargain with them, or to refrain from

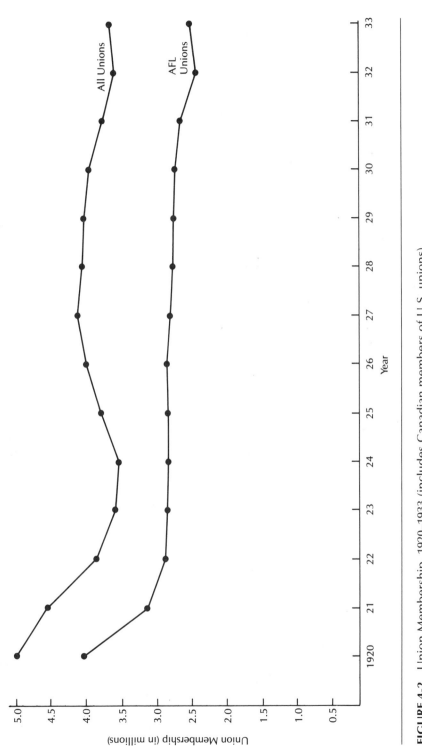

FIGURE 4-2 Union Membership, 1920–1933 (includes Canadian members of U.S. unions)

taking action against employees who belonged to them. Furthermore, the U.S. Supreme Court decision in the *Duplex* vs. *Deering* case in 1921 affirmed the power of courts to issue injunctions in labor disputes, a power most labor leaders thought had been curtailed by the Clayton Act of 1914. In addition, the court in subsequent rulings asserted its legal right to limit the number of picketers at the employer's premises during a strike (*American Steel Foundries* vs. *Tri-City Central Trades Council,* 1921) and to limit union boycotting activities (*Bedford Cut Stone Company* vs. *Journeyman Stone Cutters Association,* 1927). All these decisions limited the power of unions in their dealings with the employers; they will be discussed in more depth in Chapter 6.

Leadership Conservatism

Perhaps as much as any other factor, the limitation put upon union organizing by the craft union structure of the AFL accounted for the drop in union membership during the 1920s. As the events during the 1919 steel strike illustrated, the craft unions (each with a narrow and jealously guarded jurisdiction) were powerless in dealing with a large-scale manufacturing corporation. The craft unions were traditionally comprised of skilled workers, and many union leaders openly disdained admitting unskilled factory workers into their ranks.[96] As a result, the great mass of workers in most of the growth industries of the 1920s (steel, autos, and electrical equipment) were outside the jurisdiction of most established unions. Rather than start new unions appropriate to the interests and needs of the unskilled and semiskilled factory workers, the established unions in the AFL dissipated their energies and resources in trying to organize the few skilled workers who were employed in these industries into the existing craft unions. The inevitable result was that unions were being undermined by employer opposition in the areas where they were established, and they were failing to win any new membership campaigns they initiated. The drop in union membership during the 1920s and early 1930s is hardly surprising given these circumstances.[97]

The Rise of Industrial Unionism and the Resurgence of Trade Union Growth, 1933–1945

The factors that led to the decline in union membership during the 1920s and early 1930s were largely reversed by 1934. As the data in Figure 4.3 show, union membership increased dramatically during the 1930s and 1940s to reach a peak in 1948 that was over four times the membership levels in 1934. The United States has never seen such a sharp and sustained increase in labor union membership either before or since this time. To fully understand the factors behind this explosion in union membership we must discuss how the three factors that hindered union growth in the 1920s were changed after 1934.

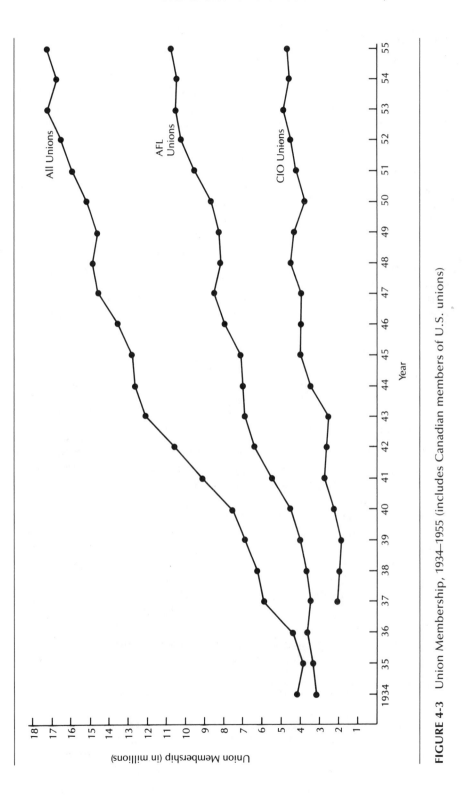

FIGURE 4-3 Union Membership, 1934–1955 (includes Canadian members of U.S. unions)

Employer Opposition

In the decade of the 1920s many employers, especially in the manufacturing sector, used three tactics to combat unions: (1) outright opposition, (2) company unionism, (3) welfare capitalism. After 1933, however, these tactics of employer opposition became less effective, and after 1935 outright opposition and company unionism had been virtually outlawed.

Overt Opposition. The use of outright or overt opposition began to decline in many major manufacturing industries after the passage of the National Industrial Recovery Act of 1933. Under the terms of Title I of the NIRA, employers were allowed to join together in trade associations (subject to government approval) to set prices and limit output in certain industries free from antitrust prosecution. It was believed that such self-regulation of industry production might help alleviate overproduction, which many people felt brought on the depression that had begun in 1929. However, before such an association would be approved all members of the association had to agree to adhere to the terms of section 7 (a) of the NIRA, which stated:

> that employees have the right to organize and bargain collectively through representatives of their own choosing, and shall be free from the interference, restraint, or coercion of employers of labor, or their agents, in the designation of such representatives or in self-organization or in other concerted activities for the purpose of collective bargaining or other mutual aid or protection.[98]

For the first time in U.S. history the right to unionize and to bargain collectively was being recognized by a federal statute that conceivably could cover any employer engaged in interstate commerce who sought its protection. Thus, with the passage of the NIRA many employers had to choose between continuing their active, overt policy of union opposition or choosing the protection against destructive business competition offered by the NIRA; many employers, particularly in manufacturing, chose the NIRA.

In the case of *Schechter Poultry Corp.* vs. *United States*, 295 U.S. 495 (1935), the U.S. Supreme Court found the NIRA to be unconstitutional. In its decision, the Court found that the NIRA gave too much power to industry councils to set prices and production levels for interstate commerce and that state power to control intrastate commerce was unconstitutionally limited by the statute. Although the NIRA itself was invalidated by the Schechter case, the spirit of section 7(a) of the act was maintained in section 7 of the National Labor Relations Act.

Company Unions. It should be noted that the NIRA section 7(a) did not outlaw company unions. In fact, it is estimated that 60 percent of those company unions in existence in 1935 had been organized since 1933, and that in 1935 over 2.5 million workers in the steel, iron, chemical, and transportation industries were in such company unions.[99] The National Labor Relations Act passed in 1935, however (after the NIRA was declared unconstitutional), did make company unions illegal. Interestingly, many union organizers in the 1930s claimed that the presence of a company union actually made easier their jobs of organizing workers into established unions.[100]

Welfare Capitalism.   When the great industrial depression began in 1929, and continued during the 1930s, many employers could not afford to pay the benefits given employees in the 1920s. Employees in many organizations observed that the first items cut at the onset of the depression were wages and benefits, not dividends.[101] Employees began to realize that the generosity of the employer was possible only when profits were high and that welfare capitalism could offer no guarantee of wages or benefits at the expense of profit. In response, workers turned to unions, which they hoped could provide them with a more secure wage and benefit arrangement through collective bargaining.

The Legal Environment

The passage of the Norris-La Guardia Act in 1932 began a new era for U.S. labor–management relations by making "yellow dog" contracts (pre-employment promises not to join a union) unenforceable.[102] In addition, the Norris-La Guardia Act strongly limited the use of injunctions in halting labor disputes. As one author observes:

> What it accomplishes is a laissez-faire setup for organized labor's economic self-help activities, on both collective bargaining and organizational angles, by requiring the courts, in their injunction-issuing capacity, to keep their hands off such activities under prescribed circumstances.[103]

Economic self-help activities such as product boycotts once again gave unions more power in dealing with management and therefore more leverage in collective bargaining.

The passage of the NIRA in 1933 and especially the passage of the NLRA in 1935 did much more to encourage union growth. In organizing coal miners in 1933, mineworkers' union officials emphasized Roosevelt's support of the NIRA by claiming "the President wants you to join a union."[104] The NLRA in its preamble (section I) states that the purpose of the law is to "encourage the practice and procedure of collective bargaining" and to "protect the exercise by workers of full freedom of association." With the establishment of the constitutionality of the NLRA by a U.S. Supreme Court decision in 1937 *(NLRB* vs. *Jones and Laughlin Steel Corp.)* the protections of the NLRA became even more secure.

The Growth of Industrial Unionism

It has been estimated that in 1929 over 83 percent of the AFL's membership was comprised of skilled craft union members.[105] In addition, the AFL executive board (its chief governing body) was comprised almost entirely of officials of skilled craft unions.

John L. Lewis.   The one major exception to the dominance of the AFL by the craft unions was the United Mineworkers Union (UMW), headed by John L. Lewis. Lewis, the son of a coal miner, had worked in the mines himself, as had most of his brothers. He spent almost his entire adult life as a union officer, and was president of the United Mineworkers from 1919 to 1960. Under Lewis's leadership the mineworkers became the largest and most powerful union in the nation. Lewis himself attained national and international recognition as the spokesman for the U.S. worker and was considered by some at one time as a serious contender for the United States presidency.[106]

For most labor historians, however, Lewis is best known for his role in promoting the growth of industrial unions — unions that organize all workers in a particular industry, regardless of their skill or craft. Under the leadership of John L. Lewis, the composition of the U.S. labor movement changed dramatically from a conservative, apolitical organization of skilled workers into a progressive, politically active organization of working people both skilled and unskilled. The main vehicle for this transformation was the Congress of Industrial Organizations (CIO), a federation of unions much like the AFL, but comprised mainly of industrial unions.

The Congress of Industrial Organizations

The CIO began in 1935 as the Committee of Industrial Organizations representing eight AFL unions representing about 1 million members.[107] The original eight members of the CIO (1935) were the United Mine Workers of America; the Amalgamated Clothing Workers of America; the International Typographical Union; the United Textile Workers; the United Hatters, Cap, and Millinery Workers of America; the International Union of Mine, Mill, and Smelter Workers; the International Ladies' Garment Workers; and the Oil Field, Gas Well, and Refinery Workers. Within one year, six more unions defected from the ranks of the AFL and affiliated with the CIO. These were the Federation of Flat Glass Workers; the Amalgamated Association of Iron, Steel, and Tin Workers; the United Automobile Workers of America; the United Rubber Workers of America; the United Electrical and Radio Workers; and the International Union of Marine and Shipyard Workers.[108] At the peak of its power, prestige, and membership, the CIO had over 6 million members and 40 affiliated unions including some (e.g., the United Steelworkers of America) that were created entirely through the organizing efforts of the CIO.

The idea to form a federation of industrial unions came from national union leaders who were dissatisfied with the conservatism of the AFL. At the time (1935) the president of the AFL was William Green, who took over the office in 1924 after Gompers's death. Ironically, Green himself was a former coal miner, former vice president of the United Mineworkers Union, and close associate of John L. Lewis. Green, however, was not a strong leader in his position as AFL president; most of the power in the federation resided in the AFL executive board, dominated by craft union leaders. Lewis was frustrated by the fact that the AFL convention refused in both 1934 and 1935 to endorse a policy of actively organizing industrial workers. Although the 1934 convention had passed a resolution in support of the principle of industrial organizing, it had done nothing to actively pursue such a policy. As Lewis critically remarked at the 1935 AFL convention:

> A year ago at San Francisco I was a year younger and naturally I had more faith in the Executive Council. I was beguiled into believing that an enlarged Executive Council would honestly interpret and administer this policy — the policy we talked about for six days in committee, the policy of issuing charters for industrial unions in the mass production industries. . . . I know better now. At San Francisco they seduced me with fair words. Now, of course, having learned that I was seduced, I am enraged and I am ready to rend my seducers limb from limb.[109]

True to his word, and illustrating the passion with which he viewed the issue of industrial unionism, Lewis was involved in a brawling fist fight with William L. Hutcheson, president of the Carpenters Union (and a well-established conservative craft unionist) on the floor of the convention hall. Hutcheson, bloodied and beaten, had to be helped from the room after his encounter with Lewis.[110] The combative, aggressive, and ambitious Lewis could not be contained by the staid, conservative leadership of the AFL. He was driven by an ambition to organize the unorganized and to expand the power and influence of the labor movement in society, in government, and in the economy. Lewis's energy, his vision, his skill as an organizer and negotiator propelled the labor movement to a position of power previously unknown.

The Growth of the CIO.   Lewis's efforts soon began showing signs of success. In 1937 the United States Steel Corporation voluntarily recognized and began negotiations with the CIO's Steelworkers' Organizing Committee (later to become the United Steelworkers of America) rather than risk a strike. In January 1937 the CIO's United Automobile Workers (UAW) conducted a sitdown strike against several General Motors plants in Ohio and Michigan. The General Motors Corporation recognized the UAW as the bargaining agent for its employees in February 1937; Chrysler Corporation recognized the UAW after a series of sitdown strikes in April 1937.[111] Ford Motor Company recognized the UAW in 1941. Within four years the CIO had been able to unionize the entire automobile and much of the steel industry, both bastions of employer opposition to unions. The wisdom of Lewis's break with the AFL needs no greater evidence than this: at the start of World War II, after only six years of existence, the CIO was close in membership to its "parent," the American Federation of Labor.[112]

Unions in the Postwar Era, 1945–1955

During World War II the labor movement continued to grow as employment expanded in the basic manufacturing industries, many heavily unionized. Unions pledged support of the war effort, and in most cases (with the notable exception of the Mineworkers in 1945) they did not engage in strikes during wartime. Much the same as during World War I, disputes between labor and management were handled by a government-appointed War Labor Board. Although there was some tension between the AFL and the CIO, particularly where they both had member unions in the same industry, generally speaking interunion peace prevailed. The CIO had lost much of its aggressive, combative character when Lewis resigned as president in 1940 to return to lead the Mineworkers in a full-time capacity. Lewis was replaced as president of the CIO by Philip Murray, former head of the Steelworkers' Organizing Committee. CIO membership increased sharply during World War II, but then stagnated after the war. The membership of the AFL, however, grew dramatically in the postwar era. Several unions (including the Mineworkers) left the CIO for a variety of reasons to reaffiliate with the AFL after World War II.

Merger of the AFL and the CIO

Negotiations to join the AFL and the CIO into one united labor federation began with Philip Murray's suggestion for a merger initiative in 1946. There had been extensive negotiations to reunite the AFL and the CIO in 1937 and 1939, and at each annual convention of the federations there were resolutions calling for "labor unity," but these attempts were all for naught.[113] In 1946, however, the unity talks appeared more promising and productive. Results were not quick in coming, however, and more reunification meetings were held in 1948, 1949, and 1950, with no real progress toward merger accomplished. In 1952, however, the situation changed drastically; Philip Murray and William Green died within a month of each other at the end of that year.

By the beginning of 1953 both federations had new leaders; George Meany was the new head of the AFL, Walter Reuther (president of the UAW) was elected president of the CIO. Both men pledged to unify the labor movement as one of their top priorities. Negotiations proceeded during 1953 and 1954, and by the summer of 1955 the two organizations agreed to a merger arrangement. It was agreed that there would be no raiding by one union of another union's membership in the new federation, that there would be no racial discrimination practiced by any member union, that craft and industrial unionism would be given equal recognition as legitimate organizational structures, and that there would be safeguards against both corruption and communist influence in the member unions.[114] In December 1955 at a convention in New York the AFL and the CIO were united into a single labor federation, almost 20 years after the split originally occurred. George Meany was elected president and Walter Reuther, secretary-treasurer. The AFL-CIO merger marked the end of a turbulent and exciting era in U.S. labor history and at the same time ushered in an era with its own challenges and rewards. With the pounding of the gavel at the 1955 unity convention, Meany and Reuther sounded the call for a new, more modern, and responsible approach to labor–management relations through a unified labor federation.

Summary

In this chapter we have discussed the earliest history of the U.S. labor movement and followed the development of this movement from the formation of the AFL to the merger of the AFL and the CIO in 1955. Beginning as local associations of skilled craftsmen, the labor movement developed slowly from workshop societies to local unions, city central bodies, national unions, and finally to federations of unions. Most of the earliest associations of workers did not endure for long. Economic depressions, employer opposition, and organizational ineptitude contributed to the demise of many of the earliest unions. The organizations that did survive, however — the national unions and the federation formed of national unions, the AFL — form the backbone of the labor movement as we know it in the United States today.

From 1886 to 1955 unions expanded their power and membership and extended their influence into virtually every industry. The development process was not easy and the leaders of the labor movement faced considerable opposition. There were many instances of violence in the history of the labor movement. Strikes of enormous proportions, such as the Pullman strike in 1894, shut down entire industries for weeks. Ideological splits and rivalries within the unions threatened to destroy the movement from within. Employer opposition and unfavorable court rulings made organizing nonunion workers difficult and threatened the security of those who were union members. Through all the turmoil, opposition, and challenge, the trade union movement grew and prospered. By 1955, when George Meany, the new president of the AFL, shook hands with Walter Reuther to seal the merger of the AFL and the CIO, it appeared that the labor movement would continue to expand indefinitely. Such was not the case. In Chapter 5 we will explore some of the contemporary events in labor history.

Discussion Questions

1. What are the differences between the craftsmen's societies of the eighteenth century and the trade unions of the nineteenth century? Can you think of an example of a craftsmen's society that exists today?

2. How important was the extension of the right to vote to members of the working class in 1824 to the development of the early unions? How did this change the character of the labor movement?

3. Some observers have commented that the utopian movements of the 1840s and 1850s represented a denial by working class people of the permanency of their status as wage earners. By contrast, the national union movement of the 1850s and 1860s represented an acceptance of working class status and an attempt at betterment. What do you think? If you had been a new immigrant to the United States in 1850 would you have stayed in the city and worked in a factory or gone to the frontier and become a farmer? Why?

4. What were the founding principles of the National Labor Union? How many of these have been incorporated into our industrial system today? Which have not?

5. Had you ever heard of the Railroad Wars of 1877 prior to reading this chapter? Why do you think that the strike turned so violent in Pittsburgh? Would the police handle a similar incident differently today? Why?

6. What were the founding principles of the Knights of Labor? How many of these are now part of our industrial system? Would any of these be considered radical today? Why?

7. Why did the Knights of Labor fail as a labor organization? Could the leaders of the Knights have done anything differently to save their organization, or were they doomed to failure from the start?

8. Reread the Preamble to the IWW Constitution in Box 4.2. Why might a union want to abolish the wage system? What type of compensation system do you think the IWW leaders would advocate?

9. Why do you think the IWW never became very popular with the mass of U.S. workers? Would the philosophy of the IWW have been better suited to the unionists in the 1860s and 1870s than to those in 1910? Why or why not?

10. Why do unions always gain members during and immediately after wars? To what extent might labor's role in the war mobilization efforts generate public support and favorable publicity for unions? How might the labor movement lose public support during wartime?

11. Why did the labor movement decline in membership during the 1920s?

12. John L. Lewis is regarded by some historians as the greatest labor leader in U.S. history. How would you contrast the trade union philosophy of Lewis with that of Gompers? Could Lewis's model of industrial unionism have succeeded as well in 1885 as in 1935? Why or why not?

Notes

[1] See Norman Ware, *Labor in Modern Industrial Society*, Boston: Heath, 1935, p. 127.

[2] See Sidney and Beatrice Webb, *Industrial Democracy*, London: Longmans, Green & Co., 1926, for a more complete discussion of the diffference between craftsmen's societies and trade unions.

[3] H. A. Millis and Royal Montgomery, *Organized Labor*, New York: McGraw-Hill, 1945, p. 19.

[4]Ware, *Labor in Modern Industrial Society*, p. 128.

[5]See Ware, *Labor in Modern Industrial Society*, p. 127, and Millis and Montgomery, *Organized Labor*, p. 21. See also J. R. Commons et al., *History of Labor in the United States*, New York: Macmillan, 1936, vol. 1, pp. 132–134, which questions whether employers' associations were a cause of or a response to early union activity.

[6]Millis and Montgomery, *Organized Labor*, p. 21.

[7]Millis and Montgomery, *Organized Labor*, p. 24; see also Ware, *Labor in Modern Industrial Society*, p. 163.

[8]Commons et al., *History of Labor in the United States*, p. 172.

[9]Millis and Montgomery, *Organized Labor*, p. 24.

[10]See Robert Dale Owen, *Threading My Way*, London: Trubner, 1874; Thomas Skidmore, *The Right of Man to Property*, New York: B. Franklin, 1964 (orig. 1829); and George Henry Evans, *The Man*, New York: 1834.

[11]Commons et al., *History of Labor in the United States*, p. 186.

[12]Millis and Montgomery, *Organized Labor*, p. 29.

[13]Ibid.

[14]Selig Perlman, *History of Trade Unionism*, New York: Macmillan, 1922, p. 19.

[15]Ibid., pp. 19, 21.

[16]Ibid., p. 26.

[17]Millis and Montgomery *Organized Labor*, p. 32.

[18]Perlman, *History of Trade Unionism*, p. 27.

[19]Millis and Montgomery, *Organized Labor*, p. 37.

[20]Ibid.

[21]Millis and Montgomery, *Organized Labor*, p. 41.

[22]Millis and Montgomery, *Organized Labor*, p. 45. See also Perlman, *History of Trade Unionism*, p. 41 and Ware, *The Worker in Modern Industrial Society*, p. 175.

[23]Millis and Montgomery, *Organized Labor*, p. 44.

[24]Ware, *The Worker in Modern Industrial Society*, p. 174.

[25]Millis and Montgomery, *Organized Labor*, p. 44.

[26]Millis and Montgomery, *Organized Labor*, p. 51. See also Ware, *The Worker in Modern Industrial Society*, p. 180.

[27]Commons et al., *History of Labor in the United States*, vol. 2, p. 90. (Some historians credit Steward's wife with writing this couplet.)

[28]Perlman, *History of Trade Unionism*, p. 48.

[29]Millis and Montgomery, *Organized Labor*, p. 50.

[30]Commons et al., *History of Labor in the United States*, vol. 2, p. 130.

[31]Commons et al., *History of Labor in the United States*, p. 13.

[32]Ware, *The Labor Movement in the U.S., 1860–1895*, New York: D. Appleton, 1929, p. 11.

[33]Perlman, *History of Trade Unionism*, p. 44.

[34]Ibid.

[35]Commons et al., *History of Labor in the United States*, p. 185.

[36]Ibid.

[37]Samuel Yellen, *American Labor Struggles*, rev. ed., New York: Monad Press, 1974, p. 12.

[38]Ibid., p. 14.

[39]Ibid., p. 17.

[40]Ibid., p. 18.

[41]Ibid., p. 35.

[42]Millis and Montgomery, *Organized Labor*, p. 62.

[43]See Terrence Powderly, *The Path I Trod*, rev. ed. 1940, New York: Columbia Univ. Press, Appendix 2 for the complete ritual ceremony.

[44]Perlman, *History of Trade Unionism*, p. 69.

[45]Millis and Montgomery, *Organized Labor*, pp. 62, 67–68; see also Perlman, *History of Trade Unionism*, pp. 70–71.

[46]For an extensive discussion of the relationship between the Roman Catholic

Church and the Knights of Labor, see Ware, *The Labor Movement in the U.S., 1860–1895*, pp. 76–77 and 96–101. It is interesting that Powderly himself was a Roman Catholic. See also Millis and Montgomery, *Organized Labor*, p. 61.

[47]Perlman, *History of Trade Unionism*, p. 83.

[48]Ibid., p. 86.

[49]Ibid., pp. 88–89.

[50]Millis and Montgomery, *Organized Labor*, p. 66.

[51]Perlman, *History of Trade Unionism*, p. 97.

[52]Millis and Montgomery, *Organized Labor*, p. 74.

[53]Ware, *The Labor Movement in the U.S., 1860–1895*, pp. 244, 247.

[54]Ibid.

[55]Samuel Gompers, *Seventy Years of Life and Labor*, New York: Dutton, 1925, p. 18.

[56]Ibid., p. 51.

[57]Leo Wolman, *Ebb and Flow in Trade Unionism*, New York: National Bureau of Economic Research, 1936, p. 16.

[58]Millis and Montgomery, *Organized Labor*, 1945, p. 79.

[59]Ibid.; Selig Perlman, *History of Trade Unionism*, pp. 135–136.

[60]Ware, *The Labor Movement in the U.S., 1860–1895*, p. xvi. Ware calls Powderly a "windbag"; Perlman calls him a "blundering amateur" (Perlman, *History of Trade Unionism*, p. 123).

[61]Millis and Montgomery, *Organized Labor*, p. 109.

[62]Ibid., p. 113.

[63]Norman Ware, *Labor in Modern Industrial Society*, p. 293.

[64]Ibid.

[65]Louis Adamic, *Dynamite, the Story of Class Violence in America*, Gloucester, MA: Peter Smith, 1963, p. 126.

[66]Ware, *Labor in Modern Industrial Society*, pp. 299–305.

[67]See Sidney Lens, *The Labor Wars*, Garden City, NY: Doubleday, 1973, pp. 123–125, for an excellent biographical description of Haywood.

[68]Ware, *Labor in Modern Industrial Society*, p. 304.

[69]Ibid., p. 307.

[70]Paul Brissenden, *The I.W.W.*, New York: Russell & Russell, 1919, pp. 76–77.

[71]Melvyn Dubofsky, *We Shall Be All: A History of the I.W.W.*, Chicago: Quadrangle Books, 1969, p. 471.

[72]Millis and Montgomery, *Organized Labor*, p. 85.

[73]Perlman, *History of Trade Unionism*, p. 164, quoting George Barnett, "The Growth of Labor Organizations in the United States, 1897–1914," *Quarterly Journal of Economics*, August 1916: 780.

[74]Perlman, *History of Trade Unionism*, p. 166.

[75]Ibid., p. 163. See also Foster Rhea Dulles, *Labor in America*, New York: Crowell, p. 205.

[76]Millis and Montgomery, *Organized Labor*, p. 85.

[77]Ibid., p. 86, quoting S. Perlman and D. Taft in Commons et al., *History of Labor in the United States*, vol. 4, pp. 15–19.

[78]Ibid.

[79]Perlman, *History of Trade Unionism*, p. 145.

[80]Millis and Montgomery, *Organized Labor*, p. 90.

[81]Lewis Lorwin, *The American Federation of Labor*, Washington, DC: Brookings Institution, 1933, pp. 76, 78.

[82]Elias Lieberman, *Unions Before the Bar*, New York: Harper and Brothers, 1950, p. 82.

[83]Millis and Montgomery, *Organized Labor*, p. 131.

[84]Perlman, *History of Trade Unionism*, p. 237.

[85]Ibid., p. 236.

[86]Lorwin, *The American Federation of Labor*, p. 165.

[87]Millis and Montgomery, *Organized Labor*, p. 144.

[88]See David Brody, *Labor in Crisis, the Steel Strike of 1919*, Philadelphia: Lippincott, 1965, for an excellent discussion of the 1919 steel strike.

[89]Perlman, *History of Trade Unionism*, p. 248.

[90]Yellen, *American Labor Struggles*, p. 253.

[91]Ibid., p. 265.

[92]Ibid., p. 269.

[93]Lorwin, *The American Federation of Labor*, pp. 200–205.

[94]See Robert Ozanne, *A Century of Labor Management Relations at McCormick and International Harvester*, Madison: University of Wisconsin Press, 1967, pp. 116–161, for an excellent discussion of company unionism.

[95]See Selig Perlman, *A Theory of the Labor Movement*, New York: Augustus M. Kelley, 1928, pp. 212–215.

[96]James Morris, *Conflict Within the AFL*, Ithaca, NY: Cornell University Press, 1958, p. 163.

[97]For a further elaboration of the decline of union membership in the 1920s see Irving Bernstein, *The Lean Years*, Baltimore: Penguin Books, 1966, pp. 83–145.

[98]Irving Bernstein, *The Turbulent Years*, Boston: Houghton Mifflin, 1970, p. 34.

[99]Millis and Montgomery, *Organized Labor*, p. 194.

[100]Jack Barbash, *Labor Unions in Action*, New York: Harper, 1948, p. 12.

[101]See Ozanne, *A Century of Labor Management Relations*, p. 144.

[102]Charles D. Gregory and Harold A. Katz, *Labor and the Law*, 3rd ed., New York: Norton, 1979, p. 185.

[103]Gregory and Katz, *Labor and the Law*, p. 186.

[104]Bernstein, *The Turbulent Years*, p. 41.

[105]Wolman, *Ebb and Flow in Trade Unionism*, p. 92.

[106]Melvyn Dubofsky and Warren Van Tine, *John L. Lewis*, New York: Quadrangle Books, 1977, p. 300.

[107]Millis and Montgomery, *Organized Labor*, p. 210.

[108]Ibid.

[109]Dubofsky and Van Tine, *John L. Lewis*, pp. 219–220.

[110]Ibid.

[111]Bernstein, *The Turbulent Years*, pp. 473, 548, 554.

[112]Arthur Goldberg, *AFL-CIO Labor United*, New York: McGraw-Hill, 1956, p. 71.

[113]Goldberg, *AFL-CIO Labor United*, pp. 50, 85.

[114]Ibid.

JOINT ECONOMIC COMMITTEE SYMPOSIUM

Prospects for significantly improving American productivity would be greatly enhanced if labor and management, as well as the Federal Government, would change certain attitudes and policies that currently inhibit progress, according to a panel of experts participating recently in a Joint Economic Committee symposium to celebrate the 40th anniversary of the Employment Act of 1946.

Labor and management would best serve the cause of productivity improvement by reversing their traditional roles, said Harvard University business professor D. Quinn Mills. "Traditionally in the United States management views productivity as its responsibility, and unions view job security as theirs. But neither is able to accomplish very much with this division of effort," he explained.

Mills contended that if unions would assume responsibility for productivity and management for job security, "American productivity, employment security and competitiveness can all be enhanced." The Harvard professor said there already are trends in this direction. "Recognizing the need to be competitive if jobs are to be saved, many union leaders are saying quietly to management about the work force, 'you get them to work; we won't object,'" he told the JEC gathering.

But in reality management can't compel people to improve, Mills added, and therefore, unions must take a more affirmative role boosting productivity. Unions, on the other hand, know that enhanced job security will not automatically result from greater productivity, he said. This means that management must make a greater effort to "plan for the productive employment of today's workers and retrain them for skills and work practices needed in a changing economy," Mills said.

The transition to new productivity-enhancing work systems featuring broader employee participation, less supervision, increased job security, and gainsharing "is made difficult by the strong attitude in this country that productivity is job destroying, not job creating," Mills observed. He added, "Managers justify proposed capital investments by citing the number of jobs they will eliminate. Unions and workers see productivity advances as displacing workers into unemployment lines. Despite some amelioration in recent years, these attitudes remain very deeply engrained in much of our management and employee work force and are a major factor in limiting the contribution which labor–management relations can make to productivity improvement."

Chapter 5

Trade Unions in the Modern Era: Contemporary Events and Issues

The remarks by D. Quinn Mills at the 1986 Joint Economic Committee Symposium highlight one of the recurring sources of tensions in labor–management relations in the United States: conflicts between the efficiency interests of the employer and the security needs of the labor force. The employer needs more productivity, more efficiency, and lower costs to compete in the market. Employees view the move to efficiency and productivity and cost saving as threatening to their jobs and to their established lifestyles. Although some flexibility has been shown by unions in allowing wage concessions and productivity enhancements at some work sites, in general these concessions have been given only when employers are in dire financial straits or on the verge of collapse. It is important to note that the security interests of the labor movement reflect not only the security needs of individual workers but also the security needs of the unions themselves. As membership levels fall, the security of unions as established institutions in society is threatened.

This chapter first discusses the growth and decline of union membership in the era since the AFL–CIO merger. In this 30-year period we have seen the number of members of organized labor swell to an all-time high in the late 1970s and drop to unexpected lows in the middle 1980s. The story of the rise and fall of organized labor during this era is to some extent told by the events that transpired. At the conclusion of this chapter some recurring themes in modern labor–management relations are identified and discussed.

Union Membership, 1955–1984

The data in Figure 5.1 summarize the trends in labor union membership during the 30-year period since the merger of the AFL and the CIO. The

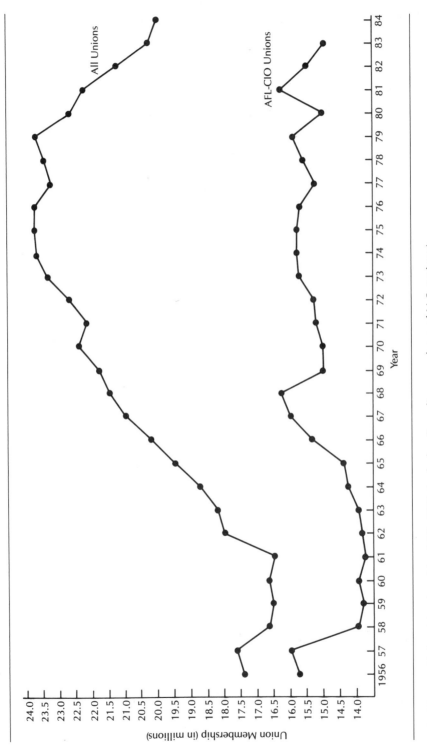

FIGURE 5-1   Union Membership, 1956–1984 (includes Canadian members of U.S. unions)

data in Figure 5.2 express union membership in the United States as a percentage of the U.S. nonagricultural labor force. The data in Figure 5.1 can be divided into five rather distinct periods: the years 1955–1957, 1958–1961, 1962–1967, 1968–1978, and 1979–1984. Each period merits separate discussion.

The immediate postmerger period, 1955–1957, was generally a time of membership expansion for most unions. The ending of jurisdictional disputes and internal union rivalries brought about by the AFL–CIO merger enabled AFL–CIO affiliates to meet the challenge of organizing nonunion workers with new vigor. The economy was generally prosperous during this period and employment was high, both favorable conditions for union growth.

The year 1958 was a bad year for union membership, especially in the AFL–CIO unions. The reasons for this decline are discussed in more detail in the next section, but generally the faltering economy, the growth in unemployment, and internal actions of the unions themselves explain this decline. It should be noted that the big drop-off in union membership as a whole did not occur until 1960. This one-year drop in membership, however, was one of the sharpest during the entire 30-year period.

The era 1962–1967 marks a recovery of membership lost during the 1958–1961 downturn. In general this was an era of growth; by 1966 total membership for all U.S. unions had reached the levels achieved in 1956, the previous peak year of union membership. By the end of 1966 union membership had rebounded from the drop in numbers experienced during the late 1950s and early 1960s.

The years 1968–1978 were a period of almost uninterrupted growth for total membership for U.S. unions; the one exception was the year 1971–1972, when a slight drop in numbers occurred. The years 1975–1976 saw the peak level of union membership ever recorded in U.S. history. Although not appreciated as such at the time, the mid-1970s may be seen in retrospect as the "golden age" for U.S. unions, at least as far as total membership numbers are concerned.

The period 1978–1986 was disastrous for U.S. union membership. Membership levels fell precipitously from 1979 to 1985 with total union membership at 17.3 million in 1985. In 1985, union membership was at its lowest point in 30 years — lower even than the previous low in 1961. The dramatic decline in union membership over this 7-year period may be the biggest event in contemporary labor relations in the past 30 years.

The data in Figure 5.2 plot total union membership in the United States as a percentage of the total U.S. nonagricultural labor force. This figure has been declining every year since 1956 with the exception of a slight increase in the years 1967–1968 and 1974–1975. As the labor force continues to expand every year, and as union membership stagnates or

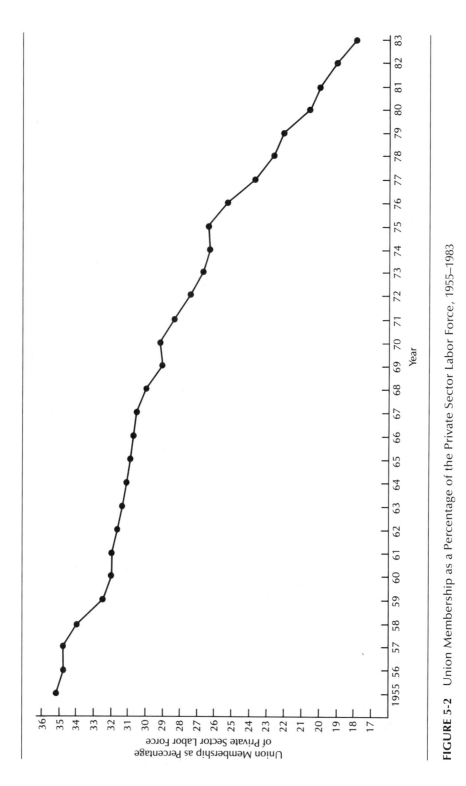

FIGURE 5-2 Union Membership as a Percentage of the Private Sector Labor Force, 1955–1983

continues to decline, the percentage of the labor force that is unionized will inevitably decline. To reverse the trend suggested in Figure 5.2, unions must grow at a rate faster than the overall rate of growth of the labor force (currently about 1 percent per year).

The Decline in Union Membership

The dramatic and sudden drop in union membership since 1979 has been of intense concern to the leaders of organized labor. As mentioned in Chapter 1, some measures are being taken by the AFL–CIO and by the national unions to reverse the decline. The drop in union membership has also prompted a good deal of thinking in the academic community about why the fortunes of organized labor have declined so precipitously in the past ten years or so. Most of the writing on this topic has focused on one or more of four factors seen as major causes of the decline in union membership: a change in the structures of the economy and of the labor force, a decline in union organizing activity, employer policies of enlightened human resource management, and a change in public attitudes toward unions.

Change in the Structures of the Economy and of the Labor Force

Many of these changes, identified and discussed in detail in Chapter 3, have been unfavorable to unions. One such change is the shift in employment from manufacturing, a traditional union stronghold, to employment in the service sector of the economy, a sector always much less a source of union membership. Another change has been a shift in population out of the states in the upper Midwest and Northeast — again, traditionally strong prolabor parts of the country and nonright-to-work states — to states in the Southeast and Southwest, states where unions are weak and also where there are likely to be right-to-work laws. A third such structural change is the growth of white collar and technical occupations, traditionally nonunion, and the decline of blue collar occupations, jobs traditionally viewed as more likely held by union members. Finally, the growth of the number of women in the labor force over the past few years has also been identified as having a negative effect on union membership because women have traditionally not been viewed as having the level of prounion sentiment that men have.

In a very innovative and insightful article published in 1985, Henry Farber of MIT performed an econometric analysis of the decline in the percentage of the labor force which is unionized from 1956–1978 using these four structural variables as the major independent variables in a regression analysis.[1] Farber's results indicate that his model can explain only about 40 percent of the decline in the percentage of the union labor force. Of the 9.4 percent decline in the percentage of the labor force unionized between 1956 and 1978, Farber found that the shift away from manufacturing accounted for about 1 percent of the total decline, that the shift toward the South and toward white collar occupations both accounted for 1.2 percent of the decline, and that the increase in the number of women in the labor force accounted for 0.5 percent of the decline. Farber concludes that while the structural changes that have been occurring in the economy and the labor force over the past few years are an important dimension of the decline in union membership over the same period, these structural changes are not the only cause for declining union membership levels and in any event are not responsible for the major portion of the decline that has occurred. It should be pointed out, of course, that the structural changes are long-term changes and may do little to explain the sharp drop in union membership since 1978.

Decline in Union Organizing Activity

One of the ways that unions grow is through organizing nonunion members of the labor force into unions. Since 1935 one of the chief methods of organizing the nonunionized has been through National Labor Relations Board (NLRB) conducted representation elections. When it wins a representation election a union wins the right to negotiate for a group of workers, and it may also win the right to enroll these workers as union members (see Chapter 8). In any event, NLRB representation elections represent a possible source of union growth. In the early 1950s unions were organizing as much as 2 percent of the labor force per year into unions through NLRB representation elections.[2] In the 1980s that figure had dropped to 0.14 percent. The decline in the number of new union members added to the ranks of organized labor through NLRB representation elections is due to four factors: the decline in the number of NLRB elections; the decline in the average size of the election unit (number of persons eligible to vote) in these elections over the past years; the decline in the percentage of elections won by unions (unions win only 45 percent of representation elections conducted today; in the 1950s, unions were winning over 60 percent of these elections); and the increase in the number of workers lost through decertification elections, in which election workers vote to revoke a union's right to represent them for collective bargaining purposes and return to nonunion status. In recent years, unions have won only about 25 percent of decertification elections.

Richard B. Freeman of Harvard University in 1985 published research investigating the decline of union success in NLRB elections over the past 30 years. He found that the level of union expenditures per worker in organizing campaigns is declining and has been declining since the 1950s.[3] Unions do not devote the amount of resources to winning representation elections today that they used to do. As dues revenues fall, there is even less money to spend on organizing campaigns in the future. Second, Freeman found that employers are much more vigorous in their campaigns opposing unions today than in the past. His data show that the volume of employer unfair labor practices increased 300 percent between 1960 and 1980; many of these unfair labor practices were in connection with union organizing campaigns. In addition, Freeman cited evidence on the increased use of management consultants employed by employers to conduct their organizing campaigns against the union as a factor in the decrease of union success in winning NLRB representation elections. Third, Freeman pointed to changes in the labor force (much the same as those identified by Farber) as a contributing factor to the decline in union success in NLRB representation elections. In closing his article, Freeman concludes that 40 percent of the decline in the union success rate of winning NLRB representation elections over the past 30 years is due to increased employer opposition, 40 percent to structural changes in the labor force, and 20 percent to decreased union expenditures or organizing campaigns.[4]

Change in Employer Policies of Human Resource Management

Many employers are union employers working to become nonunion employers; others are employers who have never had a union representing their employees. Several studies have been conducted recently on the personnel policies of successful nonunion companies and also of companies whose labor force is union at some facilities but nonunion at others. Fred Foulkes of Boston University published an extensive study of 26 predominantly nonunion manufacturing firms in 1981 and found that these nonunion firms had a variety of human resource policies that enabled them to maintain their nonunion status.[5] The nonunion firms generally provided employees with some measure of job security and provided protection against layoff. These firms provided their employees with promotion from within the system as well as job posting and job bidding schemes. The large nonunion manufacturing firms had larger than average personnel departments, the function of which was viewed as very important. Foulkes's research also showed that the nonunion manufacturing firms in his sample maintained compensation levels at the industry level or even above it, removing one of the prime motives for unionization among employees. Nonunion firms made effective use of communications to keep employees informed about company operations and also to allow employees to convey problems or complaints back to management. Finally, Foulkes found that the nonunion firms were very concerned with how managers were selected, developed, and evaluated, and encouraged managers at all levels to show concern for human resource issues.

In a related study, Anil Verma and Thomas Kochan investigated the personnel policies of a large manufacturing firm that had both union and nonunion operations.[6] This employer was expanding operations in the nonunion facilities and contracting them in the union facilities. Furthermore, the authors found that in the nonunion facilities the employer was following many of the policies identified by Foulkes to guarantee the continued nonunion status of these facilities.

Changes in the Legal System

Several recent National Labor Relations Board decisions have changed the rules of collective bargaining — rules in some cases dating back 20 or 25 years.

As of the summer of 1983, the majority of appointees to the five-person NLRB were appointed by President Reagan. Appointees to the board serve staggered five-year terms with one person's term expiring each year. By the summer of 1985, President Reagan had appointed all five members of NLRB. Two of the Reagan appointees are long-time or career NLRB officials; three of the appointees, however, are former management attorneys who have been severely criticized by organized labor for being antilabor.[7]

Some of the cases that are especially objectionable to organized labor involve decisions allowing employers to restrict union solicitation at the workplace (*Our Way Inc.*, 268 NLRB394 1983), to question employees about their union sentiments prior to NLRB representation elections (*Rossmore House*, 269 NLRB 1176 1984), and to refuse to rehire strikers who verbally threaten fellow employees while on the picket line (*Clear Pine Mouldings*, 268 NLRB 1044 1984). In addition, the NLRB has also ruled that the employer is under no obligation to obtain the union's consent when he or she relocates work from a union facility to a nonunion facility to obtain lower labor costs (*Milwaukee Springs*, 268 NLRB 601 1984). The *Milwaukee Springs* decision gives employers quite wide latitude to make relocation decisions, even during the term of the collective bargaining agreement. Many union attorneys feel that this ruling gives employers too much power to make changes at the workplace without bargaining about them and thus shifts the balance of power further to the side of the employer.

Of all the forces discussed in this section leading to the decline in union membership, this last change, in addition to employers even more vigorously opposing unions in organizing campaigns, may have the greatest short-term effect on the decline in union membership. Some authors would argue, however, that changes in NLRB policy have been responsible for at least part of the long-term decline in union influence beginning with the Eisenhower appointments to the NLRB in the 1950s.[8]

Attitudes of Workers Toward Unions

Seymour Martin Lipset used differences in public attitudes about unions to explain the divergence in union growth rates between U.S.

and Canadian unions.[9] In the 1960s, labor union density (percentage of the labor force unionized) was about the same in the United States and in Canada — about 25 percent. During the 1970s and 1980s union density declined in the United States to around 17–18 percent; in Canada, however, union density increased to 40 percent during this same time period. Lipset found that the structural changes that occurred in the U.S. labor force and economy over the past 20 years also occurred in Canada. Canadian employers opposed unions in representation elections, too — often using U.S. consultants experienced from fighting U.S. unions to aid them. Many Canadian employers used modern human resource management systems similar to those that U.S. employers might use.

Lipset believes the one major difference between the U.S. and Canadian industrial relations systems is the difference in public attitudes toward unions. Citing data from annual Gallup polls asking respondents their opinions about a variety of issues, Lipset finds that public disapproval of unions in the United States has increased from a low of 14 percent in 1957 to a high of 35 percent in the summer of 1981. Lipset found that the decline in public opinion about unions has its greatest effect on the union's ability to win NLRB representation elections, and stated at one point in his paper:

> A major, if not the major, factor affecting union growth or decline and ability to win certification elections is variation in the public estimation of unions. The opinion of workers varies almost totally in tandem with that of Americans as a whole. And knowing the distribution of public attitudes in a given year permits a fairly close prediction of the actual union density and winning percentage of unions in NLRB certification elections.[10]

Lipset reviewed several studies showing the difference in public attitudes toward unions and collectivist movements in general between the United States and Canada. U.S. citizens were found to be much more individualistic and more opposed to state intervention in virtually all aspects of their lives. Canadians were found to be more collectivistic and more accepting of state intervention in business and public welfare.

Major Events in Labor Relations, 1955–1986

Innovations in Bargaining, 1955–1957

During the short period 1955–1957 unions engaged in a variety of creative collective bargaining practices that served to stabilize their membership and to enhance their reputation as effective bargainers. In June 1955 the United Automobile Workers negotiated a pattern-setting agreement with Ford Motor Company establishing a supplementary unemployment benefit (SUB) to workers who are temporarily laid off. The SUB plan, financed by the employer, paid a supplement to the unemployment insurance benefits received by laid-off workers. SUB plans were negotiated in the steel industry in 1956.

The negotiation of the SUB benefit by the UAW in 1955 followed the negotiations of the first cost of living allowances (COLAs) for industrial workers by the UAW in its contract with the General Motors Corporation in 1950. Cost of living allowances protect the earnings power of workers during periods of inflation by granting automatic wage rate increases indexed to the cost of living. COLA clauses were adopted in other industry-wide agreements in the mid-1950s. Retirement pensions for industrial workers were first negotiated in an industry-wide agreement by the United Steelworkers of America in 1949; industry-wide pension plans became increasingly common during the 1950s in other industries as well. The large industrial unions gained a reputation as pioneers in expanding employee benefits and guaranteeing employee job security. U.S. automobile and steel manufacturers faced little foreign competition during this time period, and industry-wide bargaining imposed the same costs of labor on all employers.

A second series of events affecting the AFL–CIO in this period involved internal union policy matters. In 1956 the Brotherhood of Locomotive Firemen and Enginemen affiliated with the AFL–CIO; for the first time in over 80 years the federation enrolled one of the "big four" operating railroad brotherhoods. In 1956 the Brotherhood of Railroad Trainmen, the American Train Dispatchers Association, and the American Railway Supervisors Association all affiliated with the AFL–CIO. On the other side of the membership balance sheet, however, the AFL–CIO lost 1.6 million members when it expelled the Teamsters Union, the Bakery Workers Union, and the Laundry Workers Union for corrupt practices. The drastic decline of AFL–CIO union membership between 1957 and 1958 can largely be explained by the expulsion of these unions.

Stagnation, 1958–1961

The major events occurring during this period included the continuing investigation of unions corrupt practices by the Senate Committee on Improper Labor Activities (the McClellan Committee), which began its work in 1957, and dramatic developments in the field of collective bargaining.

The McClellan Committee continued to investigate a number of unions and union officials on charges and allegations of corrupt practices. During the committee deliberations several prominent union leaders were subpoenaed and questioned. The investigators of the committee revealed that some unions were controlled by members of organized crime, that members' dues monies were used for nonunion purposes, and that some unions were operated in an autocratic and nondemocratic fashion. The revelations of the McClellan Committee tarnished the image of union leadership in the eyes of many members of the public. Press coverage of committee hearings was extensive; few who watched the proceedings will ever forget the sullen, combative picture of Jimmy Hoffa squinting in the glare of the television spotlights, refusing to answer even the most routine questions put to him by the head legal counsel of the committee, Robert Kennedy. The major result of the committee's investigation was the passage of the Landrum-Griffin Act of 1959, which regulated the financial affairs and internal election policies of local and national unions (see Chapter 7).

The major event in the collective bargaining field during this period was the record 116-day steel strike that began in July 1959 and continued until January 1960 — the longest strike ever to take place in the steel industry. President Eisenhower invoked the national emergency strike provisions of the Taft-Hartley Act and forced the parties back to work in November 1959; the strike was settled in January during the 80-day cooling-off period. The main issue in the steel strike was not wages and hours, but the protection of workers' rights to negotiate with management concerning automation and staffing decisions.[11]

In a related development in 1960, the Pacific Maritime Association and the International Longshoremen's and Warehousemen's Union (West Coast Longshoremen's Union) negotiated the Mechanization and Modernization Agreement. This agreement relaxed certain union work rules governing the use of labor-saving machinery on the docks.[12] In exchange, the workers received protection against layoffs, a guarantee of a certain level of weekly earnings, and an employer-sponsored pension plan that encouraged early retirement. The West Coast Mechanization and Modernization Agreement was widely heralded as a progressive, responsible approach by both labor and management to the problem of automation and employee redundancy.[13] It is a good example of labor–management cooperation to solve a mutual problem through the bargaining process in an industry that traditionally had been characterized by very contentious and even violent labor–management relations.

The years 1958–1961 were generally not good years for the economy, or for the labor movement, particularly in the industrial sector. Unemployment rates, which had averaged around 3.5 percent during the early 1950s, suddenly jumped to 6.8 percent in 1958. Furthermore, unemployment rose to 10.6 percent in durable goods industries. Massive layoffs in the durable goods industries (particularly automobile manufacture) beginning in early 1960 were responsible for a large part of the dramatic drop in trade union membership in 1960–1961. Moreover, the heavy manufacturing operations were automating many of their processes during this period as well, so when the recovery began in 1962 not all employees were hired back to their old positions.

New Gains and Growth, 1962–1967

The period 1962–1967 was a period of general union growth, as the data in Figure 5.1 indicate. Major events involved three groups of employees:

railroad workers, East Coast and Gulf Coast longshoremen, and public employees.

Railroad Workers.   The railroad employees began their disputes with the railroad industry in 1959. The five operating brotherhoods (Locomotive Engineers, Firemen, Brakemen, Conductors, and Switchmen) began negotiating in that year over several issues involving pay, retirement, and work rules. After several fruitless months of bargaining, the parties agreed to submit their unresolved bargaining issues to a presidential panel for recommendations in 1960. In 1962 the presidential panel made its recommendations, which called for lowering of the retirement age, reformation of the pay structure, elimination of the fireman's position on diesel locomotives doing yard and freight work, and the use of binding arbitration to settle future disputes over technological change. The recommendation was advisory, not binding, on both labor and management.

The parties continued to negotiate after the commission's recommendations were publicized, but to no avail. The major unresolved issues involved the elimination of the fireman's position and the size of the train crew to be used. In August 1963 Congress passed legislation requiring that the parties submit their unresolved issues to arbitration. The arbitrator's report issued in November called for the gradual elimination of the fireman's position in freight and yard work, but could not rule on the size of the train crew; this issue was sent back to the parties for further negotiations. In June 1964, railroad unions and the carriers finally settled their dispute. The major issue involving the elimination of the fireman's position was to be handled gradually through encouraging early retirement as much as possible. Nevertheless, the competition by the airlines for passenger business and the competition from trucklines for freight business (made possible by an expansion of the interstate freeway system) and the continuation of antiquated staffing rules contributed to the decline in the railroad industry. As employment in the industry declined, so would membership in the railway unions.

Longshoremen.   As mentioned earlier, employers and West Coast longshoremen reached agreement in 1960 over issues involving technological change on the docks and the handling of containerized cargo. The East Coast and Gulf port longshoremen faced these same issues in 1962 but were not able to resolve them quite as easily as their counterparts on the West Coast. The initial strike called in late 1962 was halted by a Taft-Hartley national emergency strike injunction, and in January 1963 the parties agreed to go back to work pending a study of the issues in dispute by a presidential task force. The union and the employers' association, however, differed on their opinions of the task force's recommendations, and in October 1964 the union went on strike again. President Johnson intervened by requesting an 80-day cooling-off period (as President Kennedy had done in 1962) and the parties went back to the bargaining table. By January 1965 the negotiations still had not produced a resolution to the dispute and the union went on strike again. Finally, in March 1965 the parties reached an agreement acceptable to both sides. Technological change was a threat to the East Coast and Gulf dockworkers just as it had been a threat to the West Coast dockworkers earlier in the 1960s. Containerized cargo handling mechanized the docks and made unnecessary the large stevedore gangs used to unload cargo in the 1940s and 1950s. The march of technology was to diminish the numbers and strategic importance of longshoremen in the national economy.

Public Employees. One major causal factor behind the growth and development of public sector collective bargaining was the development of a legal framework that governed and promoted these activities. Probably the first step in developing such a framework came in January 1962 when President Kennedy signed Executive Order 10988, which specifically recognized the right of federal employees to join unions and to negotiate with their employer. Although it did not authorize bargaining in the federal sector to the extent that we know it today, Executive Order 10988 did mark the beginning of a new era in public sector labor–management relations (see Chapter 14).

Although the state of Wisconsin first passed a state employee bargaining law in 1959, many states did not pass bargaining laws for their employees until after the passage of Executive Order 10988. The state of New York's Taylor law passed in 1967 exemplifies the type of law passed by progressive states in regulating collective bargaining and contract negotiation for both public employers and public unions, but forbade strikes or other types of economic actions frequently found in private sector labor–management relations. The no-strike provisions of the Taylor law were tested early in 1967 when the New York City teachers went on strike, and in February 1968 when the sanitation department employees went on a nine-day strike. In September 1968 the New York teachers again went on strike until well into November, delaying opening of the schools.

This is not to say that public employees went on strike only in New York; virtually every major city in every state saw some expression of public employee militance during the era of the middle and late 1960s. Martin Luther King, Jr. was in Memphis, Tennessee, marching in support of striking garbage workers when he was assassinated in 1968. By the end of 1968 public employee unions claimed over 2.2 million members — over 10 percent of total labor union membership. The truly remarkable thing about this statistic is that in 1960 there were fewer than 1 million public employees in unions, few of them having any statutory or common law right even to belong to a union, much less to have the right to bargain with their employer.

Economic Gains and Turmoil, 1968–1978

The major events in the field of labor–management relations during the period 1968–1978 involve issues concerning internal union affairs, nationwide strikes in major industries, the passage of legislation directly affecting collective bargaining and labor relations, and experiments in nonconfrontational bargaining involving wage concessions in some instances. Labor union membership during this period generally showed a positive upward trend. As in previous periods, however, the proportion of the labor force in unions continued to decline, indicating that the labor force overall was growing faster than the union labor force.

One area that received significant media attention in the field of labor and industrial relations involved internal union affairs. As in earlier periods, the Teamsters Union was the subject of legal investigation and prosecution. The 1965 conviction of Teamsters' president Jimmy Hoffa for jury tampering was upheld in January 1966. Hoffa went to jail and served five years on his conviction, although he retained his union presidency for much of his prison term. In July 1971 Frank Fitzsimmons was elected Teamsters president. In December 1971, President Richard M. Nixon had Hoffa released from prison and commuted his sentence on the condition that Hoffa not run for union office until 1980. Hoffa was released in 1971, but appealed the restrictions on his release as unconstitutional. On July 30, 1975 Jimmy Hoffa disappeared from a restaurant in Detroit and has not been seen since. He is presumed dead and is widely believed to have been murdered by members of organized crime who sought to keep him from ever holding office in the Teamsters Union again.[14] President Frank Fitzsimmons continued to lead the Teamsters until his death from lung cancer in 1981.

A second major event was the split between George Meany and Walter Reuther in 1967 and the disaffiliation of the UAW from the AFL in 1968. The split between Meany and Reuther involved a multitude of issues ranging from support of U.S. involvement in the Vietnam War (Meany supported it, Reuther opposed it), organizing the ununionized, and conservatism in foreign policy.[15] The UAW in 1968 joined with the Teamsters and later the International Chemical Workers Union to form the Alliance for Labor Action (ALA), a quasi-federation with four million members which appeared briefly to be a viable rival to the AFL–CIO. With Reuther's death in an airplane crash in May 1970, however, the ALA ceased to be a viable organization.

The period 1968–1978 was a time of many nationwide strikes, some of them in industries in which there had never before been strikes of any kind. The four-day Postal strike in March 1970 marked the first ever national strike of federal employees. The 15-day strike of the Communications Workers of America against the Bell Telephone System in April 1968 marked the first ever nationwide telephone strike, an event that was to be repeated in 1971. Major strikes occurred in the automobile industry in 1970, 1973, and 1976. Extensive work stoppages occurred in coal mining in 1971, 1974, and 1977–1978; the latter was a 119-day strike with extensive involvement and pressure for settlement from President Jimmy Carter. The rubber industry had a 129-day strike in 1976 beginning in April and ending in August that almost bankrupted both the Rubber Workers Union and the major tire manufacturers.

Perhaps more than in any other industry, the transportation industry saw a rash of strikes in the 1968–1978 period. The East and Gulf Coast longshoremen struck in 1968 (the longest dock strike in U.S. history), 1971, and 1977; West Coast dock workers struck in 1971 and again in 1972. In 1971 Taft-Hartley injunctions were issued to stop longshore strikes on both coasts. In the rail industry strikes were either conducted briefly or averted by congressional action in 1970, 1971, and 1973. To deal with the wave of serious strikes in the transportation industry, President Nixon requested expanded presidential powers from Congress in February 1970 and in February 1971. In both cases, however, the president's proposed legislative changes to the Taft-Hartley Act and the Railway Labor Act were rejected.

A third major series of events in the 1968–1978 period involved changes in legislation that directly affected collective bargaining and labor relations. In June 1969 the Labor Department announced the Philadelphia Plan, which established guidelines for minority participation in union apprenticeship programs in the construction industry. The legality of this plan was established by court review in April 1971. In the economic arena, President Nixon instituted a 90-day wage and price freeze in August 1971 that suspended all negotiated wage increases until November 1971, and that eventually regulated negotiated wage increases until 1975. Finally, Congress passed a series of amendments to the Taft-Hartley Act in the summer of 1974 signed into law by President Nixon in July 1974, extending coverage of the National Labor Relations Act to workers in nonprofit hospitals and health care institutions.

The effects of these legislative changes on collective bargaining and labor relations were quite far reaching. With the establishment of the Philadelphia Plan, the Labor Department mandated that construction unions open up their training programs and membership rosters to qualified minority members. This in turn led to investigation of union admission policies in apprentice programs and to access to hiring hall records by the Labor Department, areas that traditionally the construction unions had operated with no outside interference from anyone. The wage and price freeze initially frustrated union attempts to catch up with inflation and led to demands for more extensive fringe benefits, relaxed work rules, and employment guarantees, all items not covered under the wage and price regulations. The Taft-Hartley amendments made possible the great growth of unions in the health care industry that was to occur between 1975 and 1980.

A fourth and final subject of major importance in the 1968–1978 period involved experiments in nonconfrontational bargaining and agreements for wage concessions in some industries. The major experiment in nonconfrontational bargaining involved the United Steelworkers of America and the major producers of basic steel. In March 1973 the Steelworkers and the steel manufacturers announced that the 1974 negotiations were going to be conducted without the presence of the union strike threat; the parties agreed in 1973 that any disputes that could not be resolved through negotiation would be arbitrated by an impartial panel of neutrals. This development marked a dramatic change in the labor relations climate of the industry that had suffered a 116-day strike as recently as 1959. True to their intentions, the parties began negotiating in January 1974 and by April had peacefully negotiated a sizable wage increase, pension benefits, and cost of living adjustments. In April 1977 a second contract was negotiated in the steel industry under the rules of the Experimental Negotiating Agreement (ENA) term of which was extended to 1980.

In 1975 news began appearing in the press of wage concessions negotiated in certain industries. In June 1975 the airline pilots agreed to forgo negotiated wage raises with Trans World Airways to forestall layoffs. In September 1975 pilots at both American Airlines and Pan American Airlines agreed to wage cuts to save jobs. Wage concessions and wage cuts were not new developments in the 1968–1978 era; wage cuts had been negotiated in many industries during the economic downturn in the 1960s.[16] What was in fact new was that the cuts were coming not in old-line manufacturing industries that had lost their competitive edge, but in the high-wage glamour occupations in the traditionally recession-proof industries. The negotiated concessions of 1975 were a bellwether of concessions to come in other industries very shortly.

Concessions and Retrenchment, 1979–1986

The period 1979–1986 was a time of business recession and recovery and also a period of almost continual union membership decline. Largely owing to the decrease in employment in the heavily unionized manufacturing industries beginning in 1980, union membership in the Autoworkers, Steelworkers, and Rubber Workers unions fell dramatically. In addition, union success in winning NLRB elections also declined somewhat during this period, further adding to the decline. Finally, employment expansion in the public sector — a factor in union growth in the 1960s and 1970s — also slowed, further exacerbating the problem of membership contraction.

Collective Bargaining Developments.   The 1980s have been a tumultuous time for labor unions and for the labor relations process. This decade may be remembered in the future as the pivotal decade for many of its industries as the United States entered a new era in the organization of its basic industries. Three industries in particular exemplify this change and perhaps give some clues as to what may lie ahead for the labor relations process.

The Automobile Industry.   The automobile industry was the earliest and one of the hardest hit industries of the recession of the early 1980s. This industry has been one of the mainstays of the U.S. industrial system. The manufacturing system perfected at Ford Motor Company during the 1920s made possible tremendous productivity gains and propelled the industry into the limelight as the pride of the U.S. industrial system. Although there were some cyclical downturns in the 1950s and 1960s, the automobile industry generally remained prosperous and profitable. In the 1970s things began to change. The dramatic rise in oil prices touched off by the OPEC oil embargo in 1973 motivated consumers to purchase automobiles that were smaller, lighter, and more fuel efficient than those they had purchased previously. In addition, there was concern for quality, value, and product innovations (such as front-wheel drive) that had not been expressed in quite the same way by automobile consumers before. Finally, fuel emission and safety standards legislated by Congress added costs to an automobile without increasing its value as a consumption good to most consumers. Foreign-produced automobiles became a much more attractive alternative to automobile consumers as a result of these factors. Cars produced in Germany and Sweden had always captured a portion of the U.S. market, but the aggressive marketing of Japanese automobiles in the 1970s brought a new type of competitor into the market. The Japanese were able to produce small, fuel efficient automobiles of high quality and low price, and they became a major source of competition in the market in a very short period of time.

The onset of the recession in 1979 brought Chrysler Corporation to the point of bankruptcy. Chrysler, the smallest of the Big Three auto manufacturers, had been losing money and laying off employees since 1977. In 1979 the crisis point was reached and the UAW and Chrysler negotiated a contract that broke with the pattern set by negotiations at GM and Ford, providing for a deferral of wage raises until March 1980. Chrysler then appealed to Congress for financial assistance in the form of loan guarantees to keep the company solvent during the crisis period. As a condition of granting the loan, Congress required that Chrysler reduce its labor costs even more than provided for in the 1979 agreement. The employees agreed and gave up 9 personal holidays and deferred wages raises even further into the future. In early 1981 Chrysler employees agreed to further concessions, giving up entirely any wage raises from the 1979 contract, surrendering any cost of living increases accrued since 1979, and forgoing any scheduled increases in the pension system negotiated in the 1979 agreement. It was estimated that these concessions saved Chrysler $1.1 billion over the life of the 1979 agreement. The employment level had fallen to 64,000 active employees in 1981, down from 251,000 employees in 1977. In addition, Chrysler was $1.5 billion deeper in debt as a result of the loans it had received in 1980 and 1981 than it had been in 1979. Douglas Fraser, the UAW president at the time, was quoted as saying that the 1981 negotiations were "the worst we've ever made, and the only thing that's worse is the alternative — no jobs for Chrysler workers."[17]

Early in 1982 the UAW negotiated new agreements with Ford and GM, even though the agreements in effect were not due to expire until September 1982. The new agreements did not contain any specific pay increase and deferred any scheduled cost of living increases for 18 months. Both agreements contained profit sharing systems that would pay workers bonuses based on increases in corporate productivity. In return for union willingness to forgo pay increases, GM agreed to reopen four of the six plants it had closed in January 1982 employing 5,000 workers. Domestic car production was at its lowest level at GM since 1948; in January 1982 there were 320,000 workers on the payroll and 140,000 laid off. The union felt that the survival of the industry and the fate of almost a million UAW members were dependent on its willingness to grant concessions to allow the automobile companies to return to a more competitive cost standing with foreign producers.

In December 1982 the UAW and Chrysler negotiated an agreement that provided for the first wage raise Chrysler employees had received since 1979 — 75 cents per hour. The differential between the hourly wage rates of employees working at Chrysler and those working at GM and Ford had increased to $2.50 by this time because Chrysler workers received no wage increases during the 1978–1982 period. The 1982 agreement also contained some provisions aimed at protecting workers' jobs in times of recession and increasing worker participation in management decisionmaking. The 1982 agreement was a short (13-month) contract.

In September 1983, Chrysler and the UAW reached a new agreement — this one also in advance of the expiration of the old contract. The reason for this early renegotiation was because the automobile industry (in general and Chrysler in particular) was beginning to show signs of recovery. Whereas the company had incurred billion dollar losses in 1979, it was making billion dollar profits in 1983 and paid off its federally insured loans seven years ahead of schedule. The 1983 contract provided for an immediate wage raise of $1.00 per hour followed by periodic 3 percent increases every six months or so to bring Chrysler employees' wages up to the level of those at GM and Ford by the fall of 1985. The package was projected to raise wage and benefit costs at Chrysler 29 percent over the two-year life of the contract.[18]

At GM and Ford, new contracts were renegotiated in September 1984. As at Chrysler in the 1983 negotiations, the 1984 negotiations at GM and Ford were set in an environment of relative profitability. GM had

profits of $3.7 billion in 1983. The auto workers had given up an esti-
mated $4,500 per person in forgone wages, had suspended cost of living
increases, and had agreed to the loss of 26 paid personal holiday days
over the life of the two year agreement negotiated in 1982.[19] The motto
for the UAW members in these negotiations was "restore and more in
84," meaning that the workers expected a restoration of their lost wages
and benefits that had been negotiated away in 1982.

The automobile companies (GM and Ford) also had some goals in
mind for the 1984 negotiations; in particular, the companies wanted a
contract that would enable them to contain or reduce labor costs per
hour, to reduce the number of hours it takes to produce a car, to maintain the flexibility necessary in production through the use of subcontracting, to move labor–management relations to a more cooperative
problem-solving arrangement, and to enhance individual commitment
to the overall goals of the corporation.[20] Interestingly, while the immediate economic circumstances were favorable to a traditional adversarial "peace at any price" contract, the corporate negotiators (especially
at GM but also at Ford) were calling for a long-term solution to labor
relations problems that had been plaguing the industry for years. In the
end the process to effect this change was made, although there was a
brief six-day strike called at some GM plants. Contrary to past strikes
in the industry, this one was only at selected plants; it was not company-wide.

Three main sections of the 1984 GM and Ford agreements deserve
special attention. One of the first areas concerns job security. After the
large layoffs of the early 1980s (many of them permanent) the union
wanted special attention paid to providing for the job security of existing members. In particular, the union wanted protection for its members against *outsourcing,* the purchase of components made by outside
suppliers — often foreign producers — that go into the finally assembled automobile. The employer, on the other hand, wanted the flexibility to outsource in situations where low-cost domestic components were
not available. The compromise was to provide job security and layoff
protection to those workers with at least one year of seniority who have
been displaced because of changes in technology, outsourcing, or productivity improvements. The layoff protection takes the form of retrain-
ing, relocation to other jobs in the company, and extra-long-term unemployment benefits. It should be noted that these benefits apply only
to those unemployed because of outsourcing — not those unemployed
because of economic recession. Further, there is no explicit reduction of
the company's right to purchase outsourced components — only an obligation to relocate, retrain, or compensate those unemployed by the
outsourcing.

In the area of wages and benefits, the UAW surrendered its time-hon-
ored 3 percent annual improvement factor wage increase for a smaller
annual increase plus an annual bonus (not incorporated into the base

wage) and the continuation of profit sharing. Some improvements were made in the pension system, some but not all holidays given up in 1982 were restored, and changes were made in the health insurance system to help curtail the ever-expanding costs of health care benefits to employers.

Many of the provisions of the 1984 GM and Ford agreements were incorporated into the 1985 Chrysler agreement. With the 1985 Chrysler settlement, wages and benefits at the Big Three automakers returned to a rough level of parity. In all three auto firms large annual wage raises were replaced by small annual increases and a combination of bonuses and profit sharing to increase worker commitment to the organization. In all instances workers were given greater protection against layoffs and job loss because of outsourcing and changes in technology, although employers were not prohibited from outsourcing or from investing in new technology.

Do the auto agreements of 1984 and 1985 signal the beginning of a new era in labor relations? No one really knows at this point.[21] It is fair to say, however, that the automobile industry has been on the leading edge of developments in the industrial relations system for almost 40 years. There is good reason to believe from recent history that the auto agreements of 1984 and 1985 may be the prototypes for major industrial contracts into the 1990s. The UAW-GM agreement for the new Saturn facility that will be operational in 1990 contains much of the spirit of the 1984 and 1985 contracts as well.

The Steel Industry.   Many of the problems faced by the automobile manufacturers in the late 1970s were also faced by the steel companies. In steel, however, the problems faced by domestic manufacturers may be worse than those faced by the automobile companies, and the prospects for the future of this industry are bleak.[22] As this chapter was being written, two of the eight largest steel producers in the nation were in Chapter 11 bankruptcy and the largest domestic producer (USX, formerly U.S. Steel) was involved in a long strike — its first strike since 1959.

The current crisis in steel can to some extent be traced back to the 116-day strike in 1959. As a result of this strike, domestic consumers of steel began switching to foreign suppliers. In 1960, only 5 percent of all steel consumed in the United States was foreign made; in 1970 it was 15 percent, and in 1985 it was 25 percent.[23] However, if we include the steel in imported automobiles, heavy machinery, and agricultural equipment produced abroad and brought into the United States as a finished good rather than as a raw material, imported steel accounts for 50 percent of all U.S. consumption.[24] There are many reasons for this: steel produced in Japan, Korea, and Brazil is often significantly less expensive than domestically produced steel because of more efficient and advanced production methods than those used in the United States.

Wages overseas are often much lower for steel workers than domestically; steelworkers in Japan make less than half as much as steelworkers in the United States; in Mexico steelworkers make only 15 percent of what a U.S. steelworker is paid.[25]

In an attempt to ensure that a strike of the magnitude of the 1959 steel strike or even of the smaller strikes of the 1960s would not occur again, the big steel companies and the Steelworkers negotiated the Experimental Negotiation Agreement (ENA) discussed earlier in this chapter.

The real crisis in the steel industry began in early 1980, when U.S. Steel announced that it would close more than a dozen plants and permanently lay off 13,000 employees. The company cited a number of reasons for the plant closings such as high operating costs, unfairly priced imports, and excessive requirements for expenditures to meet environmental standards.[26] Curiously, even though the industry was at the brink of a major downturn the negotiations of 1980 produced relatively large increases in pensions, life insurance, and health insurance. In addition, the agreement provided for a 3 percent annual wage raise for each year of the agreement plus cost of living increases. The projected estimated cost of the agreement was 24.7 percent over three years, or 7.65 percent per year compounded.[27]

In the fall of 1982, the employers who had signed the 1980 agreement wanted to reopen or to renegotiate the agreement. In the intervening two-year period the bottom had dropped out of the domestic steel industry and employers needed wage concessions to stem their losses. By October 1982 there were 130,000 steelworkers on layoff; the industry was operating at only 49 percent of capacity — its lowest operating level since 1938.[28] The proposals of October 1982 called for an industry wage freeze (eliminating the scheduled 1983 3 percent increase) and for suspension of the automatic cost of living increases due to be paid to the steelworkers in late 1982 and 1983.

The union rejected these demands, partly for political purposes and partly because of what the union viewed as greed and deception on the part of steel management. As an example, union leaders point to the purchase of Marathon Oil Company by U.S. Steel in early 1982 for $6.3 billion. How could the leaders of the union go before their members and ask them to take a $6 billion cut in wages and benefits when the largest corporation in the industry was spending billions of dollars acquiring a company that was not even in the same industry? Losses in the industry continued through 1982. U.S. Steel lost $290 million in the third quarter of 1982 and was operating at only 38 percent of capacity at year's end. Losses industry-wide were estimated at over $2 billion in 1982 and 140,000 steelworkers were laid off by the drop in demand for domestic steel during 1982.

In the spring of 1983 negotiations began anew to reach a new master agreement in the steel industry. The new agreement was reached in

March 1983 and was scheduled to be in effect for 41 months (until July 31, 1986). The new agreement provided for a 9 percent reduction in pay (averaging about $1.31 per hour), a reduction in some benefits, and a drastic reduction in cost of living allowances; and the elimination of one holiday and one week of vacation. The employers did agree to reinvest all savings from the concessions back in the steel industry and increased the employer contribution to the unemployment benefit system that supplements unemployment benefits when workers are laid off.[29] The parties agreed to abandon the Experimental Negotiating Agreement, which had governed steel negotiations since 1973. Finally, all the wage rates were to be restored to their former levels during the term of the contract, meaning that workers were to be given wage increases during the agreement that paid them back for the concessions.

The concessions in the 1983 agreement did not save the steel industry. In 1985 Wheeling-Pittsburgh Steel declared bankruptcy; in the summer of 1986 LTV Steel Company (the nation's second largest steel producer) filed for Chapter 11 bankruptcy protection. The Steelworkers union had about 700,000 dues paying members, down from 1.4 million 10 years previously. Production levels continued to be about 60 percent of domestic capacity. Some cities, once major producers of steel, are now virtually out of the steel business (Youngstown, Ohio comes immediately to mind).

The 1986 negotiations in steel were conducted quite differently than negotiations previously. The ENA was discontinued in 1983. In 1986 the large firms no longer negotiated a master agreement to be followed industry-wide. In 1986 negotiations were on a company-by-company basis.

The contracts negotiated at the six largest companies that comprise the bulk of basic steel producers vary widely. One thing that is common to all agreements in basic steel production is that they contain wage and benefit concessions. The agreement at Wheeling-Pittsburgh Steel in the fall of 1985 reduced total labor costs (wages plus benefits) from $21.40 per hour to $18.00 per hour.[30] In March 1986, LTV Steel and the Steelworkers reached agreement on a contract that would reduce labor costs from $25 to $22 per hour. At National Steel labor costs were reduced from $24 per hour to $22.50. At Bethlehem Steel costs were reduced from $24.35 per hour to about $22 per hour. At the time of this writing U.S. Steel (now called USX) had not settled with the union and the company was asking for concessions of $3.00 per hour to reduce its $25.20 per hour average labor costs down to close to $22.[31]

The collective bargaining developments in the steel industry over the past six to eight years differ markedly from those in the auto industry. The steelworkers' concessions came later than those in the automobile industry. Steel manufacturers seemed to be less aware of the coming economic crisis of the mid-1980s than did the automobile manufacturers. Negotiations focused almost entirely on wage and benefit concessions in steel — very little attention seemed to be given to increasing employee motivation and commitment through quality of working life programs or through programs designed to increase employee participation in management such as was done in the automobile industry. The domestic steel industry is in the midst of a crisis. Unfortunately for this industry, the traditional adversarial method of distributive bargaining seems to be hurting the industry and contributing to its decline rather than providing an opportunity for revitalization of the industry as has been seen in the automobile industry. The future of the domestic large-scale steel manufacturing industry and of the 300,000 workers involved in this industry appears bleak.

Trucking.   The trucking industry is a segmented industry with different economic conditions and different legal regulations for the different segments. For example, there are private trucking companies that haul freight only for one company (perhaps a manufacturer) and whose employees are paid by that company. There are for-hire trucking companies that haul freight for many different customers; these for-hire firms may haul over local routes or over long-haul intercity routes. There are common carriage long-haul companies that will haul freight for anyone, and there are also contract carriers that are exclusively under contract with particular producers.

Prior to 1980 a large segment of the trucking industry was regulated by the Interstate Commerce Commission (ICC). New firms that wanted to enter the industry had to prove to the ICC that they were providing a public service that was not being met by existing firms. Hence, few new firms entered the industry, rates were set by ICC regulation, and increased costs were passed along to the consumer in increased rates. The 500 largest firms in the industry negotiated a single National Master Freight Agreement (NMFA) with the Teamsters Union. The first National Master Freight Agreement was negotiated by Jimmy Hoffa in 1964 and represents one of the crowning achievements of this labor leader's career.[32] For the first time the Teamsters had solidified bargaining power in the hands of one negotiator; also for the first time a nationwide trucking strike became possible, a strike that could severely cripple the national freight hauling system. Such strikes were not to be seen until 1976, however. Instead the Teamsters used their power to win large economic settlements for their members. Between 1950 and 1973 Teamsters wages increased 300 percent; in all other union industries wages rose 200–250 percent.

In 1976 there was a short (13-day) national trucking strike. Negotiations in 1976 yielded a wage raise of $1.65 per hour over three years, plus a 62 cent COLA increase. The major issue in the 1976 negotiations was "uncapping" the COLA formula to allow wages to rise without limit as inflation increased.

The 1979 agreement also provided for a substantial wage increase and was won after a 10-day nationwide trucking strike. The 1979 agreement provided for a $1.50 per hour increase over the life of the agreement (3 years) plus COLA adjustments paid twice per year. In addition, employers agreed to increase health and pension insurance premium payments by $30 per week per employee. In both 1976 and 1979 the National Motor Freight Agreement led the way for national negotiations in rubber, auto, steel, and coal. The Teamsters contract usually was negotiated in the spring while the other industries' negotiations were in the fall, and the Teamsters with their National Motor Freight Agreement became the pacesetter for negotiations in other industries.[33]

In July 1980 the Motor Carrier Deregulation Act was passed, which essentially deregulated rate setting and entry of new firms into the industry. No longer were rates standardized over certain routes — no longer were new carriers discouraged from entering the industry. New firms flooded in (8,000 new firms between 1980 and 1982), rates fell, and the formerly regulated employers began to feel serious negative economic consequences.[34] The recession of 1980 exacerbated the problem and rates tumbled as trucking companies undercut each others' prices to win business.

In the fall of 1980 the employers' association that negotiated the NMFA (Trucking Management Incorporated or TMI) for the large employers asked that the agreement be reopened and that some concessions be made on wages. The agreement was not reopened as a whole, but the Teamsters did allow some local unions to negotiate exceptions to the NMFA standard wage scale for some employers on a case-by-case basis. In August 1981 negotiations began seriously to change the NMFA; the contract was finalized in February 1982, about one month before the NMFA negotiated in 1979 was due to expire. During this time 234 union trucking firms went out of business, resulting in the loss of 40,500 union members' jobs.[35] Almost one half of the firms who had been signatory to the NMFA in 1979 were bankrupt by 1982.[36] Almost half of the 300,000 Teamsters in the trucking industry were laid off in 1982.

Needless to say, the 1982 agreement contained some concessions designed to save the formerly regulated carriers some money. In particular there were no wage increases. In addition, cost of living increases were diverted to help pay increased costs of health and pension benefits. A two-tier wage system was also established paying beginning drivers 70 percent of what experienced drivers were paid; in three years this differential would be eliminated. Furthermore, significant changes were made in work rules allowing employers more flexibility in staffing certain routes and in how drivers were to be paid for certain "short hops."

The 1982 contract did not contain enough concessions to keep many large union firms in business. McLean and Spector-Red Ball, the nation's fifth and sixth largest trucking firms, went bankrupt even in the presence of employee loans and stock purchases. By the time negotiations began for the 1985 NMFA only 34 firms were represented by TMI. The 1985 NMFA provided for three annual 50 cent wage raises during its 36-month term in addition to some increases in health and pension benefits. The work rule changes and the two-tier wage schedule were retained from the 1982 agreement. Of course, the NMFA covered a much smaller segment of the industry than it had previously.

The big change in negotiations in the trucking industry has been the break-up of the power block of firms represented by TMI and signatory to the NMFA. Negotiations in trucking are becoming very decentralized, with separate agreements negotiated with each employer taking into account the financial situation of the individual employer. In trucking, much as in auto and steel, there is a break-up of the concept of a pattern and a movement to negotiate separate contracts with separate employers to accommodate their individual needs. The increasing decentralization of the bargaining structure and the accompanying loss of union power in bargaining is a significant collective bargaining development of the 1980s. It is fascinating to observe how the once powerful Teamsters Union, once feared because of its ability to disrupt the national transportation system with a nationwide strike, is now willing to abandon the concept of an industry-wide master agreement to save what is left of the industry and the union members' jobs.

Leadership Developments.   In November 1979 a momentous occasion in trade union leadership occurred: George Meany retired as president of the AFL–CIO after 24 years in the position. Meany traced his lineage back to William Green and Samuel Gompers and was one of the few people who could claim to have met personally all the presidents of the AFL (Meany met Gompers in 1924 shortly before Gompers's death). Meany was replaced by Lane Kirkland, his handpicked successor. Kirkland immediately announced a new program to organize nonunion workers and to revitalize the AFL–CIO. As an indication of the revitalization of the AFL–CIO, the UAW reaffiliated with the federation in 1981 after an absence of 13 years.

Another leadership change occurred in the Teamsters Union during this period. In May 1981 Frank Fitzsimmons died and was replaced by First Vice President Roy Williams. Fitzsimmons had been the acting president of the Teamsters since 1966 when Hoffa was jailed, and he had been recently cleared of charges alleging that he had misused union funds and had allowed organized crime figures to penetrate the union. Williams, after a very brief term in office, was indicted in June 1981 for attempting to bribe a U.S. senator (Howard Cannon of Nevada) to influence his vote on trucking deregulation legislation. In December 1982 Williams was found guilty of five counts of conspiracy to bribe a federal official and was sentenced to a federal penitentiary. The conviction of Williams marked the third of the last four Teamsters presidents to serve time in a federal jail while in office (Dave Beck, 1956; Jimmy Hoffa, 1966; and Roy Williams, 1983).

The current Teamsters president, Jackie Presser of Cleveland, has recently been cleared after a four-year investigation by the Department of Justice into embezzlement of union funds from the Cleveland Teamsters local that Presser once headed. Newspaper accounts report that Justice Department officials in Cleveland conducting the investigation recommended that Presser be indicted for his involvement in a scheme in which local union leaders padded the union payroll rosters with nonexistent employees and then pocketed the money. Newspaper accounts further reveal that Presser was acting as an FBI informant and that Justice Department officials in Washington granted him immunity from prosecution because of this activity. Presser was an active supporter of President Reagan in 1980 and in 1984. Presser also admits to having a close personal friendship with Edwin Meese, the Attorney General of the United States and the person ultimately responsible for making decisions about Justice Department prosecutions.[37]

Strikes and Industrial Conflict. There were few strikes in major industries of any significant duration during the 1979–1986 era. There was a short (10-day) Teamsters strike in 1979 and a short Coal Miners strike in 1981, a short Auto Workers strike against selected General Motors plants in 1984, and a 13-day walkout conducted by 70,000 Auto Workers against Chrysler in 1985. The largest strike in recent years was the strike involving 675,000 telephone workers in August 1983. A strike at USX is entering its third month and may prove to be one of the most important strikes of the 1980s. In general, the 1980s saw a dramatic decline in strike activity. In all 1985 there were only 54 nationwide that involved 1,000 workers or more. During the years 1969–1979, by way of contrast, there were never fewer than 200 large strikes in any given year. Only 324,000 workers were involved in strikes in 1985 and only 376,000 were involved in strikes in 1984. In the 1969–1979 era the involvement level was never less than one million workers in any one year. In 1985 only 0.03 percent of working time was lost because of strikes (three days per 10,000 workers); this is the lowest this figure has ever been in peacetime.[38]

There were some strikes, however, that received significant media attention. In the summer of 1981 professional baseball players went on strike against the owners; the strike was settled in August 1981. Also in August 1981, the Professional Air Traffic Controllers Organization (PATCO) went on strike against the Federal Aviation Administration. Under federal statute the strike was illegal and President Reagan ordered that all striking air traffic controllers be terminated from employment with the federal government; in October the Federal Labor Relations Authority decertified PATCO as bargaining representatives for the controllers. By January 1982, PATCO admitted defeat.[39] Many people feel the PATCO strike was a turning point in the labor relations climate in the United States, signaling a "get tough" attitude on the part of public officials and employers regarding union activities. The PATCO strike was an illegal strike and an unpopular one, and few voices were raised in public or in the press in defense of the air traffic controllers.

The year 1982 saw another strike in professional sports, this time in professional football. Initial demands of the union called for a fixed share of all revenue to go to the players. The employers steadfastly refused to this demand and a strike was called in September; after a nine-week strike a settlement was reached in November 1982. A one-day strike was also called in professional baseball in the summer of 1985. Although the strikes in professional sports involved a very small number of people and had a negligible effect on interstate commerce, public interest in these disputes and media attention to them made them appear to be of great importance.

The events of the 1978–1986 period indicate that collective bargaining is an enduring process responsive to changes in the economy and to the needs of the employer as well as the needs of employees. The concessions negotiated in major manufacturing industries indicate that unions will bargain a reduction in costs when faced with economic necessity. The decline in the number of strikes in major industries illustrates the belief of union leaders that industrial warfare is futile when there is no profit to divide. The decline in union membership during this era underscores a point made over 60 years ago: that to a large extent union membership is a function of the business cycle and defies even the most vigorous organizational efforts in times of economic adversity.

Contemporary and Recurring Issues

In reviewing contemporary labor history, certain issues seem to be recurring and as yet unresolved. It is the purpose of this section to identify these issues, to discuss them in a historical and contemporary context, and to present a number of options that have been suggested to deal with these issues.

Automation

Labor unions as institutional and organizational entities have struggled with the problem of automation or technological displacement for centuries. Indeed, as Ulman suggests, the need of workers to control the spread of technological innovation with its threat to job security and

craft integrity was one of the major factors behind the formation of national unions in the nineteenth century. Once formed, however, unions
must constantly deal with the problem of technological change; they
must recognize that to oppose technological innovation is almost always a self-defeating short-term strategy. On the other hand, unions
must still try to protect their members' jobs when faced with displacement and their skills when faced with tools that delete the craft component of the job.[40]

One major theme voiced by many observers of the labor relations
climate in the 1960s was the threat of automation. B. J. Widick, writing
in 1964, reports that a Gallup poll showed that people's fears about unemployment from automation were second only to their fears about the
military threat of the Soviet Union.[41] John Snyder, writing in the *New
York Times,* called automation the nation's major domestic problem in
1964 and estimated that factory automation caused the elimination of
40,000 jobs a week or 2 million jobs a year.[42] Charles Killingsworth in
a 1963 Senate testimony stated that automation in mature industries
(such as automobile manufacture) displaced workers and that "improved productivity made possible by labor saving machines simply en-
ables the industry to keep up with the normal growth of the market
while employing fewer production workers."[43]

The challenge of automation is very much a contemporary labor issue as much as it is a historical one. The concerns raised in the early
1960s about automation and its effects on the work force are repeated
in the 1980s with just as much urgency. Writing in 1981, Charles Craypo
cites changes in technology as a major factor in the decline of union
bargaining power in the late 1970s. Using contemporary examples from
meatpacking, rubber tire manufacture, coal mining, printing, building
construction, chemical refining, and steel manufacturing, Craypo shows
how technological change has displaced workers and weakened union
bargaining power.[44]

Suggestions for how unions and the public are to deal with the problem of technological displacement and the substitution of capital for
labor vary widely. Some have recommended that automation be encouraged at all costs because eventually technological change creates
more jobs than it destroys, and it makes possible the revitalization of
industry.[45] Others would recommend that government programs be established that would encourage labor mobility and sponsor training
programs for those displaced by technological change.[46] Others have
recommended the need for long-range forecasting and manpower planning to deal with problems before technological displacement becomes
a source of unemployment or skill obsolescence.[47] Still others have suggested that union political power be mobilized to control technological
displacement and to restrict the substitution of capital for labor
through protective legislation.[48]

Whatever solution is ultimately chosen, the problem of technological displacement and capital substitution is likely to remain a troubling issue for unions and for their members. Although in the long term it may be the only source for real growth and improved productivity, in the short term technology does cause uncertainty, and for some individuals unemployment and economic hardship. The task is to balance the efficiency interests of the employing community with the security interests of those employed.

Public Sector Unionism and Collective Bargaining

The subject of public sector collective bargaining is a wide and complex area covered in more detail in Chapter 14. Nevertheless, the issue of public sector collective bargaining and the issue of public sector strikes is filled with controversy and continues to be an unresolved contemporary labor issue.

Public thinking and public policy on the subject of public sector collective bargaining vary widely. On the one hand, there are examples of public policy that accept unions and collective bargaining as an accomplished fact and that establish very advanced procedures to formalize the process. On the other hand, there are also examples of public policy that sidestep the issue of public sector bargaining or that outlaw it altogether in some cases. Except for the extremes just cited, however, most of the controversy centers on the use of the strike as a weapon in negotiations. Owing to the fact that the Commerce Clause of the U.S. Constitution limits the powers of the federal legislative branch to make laws dealing only with interstate commerce, Congress was not allowed to pass laws dealing with the internal labor relations policies of the various state governments. The result has been a hodgepodge of state laws dealing with state level public sector labor relations, most of them different from each other in one or many respects (see Table 14.2).

The strike issue as much as anything divides the states and illustrates the basic underlying controversy in public sector collective bargaining today. Can meaningful collective bargaining ever occur when the union's main negotiating weapon, the strike, is outlawed? If the answer to that question is no, and the citizens of the state or city want to give their public employees meaningful bargaining rights, then the strike must be accepted, at least as a possibility.[49] If the answer to the above question is yes, and the strike is prohibited as a bargaining weapon, what measures should be taken to deal with strikes when they occur illegally?[50] Several contemporary examples come immediately to mind: the Dayton, Ohio firefighters' strike of 1977, which left the city without fire protection for weeks and during which time several homes burned to the ground; the Cleveland schoolteachers' strike of 1981, which resulted in over a month of lost classroom time; the air traffic controllers' strike of 1981, which disrupted airline traffic for months and which contributed substantially to the already precarious financial situation of several airlines, are all examples of this problem.

The question again becomes one of equity: how the rights of employees to join unions and to bargain collectively for better wages and working conditions — rights endorsed as a matter of public policy in the private sector — are balanced with the rights of the public to uninterrupted service and protection. As with automation, several alternatives are possible, ranging from outlawing all public employee strikes to allowing them whenever and wherever they occur, to restricting strikes to only certain groups of employees, to regulating them and allowing them only after a complicated series of prestrike procedures have been followed.[51] Whatever the option adopted to deal with strikes once they occur, the causes of public sector strikes will likely still remain unresolved.

Union Corruption

A third enduring and contemporary issue in labor relations involves the question of union democracy and leadership corruption. The union most often associated with this subject is the Teamsters Union, which has seen three of its past four presidents convicted on federal charges. The issue of union democracy and leadership corruption transcends the facts of cases involving particular individuals, however, and becomes a major and enduring question in the field of labor relations when one addresses the question of how much government involvement is desirable or necessary to keep unions as viable and democratic institutions and at the same time to protect their legitimate interests of independence and noninterference.

The revelations of the McClellan Committee hearing in 1957–1959 demonstrated that corruption and extortionary tactics were being used by the leaders of some major unions, particularly the Teamsters and the Operating Engineers. Robert Kennedy wrote an extensive account of these hearings and detailed illegal practices perpetrated in some unions.[52]

Many commentators would be quick to point out that corruption and criminal activity in office are not perpetrated just by leaders of labor unions but are found also in big corporations, churches, universities, and agencies of government. The problem seems to be that the public expects a high level of morality from union leaders and is shocked and indignant when it finds these expectations violated. Labor has come to be seen by many as the champion of social justice and individual rights in an increasingly bureaucratic and corrupt society.[53]

The Landrum-Griffin Act of 1959 was designed to eliminate financial corruption and dictatorial control of internal union affairs by established leadership (see Chapter 7). Unfortunately, the illegal activities the Landrum-Griffin Act endeavored to correct are still with us today.[54] The problem seems to be first and foremost that union democracy and honesty in elective office cannot be accomplished through legislation.[55] All that legislation seems to do is to make the perpetrators of illegal acts more secretive, more sophisticated, and motivated to seek higher stakes. The Landrum-Griffin Act was well intentioned, but it did not accomplish its major goal of eliminating corruption in unions. What the Landrum-Griffin Act has done is to make union election procedures more formalized, more complicated, more time-consuming, and more expensive. In addition, it has made the practice of financial record keeping a more difficult job, particularly at the local level.

The implicit problem in dealing with union democracy is motivating the membership to take an active role in participating in the governance of the organization. Unfortunately, external legislation has not been successful in doing this. The law has been successful in giving workers more freedom within their unions and perhaps more protection against unjust discrimination or discipline. But the fundamental problem remains: as long as union members are apathetic or indifferent about the affairs of their organizations, the possibility of leadership corruption is a persistent danger.

Summary

This chapter dealt with contemporary issues and events in labor management relations. One of the most important issues affecting the labor movement in recent years has been the decline in union membership. Many causes have been cited for this decline: the changing structure of the labor force, decline in union organizing activity, changes in employer policies of human resource management, changes in the legal system governing labor relations, and changes in workers' attitudes toward unions.

A second major focus of this chapter was on contemporary events and issues in collective bargaining. The chapter first briefly reviewed the major collective bargaining issues of the past 30 years and, second, analyzed recent events in collective bargaining in the steel, automobile, and trucking industry. This section of Chapter 5 also looked at recent developments and changes in the leadership of the AFL–CIO and the Teamsters union and at major strikes conducted in recent years.

Finally, this chapter examined three recurring issues in labor management relations that will likely be the focus of public concern in the years ahead: automation and technological change, public sector unionism and strike activity, and union corruption. These issues have received considerable attention from labor, management, and the public in the past 30 years and probably will continue to do so.

Discussion Questions

1. How do you react to Professor Mills's idea in the opening material where he states that unions should take responsibility for productivity at the work-

place and management should take responsibility for protecting work job security? Do you think this would strengthen or weaken union power?

2. Several factors were identified in this chapter as contributing to the decline in union membership since 1979. What single factor do you see as most important? Why?

3. Pretend for a moment that you are the president of a Teamsters Union local with 1,000 members. One of the local trucking firms in your area with 25 employees asks you for wage concessions of 20 percent. If these concessions are not granted the firm will go out of business and your membership will lose their jobs. If you do grant the concessions, all the other unionized trucking firms in your area will demand them too. What do you do?

4. Many experts and advocates of the free market economy opposed the Congressional plan to loan money to Chrysler Corporation in 1979. In retrospect the loan appears to have been a good idea. Several of the nation's large steel companies are currently facing bankruptcy and could use a federally supported loan for technological improvements. Would you support government loans in this instance? Why or why not? What would you predict to be the Steelworkers' position on this issue?

5. The Teamsters Union has been plagued for over 30 years with the issue of corruption. Surprisingly, however, this union is growing in membership and has been very effective at the bargaining table winning gains for its members. In a way, the members of this union seem indifferent to charges of corruption against their leaders. How do you explain this?

6. National unemployment levels have subsided somewhat from the double digit figures of the early 1980s to a level of about 7 percent in 1986. One proposal recently from the AFL–CIO called for a reduction in the length of the working day from 8 hours to 7 hours as a way of reducing unemployment even further. What do you think of this plan? Do you think it will produce the desired result? Why or why not?

Notes

[1] Henry S. Farber, "The Extent of Unionization in the United States." In Thomas A. Kochan, ed., *Challenges and Choices Facing American Labor*, Cambridge, MA: MIT Press, 1985, p. 22.

[2] Richard B. Freeman, "Why Are Unions Faring Poorly in NLRB Representation Elections?" in Kochan, ed., *Challenges Facing American Labor*, p. 46.

[3] Ibid., p. 51.

[4] Ibid., p. 62.

[5] Fred K. Foulkes, "Large Nonunionized Employers." In Jack Steiber, Robert B. McKersie, and D. Quinn Mills, eds., *U.S. Industrial Relations, 1950–1980: A Critical Assessment*, Madison, WI: Industrial Relations Research Association, 1981, pp. 129–158.

[6] Anil Verma and Thomas A. Kochan, "The Growth and Nature of the Nonunion Sector Within a Firm," in Kochan, ed., *Challenges and Choices Facing American Labor*, pp. 89–115.

[7] See Steven Greenhouse, "The NLRB has a New Line-up and Line," *New York Times*, April 15, 1984: 1F; see also Bill Keller, "Unions Seen on the Decline — Thanks to Reagan," *Oregon Statesman Journal*, September 3, 1984: 2.

[8] Janice Klein and E. David Wanger, "The Legal Setting for the Emergence of the Union Avoidance Strategy," in Kochan, ed., *Challenges and Choices Facing American Labor*, pp. 75–88.

[9] Seymour Martin Lipset, "North American Labor Movements: A Comparative Per-

spective." In Lipset, ed., *Unions in Transition: Entering the Second Century*, San Francisco: Institute for Contemporary Studies, 1986.

[10]Ibid.

[11]B. J. Widick, *Labor Today*, Boston: Houghton Mifflin, 1964, p. 18.

[12]Otto Hagel and Louis Goldblatt, *Men and Machines*, San Francisco: Phillips and Van Orden, 1963, pp. 42–48.

[13]Robert M. McDonald, "Collective Bargaining in the Post-War Period." In R. Marshall and R. Perlman, eds., *An Anthology of Labor Economics*, New York: 1972, p. 531.

[14]See James Hoffa and Oscar Fraley, *Hoffa, the Real Story*, New York: Stein and Day, 1975, pp. 236–242.

[15]Haynes Johnson and Nick Kotz, *The Unions*, New York: Simon and Schuster, 1972, p. 54; see also Victor Reuther, *The Brothers Reuther*, Boston: Houghton Mifflin, 1976, p. 344.

[16]See Peter Henle, "Reverse Collective Bargaining: A Look at Some Union Concession Situations," *Industrial and Labor Relations Review*, April 1973: 956–968.

[17]"Developments in Industrial Relations," *Monthly Labor Review*, March 1981; 73.

[18]"Developments in Industrial Relations," *Monthly Labor Review*, October 1983: 73.

[19]Burt Stoddard, "1984 Bargaining: Armageddon Now?" *Ward's Auto World*, June 1984: 43.

[20]Pete Kelley, *Technological Engineer*, January–February 1984: 2.

[21]For one person's opinion on this topic, see Harry Katz, "The GM–UAW Settlement: Breakthrough or More of the Same?" *Personnel*, January 1985: 21–22.

[22]Ross M. La Roe and John Charles Pool, "Steel Industry Choices: Federal Help or Bankruptcy," *Columbus Dispatch*, August 12, 1986: 2F.

[23]Janice McCormick, "Threatened Industries: Can Collective Bargaining Adapt?" In Richard Walton and Paul Lawrence, eds., *Human Resource Management Trends and Challenges*, Boston: Harvard Business School Press, 1986, p. 148.

[24]La Roe and Pool, "Steel Industry Choices," p. 2F.

[25]McCormick, "Threatened Industries: Can Collective Bargaining Adapt?" p. 150.

[26]"Developments in Industrial Relations," *Monthly Labor Review*, March 1980: 56.

[27]Ibid., June 1980: 56.

[28]William Davis, "Collective Bargaining in 1983: A Crowded Agenda," *Monthly Labor Review*, January 1983: 4.

[29]"Developments in Industrial Relations," *Monthly Labor Review*, May 1983: 47–48.

[30]"United Steelworkers Balk at Additional Concessions," *Columbus Dispatch*, June 13, 1986: 2.

[31]"Workers Off Job at USX," *Columbus Dispatch*, August 1, 1986: 1.

[32]McCormick, "Threatened Industries: Can Collective Bargaining Adapt?" p. 147.

[33]Ibid., p. 152.

[34]George Ruben, "Collective Bargaining in 1982: Results Dictated by Economy," *Monthly Labor Review*, January 1983: 30.

[35]Ibid., p. 30.

[36]McCormick, "Threatened Industries: Can Collective Bargaining Adapt?" p. 157.

[37]See Cathy Trost, "Relationship with Teamsters Chief Puts Meese in a Tight Spot on Possible Federal Prosecution," *Wall Street Journal*, April 22, 1985: 48; see also, "Teamster Chief in the Clear," *New York Times*, July 28, 1985: 4E.

[38]Kent Darr, "Strike Weapon Remains, But Unions Employing Other Tactics," *Columbus Dispatch*, September 11, 1986: 7D.

[39]Robert E. Poli, "Why the Controllers Strike Failed," *New York Times*, January 17, 1982: 1F.

[40]Lloyd Ulman, *The Rise of the National Trade Union*, Cambridge, MA: Harvard University Press, 1966, pp. 32–37.

[41]Widick, *Labor Today*, p. 3.

[42]John I. Snyder, "Automation: Threat." In Melvyn Dubofsky, ed., *American Labor Since the New Deal*, Chicago: Quadrangle, 1971, pp. 231–236.

[43]Charles Killingsworth, "Automation Is Different." In Walter Fogel and Archie Kleingartner, eds., *Contemporary Labor Issues*, Belmore, CA: Wadsworth, 1968, p. 41.

[44]Charles Craypo, "The Decline of Union Bargaining Power." In Craypo, *New Directions in Labor Economics and Industrial Relations*, Notre Dame, IN: University of Notre Dame Press, 1981, pp. 115, 153–160.

[45]Ad Hoc Committee on the Triple Revolution, "The Triple Revolution," in Fogel and Kleingartner, eds., *Contemporary Labor Issues*, pp. 43–51.

[46]Walter Heller, "The Challenge of Automation," in Fogel and Kleingartner, eds., *Contemporary Labor Issues*, p. 71.

[47]Joseph A. Beirne, *Challenge to Labor*, Englewood Cliffs, NJ: Prentice-Hall, 1969, pp. 169–173.

[48]Craypo, "The Decline of Union Bargaining Power," pp. 160–161.

[49]See for example Charles M. Rehmus, "Constraints on Local Governments in Public Employee Bargaining," *Michigan Law Review* 67 (March 1969): 919–930.

[50]See Harry Wellington and Ralph Winter, *The Unions and the Cities*, Washington, DC: Brookings, 1971, especially Chapter 11.

[51]See George Hildebrand, *American Unionism: An Historical and Analytical Survey*, Menlo Park, CA: Addison-Wesley, 1979, p. 97.

[52]See Robert Kennedy, *The Enemy Within*, New York: Harper, 1960.

[53]J. B. S. Hardman, *Labor at the Rubicon*, New York: New York University Press, 1972, pp. 49–57.

[54]"Mob-Union Ties Growing, Report Says," *Columbus Dispatch*, January 15, 1986: 1A; see also "Organized Crime Commission Proposals," *Labor Relations Reporter* 12 (29) (January 27, 1986).

[55]John Hutchinson, *The Imperfect Union*, New York: Dutton, 1970, p. 370.

JUSTICES RULE UNIONS CAN'T FINE MEMBERS WHO QUIT, RESUME WORK DURING STRIKE

By Stephen Wermiel

Washington — The Supreme Court said unions can't fine workers who resign their union membership during a strike and return to work in violation of union rules.

The 5–4 decision also strongly suggests that rules adopted by many unions to restrict or prohibit workers from resigning membership during or just before a strike are inconsistent with federal labor law.

The court, upholding the view of the National Labor Relations Board, said that imposing fines or other restrictions on workers who quit the union during a strike "impairs the policy of voluntary unionism."

Written by Justice Lewis Powell, the decision is a setback for organized labor, which has argued that unions must be able to restrict resignations during strikes to maintain their unity and bargaining power.

The case involved a seven-month strike in 1977 by the Pattern Makers' League against clothing companies in Illinois and Wisconsin. The union had a rule prohibiting resignations during a strike and enforced it by fining ten workers the approximate amount they earned after returning to work during the strike.

The NLRB in this and other cases ruled that using fines was an illegal restraint and coercion on the right of workers to join or refrain from joining a union.

A federal appeals court in Chicago agreed with the NLRB, but a federal appeals court in San Francisco ruled in another case that unions can use fines to enforce strikes.

The Supreme Court took the Pattern Makers' case to resolve this conflict and heard arguments twice, apparently because Justice Powell missed the first hearing and the court was deadlocked without him. Yesterday, Justice Powell provided the deciding vote to uphold the NLRB.

But the high court's decision may go well beyond the validity of using fines to enforce no-resignation rules. The NLRB has ruled separately that it isn't just fines that are invalid; in recent decisions the NLRB has struck down the underlying rules that prohibit resignations during strikes.

While those NLRB decisions are on appeal to different federal appeals courts, yesterday's Supreme Court decision presages the outcome. The high court repeatedly referred to "the inconsistency between union restrictions on the right to resign and the policy of voluntary unionism." Armed with the high court ruling, appeals courts may feel compelled to strike down such union restrictions.

The high court's language was so broad that John Irving, a Washington management lawyer, said it may mean unions can never restrict resignations. "It's not just in the face of a strike," said Mr. Irving, former NLRB general counsel.

Justice Harry Blackmun dissented, joined by Justices William Brennan and Thurgood Marshall. The ruling, they said, relied on the NLRB's "misplaced" view of the law and is "an affront to the autonomy of the American worker." Justice John Stevens also dissented.

Chapter 6

Labor and the Law, Part I*

The Criminal Conspiracy Trials, 1806–1842: The *Philadelphia Cordwainers* Case and *Commonwealth* vs. *Hunt*

The article from *The Wall Street Journal* summarizes an important contemporary ruling of the U.S. Supreme Court, which regularly decides cases involving labor and labor unions, usually around 10–12 cases per year. The federal district and appeals courts hear thousands of labor cases per year. In the libraries are shelves filled with books about the subject of labor law. There are large law firms in every major city that handle only labor- and employment-related cases. This was certainly not the situation when the labor movement was in its very earliest stages at the beginning of the nineteenth century. Prior to that time, of course, the legal system had no need to even address the issue of labor and the law.

It is difficult for an observer in the latter part of the twentieth century to appreciate the uncertainty judges in the early cases faced. In the very early trials the judges had nothing to guide them. The United States Constitution does not mention unions, nor does it mention anything about employer–employee relations. In addition, there were no state statutes regulating unions or workplace relations, and there were no state court decisions in the early years to guide judicial decisionmaking at the state level. Quite literally, the U.S. legal system was void of any rules or regulations covering unions or their actions when the first cases were decided.

---

*The Conspiracy Trials, the Sherman Act, and the Clayton Act (1806–1926).

The Case of the Philadelphia Cordwainers

The first court case for which there are written records was decided in 1806 in the city of Philadelphia. The case grew out of a labor dispute between an employer and his employees in November 1805. The employees were skilled shoemakers, who at that time were called cordwainers. The case is officially entitled *Commonwealth of Pennsylvania* vs. *Pullis*, but it is commonly referred to as the case of the *Philadelphia Cordwainers*.

The cordwainers in Philadelphia had been organized into a union for about 15 years, according to court records. In addition, the master cordwainers, who were the employers, had been organized into an employers' association in Philadelphia since 1789. The workers' society and the employers' association had had a history of disagreements concerning wage rates since at least 1796. The workers were well organized and had achieved a virtual closed shop status in Philadelphia, meaning that only members of the shoemakers' society could work as cordwainers in that city. In 1798 the members of the employers' association reduced the rate paid to workers to produce a pair of boots from $2.75 a pair (the price established in 1796) to $2.25 a pair. In response, the workers struck and refused to work until the price was restored to $2.75. After a short strike the wages were restored to their former levels. In 1799, however, the price was again reduced to $2.25. This time, the employers locked out the shoemakers and remained closed until the workers accepted the new lower wages, which they soon did. In 1804 there was another short strike and the price was restored to $2.75. In December 1804, however, the employers again reduced prices, this time to $2.50 per pair of boots produced. The employees accepted this wage cut for a few months, but in November 1805 they went on strike again. This time, however, the leaders of the strike were arrested on the basis of a complaint from the employers' association to the court. The strike was called off, and the strike leaders were released.[1]

In January 1806, however, the eight cordwainers who had been arrested two months earlier were indicted and charged with the crime of criminal conspiracy to raise their wages. This was a charge that had never before been applied to workers' societies in the United States, but that had been used to control the activities of labor unions in England since at least 1721.[2]

The Trial.   The trial began in March 1806. The presiding judge was a prominent member of the Federalist party, Moses Levy. The jury consisted of twelve businessmen and merchants: two innkeepers, one merchant, three grocers, one hatter, one tobacconist, one watchmaker, one tailor, one tavernkeeper, and one bottler.[3] The workers were charged with conspiring to raise their wages, with preventing other workers from working at lower wages in this trade, and with forming a society that had the purpose of forcing employers to hire only its members.[4]

The trial went on for several days and the testimony revealed that most of the charges were true. Evidence was produced from both employers and nonunion workers in Philadelphia that the cordwainers had worked together to raise wages, that they had prevented nonunion workers from working as shoemakers, and that they had agreed among themselves not to work for any employer in the city who did not abide by the union's working rules, one of which was that only union workers should be employed.

The prosecution used the evidence and testimony to build its case against the shoemakers. The prosecuting attorney Jared Ingersoll, a prominent Federalist and candidate for the U.S. vice-presidency in 1812, argued that the actions of the shoemakers' association harmed both employers and nonunion workers. He claimed that the union interfered with the natural workings of the laws of supply and demand in determining wages. In addition, the prosecution argued that combinations of workers to raise wages had been found illegal in the English court system since 1721 and that a considerable body of judicial opinion had accumulated in the English court system, most of which found unions to be illegal. Furthermore, the prosecution argued that these English decisions should be used as precedent in the United States due to the fact that there was nothing to guide judicial decisionmaking in the United States on this subject. Finally, it was argued that workers' societies, such as the cordwainers' associations, interfered with the legitimate interests of the employers and would lead to higher prices for consumers. In the interest of the society at large, it was argued that unions and their activities should be illegal.[5]

The defense position was argued by Caesar A. Rodney, a prominent Democratic Republican who was appointed as attorney general of the United States later in 1806. The defense argued that the United States Constitution allowed citizens full freedom of association for the common good. They furthermore argued that the English common law doctrine of criminal conspiracy as applied to labor unions was not binding in the United States and that it violated the spirit of the Declaration of Independence. Furthermore, it was pointed out that the English cases were all based on a statute enacted in 1348 (the Statute of Elizabeth) that specifically outlawed combinations of workers to raise wages; no such statute existed in the United States, therefore the actions of the cordwainers could not be considered illegal.[6]

In his instructions to the jury Judge Levy denounced the actions of the cordwainers' society and stated that the strike was "pregnant with public mischief and private injury"; furthermore, the judge stated that the union would demoralize the workforce and destroy the trade of the city. In his conclusion the judge stated, "A combination of workers to raise their wages may be considered from a two-fold point of view: one is to benefit themselves, the other is to injure those who do not join the society. The rule of law condemns both." The jury, after a short deliberation, made the following decision: "We find the defendants guilty of a combination to raise their wages."[7] The cordwainers were fined $8 each plus court costs.

The Importance of the *Cordwainers* Case. The ruling in the *Cordwainers* case was a dramatic one, and a shocking one to an observer in modern times. The first labor law case ever decided in the United States found that unions organized with an intention to raise wages were in and of themselves illegal. Certainly if such a rule were to exist it would doom the formation of unions in the United States.

One author has noted that "the *Cordwainers case* is important mainly for affording a distinct view of a conflict of values, interests and ideas."[8] Certainly the conflict is clearly drawn in the positions of the prosecution and the defense, positions reflecting different economic, legal, and political philosophies. In the first labor case prominent members of the major political parties argued for freedom of action and association for workers on the one hand, and argued the English doctrine of criminal conspiracy on the other. In the final poll of the jury the workers were found guilty and were fined.

The overall result, however, was not to stop the growth and development of unions. Local unions grew and developed all during the decade of the 1820s and 1830s. The reason why union growth was not stopped by the ruling in the case of the *Philadelphia Cordwainers* is that the ruling was not adopted and followed in later cases. In fact, in only one other case, *People* vs. *Fisher* (1835), did the court make the same ruling that combinations of workers to raise wages were per se violations of the law.[9] This is not to say that unions were not accused of illegality and were not found guilty in court for actions such as violence, intimidation, or coercion; indeed, 18 other criminal cases involving unions were reported before the year 1842.[10] This is also not to say that the doctrine of criminal conspiracy was no longer applied to unions; in all these cases the workers were charged with conspiracy to commit criminal acts. What is in fact different about the cases following the *Philadelphia Cordwainers* case is that in these subsequent cases some patently criminal act was alleged to accompany the union's activity: the central issue at law was not the mere act of joining together to raise wages.

✱Commonwealth *vs.* Hunt

In 1842 the Supreme Court in the Commonwealth of Massachusetts made a momentous ruling that completely disagreed with the ruling of the court in the *Cordwainers* case and that articulated a new judicial theory of labor unions and their actions. The case of *Commonwealth* vs. *Hunt* was decided in 1842 and involved a bootmakers' union in Boston, the Boston Journeymen Bootmakers Society, formed in 1835 for the purpose of protecting the wages of its members. The society collected dues, started a strike fund, and established rules of conduct for its members in the union constitution. One of the essential rules of the society was that members would not work in any shop that employed nonmembers.[11] The society conducted successful strikes in 1835 and 1836, both times resulting in wage raises.

In 1840 Jeremiah Horne, a member of the society, breached one of the constitutional rules of the association by performing extra work without receiving extra compensation from his employer. The union learned of this infraction and fined Horne for the violation. The union rescinded the fine when the employer paid Horne for the extra work. Later in the same year Horne again violated the union's rules and was again fined the sum of $1. Horne refused to pay the fine and refused to let his employer pay the fine in his behalf. Furthermore, Horne defied the leaders of the union and made defamatory remarks about them. As punishment, the bootmakers' society expelled Horne from membership and ordered him to pay a fine of $7 as a condition of readmittance; an extra fine was added for slandering the society.[12] Horne steadfastly refused to pay the fine. The society demanded that Horne be discharged and his employer complied with this demand. Very soon thereafter Horne filed a charge against the union with the district attorney of Boston, Samuel D. Parker.

The union leader, John Hunt, and six other officers of the union were indicted in October 1840 for criminal conspiracy. The charge was that the society was a criminal conspiracy to oppress and impoverish employers and nonconformist workmen, and that the defendants conspired together and agreed not to work for any employer who, after notice from the society to discharge a workman who was not a member, continued to employ him.[13] Interestingly, the central issue of the case was not in regard to a strike or boycott and did not involve an employer at all; the plaintiff was a disgruntled former union member who felt that he had been unjustly disciplined by the association.

The Trial.   The major evidence cited by the prosecutor was the union's constitution, which contained several clauses clearly prohibiting union members from working in shops with nonunion members. The prosecution charged that workers' organizations that adopted rules compelling members to pay dues and compelling employers to employ or not to employ particular workers were illegal, tyrannical, and conspiratorial.[14] Further, it was maintained that under the English common law decision in *King* vs. *Journeyman Tailors of Cambridge* (1721) and the *Philadelphia Cordwainers* case (1806), such associations of workers were illegal conspiracies. Finally, it was maintained that the object of the Boston Journeymen Bootmakers Society was to impoverish employers and nonconformist workmen and that such a society was a threat to the economic welfare of the community.

The defense maintained that the journeymen's association was not a threat to society but was merely a mutual aid association, much like the Medical Association or the Bar Association. The defense submitted evidence showing that the Medical Association had regulations concerning fees and dues and prohibited nonsociety members from practicing medicine. In addition, evidence was produced showing that the association had expelled member physicians for violating its rules.[15] Further evidence was given showing similar activities for the Bar Association.

The defense went on to maintain that the rulings in the English cases and in the *Philadelphia Cordwainers* case had no precedent value in the Commonwealth of Massachusetts. Finally, the defense maintained that there had been no illegal acts performed by the union. If there had been no illegal acts performed by its members, the defense argued, then the association could not be found to be a criminal conspiracy.

The court ruled against the bootmakers' society. While he agreed with the defense that the English and Pennsylvania cases should not be used as precedent, the judge disagreed that the union had not performed any illegal acts. He found that the union's refusal to work with an expelled member was really just an attempt to extort money from him. This extortion was an illegal act; thus the union was judged to be a conspiracy to commit criminal acts.[16] The defense appealed the ruling to the Massachusetts Commonwealth Supreme Court.

The Massachusetts Commonwealth Supreme Court heard the case in 1842. Upon reviewing the facts of the case, this court found no evidence of unlawful activity on the part of the union. The court found that the mere fact that the defendants agreed not to work for an employer who did employ a nonmember of the society was not in itself unlawful or improper because the power of the society might be exerted for honorable purposes and not necessarily for injury to society as a whole. In addition, the court found that the means used by the union were not illegal. The court did not find that the union used force or coercion or intimidation or duress to force the employer to discharge Horne.[17] The court could find no illegal purpose sought by the union, nor could it find that any illegal means had been used in pursuit of this purpose. Thus, finding no criminal activity, the charges against the union were dismissed.

The Importance of *Commonwealth* vs. *Hunt*.   The case of *Commonwealth* vs. *Hunt* is interesting because of the broad judicial endorsement given to one of organized labor's dearest goals: the closed shop. The chief justice of the Massachusetts Supreme Court could find nothing illegal in the union threatening to go on strike unless the employer fired the nonunion worker (Horne).[18] The case of *Commonwealth* vs. *Hunt* was of vital importance to unions because it clearly articulated what is today called the "means-ends doctrine"; that is, if the union uses legal means to attain a lawful objective (end), then its action is protected by the law. The *Commonwealth* vs. *Hunt* decision clearly stated that unions themselves were not illegal and that as long as they used legal means to achieve a lawful purpose they would not be prosecuted.

It is also important to point out, however, that the *Commonwealth* vs. *Hunt* decision did not do away with the criminal conspiracy doctrine as it was then applied to labor unions. One author notes that just as many, if not more, labor cases were decided after *Commonwealth* vs. *Hunt* on the basis of the conspiracy doctrine as before it.[19] The major importance of the *Commonwealth* vs. *Hunt* decision was to establish the principle that the legality of a combination of workers depends upon the purposes they seek and the means they use to attain these goals.

The Injunction in Labor Disputes

The years 1840–1870 were relatively quiet ones as far as trade union activity is concerned, and thus there were few landmark legal decisions that applied to labor during this period. The late 1870s brought with them the great railroad strikes (see Chapter 4), and soon unions were back in court more frequently. This time, however, the unions faced a new legal device heretofore not used in labor cases: the injunction.

The injunction is an order issued by the courts to protect property. As early as 1877, judges began using court orders against striking workers when they posed an imminent danger to property in receivership and under the protective shield of the court.[20] These early court orders were enforced through contempt of court actions brought against anyone who violated the court's ruling.[21] Court orders were also used to protect railroad property in receivership in the Wabash strike of 1885 and in the Southwest strike of 1886, both strikes led by the Knights of Labor (see Chapter 4).[22] In section 4 of the Sherman Antitrust Act of 1890, federal courts were given the power to restrain "combinations in restraint of trade" through the use of injunctions. After its passage the Sherman Act was frequently used as the basis for the use of injunctions in labor disputes.[23]

Actions Prohibited by Injunctions

The scope of the injunction is frequently quite broad. An injunction can have the effect of halting union leaders from engaging in all manner of activities relating to the strike. In addition, it can also restrain individual workers from supporting the strike through concerted (though not usually individual) action. Picketing may be entirely prohibited or regulated in minute detail in an injunction order. Some injunctions have forbidden the holding of union meetings and the expenditure of union funds. One injunction went so far as to "forbid the strikers to assemble on church property near the complainants' mines for the purpose of singing 'Onward Christian Soldiers.'" The court considered this action intimidating.[24]

The use of injunctions in labor disputes was a continuing source of aggravation and frustration for labor leaders all the way up until 1932, when they were sharply curtailed by federal statute. But injunctions themselves were merely a technique or tool that the courts used to curtail actions that the judges felt were illegal or improper. Of equal concern to organized labor were developments in the legislature that served to restrict union activities through statutory enactment; the first of these was the Sherman Antitrust Act of 1890.

Labor and the Sherman Act: The Pullman Strike Injunction

The Sherman Act's applicability to labor was ambiguous from the very beginning. When the initial debates on the Sherman Bill began in the U.S. Senate there was concern voiced by several senators that the proposed law might be interpreted to restrict the activities of labor organizations. At the time the bill was introduced the largest and most powerful labor organization in the United States was the Knights of Labor, and many senators argued that its activities were not to be covered by the prohibitions against the restriction of competition that the Sherman Act was designed to eliminate. The opinions of Senators Teller and Sherman on the status of organized labor under the Sherman Act are given in Box 6.1.

When serious debate began in the U.S. Senate on the Sherman Bill on March 27, 1890, several senators spoke out against provisions in the bill amendment that exempted labor organizations. The bill was rewritten by a legislative committee, and the first section of the bill was drafted to read as follows (emphasis added):

> Every contract, combination in the form of trust or otherwise or conspiracy *in restraint of trade or commerce* among the several states or with foreign nations is hereby declared to be illegal.[25]

The wording of the Sherman Bill was quite broad and clearly outlawed any combination that restrained trade in any way. The Sherman Bill was approved in the U.S. Senate on April 8, 1890 by a vote of 52–1 with 29 members absent. The House of Representatives approved the bill on May 1, 1890 without ever debating its possible application to unions.[26]

Application to Labor — Early Cases

The federal courts soon began applying the Sherman Act to restrict activities of unions. Interestingly, Senator William M. Stewart (R–Nevada) during the Senate debate in March 1890 prophesied, "it is very probable that if this bill is passed the very first prosecution would be against a combination of producers and laborers whose combinations tend to put up the cost of commodities to consumers."[27] Actually, Stewart's prediction was not too far off the mark; the *second* case prosecuted in federal court under the Sherman Act was a case involving a labor union.[28] In the case of *United States* vs. *Workingmen's Amalgamated*

BOX 6-1
The Sherman Act: Two Senatorial Opinions

Senator Henry M. Teller (R–Colorado): I believe this bill will go further than control great trusts. I believe it will interfere with the Knights of Labor as an organization. While I have never been very much in love with the Knights of Labor, because of some of their methods, yet their right to combine for their mutual protection and for their advancement cannot be denied. While in many instances I think they have gone beyond what they should have done, beyond what was legitimate and proper, yet on the whole we cannot deny to the laborers of the country the opportunity to combine either for the purposes of putting up the price of their labor or securing to themselves a better position in the world, provided always, of course, that they use lawful means. I do not believe the mere fact of combining to secure to themselves a half-dollar a day more wages or greater influence and power in the country can be said to be an unlawful combination.

Senator John R. Sherman (R–Ohio): This act shall not be construed to apply to any arrangements, agreements, or combinations between laborers made with the view of lessening the number of hours of labor or increasing their wages; nor to any arrangements, agreements, or combinations among persons engaged in horticulture or agriculture made with the view of enhancing the price of agricultural or horticultural products.

Sources: Congressional Record, 21, part 3, 51st Congress, 1st session, pp. 2561, 2611, quoted in Alpheus T. Mason, *Organized Labor and the Law,* Durham, NC: Duke University Press, 1925, pp. 122; 124.

Council of New Orleans et al.,[29] an injunction was issued in federal court under the terms of the Sherman Act halting a strike and an accompanying sympathy strike that interrupted interstate commerce in the port of New Orleans. The judge stated in his opinion that the act was meant to apply to "all combinations in restraint of commerce, without reference to the character of the persons who entered into them."[30] Thus, for the first time, a strike was enjoined under the provisions of the Sherman Act.

The Pullman Strike Injunction

The most notable application of the Sherman Act in a labor dispute was in connection with the Pullman strike.[31] The important legal question in the *Pullman* case concerns the scope and breadth of the injunction. The restraining order named certain defendants and was extended to cover "all persons conspiring with them, and all other persons whomsoever." The restraining order prohibited the persons named from "in-

BOX 6-2
Eugene Debs on the Pullman Strike

As soon as the employees found that we were arrested and taken from the scene of action, they became demoralized, and that ended the strike. It was not the soldiers that ended the strike. It was not the old brotherhoods that ended the strike. Our men were in a position that never would have been shaken, under any circumstances if we had been permitted to remain upon the field among them. Once we were taken from the scene of action and restrained from sending telegrams or issuing orders or answering questions . . . the men went back to work, and the ranks were broken and the strike was broken up.

Sources: Alpheus T. Mason, *Organized Labor and the Law*, Durham, NC: Duke University Press, 1925, p. 155; and Edward Berman, *Labor and the Sherman Act*, New York: Harper and Brothers, 1930, p. 70.

terfering with, hindering, obstructing, or stopping any mail train . . . or any other train engaged in interstate commerce, from interfering with the property of the railroads, and from using threats, intimidation, force or violence to induce employees to quit the service of the railroads or from entering the employ of the railroads."[32] Eugene Debs and the other named defendants insisted that they were doing nothing illegal by striking the Pullman company and by refusing to operate trains to which Pullman cars were attached.

Because they violated the court order — the initial restraining order — Debs and the other defendants were cited for contempt of court. In the contempt hearing it was found that the original restraining order was justified under the Sherman Act and that Debs had violated its provisions; the defendants were sentenced to jail for six months.[33] Debs applied to the U.S. Supreme Court for a writ of habeas corpus claiming that the circuit court did not have the constitutional power or the jurisdiction to issue an injunction stopping the strike. The Supreme Court disagreed and let the ruling of the lower court stand. Debs went to jail. In Debs's opinion, the injunction was the chief reason that the Pullman strike was lost by the workers (see Box 6.2). The *Pullman* case marks the beginning of the widespread use of injunctions to halt labor disputes.[34]

The Application of the Sherman Act to the Boycott: The *Danbury Hatters* Case and the *Bucks Stove* Case

The *Danbury Hatters* Case (Loewe *vs.* Lawlor)

The case that clearly tested the applicability of the Sherman Act to labor unions-boycotting activities was decided by the U.S. Supreme Court in 1908. Mason labels the *Danbury Hatters* case "second only to the Debs case in notoriety."[35] The *Danbury Hatters* decision is important not only for clarifying the relationship between the Sherman Act and labor union activity but also because it extended liability for damages down to the level of individual union members. The *Danbury Hatters* ruling was so sweeping that it caused the top level leaders of U.S. unions to fear for the very existence of the labor union as an institution in U.S. society.[36]

The Strike and the Boycott.   The events surrounding the *Danbury Hatters* case began in March 1901. At that time the United Hatters of North America, AFL requested a conference with Dietrich Loewe, the chief operating officer of the Dietrich E. Loewe and Martin Fuchs hat shops, a nonunionized manufacturer of men's hats located in Danbury, Connecticut, to discuss the unionization of his employees. Mr. Loewe refused to discuss this matter with the union representatives. During the course of the next year the union made several subsequent requests for a meeting, but each time Mr. Loewe refused to meet. In July 1902 the union declared Mr. Loewe's hat factory on strike.[37] At the time of the strike Loewe's hat manufacturing firm was one of only 12 in an industry of 82 firms that was operating as a nonunion employer.[38] In addition, Loewe worked his employees 12 to 15 hours a day and paid them a starting wage of $13 a week; the unionized shops in the industry worked a standard 8-hour day and paid a starting wage of $24 a week.[39]

Initially, the strike was quite successful; virtually all the 250 employees supported the action, and the Loewe hat company was shut down completely. In January 1903, however, Mr. Loewe reopened his factory with nonunion workers and began his hatmaking operation as if there were no strike. In response, the United Hatters asked the American Federation of Labor to publicize the fact that it was on strike against Mr. Loewe's hat company and asked that its name be placed on the AFL's "Do Not Patronize" list. This was done. In addition, the union obtained a list of Loewe's major customers, retailers and distributors, and warned them not to sell Loewe's hats under the threat of being placed on the "Do Not Patronize" list as well. Thus, the workers were on strike against the employer, they boycotted his product and urged others to do so through a national publicity campaign, and finally they used secondary boycott pressure on other employers, customers of Mr. Loewe's, urging them not to buy or sell Mr. Loewe's hats under the threat of adverse action.

District Court Suit, 1903–1906.   In August 1903 the attorneys for Mr. Loewe filed a suit for damages against the officers of the United Hatters union.[40] The suit filed in U.S. Circuit Court in Hartford claimed that the employer had lost more than $80,000 during the one year that the strike had been in progress; under the terms of the Sherman Act, anyone harmed by a combination in restraint of trade can sue for triple damages. Therefore, in the complaint Mr. Loewe claimed that the union's boycott constituted a violation of the Sherman Act, and he requested a damage judgment of $240,000 plus attorneys' fees against the union. Furthermore, at the time the suit was filed, the attorneys for Mr. Loewe submitted a list with the names of all the local union members who owned real estate or had bank accounts in the state of Connecticut and requested that the court freeze or attach these holdings as a protection against the employer's claim. The court froze the accounts and attached the real estate.[41] The union lawyers asked that the attachments against the accounts and the property be lifted. The court refused to do so. During the entire course of the litigation — 14 years — the attachment was in effect. In the end the workers lost their bank accounts, but they had their homes returned to them. Of course, while under attachment the houses stood vacant and no repairs were allowed to be made to them.

The case was somewhat complicated and took years to decide. The decision of the district court was rendered in December 1906. The district court judge found that while there may have been interference with the *manufacturing* of Mr. Loewe's hats, there was no interference with the means of transporting the product or with the product while it was transported. Therefore, the district court ruled that interstate commerce in Loewe's hats was not affected by the strike, and the case was dismissed.[42]

The U.S. Supreme Court, 1907–1908.   The case was appealed to the circuit court of appeals. Owing to the novelty of the case and to the complexity of the issues involved, the case went straight to the U.S. Supreme Court, before which it was argued on December 4 and 5, 1907. On February 3, 1908, the court handed down its unanimous decision against the union and in favor of Mr. Loewe. The decision found that the Sherman Act forbade any combination whatsoever that obstructed the free flow of commerce. The court found sufficient evidence in the case to substantiate the argument that commerce had been interfered with, and that the union was responsible for this interference. Furthermore, the court found that the Sherman Act clearly applied to the actions of the union in this case. The case was sent back to the lower courts to rule on the damages allowed the employer.[43]

The Suit for Damages, 1908–1914.   The suit for damages filed against the former employees of the Loewe Hat Company was itself quite complicated and involved decisions and appeals at the district court and appeals court levels. The case finally reached the U.S. Supreme Court again under the title *Lawlor* vs. *Loewe* and was argued on December 10 and 11, 1914. The plaintiff — the local union and its members — argued that the damage suit against the individual workers should be dropped. The attorneys for the union argued that the vast majority of the 197 surviving strikers had not been active in the union; only two of the former workers had played any active role in the strike. Most of the persons named in the suit had never attended a union meeting; many knew nothing about the nationwide boycott conducted by the United Hatters union and the American Federation of Labor.[44]

The attorneys for Loewe charged that the union had been found guilty previously of restraint of trade in violation of the Sherman Act. The workers had formed a conspiracy to commit illegal acts (restraint of trade) that had the object and effect of harming the employer. Under section 7 of the Sherman Act anyone harmed by a conspiracy in restraint of trade has the right to collect triple damages from the perpetrators of the conspiracy.

The members of the U.S. Supreme Court agreed with the employer and ordered the members of the local union to pay $252,130 in damages and costs. The American Federation of Labor appealed to all its members for contributions to help save the homes of the local union members, which were to be sold by the court to help pay the judgment. Eventually, the AFL paid $216,000 and the local union members paid $18,000 of the total settlement; the receivers of the Loewe Hat Company had agreed to settle for $234,000. It is ironic that Dietrich Loewe went bankrupt during the litigation. Paradoxically, his grandson, Matthias C. Loewe, went to work in 1947 at a hat factory in Walkill, New York; he was a member of the Hatters Union.[45]

Who Won, Who Lost?   Who won the *Danbury Hatters* case? It is not an easy question to answer. Mr. Loewe lost his business and a good deal of his fortune during the litigation. In the end, his creditors collected the damage settlement, and he died in poverty.[46] The individual union members lost their life savings and the use of their property for 14 years. In addition, they all lost their jobs during the strike. It is doubtful if any of them felt much of a sense of victory to see Mr. Loewe go bankrupt. After all, the purpose of the strike and the boycott was never to drive Mr. Loewe out of business; they merely wanted him to pay the established union wage. The public was inconvenienced by the boycott, and probably a few customers were disappointed when they could no longer buy Mr. Loewe's hats. It is difficult to find a winner in this case.

The next question that immediately arises is, Was the decision a good one — good in the sense that the case was well founded in legal precedent and that it produced a desirable outcome from the standpoint of the public? Some commentators would not agree that the decision was based on sound legal reasoning. Several authors have commented on the ruling in the *Danbury Hatters* case. Conflicting views of the decision are given in Box 6.3.

With the *Danbury Hatters* case the U.S. Supreme Court removed all doubts as to whether the Sherman Act can be applied to labor unions. The court ruled also that secondary boycotts in connection with a labor

BOX 6-3
The *Danbury Hatters* Case: Conflicting Views

Charles O. Gregory and Harold Katz state in their comment on the *Danbury Hatters* case:

> But in light of the history of the term "restraint of trade" at common law, it seems fairly obvious that the Supreme Court was in error in holding that Congress meant *any* interference with interstate commerce when it used those words at all in the Sherman Act. What this may be, then, is another instance of judicial interference with the development of national economic policy — a matter properly for the sole concern of Congress.

Edward Berman believes that the case for the workers was not well presented and that the U.S. Supreme Court made its decision on a mistaken premise — that the Sherman Act was even intended to apply to unions in the first place:

> One cannot leave the discussion of the argument of counsel in the case without calling attention to the failure of the attorneys for the workers to present their case properly. They permitted counsel for the firm to present a misleading account purporting to show that Congress intended that the Sherman Act should apply to labor; and they made no effective answer to that account. An adequate presentation of the hatters' case to the Supreme Court might have greatly changed the history of labor cases since 1908.

Alpheus T. Mason believes that the U.S. Supreme Court reached the correct decision in the *Danbury Hatters* case:

> Nothing less than the Supreme Court's decision in the Hatters case was necessary to remove all doubt concerning the application of the Sherman Act to organized labor. The court placed itself squarely on record as favoring the view that Congress must have intended that labor unions be brought within the purview of the Anti-Trust Act or else language broad enough to do that very thing would not have been used . . . the decision was quite justified not only from the point of view of legislative intent but by a common law reading of the Act as well.

Sources: Charles O. Gregory and Harold Katz, *Labor and the Law*, 3rd ed., New York: W. W. Norton, 1979, p. 209; Edward Berman, *Labor and the Sherman Act*, New York: Harper and Brothers, 1930, p. 86; and Alpheus T. Mason, *Organized Labor and the Law*, Durham, NC: Duke University Press, 1925, p. 161.

dispute affecting interstate commerce were illegal. Finally, the court ruled that damage suits may be brought by an injured employer against individual union members.[47] The *Danbury Hatters* case illustrates how great was the power of the courts under the Sherman Act to control the actions of labor unions.

Gompers *vs.* Bucks Stove and Range Company

The case of *Gompers* vs. *Bucks Stove and Range Company* is an extension of the ruling rendered in the *Danbury Hatters* case in that the U.S. Supreme Court ruled specifically on the legitimacy of the use of the "Do *not* Patronize" list in publicizing the names of employers with which AFL unions had labor disputes. The "Do Not Patronize" list was used in the *Danbury Hatters* case, but the court did not specifically rule on its legality in that case. If for no other reason, the case of *Gompers* vs. *Bucks Stove and Range Company* is important because of who the litigants were: on the one side the president of the American Federation of Labor; on the other, the president of the National Association of Manufacturers.

The facts of the case are fairly simple. On January 1, 1906, the firm announced that from that day forward employees would work a 10-hour work day. The union, the Metal Polishers Union, had negotiated and won agreement for a 9-hour day since June 1904. The employees filed a grievance with the employer over the extension of the workday, but the grievance was denied by the employer. In August 1906 three leaders of the union quit work after 9 hours. The employer fired the men. The rest of the metal polishers struck the employer. The president of the company, Mr. J. W. Van Cleave, who was also president of the National Association of Manufacturers at the time, fired all of the striking workers and replaced them with strikebreakers.[48]

In response, the union asked that the employer's product, Bucks stoves, be boycotted. The boycott was publicized at the local level, in the city of St. Louis, by members of the local Metal Polishers Union. To extend the boycott on a national level, the AFL published the name of the Bucks Stove and Range Company in its "Do Not Patronize" list in the *American Federationist,* the AFL monthly magazine. As a result of the boycott the company suffered considerable loss of business.[49]

District Court Suit.   After the boycott had been in effect for one year the employer filed suit in Washington, DC against the AFL and the Metal Polishers Union. The main charges against the union were that the union had conspired to injure the business of the company through the boycott, that it had made false accusations against Mr. Van Cleave and the Bucks Stove and Range Company, and that it was trying to force the company against its will to reduce the workday from 10 to 9 hours.[50] The employer asked for an injunction halting the union's boycott.

The union in its defense maintained that there was no conspiracy to interfere with the employer's business and that the statements made about Mr. Van Cleave by the union were true. In December 1907 the court ruled that there was a conspiracy to interfere with the employer's business through the boycott, and that this was an illegal activity. The court therefore enjoined the leaders of the AFL from restraining Mr. Van Cleave's business and ordered that the name of Bucks Stove and Range Company be removed from the "Do Not Patronize" list.[51] The union appealed the decision.

In March 1909 the appeals court ruled against the union. In the appeal attorneys for the union leaders had raised the issue that the defendants had a constitutional right to appeal to the public through the press not to patronize the employer. The appeals court ruled that freedom of speech does not legitimize an illegal action (conspiring to restrain trade).

Contempt of Court.   Meanwhile, the AFL did not take the name of Bucks Stove and Range Company immediately off of the "Do Not Patronize" list, as the court had ruled in December 1907. In fact, the January 1908 issue of the *American Federationist* (printed in December 1907) again included the name of Bucks Stove and Range Company on the list. When the attorneys for the employer saw that their client's name appeared on the "Do Not Patronize" list in the January 1908 issue of the *American Federationist,* they brought contempt of court charges against Samuel Gompers, president of the AFL; Frank Morrison, secretary of the AFL; and John Mitchell, vice-president of the AFL for violating the injunction.[52] In addition, evidence was introduced that Gompers had made speeches in Indianapolis and Baltimore urging workers not to buy Bucks stoves, also a violation of the original injunction.[53]

On December 23, 1908, the court sentenced Gompers for one year, Morrison for nine months, and Mitchell for six months in the District of Columbia jail for contempt of court. The leaders appealed the sentences. The appeal was denied in November 1909. The cases concerning the original injunction and the contempt ruling were merged and were both appealed to the U.S. Supreme Court. The merged case of *Gompers et al.* vs. *Bucks Stove and Range Company* was accepted by the court and was argued on January 27, 1911.

U.S. Supreme Court Deliberations and Decision.   In 1910, during the period of appeals, Mr. Van Cleave died.[54] The new president of Bucks Stove and Range Company, F. W. Gardner, reached an agreement with the union and all activities associated with the strike were halted. Thus the appeal concerning the original injunction against the boycott was dismissed.

The contempt of court charges, however, were litigated. In May 1911 the U.S. Supreme Court ruled that the original contempt of court order was correct and that the terms of the original injunction had been violated. The court found, however, that a technical error had been made in handling the case, and that a new investigation was necessary. In May 1914 the court ruled on technical grounds that the jail sentences against the three labor leaders should be dropped.[55] For the first time in seven years Gompers, Morrison, and Mitchell were free from the threat of imprisonment.

Importance of the Decision. The major implication of the Bucks Stove case was to severely limit the boycott as a tactic in strike conduct. The main result of the *Buck's Stove* ruling was to stop the use of "Do Not Patronize" listings in union publications.[56] At the time of the original injunction — 1907 — the *American Federationist* had about 80 names on its boycott list published monthly. After 1908 the "Do Not Patronize" list was gone.

The Clayton Antitrust Act Amendments to the Sherman Act (1914)

The judicial decision in the *Danbury Hatters* and the *Bucks Stove* cases prompted organized labor to begin a concerted political effort to amend the Sherman Act. In 1908 Gompers approached representatives of both political parties and proposed that they include a pledge to limit the use of injunctions in labor disputes and remove labor from coverage under the Sherman Act in their political platforms.[57] The Republican party refused to take such action but the Democrats adopted these proposals in their 1908 and 1912 political platforms. Woodrow Wilson campaigned for U.S. president on the basis of these political pledges and publicly supported labor's right to organize. In return, Gompers supported Wilson's successful candidacy for the presidency in 1912.[58]

In the meantime, other ominous events were occurring in the legal arena for labor. The final appeals were being argued in both the *Bucks Stove* and the *Danbury Hatters* cases, and the results could hardly be considered encouraging. In addition, a federal district court in West Virginia had ruled in December 1912 in the case of *Hitchman Coal and Coke Company* vs. *Mitchell* that the United Mineworkers Union was in and of itself a conspiracy to restrain trade and enjoined all of its organizational activities at the Hitchman Coal and Coke Company.[59] Additional injunctions were also issued against other national mineworkers' union officials in connection with organizing activities and the conduct of strikes.[60]

Gompers was plainly distressed and worried about the future of labor organizations in the United States in light of these unfavorable court decisions. Gompers is quoted as giving testimony before Congress in which he stated:

> Under the interpretation placed upon the Sherman anti-trust law by the courts, it is within the province and within the power of any administra-

tion at any time to begin proceedings to dissolve any organization of labor in the United States. . . . We do not ask immunity for any criminal act which any of us may commit; we ask no immunity from anything; but we have the right to existence, as a voluntary association of workers, organized not for profit, but organized to protect our lives and our normal activities.[61]

Prompted by Gompers's pleadings and mindful of their own campaign promises, Congress and the president slowly began developing legislation to limit the use of injunctions in labor disputes. The result of the political compromises over the issue was the passage of the Clayton Antitrust Act on October 15, 1914.

Controversy Surrounding the Clayton Act

Even before its passage, the Clayton Bill was controversial. There did not seem to be any consensus, even among the members of Congress, as to what it exactly meant. The sections of the Clayton Act that dealt with labor organizations are sections 6 and 20, reprinted here in Box 6.4.

The controversy surrounding the Clayton Act comes from whether or not sections 6 and 20 really removed unions from coverage under the Sherman Act and eliminated the use of injunctions in labor disputes. The union leaders (especially Gompers) and several congressional representatives believed that the language of the Clayton Act removed labor once and for all from coverage under the antitrust laws and curtailed the use of injunctions against the legal actions of unions. President Wilson, however, in a public pronouncement stated that section 6 did not exempt labor from the Sherman Act, but it did protect the right of labor organizations to exist.[62] An eminent spokesman for the judicial community and former U.S. president, William H. Taft, who at that time was president of the American Bar Association, delivered his opinion of the meaning of section 6 in his presidential address to the American Bar Association in 1914, reprinted here in Box 6.5.

The words of Taft should be read carefully and perhaps should be regarded as prophecy; Taft was chief justice of the U.S. Supreme Court when the first case testing the meaning of section 6 of the Clayton Act was argued in 1921.

The Magna Carta of Labor?

Unaffected by the reservations voiced by most legal scholars and many politicians as to the meaning of section 6, Gompers heralded the passage of the Clayton Act as a great victory for organized labor. Gompers called the words in section 6:

the most important [statement] ever made by any legislative body in the history of the world. It is the absolute right of man to ownership of himself and his labor power. It is a new emancipation from legalism which has in

BOX 6-4
The Clayton Antitrust Act and Labor Organizations

Section 6

That the labor of a human being is not a commodity or article of commerce. Nothing contained in the antitrust laws shall be construed to forbid the existence and operation of labor, agricultural, or horticultural organizations, instituted for the purposes of mutual help, and not having capital stock or conducted for profit, or to forbid or restrain individual members of such organizations from lawfully carrying out the legitimate objects thereof; nor shall such organizations, or the members thereof, be held or construed to be illegal combinations or conspiracies in restraint of trade, under the antitrust laws.

Section 20

That no restraining order or injunction shall be granted by any court of the United States, or a judge or the judges thereof, in any case between an employer and employees, or between employers and employees, or between employees, or between persons employed and persons seeking employment; involving, or growing out of, a dispute concerning terms or conditions of employment, unless necessary to prevent irreparable injury to property, or to a property right, of the party making the application, for which injury there is no adequate remedy at law, and such property or property right must be described with particularity in the application, which must be in writing and sworn to by the applicant or by his agent or attorney.

And no such restraining order or injunction shall prohibit any person or persons, whether singly or in concert, from terminating any relation of employment, or from ceasing to perform any work or labor, or from recommending, advising, or persuading others by peaceful means so to do; or from attending at any place where any such person or persons may lawfully be, for the purpose of peacefully obtaining or communicating information, or from peacefully persuading any person to work or to abstain from working; or from ceasing to patronize or to employ any party to such dispute, or from recommending, advising, or persuading others by peaceful and lawful means so to do; or from paying or giving to, or withholding from, any person engaged in such dispute, any strike benefits or other moneys or things of value; or from peaceably assembling in a lawful manner, and for lawful purposes; or from doing any act or thing which might lawfully be done in the absence of such dispute by any party thereto; nor shall any of the acts specified in this paragraph be considered or held to be violations of any law of the United States.

Source: 38 *Stat.* 731 and 738 (1914).

BOX 6-5
William H. Taft on the Clayton Antitrust Act

There is language in this section, especially the last clause, which, standing alone and without explanation might seem to show congressional intention to exempt such associations and their members altogether from the operation of anti-trust acts. But such is evidently not the proper construction. The representatives of organized labor applied to Congress for this provision, on the ground that they were afraid that voluntary associations for increasing wages and bettering terms of employment, where the employment was in interstate commerce, might be considered, per se, illegal restraints of that commerce and so subject them to dissolution. They, therefore, wished them declared legal. That it was not intended to make members of such associations a privileged class and free from the operation of general laws is clearly shown by the careful language of Congress, which authorizes the existence and operation of such associations and forbids the restraint of their members when "lawfully carrying out the legitimate objects thereof."

Source: William Howard Taft, "Address of the President," *American Bar Association Reports* 39 (1914); 373. The same conclusion about the application of section 6 to union activities can be found in Daniel Davenport, "An Analysis of the Labor Sections of the Clayton Anti-Trust Bill," *Central Law Journal* 80 (3) (January 15, 1915): 46–49. Davenport was a prominent attorney employed by the American Anti-Boycott Association. He was also the attorney for the employers in the case that first tested the Clayton Act before the U.S. Supreme Court in 1921, *Duplex* vs. *Deering.*

every form in the past held either directly or implicitly that anyone could have a property right in the labor power of a workman.[63]

Gompers later declared that

It [the Clayton Act] is the Magna Carta upon which the working people will rear their structure of industrial freedom.[64]

When there is so much disagreement about what the language of an act means, the Supreme Court winds up making the final determination.[65] It is interesting to note that at the same time the legal debates were raging in Congress as to whether or not section 6 of the Clayton Act exempted labor from the Sherman Act, and whether or not section 20 of the Clayton Act really limited the injunctive power of courts in labor disputes, the injunction was issued in what was to become the test case for the Clayton Act, *Duplex* vs. *Deering.*

Duplex *vs.* Deering

The manufacture of newspaper printing press machinery in the year 1913 was controlled by four companies of which only one, the Duplex Printing Press Company of Battle Creek, Michigan was not unionized.

Workers at the other companies were organized by the International Association of Machinists. At the other three companies there was a union shop, a standard 8-hour day, and a common union wage scale. At Duplex, however, the employees worked a 10-hour day and received lower wages than in the unionized firms.[66] In 1913 the other three manufacturers notified the union that unless Duplex was brought under the scope of the union's influence and was forced to pay union wages and provide union standard working conditions, they would either have to cease dealing with the union or the union would have to lower its wages and established working conditions.[67]

After some initial inconclusive meetings with the management of Duplex, the union in August 1913 called a strike against the company. Only 11 of the 200 persons employed at the Battle Creek plant went on strike; the rest kept working.[68]

In an attempt to put more pressure on the company, the union instituted a nationwide boycott against Duplex printing presses. The members of the union refused to install, repair, or do any work on Duplex presses. In addition, the union tried to prevent the exhibition of Duplex presses at a commercial trade fair in New York, threatening that all the employees at the exhibition hall would go on strike if the Duplex press was exhibited.[69]

Request for Injunction — District Court.   In April 1914 the company went to court seeking an injunction against Mr. Emil Deering, the business agent of IAM, in District 15 in New York City, and asking that the boycott be stopped.[70] A temporary injunction was issued. In April 1917, three years later, the district court ruled that it would not issue the permanent injunction sought by the company. The judge found the strike to be peaceful and lawful and conducted for a legitimate purpose.

Appeals Court Ruling.   The company appealed this ruling to the Circuit Court of Appeals. In May 1918 the appeals court affirmed the lower court ruling and refused to issue an injunction halting the strike and boycott. The majority of the judges in the appeals court ruling were of the opinion that sections 6 and 20 of the Clayton Act legalized the secondary boycott and limited the use of the injunction in halting labor disputes.[71]

U.S. Supreme Court Deliberations.   The company appealed this ruling to the U.S. Supreme Court, before which the case was argued in January 1920. The position of the employer was that the facts of this case were much like the facts in the *Danbury Hatters* case; namely, that the union was conducting a secondary boycott against the employer. The plaintiffs further argued that the limitation on injunctions found in section 20 of the Clayton Act applied only to cases where there was a labor dispute between an employer and his employees or where there was a continuing employment relationship between the parties. Finally, the attorneys for Duplex argued that the Clayton Act protected unions only in the exercise of legal and lawful activities; nothing in the Clayton Act, however, legalized the secondary boycott. Thus, the plaintiffs maintained, the court's ruling in the *Danbury Hatters* case still applied here: that secondary boycotts were illegal restraints of trade under the Sherman Act and that injunctions should be issued to halt them.[72]

The defense attorneys argued that the Sherman Act could not be applied in this case. They pointed out that the last clause of section 6 of the Clayton Act exempts labor from coverage under the Sherman Act. Additionally, the defense maintained that the Sherman Act could not be applied in this case because there had been no interference with interstate trade. Deering's activities were confined to New York City, and he did nothing to actually interfere with the trade of the Duplex Printing Press Company in two or more states.[73]

U.S. Supreme Court Ruling.   The U.S. Supreme Court ruled against the union on the grounds that the Clayton Act protections against the issuance of injunctions in labor disputes applies only where there is an established employment relationship. Because Deering was not an employee of Duplex, the language of section 20 of the Clayton Act would not prohibit an injunction being issued in this case.[74] Furthermore, the Supreme Court ruled that the congressional debates on the Clayton Bill revealed that Congress never intended to make the secondary boycott legal under the Clayton Act, and thus the acts of the Machinists union and Mr. Deering must be considered illegal. Finally, the court ruled that because Deering had conspired to restrain Duplex's business through the use of an illegal secondary boycott, it would issue an injunction halting this illegal act.[75]

Reactions to the *Duplex* Ruling.   Predictably, persons connected with the labor movement were shocked and disappointed with the ruling in *Duplex* vs. *Deering* in 1921. It appears from reading the ruling in the case that all the U.S. Supreme Court felt the Clayton Act did was to establish the fact that the Antitrust laws could not be used to forbid the existence of unions or to stop their legal activities, such as going on strike against an employer.[76] When the unions went beyond this fairly narrow scope of conflict, however, the Antitrust laws would not protect their actions. It would appear then after reading the *Duplex* decision that Gompers and the labor movement really did not achieve much through the passage of the Clayton Act. As one author puts it, "the Magna Carta vanished into thin air."[77] The noted scholar of labor law, Charles O. Gregory, says that the Supreme Court "sold labor down the river" with the *Duplex* decision.[78]

American Steel Foundries Company *vs.* Tri-City Central Trades Council

The *American Steel Foundries Company* case is important because it involves not an antitrust issue but a much more common trade union activity — a picket line. The *American Steel Foundries* case serves to clarify the rights that unions had under the Clayton Act in a fairly typical labor dispute that did not involve boycotting or a propaganda campaign conducted by labor leaders of national standing. This case involved a strike over wages accompanied by picketing. Its main legal issue involved the legality of picketing and an organization's protection from the issuance of an injunction under the Clayton Act.

The issue was one of major importance. Courts in different states had quite different views of the legality of picketing. For example, it was generally true that in 1921 picketing was regarded as illegal in many states, among them California, Illinois, Massachusetts, Michigan, New Jersey, Pennsylvania, and Washington.[79] In addition, some federal court judges said that picketing was in and of itself illegal. In the case of *Atchison, Topeka and Sante Fe Railway* vs. *Gee* (1905) the federal judge stated: "There is and can be no such thing as peaceful picketing, any more than there can be chaste vulgarity or peaceful mobbing or lawful lynching. When men want to persuade, they do not organize a picket line."[80]

On the other hand, in some states at this time peaceful picketing was not regarded as a contradiction in terms, and the right of workers to engage in peaceful picketing was specifically protected. These states were Arkansas, Arizona, Indiana, Maryland, Minnesota, Missouri, Montana, New Hampshire, New York, Ohio, Oklahoma, Oregon, and Wisconsin.[81] To add to the confusion, federal judges in some districts had found that peaceful picketing was a legal and allowable activity of unions and had issued decisions protecting workers' rights to picket.[82] The number of court cases in which the right to picket was at issue was considerable. Witte wrote in 1930 that "there have been more court decisions upon the legality of picketing than upon any other question in the law of labor combinations."[83] In addition, the conflict among decisions was dramatic and unpredictable. The U.S. Supreme Court attempted to untangle the confusing array of conflicting cases in its *American Steel Foundries* decision.

The main event precipitating the strike at the American Steel Foundries Company plant at Granite City, Illinois was a wage cut in April 1914. The factory had been shut down for six months prior to April 1914, and when it was reopened only 350 of the former 1,600 employees were recalled and these were paid wages cut from the 1913 levels.[84] The employees of the American Steel Foundries Company were not covered by a collective bargaining agreement but the local trades council, consisting mostly of members of craft local unions, interceded on behalf of the workers and asked to meet with the company management to talk about the restoration of wages to their previous levels. The company refused to meet with the union representatives. In response, the trades council organized a strike among American Steel Foundries workers. In addition, the trades council organized a picket line round the American Steel Foundries facility. Very few of the 350 employees working for the company went on strike; therefore, few of the picketers were employees of the struck employer. Some were laid-off workers who had not been rehired by the company; others were members of the local trades council who had never worked for the company.

Request for Injunction — District Court and Appeals Court.

In May 1914 the company went to federal court seeking an injunction to stop the picketing. A temporary injunction and later a permanent one were soon issued by the district court judge to halt the picketing. The testimony in the injunction hearing revealed that there was some evidence of violence connected with the picketing and that the picket line did have the effect of keeping workers out of the plant who desired to go to work. The injunction that was issued was very broad in its coverage.

The trades council appealed the ruling of the district court to the U.S. Court of Appeals, maintaining that section 20 of the Clayton Act (passed after the injunction was issued) protected the council's picketing activities from injunctions. The appeals court judges agreed and in December 1916 ruled that the original injunction halting the picketing should be lifted.[85] The company appealed this ruling to the U.S. Supreme Court.

U.S. Supreme Court Deliberations.

The case was argued before the U.S. Supreme Court in January 1919 and was reargued in October 1921. The company maintained its position that the trades council was an illegal conspiracy designed to force employees to halt work and to interfere with the company's business. In addition, the company argued that section 20 of the Clayton Act did not apply in this case because the picketers were generally not employees of the employer. Furthermore, the company voiced the opinion that picketing was not protected by the Clayton Act because the act never even mentioned the word *picketing*.

The trades council defended itself by presenting evidence that demonstrated that even though there was no collective bargaining agreement between the employer and the trades council before the big layoff in 1913, 80 to 90 percent of the former employees of the American Steel Foundries Company had been members of local unions affiliated with the Central Trades Council. Thus, the council itself had a verifiable interest in the strike.[86] The trades council argued that the temporary layoff did not sever the employment relationship and that laid-off employees should still be considered "employees" of the employer under section 20 of the Clayton Act. Finally, the council argued that the Clayton Act protected a union's right to picket an employer.

U.S. Supreme Court Ruling. The U.S. Supreme Court ruling, published in December 1921, declared that the picketing conducted at the American Steel Foundries plant in 1914 was not peaceful persuasion and was not protected under section 20 of the Clayton Act. The court found evidence of considerable violence and intimidation accompanying the trades council's activities and stated that the very use of the word *picket* indicated a militant purpose inconsistent with peaceful persuasion. The court went on to say that "picketing thus instituted is unlawful and cannot be peaceable and may be properly injoined."[87]

The court ruled that peaceful persuasion was allowable, however, but that peaceful persuasion was protected under section 20 of the Clayton Act only when it was done by employees of the struck employer. The court found that there were only two actual employees of the company on the picket line at the American Steel Foundries Company. Thus, only the peaceful persuasion of these two men was specifically protected under the Clayton Act. The peaceful persuasion of strangers to a labor dispute was not allowed and could therefore be enjoined. Finally, the U.S. Supreme Court ruled that the District Courts had the right to *regulate* peaceful persuasion even when protected by the Clayton Act. In this case the court ruled that the trades council limit the number of "peaceful persuaders" to one picketer at each point of entrance and exit from the plant. Chief Justice William H. Taft, speaking for the court, called these lone sentinels "missionaries" in his decision.[88] The trades council called this limitation on picketing "pink tea" picketing.[89]

Importance of the *American Steel Foundries* and *Duplex* Decisions. The decision in the *American Steel Foundries* case, along with the decision in the *Duplex* vs. *Deering* case, demonstrated to trade union leaders how little the Clayton Act had changed the legal status of unions. Secondary boycotts were illegal before the Clayton Act and they were illegal after it as well. Picketing had been outlawed in many jurisdictions before the Clayton Act, and the *American Steel Foundries* case did little to change the situation. The U.S. Supreme Court was willing to protect picketing only when it was conducted by one person at each entrance, and even then only when that person was a striking employee of the employer with whom the dispute was conducted. In sum, the Clayton Act did little to expand the rights of unions other than to recognize their right to exist. It became obvious to all labor leaders in the mid-1920s that the only way that unions were going to be allowed to expand their legal rights to picket, boycott, or organize the unorganized was through statutory laws that would recognize and protect certain specific activities of labor organizations. The beginning of the statutory era of labor relations law began in 1926 with a dramatic legislative enactment covering railroad employees: The Railway Labor Act.

Summary

In this chapter we have followed the development of U.S. labor law from the first recorded case, the case of the *Philadelphia Cordwainers*, through the decisions interpreting the Clayton Act. In the very early years, organized labor was regarded as conspiratorial, and the very act of joining a union was considered illegal. As judicial experience with unions and the acts of organized labor matured, unions were tried on the legality or illegality of their actions rather than on their right to exist.

The actions of unions were controlled by the judiciary through the use of the injunction. After the passage of the Sherman Act in 1890, injunctions were issued to stop many large strikes, particularly those having an effect on interstate trade. Later, injunctions were issued to halt not only strikes but also boycotts and even requests to the public not to buy products produced by certain companies.

In 1914 the Clayton Act was passed, and many persons felt that this act would exempt unions from coverage under the Sherman Act and would limit the powers of the federal courts to issue injunctions in labor cases. This was not the case. The Supreme Court decisions in the *Duplex* and the *American Steel Foundries* cases showed that the language of the Clayton Act could be interpreted in such a way that labor was not exempted from the Sherman Act and that injunctions could still be used to stop many of the activities of unions, such as the boycott and the use of the picket line. The judicial interpretation of the Clayton Act demonstrated to the labor movement the need for new legislation protecting workers' rights to engage in trade union activity.

Discussion Questions

1. Based on your knowledge of labor history gained from Chapter 4, do you find the *Cordwainers* decision surprising? Why or why not?
2. What differences do you see in the *Cordwainers* case and in *Commonwealth vs. Hunt?* What similarities do you see? If you had been on the Massachusetts Supreme Court in 1842, how would you have decided the case? Why?
3. Restraining orders (injunctions) stop strikes for only a short period of time — 9 months or so. Yet Debs in his quoted statement in Box 6.2 says that the injunction ended the strike. What steps might employers take during the period of time that the injunction is in effect to effectively end the strike?
4. Do you think the Sherman Act was intended to be applied to the actions of labor unions? Even if it was not originally intended to be applied to unions, should it have been used in this capacity? Why or why not?
5. If you were a worker in the hat industry in 1908, what effect would the *Dan-*

bury Hatters ruling have had on your attitudes toward unions? Does it make any difference in this case that Loewe's hat company was one of the few remaining nonunion companies in the industry? Would the case have been decided differently if this were the first company to be unionized rather than one of the last?

6. To what extent did the *Bucks Stove* decision compromise Gompers's rights of free speech? Where can the line be drawn between freedom of speech and protection of interstate commerce?

7. How do you interpret sections 6 and 20 of the Clayton Act? Do they, in your opinion, exempt labor from coverage under the antitrust laws and limit the use of injunctions in labor disputes? Do you agree or disagree with the interpretations of the Clayton Act given by the Supreme Court in the *Duplex* and the *American Steel Foundries* cases?

Notes

[1]Elias Lieberman, *Unions Before the Bar*, New York: Harper and Brothers, 1950, pp. 4, 10.

[2]See the *King* vs. *Journeymen Tailors of Cambridge*, 8 Modern, 10 (1721), cited in Alpheus T. Mason, *Organized Labor and the Law*, Durham, NC: Duke University Press, 1925, p. 39.

[3]John R. Commons and Associates, *History of Labour in the United States*, vol. 1, New York: Augustus M. Kelley, 1966, p. 147; originally published in 1918.

[4]Lieberman, *Unions Before the Bar*, p. 6.

[5]Ibid., p. 11.

[6]Ibid., p. 12.

[7]Ibid., p. 13.

[8]Walter Nelles, "The First American Labor Case," *Yale Law Journal* (2) (December 1931): 193.

[9]*People* vs. *Fisher*, 14 Wendell 9 (1835), New York.

[10]Edwin E. Witte, "Early American Labor Cases," *Yale Law Journal* 35 (7) (May 1926): 826.

[11]Lieberman, *Unions Before the Bar*, p. 17.

[12]Walter Nelles, "Commonwealth vs. Hunt," *Columbia Law Review* 32 (7) (November 1932): 1132.

[13]Lieberman, *Unions Before the Bar*, p. 19.

[14]Ibid., p. 19.

[15]Ibid., p. 21.

[16]Nelles, "Commonwealth vs. Hunt," p. 1147.

[17]Lieberman, *Unions Before the Bar*, p. 25.

[18]It is interesting to note that in a case decided 58 years later (*Plant* vs. *Woods* 176 Mass. 492 (1900), 57 NE 1011), the Massachusetts Supreme Court ruled that a strike used to force an employer to agree to a closed shop arrangement with a union was *not* legal.

[19]Witte, "Early American Labor Cases," p. 829.

[20]See ibid., p. 834.

[21]See Walter Nelles, "A Strike and Its Legal Consequences — An Examination of the Receivership Precedent for the Labor Injunction," *Yale Law Journal* 40 (4) (February 1931): 523. The cases in which contempt charges were imposed arising out of the strike were *Secor* vs. *Toledo, Peoria and Warsaw Railway*, 21 Fed. Cas. 968 (1877) and *King* vs. *Ohio, Mississippi Railway* 14 Fed. Cas. 539 (1877).

[22]Witte, "Early American Labor Cases," quote on p. 834.

[23]Edwin E. Witte, *The Government in Labor Disputes*, New York: McGraw-Hill, 1932, p. 84. Witte's research discloses that there were 508 injunctions issued in federal courts

and 1,364 injunctions issued in state courts prior to May 1, 1931 at the request of employers restraining the actions of labor unions.

[24]Ibid., pp. 97–98.

[25]Edward Berman, *Labor and the Sherman Act*, New York: Harper and Brothers, 1930, p. 28.

[26]Ibid., p. 31.

[27]*Congressional Record*, 21, part 3, 51st Congress, 1st session, p. 2565.

[28]The first case involved a coal mining trust, *United States* vs. *Jellico Mountain Coal and Coke Co., et al.,* 43 Fed. 898 (October 13, 1890).

[29]54 Fed. 994, affirmed in 57 Fed. 85 (June 13, 1893).

[30]Berman, *Labor and the Sherman Act*, p. 60.

[31]Alpheus Mason calls the Pullman strike "perhaps the most extraordinary contest in the history of relations between capital and labor in this country," *Organized Labor and the Law*, p. 147.

[32]Ibid., p. 149.

[33]*United States* vs. *Debs*, 64 Fed. Rep. 724 (1894).

[34]Report of the U.S. Strike Commission, Senate Executive Document, 53rd Congress, 3rd Session, vol. II, no. 7, quoted in Mason, *Organized Labor and the Law*, p. 155.

[35]Mason, *Organized Labor and the Law*, p. 156.

[36]Testimony of Samuel Gompers before the judiciary committee of the House on trust legislation, vol. I, p. 16, 63rd Congress, 2nd session, quoted in Mason, *Organized Labor and the Law*, p. 169.

[37]Lieberman, *Unions Before the Bar*, p. 57.

[38]Harry A. Millis and Royal E. Montgomery, *Organized Labor*, New York: McGraw-Hill, 1945, p. 569.

[39]Lieberman, *Unions Before the Bar*, p. 58.

[40]Berman, *Labor and the Sherman Act*, p. 78.

[41]Lieberman, *Unions Before the Bar*, p. 59.

[42]Berman, *Labor and the Sherman Act*, p. 78.

[43]See *Loewe* vs. *Lawlor*, 235 U.S. 341 (1908).

[44]Witte, *The Government in Labor Disputes*, p. 135.

[45]Lieberman, *Unions Before the Bar*, pp. 66–67.

[46]Ibid., p. 67.

[47]See Berman's conclusions, *Labor and the Sherman Act*, p. 86.

[48]Lieberman, *Unions Before the Bar*, p. 71.

[49]Mason, *Organized Labor and the Law*, p. 163.

[50]Lieberman, *Unions Before the Bar*, p. 73.

[51]Ibid., p. 74.

[52]Ibid., p. 77.

[53]Mason, *Organized Labor and the Law*, p. 164.

[54]Lieberman, *Unions Before the Bar*, p. 79.

[55]Ibid., p. 82.

[56]Witte, *The Government in Labor Disputes*, p. 119.

[57]Samuel Gompers, "The Hatters Case. The Sherman Law — Amend It or End It," *American Federationist* 17 (March 1910): 197–204.

[58]Dallas L. Jones, "The Enigma of the Clayton Act," *Industrial and Labor Relations Review* 10 (2) (January 1957): 202.

[59]Ibid., p. 204; see also the *American Federationist* 17 (November 1912): 889–893.

[60]See Berman, *Labor and the Sherman Act*, pp. 90–91. The U.S. Supreme Court was later to decide that the union itself was not per se illegal but that its activities, which included persuading workers who had previously signed pre-employment agreements *not* to join unions to join them (yellow dog contracts) was illegal. See *Hitchman Coal and Coke Co.* vs. *Mitchell*, 245 U.S. 229.

[61]Jones, "The Enigma of the Clayton Act," p. 204, quoting from U.S. Congress, House

of Representatives, Committee on the Judiciary, Hearings on the Anti-trust Legislation, 63rd Congress, 2nd Session, vol. 1, p. 16 (1913).

[62]See ibid., pp. 209–213.

[63]Quoted from ibid., p. 214.

[64]Samuel Gompers, "The Charter of Industrial Freedom — Labor Provisions of the Clayton Anti-Trust Law," *American Federationist* 21 (November 1914): 968.

[65]Felix Frankfurter and Nathan Greene state that "the Supreme Court had to find meaning where Congress had done its best to conceal it" in their discussion of the Clayton Act. See Felix Frankfurter and Nathan Greene, "Legislation Affecting Labor Injunctions," *Yale Law Journal* 38 (7) (May 1929): 888.

[66]Berman, *Labor and the Sherman Act*, p. 103.

[67]Lieberman, *Unions Before the Bar*, p. 99.

[68]*Duplex* vs. *Deering*, 254 U.S. 446 (1921).

[69]*Duplex* vs. *Deering*, 252 Fed. Rep. 737 (1918).

[70]Lieberman, *Unions Before the Bar*, p. 99.

[71]*Duplex* vs. *Deering*, 252 Fed. Rep. 748 (1918).

[72]*Duplex* vs. *Deering* 254 U.S. 447 (1921).

[73]Lieberman, *Unions Before the Bar*, p. 102.

[74]*Duplex* vs. *Deering* 254 U.S. 459 (1921).

[75]Mason, *Organized Labor and the Law*, p. 205.

[76]Lieberman, *Unions Before the Bar*, p. 104.

[77]Witte, *The Government in Labor Disputes*, p. 69.

[78]Charles O. Gregory and Harold Katz, *Labor and the Law*, 3rd ed., New York: W. W. Norton, 1979, p. 170.

[79]Witte, *The Government in Labor Disputes*, p. 34.

[80]*Atchison, Topeka and Sante Fe Railway* vs. *Gee*, 139 Fed. 500 (1905).

[81]Witte, *The Government in Labor Disputes*, p. 35.

[82]See *Allis Chalmers* vs. *Iron Molders*, 166 Fed. 45 (1908), cited in Witte, *The Government in Labor Disputes*, p. 35.

[83]Witte, *The Government in Labor Disputes*, p. 34.

[84]Lieberman, *Unions Before the Bar*, p. 108.

[85]Ibid., p. 110.

[86]Ibid., p. 111.

[87]Mason, *Organized Labor and the Law*, p. 213.

[88]Lieberman, *Unions Before the Bar*, pp. 112, 113.

[89]Gregory and Katz, *Labor and the Law*, p. 172.

UNIONS NOT CELEBRATING NLRB'S 50TH BIRTHDAY

Washington (AP) — The National Labor Relations Board is celebrating its 50th anniversary amid a torrent of criticism from organized labor, directed primarily at NLRB chairman Donald L. Dotson.

Dotson, a management attorney, has been a target of labor leaders almost from the day he took over the board as a Reagan appointee more than two years ago and began authoring decisions that overturned long-standing board policies.

In some cases, Dotson's decisions favoring employers simply reversed rulings issued by former President Carter's appointees, but other opinions reversed policy of even Republican-dominated boards.

A recent AFL–CIO study of 1,200 decisions issued in 1975–76, for example, revealed that the NLRB found employers guilty of unfair labor practice claims 84 percent of the time. The Dotson board in 1983–84, however, found them guilty 51 percent of the time.

On Monday, Dotson presided at a cake-cutting anniversary ceremony at board headquarters. Meanwhile, the AFL–CIO marked the 50th anniversary of the National Labor Relations Act, which created the board, with a four-page critique of the NLRB and Dotson in the labor federation's weekly newspaper.

"There's nothing to celebrate," said Murray Seeger, spokesman for the 13.7 million member AFL–CIO. "These people have taken a very decent law and turned it upside down."

The constant criticism has had its effect on Dotson, who in conversation with reporters Monday launched into a defense of the board's efforts to reduce substantial case backlog, another bone of contention with labor unions and Democrats on Capitol Hill.

In a recent speech to an employers' group, Dotson said "institutional labor, the working press and a large segment of the academic community" constitute a "three-ply defense" against his efforts.

Dotson says he is trying to limit government intervention in the labor relations area.

Chapter 7

Labor and the Law, Part II: Statutory Control of Labor Relations*

The passage of the National Labor Relations Act (NLRA) in 1935 revolutionized the system of labor law in the United States. The NLRA extended to almost all nonmanagerial employees who work for employers engaged in interstate commerce a federally protected right to join a union and to engage in collective bargaining. These same rights had first been given to railroad employees in 1926 under the Railway Labor Act (RLA).

Recently there has been some criticism of the National Labor Relations Board (NLRB), the federal agency responsible for administering the NLRA. Charges are being made by the labor movement that the NLRB is becoming too management-oriented and that its decisions are going against the interests of organized labor (see the *Columbus Dispatch* article). Recent decisions concerning the rights of the employer to transfer work from a unionized to a nonunion facility and to discipline employees who engage in some types of union activity at the workplace are being seen as setbacks for the rights the unions once thought they enjoyed under the NLRA. It must be pointed out, of course, that only a few years ago there were criticisms by management representatives that the NLRB decisions were too prolabor and contrary to the interests of management.

An understanding of the background behind our labor law statutes gives us an idea of why these laws were passed and what the events were in the economy and society that led up to congressional efforts to change the status of labor under the law. The contents of the statutes

*The Railway Labor Act, the Wagner Act, the Taft-Hartley Act, and the Landrum-Griffin Act (1926–1959).

themselves are important also, and in this chapter I will spend a good deal of time discussing and explaining what the laws regulating labor–management relations actually are.

The Railway Labor Act (1926)

The Railway Labor Act (RLA) of 1926 was the first federal statute passed whose sole purpose was the regulation of labor relations and collective bargaining. The act has been amended several times, but the major provision of the original legislation passed more than 55 years ago remain in effect today. One contemporary author has stated that the RLA provides "the framework for the most comprehensive control of labor relations and labor disputes on the American scene."[1] Another author, writing more than 50 years ago, stated that "we seemingly now have the best method of dealing with railroad disputes yet devised," in commenting on the RLA.[2] The RLA is a comprehensive statute and it does have a procedure for resolving labor–management disputes that goes considerably beyond anything currently existing for resolving labor–management disagreements anywhere else in the private sector. To fully understand the Railway Labor Act and to appreciate its strengths and weaknesses, it is essential to discuss its background and legislative predecessors.

The Railroad Industry

The railroad industry was the first truly national industry in the United States. With the linking of the East Coast and West Coast rail systems in 1869 the railroad industry made possible the development of the western states through providing a ready market in the East for western raw materials. In addition, the rail system carried passengers and manufactured goods west, which further aided in this development. To encourage the development of east-west trade, Congress in 1862 passed the Pacific Railroad Act, which granted guaranteed loans and large parcels of land to railroad owners willing to add more links in the east-west transportation system.

Because of the tremendous investment involved in building and operating a railroad there was always considerable pressure on the operators to produce profits to pay both employees and investors. As a result, railroad operators would sometimes collude to set rates in areas in which they competed against each other. In areas where there was little or no competition between carriers for business, the railroads would sometimes charge exorbitant rates knowing that the customers had little choice but to pay them if they wanted their products transported. Farmers were commonly the victims of such price discrimination.[3]

The result of the public outcry against the price-setting practices of the railroads resulted in the passage of the Interstate Commerce Act of 1887. This act established a federal commission, the Interstate Commerce Commission, to regulate and control rate setting practices of interstate railroads.

The press of business circumstances also forced railroad operators to economize as much as possible on the wages paid employees to control costs. The bitter and violent rail strike of 1877, discussed in Chapter 4 — the first strike ever with national impact — was precipated by a cut in wages. The rail strikes of 1885 and 1886 conducted by the Knights of Labor were also strikes over wage cuts. In much the same way that Congress deemed it necessary to control the rate-setting procedures of railroads to prevent exploitation of consumers, the labor relations practices of railroads were also regulated with the hope of preventing strikes and labor disputes. The first piece of legislation passed by Congress designed to regulate labor–management relations in the railroad industry was the Arbitration Act of 1888.[4] This was followed by the Erdman Act of 1898 and the Newlands Act of 1913, all designed to reduce strikes and to improve labor–management relations in the railroad industry.

Government Operation

The railroads were operated by the federal government during World War I, by the U.S. Railroad Administration from December 1917 until March 1920. One of the major changes that occurred immediately under federal operation was that boards of adjustment were established for each group of railway employees (e.g., skilled operators, skilled shop craft workers, and unskilled and maintenance employees). The boards were designed to deal with workers' grievances of all types; in return the employees agreed not to strike over any issue during the war. In addition, the U.S. Railroad Administration recognized and encouraged union membership and pledged that no worker would be discriminated against for union membership.

During the war years wages became standardized across different rail systems and workers enjoyed substantial wage increases (some as high as 43 percent). It is no wonder that union membership in the railroad industry grew dramatically during this period.[5] It is also not surprising to learn that the railroad unions strongly supported a legislative proposal called the Plumb Plan that would have continued government operation of the railroads after the Armistice. The Plumb Plan did not meet with the approval of the owners of the railroads, or with the majority of Congress, however.

With the end of the war and the resumption of operation of the railroads by their rightful owners, labor relations in the railroad industry deteriorated. Congress in partial response enacted the Transportation Act of 1920, which amended the Newlands Act by creating a nine-person Railway Labor Board to hear and decide wage disputes in the industry. Unfortunately, Congress did not give the Railway Labor Board, which was comprised equally of labor representatives, employer representatives and representatives of the public, any power to compel the parties to a dispute to abide by the board's decision. In addition, employees had lost their rights to join unions free from discrimination and employer interference, rights they had enjoyed during the war years. To add to the tensions in the industry, the recession that began in 1920 was forcing many railroad owners to institute wage cuts. The employers could not profitably operate in a competitive market with the wage levels left over from the wartime years.

The Shopcraft Strike of 1922

The result of all of the forces leading to a break in labor–management peace in the railroad industry was the shopmen's strike of 1922. The shop craft unions were unions of skilled workers, and they strongly resisted the wage cuts and the end of standardization of wage rates and work rules from rail line to rail line. The strike began on July 3, 1922, and involved approximately 400,000 skilled craft workers. The Railroad Labor Board regarded the strike as illegal and threatened that workers striking in violation of its orders could be replaced with no rights of rehire. By the middle of July, 1922, many other railroad workers had joined the strike in sympathy; one author estimates that as many as 700,000 railroad workers were on strike at one time. The railroads were paralyzed and no one seemed able to stop the strike, not even President Warren Harding. The strike was ended when the Department of Justice obtained an injunction against the strike leaders for interfering with interstate commerce.[6]

The main result of the Shopcraft strike of 1922 was a further breakdown of labor relations in the railroad industry. The unions generally boycotted the dispute resolution system of the Transportation Act of 1920, regarding it as biased toward management. Employers in many railroads established company unions or employer-dominated unions and refused to deal with any outside labor organization. Tensions were heightened and disputes flared, but there was no effective mechanism to deal with the problems. By 1924 it was obvious that decisive moves had to be made to restore health to labor–management relations in the railroad industry. The result of several months of planning and studying on the part of both labor and management and Congress was the Railway Labor Act of 1926.

The Railway Labor Act

The original Railway Labor Act, passed in 1926, was significantly amended in 1934. A short summary of the RLA and a brief description of its provisions, section by section, are given in Box 7.1.

The final version of the RLA passed in 1926 was the product of several events. On the one hand political forces were motivating the Congress to act. Inconvenienced by the Shopcraft strike of 1922 and frustrated by the powerlessness of the Railroad Labor Board and even the president of the United States to stop the strike, the public was demanding that something be done to deal with labor problems in the railroad industry.

BOX 7-1
Summary of the Major Provisions of the Railway Labor Act of 1926
(as amended)

Section 1

Definitions: Defines the major terms used in the legislation, such as *carrier, commerce, employee,* and *representative.* The purpose of the definitions is to clearly spell out who is covered by the legislation and who is not.

Section 2

General Purposes and Duties: This section identifies the five general purposes of the legislation as follows: (1) to avoid the interruption of interstate commerce; (2) to forbid any limitation of an employee's right to join a union; (3) to provide for the complete independence of employee labor organizations; (4) to provide for the prompt and orderly settlement of disputes concerning pay, work rules, or working conditions; (5) to provide for the prompt and orderly settlement of grievances.

The general duties of employers and unions under the act are as follows:

1. It is the duty of the carriers (employers) to make every reasonable effort to make agreements with and to settle disputes with their employees.
2. Disputes are to be settled if at all possible through the collective bargaining process.
3. Representatives of employees are to be chosen by the employees free from employer interference.
4. Employee representatives must be chosen by a majority of the employees and must not be supported, dominated, or interfered with by the employers.
5. No employer may require an employee to sign any contract requiring that he or she join or not join a union as a condition of obtaining employment.
6. Meetings to discuss grievances coming from the employees must be scheduled by the employer within 10 days from the date the request is received.
7. Employers may make no unilateral changes in wages, rules, or working conditions without first notifying and offering to meet with the union concerning these changes.
8. All disputes between labor and management must be handled in accordance with the provisions of this act. Employees must be publicly notified by the employer what their rights are under the RLA.

(continued)

BOX 7-1 (continued)

9. Questions concerning the legitimacy of an employee representative shall be decided by the National Mediation Board. The board shall have the power to conduct secret ballot elections to certify bargaining representatives.
10. Violations of items 3, 4, 5, 7, and 8 (above) by employers are to be punished by fines and jail terms.

Section 3

National Railroad Adjustment Board: Provides for the creation of a 36-member adjustment board (18 union members and 18 employer members) to settle employee grievances arising from an existing labor agreement. This section further requires that if the labor and management representatives cannot resolve the grievance themselves, a neutral third party be brought in to decide the issue.

Section 4

National Mediation Board: Provides for the creation of a three-person National Mediation Board, appointed by the U.S. president.

Section 5

Functions of the Mediation Board: The board is to assist labor and management in the disposition of disputes not resolved in negotiations through mediation and voluntary arbitration. The board will provide qualified arbitrators and mediators at the request of the parties.

Section 6

Procedures for Changing Rates of Pay, Rules, and Working Conditions: Thirty-day notice is required before labor agreements between the parties can be changed or modified. In addition, each side must offer to meet and bargain with the other party about these changes within 10 days from the time the 30-day notice is given.

Section 7

Arbitration: If the parties to a dispute over wages, work rules, or working conditions are not able to resolve their disputes through negotiation or mediation they may agree voluntarily to arbitrate the unresolved issues. The arbitration shall be conducted by a panel of arbitrators consisting of either three or six arbitrators. In either case, each party names either one or two arbitrators to the panel and these persons then select the remaining one or two members of the panel.

(*continued*)

BOX 7-1 *(continued)*

Section 8

Agreement to Arbitrate: When the parties decide to arbitrate a dispute over wages, work rules, or working conditions, they must put this agreement in writing. The agreement must state the issues to be resolved by the arbitrator and must contain a pledge by both parties that they will abide by the ruling of the majority of the arbitrators.

Section 9

Award: The award of the arbitrators shall be filed in district court, and the court shall enforce the award. The award shall not be contested unless it violates the act, unless it violates the agreement to arbitrate, or unless there was fraud or corruption on the part of one or more of the arbitrators in rendering the award.

Section 10

Emergency Boards: If in the opinion of the National Mediation Board a dispute between a carrier and its employees would cause a disruption to interstate commerce, the board may recommend to the president that an emergency board may be necessary to study the dispute. If the U.S. president deems this necessary then the parties are restrained from changing or modifying the existing agreement until 30 days after the emergency board has made its report to the president.

Section 11

Partial Invalidity: If any section of the act is found unconstitutional, only that section will be invalidated.

Section 12

Appropriations: Monies are to be appropriated annually by the legislature to meet the expenses of the Mediation Board in administering the act.

Title II (added in 1934): Section 201

Amendments to Title I: Coverage of the Railway Labor Act is extended to employees involved in interstate commerce in air transport.

Both the Republican and Democratic party platforms called for a revision in railway labor legislation in 1924.[7]

To this end, legislation was introduced in the House of Representatives in 1924. It is believed that this legislation was largely written by attorneys for the railroad unions.[8] The legislation passed the House, but was not passed in the Senate. In addition, the bill did not meet with the approval of President Calvin Coolidge, who considered it too favorable to the unions.[9] The law was rewritten by attorneys for the Association for Railway Executives in 1925 and was reintroduced into Congress. Testifying before Congress in 1926, Daniel Richberg, a labor attorney who played a major role in drafting the legislation, stated:

> I want to emphasize again that this bill is the product of a negotiation between employers and employees which is unparalleled, I believe, in the history of American industrial relations.
>
>   For the first time representatives of a great majority of all the employers and all the employees of one industry conferred for several months for the purpose of creating by agreement a machinery for the peaceful and prompt adjustment of both major and minor disagreements that might impair the efficiency of operations or interrupt the service they render to the community.[10]

The bill had full support from both the railroad employers and the representatives of the railroad employees. It passed the House in March of 1926 by a vote of 381 to 13 and the Senate in May of the same year by a vote of 69 to 13.[11] Coolidge signed the bill on May 20, 1926; it remains today as our oldest piece of legislation directly related to labor relations and collective bargaining.

Major Principles.   The major statement of principles found in the legislation is found in section 151a:

To prevent the interruption of service

To ensure the rights of employees to organize

To provide for independent organizations to represent employees

To provide for the settlement of disputes

To provide for the resolution of grievances

These purposes were mainly to be accomplished through the workings of the administrative agency created by the legislation. The original legislation provided that grievances should be settled through boards of adjustment created by the unions and the employers and overseen by the Board of Mediation created by the act. Disputes over wages, hours, or working conditions were to be resolved through mediation, also provided by the board. If the parties could not successfully resolve their dispute through mediation, voluntary arbitration was the last stage in the official impasse resolution system.

The act did provide, however, that the U.S. president could appoint an emergency board to study the facts of a dispute if it was felt that the strike would seriously affect or disrupt essential transportation service to a particular part of the country.[12] The emergency board would have the power to investigate the facts of the dispute and were to make recommendations to the president for its settlement. If the emergency board's recommendations were not accepted by the parties, these recommendations were to be made public, but there was no compulsion whatsoever for the parties to accept the recommendations. As one author points out: "Sponsors of the Railway Labor act leaned over backwards to keep out any features savoring of compulsory arbitration."[13]

The constitutionality of the Railway Labor Act was tested before the U.S. Supreme Court in 1930 in the case of *Texas and New Orleans Railroad* vs. *Brotherhood of Railway and Steamship Clerks*.[14] With this decision establishing the constitutionality of the RLA, the U.S. Supreme Court for the first time explicitly recognized the right of Congress to regulate labor–management relations in a major industry through federal statute.

The Amendments of 1934. The Railway Labor Act was significantly amended in 1934. The three major changes the 1934 amendments made in the original RLA were to:

1. establish a new board whose only function was to adjudicate grievances: the National Railway Adjustment Board.
2. rename the Board of Mediation the National Mediation Board and reduce its membership from 5 to 3. In addition, the NMB was given the power to conduct representation elections.
3. outlaw the use of "yellow dog" contracts by employers in the railroad industry.

The newly formed National Railroad Adjustment Board was a 36-member board comprised of 18 union representatives and 18 representatives of management.* These 36 members were then divided into four national boards of adjustment: one to hear grievances involving workers in operating crafts, one to hear grievances involving shopcraft workers, one to hear grievances involving nonskilled and maintenance employees, and one to hear grievances involving railway employees engaged in water transportation. The national boards were to hear worker grievances and to appoint a neutral arbitrator to resolve the issue should the representatives of the parties not be able to settle the matter themselves. If the employer did not comply with the ruling of the NRAB, the ruling could be enforced by a civil suit in federal court.[15]

The National Mediation Board was not changed much from the way the original RLA had created it. By expanding its duties through providing for representation elections, however, the 1934 amendments did

---

*The NRAB in 1986 had 34 members, 17 from each side.

have the effect of severely limiting the prevalence of company unions. The law specified that a majority of the employees in any craft or work unit had to select the appropriate bargaining agent through a secret ballot election. In no instance did a company union represent a majority of employees in a craft or a work union on any carrier. Thus, through the election process company unions were virtually eliminated in the railroad industry after 1934.

The Wagner Act (The National Labor Relations Act) (1935)

The National Labor Relations Act of 1935 is the cornerstone of private sector labor relations law in the United States. No other law, before or since, can rival the NLRA for the scope of its coverage or for its impact on the practice of labor relations and collective bargaining. Although the act was passed over fifty years ago, it is still being used today as a model for legislation regulating labor–management relations and collective bargaining.*

The Wagner Act was a product of the Depression of the 1930s and was one of the New Deal statutes that for the first time began regulating the relationship between employers and employees. Other laws following the National Labor Relations Act, such as the Social Security Act of 1935 and the Fair Labor Standards Act of 1938, were also parts of the New Deal legislative package of programs passed during the Roosevelt administration.

The Wagner Act was passed in 1935, and some authors have pointed out that it is doubtful that it could have been passed at any other time in our history.[16] It was the culmination of legal decisions and legal thinking that can be traced as far back as *Commonwealth* vs. *Hunt* (1842), where the Massachusetts Supreme Court recognized the legitimate rights of workers to join unions (see Chapter 6). More directly, however, the Wagner Act was influenced by the Railway Labor Act of 1926 and the Norris-LaGuardia Act of 1932, the National Industrial Recovery Act of 1933, and the Railway Labor Act amendments of 1934.

The Norris-LaGuardia Act (1932)

The Norris-LaGuardia Act of 1932 was one of the first federal statutes to recognize and clearly enunciate the rights of workers outside of the railroad industry to join unions. The Norris-LaGuardia Act itself was not, however, a law designed to regulate labor–management relations or collective bargaining. The Norris-LaGuardia Act cleared up much of the ambiguity surrounding the Clayton Act by clearly and strongly limiting the use of injunctions in labor disputes. The major sections of the Norris-LaGuardia Act that apply to unions are sections 2, 4, and 7 (see Box 7.2).

---

*For example, Ohio's public sector labor relations law, passed in July 1983, was patterned after the National Labor Relations Act.

BOX 7-2

The Norris-LaGuardia Act of 1932: Sections 2, 4, and 7

Section 2 states the basic philosophy of the Norris-LaGuardia Act:

> Whereas under prevailing economic conditions, developed with the aid of governmental authority for owners of property to organize in the corporate and other forms of ownership association, the individual unorganized worker is commonly helpless to exercise actual liberty of contract and to protect his freedom of labor, and thereby to obtain acceptable terms and conditions of employment, wherefore, though he should be free to decline to associate with his fellows, it is necessary that he have full freedom of association, self-organization, and designation of representatives of his own choosing, to negotiate the terms and conditions of his employment, and that he shall be free from the interference, restraint, or coercion of employers of labor, or their agents, in the designation of such representatives or in self-organization or in other concerted activities for the purpose of collective bargaining or other mutual aid or protection; therefore, the following definitions of and limitations upon the jurisdiction and authority of the courts of the United States are enacted.

In sections 4 and 7 the use of injunctions in labor disputes was closely regulated. Section 4 clearly states that injunctions will not be issued to halt any of these acts of unions:

> (a) Ceasing or refusing to perform any work or to remain in any relation of employment; (b) Becoming or remaining a member of any labor organization or of any employer organization, regardless of any such undertaking or promise as is described in section 3 of this Act; (c) Paying or giving to, or withholding from, any person participating or interested in such labor dispute, any strike or unemployment benefits or insurance, or other moneys or things of value; (d) By all lawful means aiding any person participating or interested in any labor dispute who is being proceeded against in, or is prosecuting, any action or suit in any court of the United States or of any State; (e) Giving publicity to the existence of, or the facts involved in, any labor dispute, whether by advertising, speaking, patrolling, or by any other method not involving fraud or violence; (f) Assembling peaceably to act or to organize to act in promotion of their interests in a labor dispute; (g) Advising or notifying any person of an intention to do any of the acts heretofore specified; (h) Agreeing with other persons to do or not to do any of the acts heretofore specified; and (i) Advising, urging or otherwise causing or inducing without fraud or violence the acts heretofore specified, regardless of any such undertaking or promise as described in Section 3 of the Act.

(continued)

BOX 7-2 *(continued)*

In Section 7 the procedure for the issuance of injunctions is clearly specified and the use of injunctions is clearly limited to cases where there have been illegal acts performed or threatened and where there is danger to property.

> No court of the United States shall have jurisdiction to issue a temporary or permanent injunction in any case involving or growing out of a labor dispute, as herein defined, except after hearing the testimony of witnesses in open court (with opportunity for cross-examination) in support of the allegations of a complaint made under oath, and testimony in opposition thereto, if offered, and except after findings of fact by the court, to the effect–(a) That unlawful acts have been threatened and will be committed unless restrained or have been committed and will be continued unless restrained, but no injunction or temporary restraining order shall be issued on account of any threat or unlawful act excepting against the person or persons, association, or organization making the threat or committing the unlawful act or actually authorizing or ratifying the same after actual knowledge thereof; (b) That substantial and irreparable injury to complainant's property will follow; (c) That as to each item of relief granted greater injury will be inflicted upon the complainant by the denial of relief than will be inflicted upon defendants by the granting of relief; (d) That complainant has no adequate remedy at law; and (e) That the public officers charged with the duty to protect complainant's property are unable or unwilling to furnish adequate protection.

In addition, the Norris-LaGuardia Act declared in section 3 that the courts would no longer enforce preemployment nonunion agreements (yellow dog contracts).

For all its importance, however, the Norris-LaGuardia Act cannot be regarded as a law that regulates labor–management relations. The major effect of the act was to limit the use of injunctions issued by the courts. The statement of public policy in section 2 is very poetic, but there were no enforcement powers specified in section 2 and there was no mention anywhere in the legislation of what would be done to anyone who violated someone else's right to join a union or to bargain collectively.

The National Industrial Recovery Act (1933)

The National Industrial Recovery Act (NIRA), passed in 1933, was the next statute to be considered a precursor to the Wagner Act. The NIRA, passed in the first year of the Franklin D. Roosevelt presidency and one of the first of the New Deal legislative programs, was an early attempt by the Roosevelt administration and Congress to deal with the economic woes of the nation and to reduce the level of unemployment. It allowed businesses to form trade associations on an industry-by-industry basis and to regulate prices, production standards, and labor standards free from prosecution under the antitrust statutes.[17] To protect employee rights and to gain labor support for the NIRA, section 7(a) was added to the legislation specifically recognizing and protecting workers' rights to join unions, to bargain collectively, and to refrain from joining company unions. This section was reportedly written by Donald Richberg, the author of the Railway Labor Act, and one of the draftsmen of the Norris-LaGuardia Act as well.

Section 7a reads in part:[18]

> Every code of fair competition, agreement, and license approved, prescribed, or issued under this title shall contain the following conditions: (1) That employees shall have the right to organize and bargain collectively through representatives of their own choosing, and shall be free from the interference, restraint, or coercion of employers of labor, or their agents, in the designation of such representatives or in self-organization or in other concerted activities for the purpose of collective bargaining or other mutual aid or protection; (2) that no employee and no one seeking employment shall be required as a condition of employment to join any company union or to refrain from joining, organizing, or assisting a labor organization of his own choosing; and (3) that employers shall comply with the maximum hours of labor, minimum rates of pay, and other conditions of employment, approved or prescribed by the President.

The problem with the NIRA provisions proved to be that workers' rights were established more in theory than in fact. The main problem with section 7a was that the act tried to establish broad rights of employees but it never specified a mechanism for instituting these rights. For example, there was nothing in Section 7a that instituted a procedure whereby unions established themselves as the representatives of a work group. Also, section 7a did not establish or even mention enforcement of the labor provisions of the act. Because of these shortcomings, the National Industrial Recovery Act never really did much to affect workers' rights or encourage the development of collective bargaining. As a result of its failure to cause much change in the labor–management relations system in the United States, there was not much mourning in the house of labor when the price-fixing provisions of NIRA were declared unconstitutional by the U.S. Supreme Court in 1935 in the case of *Schechter Poultry Corp.* vs. *United States.*[19] By this time, however, the Wagner Act, which was to change the labor relations system drastically, was only 11 days away from passage in the Senate.

Early Legislative Efforts

The first steps in the process of actually drafting what was to become the Wagner Act began late in 1933. Frustrated with what he saw as shortcomings in the labor provisions in the NIRA, Senator Robert Wagner (D–New York) began meetings with representatives from the American Federation of Labor (AFL) and from the National Labor Board (established in August 1933 to administer the labor sections of the NIRA) in December 1933 to establish a new law that would go substantially beyond section 7a of the NIRA in protecting workers' rights to join unions and to bargain collectively.[20] The process of actually writing the legislation as well as the political maneuvering to have it enacted were both handled almost exclusively by Senator Wagner and one assistant, Leon Keyserling.[21] The legislation that was to become the Wagner Act was not initially supported by Roosevelt or anyone in his cabinet.[22]

The Wagner Bill was written in February 1934 and was introduced into the Senate by its author on March 1. It was debated at great length, but never passed. After the congressional elections of 1934, and the tremendous gains made by the Democrats at the polls, Wagner decided to submit his bill to the legislature once again. The act was passed by the Senate in May 1935 and by the House in June of the same year.

On July 5, 1935, President Roosevelt signed the National Labor Relations Act into law; present at the signing were William Green, president of the AFL, and Robert Wagner, the bill's author. At the event of its signing Green stated, "I am confident that it will prove itself the Magna Carta of labor in the United States," — words used by Gompers at the signing of the Clayton Act, which was to prove anything but a Magna Carta.* Many experts felt that the National Labor Relations Act would be ruled unconstitutional, a fate which the NIRA met on May 27, 1935 in the Schechter case mentioned earlier.[23]

The Wagner Act

The complete text of the Wagner Act (as amended), or the Labor Management Relations Act, is given in Appendix C. In Box 7.3 all of the major sections of the act are identified. This section will discuss the four most important sections of the act, sections 1, 7, 8 and 9.

Section 1: Findings and Policy.   The purpose of this section is to establish the legal rationale for the act's passage. The first three paragraphs make a general statement about the actions of employers and include some basic assumptions about labor relations and collective bargaining — chiefly that commerce is promoted when the causes of strife are removed and when the parties sit down and negotiate about their differences as equals. The final paragraph of section 1 is a strongly prolabor policy statement (see Appendix C). As one author states, "the Wagner

---

*In all truth, the term *Magna Carta* was a poorly chosen one for each to use. The *Magna Carta* only codified or wrote down what were the already existing rights of English citizens — it added nothing in and of itself to those rights. A better term would have been to proclaim the Wagner Act as the "Bill of Rights" of U.S. labor.

Act was one-sided in theory is beyond dispute."[24] There can be no question after reading its preamble that the reason the NRLA was passed was to promote commerce, and the method proposed for promoting commerce was to restrain certain acts of employers and to encourage the growth of unions and the process of collective bargaining.

BOX 7-3
Summary of the Major Provisions of the Wagner Act of 1935

Section 1

Findings and Policy: Defines the founding assumptions behind the legislation. States the purpose of the new law.

Section 2

Definitions: Defines the major terms used in the legislation, such as *employer, employee, labor organization, commerce, affecting commerce* and *labor dispute,* among others. This section specifically excludes government employees, agricultural workers, workers covered by the Railway Labor Act, and domestic servants from coverage.

Section 3

National Labor Relations Board: Officially creates the National Labor Relations Board (NLRB), a three-person board chosen by the president of the United States.

Section 4

Sets the salary of NLRB members and provides for the appointment of a support staff for the NLRB.

Section 5

Establishes Washington, DC as the home office for the NLRB.

Section 6

Gives the NLRB the power to make rules and regulations necessary to carry out the purposes of the act.

Section 7

Rights of Employees: Gives employees the right to self-organization, to form, join or assist labor organizations, to bargain collectively through

(continued)

BOX 7-3 *(continued)*

representatives of their own choosing, and to engage in concerted activities for the purpose of collective bargaining or other mutual aid or protection.

Section 8

Unfair Labor Practices of Employers: (1) To interfere with, restrain, or coerce employees in the exercise of rights guaranteed in section 7; (2) to dominate, or to interfere with, the formation or administration of a labor organization, or to contribute financial support to it; (3) to discriminate in regard to hiring or tenure of employment or any term of condition of employment to encourage or discourage membership in a labor organization; (4) to discharge or discipline an employee for giving testimony or for filing charges under the act; (5) to refuse to bargain collectively with the chosen representatives of employees.

Section 9

Representatives and Elections: (1) Provides for exclusive representation by a union if a majority of employees chooses representation for the purposes of negotiating wages, hours of employment, or other conditions of employment; (2) allows the NLRB to decide on a case-by-case basis the composition of the election unit; (3) gives the NLRB the power to conduct hearings and to hold elections for the purpose of certifying a bargaining representative.

Section 10

Prevention of Unfair Labor Practices: (1) The NLRB is given exclusive enforcement powers to prevent unfair labor practices. (2) The NLRB is given the power to issue complaints and to conduct hearings where unfair labor practices have been alleged against employers. (3) The NLRB is given the power to issue cease and desist orders where the investigation reveals that unfair labor practices have been committed. The board is further given the power to order the reinstatement with back pay of employees who have been unfairly discharged or disciplined. (4) The NLRB has the power to modify its own rulings. (5) The NLRB has the power to petition any federal circuit court of appeals to enforce its rulings. (6) NLRB rulings may be appealed at the federal circuit court level. (7) Appeals will not stop NLRB orders until they are decided. (8) The jurisdiction of the courts to enforce the NLRB rulings shall not be limited by the provisions of the Norris-LaGuardia Act. (9) Petitions filed under the Act shall be heard within 10 days.

(continued)

BOX 7-3 *(continued)*

Section 11

Investigatory Powers: The NLRB and its agents have the power to subpoena witnesses and to compel the production of evidence necessary to conduct any investigation.

Section 12

Interference with the conduct of NLRB investigations will be punished by fines and jail sentences.

Section 13

Limitations: Nothing in the act shall be construed as to interfere with or to diminish in any way the right to strike.

Section 14

The Wagner Act supersedes all possibly conflicting federal relations statutes.

Section 15

If any section of the law is found unconstitutional, the remainder of the law will remain valid.

Section 16

The official title of the act is the National Labor Relations Act.

Section 7: Rights of Employees.   Section 7 of the NLRA was inspired by section 7(a) of the NIRA. In section 7 Congress specifically stated that the act of joining a union, the process of collective bargaining, and actions in support of bargaining were to be recognized as legitimate and worthy of statutory protection. Certainly this kind of protection stands in sharp contrast to the vaguely written provisions of the Clayton Act. In the Wagner Act unions are recognized as legitimate institutions in society and workers have a federally protected right to join them and to actively support them.

Section 8: Unfair Labor Practices of Employers.   Section 8 of the Wagner Act outlines a list of five prohibited practices of employers and calls them unfair labor practices (see Box 7.3). No longer, for example, could employers legally fire workers for joining unions. No longer could employers legally refuse to bargain with a union if that union represented a majority of the work force. No longer could employers set up company unions to represent their employers. The limitations on employers' actions outlined in section 8 were the most controversial section of the Wagner Act, and continue to be the source of most litigation arising under the NLRA today.

Section 9: Representatives and Elections.   The provisions in section 9 of the Wagner Act establish a procedure for selecting a bargaining representative, usually through a secret ballot election supervised by the NLRB. The election procedure in section 9 establishes a process for the selection of employee representatives at the workplace that is somewhat similar to the selection of a political representative in Congress. For example, section 9(a) requires that the union selected as a bargaining representative serve as the exclusive representative for employees in a particular work group. For any one group of employees there can be only one bargaining representative. In section 9(b) the Act gives the NLRB the power to determine the composition of the work group which will be voting in the representation election. The determination of the voting group is called *unit determination* and that is analogous to the determination of voting district boundaries in a congressional election. One of the major functions performed by the NLRB in the election procedure, this is one of the most complex issues in the field of labor law. Even drafting the language in section 9(b) involved study and careful choice of terms; Senator Wagner said that the drafting of section 9(b) gave him more trouble than any other section of the act.[25] Unit determination will be further discussed in Chapter 8.

In section 9(c) the Wagner Act gives the NLRB the power to conduct secret ballot elections for the purpose of certifying labor organizations as collective bargaining representatives. The right to act as a collective bargaining representative for a group of employees begins only when a labor organization has been selected (elected) by a majority of that group of employees for the express purpose of representation.

The provisions in section 9 are unique to the U.S. system of industrial relations and express a belief in the democratic process. No longer do workers have to strike to force their employers to bargain. With the process set forth in section 9, workers need only to start the election procedure in motion, and the question of whether or not the employees will be represented at the bargaining table by a union is decided at the ballot box, not in the streets. If a majority of employees vote to have the union represent them, then the employer must come to the table and bargain. If the union is not selected, then the employer is prohibited by law from negotiating with that union. In the deliberations on the Wagner Act in the Senate, several senators pointed to section 9 as one of the chief strengths of the legislation. As Senator Garrison remarked, "Give

workers a means of expressing and redressing their economic grievances and they have no inducement to overthrow the social system."[26]
The conduct of representative elections will be discussed in much more
depth in Chapter 8.

National Labor Relations Board *vs.* Jones and Laughlin Steel Corporation

As soon as the Wagner Act became law, many experts claimed that it
was unconstitutional. One group of very prominent attorneys, who
formed what was known as the National Lawyers' Committee of the
American Liberty League, issued a report in September 1935 stating
that in their opinion the Wagner Act was not constitutional.[27] As a result
of this report many employers openly violated the requirements of the
NLRA. It was obvious that the Wagner Act was never going to be obeyed
until its constitutionality was established.

The test case before the U.S. Supreme Court that established the
Wagner Act's constitutionality was the case of *National Labor Relations
Board* vs. *Jones and Laughlin Steel Corporation.*[28] The major issue raised
by the attorneys for the company in this case was that Congress had
gone too far in passing the Wagner Act. The company maintained that
the effect of industrial relations issues on interstate trade arising in one
company that manufactured a product in one state was too remote to
warrant federal intervention.[29] While the company felt that the state of
Pennsylvania may have some right to regulate its industrial relations
system (the case originally arose out of a labor dispute at Aliquippa,
Pennsylvania), it felt also that the federal government did not have the
right under the U.S. Constitution to do so.

The case was argued before the U.S. Supreme Court in February 1937
and the decision was made public on April 12, 1937. In a five-to-four
decision, the court found that the Congress does have the power to regulate industrial relations matters where it can be proved that such matters substantially affect the operations of a firm that is large enough
itself to affect interstate commerce. The court ruled that a firm need not
trade goods across state lines to be covered by the NLRA; if a company
is big enough to *affect* interstate trade (through either its sales or its
purchases) then it is covered by the act. In addition, the court ruled that
the rights to organize and bargain under the NLRA were fundamental
rights and that Congress has the constitutional authority to recognize
and codify these rights in a statute.[30] Finally, the court ruled that the
NLRB was acting within its powers when it ordered the employer to
cease and desist from certain unfair labor practices and when it ordered
the employer to reinstate discharged employees with back pay.[31] In this
very broad ruling the U.S. Supreme Court validated the scope of coverage of the NLRA, it legitimized the basic rights guaranteed by the
Wagner Act, and it recognized the power of the NLRB to administer that
act. As one author so eloquently observes:

The Wagner Act cases mark the end of the "old Constitution" which was composed largely of doctrines protective of property rights as defined by classical economic theory and which had been erected through the re-shaping of constitutional law by the forces of industrialism following the Civil War. After 1937, business groups placed on the defensive in the political process could no longer retreat to this body of law as a final refuge, as they had following the passage of the Wagner Act. The Wagner Act cases opened the floodgates of national power and henceforth the conflict over its exercise would generally be resolved in the legislative and administrative processes.[32]

The Taft-Hartley Act (The Labor Management Relations Act) (1947)

Almost from the moment that the constitutionality of the Wagner Act was established on April 12, 1937, a movement was started to change the law. On April 28, 1937 the U.S. Chamber of Commerce announced a campaign to amend the Wagner Act by adding a list of union unfair labor practices to Section 8.[33] In May 1937 the National Association of Manufacturers (NAM) began a long-range educational program designed to influence public opinion concerning the need to amend the Wagner Act.[34] The NAM campaign incorporated the use of radio, newspapers, pamphlets, and leaflets in its appeal to the public. The campaign to amend the Wagner Act did not have any immediate payoff in Congress, although a bill was passed in the House of Representatives in 1940 (the Smith Act) that did include some provisions to change the NLRA. The Smith Act never received serious consideration in the Senate, however.[35]

State Legislation

The major area where there was a movement to amend the Wagner Act was at the level of the states. Beginning in 1939 and continuing right up to 1947, state legislatures passed laws that included provisions for unfair labor practices of unions, outlawed union security agreements (such as the closed shop and union shop), limited internal union discipline procedures (such as fines or expulsions), limited strikes and picketing, banned secondary boycotts, and outlawed jurisdictional and wildcat strikes. By the time the Taft-Hartley Act was passed in 1947, more than 30 states had passed some sort of statute limiting the activities of labor unions. Of particular importance is the fact that the provisions of many of the state laws found their way into the final version of the Taft-Hartley Act. As Mills and Brown observe, the legislative developments in the states foreshadowed the inevitable passage of legislation amending the Wagner Act at the national level.[36]

At this point the question may be asked, "What forces motivated the change in labor policy at the state level, and how were these forces to later affect a change in the Wagner Act at the national level?" The factors that contributed to a change in the Wagner Act may be divided into two categories: industrial relations factors and political factors.

Industrial Relations Issues (1935–1947). As already described in Chapter 5, the labor movement was in an upheaval beginning in 1935 with the formation and rise to power of the Congress of Industrial Organizations (CIO), led initially by John L. Lewis. The CIO was from the very beginning a much more activist organization than was the AFL. It did not hesitate to use radical tactics in organizing and in strike activity such as the sit down strike used so successfully against the General Motors Corporation in 1937. The CIO also employed persons who were known members of the Communist party and who had once participated in the Communist-dominated Trade Union Unity League.[37] In addition, the AFL and the CIO often became entangled in jurisdictional disputes and in campaigns to raid each other's memberships through rival organizing campaigns.[38] Many unions, particularly in the construction industry, used the closed shop as a way of extracting exorbitant dues money from their members and as a way of exerting almost total control over them. Some unions abused the use of the boycott and entered into collusive arrangements with employers to control access to certain product markets. All these union activities led to a change in public acceptance of union goals that found its earliest expression in state laws controlling the actions of unions and a later expression in the Taft-Hartley Act. As an extreme example, the voters in the state of Oregon, angered by a rash of jurisdictional disputes between rival AFL and CIO woodworker unions in 1938, passed by popular referendum a law that specifically outlawed strikes and picketing associated with disputes among unions.[39]

Of all the industrial relations factors leading up to the passage of the Taft-Hartley Act, however, probably none is as important as the wave of strikes that followed World War II. Reacting to a reduction in overtime, an increase in prices, and an end to wartime prohibition on striking, workers struck in record numbers in 1946 and 1947. In February 1946, for example, over 23 million worker days were lost to strikes. By comparison, in February 1945 (while the war was still on) only 388,000 worker days were lost to strikes. Major lengthy strikes were conducted against General Motors (113 days), General Electric (56 days) and Westinghouse (115 days). In addition there were nationwide strikes in the steel, rail, and coal industries, all in 1946. In the steel, rail, and coal disputes President Harry S. Truman intervened personally, seizing control of the industries and attempting to settle the disputes, all of which had the potential for causing a national emergency. The coal and rail strikes particularly caused public concern and public outrage at the activities of the unions.[40]

Political Issues. The political factors associated with the passage of the Taft-Hartley Act are mainly related to the decline in prominence and power of the Democratic party following the end of World War II. With the death of Franklin D. Roosevelt in April 1945, the Democratic party lost its most powerful and popular leader. Harry S. Truman, Roosevelt's vice president, who succeeded him in 1945, was scorned by many and did not initially have a large national following. The result was that with the congressional elections in 1946, the Democratic party lost its majority in both the House and the Senate for the first time since 1930. The balance was such that there were 249 Republicans and 185 Democrats in the House and 51 Republicans and 45 Democrats in the Senate.[41]

Many of the newly elected representatives and senators felt that they had a mandate from their constituents to change the Wagner Act. As a result, one of the first orders of business of the newly elected 80th Congress was to begin the legislative process to change the regulation of labor–management relations. Over 17 separate pieces of labor legislation were introduced into Congress during the first day of the legislative session beginning in 1947.[42]

This is not to say that there was not a movement in Congress to amend the Wagner Act before 1947; 169 different pieces of legislation were introduced into Congress to change the National Labor Relations Act in the 10-year time period 1937–1947.[43] One of these, the Case Act, was passed by both houses of Congress in 1946 but was vetoed by President Truman. The supporters of the Case Act did not have enough votes to override the president's veto in 1946.

With the change in the balance of power in Congress beginning in 1947, however, the movement to amend the Wagner Act began anew. In fact, this was one of the first orders of business of the 80th Congress and its major concern until the Taft-Hartley Act was passed in June 1947. Committee hearings to consider new labor legislation began in the Senate in January under the leadership of Senator Robert Taft (R–Ohio). In the House, committee hearings began in early February under the leadership of Representative Fred Hartley (R–New Jersey). Because of the plethora of bills introduced, the committee chairmen in both the House and the Senate were required to prepare proposals that reflected the best parts of all the legislative initiatives they received and to present these to the full House and Senate.

Legislative History. The bill from the House Committee on Labor and Education was introduced to the House of Representatives by Representative Hartley on April 15. After only six hours of debate the bill was passed on April 17 by a vote of 308 to 107; a majority of voters from both major parties voted for the bill.[44] On that same day, April 17, Taft reported to the Senate the bill devised by his committee, the Senate Committee on Labor and Public Welfare.[45] Debate on the Taft Bill in the Senate was loud and acrimonious. Even the staff of the NLRB entered the deliberations by preparing a report that objected to virtually every change in the Wagner Act proposed by the Taft Bill.[46] After nine full days of debate, however, the Senate bill was passed on May 13 by a vote of 68 to 24, again reflecting considerable bipartisan support for the legislation.[47]

Because the Senate and the House bills differed considerably, a conference committee was necessary to reconcile the differences. In early June the conference committee bill, now known as the Taft-Hartley Bill, was voted upon and approved by both the House and the Senate and on June 5 it was sent to the president for his signature.

After 15 days of deliberation and tremendous pressure from organized labor, Truman refused to sign the legislation. Although Truman had asked Congress in his State of the Union message in early January 1947 to amend the Wagner Act, he did not like the form of the changes as reflected in the Taft-Hartley Bill. In a long and detailed veto message to Congress Truman listed several specific objections to the Taft-Hartley Bill, among them the charge that it would increase strikes and that it would deprive workers of their rights. In concluding his message to Congress, Truman wrote:

> The most fundamental test which I have applied to this bill is whether it would strengthen or weaken American democracy in the present critical hour. This bill is perhaps the most serious economic and social legislation of the past decade. Its effects — for good or ill — would be felt for decades to come.
>
> I have concluded that the bill is a clear threat to the successful working of our democratic society.[48]

To underscore the strength of his convictions, Truman delivered his veto message to the general public in a nationwide radio broadcast on the same day, June 20, 1947.

The sense of urgency conveyed in the president's veto message did little to affect the votes of Congress. In the House, the veto message was received at 12:05 on June 20. One minute after receiving the message, the clerk of the House began reading it to the legislative assembly. Immediately after reading the veto message, without a word of debate, the vote began to override the veto; the vote was 331 to 83, a greater majority than when the bill was passed in the House originally.[49]

In the Senate there was lengthy debate on the veto but the result was the same as in the House: The president's veto was overridden. Even the pleadings of the ailing Robert Wagner were to no avail; on June 23, 1947, the Senate voted 68 to 25 to pass the Taft-Hartley Act over the presidential veto.[50]

The Taft-Hartley Act: Amendments to the Wagner Act

It is difficult to summarize an act as complex and as lengthy as the Taft-Hartley Act in a few pages. A summary of the major provisions of this act are given in Box 7.4.

BOX 7-4
Summary of the Major Provisions of the Taft-Hartley Act of 1947

Title I: Amendment of National Labor Relations Act

Section 2

Definitions: Changes the definition of *employee* found in the Wagner Act to explicity exclude supervisors and foremen from coverage under the act.

Section 3

National Labor Relations Board: (1) Increases the number of NLRB members from 3 to 5; (2) allows panels of 3 members to make decisions; (3) creates the office of General Counsel, who is given the authority to investigate charges, issue complaints, and prosecute cases before the NLRB.

Section 7

Rights of Employees: Amends Title 7 of the Wagner Act to specifically recognize the rights of employees not to participate in the activities of labor organizations.

Section 8(a)3

Unfair Labor Practices (of Employers): (1) Employer unfair labor practices 8(3) of the Wagner Act is amended to make the inclusion of closed shop clauses illegal in labor agreements. (2) An employer may not terminate an employee who is not a union member, even if union membership is required, if the employee has been denied union membership for any reason other than the nonpayment of dues.

Section 8(b)1

Unfair Labor Practices (of Unions): It is unfair labor practice for a union to deny anyone's section 7 rights.

Section 8(b)2

It is an unfair labor practice for a union to cause an employer to discriminate against an employee because of his or her union activity.

Section 8(b)3

It is an unfair labor practice for a union to refuse to bargain collectively with an employer.

Section 8(b)4

It is an unfair labor practice for a union to engage in an secondary boycott for the purposes of: (a) forcing an employer or self-employed person to join a labor organization or to cease doing business with

(continued)

BOX 7-4 *(continued)*

anyone else; (b) forcing an employer to recognize a union that has not been certified as the bargaining representative of his or her employees; (c) forcing an employer to recognize a union where his or her employees are already represented by another union; (d) forcing an employer to assign work to members of one union rather than to members of another union.

Section 8(b)5

It is an unfair labor practice for a union to charge excessive dues.

Section 8(b)6

It is an unfair labor practice for a union to extract payment from an employer for work not performed or not to be performed (featherbedding).

Section 8(c)

It shall not be considered an unfair labor practice to express views and opinions in either written or verbal form as long as these views and opinions do not contain threats of reprisal or force or promises of benefit (free speech amendment).

Section 8(d)

(1) *Collective bargaining* is defined as the "mutual obligation of the employer and the representative of the employees to meet at reasonable times and to confer in good faith with respect to wages, hours, and other terms and conditions of employment." (2) Each party is required to notify the other party 60 days before contract expiration if it wishes to terminate or modify the contract. (3) The Federal Mediation and Conciliation Service must be notified 30 days before contract expiration if no agreement has been reached.

Section 9(c)

Representatives and Elections: (1) Employees may file a petition to decertify a union as a bargaining representative. (2) Employers may file petitions when they have been requested to recognize a union. (3) The number of elections in any bargaining unit is limited to one in any 12-month period.

Section 9(e)

Employees by a secret ballot election may rescind a union shop clause in a labor agreement (union shop deauthorization).

Section 9(f)

Unions must file a copy of constitution, by-laws, and financial reports with the U.S. Secretary of Labor.

(continued)

BOX 7-4 *(continued)*

Section 9(g)

All information required in 9(f) must be updated annually.

Section 9(h)

Coverage of the NLRA is denied members of any union whose officers do not file non-Communist affidavits.

Section 10(a)

Prevention of Unfair Labor Practices: The NLRB may cede jurisdiction in some labor relations matters to the states where the states have statutes that are consistent with the NLRA.

Section 10(j)

The NLRB has the power to petition courts for injunctions to stop unfair labor practices.

Section 10(k)

The NLRB has the power to adjudicate disputes where they violate section 8(b)4D.

Section 10(l)

Unfair labor practices in section 8(b)4 have priority in case handling. Injunctions must be sought to prevent secondary boycotts.

Section 14(b)

Limitations: States may outlaw agreements requiring membership in labor organizations as a condition of employment (right-to-work amendments).

Title II: Conciliation of Labor Disputes in Industries Affecting Commerce: National Emergencies

Section 202

Creates the Federal Mediation and Conciliation Service as an independent agency.

Section 203

Function of the Service: (1) The mission of the FMCS is established to prevent or minimize labor disputes through conciliation and mediation. (2) The FMCS may assist the parties in settling grievances arising under the interpretation of an existing labor agreement in exceptional areas.

(continued)

BOX 7-4 (continued)

Section 206

National Emergencies: The U.S. president may appoint a board of inquiry to study disputes that may have the effect of imperiling the national health or safety.

Section 208

If the Board of Inquiry report reveals that a dispute will cause a national emergency, the U.S. president has the power to direct the attorney general to petition the district court to issue an injunction halting the strike for 80 days.

Section 209

(1) The parties must attempt to settle their dispute through negotiations assisted by a federal mediator for 60 days. (2) At the end of the 60-day period the Board of Inquiry must report to the U.S. president and the public the position of the parties. (3) If no agreement has been reached during the 60 days of negotiation, the NLRB must conduct a poll of the employees allowing them to vote on the employer's final offer. This poll must be conducted within 15 days after the 60-day negotiating period. (4) The NLRB must report the results of the poll to the attorney general within five days after the vote is completed.

Section 210

Upon receiving the results of the poll the attorney general must ask that the injunction be lifted. The president, at this point, must make a report to the Congress outlining all events which have transpired during the 80-day period.

Title III: Suits by and Against Labor Organizations

Section 301(a)

(1) Suits for violation of contracts between an employer and a union may be brought in district court. (2) Suits for damages against labor organizations shall be limited to the assets of the organization only.

Section 304

Restriction on Political Contributions: Amends section 314 of the Federal Corrupt Practices Act to make it illegal for labor organizations to make direct contributions of dues money to support candidates for national political office.

Section 305

Strikes by Government Employees: Makes strikes by federal government employees illegal.

The first section of the Taft-Hartley Act is a series of amendments to the Wagner Act; when we speak of the National Labor Relations Act today we refer to it as the National Labor Relations Act, as amended.

Wagner Act Section 1: Findings and Policies. Section 1 of the Wagner Act was amended to add a new paragraph between the third and fourth paragraphs of the old Wagner Act; the new paragraph states that the actions of unions as well as those of employers can have the effect of interrupting commerce and states, that it will now be part of the public policy of the United States government to eliminate obstructions to commerce when they are caused by unions as well as when they are caused by employers.

From the very first section, the Taft-Hartley Act states that it is the intention of this law to regulate the actions of unions as well as the actions of employers. To a large degree this may be considered the real purpose of the Taft-Hartley Act — to control some of the actions of labor unions through the regulatory mechanism of the NLRA. Congress recognized in 1947 that the passage of the Wagner Act 12 years earlier had allowed unions to grow and prosper; in 1947 there were 12 million union members in the United States as against less than 4 million in 1935. Congress further recognized that it had a responsibility to the public and to the employers to regulate the power of organized labor, power the unions would not have possessed had it not been for the protections given in the Wagner Act.

Wagner Act Section 2: Definitions. The next important change in the Wagner Act made by the Taft-Hartley Act was to exclude supervisors and foremen from the coverage of the NLRA. This change was accomplished by specifying in section 2, Definitions, that supervisors and foremen were to be specifically excluded from coverage. The reason for this change was that the NLRB since 1942 had been recognizing units of foremen and had been certifying them as bargaining representatives. Employers, as might be expected, reacted strongly against this position and argued that unions of foremen and supervisors would divide the loyalty of this "front line of management." Congress agreed with this position and specifically excluded foremen and supervisors from coverage.

Wagner Act Section 3: National Labor Relations Board. The third major amendment to the Wagner Act deals with the size and the administration of the National Labor Relations Board. The Taft-Hartley Act made two important changes in the administration of the NLRB: to increase the board's size from three members to five members, and to allow three-person panels to make rulings on cases. The second important change in section 3 of the Wagner Act was to create a whole new administrative body within the National Labor Relations Board, the office of the General Counsel. The general counsel was given the power to investigate all complaints, and was to represent the government's position in NLRB cases. Thus, the general counsel became like a district attorney in the municipal court process. The five-person board became more like a panel of judges; it heard those cases presented by the general counsel for the public (prosecution) and those cases handled by private attorneys for the defense (either a union or an employer).

Wagner Act Section 7: Rights of Employees.   The Taft-Hartley Act added a very important clause to the statement of basic workers' rights under the law by adding that workers have the right to refrain from union activity, although not from union membership if there is a union shop provision in the labor agreement. The importance of this section 7 change was quite profound, for under section 8 an employer or a union, as we shall soon see, could violate someone's basic rights under the law if these rights interfered with a worker's right to join or not to join a union. Very importantly, Congress recognized that it was important to protect workers' rights and freedom of choice. To protect the freedom of choice it is not enough to protect only one position; both sides, the affirmative and the negative, must equally be protected.

Wagner Act Section 8: Unfair Labor Practices of Employers.   *Outlawing of the Closed Shop.*   Section 8(a)3 of the Wagner Act was rewritten; before the change an employer could require that an employee be a member of a labor union before the person was even hired (closed shop); after the change an employee can be required to be a union member 30 days after he or she is hired (union shop), but not before. Thus, the closed shop was outlawed.

Union Unfair Labor Practices.   The sixth major change that the Taft-Hartley Act made in the Wagner Act was truly of landmark proportions and may be considered the most important and most needed contribution of the act: the addition of union unfair labor practices to section 8 of the Wagner Act. The union unfair labor practice section of the amended NLRA is called section 8(b). The employer unfair labor practice section became section 8(a).

Section 8(b) as passed in 1947 contains six union unfair labor practices (see Box 7.4); a seventh unfair labor practice regulating recognition picketing was added in 1959. (Recognition picketing is picketing for the purpose of forcing an employer to recognize a union without an election.) The union unfair labor practice provisions of section 8 do much to equalize the obligations of employers and unions under the law. A close look at the list reveals that union unfair labor practices 8(b)1, 8(b)2, and 8(b)3 are virtually the same as employer unfair labor practices 8(a)1, 8(a)3, and 8(a)5. Unfair labor practices 8(b)4, 8(b)5, and 8(b)6 are aimed at particular actions of unions: the secondary boycott, union dues, and work rules relating to staffing levels.

Employer Free Speech.   A new clause (c) to section 8 is sometimes called the free speech amendment. Section 8(c) specifically allows employers and unions to express their views and opinions about each other freely and without fear that this expression of opinion would constitute an unfair labor practice. Neither party in its expression, however, is to threaten or to coerce or to promise benefit to the other party.

Bargaining Defined.   Paragraph 8(d), defines collective bargaining and requires a 60-day notice to the other party before a collective bargaining agreement can be terminated or modified. A further requirement in section 8(d) is that the parties must meet and confer in "good faith" in their dealings with each other. The definition of what good faith actually means is a key determinant of whether or not the parties have met their obligations under 8(a)5 (employers) or 8(b)3 (unions). Furthermore, section 8(d) requires that the parties notify the Federal Mediation and Conciliation Service (FMCS; see below) and any state mediation agency 30 days before changing or terminating the contract. The major reason section 8(d) was passed was to eliminate surprise strikes or lockouts and to eliminate unanticipated changes in the contract. The notification requirements to the FMCS and state agencies guarantee that there will be at least some chance to have a skilled mediator offer his or her services to the parties in an attempt to avert strikes or lockouts.

Wagner Act Section 9: Representatives and Elections.   An addition to section 9 of the Wagner Act allows for election petitions to be filed by employees who wanted to be free of union representation *(decertification)*, and allows for election petitions to be filed by employers when a union requests representation without participating in an election. Section 9 was also changed to allow for only one election in a bargaining unit in each year. Thus, if a union loses an election in a particular unit it has to wait 12 months before trying again. The changes in section 9 election procedures are important and have had a major impact on the labor relations process. The provision for decertification elections (section 9(c)1(A) is especially important for a unionized work group that wants to become union-free. Presently there are about 800 decertification elections conducted every year in the United States. In over 75 percent of these cases, the union is decertified.

Wagner Act Section 10: Prevention of Unfair Labor Practices.   In section 10(l) the Taft-Hartley Act requires that whenever the NLRB receives a secondary boycott complaint alleging a violation of section 8(b)4 it is required to give priority to these cases and to seek an injunction in federal court halting the boycott if a boycott is found to exist. The importance of these changes in section 10 of the Wagner Act is to give the NLRB more power in enforcing the act. In particular, the NLRB is given the power to seek injunctive relief from the courts to stop unfair labor practices immediately, rather than having the whole complaint appealed and relitigated — a process that can take months.

Wagner Act Section 14: Limitations.   The final major amendment to the Wagner Act was the addition of section 14(b) to the original NLRA. Section 14(b) allows for the passage of what we today call state right-to-work laws. The law specifically allows states that had passed laws outlawing all forms of union security to keep these laws and allows for other states to pass new right-to-work laws. It was mentioned above that at the time the Taft-Hartley Act was passed more than 30 states had passed some sort of statute limiting the activities of unions; of these, 13 states had specific state laws outlawing all types of union security.[51] In 1986 there are 21 right-to-work states: Alabama, Arizona, Arkansas, Florida, Georgia, Idaho, Iowa, Kansas, Louisiana, Mississippi, Nebraska, Nevada, North Carolina, North Dakota, South Carolina, South Dakota, Tennessee, Texas, Utah, Virginia, and Wyoming. The right-to-work issue is a major source of controversy, and section 14(b) is one of the sections of the Taft-Hartley Act most vehemently opposed by organized labor.

The Taft-Hartley Act: New Provisions

Federal Mediation and Conciliation Service.   In addition to amending existing sections of the Wagner Act, the Taft-Hartley Act also added some new provisions to the law. One of these provisions was found in Title II of the Taft-Hartley Act, in section 201–204, where Congress created a new independent agency entitled the Federal Mediation and Conciliation Service, or FMCS. The FMCS was created out of the existing Conciliation Service of the U.S. Department of Labor. The new FMCS was given the statutory obligation to prevent or minimize interruptions to the flow of commerce growing out of labor disputes. The legislation is written in such a way that the FMCS is portrayed in a helping role rather than in an adjudicatory one. The law does not give the FMCS the power to arbitrate labor disputes or to compel a settlement to a dispute through any means. Labor and management are under no obligation to follow the suggestions made by a federal mediator to resolve the dispute.

National Emergency Disputes.   In section 206–210 of Title II there are procedures established for dealing with disputes that cause a national emergency. A *national emergency dispute* is defined as a strike or lockout that affects an entire industry or a substantial part of an industry such that if the strike were to continue it would imperil the national health or safety. Strikes in industries such as longshoring, coal mining, atomic energy production, and steel (among others) have been halted by the national emergency disputes provision of the Taft-Hartley Act. The procedure allows the president of the United States to investigate the facts of the dispute through a special board of inquiry. If the board of inquiry finds that a national emergency is or would be caused by the strike or lockout, the president can request that an injunction be issued stopping the dispute for a total of 80 days — the so-called 80-day cooling-off period. It has been used 34 times between 1947 and 1986, with varying degrees of success.

Unions as Legal Corporations.   The final major additions to the Wagner Act added by the Taft-Hartley Act discussed here are found in Title III. In section 301 the law provides that unions are legal entities and that they may sue and be sued as legal entities. The law further limits the liability in a suit against a labor organization to the assets of the organization itself. The rights granted to unions in section 301 may be viewed by unions as a mixed blessing. On the one hand, unions can sue employers if employers do not live up to the terms of a collective bargaining agreement, which may be viewed positively by some unions, although the more normal route is to file a grievance or in some rare cases to go on strike or to file an unfair labor practice charge with the NLRB if the contract is violated. On the other hand, the union itself can be sued if its agents violate the contract in some way, a prospect that might not be viewed so positively by labor leaders in some industries. While this change in the law may be defended as promoting responsible, businesslike dealings between labor and management, it can also be viewed as an attempt to limit rank and file militancy by others. It is interesting to note that the advantages and disadvantages of union "incorporation" have been debated among legal scholars and labor leaders since at least 1900.[52]

Political Contributions.   In section 304 of the Taft-Hartley Act unions are prohibited from making direct political campaign contributions to candidates for national political office such as the president, senators and representatives. This same restriction was first applied to business corporations in 1925, and section 304 of the Taft-Hartley Act merely extended this restriction to labor organizations. Actually, the law has had little effect on limiting the political activities of unions. Labor organizations merely organize political action committees (PACs) among their politically active members and establish specifically designated funds (separate from dues monies) out of which political contributions are made. This type of activity and the voluntary donation of time by union members to support political candidates is perfectly legal within the limits of the law. The same is true for companies that organize political action committees among employee groups.

Strikes by Federal Government Employees. In section 305 of the Taft-Hartley Act, strikes by federal government employees are specifically outlawed. The penalty for striking is immediate discharge from federal employment and no possibility of reemployment for three years. In 1947 there were several strong unions among federal employees, particularly in the Postal Service. The purpose of section 305 is to serve notice to these unions and any other unions that strikes against the government are not to be tolerated. This section of the law and its strike prohibitions also apply to any corporation operated by the government in times of national emergency, such as the railroads during World War I.

Conclusion. The Taft-Hartley Act made tremendous changes in the legal system regulating labor relations and collective bargaining — changes that the members of organized labor have actively resisted. In addition to specifically outlawing certain actions of unions such as secondary boycotts and jurisdictional strikes, the act outlawed the closed shop, allowed states to outlaw the union shop and gave the U.S. president the power to intervene in certain strike situations. But the Taft-Hartley Act did more than merely limit the collective bargaining activities of unions. In some sections it regulates the actual functioning of unions and even puts limits on external activities such as political contributions. Interestingly, the next change in the statutory body of labor relations law, the Landrum-Griffin Act, was to put even more emphasis on controlling and regulating unions as organizations, and less emphasis on controlling their bargaining activities than had the Taft-Hartley Act.

The Landrum-Griffin Act (Labor Management Reporting and Disclosure Act) (1959)

Attempts to Repeal the Taft-Hartley Act

With the surprise election of Harry Truman (who was backed solidly by the labor movement) to the U.S. presidency in 1948, many people predicted that the Taft-Hartley Act would soon be repealed or significantly amended.[53] Truman himself, in his State of the Union message to Congress in January 1949, called for a repeal of the Taft-Hartley Act and a return to the rules of the Wagner Act with certain amendments limiting secondary boycotts, jurisdictional disputes, and national emergency strikes.[54] The labor movement called for an immediate repeal of the Taft-Hartley Act and would not settle for any legislative compromise short of the elimination of what was regarded by union leaders as the "slave labor act."

The Taft-Hartley Act was not repealed in 1948; it was not even changed. Although several measures were introduced into Congress in 1948 calling for significant alterations to the Taft-Hartley Act, none of these was passed. A coalition of Republicans and southern Democrats led by Senator Taft frustrated all attempts to alter the basic regulations governing labor relations and collective bargaining in the 81st Congress.

Incensed at Taft's open challenge to their legislative agenda, labor leaders from both the AFL and the CIO vowed to use their political muscle to secure his defeat for reelection to the Senate in 1950. To no one's surprise in Ohio, however, Taft was reelected in a landslide in 1950, beating his opponent by more than 430,000 votes. In other parts of the country also, senators who had been targeted for defeat by the union because of their support of the Taft-Hartley Act were reelected in 1950. One author calculated that after the elections of 1950 the Senate was composed of 55 members who openly supported Taft-Hartley and 41 who opposed it.[55] Thus, for the legislative session in the years 1951–1952, there was little possibility that the Taft-Hartley Act would be changed and there were virtually no legislative initiatives forthcoming to do so.

Election of Eisenhower

In the presidential campaign of 1952 the Democratic candidate, Adlai Stevenson, called for the repeal of the Taft-Hartley Act, and the Democratic party platform in 1952 included a provision calling for its repeal.[56] The Republican candidate, Dwight D. Eisenhower, made no promises to repeal or even to significantly amend the Taft-Hartley Act during the campaign. With the election of Eisenhower in 1952 — the first Republican president to hold office in over 20 years — the labor movement lost all chances of receiving any help from the White House in securing any favorable changes in labor legislation. In fact, the administration initiated legislation in 1954 that was even more restrictive than was the Taft-Hartley Act. This bill was defeated, but only by a narrow margin and only after a determined defensive fight backed by the unions.

For the next three years no serious attempts were made by either side to repeal or to strengthen the Taft-Hartley Act. The efforts of the AFL and the CIO were more directed toward finding a common ground upon which to base their merger than to legislative reform. With the merger completed in December 1955, however, the federation was ready to mount a new effort to repeal the Taft-Hartley Act, but this new effort was doomed to failure.

Union Corruption

The merger negotiations between the AFL and the CIO brought to public attention many examples of corruption among AFL union leaders.[57] As a result of an internal investigation beginning in 1956, the AFL charged six national unions with violating the federation's ethical practice code; these unions were the United Textile Workers, the Allied Industrial Workers, the Distillery Workers, the Teamsters, the Laundry Workers, and the Bakery and Confectionery Workers unions. The Textile Workers, Allied Industrial Workers, and the Distillery Workers elected new leaders and were allowed admission to the united AFL–CIO. The Teamsters, Laundry Workers, and Bakery and Confectionery Workers, however, did not do anything to change their corrupt ways, and they were expelled from the AFL–CIO in 1957.[58]

The problem of corruption in some local and national unions had been common knowledge for some time. The AFL in 1953 expelled the International Longshoremen's Association for corrupt practices. The problems of racketeering on the docks had been publicized in the popular press in Malcolm Johnson's *Crime on the Labor Front* (1950) and in the film *On the Waterfront* starring Marlon Brando in 1954. It was not until the mid-1950s, however, that the issue of corruption in labor unions was to become a major source of public concern.

The McClellan Committee

In early 1956 the Senate Permanent Subcommittee on Investigations of the Senate Government Operations Committee was investigating military clothing procurement contracts. The chief counsel of the committee, Robert F. Kennedy, became aware of labor union violence and corruption during the course of this investigation.[59] As later discoveries were made regarding massive corruption and financial malfeasance, particularly in the Teamsters union, a special Senate committee was formed in January 1957 to study the problem. The committee, named the Select Committee on Improper Activities in Labor or Management Fields, was composed of four Democratic senators, John L. McClellan of Arkansas, Samuel J. Ervin of North Carolina, John F. Kennedy of Massachusetts, and Patrick V. McNamara of Michigan; and four Republican senators, Joseph R. McCarthy of Wisconsin, Karl E. Mundt of South Dakota, Irving Ives of New York, and Barry M. Goldwater of Arizona.[60] The chairman of the committee was Senator McClellan and it was popularly known as the McClellan Committee. The chief legal counsel of the committee was Robert F. Kennedy.

The McClellan Committee hearings began officially in February 1957. By the time the committee had concluded its investigation in 1959 it had called 1,526 witnesses to testify, had met for 270 hearing days, and had filled 58 volumes totaling 20,432 pages with evidence and testimony. In addition, the committee received about 200,000 letters from the public during the course of its investigations.[61] The main result of the committee's investigation was to produce conclusive evidence of corruption, racketeering, and undemocratic practices in the affairs of many national unions, among them the Teamsters, the Bakery and Confectionery Workers, the Operating Engineers, the United Textile Workers, the Allied Industrial Workers, the Carpenters, and the Laundry Workers. All these unions were AFL–CIO affiliates at the start of the

McClellan Committee investigations, although as mentioned above, the Teamsters, the Bakery and Confectionery Workers, and the Laundry Workers were expelled from the AFL–CIO in late 1957 as a result of the federation's own investigations.

The McClellan Committee hearings quickly became a source of intense public interest and attention. As shocking revelations of corruption, massive financial misdealings, and gangster involvement in unions became known, the public was outraged. Television cameras were present at many of the hearings, and the public could see firsthand the arrogance and defiant attitude exhibited by some union leaders under investigation. Even George Meany, president of the AFL–CIO, was shocked at the committee findings. He is quoted as saying, "We thought we knew a few things about trade union corruption, but we didn't know the half of it, the tenth of it or even one-hundredth of it."[62]

The major recommendation to come out of the McClellan Committee was for legislation to regulate the five areas in which the committee had found most of the problems in the administration of local and national unions: (1) regulation of pension and welfare funds, (2) control of union financial affairs, (3) control over internal democratic practices, (4) control of the activities of labor and management consultants, and (5) a clearer definition of the jurisdiction of the NLRB and the courts in dealing with problems arising under the labor law statutes.[63] The process of translating these recommendations into legislation was the next logical step, one that began with a legislative initiative in the Senate by John F. Kennedy (D–Massachusetts) in 1958 and ended with the passage of the Landrum-Griffin Act in 1959 (see Box 7.5). What started as a liberal Democratic bill to control some of the corrupt practices of unions, but also to weaken the Taft-Hartley Act restriction on unions, became a much more conservative piece of legislation that closely regulated the internal affairs of unions.

BOX 7-5
Major Provisions of the Landrum-Griffin Act of 1959

Title I

Section 101

Bill of Rights of Members of Labor Organizations: (1) Union members have the right to participate equally in all official affairs of their organization. (2) Union members have the right to assemble freely and express their views verbally. (3) Union members have the right to vote on dues increases and assessments. (4) Union members have the right to sue their own unions in civil courts. (5) Safeguards are established against disciplinary actions of unions against members.

(continued)

BOX 7-5 *(continued)*

Section 104

Establishes rights for every member to have a copy of any collective bargaining agreement which covers that employee.

Title II

Section 201

Reporting of Labor Organizations Officers and Employees of Labor Organizations and Employers: (1) A copy of union by-laws and constitution must be filed with the U.S. Secretary of Labor. (2) Every local and national union must file an annual financial statement with the U.S. Secretary of Labor showing assets, liabilities, sources of income, and expenditures. (3) Financial reports must disclose the salaries, allowances, and expenses of all union officers and employees.

Section 203

Requires employers to disclose any payments to union officers and to labor relations consultants.

Title III

Section 301

Trusteeships: Requires national unions to file a report with the U.S. Secretary of Labor within 30 days of trusteeing a local union.

Section 302

Allows the use of trusteeships only: (1) to correct corruption or financial malpractice; (2) to assure the performance of collective bargaining agreements; (3) to restore democratic procedures; (4) to carry out the legitimate objectives of the labor organization.

Section 304

Gives the U.S. Secretary of Labor the power to investigate and to take legal action against national unions where violations of the trusteeship regulations have been found to exist.

Title IV

Section 401

Elections: (1) National unions must have an election of officers at least once every five years. (2) Local unions must have an election of officers at least once every three years. (3) All candidates for union office must have access to the names and addresses of all eligible voters. (4) Members must be notified by mail 15 days in advance that an election is going to be held.

(continued)

BOX 7-5 *(continued)*

Section 402

Gives the U.S. Secretary of Labor the power to investigate complaints made by union members regarding the fairness of internal union elections. If the secretary finds a violation of the election regulations, he or she may petition the courts to invalidate the election and to order that a new election be held under his or her supervision.

Title V

Section 501

Safeguards for Labor Organizations: Details the fiduciary responsibilities of labor union leaders.

Section 502

Requires that all union officers who are responsible for the financial affairs of any local or national union be bonded for up to $500,000.

Section 503

Limits loans from the union to officers and employees of the union to $2,000.

Section 504

Prohibits felons and members of the Communist party from holding union office for a period of five years after imprisonment or after disavowing Communist affiliation.

Title VI

Section 601

Miscellaneous Provisions: Gives the U.S. Secretary of Labor broad powers to enforce the Act.

Section 602

Outlaws extortionate picketing.

Title VII

Section 701

Amendments to the Labor Management Relations Act of 1947: Allows state courts or state labor relations agencies to assert jurisdiction in cases where the NLRB declines to assert jurisdiction.

Section 702

Allows economic strikers who have been replaced by the employer the

(continued)

BOX 7-5 *(continued)*

right to vote in NLRB elections for a period of up to one year at their former place of employment.

Section 704

(1) Secondary boycott activity as described in section 8b(4) of the Taft-Hartley Act is redefined. (2) A new subsection (e) to section 8 of the NLRA that outlaws hot cargo contracts is added. (3) A new paragraph (7) to section 8(b) of the NLRA that limits recognition picketing to 30 days is added.

Section 705

Adds a new subsection (f) to section 8 of the NLRA allowing the use of prehire agreements in the construction industry.

Major Provisions of the Landrum-Griffin Act

The Landrum-Griffin Act, officially titled the Labor-Management Reporting and Disclosure Act, has been summarized in Box 7.5. This section highlights its major provisions. As stated in its preamble, the purpose of the LMRDA is to control the activities of unions and employers that interfere with employee rights under our existing labor laws. Note that the LMRDA specifically covers unions and employers in the railway and airline industries; these employees are *not* covered under the provisions of the Wagner and Taft-Hartley acts.

Title I of the Landrum-Griffin Act contains the "Bill of Rights" of union members added by Senator McClellan to the act during the Senate debates (see Box 7.5). Title I also guarantees members the equal right to meet and assemble freely with other members, and to express their opinions openly at meetings. In addition, Title I gives union members the right to vote on dues increases, gives them the right to sue their own unions, and gives them protection against unjust disciplinary action (such as fines or suspensions). The Act further provides that enforcement of Title I rights are to be handled through the court system.

Title II of the Landrum-Griffin Act requires reporting to the Secretary of Labor the constitution and by-laws of all labor organizations, names and titles of all officers, and detailed financial reports. All reports filed under Title II are public information. Enforcement of Title II is through the courts, and the statute provides for fines and imprisonment for anyone violating the provisions of this section.

Title III limits trusteeship activities of national unions. The imposition of trusteeship is normally to be only for the purposes of correcting corruption, restoring democratic procedures, remedying financial malfeasance, or assuring the performance of collective bargaining agreements. In most cases, trusteeships are not to exist for longer than 18 months, or the national union must show cause in court why it is necessary to extend the period of trusteeship for longer than this period.

Title IV of the LMRDA regulates the election of union officers, and Title V outlines the financial responsibilities of union officers. Officers who violate their financial responsibilities are subject to imprisonment and fines under Title V.

Title VI of the Landrum-Griffin Act gives the Secretary of Labor the power to conduct investigations.

The final section of the LMRDA, Section VII, contains a series of amendments to the Taft-Hartley Act. The specific amendments specify more clearly the role of the states in regulating labor relations, restore voting rights in NLRB elections to economic strikers, and limit recognition picketing to a period of not longer than thirty days. In addition, Title VII outlaws "hot cargo" contracts in all but the construction and garment industries. Finally, section VII allows the use of preferential hiring provisions in labor agreements in the building and construction industries.

Summary

Over a period of 33 years the legal system governing labor matters changed from one based almost totally on common law to one based almost totally on statutory law. The forces that shaped the development of the statutes were partly economic, partly social, and partly political. The statutory system, once established, became more and more comprehensive so that by 1959 even the internal affairs of unions were controlled by it, in addition to the guarantees to organize granted by the Wagner Act and the controls on collective bargaining activities detailed so explicitly in the Taft-Hartley Act.

Discussion Questions

1. The railroad industry has always been accorded special treatment by Congress. The labor relations history of the railroad industry likewise stands in contrast to the history of labor relations in other industries. To what extent have the events in history shaped the nature of labor law in the railroad industry?
2. Read over the material in Box 7.2 again. Why is the Norris-LaGuardia Act not a comprehensive labor relations statute? How does it differ from the Wagner Act?
3. In the preamble of the Wagner Act the stated purpose is to reduce strikes and industrial unrest by allowing workers the right to organize free from employer interference. Has the Wagner Act reduced or increased strikes and industrial unrest? How has the nature of disputes between labor and management changed in the post-NLRA era?
4. How did section 9 of the NLRA change the process of union recognition?

What advantages and disadvantages might the election procedure have over striking for recognition?

5. If the U.S. Supreme Court were to review the constitutionality of the Wagner Act today, how do you think it would rule? Could legislation like the Wagner Act be passed in today's political environment? Why or why not?

6. The issue of right-to-work laws is a controversial subject and one that appears to be gaining some renewed popularity. Does your state have a right-to-work law? What advantages and disadvantages can you see for a state that has a right-to-work law?

7. How well would you judge the Landrum-Griffin Act has done to eliminate corruption in labor unions? Do you feel that this problem can ever be effectively dealt with through legislative efforts? Why or why not?

Notes

[1]Herbert R. Northrup, "The Railway Labor Act: A Critical Reappraisal," *Industrial and Labor Relations Review* 25 (1) (October 1971):3.

[2]Edwin E. Witte, *The Government in Labor Disputes*, New York: McGraw-Hill, 1932, p. 244.

[3]Charles M. Rehmus, "Evaluation of Legislation Affecting Collective Bargaining in the Railroad and Airline Industries." In Charles M. Rehmus, ed., *The Railway Labor Act at Fifty*, Washington, DC: National Labor Relations Board, 1977, p. 2.

[4]Joshua Bernhardt, *The Railroad Labor Board*, Baltimore: Johns Hopkins University Press, 1923, p. 11. Actually the federal statute of 1888 was preceded by state laws in Maryland (1878), New Jersey (1880), Pennsylvania (1883), Ohio (1885), and Iowa, Kansas, Massachusetts, and New York (1886). All these laws provided mechanisms for the settlement of labor disputes.

[5]Leonard Lecht, *Experience under Railway Labor Legislation*, New York: Columbia University Press, 1955, p. 34. Lecht (p. 32) estimates that by the end of the era of government operation virtually all the operating personnel, 90 percent of the skilled craft employees, and 80 percent of the unskilled and maintenance employees were union members. At the beginning of the war fewer than 20 percent of the skilled craft employees and virtually none of the unskilled employees were unionized.

[6]Lecht, *Experience under Railway Labor Legislation*, p. 43.

[7]Ibid., p. 48.

[8]Rehmus, "Evaluation of Legislation Affecting Collective Bargaining in the Railroad and Airline Industries," p. 7.

[9]Lecht, *Experience under Railway Labor Legislation*, p. 49.

[10]"Railroad Labor Disputes," hearings before the House Committee on Interstate and Foreign Commerce, 69th Congress, 1st session (1926), p. 9. Quoted in Rehmus, "Evaluation of Legislation Affecting Collective Bargaining in the Railroad and Airline Industries," p. 8.

[11]Rehmus, "Evaluation of Legislation Affecting Collective Bargaining in the Railroad and Airline Industries," p. 8.

[12]Lecht, *Experience under Railway Labor Legislation*, p. 53.

[13]Ibid., p. 54.

[14]50 U.S. 427 (1930).

[15]Lecht, *Experience under Railway Labor Legislation*, p. 84.

[16]Leon H. Keyserling, "Why the Wagner Act?" In Louis G. Silverberg, ed., *The Wagner Act: After Ten Years*, Washington, DC: Bureau of National Affairs, 1945, p. 6.

[17]Irving Bernstein, *The New Deal Collective Bargaining Policy*, Berkeley: University of California Press, 1950, p. 29.

[18]Public Act No. 67, 73rd Congress 48 Stat. C. 90 (1933), quoted in Edwin Witte, "The Background of the Labor Provisions of the NIRA," *University of Chicago Law Review* 1 (4) (March 1934): 575.

[19]205 U.S. 495 (1935).

[20]Bernstein, *The New Deal Collective Bargaining Policy*, pp. 62, 63.

[21]Leon Keyserling, "The Wagner Act: Its Origin and Current Significance," *George Washington Law Review* 29 (2) (December 1960): 201.

[22]Bernstein, *The New Deal Collective Bargaining Policy*, p. 62.

[23]Ibid., p. 128.

[24]R. W. Fleming, "The Significance of the Wagner Act." In Milton Derber and Edwin Young, eds., *Labor and the New Deal*, Madison: University of Wisconsin Press, 1957, p. 140.

[25]Bernstein, *The New Deal Collective Bargaining Policy*, p. 125.

[26]Quoted in Bernstein, *The New Deal Collective Bargaining Policy*, p. 102. Fleming in his discussion of the significance of the Wagner Act details extensively Senator Wagner's belief in the value of industrial democracy in preserving overall political democracy. See Fleming, "The Significance of the Wagner Act," p. 135.

[27]Jerold S. Averback, *Labor and Liberty: The LaFollette Committee and the New Deal*, Indianapolis: Bobbs-Merrill, 1966, p. 54.

[28]301 U.S. 1 (1937).

[29]Elias Lieberman, *Unions Before the Bar*, New York: Harper and Brothers, 1950, p. 191.

[30]Richard C. Cortner, *The Wagner Act Cases*, Knoxville: University of Tennessee Press, 1964, p. 174.

[31]Lieberman, *Unions Before the Bar*, p. 198.

[32]Cortner, *The Wagner Act Cases*, p. 188.

[33]*New York Times*, April 28, 1937, cited in H. A. Millis and Emily Clark Brown, *From the Wagner Act to Taft-Hartley*, Chicago: University of Chicago Press, 1950, p. 282.

[34]Millis and Brown, *From the Wagner Act to Taft-Hartley*, p. 283.

[35]Gerard D. Reilly, "The Legislative History of the Taft-Hartley Act," *George Washington Law Review* 29 (2) (1959): 287.

[36]Millis and Brown, *From the Wagner Act to Taft-Hartley*, pp. 328, 332.

[37]Reilly, "The Legislative History of the Taft-Hartley Act," p. 287.

[38]See Herbert Harris, *Labor's Civil War*, New York: A. A. Knopf, 1940, for an excellent account of these rival organizing campaigns.

[39]H. A. Millis and Royal A. Montgomery, *Organized Labor*, New York: McGraw-Hill, 1945, p. 617. This law was found unconstitutional by the Oregon Supreme Court in the fall of 1940. See *AFL* vs. *Bain*, 106 Pac (2d.) 544 (1940).

[40]Millis and Brown, *From the Wagner Act to Taft-Hartley*, p. 313.

[41]Lieberman, *Unions Before the Bar*, p. 310.

[42]Millis and Brown, *From the Wagner Act to Taft-Hartley*, p. 363.

[43]Ibid., p. 333.

[44]Reilly, "The Legislative History of the Taft-Hartley Act," p. 294.

[45]Millis and Brown, *From the Wagner Act to Taft-Hartley*, p. 364.

[46]Reilly, "The Legislative History of the Taft-Hartley Act," p. 297.

[47]Millis and Brown, *From the Wagner Act to Taft-Hartley*, p. 380.

[48]Daily Congressional Record, 93:7503, cited in Millis and Brown, *From the Wagner Act to Taft-Hartley*, p. 390.

[49]Lieberman, *Unions Before the Bar*, p. 311.

[50]Millis and Brown, *From the Wagner Act to Taft-Hartley*, p. 392.

[51]Ibid., p. 330.

[52]Millis and Montgomery, *Organized Labor*, pp. 657–661.

[53]See Sumner H. Slichter, "The Taft-Hartley Act," *Quarterly Journal of Economics* 63 (1) (February 1949): 1.

[54]Benjamin Aaron, "Amending the Taft-Hartley Act: A Decade of Frustration," *Industrial and Labor Relations Review* 11 (3) (April 1958): 328.

[55]Ibid., p. 331.

[56]Ibid., p. 333.

[57]Arthur J. Goldberg, *AFL–CIO Labor United*, New York: McGraw-Hill, 1956, p. 86.

[58]Sar Levitan and J. Joseph Loewenberg, "The Politics and Provisions of the Landrum-Griffin Act." In Marten Estey, Philip Taft, and Martin Wagner, eds., *Regulating Union Government*, New York: Harper and Row, 1964, p. 39.

[59]For a complete account of how Kennedy first learned about corruption in the Teamsters Union, see Robert F. Kennedy, *The Enemy Within*, New York: Harper and Brothers, 1960, pp. 3–16.

[60]Alan K. McAdams, *Power and Politics in Labor Legislation*, New York: Columbia University Press, 1964, p. 37.

[61]Levitan and Loewenberg, "The Politics and Provisions of the Landrum-Griffin Act," p. 35.

[62]Ibid., p. 36. Quote found in *The Congressional Digest*, November 1958: 260.

[63]Levitan and Loewenberg, "The Politics and Provisions of the Landrum-Griffin Act," p. 36.

UNIONS AND NLRB ELECTIONS

Since the 1950s, private sector unions have experienced a substantial decline in the number of workers organized through National Labor Relations Board (NLRB) representation elections. In the mid-1950s through the mid-1960s, unions were victorious in over 60 percent of NLRB elections, organizing 50 to 75 percent of the work force annually through the election procedure. In the early 1980s, unions were winning a bare 45 percent of elections and engaged in so few elections that just 0.14 percent of the unorganized work force became organized via NLRB elections — a percentage less than that needed for unions to maintain their share of the work force, much less to grow proportionally with it. The decline in union success in NLRB elections, coupled with a "natural" attrition of membership, underlies the precipitous fall in union density in the United States — a fall that contrasts sharply with increases in unionism in most other western countries, including Canada. What has caused this drop in union success in NLRB elections? Studies of the causes of the decline suggest that perhaps 40 percent is due to increased management opposition; perhaps 20 percent is due to reduced union organizing effort per nonunion worker; the remaining 40 percent is due in part to structural changes in the economy and in part to unknown forces. To some extent both management opposition and union organizing effort are responses to a changing economic and legal environment. What the calculations and studies underlying them show is that success or failure in NLRB elections, and thus the future of unionization in the United States, can be traced back to specific activities by labor and management rather than to amorphous general social developments.

Chapter 8

Representation Elections

Representation elections are one of the major innovations introduced into the U.S. industrial relations system by the National Labor Relations Act (NLRA). Responsibility for conducting representation elections is in the hands of the National Labor Relations Board (NLRB); the powers of the NLRB in this capacity are outlined in section 9 of the NLRA, as amended (see Appendix A). It can be seen from reading this section of the law that the board has almost total control over the representation process. The NLRB makes decisions about the size of the election unit; the time, date, and place of the election; and the eligibility of individual voters. It also conducts the election; counts the ballots and certifies the results; rules on any appeals concerning the election; and has the power to invalidate an election and order that it be rerun.

Prior to 1935 there was no established process to choose a union as the bargaining representative for a group of workers. The procedure that most unions used before 1935 was to call a strike against the employer and then picket the premises until the employer was forced through economic action to recognize the union. The recognition strike, the recognition picket, and the use of secondary boycotts in the recognition process were commonplace before 1935. The strikes and boycotts in the *Danbury Hatters* and the *Duplex Printing Company* cases (see Chapter 6) were both for the purpose of forcing the employer to recognize the union as the employees' bargaining agent. The 44-day sit-down strike at the General Motors Fisher Body plant in Flint, Michigan in 1937 was also a strike for recognition, but generally the use of recognition strikes declined after the Wagner Act was passed. The Taft-Hartley Act made the use of secondary boycotts an unfair labor practice if used for the purpose of recognition (sections 8b4 (B) and 8b4(C)); the Landrum-Griffin Act limited recognition picketing to a period of not more than 30 days, where it was allowed at all (section 8b7).

The most common method of achieving recognition today is through an NLRB-administered representation election. Unfortunately for the labor movement, the number of representation elections held, and the number of new members added through the representation process, are falling. During the decade of the 1970s about 8,000 NLRB representation elections were conducted every year and about 400,000 workers voted in these elections annually. The unions usually won about 50 percent of these elections. The National Labor Relations Board Annual Report stated that 7,512 representation elections were conducted in fiscal 1982 and that 392,157 workers participated in these elections. The unions won 45 percent of these elections. Most recent NLRB election data reveal that between April 1984 and March 1985 only 3,673 elections were held involving only 213,182 employees. Unions won 46.4 percent of these elections and added a potential 81,891 new members through the election process.

The Organizing Process

The drop in the number of representation elections in recent years and the increase in decertification elections during the same time period point out one of the causes of the decrease in union membership discussed in Chapters 1, 3, and 5. The representation election procedure represents an important potential source of union growth. For this potential to be realized, however, unions must aggressively pursue non-union workers who have an interest in unionization, motivate an interest in unionization among those workers, convince the workers to vote for the union in a representation election, and represent the workers to their satisfaction so they will maintain their unionized status. The difficulty of organizing nonunion workers remains one of the greatest challenges facing unions today; yet it is a challenge that the labor movement must face if it is to remain a viable force in the economy.

For most union members, voting in a representation election is about as active as they ever become in worker activism or in trade union affairs. For the trade union leader, however, and for the management official representing the employer in the representation process, the organizing process is time-consuming, oftentimes frustrating, and tightly controlled by the legal system. Many organizational campaigns seem to proceed in a step-by-step progression, a process that we will describe below.

Contact with a Union Organizer

Although sometimes a company is targeted by a union and organizers attempt to win representation rights by working on the outside of the work group, the much more common practice is for a group of disgruntled employees to contact the union organizer and for organizing to be conducted by a group of insiders.[1] The motivation to contact the union organizer may come from one of several sources. Perhaps employees feel that they are underpaid relative to what they feel they should be making, perhaps they are being subjected to arbitrary and unjustified discipline by supervisors, perhaps they are insecure about their job tenure, perhaps they are dissatisfied with the safety of the workplace; or perhaps it is the need for a mechanism to communicate with management about worker needs that motivates the employee group.[2] Whatever the reason, the contact is made and the organizer, who may be a local union business agent or officer or an employee of an international union — such as a district representative — will explain to the employee group the advantages of unionization and the procedure to be followed in choosing a bargaining representative.

If the organizer is successful in persuading the employee group to go ahead with their plans to join a union, the employees may form an organizing committee. It is possible that the organizer may want to play a very active role in the activities of this committee; it is also possible that at this stage of the process the organizer may let the employees handle most of the work until the process reaches its later stages. In some cases the international union may send someone out from national headquarters to spearhead the organizing effort, particularly if the election unit is large and the prospects of winning the election look good from the outset.

Solicitation of Signatures on Authorization Cards

The next step in the representation process is to secure employee signatures on union authorization cards (Figure 8.1). Section 9c(1)(A) of the NLRA requires that before the NLRB will become involved in any election the union must prove that a "substantial number" of employees want to be represented for purposes of collective bargaining. Under the rules currently followed by the NLRB at least 30 percent of the employees in a unit must sign authorization cards before the board will direct that an election be held.[3] This demonstration of support among a work group is called a *showing of interest* by the NLRB, and it is analogous to the requirement in political campaigns that candidates obtain a certain number of signatures on a petition before their names can appear on the ballot.

Signatures on authorization cards may be obtained at special organizing meetings, at informal after-work meetings between union activists and their fellow workers, and at the workplace itself during nonwork hours.[4] Employers may have rules limiting solicitation during nonwork hours in some industries, however, where the employees are in contact with customers or patients during nonwork hours, such as in retail stores or hospitals. Generally speaking, nonemployees (such as organizers) can be banned from the workplace, particularly when other

United Paperworkers International Union

DESIGNATION FOR REPRESENTATION

I hereby designate the United Paperworkers International Union, AFL-CIO, and or its Local Union, as my collective bargaining representative with respect to wages, hours and conditions of employment. I authorize the Union to seek recognition from my employer as bargaining representative.

PRINT NAME_____ DATE _____

SIGNATURE _____

ADDRESS_____ PHONE NO. _____

CITY_____ STATE_____ ZIP_____ SHIFT_____

JOB_____ DEPT. _____

EMPLOYED BY_____

            (COMPANY)   (PLANT)

United Food & Commercial Workers International Union

Affiliated with AFL-CIO-CLC

AUTHORIZATION FOR REPRESENTATION

I hereby authorize the United Food & Commercial Workers International Union, AFL-CIO-CLC, or its chartered Local Union(s) to represent me for the purpose of collective bargaining.

_____ (Print Name) _____ (Date)

_____ (Signature) _____ (Home Phone)

(Home Address) _____ (City) _____ (State) ___ (Zip)

(Employer's Name) _____ (Address)

(Hire Date) _____ (Type Work Performed) _____ (Department)

        Day   Night   Full   Part-

        Shift ___   Shift ___   Time ___   Time ___

(Hourly Rate) _____ (Day Off)

Would you participate in an organizing committee? Yes ____ No ____

FIGURE 8-1 Union Authorization Cards

channels are available to contact employees and when the employer has a uniformly applied nonsolicitation rule that applies to all nonemployees, not just to union organizers. Likewise, a policy of barring access to company property to off-duty employees has also been allowed by the NLRB.[5]

It is possible also to use other evidence of employee interest such as membership applications or dues check-off authorizations as well as specific authorization cards. In most cases, however, employees will not become members of the union or pay dues to the union until that union is certified as the bargaining agent. Thus authorization cards are used as evidence of employee interest in unionization, though signing such a card does not obligate the employee to join the union or to pay any money to it at the time of signature.

Although the signatures of a minimum of 30 percent of employees in a unit are required before the union can request that the NLRB conduct a representation election, most unions want to have a significantly larger showing of interest than this before proceeding any further with the election process. The main reason for this is that organizing is expensive, from the union's perspective, and the union does not want to participate in an election unless it feels it has a good chance of winning. Under section 9(c)(3) of the Taft-Hartley Act, if a union loses an election in a unit it must wait a year before another election can be conducted. Because authorization cards must be used within one year of signature, this means that the union has to start its organizing efforts from scratch once it has lost an election. Also, losing the election may cause the disillusionment of the organizing activists within the unit and may cause the union to lose prestige in the eyes of its supporters. This is not to say that unions do not sometimes request elections in units where they have only the required minimum level of showing of interest, but they usually do not seek such elections. Research evidence has shown that unions win about 50 percent of elections when 65 percent of the work group sign authorization cards and only about 10 percent of elections when only 30 percent of the work group sign authorization cards.[6] In most cases, at the very least the union will want to have more than a majority of the work group sign cards before proceeding to the next step in the organizing process.

Notification to the Employer

If the union does possess a majority of signatures from the employees in the work group, the union can request at this point that the employer recognize the union and begin bargaining, a procedure called a *request for voluntary recognition*. The union commonly will offer to let a third party check the authorization cards against a payroll roster to prove to the employer that it does represent a majority of the employees in the work group. This procedure is known as a card check and is allowed by the NLRB. Much more commonly, however, the employer will refuse the union's request for recognition without an election. This is perfectly within the employer's right to do and it requires no explanation or justification to the union on the employer's part.[7] Employers should be cautioned, however, that if they do check the authorization cards (or if they have someone else check them) and find that a majority of employees have signed them, then it is incumbent upon the employer to recognize the union and to begin bargaining. The employer may not insist upon union certification through an election once he or she has verified union majority status through a card check.[8]

Petition to the NLRB

If the employer has refused the union's request for recognition without an election, the next step is for the union to petition the NLRB to conduct a representation election. The union does this through filing a petition with one of the 38 regional offices of the NLRB that have the duty to administer elections in that area, including in that petition all relevant information about such topics as the composition of the unit, the employer's name, and the union's name[9] (Figure 8.2). Two or more unions may submit petitions to the NLRB at the same time.

When the regional director of the NLRB receives the petition, he or she will first check to make sure that it is supported by the required "showing of interest" by checking the signed and dated authorization cards against a payroll list from the employer. The cards must be given to the regional director within 48 hours after the petition is filed. Once the validity of the petition is established the regional director must check several other things before processing the petition. For example, the petition cannot be accepted if the workers voting in the election work in an industry that is excluded from coverage under the NLRA, such as the railway or airline industries (covered by the Railway Labor Act); state, local, or federal government (covered by state or federal public employee bargaining laws); workers in domestic service; or workers in agriculture. In addition the NLRB will not assert jurisdiction over employers who do not affect interstate commerce; generally employers that do a small volume of business annually (less than $250,000 in manufacturing, for example) will not be covered under the NLRA. In these instances, if the state has a "little Taft-Hartley Act" applying to employers falling outside the NLRA's jurisdiction, then the state law controls labor relations issues for these employers and unions.

The petition may be rejected by the regional director for a variety of other reasons as well. For example, the petition will not be processed if there has been an election among this work group in the past 12 months; section 9(c) of the NLRA limits elections to one every 12-month period. The petition will not be accepted if there is already another union representing the work group; this is called the *contract bar doctrine*. A valid collective bargaining contract bars any election for up to a three-year period of time. If the collective bargaining agreement is about to expire, however, an election can be held during a period of no more than 90 and no less than 60 days before expiration.[10]

Once the regional director has concluded that the NLRB has jurisdiction over this industry, that there has been no other election in this work group within the past 12 months, and that there is no contract bar to the election being held, then the petition can advance to the next step of the process.

The Election

Establishment of Ground Rules

Most of these rules, of course, are established by NLRB regulations, but there are some items that can be decided mutually between the parties.

UNITED STATES OF AMERICA
NATIONAL LABOR RELATIONS BOARD

PETITION

FORM EXEMPT UNDER
44 U.S.C. 3512

DO NOT WRITE IN THIS SPACE
CASE NO.
DATE FILED

INSTRUCTIONS.—Submit an original and four (4) copies of this Petition to the NLRB Regional Office in the Region in which the employer concerned is located.
If more space is required for any one item, attach additional sheets, numbering item accordingly.

The Petitioner alleges that the following circumstances exist and requests that the National Labor Relations Board proceed under its proper authority pursuant to Section 9 of the National Labor Relations Act.

1. Purpose of this Petition *(If box RC, RM, or RD is checked and a charge under Section 8(b)(7) of the Act has been filed involving the Employer named herein, the statement following the description of the type of petition shall not be deemed made.)*

(Check one)

☐ **RC-CERTIFICATION OF REPRESENTATIVE** —A substantial number of employees wish to be represented for purposes of collective bargaining by Petitioner and Petitioner desires to be certified as representative of the employees.

☐ **RM-REPRESENTATION (EMPLOYER PETITION)**—One or more individuals or labor organizations have presented a claim to Petitioner to be recognized as the representative of employees of Petitioner.

☐ **RD-DECERTIFICATION** — A substantial number of employees assert that the certified or currently recognized bargaining representative is no longer their representative.

☐ **UD-WITHDRAWAL OF UNION SHOP AUTHORITY**—Thirty percent (30%) or more of employees in a bargaining unit covered by an agreement between their employer and a labor organization desire that such authority be rescinded.

☐ **UC-UNIT CLARIFICATION**—A labor organization is currently recognized by employer, but petitioner seeks clarification of placement of certain employees: *(Check one)* ☐ In unit not previously certified
☐ In unit previously certified in Case No. _____

☐ **AC-AMENDMENT OF CERTIFICATION**—Petitioner seeks amendment of certification issued in Case No. _____

Attach statement describing the specific amendment sought.

2. NAME OF EMPLOYER	EMPLOYER REPRESENTATIVE TO CONTACT	PHONE NO

3. ADDRESS(ES) OF ESTABLISHMENT(S) INVOLVED *(Street and number, city, State, and ZIP Code)*

4a. TYPE OF ESTABLISHMENT *(Factory, mine, wholesaler, etc.)*	4b. IDENTIFY PRINCIPAL PRODUCT OR SERVICE

5. Unit Involved *(In UC petition, describe PRESENT bargaining unit and attach description of proposed clarification.)*

Included

Excluded

6a. NUMBER OF EMPLOYEES IN UNIT
PRESENT _____
PROPOSED (BY UC/AC)

6b. IS THIS PETITION SUPPORTED BY 30% OR MORE OF THE EMPLOYEES IN THE UNIT?*

☐ YES ☐ NO

*Not applicable to RM, UC, and AC

(If you have checked box RC in 1 above, check and complete EITHER item "a or "b, whichever is applicable)

7a. ☐ Request for recognition as Bargaining Representative was made on .... and Employer
(Month, day, year)
declined recognition on or about .... *(If no reply received, so state)*
(Month, day, year)

7b. ☐ Petitioner is currently recognized as Bargaining Representative and desires certification under the act.

8. Recognized or Certified Bargaining Agent *(If there is none, so state)*

NAME	AFFILIATION
ADDRESS	DATE OF RECOGNITION OR CERTIFICATION

9. DATE OF EXPIRATION OF CURRENT CONTRACT, IF ANY *(Show month, day, and year)*	10. IF YOU HAVE CHECKED BOX UD IN 1 ABOVE, SHOW HERE THE DATE OF EXECUTION OF AGREEMENT GRANTING UNION SHOP *(Month, day, and year)*

11a. IS THERE NOW A STRIKE OR PICKETING AT THE EMPLOYER'S ESTABLISHMENT(S) INVOLVED? YES .... NO	11b. IF SO, APPROXIMATELY HOW MANY EMPLOYEES ARE PARTICIPATING?

11c. THE EMPLOYER HAS BEEN PICKETED BY OR ON BEHALF OF .... A LABOR
(Insert name)
ORGANIZATION, OF .... SINCE ....
(Insert address) *(Month, day, year)*

12. ORGANIZATIONS OR INDIVIDUALS OTHER THAN PETITIONER (AND OTHER THAN THOSE NAMED IN ITEMS 8 AND 11c), WHICH HAVE CLAIMED RECOGNITION AS REPRESENTATIVES AND OTHER ORGANIZATIONS AND INDIVIDUALS KNOWN TO HAVE A REPRESENTATIVE INTEREST IN ANY EMPLOYEES IN THE UNIT DESCRIBED IN ITEM 5 ABOVE. (IF NONE, SO STATE.)

NAME	AFFILIATION	ADDRESS	DATE OF CLAIM *(Required only if Petition is filed by Employer)*

I declare that I have read the above petition and that the statements therein are true to the best of my knowledge and belief.

....
(Petitioner and affiliation, if any)

By...   ....
(Signature of representative or person filing petition)   *(Title, if any)*

Address ....
(Street and number, city, State, and ZIP Code)   *(Telephone number)*

WILLFULLY FALSE STATEMENT ON THIS PETITION CAN BE PUNISHED BY FINE AND IMPRISONMENT (U.S. CODE, TITLE 18, SECTION 1001)

☆ U. S. GOVERNMENT PRINTING OFFICE: 1980-623-083

FIGURE 8-2 An NLRB Petition for Election

If the parties fail to agree on these issues, of course, the NLRB will make the final decision for them.

The Election Unit

Which employees will actually vote in the election? The *election unit* is a point on which labor and management may disagree. For example, assume that a union has been soliciting signatures on authorization cards in an auto parts manufacturing plant that has 300 employees. Assume further that the plant's 300 employees are divided into equally sized work groups of 100 production and maintenance personnel, 100 warehouse and truck driving workers, and 100 clerical and sales workers. The union (say the United Auto Workers) wants to represent only the production and maintenance employees, and it has authorization cards signed from 55 of these employees. The employer disagrees with this and says that if the union wants to represent the work group it should represent not only the maintenance and production workers but the truck drivers and warehouse workers too. The employer's position may be based on the fact that he or she does not want the labor force fractionalized into competing groups and that he or she would rather deal with one union for all employees rather than face the possibility that there may be two unions in the shop at some later point in time.

The determination of what the appropriate election unit is in this case will be extremely important. If the larger unit (200 employees) is determined to be the appropriate unit, then the union does not have enough authorization signatures (with only 55) for the election even to be conducted (the minimum number of cards required in a unit of 200 would be 60). In addition, the union may not have much support among the truck drivers and warehouse workers, which would almost guarantee a defeat for the union if the election were to be held in the larger unit.

In a situation such as this, when the employer and the union disagree about the unit, the NLRB regional director will have to make a decision to resolve the issue. In most cases the regional director will schedule a hearing and allow both parties to present their positions on the issue. In making the decision about the unit the regional director will rely on the following criteria to guide his or her decision.

> The extent and type of union organization of the employees
>
> The bargaining history in the industry as well as those of the union and of the employer
>
> The similarity of duties, skills, interests, and working conditions of the employees
>
> The organizational structure of the company
>
> The desires of the employees[11]

If the union can prove that the tradition in the auto parts industry is for truck drivers to be separated from production workers for bargaining purposes, that the truck drivers have widely different job duties and skills than the production workers, that the truck drivers function under a different system of work rules than the production workers, and that the truck drivers and the production workers do not want to be represented by the same union, then the union will likely prevail and there will be two units. If, on the other hand, the employer can prove that the tradition in this industry is to lump production workers and truck drivers together in one big unit, that the job skills and duties of the two groups are quite similar, that the same personnel rules and policies apply to both groups, and that the employees really do want to be put together in a combined unit, then the employer will prevail and the larger unit will be considered the appropriate unit. The NLRA specifically states only that the unit must not mix plant guards with a unit of nonplant guards and that professional employees must not be mixed in a unit of nonprofessional employees unless a majority of the professionals vote to be included in that nonprofessional unit.

Basically, the union wants the election boundaries defined in such a way that the election unit includes the maximum number of prounion workers. The employer wants these boundaries defined in such a way that the election unit is diluted with employees who are not union supporters. The regional director of the NLRB must make a judgment based on the facts of the case and on the criteria for unit determination as established by NLRB policy and procedures.

Other Issues

If there is no dispute about the unit, however, the parties may expedite the election process considerably by entering into a *consent agreement*. In a consent agreement the parties agree mutually to all the ground rules of the election in advance (without a hearing) and agree to let either the regional director or the five-person NLRB in Washington, DC resolve any issues that may arise after the consent agreement is signed. The majority of elections are held without a hearing.

In establishing the ground rules of the election, either through a hearing or through a consent agreement, the following issues must be resolved.

The definition of the appropriate election unit

A list of employees who are eligible to vote

The date, time, and place of the election

The name(s) of the union or unions that will be on the ballot

How and where election notices will be posted so that employees will know the details of the upcoming election

Usually the election is held within 30 days from the time that the above details are resolved by the parties. The election can be held either on company time (with the employer's agreement) or off company time. The election may be — and usually is — held on the company's property, but this is not required. In rare cases when the voters are widely scattered, voting is conducted through the mail, but this is not the common practice. The goal in scheduling the election is to give all eligible employees an equal and adequate chance to vote with a minimum of interference with the workday.[12]

At the time the parties enter into a consent agreement, or at the time the regional director makes a decision on the unresolved ground rules in a hearing, the regional director will require the employer to prepare a list of the names and addresses of all the eligible voters. This list must be given to the regional director of the NLRB within seven days from the time that the consent agreement is signed or the decision in the hearing is reached. When the regional director receives the list he or she will then forward it to the union. Called the *Excelsior list,* this list was first required in the case of *Excelsior Underwear, Inc.*[13] It becomes the official roster of the election and is used to monitor the election to make sure that only eligible voters actually vote and that each voter casts only one ballot. The union also uses this list in its campaign to identify the voters and also to contact them. With the filing of the Excelsior list, the election process moves to perhaps the most interesting phase, the election campaign.

The Campaign

The election campaign in a representation election is much like the election campaign in an important partisan political contest. Both sides believe strongly and passionately in their positions, and each is willing to go to great lengths to publicize its opinions. The campaigns in both cases are conducted by a relatively small group of activists. The real purpose of the campaign is to win the votes of those people who do not feel strongly about either side and who have not made up their minds about which side to vote for in the election. In representation campaigns, as in political campaigns, most people have their minds made up long before the organizing process reaches the campaign stage. People's attitudes about unions, just like their attitudes about politics, are a product of their own life and work experiences, family background, socioeconomic status, and demographic characteristics. Union election campaigns and political campaigns probably do little to change the long-standing attitudes and beliefs that most people have. But, nevertheless, the campaigns in each instance are conducted with enthusiasm and intensity.

Increasingly, it seems, both union and management campaigns (but most especially management campaigns) during representation elections are conducted by outside experts (or consultants) who make a living out of conducting and resisting organizing campaigns. The influence of outside professional experts in organizing campaigns, many of whom have little real affiliation with the particular management or union in a campaign, is again a parallel to political campaigns orchestrated by consultants who may have little or no ideological connection with the candidate they are working for.

But there is at least one main difference between organizing campaigns and political campaigns. For the participants in the union representation election the outcome of the vote is likely to have great immediate personal effect. For most people voting in political campaigns the outcome is likely to have little immediate personal effect.

The Employees' Perspective. If the union is selected as a first-time bargaining representative there will begin a flurry of activity among the work group. Negotiations with the employer to bargain a contract will commence immediately after the election is won, workers' demands will be solicited by the bargaining committee, stewards and grievance committee persons will be chosen, local officers will be elected. If a contract is negotiated, wages may rise, new fringe benefits may take effect, and very likely employees will begin paying monthly dues to the union; an amount of $25 to $30 a month would not be at all uncommon. (In some craft unions of construction workers, the dues may be much higher, however). The point is that the selection of the union will generally bring about a change in the status quo at the workplace; some changes may be good, others not so good.

The Union's Perspective. The outcome of the election will also have some immediate effects for the union. Winning brings a new source of revenue and growth in the organization, something most organizations enjoy. It may mean that a low-wage employer who has been making business too competitive for unionized firms in the market has been "brought into line." Victory will also build up the reputation of the organizer and may enhance the prestige of all union officers.

The Employer's Perspective. The selection of a union as a bargaining representative by the work group will also bring about some change for the employer, almost all of it perceived to be bad and perhaps even disastrous. The commencement of negotiations with the union means that management's unilateral control of the work group is gone. It means that the employer is no longer free to make uncontested decisions about wages and fringe benefits. It may mean that the employer will lose some competitive edge in the marketplace, threatening the economic well-being of the company. It will almost certainly mean that the employer will lose a good deal of flexibility in managing the activities of the work group and perhaps some efficiency in the production process. It may also mean a loss of personal prestige for the employer and the end of a career from some middle and upper-level managers who failed the corporation by losing the campaign to the union. The point here is that from the employer's point of view the stakes of the outcome of the election are very high. Given the circumstances, is it any wonder that the campaigns are fought so vigorously?

In some cases so-called union busters may be hired by the employer to manage the employer's campaign. *Union buster* is the term given by labor sympathizers to management consultants who orchestrate and manage employer responses to union organizing campaigns. These consultants are the employer's counterpart to the union organizers, and they employ a variety of tactics to help thwart or frustrate the organizing process. A recent issue of the AFL–CIO's *Report on Union Busters* (a monthly report published by the AFL–CIO's National Organizing Coordinating Committee) described the activities one consulting firm. According to the report, this firm advises employers to delay elections as long as possible by filing objections and appeals to rulings made by the NLRB regional director at the pre-election hearing. The firm is reported to advocate instilling fear in workers and their families by sending letters to workers' homes warning them against strike violence and of loss of pay and benefits if the union is successful in the organizing campaign. The firm reportedly advises its clients to "throw union organizers out and to worry about the NLRB later," urges employers to actively oppose authorization card-signing campaigns among workers, and allegedly tells employers that "no company ever lost an election which wasn't held."[14] This firm also reportedly urges employers to interrogate workers about their sympathies regarding the union prior to the election — a tactic allowed by the NLRB following the *Rossmore House* ruling (see Chapter 5) — and to classify them as red (prounion), yellow (undecided), or green (promanagement).

The AFL–CIO report also identified management consultants who orchestrate decertification campaigns — election campaigns to rescind union recognition once a union has been certified as a bargaining representative. The report mentions one management consultant who offers to manage decertification campaigns for employee groups free of charge. Once the union is decertified, the consultant reportedly offers to provide his services to employees as a permanent mediator-arbitrator for a fee ranging from $4 to $10 per employee per month. The consultant reportedly tells employees that "this approach allows employees continual representation without international union domination, and it permits a neutral third party to permanently represent the needs and interests of the employer and the employees without the likelihood of pride, ego, international policies, and the threat of strikes disrupting the work situation."[15]

Management consultants advising employers on organizing campaigns may be found in almost any representation election. In some cases these consultants are affiliated with large consulting firms that specialize in labor relations matters (for example, Modern Management Methods of Chicago); in other instances they may be attorneys working for large and prestigious management law firms (for example, Seyfarth, Shaw, Fairweather, and Geraldson, also of Chicago). In other instances they may be independent sole proprietors who offer a variety of services to employers including election campaigns, negotiations, grievance handling, attitude surveys, and more general personnel consulting. It has been estimated by some observers that management consultants may be involved in as many as two of every three representative elections.[16] The presence of management consultants in organizing campaigns has been found by some researchers to significantly reduce the probability that a union will win a representation election[17] and to further reduce the chances of successfully negotiating a contract once a representation election has been won.[18]

The National Labor Relations Board is in the middle of all this intense emotional activity. It is up to the board to regulate the campaign and to see to it that the fight is as fair as possible. The board in a leading decision in 1948 *(General Shoe Corporation)* summed up its role in regulating the election process as follows.

> In election proceedings, it is the Board's function to provide a laboratory in which an experiment may be conducted, under conditions as nearly ideal as possible, to determine the uninhibited desires of the employees.[19]

To effect its role as the umpire in the election process the NLRB has promulgated extensive rules on the conduct of the campaign.

Campaign Literature

For both management and labor the contest for the votes of the work group is often waged through a "paper war" of campaign literature (Figure 8.3). Because the union has the names and addresses of the eligible voters from the Excelsior list, it will often use extensive mailings of campaign material to get its message to the voters. Although every election is different, there are some very similar themes that occur and recur in almost every campaign. As Derek Bok observes, there are three issues that are fundamental in every campaign: (1) Are the working conditions at the work site unsatisfactory? (2) Can the union improve on these conditions? and (3) Will representation by the union bring disadvantages that will outweigh the advantages of representation?[20]

Union Campaign Issues. In its campaign literature the union will address all these issues at one time or another. The union will stress whatever negative factors it can about current working conditions. It may relate past or present examples of injustices against workers, such as arbitrary discipline or discharge, examples of favoritism or discrimination, indiscriminant firings, safety violations, inadequate wages or fringe benefits, and so forth. The union will also stress the victories it

It takes a strong union to win justice on the job

Thousands of public employees around the country belong to CWA—the Communications Workers of America.

We'd like to tell you why.

We chose CWA because it's a strong, democratic union with a proven record of achievement for public employees.

Some of us in CWA are white-collar workers. Others have blue-collar jobs. We include clericals, professionals, technicians, and maintenance and craft workers.

We work for state, county and municipal governments in offices, schools, libraries, welfare agencies, hospitals, parks, highway and maintenance departments.

We come from cities and towns all across America, in places like Trenton, N.J., Sioux City, Iowa, Gainesville, Fla., and Albuquerque, N.M. But no matter where we work, we all have one thing in common: **CWA has made our jobs better.**

With only an employee association or with no union at all, we had little say about our pay, benefits, hours and working conditions.

Now, with CWA, we speak with a united voice, and our employers have to listen.

CWA negotiates strong contracts and makes sure that our employers live up to them.

In states where there is no law giving public employees the right to bargain for a contract, CWA works for such a law. In the meantime, it helps us get fair treatment on the job and lobbies for increases in salaries and benefits and for other improvements.

A union we can turn to for help

With CWA, we have someone to turn to when we are treated unfairly.

CWA contracts spell out procedures which protect us from unfair firings or discipline and from favoritism in promotions, distribution of overtime, layoffs and assignment of work.

We have union "stewards" at each job site and trained union officers to represent us if our contract rights are violated.

We have effective grievance procedures, often with a system for arbitration of deadlocked disputes by a neutral outside person chosen by both sides.

We have real impact on policy decisions affecting budgets, job security and pay levels.

Backed by CWA's professional negotiators, researchers, field representatives, organizers and legal staff, we're able to establish strong local unions and to win our rights in meetings with management, civil service commission hearings, and public employee labor relations board cases.

A union with experience in bargaining for public employees.

CWA has the experience and skill to win improvements for public employees. Here are a few of the gains made by CWA members in the public sector around the country:

- **Wage increases and cost-of-living pay** comparable to the private sector.
- **Re-evaluation of job titles** and upgrading of salary levels.
- **Better promotional opportunities** and career ladders.
- **Expanded educational programs** including job training and employer-paid tuition for continuing education courses.

- **More time off** in the form of paid holidays, longer vacations and comp time.
- **Improved medical insurance and pension plans,** plus new health benefits such as dental coverage and fully-paid dependent coverage.
- **Special pay** such as bonuses, uniform allowances, shift differentials, stand-by pay, and premium pay for work on holidays and weekends.
- **Safety and health committees** and contract protection against unsafe equipment and other job hazards.

A union that gives us real strength

CWA has been able to win good contracts because of its strength.

In addition to its public employee members, CWA represents more than half a million workers at Bell Telephone and thousands of others in private industry. No matter where you live and work, there are probably CWA members nearby.

These CWA members actively support us at the state, local or national level so that we don't become scapegoats for government budget crises. They fight alongside us for adequate funding for public services.

They also help us win strong contracts without strikes. CWA has a multi-million dollar defense fund that provides financial assistance to CWA members who find it necessary to strike.

In the public sector, management is a lot more likely to settle with a union when it knows the members have this kind of backing.

CWA's private sector experience also helps us close the gap between our pay levels and those in private industry. A union that can bargain on an equal footing with Ma Bell—the largest employer in the world—has the strength we need to bargain effectively with public employers.

A democratic union that belongs to the members

We, the members, are CWA.

We elect local people who represent us, who choose our national officers and determine union policies, and who set our dues level.

We decide our bargaining demands, and we vote on proposed contracts before they can be signed.

CWA knows that it takes all of us to build a strong union. That's why it provides training for members in winning grievances, labor law, public speaking, public relations, health and safety, and other subjects.

CWA – The Communications Workers of America

For more information, contact the nearest CWA local or district office. If you can't locate them, write to the CWA Organizing Department or Public Employee Department, 1925 K St. N.W., Washington, D.C. 20006. Or call 800-424-2872 (toll-free).

FIGURE 8-3   Union Campaign Literature

has made at other workplaces and even may reproduce the paychecks of workers at unionized facilities to show the high wages of some unionized employees. The union will stress the power of collective action and will go to great lengths to stress that "you are the union" and that the union is like one big happy family held together by a common bond of mutual protection. The union will stress positive statements about unions made by many national political and religious leaders, such as President Eisenhower (who once remarked that only a fool would try to deprive working men and women of the right to join a union of their choice), President Kennedy, Martin Luther King, Jr. (who was assassinated while in Memphis supporting a garbage workers' strike), Pope Pius XII, and Pope John XXIII. The union will stress its democratic procedures and will emphasize that strikes are called only after a strike vote is held, that dues are raised only if the members vote to raise them, and that every local draws up its own constitution and by-laws and makes its own rules regarding fines and discipline of members.

Employer Campaign Issues.   The employer, of course, also wages a propaganda campaign to influence the voters. The employer will emphasize the positive factors about the current working conditions and the improvements in wages and fringes that have occurred over the past few years. The employer also will emphasize that wages are paid out of profits and that only higher profits make higher wages possible, not unionization. The employer may tell of firms in this industry that have gone bankrupt or have relocated because of union pressure. The employer will question the motives of the union organizers, will publicize the financial dealings of the national union, and will point out the large salaries and expense accounts enjoyed by many national union officials. In the campaign the employer may bring up evidences of union corruption and racketeering, particularly if the Teamsters Union is the opponent. The employer will emphasize in the course of the campaign that the union organizers are "outsiders" and that, if elected, the union will come between the employer and the employees and destroy the friendly, harmonious, "one on one" nature of interpersonal dealings at the workplace. The employer may point out the losses that employees could suffer if a strike were called and may note that employees can be fined by the union for refusing to walk the picket line or for crossing the picket line. Finally, the employer will emphasize that bargaining is a two-way street and that the union cannot guarantee that there will be any improvement at all in wages or working conditions as a consequence of their activities.

The NLRB has the unenviable job of regulating and controlling the conduct of the parties during the organizing campaign. One area of campaign regulation that the NLRB has had a considerable (and vacillating) experience with is the regulation of this campaign literature.

Hollywood Ceramics. The NLRB first began regulating the material in campaign literature with the *Hollywood Ceramics* case decided in 1962.[21] In this case the board said that substantial misrepresentations made in literature distributed during the campaign could be grounds for invalidating the results of the election. The *Hollywood Ceramics* rule invalidated elections when either the union or the employer made misleading statements about such topics as employee earnings elsewhere, company profits, and the advantages of unions that could have a substantial effect on the outcome of the election. When an election was invalidated because of misleading campaign literature the usual remedy was to schedule a new election.

Shopping Kart. In 1977 the NLRB changed its long-standing policy of setting aside elections based on misleading campaign literature in the *Shopping Kart Food Market Inc.* case.[22] The board's decision in *Shopping Kart* was influenced by the results of an empirical study conducted by three university professors, Julius Getman, Stephen Goldberg, and Jeanne Herman, published in the *Stanford Law Review* in January 1976.[23] The results of the research showed that campaign literature had little effect on the way workers voted in NLRB elections. The authors concluded their article with a recommendation that the *Hollywood Ceramics* rule be overturned; the NLRB did just that in the *Shopping Kart* decision.

General Knit. In *Shopping Kart* the board said that only if statements were made that implied NLRB favoritism for one side or another, or if forged documents were used as campaign literature, would it set aside elections. Late in 1978, however, the NLRB reversed itself and said that it would go back to the *Hollywood Ceramics* rule and that campaign literature would again be monitored for falsehoods. This was the *General Knit of California* case decided in 1978.[24] The board decided, after a year's experience, that the *Hollywood Ceramics* rule enhanced employee choice and fairness in elections better than the hands-off approach of *Shopping Kart*.

Midland National Life. In August 1982, however, the board again changed its mind, overruled *Hollywood Ceramics* and *General Knit*, and decided to go back to the *Shopping Kart* rules in the *Midland National Life Insurance Company* case.[25] At the present time the *Shopping Kart* rule as reestablished in the *Midland National Life* case still stands; that is, the NLRB will not overturn the results of a representation election based on allegations of false or misleading campaign literature. The only times an election will be invalidated because of the literature used is if forged documents are used, or if material is distributed that has the appearance of an official NLRB document that endorses the position of one party over the other in the election.

The Polling Place

The election is conducted by a representative of the NLRB. The parties to the election are allowed to have observers at the polls who may assist the person conducting the election, but these observers mainly serve to verify that the election is conducted in a fair and impartial manner. The observers also serve the function of challenging ballots in some cases. If someone votes who is not listed on the eligibility list, or if a supervisor should cast a ballot, these votes would be challenged by one party or the other.

The ballots themselves are handled only by the NLRB representative and the voter. The ballots in some cases may be printed on colored paper to foil any attempts at duplication of the ballot or ballot box "stuffing." Voters are required to identify themselves to the NLRB agent and when they receive their ballots their names are striken from the list of eligible voters.

The ballots are marked in a voting booth according to strict rules. For example, no ballot will be counted if the identification of the voter is possible (if someone were to sign his or her ballot, for instance). A voter's ballot will not be counted if it is shown to another voter after it is marked,[26] or if it contains an unauthorized write-in choice. An unmarked ballot also will not be counted.

A challenged ballot is placed in a special envelope inscribed with the voter's name, the reason for the challenge, and the name of the challenging party. When the voting is concluded, the NLRB representative will open the sealed ballot box and will separate out the challenged ballots. All nonchallenged ballots are counted first and the challenged ballots will be opened only if they will make a difference in the outcome of the election. In cases where the challenged ballots do make a difference, however, the regional director or the five-person board in Washington, DC will have to rule on their admissability before the results can be certified.

Appeals and Post-Election Procedures

After the election is over and the ballots have been counted, the parties are given five days to appeal the results of the election. In some cases the results of the appeal will necessitate that the election be rerun. In other cases the NLRB may disregard the results of the election and order that bargaining take place between the parties immediately.

It sometimes happens that the election is inconclusive, that is, that no clear winner emerges from the contest. An inconclusive result occurs when there is more than one union on the ballot. If no choice on the ballot receives a majority of the votes cast, then it will be necessary to have a runoff election between the two choices receiving the most votes. Assume that an election was held at the hypothetical car parts manufacturing facility mentioned earlier in this chapter within the unit of

100 employees. Assume further that the Teamsters Union collected signatures from a few employees and that it intervened on the ballot, meaning that its name, as well as that of the United Auto Workers, appeared on the ballot. The choice "no union," of course, also appeared on the ballot as well. When the ballots were counted the results were as follows:

United Auto Workers	40 votes
Teamsters	35 votes
No union	25 votes

In this case the NLRB would order a runoff between the two choices getting the most votes — the UAW and the Teamsters. What if the two unions had tied at 25 votes each and the no-union choice got 50 votes? In this case the election results are nullified and the election is rerun. If the same result occurs again, that is, 25 votes for the Teamsters, 25 for the UAW, and 50 for no union, the petition will be dismissed.[27] For it to be certified as the bargaining representative the union must win a majority of the votes cast; if there is a 50–50 tie between the UAW and no union in our example, the election will not be rerun. In this case the union would lose the election.

Elections can be invalidated and ordered rerun if there is evidence to prove that the election was not conducted in a fair manner, for example, if employees were not permitted an opportunity to vote through the action of either the employer or the union. The board has strict prohibitions on campaigning around the polling place by either party; even prolonged conversation between observers and voters has been held to be improper and has been grounds for overturning an election.[28] A ballot box left unattended for any period of time can also be grounds for invalidating the election. Finally, any statements by the NLRB representative at the election that can be considered as indicating NLRB endorsement of one party or the other can also be possible grounds for overturning the election. It should be pointed out that objections about the conduct of the election itself are not the most common type of appeal to be made. A more common ground for appeal is based on other factors that have an effect on the overall nature of the representation campaign rather than just on the conduct of the election itself on election day.

Board-Ordered Recognition

The *Gissel* Rule.   In some instances, however, where there is a substantial interference with free choice the board will disregard the results of an election or perhaps intervene in the process before an election is even held. In cases where major unfair labor practices have occurred that made the exercise of free choice impossible, the NLRB has intervened in the procedure and granted the union bargaining rights.

The leading U.S. Supreme Court case that authorized this practice of granting automatic recognition was the case of *NLRB* vs. *Gissel Packing Co. Inc.*, decided in 1969.[29] The NLRB had been allowing recognition based on authorization card signatures since 1949 with the *Joy Silk Mills, Inc.* decision.[30] In cases like *Joy Silk*, where the union could prove that it once held a majority of employees signing authorization cards, and that the employer had destroyed this majority through unfair labor practices, the board would issue bargaining orders certifying the union as the representative of the employees. As redefined in the *Bernel Foam* decision, this bargaining order could be issued even if the union participated in an election and lost the election and then filed an appeal.[31] Employers objected strongly to the *Joy Silk* rule, charging that signatures on authorization cards were not a reliable expression of employee interests and that the board should not issue bargaining orders based on them.

The U.S. Supreme Court resolved this issue in the *Gissel* decision, and went considerably beyond the limits that the NLRB had imposed upon itself up to that time.[32] In its decision the Supreme Court allowed recognition and would impose a duty to bargain upon the employer when a majority could be proved by the union even without an election. It affirmed the NLRB's confidence in the validity of authorization cards to prove majority standing.[33] Finally, the decision allowed the board to issue bargaining orders where there was evidence of employer unfair labor practices in the pre-election period.[34]

The major effect of the *Gissel* decision was to affirm the NLRB's *Joy Silk* procedures, which had been in effect for more than 20 years. A secondary effect, and one unused until recently, was to give the NLRB the power to issue bargaining orders even when the union never had a majority of the employees signing authorization as a remedy for massive employer unfair labor practices. The NLRB historically has been very reluctant to issue bargaining orders in cases where the union never had majority support. In 1981, however, as ordered by the Third Circuit Court, the NLRB reexamined this policy and determined in the *United Dairy Farmers Cooperative Association* case that bargaining orders can be issued without the union's ever demonstrating a majority.[35] In another decision a year later the NLRB again issued a bargaining order when the union did not have a majority of card signatures and when there was evidence of "massive and unrelenting" employer unfair labor practices that would have made the conduct of a fair election impossible.[36]

The *Gissel* Rule in Practice — *Conair Corporation*.   The official account of the employer's actions taken from the *Conair Corporation* case decided by the NLRB in 1982 gives some idea of what is meant by "massive and unrelenting" unfair labor practices.

The NLRB in its decision specifically cited the employer for 14 separate unfair labor practices, all violations of sections 8(a)(1) or 8(a)(3) of the NLRA in this case. These included:

Interrogating employees concering union activities and sympathies toward unions.

Creating the impression that union activities were under surveillance.

Soliciting employee grievances and complaints during the union organizing campaign and indicating that these grievances and complaints would be adjusted.

Expressly and implicitly promising employees benefits.

Warning employees that existing benefits would be taken away or reduced.

Threatening employees with plant closure and loss of employment.

Granting improved benefits in an attempt to undermine union support.

Threatening to discharge employees if they engaged in a protest strike.

Discharging employees who did engage in a protest strike.[37]

The NLRB in this case found the employer guilty of committing "outrageous" and "pervasive" unfair labor practices and issued a bargaining order granting the union the right to represent the employees even though the union possessed authorization cards from only 46 percent of the employees and received only 33 percent yes votes in the election.

It is interesting to note that the Court of Appeals for the District of Columbia in 1983 refused to enforce the NLRB's ruling in the *Conair* case. The appeals court would not stand behind the NLRB's issuance of a bargaining order that was not supported by some evidence of majority support for the union by the employees in the work group.[38]

In light of the appeals court ruling, and perhaps also because of the changing composition of the NLRB itself (since 1983 the majority of the NLRB members have been Reagan appointees; since 1985 all NLRB members are new Reagan appointees), the NLRB reversed its 1982 *Conair* decision and declared on May 14, 1984 in the case of *Gourmet Foods Inc.* that it will no longer issue bargaining orders unless there has been some evidence that the union was supported at some time by a majority of employees in the bargaining unit.[39] At the present time the NLRB will not issue bargaining orders giving the union the right to represent a group of employees unless the union either wins an NLRB-supervised election or demonstrates to the NLRB that it at one time did represent a majority of employees in a unit and that the employer destroyed this majority through unfair labor practices.

The practical result of the *Gourmet Foods* decision is that unless it can collect a majority of employee signatures on authorization cards, a union has no chance of winning any appeal following an election other than by holding another election. This ruling gives employees less protection from employer unfair labor practices in the initial stages of union organizing activities (before the election) and limits the power of the NLRB to punish employers who violate the law. However, this decision also guarantees that no union will be certified that does not represent a majority of employees in a particular unit — a purpose that is certainly within both the letter and the intent of the law.

Decertification Elections

In some instances employees may desire to be free of the union — to disavow the union's right to represent them for purposes of collective bargaining. When a union is decertified employees follow much the same procedure of collecting signatures and petitioning the NLRB for an election as they did when the union was originally certified as the bargaining representative in the first place. The Taft-Hartley Act amendments to section 9 of the NLRA (9(c)(1)(A)(ii)) allow for employees to petition the NLRB to decertify a union. The same 30 percent of the bargaining unit is necessary to substantiate a petition to hold a decertification election as was necessary to substantiate a certification election. The same type of secret-ballot election is held to decertify a union as was held to certify it.

There are, of course, some differences between decertification election campaigns and certification election campaigns. In decertification elections the employer is not in opposition to the election activists but is probably in total support of their activities. Legally, the employer is not allowed to sponsor a decertification campaign although the NLRB will allow the employer to "support" such activities that may lead up to the decertification election.[40] Once a petition for decertification has been filed by a group of workers and the election is scheduled, however, the employer is given full freedom to state his or her position on the question of voting for or against the union. As in certification elections, neither the union nor the employer is allowed to make promises of benefit or to threaten or coerce employees to influence their vote.

Decertification elections can be held only at certain times during the labor–management relationship. For example, once a union is certified as a bargaining representative through an NLRB election, the union may not be decertified for one year. Board regulations allow only one election (not counting rerun or repeat elections) in any unit in any 12-month period. Likewise, if a union has been decertified a new union may not be certified to represent employees until a year has passed.

Furthermore, the existence of a collective bargaining agreement between labor and management serves to bar holding decertification elections while the contract is in effect, up to three years. While a contract is in effect, decertification petitions may be submitted only during a period no longer than 90 days and no shorter than 60 days before the contract expires.[41] The purpose of this rule is to give the parties some sense of stability in their relationship during the period of intense negotiations leading up to a new contract. The union knows that if no decertification petition has been filed during this 30 day period that none will be filed during the last 60 days of the existing agreement. Of course, if the agreement expires and a new agreement is not immediately signed, a decertification petition can be filed by employees at any time until a new agreement is reached.

Decertification elections represent a problem for the labor movement. When a decertification petition is filed by a group of employees it indicates a show of dissatisfaction on the part of employees. When a decertification election is lost by the union it represents a loss of union membership. For the most recent period for which data are available (April 1984–March 1985), NLRB records indicate that 878 decertification elections were held; the unions won only 24.9 percent of these and lost 75.1 percent. In total, 31,210 workers were eligible to vote in these 878 elections representing a potential loss in membership of that many people. During this time, the 878 decertification elections accounted for 19 percent of all NLRB-supervised elections. By way of contrast, during the 1960s there was an average of about 250 decertifications per year; during the 1970s there was an average of 560 decertifications per year. During the 1980s the average will probably be around 880 or 900 per year.[42] Of even greater significance, however, is the fact that in the 1960s and 1970s decertification elections amounted to a small percentage of the NLRB's election volume — always less than 10 percent. Today the percentage of decertification elections is 19 percent of the NLRB's election caseload, and the 31,210 workers in the decertified units represent a sizable number of lost potential members. No longer can unions view decertification elections as a minor burden.[43]

Research on Representation Elections

A 1983 review noted that over 60 empirical studies have been conducted on the topic of representation elections or have used representation election data in studying some issue in labor–management relations.[44] More than 50 of these studies were conducted during the 1970s and 1980s; and, of course, more have been written since 1983. The review categorizes this research into two general types: studies that use the individual and his or her attitudes as the unit of analysis, and studies that use the election itself as the unit of analysis. The research evidence demonstrates that factors associated with the individual and with the characteristics of the election process itself both influence election outcomes.

Individual Studies

The results of eight studies that use the individual as the unit of analysis were summarized in the Heneman and Sandver review. Individual-level studies gather their data through questionnaires filled out by employees in the election unit, usually after the election was over. Employees were asked questions about their attitudes toward their jobs and toward unions; some demographic data was usually collected; and, of course, workers were asked how they voted in the election. The results of virtually all this research shows that workers tend to vote for unions when they are dissatisfied with their jobs and when they feel that the union can do something to solve the problems.

The specific studies show this result again and again. Brotslaw in a study of retail store employees found that prior union membership and prounion sentiment often resulted in votes for the union, and that low levels of job satisfaction also gained prounion votes.[45] Muczyk, Hise, and Gannon in a study of college faculty members found that those unhappy with their compensation voted for the union, and that these professors' attitudes toward unions were positive.[46] Getman, Goldberg, and Herman, in the most comprehensive study ever of representation elections in 31 different settings involving over 1,000 workers, found again that if workers hold positive attitudes about unions and their activities, then these workers tend to vote for unions in representation elections. Also they found that negative feelings about the job are associated with voting for the union in elections.[47] Jeanne Brett in a later study, using the same data as Getman and Goldberg, found that dissatisfaction with wages, supervisory style, type of work performed, fringe benefits, promotion prospects, and job security were all associated with voting for the union in representation elections.[48] Similar results to those summarized here have been obtained in research conducted on groups of white collar retail employees,[49] production employees in a manufacturing firm,[50] nurses,[51] and faculty members in a private college.[52]

Election Studies

The second category of empirical research studies conducted on representation elections reviewed by Heneman and Sandver used the characteristics of the election itself as the unit of analysis and related election unit factors with the outcome of the election. Because not all the 19 studies reviewed used the same data set or employed similar research methodologies, the results of this type of research are not as clear-cut as are the results for the studies of individual voting behavior. The election-level studies generally show that the outcomes of the election are related to the size of the election unit, with employees in large units being less likely to vote for unions than those in smaller election units. One study conducted in 1982 showed that unions won 52.3 percent of all elections conducted in units of less than 40, but only 36 percent of elections conducted in units of more than 40, and only 29 percent in units of 100 or more employees.[53] Other studies have found that union election victories are related to the general health of the economy, with unions winning more elections in times when production is rising[54] and when prices are rising as well.[55] It has been found in several studies that the shorter the time span between the filing of the election petition and the actual conduct of the election, the greater the union's chances of winning the election.[56] Voter turnout has been found to be a factor in election outcomes with a high voter turnout associated with a lower probability of the union winning the election.[57] The presence of labor relations consultants who are paid to run an election campaign for the employer has been found to be negatively associated with the union winning the election.[58] Finally, it has been found that win rates in elections vary dramatically among different unions, with some unions winning as few as 10 percent of the elections they have participated in over the last 10 years, and others winning over 60 percent of the elections they have participated in over the same period of time.[59]

A Model of Election Outcomes

In Figure 8.4 a framework is proposed to integrate the research findings from both categories of research into one model of election outcomes. The outcome of representation elections is the product of a complex series of interrelated forces. There are psychological forces operating with the individual worker that determine his or her attitudes toward work and toward unionization. There are legal factors at work in the process that determine the size of the election unit and how long the

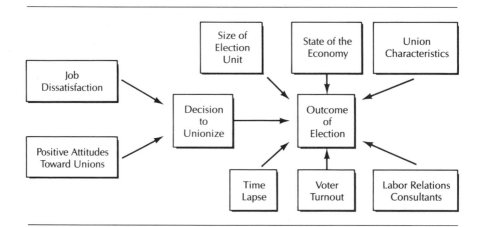

FIGURE 8-4 A Model of Union Representation Election Outcomes

election process will take, and that control how the parties may act during the campaign. There are economic factors at work as well that may influence workers' perceptions of both the benefit and the cost of unions and also that will impose some limit on how many resources the union and the employer can devote to the campaign. In short, the election process is a complex activity; the outcomes of elections depends on the interrelation of a number of competing and complementary forces. If the research on this subject has shown anything, it has demonstrated the importance of appreciating the interplay of a variety of forces in determining election outcomes.

Summary

The conduct of representation elections is one of the major activities of the NLRB. Not only does it involve time and effort on the part of the field staff to supervise over 3,500 elections every year, but the volume of litigation associated with elections comprises one of the major activities of the NLRB legal staff as well.

There is much at stake in an NLRB election. The union, the employees, and the employer are all affected directly and immediately by the outcome of the representation election. This chapter has discussed research findings on this topic and has proposed a theoretical model that can be used to understand how a number of independent factors work together to determine the outcomes of representation elections.

Discussion Questions

1. How does the representation election procedure change the process of union recognition from what it had been prior to the passage of the Wagner Act?
2. What does the term *voluntary recognition* mean? When might it be in the employer's best interest to grant the union voluntary recognition? When should the employer refuse voluntary recognition?
3. What criteria does the NLRB hearing officer use to resolve differences between the union and the employer over the determination of the election unit? Why do some experts believe that the determination of the bargaining unit is the most important factor in determining the outcome of the election itself?
4. What might be the advantages and disadvantages of grouping production employees and warehouse employees together into the same bargaining unit?
5. Develop a list of five arguments that an employer may use to persuade employees that they should not vote for the union. Develop a list of five arguments that a union may use to persuade employees that they should vote for the union.
6. Do you believe that the truth or falsity of campaign literature should be regulated by the NLRB? Why or why not?
7. How do you feel about the controversy surrounding minority bargaining or-

ders? Do you feel the NLRB should have the power to issue bargaining orders in cases such as *Conair?* How do you think the U.S. Supreme Court would resolve this controversy?

Notes

[1]Julius G. Getman and John D. Blackburn, *Labor Relations: Law, Practice, and Reality,* 2nd ed., Mineola, NY: Foundation Press, 1983, p. 73.

[2]See Jeanne M. Brett, "Why Employees Want Unions," *Organizational Dynamics,* Spring 1980: 51.

[3]See *NLRB Rules and Regulations and Statements of Procedure,* Washington, DC: U.S. Government Printing Office, 1976, section 101.18.

[4]See Charles Morris, *The Developing Labor Law,* Washington, DC: Bureau of National Affairs, 1983, p. 91.

[5]Ibid., p. 90, 92 nn. 119, 120, and 102. The leading decision in the health care industry relating to this issue is *Beth Israel Hospital* vs. *NLRB,* 437 U.S. 483 (1978).

[6]Marcus Sandver, "The Validity of Union Authorization Cards as a Predictor of Success in NLRB Certification Elections," *Labor Law Journal,* November 1977: 699.

[7]*Linden Lumber Division, Summer and Co.* vs. *NLRB,* 419 U.S. 301 (1974).

[8]*Jerr-Dan Corp.* vs. *NLRB,* 237 NLRB 302, enforced in 601 F2d 575 (CA3, 1979).

[9]K. McGuiness, *How To Take a Case Before the National Labor Relations Board,* 4th ed., Washington, DC: Bureau of National Affairs, 1976, p. 69.

[10]Morris, *The Developing Labor Law,* p. 374.

[11]Ibid., p. 414.

[12]Ibid., p. 382.

[13]*Excelsior Underware Inc.* vs. *NLRB,* 156 NLRB 1236 (1966).

[14]AFL–CIO National Organizing Coordinating Committee, *Report on Union Busters* #48, Washington, DC, May 1985, p. 5.

[15]Ibid., p. 7.

[16]Stephen Schlossberg and Judith Scott, *Organizing and the Law,* Washington, DC: Bureau of National Affairs, 1983, p. 115.

[17]John Lawler, "Labor Management Consultants in Union Organizing Campaigns: Do They Make a Difference?" *Industrial Relations Research Association Proceedings,* 1981:374–380.

[18]AFL–CIO National Organizing Coordinating Committee, *Report on Union Busters,* p. 3.

[19]*General Shoe Corporation,* 77 NLRB 124 (1948).

[20]Derek C. Bok, "The Regulation of Campaign Tactics in Representation Elections Under the National Labor Relations Act," *Harvard Law Review* 78 (1) (1964):49.

[21]*Hollywood Ceramics Co., Inc.,* 140 NLRB 224 (1962).

[22]*Shopping Kart Food Market, Inc.,* 228 NLRB 1311 (1977).

[23]Julius Getman and Stephen Goldberg, "The Behavioral Assumptions Underlying NLRB Regulation of Campaign Misrepresentations: An Empirical Evaluation," *Stanford Law Review* 28, (January 1976): 279–284.

[24]*General Knit of California Inc.,* 239 NLRB 619 (1978).

[25]*Midland National Life Insurance Co.,* 263 NLRB 27 (1982).

[26]Morris, *The Developing Labor Law,* p. 396.

[27]Ibid., p. 410.

[28]Ibid., p. 402.

[29]*NLRB* vs. *Gissel Packing Co., Inc.,* 395 U.S. 575 (1969).

[30]*Joy Silk Mills Inc.,* 85 NLRB 1263 (1949).

[31]*Bernel Foam Products Co., Inc.,* 146 NLRB 1277 (1964).

[32]*NLRB* vs. *Gissel,* p. 579.

[33]See Morris, *The Developing Labor Law,* p. 502 for a lengthy discussion of this issue.

[34]*NLRB* vs. *Gissel,* p. 613.

[35]*United Dairy Farmers Cooperative Association*, 240 NLRB 1026 (1979), affirmed and remanded for reconsideration 633 F2d 1054 (CA3, 1979). Bargaining order issued 257 NLRB no. 129 (1981).

[36]*Conair Corporation*, 261 NLRB 1189 (1982).

[37]Ibid., pp. 1262–1290.

[38]*Conair Corp.* vs. *NLRB* 114 LRRM 3169 (DC Cir. 1983).

[39]*Gourmet Foods Inc.*, 270 NLRB No. 113 (1984).

[40]Ken Gagala, *Union Organizing and Staying Organized*, Reston, VA: Reston Publishing Co., 1983, p. 201.

[41]Schlossberg and Scott, *Organizing and the Law*, pp. 265, 268.

[42]Marcus Sandver and Kathryn Miller, "Union Decertification: Contemporary Issues and Research," paper presented to the Industrial Relations Research Association, Dallas, December 27, 1984.

[43]Joseph Krislov, "Decertification Elections Increase but Remain No Major Burden to Unions," *Monthly Labor Review*, November 1979: 30–31.

[44]Herbert G. Heneman III and Marcus H. Sandver, "Predicting the Outcome of Union Certification Elections: A Review of the Literature," *Industrial and Labor Relations Review* 36 (4) (July 1983): 537–559.

[45]Irving Brotslaw, "Attitude of Retail Workers Toward Union Organization," *Labor Law Journal* 18 (3) (1967): 149–171.

[46]Jan Muczyk, R. T. Hise, and Martin Gannon, "Faculty Attitudes and the Election of a Bargaining Agent in the Pennsylvania State College System," *Journal of Collective Negotiation in the Public Sector* 4, (1975): 175–189.

[47]Getman and Goldberg, "The Behavioral Assumptions Underlying NLRB Regulation of Campaign Misrepresentation," pp. 263–284.

[48]Brett, "Why Employees Want Unions," pp. 47–59.

[49]W. Clay Hamner and F. J. Smith, "Work Attitudes as a Predictor of Unionization Activity," *Journal of Applied Psychology* 63, (1978): 415–421.

[50]Chester A. Schriesheim, "Job Satisfaction, Attitudes Toward Unions and Voting in a Union Representation Election," *Journal of Applied Psychology* 63, (1978): 548–552.

[51]J. Y. LeLouren, "Predicting Union Vote from Worker Attitudes and Perceptions," *Industrial Relations Research Association Proceedings*, 1979: 72–82.

[52]T. H. Hammer and M. Berman, "The Role of Noneconomic Factors in Faculty Union Joining," *Journal of Applied Psychology* 66, (1981): 415–421.

[53]Marcus H. Sandver and Janina C. Latack, "Unit Size and Outcomes in NLRB Elections: An Empirical and Conceptual Analysis," paper presented at the National Academy of Management Annual Meetings, New York, August 18, 1982.

[54]Irving Krislov, "Union Organizing of New Units, 1955–1966," *Industrial and Labor Relations Review* 21, (1967): 31–39.

[55]Myron Roomkin and Harvey Juris, "Unions in the Traditional Sectors: The Mid-Life Passage of the Labor Movement," *Industrial Relations Research Association Proceedings*, 1978: 212–222.

[56]Richard Prosten, "The Longest Season: Union Organizing in the Last Decade," *Industrial Relations Research Association Proceedings*, 1978: 240–249.

[57]Marcus H. Sandver, "Predictors of Outcomes in NLRB Certification Elections," *Midwest Academy of Management Proceedings*, 1980: 174–181.

[58]John Lawler, "Labor–Management Consultants in Union Organizing Campaigns: Do They Make a Difference?" *Industrial Relations Research Association Proceedings*, 1981: 374–380.

[59]Marcus H. Sandver, "Inter-Union Differences in NLRB Election Outcomes, 1973–1980," paper presented at the National Academy of Management meetings, San Diego, 1981.

DRIVING A HARD BARGAIN IN DETROIT

The meetings go on almost every day now in a guarded suite of wood paneled offices on the fifth floor of the General Motors Building in Detroit. On one side of the table are rows of GM executives, conservatively clad in dark, pin-striped suits. Facing them are burly men in open-necked shirts whose large callused hands bespeak of a lifetime of physical work — the rank and file bargaining committee of the United Automobile Workers — and members of the union's highly regarded professional staff, as impeccably dressed as their corporate adversaries.

They pass position papers back and forth and argue, occasionally at eye glazing length, about the rightness of their stands. Sometimes voices rise and tempers flare, but for the most part the discussions remain civil at this point. The real pressure will come as the September 15 strike deadline draws near. "In the first six weeks of bargaining you make a determination of areas in which an agreement can be made," said B. Patrick Crane, Jr., GM's general director of labor relations. But serious bargaining does not commence until the companies make economic offers and the union picks a principal negotiating target.

If past practice holds, Mr. Donald Ephlin, head of the UAW's GM division, will manage the talks until Labor Day when Mr. Owen Bieber, President of the UAW, will arrive for the final push for the deadline. Typically, the hard issues are put off until the round-the-clock sessions of the last day or two of negotiations. It is easier to put off difficult decisions until the shortage of time leaves no choice and because it gives the membership the impression that their negotiators have been scrapping for the last penny.

When the crunch comes and the strike deadline approaches, the man on the spot will be Owen Bieber. He is the one who will probably end up in the big corner office of GM's chairman Roger B. Smith, in the final hours before midnight, hammering out a deal or deciding to call 350,000 General Motors workers out on strike.

Chapter 9

The Structure of Collective Bargaining

Chapter 8 discussed the process of organizing and conducting union representation campaigns. This chapter describes the structure of collective bargaining. As the material in the box indicates, bargaining takes place within a well-structured system of relationships between labor and management and it proceeds in a process that appears almost ritualistic. Collective bargaining may be defined as the mutual determination by labor and by management of the wages, hours, and other terms and conditions of employment for employees within a certain work group or bargaining unit. It is no accident that this discussion of bargaining begins after that of organizing campaigns, for bargaining can begin only after the union has been certified as the bargaining agent by a particular group of employees. Once the union is certified, then bargaining must begin. However, collective bargaining cannot occur between representatives of labor and management until this certification step has been completed.

The vote to certify a union as a bargaining agent takes place within a group of employees called the *election unit* (see Chapter 8). It is important to note that the election unit may or may not be the unit that actually negotiates the labor agreement. It is possible that the employees in the original election unit may be united with other employees represented by the same union; it is then the union that bargains with the same employer in what is called a *multiplant bargaining unit*. It is possible that the employees in the election unit may be united with other employees who are represented by the same union but who work with different employers in what is called a *multiemployer bargaining unit*. The structure of the bargaining unit depends largely upon the structures of the union and of the employer that are entering into the bargaining relationship. The structure of the bargaining unit is an important factor in determining the content of negotiations and may have an effect on the goals and the behaviors of the negotiators as well.

The Union Structure

Any discussion of union structure must begin with the basic structural distinction between craft and industrial unions. The main distinction between these two types of union is that craft unions are defined as including all workers with a particular skill or trade (such as carpenters or electricians or typographers) while industrial unions are defined as including all workers in a particular industry regardless of their skill or trade or occupation (e.g., all steelworkers, all rubber workers, all automobile workers). However, very few unions today fit perfectly the traditional definition of a craft or an industrial union. Although exceptions to this basic categorization of craft and industrial unions abound, it is still useful to retain the craft–industrial distinction for explanatory purposes.

Craft Unions

Craft and industrial unions differ dramatically from each other in a number of dimensions, including the environment in which they operate, the power balance of local versus national leaders, and their goals in bargaining. Barbash points out that craft unions operate predominately in a nonfactory worksite marked by a low level of technology, a local labor market, a local product market, a casual labor market, and employers who operate relatively simple entrepreneurial operations.[1]

What this means is that craft unions most often represent in bargaining the interests of members who possess a skill or a trade, who commonly work at a worksite that is not permanent, and who compete with each other for jobs in a local labor market area. The products or services supplied by craft workers are frequently labor intensive (a relatively high proportion of the total cost of the product or service is attributable to labor costs); the products or services are consumed in a local product area; and the craft workers' casual labor market consists of one where there is frequently not a long-term employment relationship between workers and employers. In some cases the craft worker may work for one employer one week and another employer the next. Finally, the craft worker often works for an employer who is in a very competitive product market and who operates a small-scale enterprise with few levels of bureaucracy and shortened lines of authority.[2] Additionally, it is not uncommon to find that the employer of the craftworker has at one time been a member of the craft union or at least has a very good working knowledge of the skills or trade involved in the occupation.

Industrial Unions

The industrial union member works in an environment quite different from that of the craft union member. The industrial union member is more likely to work in a fixed or factory worksite for a firm that requires complex technology and that produces a capital intensive product.[3] Further, the products supplied by the industrial union member are likely to be sold in a national or international market. The nature of competition in the product market for goods produced by industrial workers is likely to be oligopolistic, with a few large firms dominating the market. Finally, the firm that employs the industrial worker is more likely to be large-scale, bureaucratic, and more functionally complex than the firm employing the craft worker.

The Employer Structure

In much the same way that unions may be divided into craft and industrial types, employers may be divided into two general structural types as well: *centralized* and *decentralized*. Unfortunately, the complexities of industrial organizations and the constant change in corporate structure because of mergers, acquisitions, and conglomerations make difficult a clear-cut distinction between centralized and decentralized employers.

Centralization

A company that has a centralized structure is one that concentrates decisionmaking power in a corporate office or headquarters. In a centralized corporate structure, power over policy and decisionmaking are concentrated in the hands of top management. The determinants of the centralization of power come primarily from the nature of the market for the products; firms with a national or international market for their products are usually more centralized than firms with a local market for their products.[4]

Decentralization

Cushman notes that the central determinant of the organization's structure is "the point in the company where administrative control is related to economic facts and decisions."[5] Thus, decentralized companies are those having a local market for the product or those organized in such a way as to give decisionmaking power to managers in certain diversified profit centers, usually corresponding to different product lines.

A simple extension of the concept of centralization and decentralization leads to a description of the most typical types of management bargaining unit. Employer organizations having a centralized bargaining structure are usually those characterized as having a multiplicity of worksites or workplaces. The multiplant employer, for example, is usually thought of as having a centralized structure enabling the employer with many different worksites to standardize and coordinate personnel and labor relations policy companywide. This is particularly true if the same product is produced at each plant or worksite or if the plants or worksites are integrated into a production network to produce a common product.[6] A good example would be the General Motors Corporation, which has 140 separate worksites in the United States, all of them parts of an integrated production network to produce cars and trucks.

Employers having a decentralized bargaining structure, on the other hand, are commonly thought of as single plant or single worksite production operations. In these operations the control over bargaining is at the local or worksite level. Examples of employers having a decentralized structure may be found in the construction industry (Table 9.1), in the printing industry (especially newspapers), in public education, and in public safety such as police and firefighting.

Multiemployer Bargaining

In some industries employers join together in employer associations and bargain as a multiemployer bargaining unit, enabling employers in a particular locality or in a particular industry to speak as one voice in negotiations with unions. These associations may serve other useful functions to their members in addition to collective bargaining. Through these associations employers may engage in such activities as political lobbying, information sharing, or conducting educational seminars. Multiemployer bargaining is common in such decentralized industries as construction, hotels and restaurants, wholesale and retail trade, and printing. In these industries the employer associations are usually local and negotiate labor agreements with unions on a city-by-city basis. Bargaining through employer associations is done on the national level in the bituminous coal mining industry and also in truck driving and longshoring.

The Bargaining Structure

The bargaining structure can be described as "how unions and employers organize the collective bargaining relationship internally and with each other."[7] One of the best descriptions of the types of bargaining unit is given by Chamberlain, who observes:

> The type of the bargaining unit is given by the configuration of the employees on a spectrum ranging from pure craft groups at one end to the comprehensive (industrial) group at the other. Most bargaining unit types fall somewhere in between, including more than a pure craft and less than all the employees. Without trying for unnecessary precision, however, we

TABLE 9-1   Bargaining Structure in Building Construction: Major Employer Associations and Unions

Employer Association	Principal Unions	Geographic Coverage of Agreement
Associated General Contractors (AGC)	Carpenters Laborers Operating Engineers Teamsters Ironworkers (rod-men)	Local or state
National Association of Homebuilders (NAHB)	Carpenters Laborers Bricklayers	Local or state
Mason Contractors Association of America (MCAA)	Bricklayers	Local
National Electrical Contractors Association (NECA)	Electricians (IBEW)	Local
Elevator Constructors Employers Association	Elevator Constructors	National (except NYC)
Mechanical Constructors of America (MCA)	Pipefitters	Local
Sheet Metal and Air Conditioning Contractors National Association (SMACNA)	Sheet Metal Workers	Local
National Erectors Association	Ironworkers (structural)	Local
International Association of Wall & Ceiling Contractors (IAWCC)	Plasterers	Local
National Insulation Contractors Association (NICA)	Asbestos Workers	Local
Painting and Decorating Contractors Association (PDCA)	Painters	Local
National Roofing Contractors Association (NRCA)	Roofers	Local
Plumbing, Heating, and Cooling Contractors National Association (PHCCNA)	Plumbers	Local

Source: D. Quinn Mills, "Construction." In Gerald G. Somers, ed., *Collective Bargaining: Contemporary American Experience,* Madison, WI: Industrial Relations Research Association, 1980, p. 65.

may think of the two basic types as tending toward one or the other of these extremes.

By the area of the bargaining unit we mean the configuration of the employer groups comprising it whether a single department of a plant, the plant itself, the company that has more than one plant or multi-company units.... there may be craft type units in a plant wide area, comprehensive-type units in a company wide area and so on in various combinations.[8]

As Chamberlain suggests, there are additional complexities within this simple distinction of craft versus industrial and centralized versus decentralized bargaining. Table 9.2 identifies eight types of bargaining units and gives an example of at least one industry that fits each type of bargaining configuration.

Table 9.2 gives us an idea of the complexity of the bargaining structure concept. By combining the type of employer structure (or the area of the bargaining unit) that may be (1) single employer-single plant, (2) local multiemployer, (3) single employer, multiplant, or (4) national multiemployer with the two types of union structure, we get eight possible types of bargaining structures. We can infer from Table 9.2 that the general discussion of craft and industrial unions developed earlier may not be precisely accurate. Table 9.2 shows that some craft unions negotiate with employers on a national multiemployer basis and that some industrial unions negotiate with employers on a local and sometimes even plant-by-plant basis.

The concept of the bargaining structure is important for the bargaining process because the definition of the bargaining structure will determine who is covered by the agreement (both employees and employers) and who will be the signatory parties to the agreement (representatives both of labor and of the employer). The definition of the bargaining structure may determine who actually sits at the bargaining table representing each side. In highly decentralized bargaining a representative of the local union may represent the employees; an attorney or a local management consultant or someone from the industrial relations staff of the company may represent the employer. In

TABLE 9-2 Bargaining Units

	Decentralized		Centralized	
Unit	Single Employer, Single Plant	Multiemployer (Local)	Single Employer, Multiplant	Multiemployer (National)
Craft	Hospitals Firefighting Police Education	Construction Printing and publishing	Airlines Railroads	Trucking Longshoring
Industrial	Chemicals Oil refining	Retail trade Wholesale trade Hotels and restaurants	Automobiles Rubber Steel Communications Agricultural implements	Coal mining

highly centralized negotiations, the representatives from each side are more likely to be someone from the international union staff on the union's side and someone from the corporate headquarter's labor relations staff on the side of the employer.

The subject matter of negotiations may be somewhat different in decentralized bargaining than in centralized bargaining. Plant level issues such as wages and benefits occupy a more important role in local negotiations; corporate policy regarding subcontracting, retaining of displaced workers, and even union participation on the corporate board of directors may be more important topics at national level negotiations.

Finally, the determination of the bargaining structure may affect the relative power of the parties at the bargaining table. A local union negotiating with a representative of a single plant that is part of a large multiplant employer may fear that a strike against that employer may not be very effective. If that one plant goes on strike, the employer can keep operating the other plants and can still be producing goods and earning revenue. In contrast, if the union is able to negotiate with the employer on a corporate-wide or a multiplant basis, the threat of a strike that would idle the entire organization may have much more effect on the bargaining behavior of the employer than the threat of a strike that would shut down only one plant.

There are forces that seem to shape the bargaining structures of particular industries. Of course, as these forces change, the bargaining structures within these industries also change.[9]

The Labor Market

In the decentralized craft bargaining that takes place in the construction industry, for example, the labor market for construction workers is local, because of the small scale of most construction contractors. However, as some construction firms grow in size and become competitors in a national market, the bargaining structure also expands and becomes more centralized. There appears to be a trend towards centralization in the construction industry. Four large construction firms (Brown and Root, Fleur, Parsons, and Bechtel) are now estimated to control 10 to 15 percent of U.S. construction sales.[10] As this trend continues, the unions will negotiate master or regional contracts with the unionized large firms to standardize wages. Some local unions in some construction unions have already increased their boundaries to cover an entire state. There is only one Operating Engineers local in the state of Ohio, for example, and one statewide Operating Engineers construction agreement that covers all unionized heavy equipment contractors statewide. To some extent, the labor market for the workers in a particular industry determines the nature of the bargaining structure in that industry.

The Product Market

Generally speaking, the more local the product market for goods and services produced by unionized workers, the more local and decentralized will be the bargaining structure; the more national or regional the product market becomes, the more centralized the bargaining structure becomes.[11] For automobile manufacturing, for example, the national scope of the product market creates pressures for a centralized national bargaining structure. In construction, newspaper printing, or health care the local scope of the product market leads to local level bargaining. Wages can differ widely even within the same craft or trade from city to city because of the prevalence of local bargaining over wages.

Technological Change

Technological change can affect the structure of bargaining. Improved transportation and communication make it possible for firms in a wide geographic area to compete with each other, thus widening the product market and possibly transforming the bargaining structure from a local structure to a regional or national structure. Technological change also may have the effect of making some crafts or trades obsolete and may transform the bargaining structure from a craft structure to a more industrial or comprehensive one. Such a change has occurred in the railroad industry, where technological change and the use of new equipment have eliminated many of the traditional railroad crafts (firemen are a particularly good example) and have prompted many union mergers (such as that of the Firemen and Enginemen's Union, the Trainmen's Union, the Conductors and Brakemen's Union, and the Switchmen's Union into the United Transportation Union in 1969; and the merger of the Sleeping Car Porters, Freight Handlers, and Express and Station Employees with the Brotherhood of Railway Clerks in 1978).[12] Bargaining on the railroads still does not truly fit the industrial union model, but it is moving in that direction. A similar type of change is occurring in the newspaper publishing industry, where technological change is making craft distinctions in the publishing industry obsolete. The response from the unions has been much as in the railroad industry, with unions merging and the bargaining structure moving more toward an industrial comprehensive structure.[13] Interestingly, in the health care industry technological change is creating more specialized technical occupations and the pressure in this industry is to create within hospitals narrow specialized craft bargaining units that can accommodate the needs of these special occupational groups.[14] Thus, technological change can both widen and constrict bargaining units.

The State of the Economy

The recession of the 1980s forced a number of employers to withdraw from multiemployer bargaining units and to bargain in separate contracts with unions on a company-by-company basis. This has certainly been true in the steel industry, where since 1985 the major steel producers now negotiate separately rather than as a nationwide group.[15] The breakup of the coordinated steel industry bargaining group marks the first time in 30 years that the separate steel companies have negotiated separate contracts with the Steelworkers Union. One reason for the breakup of the multiemployer bargaining unit was the bankruptcy of the Wheeling Pittsburgh Steel Company in 1985. After declaring Chapter 11 bankruptcy the company drastically cut wages and benefits but still continued to operate. The union struck Wheeling-Pittsburgh for 88 days but eventually the strike was settled and the employees took a 16 percent cut in wages and benefits.[16] Other steel producers demanded similar or even greater wage reductions to stay competitive with Wheeling-Pittsburgh. Steelworkers leaders made the decision to negotiate in 1986 on a company-by-company basis rather than nationwide because not every company in the industry was in the same financial position. Concessions negotiated in the steel industry in 1986 varied widely from company to company. For example, concessions at LTV Steel reduced wages and benefits by $3.60 per hour to $22 per hour. At National Steel the concessions were $1.50 per hour, and at Bethlehem Steel the concessions totaled $2.35 per hour.[17]

Economic pressures on employers in the construction industry have prompted many employers to withdraw from local contractors' associations and to negotiate individual labor agreements with the building trades unions. Employers who are unable to pay union wages and operate at a profit ask for concessions and reductions in the union rate. If the union leader wants to maintain jobs for his or her members, concessions need to be made. Of course, once special concessions are made to accommodate the needs of one employer, other employers soon begin demanding special considerations and the bargaining structure changes from a coordinated multiemployer structure to an individual employer structure.

Advantages and Disadvantages of Alternative Bargaining Structures

It is possible to discuss some of the advantages and disadvantages of the alternative types of bargaining structure identified in Table 9.2

Craft Units

Single Employer–Single Plant.   This is the narrowest, most decentralized type of bargaining unit, encompassing all the employees of a particular employer at a particular workplace who possess a certain craft or skill. Some examples include a unit of nurses in a municipal hospital, a unit of teachers in a school system, or a unit of police or firefighters in a city. The advantages of this type of bargaining unit are the solidarity and cohesion that can result from a group of people with similar interests and skills who work together. The jurisdiction of the craft can be best protected by narrow craft bargaining with the employer. The community of interest among the bargaining unit members should reduce internal organizational conflict. The small scale of the unit may give individual members more opportunity to participate in the affairs of the local union and perhaps to have personal input into the bargaining process. If the skills of the members are unique and the employer is not able to replace the workers easily in the event of a strike (firefighters, for example), the bargaining unit may possess considerable bargaining power.

On the other hand, craft units negotiating for their members with a single employer may suffer some disadvantages, too. Craft bargaining is to some extent destabilizing to the employer. Rivalries may develop among crafts at the worksite over both jurisdiction and wage levels. If the crafts negotiate agreements at different times there may be increased pressures on the employer, who faces strike threats from each of the crafts he or she negotiates within each contract round.

Multiemployer Local. Craft units negotiating contracts with multiple employers usually negotiate with employer associations such as the Associated General Contractors in the construction industry. There are many advantages both to employers and to the craft unions of negotiating within such a bargaining structure. The most important advantage to employers is that negotiating within such a structure prevents "whipsawing" by the union, or targeting one employer in a competitive industry (usually the weakest or most vulnerable employer), negotiating a contract with that employer, and then imposing this contract on other employers in the industry one at a time. The individual employers are afraid to risk a strike in such a situation because they know that their competitors will continue to operate and may steal away some business or customers while the targeted employer is on strike.

For the craft unions, multiemployer bargaining helps standardize wages and working conditions in a local area and thus helps the union protect its jurisdiction from rival unions. In addition, negotiations can be consolidated into one agreement covering a number of often small employers, thus reducing greatly time spent in negotiation. Because they pay the same wage levels and benefits, all employers in the industry can regard wages as fixed and know that all other employers in a local area will be paying their employees the same wage level for the same work. Thus, when bidding on jobs in construction or printing, all bidders know that their competitors will be paying the same price for labor — the union rate.

The disadvantage of such a bargaining structure is that the craft unions may sometimes face a situation where an employer needs to pay less than the union rate to stay in existence. If the union refuses to grant the lower rate the employer may go out of business and the union loses work for its members. If the union does grant concessions to a particular employer, however, the other employers — even those in a healthy economic situation — will demand them too. Multiemployer bargaining may inhibit the flexibility necessary to unions and employers in their bargaining relationship.

Single Employer–Multiplant.   Employers in such industries as railroads and airlines are frequently characterized as having an oligopolistic market for the service they provide. Because the employers in these industries are large corporations operating in national markets, the union must have a bargaining structure appropriate to these circumstances. Thus, wages are standardized nationwide for each employer although wages and benefits may vary from employer to employer. Individual employers maintain the flexibility they need to negotiate labor costs; the unions are able to maintain their separate craft identities through craft-by-craft bargaining, and members know that wages and working conditions are standardized companywide for persons doing the same jobs with the same skills and experience. Further, the union is able to achieve some degree of bargaining power over the employer because any strike action against the employer will be nationwide in scope.

Multiemployer National.   This bargaining unit is found where there is a nationwide industry with many competitive employers who employ workers of a particular trade or craft. Although not commonly regarded as such, truck driving is a craft or trade, and the National Master Freight Agreement negotiated by the Teamsters Union can be regarded as a national multiemployer agreement covering a craft group. The longshoremen's contracts actually are regional contracts with one union (the International Longshoremen's and Warehousemen's Union) negotiating a contract covering employees in the Pacific ports and another union (the International Longshoremen's Association) negotiating with employees in the Atlantic and Gulf of Mexico ports. This negotiating structure has the advantage of standardizing wages and benefits across all employers nationwide. It helps the unions achieve consistency in wages for its members in these industries. The disadvantages of this type of unit are that individual units are very large; the interests of the individual employers and individual local groups are frequently submerged for the good of the larger group. There is constant danger that nonunion competitors will undercut the labor costs of unionized firms and drive them out of business. It is difficult to police contracts with such a large scope, and firms may subvert the national agreement through starting their own nonunion "alter ego" companies (this practice is known as double breasting) to escape the high labor costs imposed by the national multiemployer agreement. The deregulation of the trucking industry has put considerable pressure on the Teamsters Union and the unionized employers signatory to the National Master Freight Agreement by allowing virtually free entry into the market to employers. Most of the new entrants into the trucking industry are nonunion.

Industrial Units

Single Employer–Single Plant.   This negotiating unit is most appropriate to single plant manufacturing operations or to firms that allow considerable autonomy over labor relations matters to managers of separate plants within the corporation. Its advantages are adaptability of the contract to local conditions and the fact that local union members have the prospect of providing some input into how the contract is negotiated and to what it may contain. This negotiating unit may put the union at a disadvantage, however, if the owner of a multiplant operation can easily shift work from one plant to another in the event of a strike. Plant-by-plant negotiations may make it difficult for a corporation to establish a corporation-wide human resource policy, as well.

Multiemployer Local.   These bargaining units are found most often in the retail and wholesale trade and in the hotel and restaurant industries. Their agreements cover all unionized workers in a particular geographic area who work in the industry, and all employers who employ these workers, as well. They have the advantage of standardizing wages and benefits in a particular industry and area, and also eliminate the strife and conflict that can arise from craft-by-craft negotiations. When the Meatcutters Union and the Retail Clerks International Association merged in 1979 to form the United Food and Commercial Workers Union (UFCW), industrial unionism in the retail food industry became an accomplished fact. The merger helped alleviate rivalry that sometimes developed between unionized meatcutters who worked in the butcher section of food stores and retail employees who worked the cash registers and stocked the shelves. Prior to the merger, the butchers were regarded as skilled craft unionists who negotiated separate contracts with the employers.

The UFCW negotiates with many small retail stores through employer associations. This type of multiemployer bargaining protects employers from whipsawing in this competitive industry and helps standardize wages in an area for the employees. Bargaining is conducted at the local level, although input into negotiations from each individual worksite may be limited because of the number of worksites that may be represented in the negotiations. The major advantage of this type of structure for the union is the increased bargaining power that the union is able to attain by bargaining for a larger portion of the industry in an area, thus reducing nonunion competition in the event of a strike.

Single Employer–Multiplant. This unit is the one most commonly found in U.S. manufacturing. True industry-wide agreements are rare in the United States. Much more common are agreements that cover all plants or operating facilities of a particular company nationwide. Agreements negotiated with large-scale, well-known leaders in the industry may become part of a pattern of bargaining in that industry for the union, which may attempt to impose that pattern agreement on all employers in that industry. Such was the case in the automobile industry for many years. The United Automobile Workers would choose one of the Big Three automobile manufacturers as the target employer, negotiate an agreement with that employer, and then use this contract as the pattern to achieve in negotiations with the other two automobile companies. The same type of pattern bargaining was also followed in the rubber industry. Negotiations in both industries have always been with individual companies — not with associations of employers.

This bargaining structure offers many advantages both to the union and to the company. For the union, the resources of the entire organization can be used to support a strike against a particular company. The union in negotiations of this type can afford to provide monetary support (strike funds) to workers on strike. The union negotiators will be the most experienced and most expert available in the organization. For the company, centralized negotiations provide an opportunity to standardize wage and benefit packages corporation-wide and also permit the establishment of a unified corporate labor relations and human resource policy. If the union is able to establish a pattern of bargaining and is able to enforce this pattern through the industry, this may help stabilize competition in the industry as well.

The major disadvantage of this bargaining unit involves the distancing of negotiations from the individual member and from the concerns of particular worksites or work groups. The possibility for conflict within the union increases as groups of workers have less and less chance of individual input. Individual members may feel alienated and estranged from the bargaining process. Interests of particular groups (skilled workers or older or younger workers, for example) may be sacrificed or ignored by the union leaders negotiating the contract.

In some instances an attempt has been made to deal with the problems of national multiplant negotiations by establishing what are known as *two-tier negotiations*, in which negotiations over some major issues such as wages, benefits, corporate labor relations policy, and management rights are negotiated at the national level, and the results are included in a master agreement that covers all workers in the corporation. On some other issues such as local working conditions, hours of work, and plant rules, however, there will be negotiations on the local level.

Two-tier bargaining sometimes creates problems in negotiations, however.[18] It is often difficult to coordinate between the national level and the local level negotiators. In some instances local union militancy may create pressures for a strike at the local level that are not present at the national level. Local level negotiations may drag on long after national level bargaining is completed. The 1984 GM and the 1986 Bell System settlements were both delayed by strikes over local issues. However, two-tier negotiations will probably expand in years to come. The combination of national level and local level bargaining creates a very logical and smoothly functioning bargaining relationship.

Multiemployer National.   This is the most comprehensive and most centralized type of bargaining structure. In this bargaining unit, all workers who work in the same industry are covered by the same agreement. Known as industry-wide bargaining, the best example used to be in basic steel production, where the "Big 8" steel firms would negotiate together with the United Steelworkers of America to negotiate a master steel contract. As mentioned above, this type of structure no longer exists in the steel industry; the big steel companies now negotiate on a company-by-company basis. Industry-wide bargaining still exists to some extent in bituminous coal production, however. At least the major producers of bituminous coal still bargain through the Bituminous Coal Operators Association, although some operators negotiate separate company-by-company contracts. Industry-wide negotiations in coal were largely brought about through the efforts of John L. Lewis in the 1950s. There is good reason to believe that industry-wide negotiations probably will not continue for too much longer even in the bituminous coal mining industry.

The major disadvantage of industry-wide negotiations is the loss of flexibility that is increasingly necessary in modern labor negotiations. The imposition of an industry pattern through national multiemployer bargaining is really viable only if the industry is profitable and if the producers are reasonably free from domestic nonunion or international competition. Once they lose their competitive advantage, employers need flexibility to restore themselves to profitability. Industry-wide bargaining reduces or eliminates this flexibility for individual corporations. In addition, industry-wide bargaining carries with it all the problems generally associated with national level bargaining, such as conflict over items to be negotiated, the estrangement of local union members from the bargaining process, and the centralization of power in national union leaders.

Union Bargaining Goals

The differences in union structure leads to differences in union bargaining goals and bargaining activities (Table 9.3). For both craft and industrial unions, a major goal in bargaining is establishing a price for labor, in most cases measured by so many dollars and cents per hour worked or, in some cases, by some type of piece rate (so many dollars or cents for each unit of output produced). The price of labor includes overtime payment, shift premiums, production business, and cost of living adjustments. In addition, the general category of price of labor includes fringe benefits. Bargaining over fringe benefits may be quite different in industrial union negotiations from that in craft union negotiations. The reason for this lies in the difference in the employment relationship for craft workers and industrial workers with the employer.

Craft Unions

Wages and Benefits. For craft workers the casual and intermittent nature of the employment relationship necessitates in many cases that the union itself maintain and administer the pension, life insurance, and health insurance benefits for the members. Because the employment relationship between craft workers and their employer is often short term and unstable, the union must provide the stability in the administration of the benefits for their members. The goal in negotiations for the craft union is to increase the level of contribution from the employer going to pay fringe benefits, but not necessarily to expand the scope of benefits. In cases where the employment relationship between the employer and the craft union worker is not casual but is more permanent and long term, the employer may play a larger role in determining and administering workers' benefits, however.

Quality of the Craft. For craft unions a second major goal in bargaining is to maintain the quality and integrity of the craft or the trade and to protect the union's jurisdiction. Hence the union is concerned that only union members do certain types of work and that the work that is

TABLE 9-3 Union Goals

Craft Union	Industrial Union
1. Price of labor (wages)	1. Price of labor (wages, fringes)
2. Quality of trade/jurisdiction	2. Individual worker protection
3. Level of employment and supply of labor	3. Job and income security
4. Union security	4. Union security

within the control of the union remain within its control. Through this control of the workplace the union can help protect the jurisdictional rights of the union to do certain types of work and can at the same time protect the amount of work available for its members. The craft union will be very concerned, for example, that nonmembers not encroach on the work members would normally do. In addition, craft unions commonly promulgate rules in bargaining that regulate the type of tools and materials to be used, and the level of staffing. As an example, a common goal of most local teachers' unions is to reduce class size to a reasonable level (in many districts down to 24 to 26 students). The rationale of reducing class size is usually justified on the basis of enhancing the quality of the educational experience for both the student and the teacher.

Labor Entrance Requirements.   A third goal of craft unions in bargaining is to control the supply of craft workers to fit the supply of available jobs and to regulate the supply of jobs available to members. The regulation of the labor supply can be accomplished through entrance requirements into the local union. The union may perhaps require that admission be obtained only through completion of a union-controlled apprenticeship program. This type of regulation complements the goal of maintaining craft quality in that the union is assured that all members meet some established level of educational attainment relating to the trade. In addition, some unions in the past have controlled access to their apprenticeship program such that only sons, grandsons, or nephews of current members were admitted. Thus, not only are numbers controlled, but those who are admitted may have more of an ideological commitment to the union than others because of their family background. It should be pointed out that such restrictive entrance practices once used in the past are now generally illegal.

The Hiring Hall.   A second facet to the goal of controlling the labor supply and controlling the supply of work includes acting as an active participant in the labor market for members. The mechanism for participation in the labor market is through the union hiring hall. Many craft union locals maintain hiring halls for their members.[19] The union hiring hall is a clearinghouse that acts to match employers seeking workers with union members who are skilled, experienced, and ready to go to work. The benefit to the employer of the hiring hall is that the employer knows that he or she can obtain highly qualified union workers with no more than a phone call to the local union office. The advantage to the union of the hiring hall is that the union can spread out the opportunities for employment among its members and that it can standardize and enforce the payment of union wage rates to its members as well. If the hiring hall is operating at equilibrium, then all those workers who are seeking employment will find it and all those employers who are seeking workers will find them as well. In times of great labor demand the local union leaders may find it necessary to add some people to its hiring roster who have not met the criteria for admission into the union but who are allowed to work temporarily on union jobs by virtue of experience they have gained elsewhere. Such workers are called *permit holders*. Occasionally members from other local unions of the craft may come to a city with a high demand for labor and ask to be placed on the hiring hall roster. Such requests are usually honored. These persons are called *travelers*.

Union Security.   The final goal of union security can be obtained through bargaining by requiring that all workers on a union job site (that is, working for a contractor signatory to a union agreement) be members of the union. Obviously, the union will see to it that these workers who find employment through the hiring hall have their dues paid up. In addition, the union will require that only dues-paying union members be allowed on union construction sites and that union members refuse to work with nonunion workers. If the union can control the acquisition of skill by nonunion members, and can keep nonunion members off unionized projects and force employers to hire only dues-paying union members, the security of the union and its stream of income from dues money is enhanced.

Industrial Unions

Fringe Benefits.   The industrial union also has goals in bargaining that are in some cases different from those of the craft union. For example, the goal of expanding the scope of fringe benefits is very important for industrial unions. For these unions, fringe benefit contributions are not the central focus of negotiations; costs are left to the employer to worry about. For industrial unions it is the level of benefit, the type of benefit, and in some cases the provider of the benefit that is most important to negotiate. Because for the industrial worker the employer pays for and administers the fringe benefits program, the focus is on coming up with new and expanded types of benefits and increasing the coverage of existing benefits. It should be pointed out, however, that in some cases the union may be very concerned with how the employer's pension money is invested, particularly if it is invested in nonunion companies or invested in countries with repressive social systems with which the union leaders disagree (such as South Africa).

Protection of Individual Rights.   Industrial unions are very concerned with protecting individual workers' rights on the job through restriction of the employer's rights to take disciplinary action against employees. Individual worker protection is not quite so important to craft unions, because craft workers know that if they get dismissed from one job through a disagreement with the foreman or for some infraction of the rules, they can obtain another job quickly through the hiring hall. The industrial worker, by contrast, has no such guarantee of finding another job if he or she should be terminated. As a result, elaborate rules are negotiated in industrial union labor agreements establishing due process and just cause requirements for employer actions concerning individual workers. The rights of individuals are protected through the grievance procedure in the agreement (see Chapter 13), a process that is much more elaborate and formalized in industrial union agreements than in those of craft unions.

Job and Income Security.   Industrial unions are very concerned that their members have the right to be protected against layoff and have the right to recall once they have been laid off. As a result seniority is a major bargaining item in industrial worker labor agreements. Seniority provisions commonly require that the least senior members of a work group be the first to be laid off and that the most senior workers who are laid off are the first to be recalled. Through this mechanism workers receive some job security with the acquisition of seniority. In addition, industrial unions may negotiate provisions into agreements that specifically protect union members when they are laid off through monetary supplements to a worker's unemployment benefits called *supplementary unemployment benefits* (SUBs).

Employer Bargaining Goals

Employer bargaining goals are easier to identify and discuss than are union bargaining goals, possibly because we have better information and data on company bargaining goals than on union bargaining goals, and possibly because the constituency of management (the owners of the business or the stockholders) have a less active role to play in negotiations than does the constituency of the labor negotiator. The stockholders and the owners of the firm want to receive the best possible return on their investment. Thus, management will be interested in controlling costs, increasing productivity, protecting profits, minimizing losses from strikes or slowdowns, and remaining competitive with other firms in the industry.[20] The relative importance of these factors may change, however, as business and economic conditions change over time.

Wages

In 1978 and 1983 the Conference Board conducted major studies of the management of labor relations within U.S. industry.[21] The major data source upon which the study was formed was responses to a survey mailed in both years. In 1978, responses were received from 778 companies; 668 of these had some unionization present. In the 1983 study responses were received from 504 companies, of which 302 had at least one union present. Of the 1983 survey respondents, 197 had also responded to the 1978 survey. One of the survey items asked employers to identify the criteria or considerations they used in formulating the company's goals regarding wages. The rank order of the responses from the unionized companies responding to this question in 1978 and 1983 are given in Table 9.4.

The results of the two Conference Board reports show a movement in employer objectives in wage bargaining away from a concern with patterns of settlement within a particular industry or with a particular labor market to more concern with productivity of the individual firm and profits. Employers during the late 1970s and early 1980s seem to be turning away from comparing themselves and their wage rates with other employers in the same industry or same locality and seem much more introspective about productivity, labor cost levels, and profits, as indicated especially by the rankings off the first five items in Table 9.4. In addition, potential losses from a strike dropped from seventh place in 1978 to ninth place in 1983. Apparently the strike is declining in im-

TABLE 9-4 Criteria Used in Formulating Company Wage Objectives

1978 *(N = 659)*	*1983** *(N = 197)*
1. Industry patterns	1. Productivity of labor cost trends in company
2. Local labor market conditions	2. Expected profits
3. Expected profits of company	3. Local labor market conditions
4. Productivity or labor cost trends in company	4. Industry patterns
5. Consumer price index increases	5. Consumer price index increases
6. Influence of this settlement on other settlements	6. Company wage patterns (historical)
7. Potential losses from a strike	7. Influence of this settlement on other settlements
8. Company wage patterns (historical)	8. Company benefit patterns (historical)
9. Company benefit patterns (historical)	9. Potential losses from a strike
10. Union settlements in other industries	10. National labor market conditions
11. National labor market conditions	11. Major union settlements in other industries

*All 197 respondents had also responded to the 1978 survey.

Source: Audrey Freedman, *Managing Labor Relations,* New York: The Conference Board, 1979, p. 37, and *The New Look in Wage Policy and Employee Relations,* New York, The Conference Board, 1985, p. 10.

portance as a threat to management. Losses because of strikes have been declining steadily in the past few years and we are presently at one of the lowest strike rates in U.S. history. Union settlements in other industries were tenth in 1978 and eleventh in 1983. This along with the decline in the importance of local labor market conditions and the decline in importance in industry patterns all suggest a decline in the relative importance in pattern bargaining in general over this time period. This decline in the importance of pattern bargaining had been noted by Freedman and Fulmer earlier,[22] and the 1983 Conference Board survey seems to verify this trend. Apparently the recession of the early 1980s has caused companies to be much more concerned about internal conditions and costs and less concerned about what is going on in the industry and in the local labor market, and much less concerned about what is happening in other industries.

Fringe Benefits

The Conference Board survey also asked employers in 1978 and 1983 to rank their most important nonwage, or fringe benefit, goals in bargaining. The rank order of the number of responses to this question are given and summarized in Tables 9.5 and 9.6 on the basis of whether a company responded that an item was one that it wanted to tighten (reduce), maintain (stay the same), or liberalize (increase).

Overall it appears that insurance of all types has increased in importance as a management goal over the 1978–1983 period. Cost of living and the duration of the agreement have both declined in importance somewhat as management goals over the same period. The increase in the importance of insurance as a bargaining item is undoubtedly re-

TABLE 9-5 Company Fringe Benefit Objectives, 1978

Item	Mention (N = 568)	Tighten	Maintain	Liberalize	Achieve
1. Time off with pay	84%	12%	55%	33%	85%
2. Flexibility in assignment	82	55	42	3	76
3. Pensions	82	11	43	46	88
4. Health insurance	80	11	47	41	87
5. Cost of living	78	13	76	10	86
6. Duration of agreement	75	23	64	11	92
7. Life insurance	75	7	52	40	91
8. Dental insurance	72	5	70	25	91
9. Subcontracting	68	17	80	2	94
10. Layoff and recall	68	33	58	9	87
11. Union security	55	10	86	4	94
12. Income security	50	6	84	10	89

Source: Audrey Freedman, *Managing Labor Relations*, pp. 19–23, © 1979 The Conference Board.

TABLE 9-6   Company Fringe Benefits Objectives, 1983

Item	Mention (N = 197*)	Tighten	Maintain	Liberalize	Achieve
1. Health insurance	81%	57%	33%	10%	79%
2. Time off with pay	76	34	59	7	84
3. Flexibility in assignment	68	69	28	3	80
4. Pensions	67	16	55	28	86
5. Life insurance	61	16	52	31	82
6. Dental insurance	59	20	63	17	84
7. Cost of living	57	51	46	4	85
8. Subcontracting	53	26	74	less than 1	86
9. Duration of agreement	53	30	62	8	90
10. Layoff and recall	50	40	52	8	83
11. Union security	37	14	84	3	81
12. Income security	35	9	80	11	88

*All responses were from firms which had responded to the 1978 survey.

Source: Audrey Freedman, *Managing Labor Relations,* pp. 19–23, © 1979 The Conference Board.

lated to the increase in the cost of insurance (especially health insurance) over this time period. The decline in cost of living as a bargaining goal can be related to the fact that cost of living moderated during the early 1980s.

Not only have management nonwage goals in bargaining changed in recent years, but also employers' orientation toward these goals. The results from the 1978 and 1983 surveys can be roughly summarized as follows:

	1978	1983
Tighten	18%	34%
Maintain	61	55
Liberalize	21	11

The shift in emphasis overall has clearly been toward tightening or reducing benefits and away from liberalizing or giving more benefits. The results of this survey will not come as a surprise to most union negotiators who were negotiating contracts during this time period.

Summary

The bargaining structure concept is important in industrial relations because it determines who will be covered by the labor agreement. The bargaining structure is a complex concept determined by a variety of factors such as the nature of the product market, the labor market, technology, and the general health of the economy. The bargaining structure in the steel industry is different from that in the chemical industry — even though these industries have some things in common (advanced technology, for example). The markets for the products supplied by these industries are sufficiently different to cause a difference in the structure of the bargaining relationship between labor and management. As the factors that determine the nature of the bargaining structure in an industry change, the structure itself changes, too. The change from multiemployer to single employer bargaining in the steel industry in 1985 is a good example.

Both unions and employers with different types of bargaining structures may have different goals. Recent data from the Conference Board suggests that employer goals in bargaining may be changing. The Conference Board data suggest that employers are less concerned about patterns of bargaining in setting wage goals in their industries or in their local areas, and are more concerned today about conditions in their individual worksites and corporations as determining objectives or targets in bargaining. If this is true we may expect to see greater disparity in wage rate settlements in years to come as companies increasingly "go their own way" and disregard external forces in determining wage rates. In the fringe benefit area, employer goals appear to be oriented, increasingly, to tightening up on health insurance costs, to holding the line on time off with pay (vacations and holidays), and to gaining greater flexibility in assignment of employees. As collective bargaining moves through the 1980s and into the 1990s, it will be interesting to see how successful employers are in achieving these goals.

Discussion Questions

1. Compare and contrast the characteristics of the workplace and the structure of the employer for craft and for industrial workers.
2. What do we mean by the term *casual labor market?* How do you think this may affect the worker's loyalty to the employer? How may this affect the worker's loyalty to his or her union?
3. Why is the grievance procedure more important to industrial union members than to craft union members?
4. Why are craft unions so concerned about protecting their jurisdiction?
5. Why is the hiring hall such an important aspect of local union power in the construction industry?
6. How may management bargaining power be enhanced through a decentralization of the bargaining structure? How may it be enhanced through a centralization of the bargaining structure?

Notes

[1]Jack Barbash, *The Elements of Industrial Relations*, Madison: University of Wisconsin Press, 1984, p. 53.

[2]John T. Dunlop, "The Industrial Relations System in Construction." In Arnold Weber, ed., *The Structure of Collective Bargaining*, New York: Free Press, 1961, p. 259.

[3]Barbash, *The Elements of Industrial Relations*, p. 53.

[4]Arnold Weber, "Stability and Change in the Structure of Collective Bargaining." In Lloyd Ulman, ed., *Challenges to Collective Bargaining*, Englewood Cliffs, NJ: Prentice-Hall, 1967, p. 15.

[5]Cushman, "Management Objectives in Collective Bargaining," in Weber, ed., *The Structure of Collective Bargaining*, p. 64.

[6]Weber, "Stability and Change in the Structure of Collective Bargaining," p. 21.

[7]Barbash, *The Elements of Industrial Relations*, p. 96.

[8]Neil Chamberlain, "Determinants of Collective Bargaining Structures" in Weber, ed., *The Structure of Collective Bargaining*, p. 4.

[9]For an expansion of this theme see John R. Commons, "American Shoemakers, 1648–1895: A Sketch of Industrial Evolution," *Quarterly Journal of Economics* 24 November 1910: 39–84. Additional insight on this topic can be gained from reading Lloyd Ulman, *The Rise of the National Trade Union*, Cambridge, MA: Harvard University Press, 1955.

[10]Charles Craypo, *The Economics of Collective Bargaining*, Washington, DC: BNA Books, 1986, p. 100.

[11]George Brooks, "Unions and the Structure of Collective Bargaining," in Weber, ed., *The Structure of Collective Bargaining*, pp. 12–14.

[12]Neil Chamberlain and James Kuhn, *Collective Bargaining*, 3rd ed., New York: McGraw-Hill, 1986, p. 268.

[13]Craypo, *The Economics of Collective Bargaining*, pp. 82–100.

[14]Chamberlain and Kuhn, *Collective Bargaining*, p. 268.

[15]Donald F. Cuff, "Forging a New Shape for Steel," *The New York Times*, May 6, 1985, p. 4F.

[16]A. H. Raskin, "The Steelworkers: Limping at 50?" *The New York Times*, June 15, 1986, pp. 1F, 29F.

[17]"United Steelworkers Balk at Additional Concessions," *Columbus Dispatch*, June 13, 1986, p. 2H.

[18]See Thomas Kochan, *Collective Bargaining and Industrial Relations*, Homewood, IL: Irwin, 1980, for a more detailed discussion of these problems.

[19]Weber, "Stability and Change in the Structure of Collective Bargaining," p. 15.

[20]Thomas Kochan, *Collective Bargaining and Industrial Relations*, p. 231.

[21]Audrey Freedman, *Managing Labor Relations*, New York: The Conference Board, 1979; and Audrey Freedman, *The New Look in Wage Policy and Employee Relations*, New York: The Conference Board, 1985.

[22]Audrey Freedman and William E. Fulmer, "Last Rites for Pattern Bargaining," *Harvard Business Review*, March–April 1982: 30–50; see also Audrey Freedman, "A Fundamental Change in Wage Bargaining," *Challenge*, July–August 1982: 14–17.

U.S. STEEL PLANS NAME CHANGE, RESTRUCTURING

By J. Ernest Beazley,
Staff Reporter of *The Wall Street Journal*

U.S. Steel Corp., in a move that would ease the ultimate disposal of its steel operations, plans to rename itself and to restructure its troubled steel and iron ore assets as a stand-alone unit.

Sources close to the nation's largest steelmaker said the move probably will be announced within a few days.

It is understood that U.S. Steel will retain its 85-year-old name for the marketing of its steel. The new name for the parent concern isn't known though the company for over a year has been promoting the USS logo. U.S. Steel officials wouldn't comment.

The company's steel operations are currently part of its steel and related resources division, which also includes its Great Lakes shipping, coal and limestone mining activities. U.S. Steel recently said that if its steel and iron ore operations had been set up separately, without the parent absorbing large interest and staff costs, the operations would have had pretax losses of $2.37 billion since 1980.

Pressure on Union

U.S. Steel's move would fall amid an impasse in bargaining for a new labor contract with the United Steelworkers union. Union officials and other steel makers see the restructuring as an effort to bring pressure on the union, from which U.S. Steel has sought deep concessions.

The threat of a spinoff is perhaps the biggest weapon in U.S. Steel's arsenal. Reorganizing its troubled steel and iron ore operations into an independently owned company might eventually force the union to consider givebacks of the magnitude granted other troubled producers such as Wheeling-Pittsburgh Steel Corp. Just restructuring the operations as a unit draws more attention to steel's lack of profitability, some analysts have said.

Though U.S. Steel's labor contract doesn't expire until August 1, the steelmaker faces a self-imposed deadline Friday for reaching a settlement with its 21,213 workers. Neither side has reported substantial progress, with one negotiator terming the talks as "not at a total standstill but awfully slow going." Both sides expect to recess talks later this week. The latest snag: A ban on nonunion contractors that has been agreed to by other steelmakers would force U.S. Steel to recall about 2,000 laid-off union workers.

U.S. Steel, taking a tough stance, was the last of the nation's six major steelmakers to open bargaining. But the company has become increasingly vulnerable as customer pressures and concerns over lost market share have multiplied.

Weaker Hand

Four steelmakers already have signed new labor accords while a fifth has secured a three-month extension of the current pact in an effort to assuage customer fears of a walkout. As a result, U.S. Steel's hand has weakened. General Motors Corp., the industry's single biggest customer, has canceled the steelmaker's August deliveries and placed the orders with competitors.

Other big buyers, including Ford Motor Co. and Chrysler Corp., have instructed U.S. Steel to build as much as six weeks of added inventory as a strike hedge. Ford currently has sought a 30-day hedge.

Lost business from jittery customers falls at an especially difficult time for U.S. Steel. The steelmaker reportedly lost 20% to 30% of its share of GM's steel business in bidding for the 1987 model year, and steel markets have turned down since spring.

Chapter 10

The Process
of Bargaining

The material at the beginning of this chapter illustrates a type of tactic that may be used in bargaining. In this case a large multinational producer of steel leaks information to the press during a very critical stage of negotiations, hinting that it will spin off or divest itself of its steel operations sometime in the near future. The purpose of this disclosure is to put pressure on the union to grant additional concessions to the employer during negotiations. The article points out that the steel division of U.S. Steel is losing money — losses that other, more profitable divisions of the company (such as its $5.9 billion Marathon Oil division) have to cover. The divestiture of the steel division of U.S. Steel would cap the trend that has been occurring in this employer's organization over the last few years. Today, steel accounts for only 30 percent of U.S. Steel's sales; in 1979 it accounted for 79 percent. U.S. Steel knows that this press release and the union's knowledge of the change in its corporate configuration will enable the employer to gain some advantage at the bargaining table. The question is how much advantage it will bring and whether this will be enough to enable U.S. Steel to force the Steelworkers Union to grant it concessions sizable enough to return the steel divisions to profitability.

This chapter discusses theories of bargaining, in particular the concept of bargaining power, and includes a description of tactics and persuasion in labor negotiations. Finally, it delineates the stages of bargaining and identifies how the collective bargaining process changes as the parties move from one stage of bargaining to another.

Theories of the collective bargaining process attempt to analyze, to explain, and to predict movements in and outcomes of bargaining based on characteristics of the situation or of the negotiators themselves. Historically there have been two approaches to theorizing about the negotiations process: an economic perspective and a behavioral perspective. More recently a third viewpoint has emerged — an integrated perspective that attempts to draw upon the strengths of both the economic and the behavioral models in order to improve the analytic quality of theories of the collective bargaining process.

Economic Theories: The Zeuthen Model

One of the earliest economic theories of the bargaining process was developed by F. Zeuthen in the 1930s.[1] Although not specifically developed to explain labor–management negotiations, the Zeuthen model has much to offer for analyzing these negotiations and it has been used as a foundation for many subsequent theories.[2] The Zeuthen model begins with two parties facing each other in negotiations with conflicting goals. Party A initially seeks to achieve a wage rate of A_n and party B initially seeks to achieve a wage rate of B_n. In this example, let us label party A the union and party B the employer, and let us assume that the quantity of wages the union is seeking in A_n is higher than the level of wages the company is offering in negotiations B_n, but that the parties are interested in reaching a settlement. The central question is, how can we explain why the parties reached the wage rate they did in negotiations, given the distance separating them when negotiations began?

In Zeuthen's model it is assumed that each party has a certain goal in bargaining — a goal that it will not sacrifice even if that means calling the members out on strike (union) or facing the strike (company). These goals we can label C_a and C_b; these are the goals the parties will be willing to strike over if achieved. For the sake of example, let us assume that the company goal C_b (the absolute maximum that the company can afford to pay its employees) is $8.00 per hour. Let us assume that the union's goal C_a is $7.50 per hour, meaning that the union would go on strike rather than accept any wage offer of less than $7.50. When negotiations begin, the company makes an initial offer of a wage rate of $7.00 per hour. The union begins negotiations with a demand of $9.00 per hour. These initial wage demands and offers are quite far apart and they are quite far from the real goal each party has in bargaining.

The union and the employer both know that if they stay with their original bargaining demands, a strike or a lockout will occur. The union knows that it can receive $7.00 per hour by merely capitulating to the company when bargaining begins. The union knows that if it insists on the $9.00 wage rate that conflicts will be a near certainty — say, 90 percent certain. So the union negotiator begins the calculations in the following way: if I insist on $9.00, I will gain the difference between what I am asking for ($9.00) and what I know I can have right now ($7.00) with a 10 percent chance of assurance. In other words, I'm 90 percent sure that a strike will occur and I will not get what I really want. At the same time, I'm losing the difference between what the company is offering ($7.00) and what I really want ($7.50) with a 90 percent probability. In Zeuthen's model, the union will stick with its initial demand of $9.00 only if the potential gains from this bargaining position times the probability that it will be achieved exceeds the potential loss from this position times the probability that this will be achieved. In Zeuthen's model this can be expressed as follows:

A will not move in bargaining if

$$(A_n - B_n) (1 - p_n) > (B_n - C_a)p_n$$

where

A_n = union's initial demand ($9.00)

B_n = company's initial offer ($7.00)

C_a = union's goal in bargaining ($7.50)

p_n = probability of conflict occurring over this demand (90%)

In this case the union will not stick to its initial demand and it would move in negotiations.

The company also has to make calculations on its side of the table. The company's chief negotiator also has some ideas about the probability of conflict in this case. The company negotiator feels that if he or she insists on a $7.00 wage rate, conflict will be 50 percent probable. How likely will the company be to move in negotiations? In the Zeuthen model the company would not move in negotiations if

$$(B_n - A_n) (1 - q_n) > (A_n - C_b) (q_n)$$

where

B_n = company initial offer ($7.00)

A_n = union initial demand ($9.00)

C_b = company absolute goal ($8.00)

q_n = probability of conflict (50 %)

In this case the company will stick to its initial bargaining position and will not make any concessions. As one can see from the equations, however, if the company negotiators had felt that the probability of conflict associated with sticking to their initial offer was as high as the union's estimation (90 percent), then the company negotiators would have modified their initial wage offer.

In the Zeuthen model this process will continue until the perceived gains from not moving off a bargaining position exceed the gains to be made from capitulating with the other side's offer. As negotiations continue, demands are modified and the perceived probability of a strike also changes. As the union's perceived chance of conflict decreases over a particular issue, its concession rate also decreases. For example, in this bargaining scenario the union would not move in bargaining if it had calculated that the chance of a strike occurring over the $9.00 wage demand was only 50 percent.

The Zeuthen model has been expanded and modified over the years in many different ways, but the essential characteristic of most of the economic theories of the bargaining process involves some calculation of utility by the negotiators. The bargaining process is conceptualized as an exercise in utility maximization, with each party making decisions to move or to stand firm in negotiations depending on an economic calculation of costs and benefits.

Behaviorally Based Theories: Walton and McKersie

Behaviorally based theories of the bargaining process attempt to incorporate a wider range of explanatory variables into models that attempt to analyze the bargaining process. In particular, behavioral theories of bargaining attempt to incorporate factors that measure among other things the attitudes of the negotiators, the personalities of the negotiators, the relationship between the negotiators and their constituents, and the strategy and tactics used by the negotiators in explaining the outcome of bargaining.

One of the first widely accepted behaviorally based theories of the collective bargaining process was authored by Richard Walton and Robert McKersie and was presented in their pioneering work *A Behavioral Theory of Labor Negotiations*.[3] In this work, Walton and McKersie propose that collective bargaining can best be understood not as a single process but rather as an exercise involving four distinct and conceptually different subprocesses labeled (a) distributive bargaining, (b) integrative bargaining, (c) attitudinal restructuring, and (d) intraorganizational bargaining. Each of these aspects of the bargaining process demands different behaviors and tactics on the part of the negotiators, and these subprocesses may have competing goals that need to be recognized and balanced by the negotiators.

Distributive Bargaining

In the Walton and McKersie model, distributive bargaining is that aspect of the bargaining process that involves the distribution of scarce rewards between labor and management. Distributive bargaining is sometimes called *zero sum bargaining* because what one party gains the other party loses. Distributive bargaining is that aspect of the bargaining process that is described by most of the economic theories of the bargaining process, such as Zeuthen's theory described earlier. In the

Walton and McKersie framework the movements during negotiations are motivated by the subjective expected utility (SEU) of each issue in negotiations as evaluated by the chief negotiator for each side. In their model, the SEU of each particular issue in negotiations is determined by the utility or value of a particular item (say, a $1.00 pay raise) that we can label U_I, the probability that the other side will accept the item, which we can label P_A, the probability that the other side will not accept the item $(1 - P_A)$, and the utility of the strike U_S. The Walton and McKersie model may then be expressed as follows:

$$SEU = (U_I \times P_A) + ([1 - P_A] \times U_S)$$

Negotiators will seek to maximize their SEU from negotiations by balancing in negotiations issues and items that have the greatest utility payoff for negotiators. In many respects this aspect of the Walton and McKersie model is similar to the Zeuthen model.

Integrative Bargaining

Going beyond the Zeuthen model, however, Walton and McKersie next introduce the idea that collective bargaining can have the possibility of a variable payoff in addition to a zero sum payoff. The variable payoff means that both sides can benefit from particular items in negotiation, and that one party's gain is not necessarily the other party's loss. This component of the bargaining process Walton and McKersie label integrative bargaining. Integrative bargaining most often involves mutual problem solving about issues of joint concern. Requiring cooperation, information sharing, trust, and commitment to a mutual goal on the parts of both labor and management, it is most often found in mature bargaining relationships or perhaps in cases where the employer is in dire financial peril and needs help from the union to survive. Examples of integrative bargaining may involve labor–management committees to improve such conditions as safety and health at the workplace, joint efforts to reduce cost and waste, and efforts to provide joint employee assistance programs for alcoholism and drug abuse. Integrative bargaining is sometimes called *win-win bargaining*, and there are frequently items discussed in negotiation that are negotiated within the integrative framework rather than the distributive.

Attitudinal Structuring

The attitudinal structuring aspect of negotiations refers to the actions and behaviors of the parties at the table that are designed to change their attitudes toward one another. These attitudes may be categorized as six types, ranging from conflict to containment, aggression to accommodation, cooperation to collusion. The process of attitudinal structuring involves efforts of the negotiators to move the parties' relationship from one type of relational pattern to another.

For example, an employer may want to build a closer relationship with a union than what currently exists. At the moment the employer and the union are at a stage of accommodation in their relationship, meaning that the employer recognizes the union and negotiates with it as the law requires but that the parties are no better than neutral in the overall nature of their relationship. If the employer desires a movement toward a more cooperative and positive relationship with the union, the employer may signal a desire to move the relationship in such a way at the bargaining table. The employer's representative will probably not come out and boldly say "Let's be friends" to the union negotiator (such a move would be regarded as a sure sign of weakness by the union negotiator and would likely be exploited), but the negotiator may subtly change his or her behavior in bargaining to indicate more trust in the union, more friendliness, more appreciation of the union's legitimacy. If the attempts at changing the relationship through these changes in behavior fail (either because the union does not want to change the relationship or because the union negotiator did not correctly interpret the signal the management negotiator was sending), the management negotiator may abandon the effort and revert back to the old type of behavioral interaction. Nevertheless, the point that Walton and McKersie are making is that some of what goes on in bargaining is related not so much to wages and working conditions but to changing the nature of the day-to-day relationship between labor and management, an aspect of negotiations not captured in purely economic models.

Intraorganizational Bargaining

Walton and McKersie's concept of intraorganizational bargaining refers to the negotiations that occur within a particular bargaining team. As negotiations progress, compromises are made and the number of issues on the bargaining agenda are reduced. During this process of compromise and trade-off there is often conflict within a bargaining team as to what items to drop off the list of demands and how to best trade off one issue against another. The members of the bargaining team, particularly on the union side, see themselves as representing the interests of their constituents. For this reason one member of the bargaining team may disagree strongly with a proposal to drop a particular demand. For example, more senior members of the team may push for seniority to play a larger role in determining rights for promotion. Younger workers may push for higher wages. Workers with families may push for increased health insurance and benefits. The competing interest of the work group are expressed by different members on the bargaining team. Before consensus can be reached to drop or modify a particular issue, negotiations must go on among team members. The same type of intraorganizational bargaining may go on among members of the management negotiating team as well.

The Walton and McKersie model has been widely accepted and attempts have been made to test the model empirically and to unify the four subprocesses into one integrated model of the bargaining process. Results to date seem to indicate that collective bargaining is a multidimensional process involving more than merely the calculation of economic utility from a particular wage rate.[5] The empirical results almost always stress the importance of the behavioral aspects of bargaining in determining bargaining outcomes, although it is fair to say that we do not yet have a general theory of collective bargaining that integrates all the economic and behavioral components of negotiations. Perhaps we never will.

An Integrative Theory: Chamberlain's Bargaining Power Theory

In a bargaining power model the ability to move the other party in negotiations is related to bargaining power possessed to a greater or lesser degree by each party in the bargaining interaction. One of the best formulations of the bargaining power concept was given by Neil Chamberlain,[6] was restated in Chamberlain and Kuhn's work *Collective Bargaining* in 1965, and was published again in 1986. In the bargaining power model the participants to the negotiations process are motivated to make concessions in bargaining based on their perceptions and calculations of costs of agreement and disagreement. For Chamberlain, the union's bargaining power (U_{BP}) can be expressed as follows:

$$U_{BP} = \frac{MC_D}{MC_A}$$

where

MC_D = management's cost of disagreeing with the union

MC_A = management's cost of agreeing with the union

The bargaining power of management (M_{BP}) can also be expressed as:

$$M_{BP} = \frac{UC_D}{UC_A}$$

where

UC_D = union's cost of disagreeing with management

UC_A = union's cost of agreeing with management

Chamberlain's model theorizes that both management and the union make some calculations about the economic and political costs and consequences of agreeing with the other party and settling the dispute, or sticking to their own positions and prolonging the dispute by continuing to disagree with the adversary's position.

The Consequences of Disagreement

In coming to a decision about whether to agree or disagree with the other party in negotiations, each negotiator must identify what the likely consequences of agreeing or disagreeing with the other party will be.[7]

Management.   In evaluating a union's eleventh-hour final proposal, the management negotiator might consider a number of factors in deciding whether to agree with the union's final proposal (accepting the contract on the union's terms and avoiding conflict) or to disagree with the union's final proposal and therefore guarantee the increased probability of conflict with the union. Some of the consequences of disagreement are psychological. The management negotiator may disagree with the union, for example, to show the union negotiators that management is really tough and that it cannot be backed down in negotiations. Thus, management may be attempting to show its strength in negotiations by sticking to its own position and not accepting the union proposals on a particular issue. This reputation of toughness may be an asset to management in future negotiations. There may also be a personal benefit to the individual negotiator who holds firm to his or her position and who acquires a reputation as a "tough battler." Some consultants and attorneys have spent years building reputations as tough negotiators who never back down under pressure. In some cases this bargaining behavior is very appropriate to certain situations, and these negotiators are in great demand.

There are, of course, economic advantages to the employer by holding firm and not acceding to union demands in bargaining. The employer may save himself or herself some money by standing firm on wages and benefits and not giving in to the union's demands. If the employer has a target wage rate and cannot afford to go above that target, the negotiator may be protecting the employer's competitive standing in the market by refusing to accede to union demands.

There are also negative consequences to the employer of disagreeing with the union, as well. If the disagreement causes a strike there will likely be disruption at the workplace. The volume of production and quality of service are likely to decrease. There may be a disruption in the employer's ability to provide the product or service to customers; this could result in a decrease in market share and decline in the number of customers as customers shift to alternative sources for the product or service. Sometimes disputes with the union may cause violence or property damage. It is possible that a dispute with the union may have a negative effect on worker attitudes and morale. The dispute or disagreement may create an additional type of tension at the workplace and may damage day-to-day working relationships between supervisors and employees; this is so particularly if the supervisors continue to work and operate the facility once a strike has been called.

The Union. There are positive and negative consequences to the union also in disagreeing with management. For the union leader, several positive and negative outcomes from disagreement need to be balanced in making a decision either to accept the employer's final offer or to reject it. In coming to his or her decision, the union representative must consider a number of issues. On the one hand, the union leader knows that there are some political benefits to standing firm and to disagreeing with the employer. The union leader is an elected official. He or she must stand for reelection periodically (once every three years for local officials and once every five years for national officers) and knows that there is no greater political liability than to be regarded as weak or a person who "sells out" the membership to management.[8] The need to maintain an image of toughness to protect their political standing may be especially strong for those facing some political opposition in their organizations. Many members want a strong union leader, one who is not afraid to stand up to management.[9] Disagreeing with the employer in negotiations and not backing down even in the face of conflict is a way of acquiring such a reputation.

In addition to political advantages there may be economic advantages to disagreeing with the employer. The union may demonstrate to the employer its strength and solidarity and may be able to scare the employer into granting concessions because of the union's apparent militancy. The union may be able to force the employer to pay higher wages through a show of strength in negotiations.

There are, of course, negative consequences to disagreement. The disagreement may force the union into striking to prove its militancy. The strike will cause some loss of income to the members. It will also mean a loss in dues money to the union and perhaps some outlay of strike fund monies to striking workers, as well. The strike may result in the replacement of some workers by management. It may motivate the employer to transfer some work to other facilities, resulting in loss of employment to union members. It may result also in a loss of customers to the employer and in a loss of work for union members — a loss that may be long term. The strike may imperil the financial health of a weak employer to the point of bankruptcy. Finally, the dispute may give the union a negative public image as being selfish, greedy, and unconcerned with the needs of the public.*

*The strike of municipal workers in Philadelphia during the July 4, 1986 weekend caused the cancellation of many events during the three day weekend. It is fair to say that the strike did not enhance the public's image of the union when swimming pools were closed and activities canceled because of the strike.

The Consequences of Agreement

Management.   The employer may decide to agree with the union's position in negotiations and to settle on the union's terms to avoid conflict. There are both positive and negative consequences from such a decision. On the positive side, of course, the dispute is settled, conflict is averted, and peace and harmony return to the relationship. The employer is assured for some fixed term (the length of the contract) that conflict is reduced and that stability will return to labor–management relations.

On the negative side, the employer may acquire a reputation as an "easy touch" in negotiations and may be setting the stage for extreme union demands and behaviors in future negotiations. The employer may find that the price of peace is dear and may face a loss of competitive standing in years ahead by negotiating a contract too favorable to the union. The employer may find that groups of workers in the organization currently not unionized (e.g., clerical or sales workers) may threaten unionization or actually seek union representation once the power of the union is demonstrated in winning gains for a group of employees in the organization.

The Union.   Agreeing to management's terms, even if these terms are less than what the union really wants, has some positive and some negative consequences for the union as well as for the employer. On the positive side, the threat of the strike may be averted, although this cannot really be guaranteed because most unions require that any agreement be ratified by the membership (voted on by the membership) before it takes effect. It is possible — and it does happen — that a tentative agreement negotiated at the bargaining table is subsequently turned down by the membership when a ratification vote is taken.

On the negative side, of course, the union leader realizes that he or she may be perceived by management as weak in future dealings and may be manipulated by management in future interactions. The membership may see the union leader as cowardly in the face of adversity. Agreeing to a wage level or benefit level less than what the union really wants may create pressures from other employers. This is especially true when concessions are given. Employers may pressure the union for concessions given to other, weaker employers even when the financial health of their own organizations is quite different. Finally, agreeing to management's terms even when they are really below the union's target settlement may create tensions among the work group to decertify that union and to select a rival organization as the bargaining agent.

Costs of Agreement and of Disagreement

In the Chamberlain model, to the extent that $MC_D/MC_A \geq 1$, then the union possesses leverage or bargaining power over the employer and the employer will probably move toward accommodation with the union's demands. If $UC_D/UC_A \geq 1$, then the union will probably make concessions and move toward the position of the employer. According to the Chamberlain model, the way that the union can increase its bargaining power is to increase MC_D and to decrease MC_A. The employer likewise will engage in tactics designed to increase the union's perception of UC_D and to decrease the union's perceptions of UC_A. Carl Stevens in his classic work *Strategy and Collective Bargaining Negotiations* refers to these tactics in an approach avoidance framework and labels attempts to increase the costs of disagreement as class I tactics in bargaining, and attempts to decrease the cost of agreement as class II tactics in negotiations. Class I tactics are designed to prevent the opposing party from insisting on his or her own position. Class II tactics are designed to encourage the opponent to agree on the negotiator's terms.[10]

Union Tactics Designed to Raise the Costs of Disagreement to Management. *The Strike.* When they think about the costs of disagreement, most people immediately think about the costs associated with a strike. For most employers who negotiate with unions in the private sector, the concern about costs associated with strikes is valid. When there is a strike the output from a production facility is usually diminished. Sometimes the facility may be shut down entirely because of the strike (such as happened during the 1981 Baseball strike). Sometimes the facility may be operated at reduced levels by a crew of supervisors or replacements for the strikers (such as happened in the 1981 Air Traffic Controllers strike). Some production facilities are automated to such a degree and the level of service provided by supervisors is so complete that the public may not even be aware that a strike is in progress (such was largely the case during the 1986 AT&T telephone strike conducted by the Communications Workers of America). The strike is costly to management because production is reduced and to a degree revenue or income is also reduced. The employer still has to meet certain fixed costs during the strike (interest, wages of some managerial and clerical employees who work during the strike, some utility costs), but revenue and production are decreased. As Chapter 12 will demonstrate, strikes destabilize the relationship between the employer and his or her customers and may be disruptive to peaceful and cooperative relations with the union in future years as well. Strikes are sometimes accompanied by violence and property damage, especially when the employer continues to operate the facility with strikebreakers.[11]

The Picket Line. A picket line usually goes along with the strike. When they picket, union members march around the points of access to the worksite with signs advising the public that a labor dispute is in existence. Picketing usually has the effect of discouraging people from entering the employer's place of business. The goal of picketing is to enforce the power of the strike by discouraging strikebreakers from going to work, discouraging customers from buying from the employer, and by discouraging those with items to deliver or to pick up from entering the worksite.

The Boycott.   The union may boycott the employer's product or service during the strike and may urge all its members and sympathizers nationwide to do the same. The boycott may be an effective tool against the employer because it disrupts revenue from sales of the product that is already on the dealer's shelves; because it threatens the employer with a decrease in market share and sales in the future because of product switching once customers have tried a competitor's product and become used to it; and because some products require continuous purchase of replacement parts from the employer after the original sale is made (e.g., we continue to purchase Ford or GM replacement parts from the manufacturer during the entire period we own a Ford or GM automobile).

The Corporate Campaign.   The corporate campaign is most often associated with a union consultant by the name of Ray Rodgers,[12] who successfully used this tactic against J. P. Stevens Co. in 1978. The corporate campaign is a modern, sophisticated version of the secondary boycott. It involves pressuring high level executives in a neutral company with threats of withdrawing union funds (from financial institutions) or of boycotting the producer's product unless the neutral organization pressures the target company into acceding to the union's demands. In the case of J. P. Stevens, the Clothing Workers Union threatened to withdraw union pension funds from Manufacturers Hanover Bank in New York, a major financier to J. P. Stevens. J. P. Stevens soon reached a peaceful agreement with the union largely as a result of this pressure. The corporate campaign has been used less successfully since the J. P. Stevens incident, but it is looked upon as a possible union negotiating tool in some instances.

Union Tactics Designed to Decrease the Costs of Agreement to Management. *Productivity Bargaining.*   The union in its negotiations must also reduce management's perceived costs of agreeing to the union's terms, Stevens's class II tactic in negotiations. The union can do this in a variety of ways; perhaps the most often used tactic is to promise to management that if the agreement is signed, the union members will increase productivity. This means that employers will receive more output per employee and more output per dollar of labor cost expended as well. Some unions have engaged in specific negotiations called productivity bargaining. In these negotiations the union agrees to trade certain restrictive work rules (such as limitations on technology or controls on certain types of worker doing certain types of work) in exchange for increases in wages.[13] This can be a very effective tactic in negotiations and of great value to the employer in reducing labor costs. Related to this, the union may offer to reduce the number of job classifications in the organization to allow the employer more flexibility in transferring workers from one job to another depending on where workers are needed most.

Backloading.   In some cases the union can help the employer reduce labor costs by backloading the wage increases provided for in the contract. Backloading involves putting off the payment of wage increases until some time later in the contract period rather than immediately. For example, if the union had negotiated a 15 percent pay raise over the life of a three year contract, the impact on labor costs to the employer can be quite different depending on when the wage raises go into effect. For example, an employer currently has a payroll of $100,000. What would be the difference in total labor costs over the three years if (a) the 15 percent wage raise was instituted immediately and remained in effect the entire three years; (b) the wage raise was divided into 5 percent the first year, an additional 5 percent the second year, and an additional 5 percent the third year; or (c) if the wage raise was 0 percent the first year, 5 percent the second year, and 10 percent the third year? In the first case the employer would pay $115,000 the first year of the contract, $115,000 the second year and $115,000 the third year for a total labor cost of $345,000. In the second case the employer would pay $105,000 the first year, $110,250 the second year ($105,000 + 5 percent) and $115,726.50 the third year ($110,250 + 5 percent) for a labor cost of $330,976.50 over the three years. In the final example, the employer would pay $100,000 the first year, $105,000 the second year and $110,500 the third year for a total labor cost of $315,500. Obviously, it is to the advantage of the employer to defer labor costs into the future. In each instance the union may claim to have won a 15 percent wage raise for its members over the life of the contract, but the timing of these raises may have drastic effects on labor costs for the employer.

Contract Length.   Negotiations are expensive and time consuming, and they interfere with the normal course of business operations. Employers generally prefer to negotiate long-term contracts to reduce the costs and disruptions associated with the negotiation process. The union can offer to lengthen the contract term to decrease the employer's cost of agreement. The union may offer to go from a two year to a three year contract, for example. A long-term contract with backloaded wage raises can produce considerable labor and negotiating cost savings to the employer as compared to a shorter term contract with frontloaded or equally spaced wage raises.

Withdrawal of Grievances.   In some cases the union may offer to withdraw grievances that have accumulated at various stages in the grievance procedure in exchange for management concessions (the grievance procedure is discussed in detail in Chapter 13). Some unions engage in the practice of filing many grievances shortly before contract expiration. Some of these grievances may have merit, and some may not. In any event, written grievances submitted to management require answers. Under the agreement, management is required to investigate the facts of each grievance and to respond to the union, a time-consuming and thus expensive procedure for management. The union may offer in negotiations to withdraw grievances and to save the employer time and money. This reduces costs for the employer and thus reduces the costs of agreement with the union. The union will likely expect something in return for this favor, however.

Product Promotion. In some instances the union may gain visibility by offering to help the employer promote his or her product in some way or other in return for favorable terms in the contract. The United Automobile Workers are prominently displayed in television ads for Ford declaring that "quality is Job One" at Ford. Some unions will allow employers to place the union label on products such as clothing. The union then promotes union-made products through national advertising such as the International Ladies' Garment Workers Union's "look for the union label" television and magazine advertising campaign.

Management Tactics Designed to Raise the Union's Perceived Costs of Disagreement. Just as the union can use what Stevens calls class I tactics to increase the employer's perceived costs of disagreement and thus increase its own bargaining power, the employer can engage in a strategy to increase the union's perceived costs of disagreement and increase its own bargaining power.

Stockpiling the Product. One way the employer can do this is to impress upon the union the high costs associated with the strike. The employer may make preparations to stockpile the product in warehouses away from the worksite so the product can be shipped to customers (and thus guarantee a stream of revenue) even if a strike is called. This will protect the employer from loss during the strike and will likely lengthen the strike and increase the losses in income to the strikers, thus increasing the union's cost of disagreement.

Automation. The employer may hint to the union in negotiations that it may be forced to automate some operations, or even to relocate the production facility, if labor costs are raised too high as a result of negotiations. If the union goes on strike and imposes big losses on the company, the employer may be forced to liquidate a particular part of the company or to divest itself of a particular operation. The announcement by U.S. Steel (now officially USX Corporation) that it may divest itself of its steelmaking operations entirely unless they can be operated profitably is a not-so-subtle hint to the Steelworkers Union that the costs of disagreeing with this employer at this particular time may be very high indeed. How likely would you be to call a strike against a firm that may be forced out of business as a result of the losses it may incur as a result of a strike?

Continuing Operations.   If the employer can successfully operate the production facility with supervisors and replacement workers while the strike is in effect, the employer may lose all incentive to negotiate with the union. The employer may thus impose the ultimate cost on the union for disagreement: to replace all the strikers with nonunion workers and to continue operation as a nonunion employer. The union in this case loses everything — the members lose their jobs and their incomes, the union loses all its members at the worksite and may even lose the right to negotiate with this employer if the replacement workers decertify the union. This is essentially the situation the flight attendants at TWA faced in their strike of 1986. All the strikers were replaced with newly hired flight attendants shortly after the strike was called. After a few months there were no jobs to return to, even if the flight attendants had voted to end the strike and accept management's final offer.

Management Tactics Designed to Decrease the Union's Costs of Agreement.   In much the same way that the union tries to decrease the employer's perceived cost of agreeing with the union in order to increase its bargaining power, the employer seeks to lower the union's perceived cost of agreeing with the employer to increase its bargaining power. The employer will try to "sweeten" or enrich the offer so there are benefits for the union in agreeing with management that might not be readily apparent.

Profit Sharing.   The union leaders may hesitate to agree to a contract that does not contain substantial wage increases, for example. The union leader knows that if his or her members do not receive the wage increases they want or expect in negotiations, there may be negative consequences for the leader's political future in the union. The employer may offer profit sharing or stock ownership plans as a way of providing more income to employees in the future if profits increase. One advantage of this course of action from the employer's perspective is that profit sharing does not become part of the fixed costs of employing labor (as are hourly wages or benefits), and it is paid only if there are actually profits to distribute. Additionally, profit sharing and employee stock ownership plans may have some motivational impact on the employees, thus resulting in productivity gains as well.*

The Bonus.   A second way the employer can decrease the union's cost of agreement is through providing bonuses to the employees. A bonus is a way of giving employees an increase in income without adding to the wage rate. A bonus can be paid in years that the employer is making profits and withheld in years when the employer is losing money. Agreements that contain provisions for a one-time or periodic bonus that does not become part of the hourly wage are increasingly common. The employees are better off financially when the bonus is paid, yet the employer is spared the problem of increasing hourly wages that may have to be pared back at some later time to maintain competitive standing. Bonuses give employers the flexibility to provide rewards to employees when they are best able to finance them. Changes in the hourly wage rate create a continuing wage liability that has to be paid. The only way to control costs in such a fixed wage system is either to negotiate concessions in the wage rate or to lay off employees.

The Two-Tier Wage System.   In a two-tier wage system those who are presently employed are shielded from excessive wage cuts or concessions; however, those who are newly hired will receive substantially less in starting wages than those currently employed in the same job. The two-tier system reduces the cost of agreement because current union members are not affected and thus should not be displeased that this concession was negotiated. New employees or those yet to be hired are the ones who will absorb the wage cuts, not those currently employed. The union leader does not have to worry about the political wrath of current members — in fact, these members may be happy that they do not have to absorb the costs of the wage cut or take a layoff. The newly hired employees probably constitute a small minority of the bargaining constituency.

The Cost of Living Allowance.   A cost of living allowance (COLA) triggers an automatic wage raise as the cost of living increases. It is paid only when inflation actually has risen, and often a cap or limit is placed on how much the COLA can increase in any one year. The advantage of the COLA to the worker is that wages are protected against the eroding influence of inflation. Employees perceive COLAs as an advantage and may be willing to take less in actual wage increases now if they know

*Profit sharing is one of the key components to the new General Motors/United Autoworkers Saturn agreement. Under this agreement workers at the Saturn plant are to receive only 80 percent of what other GM workers receive in wages. The rest of their earnings will be made up of profit sharing and productivity bonuses that may give them higher or lower earnings than other automobile workers depending on the profitability of the new facility.

that their purchasing power is protected against inflation in the future. Of course, COLAs are not so important in time of low inflation, and their frequency has declined with the low inflation rates of the mid-1980s.

Behavioral Strategy and Tactics

There is some danger in discussing the bargaining power model that we overemphasize the role that economic power, strikes, and boycotts have on the outcome of negotiations. Persuasion and communication are also vital aspects of the negotiation process as well.[14] The labor negotiator and the management negotiator are continually using factual data, logic, emotion, and sometimes deception to change the opponent's mind and his or her position in bargaining. Through persuasion, the negotiator seeks to manipulate the opponent's perceptions about costs and benefits of conflict and costs and benefits of agreement. In addition, through the behavioral process, the negotiator seeks to manipulate the opponent's perceptions of the negotiator's costs and benefits of agreement and disagreement.[15]

The communication process involves three elements: the message (what is said), the sender, and the receiver. Persuasion involves manipulating one or more elements of the communication process to bring about perceptual change in the other party. The message that is being conveyed should stress the importance of an issue to the other party and the attractiveness of the negotiator's proposal to the opponent. Related to this is the fact that once agreement is made on an issue — even a small one — agreement becomes easier on a second issue. It is much easier to persuade with positive momentum than it is through fears and threats. "Keep the ball rolling" is a common expression that negotiators use to describe this force of positive momentum. Often this momentum will begin with getting the other party to agree to a "point in principle," or "just for the sake of agreement" or "hypothetically speaking." Tailoring the message to maximize the attractiveness of the issue to the other party and building the positive momentum are ways to move negotiations in a particular direction.

The sender of the message is an important part of the persuasion process. People are best persuaded when they feel that they are not being persuaded but rather that they reached a conclusion through their own logical processes. The sender of the message must not appear to be involved in persuasion or "pulling the wool over someone's eyes." The ability to communicate natural enthusiasm, sincerity, and spontaneity are a big plus for the negotiator.[16] In addition, it is important that the negotiator be perceived by the opponent as trustworthy and credible for persuasion to be most effective. The need for credibility and expertise is one reason why so much emphasis is put on experience in choosing a negotiator.[17] Negotiators for both management and the union know that an inexperienced negotiator will not be perceived as credible by the other side and that the inexperienced negotiator will be at a disadvantage in an attempt to persuade the opponent on virtually any issue.

A third way to facilitate movement in negotiations through persuasion is through breaking down the barriers or defenses that the opponent has erected around himself or herself that may prevent communication and thus persuasion from taking place. As Lewicki and Litterer point out, the objective in communications as it relates to the opponent is to diffuse defensiveness and combativeness and to make the other party feel that he or she has been heard and understood. In other words, the negotiator receiving the message should be a good listener. The good listener maintains natural eye contact with the sender of the message, maintains an attentive body position, faces the sender directly, and participates in the communication process by taking notes of major points and by gesturing and nodding to indicate understanding during the conversation. The good listener will paraphrase the conversation occasionally to let the sender know that he or she understood and remembered what was being said. In addition, the persuasive listener asks questions about any points that are confusing and looks for things (however small) to agree with in the opponent's presentation. The good listener must, of course, realize that he or she is representing a position that is contrary to that of the sender and must be careful to resist the appearance of agreeing to the opponent's position when agreement has not been reached yet. Lewicki and Litterer call this "innoculating oneself against the other's arguments."[18]

Gambits.   There is a continuing interest in gambits or tricks that negotiators play to persuade the opponent in negotiations. The skilled negotiator has seen all the tricks and uses them or defends himself or herself against them as the occasion demands. The list below is borrowed mostly from Kennedy, Benson, and McMillan, but these negotiating tactics are well known to most negotiators.[19]

Off Limits.   The off limits tactic is a way of signaling to the opponent that a particular item is nonnegotiable. It establishes the outside of the bargaining range and indicates to the opponent that it would be a waste of time to explore this issue further. Responses to off limits issues are usually accompanied by emphatic language: "The demand for the four-day week is totally unacceptable to us. We do not have it at any of our other facilities and we do not want it here. Our operation demands staffing five days a week — we will never accept a four-day week, not today, not tomorrow, not next week, not ever."

Tough Guy–Nice Guy.   In some police precincts this tactic has been elevated to an art in dealing with criminals and making plea bargains. In labor negotiations it often involves an interplay between a local union official who may be playing the role of the militant, hot-headed "tough guy" and the representative of the international union who may play the nice guy role. The interplay between the two roles is critical. The tough guy must be careful not to intimidate or provoke the opponent into a hostile response; the nice guy must not appear to contradict or overrule the tough guy as this may compromise the original position unnecessarily. An example may be:

> Tough guy: All right, get this and get this straight. The four-day week is our number one bargaining priority. If we don't reach agreement on this issue we'll see you on the picket line. Our members will go to any lengths to achieve this change. I can't be responsible for what they might do if you throw this proposal back in their faces. All I do know is that you'll be sorry for the actions you've taken here for years to come. Come on, Charlie, let's clear out of here — these negotiations are over.

> Nice guy: In a minute, Tom. What we're trying to say here is that the four-day week is an important demand to many of our members. A demand they feel strongly attached to. How about this, what if we implement the four-day week in one department, on a trial basis for six months and then assess its effectiveness? We could agree to certain criteria in an amendment to the contract that could be used to evaluate the change. If it's effective it could be continued and expanded into other departments. If not, it could be discontinued.

The tough guy makes a "high demand," an extreme position. The nice guy makes a reasonable demand and one that seems very palatable compared to the tough guy position. The first alternative, a company-wide four-day week, is totally unacceptable — off limits to the company negotiator. However, a limited experiment in one department seems pretty reasonable, even attractive by contrast.

The Salami Tactic. Salami does not taste good in big chunks; it tastes best in thin slices eaten one at a time. The salami tactic in negotiations is a gradualist tactic. The nice guy in the above exchange was using the salami tactic in the four-day work week discussion: begin small and keep moving in small steps, and eventually the salami will be consumed. Start with a limited goal, next move to implementation in one part of one department, then move to implementation in the whole department, then implementation for a whole shift.

The Blockbuster Tactic. This tactic is sometimes also called the "logic of the big demand." The blockbuster tactic involves demanding something that is unheard of and even outrageous in the hopes of getting something else that is really wanted. This has also been labeled by some as "the Russian front tactic" (anything but the Russian front!). The blockbuster might be something like a "guaranteed annual wage" where the union demands that everyone is guaranteed a certain level of earnings during the life of the contract — whether there is work to do or not. The employer is stunned that the union would ask for such a thing and begins to explore ways to counter such an extreme demand. Proposals for changes in the layoff system may be a way of countering such a demand, perhaps spreading layoffs around equally so that the burden of layoff is not disproportionately felt by the less senior employees only. By opening with an outrageous demand, the union has motivated the company to begin thinking about this issue and to come up with a solution to the problem that is better than the union had hoped for. When it works, the blockbuster motivates an initial position on the opponent's part that is much more favorable and a much better place to begin negotiations on an issue than originally expected. There is a danger in overplaying the blockbuster, and skilled negotiators know that it can be used only infrequently.

Who's Your Friend.   This tactic attempts to build on past positive associations and the tradition of cooperation that has prevailed between the parties (if any). It also has an element to it of looking out for the other side. For example:

> Company negotiator: There's been a steel mill owned by XZ Corporation in this town for over 50 years. Your fathers worked here, your grandfathers worked here, you grew up going to company picnics and your Christmas presents were purchased with the Christmas bonuses provided your families by this company. There is no guarantee that this mill will be here for your children to work in — or your grandchildren. This company is facing a crisis — we need wage concessions of major magnitude to keep this mill operating. We've helped you in the past when times were good — now you've got to help us through the bad times by agreeing to wage concessions and a quick settlement without a strike.

The Mandate Demand.   Union leaders are to a large extent politicians. They are elected to lead their constituencies and to represent them. Often new leaders are elected to their positions because of a promise they have made to the members — "no more concessions," "30 and out," "restore and more in '84," and so forth. If elected because of a stand on a particular issue, the leader may feel that this is a mandated demand — a demand that cannot be surrendered. The leader is publicly bound to a mandated demand; no agreement is possible without some element of the mandated demand being included in the contract. There are ways of compromising on the mandated demand, such as achieving the demand in principle if not in fact. The demand can be traded off for something perhaps more tangible that the members would be just as happy with. But in any event, the mandated demand is a way the union or the company can demonstrate to the other party the importance of a particular issue.

Pointers for Negotiators

Charles Loughran, an experienced management negotiator, has developed a series of tips for management negotiators in labor negotiations.[20] These tips apply equally well to labor or management negotiators and illustrate many of the points brought out earlier in the Behavioral Strategy and Tactics section of this chapter.

In presenting offers and proposals, Loughran suggests:

> Offers and counteroffers should be written — not verbal. Written offers carry a tone of seriousness that verbal offers do not.

> When offers are being made they should be read aloud — not merely distributed.

> Explain your position and how you arrived at it on key issues. Use logic and data to bolster your position.

> Accentuate the positive, but avoid the hard sell. The features of a proposal that are attractive to the opposite party should be pointed out.

> Have confidence that your offer will be accepted. If you believe in the rationality of your position on an issue, defend it with confidence; expect acceptance, not rejection.

> Invite questions. This shows confidence and pride in your position and allows the other party to discuss your proposal openly.

In general Loughran finds that successful negotiators have the following characteristics.

> They are well prepared. They have reviewed all their preparatory material in advance and they know where they want the negotiations to go.

> They know the territory. They know the industry and the employer's place in it — they know the economic environment and how it is changing.

> They have patience. They realize that labor negotiations can sometimes drag on for months and that bargaining is sometimes filled with discussions of minute detail.

> They inspire confidence. They convey to other team members that their position is right and they inspire their opponents to believe an agreement will be reached.

> They do not burn the candle at both ends. They pay careful attention to getting the proper amount of rest and to moderation in eating and drinking before and after negotiations. To be an effective bargainer, you must be on your toes constantly.

> They are congenial. They are friendly and even-tempered with colleagues and opponents.

They are organized. They have a system for organizing all the bargaining issues, and they maintain files of backup data for those demands that need such data.

They talk straight. They use plain and straightforward language.

They are positive. They are oriented to positive statements and expressions — they are more likely to see the glass as "half full" rather than "half empty."

They know their own limits. Effective negotiators know when to call on expert advice or assistance. They avoid "shooting from the hip."

They have integrity. An effective negotiator keeps his or her word once a deal has been made.

They avoid unnecessary confrontations. Effective negotiators accept conflict as part of the business but they do not provoke confrontations unnecessarily.

They are magnanimous. They are good winners when the other party is forced into making a concession. They do not "rub it in" when the opponent backs down.

They deal with pressure. Pressure is part of labor negotiations — particularly in the final stages. The negotiator should try to be calm under pressure and use pressure constructively.

They keep their eye on the ball. An effective negotiator keeps track of the essential issues and does not allow himself or herself to be sidetracked or distracted by peripheral issues.

They are flexible. It is important to have a game plan or overall strategy, but it is just as important to realize that there may be several alternative ways to meet that overall plan.

They are tenacious. The effective negotiator is not discouraged by minor road blocks or impedances to progress.

They take prudent risks. The effective negotiator knows that bargaining involves risks and takes these risks when the situation demands it.

They are educators. Effective negotiators educate their constituencies of the realities of life. They let those they represent know the costs and benefits of alternative paths of action.

The Bargaining Process

Many authors have commented that bargaining seems to progress through steps or stages during the course of negotiations, with different types of behaviors and activities being exhibited by both labor and management at each step or stage.[21] The number of stages or steps is open to some debate; Stevens talks about "earlier" and "later" stages of negotiations without ever enumerating a number of stages or steps.

Douglas has a three-stage theory of the negotiations process. Morse talks of a three-stage negotiations process.[22] Kennedy, Benson and McMillan describe negotiations as involving an eight-step process.[23] This chapter develops a four-step description of the bargaining process. The four steps are labeled (1) the preparation stage, (2) the public relations stage, (3) the hard bargaining stage, and (4) the settle-or-strike stage.

The Preparation Stage

Preparations for bargaining begin long before the parties come to the bargaining table and long before the contract expires. It is difficult to say exactly when preparations for negotiations begin, but many people in the field would say that six months in advance of contract expiration is about when serious preparations begin. The activities of labor and management are quite different during the preparation stage.

Management Preparations.   On the management side the key to preparing for bargaining is the assembly of data — hard economic data about labor costs, settlements among competitors, costs of benefits, costs of possible wage increases. In its study of labor relations, the Conference Board received the following outline of management preparations for bargaining in a manufacturing firm.[24]

1. Review of current contract
2. Collection of backup data
3. Identifying anticipated union demands
4. Selecting the company negotiating team
5. Developing company negotiating objectives
6. Preparing a bargaining manual for company negotiators
7. Developing a strike plan
8. Developing a customer contingency plan in the event of a strike
9. Developing a negotiations communications program
10. Formulating corporate strategy
11. Sending formal notification of contract termination to the union
12. Determining physical arrangements for the negotiations meetings

In large companies the preparation of all the data and the coordination of the preparations will likely be handled by the staff of the labor relations department. In smaller companies the preparations may be handled by the personnel department, or perhaps by a private consultant or attorney who is brought in specifically to handle the negotiations.

Union Preparations.   On the union side, preparations will also begin for negotiations well in advance of the first meeting between the parties. Because the union is usually the "moving party" in the process (meaning that the union is usually the party with the most changes to propose in the current agreement), the union will begin early to identify its proposals for the upcoming negotiations. Some large unions preparing for national negotiations begin by calling a bargaining convention at which the delegates identify and vote on crucial items to be addressed in negotiations. In smaller unions, or for negotiations to be conducted at the local level, the union may survey its members with a questionnaire to identify the members' goals in negotiations. The union will undoubtedly review past grievances filed during the past agreement period to identify problem areas in the contract, or areas where the language of the contract is unclear. At this stage in negotiations, the members of the union will likely be given the chance to vote on a bargaining committee and to choose the people who will represent them in bargaining.

The union will also, if possible, review data concerning the employer's finances during the preparation stage of negotiations. This is becoming increasingly common, as the report in Box 10.1 indicates. Although the employer's ability to pay may not be the most important determinant of the outcome of bargaining, the wise union official will at least take a look and consider changes in the employer's financial situation since the parties have last negotiated. At the close of the preparation stage of bargaining, both sides know who their negotiators will be, and both sides have some idea of what their goals and objectives will be in the upcoming negotiations.

The Public Relations Stage

The public relations stage of bargaining begins about 60 days before the contract expires in national negotiations and perhaps 30 days before the contract expires in local negotiations. Under section 8d of the National Labor Relations Act (NLRA) (as amended) the parties are required to give each other 60 days' notice prior to contract expiration if they intend to use the strike or the lockout once the contract does expire. Also under section 8d of the NLRA, the parties are required to give the Federal Mediation and Conciliation Service (FMCS) 30 days' notice before contract expiration. It is common to see the parties begin initial meetings sometime during this 60 or 30 day period. Many times the union will present its initial list of demands during this stage, a list of demands that may be very long and that reflects the wishes of as many members as can be accommodated. Sometimes the union will present a large initial demand for wages during the public relations stage, a demand that is met with disbelief by the employer and that is stoutly and firmly defended in public by the union. It is also common to see both labor and management begin to make plays to the press for public support during this period. Union leaders may release statements notifying the public about the importance of certain union demands. The employers may also go to the press and may make statements about their concern for their employees and their wishes for a peaceful and productive negotiations.

BOX 10-1
Labor and the Bottom Line

More and more, labor unions are scrutinizing the significance of the bottom line, and pressing management to disclose sensitive financial and marketing information before sitting down at the bargaining table. And they are even sending their members to school to acquire a basic education in corporate finance and analysis, all in an effort to achieve a stronger bargaining position in the face of greater corporate demands for wage concessions and givebacks.

"Unions have been looking for a new kind of clout and you can expect this thrust for information to increase and intensify," said B. J. Widick, a senior lecturer on labor at the Columbia University Business School.

Labor's quest for financial data has come a long way since Walter Reuther and the United Automobile Workers first tried, unsuccessfully, to "look at the books" of the General Motors Corporation in the late 1940s. The drive by the Amalgamated Clothing and Textile Workers Union to unionize J. P. Stevens in the late 1970s was a turning point in labor's campaign to divine corporate America's financial secrets. After thorough research the union was able to exert pressure on the company by trying to influence its directors and other business interests. "That's when unions really started thinking they ought to know more about finance," Mr. Widick said.

And in a more recent example, the Communications Workers of America, since the breakup of the American Telephone and Telegraph Company, have begun to monitor public documents submitted to the Federal Communications Commission and to track rate increases. The United Electrical, Radio and Machine Workers of America has used the Boston-based Industrial Cooperative Association, a nonprofit consulting group, to investigate the financial condition of companies it bargains with.

The recession has contributed to the trend, bringing about major contractions in basic industries such as autos, steel and chemicals and propelling unions into the financial sphere in their effort to understand why such woes came upon them and just how great the problems were.

For labor leaders like Mr. Charles E. Bryan [a machinists' union local union president at the Eastern Airlines facilities at Kennedy and LaGuardia Airports] who believe that "employees of any company have an investment of their lives in that company and have a right to know as much about the company as someone who owns stock in it or lends it money," access to financial data is a critical issue.

Moreover, labor officials contend that in some cases their push for financial data can help the company as well. "There have been instances involving small companies, particularly in the garment industry, where the company's business expertise is probably less than that of the union," said Richard Prosten, research director of the Industrial Union

(continued)

BOX 10-1 *(continued)*

Department of the AFL–CIO, "and a look at the books can enable the
union to offer friendly advice."

Audrey Freeman, chief labor economist for the Conference Board,
confirmed that "management wants to get employees more involved in
the business as a business."

Source: Wendy Cooper, "Labor's New Drive to Learn About the Bottom Line,"
The New York Times, July 24, 1983, pp. 8F. Copyright © 1983 by The New York
Times Company. Reprinted by permission.

The Hard Bargaining Stage

At some point the parties begin the real serious work of negotiations.
This may begin anywhere from 7 to 14 days before the contract expires,
depending on the number of issues to be resolved. The hard bargaining
stage is characterized by a much more serious pattern of negotiating
behavior on the part of the negotiators than during the public relations
stage. During hard bargaining, the parties will most likely be meeting
on a daily basis. They will commonly declare a news blackout during
this stage and will withhold information from the press. The parties will
now be exchanging written proposals and counterproposals and will
begin to make some interim agreements on some (usually noneconomic)
items.

On the union side of the bargaining table, the members of the committee will begin to rescale the bargaining agenda. The long list of initial demands will begin to be reduced in number. Some items will be
agreed to by management; some will be quietly dropped until a later
round of negotiations (possibly three to five years in the future). On both
sides of the bargaining table there will be a good deal of intraorganizational bargaining away from the bargaining table in private small
group meetings and caucuses. Sometimes these intraorganizational
bargaining sessions can produce a great deal of tension and conflict
among members on a team. No one wants to see his or her "pet" bargaining demand dropped or sacrificed; concern with how the constituents will perceive the dropping or the rescaling of a previously stated
goal in bargaining will be expressed.

The Settle-or-Strike Stage

The final stage of bargaining is the settle-or-strike stage. This stage of
bargaining begins between 24 and 48 hours before the contract expires
or before the bargaining deadline. In the settle-or-strike stage the parties know that the end of negotiations is rapidly approaching and both
begin to mentally calculate the costs and benefits of agreement and disagreement. On both sides of the table there will probably be prepara-

tions for a strike during this stage. The union leaders will already have taken a strike vote of the members authorizing them to call a walkout if the negotiations are not concluded successfully. On the employer's side of the table, preparations must begin for closing the plant during the strike, for operating the plant during the strike with supervisors, or for operating the plant with temporary strikebreakers or even permanent replacements.

The settle-or-strike stage will end with either a settlement or a strike or in some instances an agreement to continue working without a contract by the union (usually given on a day-by-day basis). The parties will probably be meeting continuously during this final stage of bargaining; perhaps a federal mediator will be in attendence attempting to assist the parties in finding an agreement. In all likelihood the representatives of both labor and management will begin constant telephone contact with their supervisors checking on the acceptability of alternative offers and counteroffers. The pace is frantic, the stress level is extreme, and the long days of bargaining and arguing begin to wear on everyone. In the end, the employer makes a final offer; the union team recesses to consider the final offer. Perhaps some changes are recommended, the employer's team recesses to consider these and makes an amended final offer; the seconds tick away and the deadline approaches. The union team returns from its meeting and in the final minutes of the existing agreement a decision is made by the union to either settle or strike.

If a decision to settle is made, there is a great sigh of relief from all involved and the union then takes the contract to its members to be ratified. If the members agree that the contract is the best obtainable, they will ratify it by a vote and the negotiations process is over. If the members reject the contract, then the parties must go back to the bargaining table. If the contract is not ratified the members of the union usually strike. This means that bargaining begins again — usually at a level of intensity that the parties experienced during the hard bargaining stage. The difference now, of course, is that the employer's final offer is taken as the beginning point of negotiations, not the end. Fortunately, strikes are a relatively rare occurrence in U.S. industrial relations. The most likely outcome is that the parties will reach agreement during negotiations. The document that contains the elements of this agreement is called, appropriately enough, the labor agreement.

Summary

This chapter has focused mainly on what actually happens when labor and management face each other across the bargaining table. Several people have had theories of the bargaining process; some from an economic perspective, some from a more behavioral or psychological perspective. Because bargaining is a process involving two parties with conflicting goals, conflict is often a possibility. There are costs and benefits to conflict, and the parties in bargaining weigh these risks and potential payoffs in making their decisions about accepting the other party's position on an issue or disagreeing with it and causing conflict. The causes and consequences of agreement and disagreement in labor disputes were discussed at length.

Negotiations involve an element of interpersonal relations, and one of the most important characteristics a negotiator needs to have is persuasiveness through effective communication and effective listening. A negotiator must also be familiar with specific gambits (tactical maneuvers). The characteristics of an effective negotiator are listed.

Finally, this chapter has discussed the stages of bargaining, from planning for bargaining to begin to the narrowing of demands once bargaining has begun, to making decisions whether to prolong the conflict or to reach agreement at the conclusion of negotiations. Labor negotiations are a complex set of interactions, and they involve elements of all the social sciences including economics, psychology, sociology, and politics. No wonder this subject attracts the attention of researchers from so many academic disciplines. Virtually all the complexities of business and social relationships can be found in some element of the collective bargaining process.

Discussion Questions

1. Reread the boxed material at the beginning of this chapter. As a union negotiator, how would you approach a situation in which you are negotiating with a highly profitable company that is losing money in only one component — the unionized component? Are wage concessions called for in a situation like this? How would you try to justify such concessions to your members?
2. What do you see as the major contribution to our understanding of the collective bargaining process that is made by economic theories of the process?
3. What do you see as the major shortcomings of economic theories of the collective bargaining process?
4. Suppose for a moment that you were contacted by a local employer who is busy preparing for negotiations with a local union in your area. The employer wants your assistance in gathering information regarding wage rates in comparable-sized companies, industry wage and benefit trends, and cost of living information. Where would you direct this employer to find these data?
5. Sometimes collective bargaining seems like a big ritual with the parties going through a long, drawn-out process to reach a settlement that could have been bargained in a much shorter period of time. Why does bargaining take such a long time? Why don't the parties just sit down and reach an agreement as quickly as possible?
6. How useful are tricks or gambits in negotiations? In which instances might such "tricks of the trade" be especially useful? In what instances might they be detrimental to the negotiation process?

Notes

[1] F. Zeuthen, *Problems of Monopoly and Economic Warfare*, London: Routledge and Sons, 1930.

[2] Richard B. Peterson and Lane Tracy, *Models of the Bargaining Process: With Special Reference to Collective Bargaining*, Seattle: University of Washington Monograph Series, 1977, p. 4. Additional economic theories of the bargaining process inspired by Zeuthen's work include Jan Pen, "A General Theory of Bargaining," *American Economic Review* 42 (1952): 24–42; J. F. Nash, "The Bargaining Problem," *Econometrica* 18 (1950): 128–140; J. G. Cross, "A Theory of the Bargaining Process," *American Economic Review* 55 (1965): 67–94; and Alan Coddington, *Theories of the Bargaining Process*, Chicago: Aldine, 1968.

[3] R. E. Walton and R. B. McKersie, *A Behavioral Theory of Labor Negotiations*, New York: McGraw-Hill, 1965.

[4] See Peterson and Tracy, *Models of the Bargaining Process*, p. 49.

[5] See R. B. Peterson and L. Tracy, "Testing a Behavioral Theory Model of Labor Negotiations," *Industrial Relations* 16 (1977): 35–50; or Bevars Mabry, "The Pure Theory of Bargaining," *Industrial and Labor Relations Review* 18 (1965): 479–592; or Tom Kochan and Hoyt Wheeler, "Municipal Collective Bargaining: A Model and Analysis of Bargaining Outcomes," *Industrial and Labor Relations Review* 29 (1975): 46–66.

[6] Neil Chamberlain, *Collective Bargaining*, New York: McGraw-Hill, 1951.

[7] See Ross Stagner and Hjalmar Rosen, *Psychology of Union–Management Relations*, Monterey, CA: Brooks-Cole, 1965, p. 103.

[8] Neil Chamberlain and James Kuhn, *Collective Bargaining*, 3rd ed., New York: McGraw-Hill, 1986, p. 204. Sam Church, United Mineworkers of America's president, was labeled "Sell-out Sam" by his opponents after the 1981 coal negotiations.

[9] See Ross Stagner, *Psychology of Industrial Conflict*, New York: Wiley, 1956, p. 414–448.

[10] Carl Stevens, *Strategy and Collective Bargaining Negotiations*, New York: McGraw-Hill, 1963, p. 21.

[11] William Serrin, "The Copper Miners May Be at the Point of No Return" *The New York Times*, July 29, 1984, p. 1E.

[12] "Labor's Blacklist," *The Wall Street Journal*, March 24, 1978, p. 6.

[13] See Robert B. McKersie and Lawrence C. Hunter, *Pay, Productivity, and Collective Bargaining*, London: MacMillan, 1973.

[14] Charles S. Loughran, *Negotiating a Labor Contract: A Management Handbook*, Washington, DC: BNA Books, 1984, p. 172.

[15] Roy J. Lewicki and Joseph Litterer, *Negotiation*, Homewood, IL: Irwin, 1985, p. 82.

[16] Lewicki and Litterer, *Negotiation*, p. 194.

[17] Loughran, *Negotiating a Labor Contract*, p. 172.

[18] Roy J. Lewicki and Joseph Litterer, *Negotiation*, p. 206.

[19] Gavin Kennedy, John Benson, and John McMillan, *Managing Negotiations*, Englewood Cliffs, NJ: Prentice-Hall, 1982, pp. 143–161.

[20] Loughran, *Negotiating a Labor Contract*, pp. 184–189.

[21] See for example Ann Douglas, *Industrial Peacemaking*, New York: Columbia University Press, 1962; or Stevens, *Strategy and Collective Bargaining Negotiations;* or Walton and McKersie, *A Behavioral Theory of Labor Negotiations*.

[22] Bruce Morse, *How to Negotiate the Labor Agreement*, South Bend, MI: Trends, 1981.

[23] Kennedy, Benson, and McMillan, *Managing Negotiations*, p. 14–22.

[24] Audrey Freeman, *Managing Labor Relations*, New York: The Conference Board, 1978, pp. 19–23.

ILA ENDS WALKOUT AT EAST COAST PORTS BUT STILL MUST FACE SHIPPERS' DEMANDS

By Daniel Machalaba

An agreement Friday that ended a three-day strike by the International Longshoremen's Association at East Coast Ports may prove to be a short-lived victory for the union, which faces mounting pressure for wage cuts and work rule changes.

Competition in the depressed maritime industry among carriers, ports and union and nonunion crews is putting the ILA on the defensive. A proliferation of non-ILA labor — receiving 40% less in wages and benefits — on the Gulf and Atlantic coasts is encouraging ports further north that use ILA dockworkers to challenge the union for cost savings.

The agreement extended an expired contract for 45 days, thus ending a walkout that shut ports from Maine to Virginia. In reaching the accord, a management group bowed to the ILA and withdrew demands that any contract extension include a two-tier wage system.

The Council of North Atlantic Shipping Associations, which represents waterfront employers in Philadelphia, Baltimore, Providence, R.I., and Hampton Roads, Va., cited resistance by ship owners who feared that the strike would deepen their financial problems. "We felt it was time to take a stand, but the (ship) lines apparently didn't," said Edward J. Adams, vice president of International Terminals Operating Co. and a member of the Hampton Roads employers negotiating committee.

When negotiations between the ILA and management for a new three-year contract resume, the Council of North Atlantic Shipping Associations vows to press for a two-tier wage system with pay cuts for some crews. "There's tremendous pressure on us," said Francis A. Scanlan, the group's chief counsel, who points to the growth of non-ILA dockworkers with wages lower than those of ILA members and without expensive ILA-fringe benefit packages.

Under the extended three-year IA master contract, the union's members on the Atlantic and Gulf coasts received a base wage of $17 an hour. But fringe benefits, including vacation pay, contributions to pension and welfare funds and the guarantee of a certain number of hours of work each year, boosted total ILA compensation costs in some ports to more than $35 an hour.

"The ILA continued to take, take, take," said J. Durel Landry, president of the Association of Independent Stevedores and Terminal Operators, a group promoting the use of non-ILA labor on the Gulf coast. By employing non-ILA workers whose compensation rate reaches a maximum of $25 an hour, these stevedores are dropping rates and winning customers. "The ILA had a monopoly on the waterfront but now it has competition," said Mr. Landry.

Chapter 11

The Labor Agreement

Theories

The labor agreement represents the codification or the solidification of the rules of the workplace discussed by labor and management during the collective bargaining interaction. By tradition the labor agreement is a written document, and by law most of the terms of this agreement are enforceable in court.[1] The labor agreement is a common product of the collective bargaining process. In 1980, the most recent date for which data are available, about 190,000 labor agreements were in effect.[2] Each year over 60,000 new agreements are negotiated although no more than 350–400 of these can be classified as major, meaning that they cover 500 or more employees.[3] The labor agreement has a long history in U.S. labor relations. The first comprehensive industry-wide written contract is believed to have been drafted between the Stove Molders Union and the Associated Stove Manufacturers in 1891.[4]

However, it has not been until the last 30 years or so that concern has developed about exactly what the labor agreement represents. For example, in the early years of the twentieth century the theory was popular that the labor agreement was an amalgamation of individual contracts of employment by the employees with the employer negotiated by the union. Failure by the employer to pay an employee his or her proper wage rate was regarded as a breach of contract.[5] A second view was that the labor agreement is a third party contract with the employer as the promisor, the union as the promisee, and the employees as beneficiaries.[6] A third view was that the labor agreement is a trust negotiated between the labor organization and the employer for the benefit of the employees, with the union playing the role of the fiduciary.[7] The purpose of all these theories is to establish a relationship between the labor agreement and the traditional commercial contract and to delineate the rights of employees, labor organizations, and employers to take legal action against each other in the event of the breach of such an agreement.[8] The continuing attempt by the judicial system to establish an ironclad relationship between commercial and labor agreements has prompted Clyde Summers to write:

> . . . the collective agreement differs as much from the common contract as Humpty Dumpty differs from a common egg. The failure of the courts to see and remember the differences causes confusion and leads them to blunder.[9]

Archibald Cox proposes that the labor agreement

> serves a function fairly comparable to the role of the Federal Trade Commission Act or the National Labor Relations Act in the whole community. It is an instrument of government as well as an instrument of exchange.[10]

Cox comments that labor agreements, unlike most other contracts, are an instrument of government because they regulate diverse affairs of many people with conflicting interests over a substantial period of time. In his view, the collective bargaining agreement has the nature of an armed truce in a continuing struggle. Cox concludes that labor agreements and commercial contracts are quite different and that the general rules of contract law developed in the courtroom may not be totally applicable in interpreting and enforcing agreements between labor and management.[11]

Further reflections on the nature of the labor agreement have produced valuable new insights into the functions of the labor agreement and how that agreement is to be interpreted and enforced. Drawing on Dunlop's seminal *Industrial Relations Systems*, David Feller has devised a theory of the labor agreement as the embodiment of the rules of the workplace. He argues, as Cox did earlier, that collective bargaining's largest significance is the creation of a system of private law to govern the employer–employee relationship. According to Feller, the labor agreement assures both management and labor consistency of action, and it defines the limits of power and subordinate members of management over the workers. Feller notes that the labor agreement produces several benefits to the employer. The agreement gives the employer stability in the labor–management relationship for a fixed period of time; it helps assure compliance with top management policies by both management and labor throughout the organization; and, finally, it gives the company the right to take unilateral unchallenged action in some areas free from interference from employees.[12] Of course, the labor agreement offers substantial benefits to employees too, in Feller's own words:

> The employees' interest seems plain enough. It is not only that collective bargaining offers, or at least appears to offer, a method of obtaining a larger share of the economic pie. Even where this is not so, as in the case

of plants and industries which traditionally follow wage patterns set elsewhere, the collective agreement provides a system of law to govern matters much more important to the employee than those governed by most public law: his right to a job and to a promotion, the hours at which and the conditions under which he is required to work, his right to refuse or to share in the opportunity to work overtime, the length and scheduling of his vacations and so forth.[13]

As a result of his reflections on the labor agreement Feller, like Cox before him, concludes that the labor agreement is not a contract between the employer and the employee and that neither should have the right to bring suit against the other for its breach. Feller does believe, however, that there are some contractual obligations for both the union and the employer that may be embodied in the labor agreement. In particular, he points to the employer's contractual obligation to process workers' grievances and to the union's contractual obligation not to strike during the term of the labor agreement. Feller feels that the breach of either of these obligations should be subject to court suit.[14]

Contents of a Typical Labor Agreement

The Recognition Clause

Most labor agreements begin with a recognition clause, one purpose of which is to state the coverage of the agreement as applied to the employer. The employer as a party to the agreement will be clearly identified as a single employer or as an association of employers. A second function of the recognition clause is to establish the union as the sole and exclusive representative for a group of employees. The recognition clause establishes the union's contractual rights to act on the employees' behalf for the purpose of determination of wages, hours, and other terms and conditions of employment. The employer agrees not to deal with any other group claiming to represent his or her employees in this particular bargaining unit during the term of the contract. Finally, the recognition clause defines the bargaining unit, very carefully spelling out what group of employees are covered by the contract and what other groups are excluded. The recognition clause thus outlines the boundaries of the bargaining structure and gives a specific union the right to represent employees so named.

Management and Union Rights Clauses

The management and the union rights clauses in the agreement state in concrete terms the activities of the employer and the union that are specifically recognized and sanctioned by the other party during the terms of the agreement. These clauses set the limits to the employer's power to direct and maintain the operations of the company and define the limits of the union's power to represent its members at the workplace.

Management Rights. The management rights clause is found in a very high percentage of labor agreements. A survey conducted by the Bureau of National Affairs (BNA) in 1985 found a statement of management and union rights in all but one of the 400 labor agreements surveyed.[15] The management's rights clause commonly identifies two types of management right: reserved rights and shared rights. Reserved rights are items that are reserved solely for decisionmaking by management. Shared rights are those that the union and the employer are allowed to determine mutually, usually subject to the union's rights to file a grievance protesting a particular act of management.

The employer generally wants as broad a definition of management rights as possible. Most employers view much of what goes on in collective bargaining as a limitation on management from the outset.[16] Thus employers are careful in how much discretion they give away in negotiations. In most contracts the employers reserve for themselves the exclusive right to manage the business, to control production, and to determine the number and location of plants, the method of production, the price and other such decisions dealing with the product, as well as the acquisition, disposal, and control of company property. These are called *exclusive rights*. Company actions and decisions about these issues cannot be protested by the union through the grievance process.

Decisions dealing with people, however, are often shared with the union or are decisions that the union may have the right to protest through the grievance procedure (see Chapter 13). These rights, so-called *shared rights*, relate to decisions that management may make regarding such matters as discipline, discharge, promotion, transfer, and classification of employees. In some instances some decisions relating to "people issues" are reserved solely for the decisionmaking of management. The employer may insist, for example, that decisions regarding hiring of new employees should be an exclusive management right because yet-to-be-hired employees are not members of the bargaining unit and have no rights under the contract until they are hired. Similarly, the employer may argue that the evaluation of employees should be solely the responsibility of management and not shared with the union because of the subjectivity inherent in performance evaluation and the need for confidentiality in conducting performance evaluation.

The union feels that its duty is to protect its members' rights on the job. Thus it would like to be able to bargain about any decision and to protest through the grievance procedure any act of management having negative consequences for the workers. Subcontracting is an issue that is often debated by unions and employers when the management's rights clause is negotiated. Employers generally want freedom and flexibility in operating the workplace; if it is cheaper to subcontract out a particular aspect of the operation than to do it in house, the employer will want to have the opportunity to take advantage of this saving. For example, an employer currently pays custodians $9.00 an hour under a union contract to keep tidy the washrooms and locker rooms at the workplace. If the employer subsequently discovers that a janitorial service can provide these same services for $6.00 per hour, the employer will likely want to use the janitorial service and lay off or reassign his or her $9.00-an-hour custodians. The union will resist this reassignment and will want language in the contract restricting management's right to subcontract out the work done by bargaining unit members. In most cases the union will not be successful in totally prohibiting the employer's use of subcontracting, but the union may get in the agreement language that requires advance notice of subcontracting or that prohibits subcontracting if there are employees on layoff.

Union Rights.   The statement of union rights covers a number of items of special importance to the union in discharging its activities as the representative of the work group, such as outlining the contractual rights of union representatives to conduct union business during working time. Another union concern is the contractual rights of union representatives to gain access to the workplace and to talk to members about their problems. A third issue is the right of the union to communicate with its members at the workplace through the use of bulletin boards or the distribution of union literature.

The union rights clause is important to the union because the union wants to have the right to access the workplace and talk to members about grievances or other matters of business where the members are most accessible: at work. Once the workday is over, employees want to go home. The union rights clause is important to the employer because the employer needs to have control over the workplace. The employer pays his employees to work — not to conduct union business on company time. If union business must be conducted during the workday, the employer may want to limit the number of hours to be spent on these activities per month or the number of people who are allowed to participate. Additionally, the employer may want to require that employees go "off the clock" or "punch out" when they are conducting union business at the workplace to guarantee that the employer is not paying for time spent on these activities.

Union Security

The concept of union security involves the obligations that workers have to become a member of or to provide financial support to a union. Most labor agreements include some type of union security provision. In the 1985 BNA survey of 400 agreements, all but 3 provided for some type of union security, the most common being the *union shop,* a provision that requires all bargaining unit members to become union members 30 days after employment; the *modified union shop,* which requires newly hired members of the unit to become union members but not those hired before a certain date; the *agency shop,* which requires employees to pay a service fee to the union but does not require union membership; and maintenance of membership, which requires all present union members to retain their membership during the term of the agreement but does not require newly hired employees or those not presently union members to join.[17]

In addition to obligations to enter into and retain union membership, labor agreements also contain provisions guaranteeing the payment of union dues to the union, mainly by checkoff provisions in the labor agreement. The *checkoff* is an authorization that an employee gives his or her employer to deduct his or her union dues directly from the paycheck. Under a checkoff arrangement the employer collects the union's dues and initiation fees from the employees and forwards the money to the union. At first glance it may appear odd that the employer may be willing to provide such a service for the union. However, many employers see real advantages to the checkoff, the main one being elimination of the need for the union steward to collect money from the work group, an activity that can be very disruptive to work activity. In the BNA 1985 survey 90 percent of the sampled labor agreements contained provision for a checkoff.[18]

Union security provisions are extremely important to labor organizations. Because it is obligated to represent all members of the bargaining unit fairly and equally and without discrimination regardless of their membership status, a union assumes the duty to represent everyone in the unit once it is certified as the bargaining representative. This means that all workers' grievances must be processed in the same way for members and nonmembers alike. Processing grievances, negotiating contracts, and representing workers takes time and money. The union wants to ensure that everyone who receives these services from the union pays for them. Workers who are covered by the contract but who do not pay dues are called *free riders;* the cost of representing these workers is subsidized by those workers who do pay dues.

The union security issue is important both to management and to many workers who are philosophically opposed to this aspect of unionism. Even workers and managers who do not disagree with the concept of unionism per se will recoil at the thought of being forced to pay money to a union as a condition of employment. Under the union shop or the agency shop, the payment of dues to the union is a condition of employment and workers can be terminated for violating it. In addition to resisting the general coercive nature of the union shop, many people disagree with how the union spends the money it extracts involuntarily from the people it represents. Members may object to unions using their dues money to support charitable organizations (e.g., environmental or religious organizations), or to support political causes (e.g., voter registration campaigns or voter educational campaigns) that the members may not support.

In many states, union shop and agency shop provisions are illegal — these are the so-called "right-to-work" states discussed and identified in Chapter 3. In these states, obligatory payments of dues monies to unions are prohibited. In 1982 and in 1986, the U.S. Supreme Court has ruled that union members can get a rebate on their union dues when these monies are spent for activities outside normal representation duties such as negotiation and grievance processing.[19]

Discharge and Discipline

Over 98 percent of the 400 agreements in the 1985 BNA survey had some statement regarding discipline and discharge. The discharge and discipline statements in a labor agreement usually discuss three items: the grounds for discharge and discipline; the process to be followed in discharging and disciplining an employee; and the procedure that an employee must follow to appeal a discharge or discipline decision.

Grounds. The grounds for discharge and discipline may be stipulated in one of two ways: to require that discharge and discipline be used only where there is "just cause" for the action, or to specify very clearly in the language of the agreement what types of conduct will subject an employee to discharge and discipline (common grounds are dishonesty, theft, intoxication, or insubordination).

Process and Procedure. Various procedures may be followed when action is taken against an employee. Very commonly the agreement will require that an employee be warned before he or she can be discharged. Also common is a procedure for progressive discipline providing one type of discipline for the first infraction of a rule (a written warning or reprimand) and a more stringent type of punishment for the second (perhaps a 7-day suspension) and third (perhaps a 30-day suspension) offenses.

Appeal. Most contracts allow the union to appeal a management discipline or discharge decision through the grievance procedure. In the majority of contracts the employee must appeal the reprimand or termination within 5 or 10 days. If the employee waits longer than this, his or her rights of appeal are assumed to be waived.

The discipline and discharge portion of the agreement is extremely important both to management and to the union. The employer needs to ensure that workers come to work on time, that they work up to their full potential, and that they follow the rules of the workplace. Employees who break the rules are disciplined as a lesson to themselves and as an example to other employees that the employer will not tolerate those who will not or cannot follow the rules of the workplace.

Limitations on the employer's unilateral right to make discharge and discipline decisions are important to the union, too. One of the greatest benefits a union can offer to its members is protection against unjust termination or punishment. By appealing a disciplinary action through the grievance procedure the union may be successful in having the action rescinded or having the severity of discipline reduced.

Seniority

Clauses providing that some role be played by seniority in making decisions about bargaining unit employees were found in 90 percent of the contracts surveyed by the BNA in 1985.[20] In 93 percent of these agreements seniority was measured as the length of the employee's continuous service with the company. For the union seniority provides a measure of protection for workers against layoff (discussed in the next section) and also can give workers priority for benefits such as promotion. In most agreements (73 percent), seniority plays some role in making promotion decisions, although in only 5 percent of the agreements in the BNA survey was seniority the *only* factor in determining promotion. In most cases (68 percent), seniority was one of several factors to be considered in making promotion decisions.

Seniority is one of the cornerstones of trade union philosophy. Union leaders will argue that seniority is the fairest way to make distinctions among members of the bargaining unit because it is the only true, unambiguous way to distinguish among workers. Seniority is measurable — it is quantitative and objective. If one worker has 10 years of seniority on a particular job and others have 8, then the worker with more seniority should be the first in line for promotion and the last in line to be laid off. For the union, acquiring more and more seniority is like acquiring greater and greater rights at the workplace. Furthermore, union leaders argue that by allowing promotion to be made on any criteria other than seniority, it is too easy for supervisors to discriminate among workers and to pick their favorites for promotion.

For the employer, seniority is not usually the favored way to make personnel decisions. Most employers would prefer to make these decisions on the basis of ability or merit. Employers want to promote the "best" people — not just those who have been there the longest. Likewise, in making layoff decisions, the employer will want to lay off the poorest performers first and let the more productive employees keep working. The employer knows that if young people feel that they are going to have to wait forever to get promoted, the really ambitious people will leave the organization. To maintain vitality and vigor the organization may feel it needs the flexibility to promote whomever it wants, whenever it wants. The resolution of the differences in the union's and management's perspectives on seniority will have to be negotiated at the bargaining table.

Personnel Movement — Layoff, Recall, Transfer

The BNA survey in 1985 found that layoff provisions were found in 91 percent of the labor agreements studied. With the recession of 1979–1983 in manufacturing, and with the massive layoffs that occurred and still exist in the auto, steel, and rubber industries, layoff provisions became extremely important to workers, unions, and employers. In most agreements (89 percent of those surveyed), seniority plays some role in determining who will be laid off; in 49 percent of the agreements seniority is the only factor to be considered in laying off an employee. In most agreements (60 percent of those surveyed) an employee is allowed to "bump" a junior employee when the senior employee has been targeted for layoff — that is, to displace a less senior employee in a department or in a job classification so that the more senior employee can continue to work rather than be laid off.

Recall is commonly provided in labor agreements (82 percent), and usually is incorporated into the layoff procedure. Recall rights are usually in the order of seniority, meaning that the most senior laid-off employee in a job classification will be the first one called back to work once the layoff is over. In most labor agreements, laid-off employees must be recalled before the employer may hire any new employees.

When layoffs occur, a method has to be found to determine who will be laid off and who will continue working. Likewise, when it is time to recall employees, a way is needed to determine who gets recalled and in what order they are recalled. The union's perspective on layoff and recall is usually that seniority should be the only factor guiding these decisions. The union would usually prefer, also, that employees be given wide rights to "bump" other less senior employees in other jobs to keep the more senior employees working. The only deviation from the principle of seniority that most unions will condone is to provide *superseniority* for union offers and stewards at the workplace to protect these persons against layoff. Superseniority means that union officers and stewards automatically move to the top of the seniority roster in their jobs or departments. If layoffs do occur, the stewards and officers will be the last laid off. The argument made to defend superseniority is that the stewards and officers represent the bargaining unit — they cannot protect workers' rights if they are laid off and not working. Therefore, superseniority is necessary to maintain continuity in representation.

The employer usually prefers to lay off the least productive person first and to recall the most productive person first. This helps the employer maintain production and gives the employer some flexibility on making layoff decisions. The employer will not usually want to see wide bumping rights — bumping causes disruption throughout the workplace and often results in inexperienced workers taking on new positions with which they have little direct or recent experience. Finally, the employer may oppose the superseniority concept as a way for the union to provide a benefit to its leaders, a benefit the employer pays for without any gain or return. The employer may also see superseniority as a divisive source in the workforce and a threat to efficiency.

Hours and Overtime

Provisions in labor agreements covering hours of employment and overtime were found in 99 percent of the 400 contracts in the 1985 BNA survey. As mentioned in Chapter 7, hours of work are one of the three mandatory items of bargaining specifically mentioned in the National Labor Relations Act. The hours and overtime section of the labor agreement will usually contain four provisions, each covering a separate aspect of hours and overtime: daily and/or weekly work schedules; overtime work and overtime pay; weekend work and weekend pay; and lunch, rest, and cleanup periods.

Work Schedules.   The vast majority of labor agreements surveyed by the BNA in 1985 (83 percent) specified some statement of daily work hours and weekly work schedules. In 94 percent of these contracts the 8-hour day was the standard work day. In most agreements (93 percent) the weekly work week was specified as 40 hours. Shorter work weeks were predominant only in the apparel industry.

Overtime.   The most common type of overtime provision (99 percent of the contracts surveyed) is the payment of time and a half (1½ times the hourly rate of pay) for all work performed in excess of 8 hours a day. It is also common to see a statement in the contract that it is the policy of the company to distribute overtime as equally as possible among members of the work group.

Weekend Pay.   Weekend pay was discussed in 70 percent of the contracts surveyed by the BNA in 1985. Weekend pay is commonly paid in much the same manner as overtime. In a majority of the agreements surveyed, the premium pay for Saturday work is time and a half; the most common premium for Sunday work is double time pay.

Lunch Periods and Breaks.   Lunch periods were specified in a majority of labor agreements surveyed by the BNA (60 percent) but in only 25 percent of these was the lunch period paid. Interestingly, rest periods or breaks were specified in only 43 percent of the agreements surveyed in 1985. The most common type of break arrangement is for two 10-minute breaks a day, although two 15-minute breaks a day are also commonly found.

Control of the length of the working day has been a concern of U.S. unions since earliest times. Chapter 4 described the movement for the 10-hour day in the 1830s and the movement for the 8-hour day that began in the 1860s. It is easy to see the union's motivation in wanting to control the length of the working day and in limiting overtime. A good argument can be made that a workday of 10–12 hours in manual labor occupations "burns out" workers; such a workday exhausts people physically, creates a safety and health hazard because of fatigue, and impairs the chance for a normal family life when a member of the family is always at work. It can also be seen from the union's perspective that an overly long workday restricts the number of union members at the workplace. Afterall, if it takes 100 people 12 hours a day to staff the workplace, it would take 150 people working 8 hours a day to do the same work. If workers pay $20 a month in union dues, the union will increase its dues revenue from $2,000 a month to $3,000 a month as a result of the shorter work day. The same logic applies to overtime work. The union would prefer that the employer not work existing employees overtime but instead hire additional employees to do the work.

The employer has a different perspective on the issues of hours of work and overtime. The employer would generally prefer to work existing employees longer hours in the face of a rising demand for the product rather than hire new employees, for a number of reasons. It is expensive to hire new employees — recruiting must be undertaken, people have to be interviewed, references have to be checked. New workers have to be trained or at least oriented to the workplace. More employees mean that more supervisors have to be hired, and new tools and equipment have to be purchased for the new employees to use. Furthermore, the employer has to provide these new employees with health insurance and make contributions to the pension fund for them. These "fixed costs" are already paid for existing employees. Finally, the employer knows that if he or she must lay them off at some point in time, the newly hired employees will likely collect unemployment benefits from the unemployment insurance fund maintained by the state department of employment services. The level of contribution that an employer must make to the fund depends on the firm's "experience rating." An employer that has many workers on layoff collecting from the fund will have to pay a higher premium or make a larger contribution to the fund than an employer that has no workers on layoff collecting benefits. Hence, the employer will generally resist hiring new employees if possible.

Wages

To many people wages seem to be the only thing that unions negotiate over (of course, this is far from true). Contract provisions relating to wages were found in almost all the 400 agreements in the BNA 1985 survey. The wage section of a labor agreement usually addresses three separate aspects of the wage issue: deferred or scheduled wage increases, cost of living adjustments, and supplementary pay.

Deferred or Scheduled Wage Increases.   Because most contracts are for more than one year, the wage section of the agreement will detail how much wages will rise (or fall in the case of a concession contract) over the life of the agreement. In most cases, the increases begin at the signing of the contract and scheduled increases occur at the anniversary date of the agreement (e.g., one year from the date of the signing of the agreement). Scheduled increases may be expressed in percentage terms (*X* percent per year) or in flat-rate terms (*X* cents per hour per year).

Cost of Living Adjustments.   The cost of living section of the labor agreement will detail how the general level of wages will be adjusted for increases in the cost of living (usually measured by the Consumer Price Index or CPI). In the 1985 BNA contract survey, 42 percent of the agreements had a provision for adjusting the wage level for increases in the cost of living, down from 48 percent in 1983. Virtually all the cost of living adjustments were keyed to changes in the CPI. The most common type of cost of living adjustment (COLA) is a one cent per hour increase in wages for every 0.3 percent increase in the CPI — if the CPI increases 6 percent in a year, wages rise 20¢ per hour at the end of that year to compensate workers for this increase. The computation of the raise would be as follows:

$$\frac{6\%}{0.3\%} = 20 \times 1¢ \text{ per hour} = 20¢ \text{ wage increase per hour}$$

It is important to remember that COLA adjustments are an addition to the scheduled wage increases. COLA adjustments are affected by both the amount of increase in the CPI and by the formula used to compensate the COLA increase. If the contract specified a 1¢ per hour increase for every 0.2 percent increase in the CPI, a 6 percent annual CPI increase would result in a 30¢ per hour wage adjustment; contrastingly, if the agreement provided for a 1¢ per hour increase for every 0.4 percent increase in the CPI, wages would be adjusted only 15¢ per hour for a 6 percent increase in the CPI.

Wage Supplements.   Wage supplements can take many forms but generally they are provided either for shift work or for call-in or reporting pay. Shift differentials are a supplement to the straight time hourly wage that are designed to compensate employees for the inconvenience of working at a time other than day shift. A large number of agreements in the 1985 BNA survey (86 percent) provided for some type of shift differential, most commonly 25¢ per hour for employees on the second shift (3–11 P.M.) and 30¢ per hour for employees on the third shift (11 P.M.–7 A.M.). Call-in pay and reporting pay were also provided for in a large number of the contracts in the BNA survey (68 and 74 percent, respectively). Call-in pay refers to a pay guarantee to be given to workers who are called back to work at a time other than their regularly scheduled work time. The most common amount of pay guaranteed for a call-in was four hours. Reporting pay is the amount of pay that is guaranteed to a worker who shows up for work, but for whom there is no work available. As with call-in pay, the most common amount of pay specified for reporting pay was four hours.

It is not hard to see why the wage section of the agreement is important to the union. The union wants to provide good wages for its members, to see these wages increase over time to provide for a progressively better standard of living, and to protect this standard of living from erosion because of inflation. Union leaders often point out that high wages make it possible for union members to have the purchasing power to buy the products they produce, such as cars, appliances, and new homes. After all, robots do not buy cars.

The employer is also vitally concerned about wage rates. Wages constitute one of the largest outlays of expense that the employer will make during the year. For some employers in service occupations, wages constitute 70–75 percent of total case outlays per year. Wages are also an immediate and constant drain on cash. They are paid weekly or biweekly and cannot normally be deferred when the cash flow is tight. There is little the employer can do to control this drain on the cash flow other than to lay off employees. This, of course, decreases output and eventually revenue, which also reduces cash flow. To remain competitive and to keep a healthy balance between revenue and expenses the employer must control wage rates. In very competitive industries where profit margins are tight, controlling wage rates may be the key to survival for the organization. In times of intense competition from low-wage foreign or domestic competitors wages are often negotiated downward in labor agreements (concession bargaining).

Fringe Benefits

Fringe benefits, or *indirect compensation,* are an increasingly important part of the labor agreement. For the past 50 years labor unions have led the way in pioneering new types of fringe benefits and in expanding the coverage of existing benefits for workers covered by labor agreements. Although it is difficult to summarize the types of benefits in labor agreements because of their complexity, it is possible to categorize the following four types: pensions, insurance, holidays, and vacations.

Pensions.   Pension benefits were provided for in virtually all the labor agreements surveyed by the BNA in 1985. The pension section of the contract will usually specify the basic details of the pension package provided for workers covered under the agreement. Items commonly addressed include some mention of normal retirement age (customarily, 65 years) and also provisions for early retirement (usually, at 55 years). In addition, the pension section discusses payment arrangements should employees become disabled before they are eligible for retirement. Finally, this section of the agreement addresses the issue of benefit levels. A common formula for computing pension benefits is to provide a specified amount of benefit for every year of service. The most common level of benefit found in the 1985 BNA survey was $20 per month pension benefit for each year of service. Thus, for an employee with 20 years of service the pension benefit is $400 per month; for 30 years of service, $600 per month. In most cases the pension is in addition to the benefits workers receive from Social Security. In the vast majority of contracts surveyed, the contribution to the pension fund was financed totally by the employer.

Insurance.   Many types of insurance may be provided employees in a collective bargaining agreement, most commonly life insurance, found in 96 percent of the contracts in the 1985 BNA survey usually for $10,000.00 upon the death of an employee. Most labor agreements (more than 83 percent of those in the BNA survey) also provide for some type of sickness and accident insurance, hospital and surgical insurance. In addition, over 79 percent of the surveyed contracts now provide for dental insurance, up from 65 percent in 1983 and 15 percent in 1975.

In most cases the employer pays the cost of the premium for health care insurance, and also in most cases the health insurance covers not only the employee but also his or her dependents. Health insurance costs have been escalating quite rapidly in the past five years and even the very largest employers are finding health insurance to be one of the most, if not the most, expensive benefit offered to employees. Health care cost control promises to be one of the major issues in collective bargaining in the future.

Holidays.   Virtually all the contracts in the BNA survey (99 percent) provide for some type of holiday schedule. The average number of holidays in union labor agreements in 1986 was 10 days. In the vast majority of cases (90 percent) employees are paid 8 hours of straight time hourly wage for holiday pay. The most commonly listed holidays in the BNA survey are listed in Table 11.1.

Vacations.   Vacations were provided in 92 percent of the contracts included in the 1985 BNA survey, which revealed that the majority of labor agreements provide for vacations up to five weeks in duration. In the great majority of cases (89 percent) the length of vacation is directly tied to the employee's length of service; that is, as seniority increases, so does the length of the vacation benefit provided. The most common

TABLE 11-1 Most Commonly Observed Holidays (frequency expressed as percentage of contracts)

Holiday	All Industries	Manufacturing	Nonmanufacturing
Thanksgiving	98	100	96
Labor Day	98	100	96
Christmas	98	99	96
Independence Day	97	98	96
New Year's Day	97	98	96
Memorial Day	95	96	94
Day after Thanksgiving	56	76	25
Good Friday, including ½ day	52	72	20
Christmas Eve	51	72	18
Washington's Birthday	38	33	45
New Year's Eve	29	45	7
Employee's birthday	26	17	39
Veterans' Day	20	14	30
Floating day	17	20	12
Personal day	12	7	19
Christmas-New Year's week	11	18	—
Columbus Day	10	7	14
Election day	7	6	8
Other days during Christmas week	7	11	1
Martin Luther King's Birthday	5	5	7
Lincoln's Birthday	4	1	8
Day chosen locally	4	4	3
Easter Monday	4	7	1
Christmas Eve, ½ day	3	2	3
New Year's Eve, ½ day	2	2	1

Source: Reprinted by permission from *Collective Bargaining, Negotiations, and Contracts,* copyright 1986 by the Bureau of National Affairs, Inc., Washington, DC.

relationship between length of service and length of vacation found in the BNA survey was 1 week of vacation for 1 year of service, 2 weeks of vacation for 2 years of service, 3 weeks of vacation for 8 years of service, 4 weeks of vacation for 15 years of service, 5 weeks for 22 years of service, and 6 weeks of vacation for 26 years of service.

Benefits are high on the bargaining agenda for almost every union. They are a continuation of income and are related to increases in wages. A good pension system will guarantee a fairly high level of earnings in retirement without requiring that the worker scrimp and save during the years that he or she is working. The pension plan and the insurance plans provide the worker and his or her family with a sense of security against income losses because of illness or disability. The vacations and holidays found in the contract give the employee and his or her family time to enjoy the good things in life and time to spend the money which has been worked long and hard for. An additional advantage of benefit plans are that they provide a tax-free source of compensation. At the present time contributions to benefits plans made by employers are not taxed. Thus, if the employer provides a worker with a $200 per quarter health insurance plan, this is like an equivalent increase in wages that is not taxed. If they had to purchase the plan, employees would do so with income already taxed (after-tax dollars).

For the employer, fringe benefits are a concern because of their cost. For some employers, benefits now constitute an expense equal to 50 percent or more above hourly wages (see introductory material to this chapter) if wages are $8.00 per hour, total labor costs may be $12.00 per hour; $4.00 goes to pay benefits such as pensions, health and life insurance, and vacations. One major concern of employers is that benefits costs are increasing and that there is little employers can do to control these costs. Health insurance costs are escalating as the costs of health care rise. There is not much the employer can do without reducing the type of benefit provided when insurance costs increase. Likewise, legal controls under the Employee Retirement Income Security Act (ERISA) of 1974 require that employers make annual contributions to pension plans and that these plans be fully funded, meaning that the amount of contribution to the plan each month equals the amount of benefit provided to the employee that month. This requirement now makes pension plans virtually the same type of immediate monthly expense as wages.

Working Conditions, Safety, and Nondiscrimination

Most labor agreements (over 84 percent of those surveyed) contain pledges by the employer and by the union to protect the health and safety of the individual employee. In addition, there is also commonly a provision in which the employer agrees to provide safety equipment (such as safety goggles and safety shoes) at no or greatly reduced cost to the employee. In the nondiscrimination section of the contract the employer and the union agree that neither will discriminate against any employee on the basis of race, color, creed, sex, national origin, or age. This statement was found in 96 percent of the labor agreements surveyed by the BNA in 1985.

Statements of safety and of nondiscrimination are important to the union largely because of the principle they enunciate. Some people may question whether such provisions are really necessary in the agreement; after all, the Occupational Safety and Health Act of 1970 requires employers to provide employees with a safe workplace, and the Equal Employment Opportunity Act of 1972 prohibits discrimination at the workplace. Union leaders know this, of course, but they are quick to point out that sometimes it is much better to have these provisions in the contract than to rely on federal legislation. Grievances over safety issues can usually be resolved much more quickly through the grievance procedure than by going to the Occupational Safety and Health Administration.

Employers seldom object to negotiating safety and nondiscrimination provisions in agreements. The employer usually welcomes the union's involvement in safety programs and may recommend the establishment of a joint labor–management safety committee to identify and resolve safety problems. Similarly, the employer will seldom disagree to an affirmation of its own corporate nondiscrimination policy in the labor agreement.

Grievance Procedure and Arbitration

A provision for resolving workers' grievances under the collective agreement was found in all 400 contracts in the 1985 BNA survey. Most grievance procedures have a fairly standardized format. They identify who represents labor and management at each step in the grievance process and specify time limits for the processing of grievances from one step to another. Finally, the great majority of labor agreements (99 percent of those surveyed) provide for the adjudication of unresolved grievances by a neutral third party chosen mutually by labor and by management.

The most common type of grievance procedure in labor agreements is a three-step procedure, in which the employee is represented by a shop floor union representative (steward) at the first step and the employer is represented by the shop foreman. In the majority of contracts (55 percent) the grievance must be written at the first step. In the second step the employee's grievance is usually handled by a representative of the local union grievance committee; the employer representative at the second level is usually from the corporate industrial relations staff.

If the parties are not able to resolve their dispute through the grievance procedure, then someone from outside the workplace will usually be called upon to make the decision as to how to resolve the grievance. This process is called *grievance arbitration* and will be covered in more detail in Chapter 13. In the BNA survey, 99 percent of the labor agreements used arbitration as the final method of resolution of grievances. In most cases, the parties mutually select the arbitrator and share equally the costs of the arbitrator's fees and expenses.

The grievance procedure portion of the labor agreement is important to both labor and management because through this procedure the contract is applied to real-life situations that may arise at the workplace. Generally the grievance procedure is the forum that the union uses to protest some action of management that it disagrees with (e.g., subcontracting) or to allow a second look at some action of a supervisor regarding an individual covered by the agreement (e.g., discipline or discharge). If the parties cannot agree over an issue while going through the steps of the grievance procedure, then a third-party neutral, an arbitrator, is brought in to resolve the problem. The grievance procedure provides a rational, logical, quasi-legalistic forum for resolving labor–management disputes while the contract is in effect. By agreeing to submit issues in dispute to the grievance procedure, the employer is giving up his or her right to take unilateral action regarding the workforce and the union is giving up its right to strike over actions of management that it disagrees with.

No Strike–No Lockout.   The no strike–no lockout provisions of the labor agreement contain a guarantee from both parties that neither will take economic action against the other during the terms of the agreement. Strike and lockout clauses appear in 95 percent of the agreements in the BNA 1985 survey. The no-strike clause is viewed as a concession by the union that it will not use its ultimate weapon (the strike) during the term of the agreement. The union usually views the agreement by management to process workers' grievances through the grievance procedure and to arbitrate them if they are unresolved as a trade-off for the no-strike pledge. The union gives up its right to strike during the contract if the employer is willing to submit unresolved workers' grievances to arbitration. Sometimes in labor agreements the union's pledge not to strike is conditional on the employer's agreement to arbitrate disputes and to abide by the arbitrator's award. In contracts such as these, the union's obligation to live up to its no-strike pledge is rescinded if the employer refuses to abide by an arbitrator's award or if he or she refuses to process a grievance in the first place.

The no-lockout clause is the employer's equivalent of the union's no-strike clause. The employer agrees in the vast majority of cases (90 percent of the contracts surveyed) not to use the lockout or the plant shutdown as a weapon or tactic against the union. The no-lockout pledge can also be conditional, usually on the union's agreement to process grievances and to abide by arbitrated rulings.

The no strike–no lockout clauses in the contract are probably of most importance to management. The no-strike pledge on the union's part guarantees the employer a period of labor peace for a certain fixed period of time. The employer can make commitments for the future and know with a high degree of certainty that the production schedule will not be interrupted by a strike as long as the contract is in effect. If the union violates its no-strike promise, the employer can go to court and under section 301(a) of the Taft-Hartley Act sue the union for breach of contract, provided the employer has offered to submit the issue in dispute to the grievance procedure. Alternatively, or in addition, the employer may also petition in federal court for an injunction to stop the strike.

Duration

The final section in most labor agreements is the duration clause. The majority of labor agreements in the BNA survey were three-year agreements (79 percent); one-year agreements comprised only 3 percent of the sample; two-year agreements comprised 13 percent, and agreements longer than three years comprised 5 percent of the sample. The duration clause will sometimes contain a provision, called a *reopener*, that allows the parties to renegotiate a certain portion of the contract while the rest of the agreement remains in effect. Sometimes wage reopeners are included in the contract if either the company or the union feels that events at the current time are not representative of what events may be like over the next three years. For example, if the union is negotiating with an employer over wages during the low point of an unusually sharp recession, the union may settle for a low wage at the time of negotiation and ask for the right to reopen or renegotiate the wage level at some time in the near future (usually within a year). In most cases, when reopener negotiations are conducted the union has the right to strike if the reopened issue is not satisfactorily resolved. In reopened negotiations, only items covered by the reopener agreement are negotiated.

The duration clause of the agreement is important because it will determine how long the agreement is in effect and how long the parties are bound by it. In most cases the contract is fully binding on the parties and the agreement is not normally changed or amended while it is in effect. The union usually will agree to a long-term contract only if it feels it has achieved all its goals in negotiations; otherwise it will be reluctant to sign an agreement of three years or longer. Often the duration of the agreement will be used as a trade-off for something the union wants to achieve in negotiations. For example, the union may agree to a three-year contract if the employer will agree to a COLA clause protecting workers' wages from the eroding effects of inflation.

Generally speaking, the employer will prefer a long-term contract. Negotiations are expensive and time consuming; the longer the employer can go between periodic renegotiations of the agreement, the better.

Administration

Once the agreement is negotiated and all the terms within it are settled, and it is ratified by the union membership, the contract is printed and distributed to all the members covered by it and all the supervisors and foremen who will be working with it. Usually the union will conduct educational programs for its stewards and grievance committee members to let them know exactly what the new contract says. Likewise, the employer will conduct educational programs with the foremen and supervisors to advise them how the new contract changes the rules and regulations of the workplace.

The employer will immediately need to implement the changes in the workplace required by the agreement. If new wage rates have been negotiated, they will take effect immediately. This, of course, will change workers' earnings so all payroll accounts have to be changed; the employer will also have to recompute his or her contribution to the Social

Security system (the employer and the employee each contribute 50 percent of the total Social Security contribution) because of the increase in hourly wages. If there has been a change in the medical insurance system or the retirement system, new contribution levels will have to be calculated and new contracts negotiated with the companies that provide the health insurance or administer the pension plan. Negotiating the agreement is one thing — actually putting it into effect and implementing the changes is another. There is a tremendous amount of time and effort necessary to actually change the terms and conditions of the workplace as stipulated in the agreement. Most of the burden of implementing the changes negotiated falls on management.

The union's role in contract administration is to make sure that the negotiated changes are implemented and that the employer makes these changes consistent both with the intentions of the parties when negotiations were taking place, and also with what the contract actually says. A crucial determinant of good contract administration is making sure that the contract says what the parties mean it to say. This means that the people writing the contract need to be very clear about what they actually mean. They need to avoid ambiguous words; they need to be precise about numbers and units of time and exact about the effective dates of new contract terms. A good example of ambiguity in contract language concerns the use of the word "days." The grievance procedure may say, for example, that a worker must appeal a disciplinary action within 10 days from the time the disciplinary action is taken. Does this mean 10 working days or 10 calendar days? The contract must be explicit or the administration of the agreement will be problematic and likely a source of grievances for months to come. Effective administration of the agreement is dependent on clear and precise contract language.

Effects of Collective Bargaining

Up to this point the process and products of bargaining have been described without reference to their effect on workers or on employers. At this point some attention will be given to the effect that collective bargaining has had on the people directly affected by the process and products of negotiations.

Wages

It seems logical to believe that unions have had an effect on wages, but the difficulty is in identifying just how large the effect is. Labor economists have been researching this topic over the past 25 years and are now able to answer this question with some degree of confidence. Over the period of time for which we have reliable wage data, the union wage level is usually estimated to be around 20 percent above the nonunion wage level, all else being equal. This means that, controlling for the type of work being done, the length of the work year, worker quality, company size, and other factors, unions raise the wages of their members about 20 percent above what wages would have been in the union's absence.[21] Recently, unions have been negotiating concessions and union wages have been falling. In 1986 wages for union workers in manufacturing actually declined by an average of 1 percent.[22] Researchers in years ahead looking at wage data for the 1980s may find that the union effect on wages decreased below usual levels for this decade.

Two of the most interesting findings to come out of the vast literature attempting to measure the effects that unions have had on wages deal with the wage effects over time and with the differential effect that unions have had on the wages of certain groups of workers. The estimation of union wage effects is given in Figure 11.1, which illustrates the great variability of the estimated union effect — greatest during the years of the Great Depression (1930–1935); smallest during the years of high inflation immediately following World War II. Since 1975 the union wage level effect is estimated to be about 30 percent, slightly above the 60 year average.

For certain occupational and demographic groups the effects that unions have had on wage rates are even higher than for other groups. For example, research evidence shows that union wage effects are larger for younger people than for older people, for nonwhites than for whites, and for those with less than a high school education than for those with a college degree. What the figures are stating, of course, is not that workers with less than a high school education make more money than workers with a college education but that compared to other workers with similar educational backgrounds in nonunion establishments, workers with less than a high school education make 27 percent more in union firms than in nonunion firms. A summary of differences in union wage levels is given in Figure 11.2. The finding from the research on the effects of unions on wages leaves little to debate about whether or not unions raise wages. The answer is that unions do raise wages above what they would have been in their absence.

Fringe Benefits

The issue of fringe benefits is one of the most important compensation issues of our time; in 1980 expenditures on employee benefits exceeded $400 billion. Results of fringe benefits research reveal that unions increase fringe benefits substantially, about 30 percent higher in union firms. For the value of total compensation — wages plus fringe benefits — the union's effect was 25 percent. The areas where the greatest union effect was found was on pensions; life, accident, and health insurance; vacation pay; and holiday pay.[23] Studies of worker perceptions of fringe benefits show that generally union workers have a greater awareness of the benefits that are available to them than do nonunion workers, and that union workers are more satisfied with the benefits they do receive

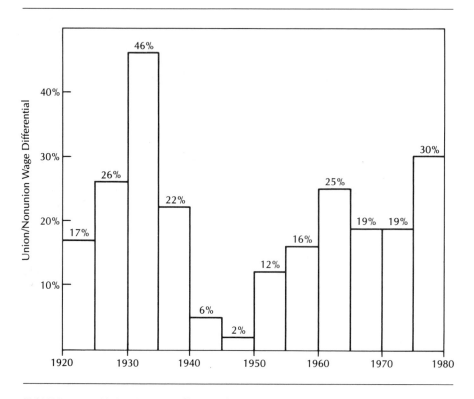

FIGURE 11-1   Union Wage Differential Over Time

than are nonunion workers. Perhaps this is not surprising, given the magnitude of the difference in the amount of fringe benefits received.

Employee Turnover

It is estimated that employee turnover involves as much as 5 percent of the labor force every year, often at great expense to organizations. For every employee that quits, a new one usually needs to be hired. Expenses relating to the costs of recruitment, selection, testing, and placement all rise as turnover rates rise. In addition, investments the employer may have made in training employees are lost when an employee quits. Freeman and Medoff estimate that turnover is between 31 and 65 percent lower in union than in nonunion firms, meaning that the average worker's tenure (length of service) is longer in union than in nonunion firms. These authors were able to estimate from statistical controls that even if the union's effect on wages of 20 percent were eliminated the union work force would still have a 5–12 percent lower turnover rate than the nonunion work force.[24]

When they contemplate the turnover decision, individual workers are often portrayed as considering two questions: (1) How easy will it be

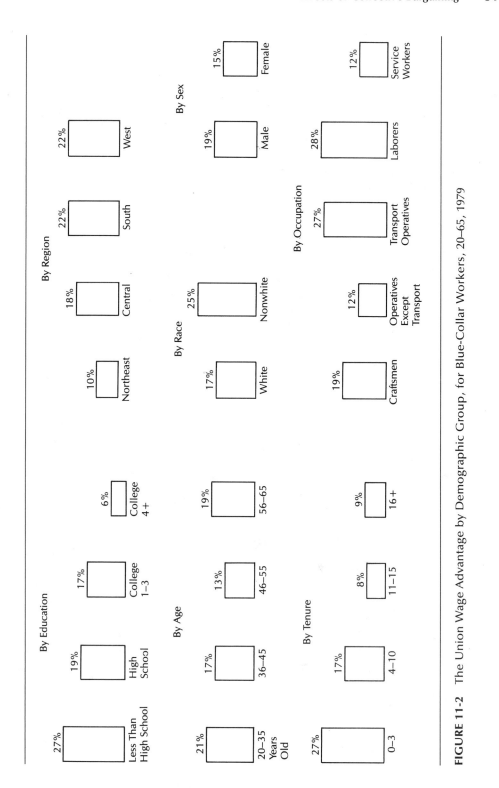

FIGURE 11-2   The Union Wage Advantage by Demographic Group, for Blue-Collar Workers, 20–65, 1979

for me to leave this job and find another one that's comparable? and (2) How badly do I want to leave this job in the first place? This formulation of the turnover decision, called the March and Simon model,[25] views turnover as functions of both ease of leaving and desirability of leaving. If a union job pays higher wages and benefits than do other jobs in the local area or industry, the worker may not have an easy job finding a comparable job if he or she quits. In addition, if the union is able to provide a better working experience at the workplace than the worker might experience at a nonunion shop, or if the union is able to diffuse the tensions of the workplace, then the desirability of leaving may be further reduced at a union place of employment.

Job Attitudes

Whether unions have a positive or negative effect on workers' attitudes is an interesting question. In the discussion on turnover we could speak with conviction on the topic of ease of leaving because we knew fairly well that unions raise wages above the level of nonunion firms. The question of workers' attitudes, however, is open.

The research in the field shows that union members report themselves as *less satisfied* with their jobs than do nonunion workers. One interesting finding of job attitude surveys is that although union workers report themselves less satisfied than nonunion workers,[26] their turnover rates are still lower. A number of explanations have been offered for this paradox. The March and Simon model may give the answer: the ease of leaving factor outweighs the desirability of leaving factor. Another explanation is that union members see themselves as *expected* to criticize management and to constantly agitate and demand changes in the employment relationship.[27]

By breaking down the general attitudes of workers into facets of satisfaction, we can better understand what causes workers to feel dissatisfied. In his *Collective Bargaining and Industrial Relations* (1980), Thomas Kochan provides data on union workers' attitudes by facet (or component) of job satisfaction. The Kochan analysis of the data reveals that union workers are generally positive about the "bread and butter" aspects of their jobs but are generally negative about satisfaction with their supervisors, with promotion prospects, with job content, and with the adequacy of resources and information necessary to do the job.[28] It may be that workers in a union job are subjected to different stresses than are workers in a nonunion job. It may be, for example, that supervisors push workers harder and expect more of them in a union than in a nonunion shop. Given the significant wage premium given to union workers, it would not be surprising to find that supervisors expect more of them. In addition, it may be that workers are expressing dissatisfaction with the promotion system because the labor agreement allows promotion only for senior employees or limits promotion possibilities to a department-by-department line of progression. These answers are tentative and partial, but they may help gain some insight into the paradox of the partially satisfied, partially unsatisfied union worker. It is interesting to note as well that the vast majority of unionized workers (over 75 percent) report themselves as being generally satisfied with their unions.[29]

Productivity

Most people would unhesitatingly speculate that unions have a negative effect on overall productivity of organizations. Interestingly, research results show just the opposite — that union firms in general show higher levels of productivity per worker hour than comparable non-union firms. The results vary by industry and over time, from 15 to 25 percent in manufacturing, 21 to 28 percent in construction, 6 to 8 percent in cement production, and −14 to −18 percent in coal mining.[30]

There are a number of factors that can explain this general increase in productivity of union over nonunion firms. One that comes immediately to mind is the effect of unions on turnover. If union workers have longer job tenure they have more job experience and they may be more productive overall. The stability of the union work group may contribute to increased productivity. In addition, it may be that the quality (ability) of the union work group is higher because higher paying union firms are able to attract the very best workers in an area. Additionally, it may be that union workers are more skilled than nonunion workers because of skills acquired by the union workers through union apprenticeship programs. It may be that union employers are more likely to substitute capital (machinery) for expensive union labor in an attempt to save money, and to increase productivity in order to stay competitive. Finally, it may be that union workers are more productive than nonunion workers because of the closer and more positive relationship between workers and employers in an organized enterprise.[31] Whatever the reason, the research on union effects on productivity offers interesting and valuable evidence on the nature of the employment relationship at the union firm.

Profits

The research evidence on this topic tends to reinforce the conventional wisdom of the public. Research on the profitability of union versus nonunion firms consistently shows that union firms have lower levels of profitability than do nonunion firms. The magnitude of the effect is quite large in some cases, ranging from −9 to −32 percent depending on the industry studied, the time period used, and the definition of profit employed. Additional information reveals that stock prices fall on average from 2.7 to 3.8 percent as the result of a successful union organizing campaign conducted at a company.[32] The results from the profitability studies show that the effect of unions on profits is greater for highly concentrated industries (oligopolized industries) than for less centralized competitive industries. Indeed, the argument can be made that unionism has the effect of reducing profits to the level they should have been in a competitive market anyway. Again, no matter what rationale one wants to give for the finding, the results rather consistently show a negative relationship between unionization and measures of corporate profits.

Summary

At the beginning of this chapter, the concept of the theory of the labor agreement was introduced and discussed. In the middle section, the components of the labor agreement were identified and discussed in some detail. Finally, in the last section an investigation was made of the effect that bargaining has had on outcomes of importance to the organization such as wages, fringe benefits, turnover, job attitudes, productivity, and profits.

Discussion Questions

1. To what extent is a labor agreement a contract? To what extent does it differ from a traditional commercial contract? How would the collective bargaining process be changed if the courts treated the labor agreement like any other commercial contract?
2. What does the employer "get out" of the collective bargaining process and the labor agreement? Is the collective agreement nothing more than a limitation on management's right to manage?
3. What do you see as the advantages and disadvantages of a promotion system based on seniority? What are the advantages and disadvantages of a merit-based system? How do you think the opinions of older workers may differ from those of younger workers on this issue?
4. It's easy to see why the management rights clause in the agreement is important to management. Why might the management rights clause be important to the union? Are there some aspects of running the business that the union would prefer not to become involved with? Which aspects? How might this differ from industry to industry?
5. How did you react to the research findings that showed that union workers are more productive than nonunion workers? Can you think of industries or particular workplaces where this would not be true? Give examples of what you feel are inefficiencies fostered by unions. Give examples of contributions to productivity that unions have been responsible for.
6. Why do you think unionized workers have lower levels of job satisfaction than nonunion workers? How might this vary from industry to industry or over time?

Notes

[1] National Labor Relations Act (as amended), section 301(a).
[2] Thomas Kochan, *Collective Bargaining and Industrial Relations* (Homewood, IL: Irwin, 1980) p. 85.

[3]Bureau of National Affairs, *The 1985 Calendar of Negotiations* (Washington, DC, 1984).

[4]Harry Millis and Royal Montgomery, *Organized Labor* (New York: McGraw-Hill, 1945), p. 93.

[5]*Hudson* vs. *Cincinnati*, N.O. & T.P. R. Co. 154 Ky 711, 154 S.W. 47 (1913), quoted in Archibald Cox, "The Legal Nature of Collective Bargaining Agreements," *Michigan Law Review* 1 (November 1958): 19.

[6]*Leahy* vs. *Smith*, 137 Cal. App. (2nd) 884, 290 P. (2d) 679 (1955), quoted in Cox, "The Legal Nature of Collective Bargaining Agreements," p. 20.

[7]*Springer* vs. *Powder Power Tool Corp.*, 220 Ore. 102, 348 P. (2d) 1112 (1960), quoted in David Feller, "A General Theory of the Collective Bargaining Agreement," *California Law Review* 6 (3) (May 1973): 663.

[8]Cox, "The Legal Nature of Collective Bargaining Agreements," p. 21.

[9]Clyde Summers, "Judicial Review of Labor Arbitration," *Buffalo Law Review* 2 (1) (1952): 17–18.

[10]Cox, "The Legal Nature of Collective Bargaining Agreements," p. 22.

[11]Ibid., pp. 23, 30.

[12]Feller, "A General Theory of the Collective Bargaining Agreement," pp. 721, 723, 761. See also John T. Dunlop, *Industrial Relations Systems* (New York: Henry Holt, 1958), Ch. 1, 2.

[13]Ibid., p. 761.

[14]Ibid., p. 773.

[15]Bureau of National Affairs, *Collective Bargaining Negotiations and Contracts* (Washington, DC, 1986), p. 65:1.

[16]Charles L. Loughran, *Negotiating a Labor Contract: A Management Handbook* (Washington, DC: BNA Books, 1984), p. 272.

[17]Bureau of National Affairs, *Collective Bargaining Negotiations and Contracts*, pp. 87:1, 87:2.

[18]Ibid., p. 87:4.

[19]See *Howard Ellis* vs. *Brotherhood of Railway, Airline and Steamship Clerks* 104 S. CT. 1883 (1982) and *Chicago Federation of Teachers* vs. *Hudson* 89 L. Ed. 2, 232 (1986).

[20]Bureau of National Affairs, *Collective Bargaining Negotiations and Contracts*, p. 75:1.

[21]Richard Freeman and James Medoff, *What Do Unions Do?* (New York: Basic Books, 1984), p. 46.

[22]Cathy Trost, "Pay Raises Shrank in Labor Pacts Set in 1986 First Half," *The Wall Street Journal*, July 29, 1986, p. 7.

[23]Freeman and Medoff, *What Do Unions Do?* pp. 64–65.

[24]Ibid., p. 96.

[25]Ibid., p. 96.

[26]Ibid., p. 140.

[27]George Borjas, "Job Satisfaction, Wages and Unions," *The Journal of Human Resources* 44 (1) (Winter 1979): 21–39.

[28]Thomas Kochan, *Collective Bargaining and Industrial Relations* (Homewood, IL: Irwin, 1980), p. 374.

[29]Freeman and Medoff, *What Do Unions Do?*, p. 143.

[30]Ibid., p. 166.

[31]Ibid., p. 177.

[32]Ibid., pp. 183, 184.

BASEBALL PLAYERS GO OUT ON STRIKE; GAMES CANCELED

By Murray Chass

The second baseball strike in five seasons officially began yesterday as 650 players stayed away from major league parks and forced the cancellation of 13 games.

"As far as games tonight," Donald Fehr, the players' chief negotiator, said yesterday, "there aren't going to be any unless something changes very quickly."

Representatives of both sides met in secrecy yesterday with the memory of a 50-day strike during the 1981 season fresh in their minds. According to a source familiar with the seven-hour meeting, the negotiators spent much of the time "brainstorming ideas." The focus of some of that discussion was salary arbitration, the procedure by which qualifying players can have disputes settled by an arbitrator and which has become the primary issue in the strike.

The source said they conducted "a deeper exploration of the salary arbitration thing than they had before" and came away perhaps with "a greater understanding of each other's position."

"My hope is we'll find a way through it," Mr. Fehr said between bargaining sessions. "We haven't found it yet. Maybe we'll find it in the next 24 hours."

Lee MacPhail, the owners' chief negotiator, had little to say as word of the strike spread. At his office, before the start of the evening negotiations, he said, "It could all fall apart in two minutes or it could last all night."

The owners' contribution to the players' benefit plan had at one time been the most difficult issue, but in recent days it had been eclipsed by salary arbitration. The owners have said they want to slow the escalation of player salaries, which have risen from an average of about $51,500 in 1976 to an average of about $360,000 this year, and they have targeted the arbitration procedure as perhaps the most troublesome factor in that escalation.

As a result, they have proposed raising the eligibility requirement from two years of major league service to three years and restricting a player in arbitration to a 100 percent raise over the previous year's salary. The current procedure is for a player and his club each to submit a salary figure, and an arbitrator hears their arguments and selects one figure or the other. He cannot pick a compromise salary. . . .

In recent days, the two sides seemed to grow even firmer in their positions, and their comments after Monday's meeting left virtually no doubt that their efforts would result in a strike. Mr. Fehr, in fact, said late Monday night that he considered the strike to be on at the conclusion of games that evening.

No Optimism Voiced

At his office yesterday afternoon, he said, "I can't say that I expect anything positive that will end the strike quickly."

Some owners seemed to indicate that as well. Emerging from a meeting of the Player Relations Committee Executive board late yesterday afternoon, John McMullen, owner of the Houston Astros, said the two sides were "making movement" on the issue of the owners' contribution to the benefit plan, but he said, "No, no way," when asked if the owners would compromise on their salary arbitration position.

Meanwhile, in San Diego, Ballard Smith, president of the Padres, said management was prepared "to lose the rest of the season" if necessary.

Chapter 12

Outcomes of Bargaining: Strikes and Industrial Conflict

Anyone involved in the field of labor relations and collective bargaining for any length of time probably will become involved in a strike or some other type of industrial conflict at some point. For many members of the public the strike is the most widely noticed and most worrisome issue in labor relations. It seems that the press is most eager to report on labor relations matters when a strike is imminent or when one has just been called. The 1985 baseball strike had been rumored for months and when it officially began it was front page news in all the major newspapers of the country, even though it lasted only two days. Even a strike involving a small number of workers will find its way onto the pages of the local newspaper or will be talked about during the local nightly news.

Why all the interest in strikes and industrial conflict? What is it about the concerted refusal to work on the part of a group of organized workers that attracts so much interest and warrants so much attention? Is there a general problem with strikes in the United States that the public should be aware of and that the government (perhaps) should deal with? What causes strikes, and what role do they play in the industrial relations system? Are there better ways to resolve differences between labor and management other than through the use of force and refusals to work? These are just a few of the issues addressed in this chapter.

The Role of the Strike in the Bargaining Process

The Bargaining Position of the Opponent

It is important to note that the strike can serve a variety of purposes. In most instances the strike is seen as an attempt on the part of unions to impose costs of disagreement on the employer, the role that strikes played in the bargaining power model discussed in Chapter 10. The longer the employer disagrees with the union, or refuses to abide by or agree with the union's position in bargaining, the greater costs the employer incurs.

The Hicks Model.   In the Hicks model of wage determination in bargaining, the strike plays the primary role of forcing the employer to accede to the union's demands by reducing the employer's resistance to the union. The strike correspondingly forces the union to reduce its demands in bargaining over time. The union's resistance to agreeing with the employer declines as the projected length of the strike necessary to force the employer to agree to a particular position increases. The concessions that the employer is willing to make to the union increase as the length of the prospective strike increases as well. In short, the union will attain large wage gains only if it is willing to strike for a long time to achieve them and if the strike can be maintained during this time, meaning that the employees are not replaced by strikebreakers, and that the employer does not relocate or go out of business. Employers will pay high wages only if forced to as a result of the long strike by the union (see Figure 12.1).

The strengths and the weaknesses of the Hicks model have been discussed in many other places and at great length. The model makes certain assumptions about the amount of information the parties possess at negotiations. The utilitarian costs and benefit analysis that Hicks envisions going on at the bargaining table probably are not nearly as precise as he would lead us to believe. It is doubtful if either side really calculates in the manner Hicks describes the costs and benefits from strikes of a particular length. The model perhaps does a better job of explaining retrospectively why a particular move was made in bargaining than in predicting for the future how the parties will move given certain demands from each party.[1]

The real strength of Hicks's model is not in predicting the level of wages as a result of strikes, however, but to demonstrate that strikes have the effect of moving the parties off established bargaining positions and closer to a point of agreement as they increase in length. This is one of the major functions of the strike — to motivate the parties to reach agreement as the costs of disagreement escalate. Unions use the strike to force the employer to move up his or her concession curve; the employer takes a strike of a particular length to force the union down its resistance curve to a point more acceptable to management than one previously demanded.

The Bargaining Range Model.   Another way to look at the role of the strike in contract negotiations is to imagine the parties entering the dispute with certain ranges of acceptable settlements. For example, the

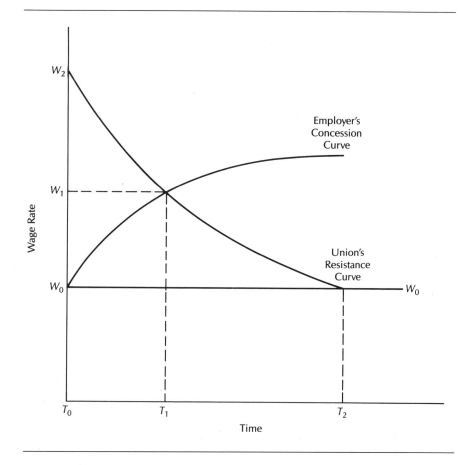

FIGURE 12-1   The Hicks Bargaining Model

employer may have the acceptable range of settlements on wages illustrated in Figure 12.2.

In this instance the employer has a bargaining range of 50 cents per hour. The employer is willing to make an initial offer in bargaining of a $5.00 per hour wage rate. The employer is willing to raise this wage rate to $5.50 per hour in negotiations but will go no higher. The union leaders also have a bargaining range in negotiations. The union may have the target wage range also illustrated in Figure 12.2, with a $7.00 per hour maximum goal and a $6.00 per hour minimum goal.

The problem that employer and union negotiators will eventually discover is that there is no overlap between the two bargaining ranges, and thus no possible agreement on wages. At this point a strike is called and as a result of the strike the parties rescale their expectations and revise their bargaining goals to the levels illustrated in Figure 12.3. The parties now do have an overlap in their bargaining ranges and a settle-

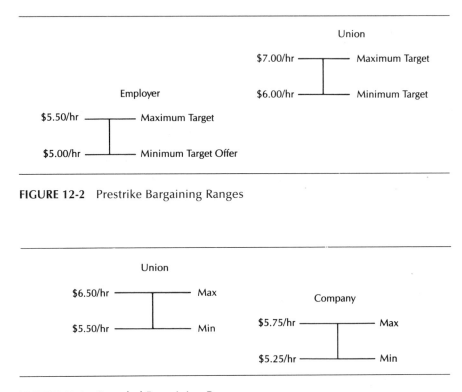

FIGURE 12-2 Prestrike Bargaining Ranges

FIGURE 12-3 Rescaled Bargaining Ranges

ment can be reached somewhere in the $5.50–$5.75 range. In this example both parties changed their target positions as a result of the strike. This is not always true in bargaining, nor, of course, is it necessary for a settlement to be reached. All that is necessary is that *one* of the parties readjust his or her target positions to overlap with the bargaining range of the opponent.

The Locus of Power

Not all strikes are used to move an opposing party into or out of a bargaining range. Some strikes are called over issues that are not really about wages but are about the change of the current bargaining relationship and the power balance in that relationship. Dunlop gives several examples of strikes to change the structure of bargaining from a local single-employer structure to a multiemployer structure or from local level bargaining to national level bargaining.[2] The point here is that the parties may not be in a dispute about wages at all. At the extreme, the strike may be provoked by the employer in the hope that as a result of the strike the employer can become free of the union and of union workers. After a strike is called, the employer is free to hire replacements for the strikers. In some cases employees vote to decertify the union — to rescind the union's right to represent the employees — when a strike has continued for a long time.[3]

Related to this may be strikes that are called for the purpose of escalating the level at which the strike is settled. In some industries, particularly railroads or airlines or national defense industries, the strike brings the government into the process as a participant. Either party may use the presence of the government as a power lever in bargaining. Without the strike no crisis would have been precipitated and the intervention of the government into the dispute would have been unnecessary.

The Relationship Between the Negotiators and Their Own Constituents

Not all strikes are called for the purpose of moving the other party toward agreement. Some strikes are called for political purposes on the part of negotiators, particularly union negotiators.[4] Strikes in some instances can be seen as an example of mass protest. The leader of a mass protest strike acquires a certain stature, a certain heroic standing among his or her fellows. Some union leaders use the strike to demonstrate to their members that they are brave and courageous negotiators and that they are not afraid to use the power that their position gives them if necessary. The coal strike of 1974 was the first national negotiations conducted by Arnold Miller, the newly elected president of the Mineworkers' Union. The long auto strike of 1970 was led by Leonard Woodcock, a man who assumed the presidency of the United Automobile Workers (UAW) in 1970 after Walter Reuther's death in an airplane accident. Union leaders, like national leaders, must sometimes exercise their power to show their constituents the power and force of their convictions and resolve.

A second component of the political strike is to force union members to rescale unrealistic demands. A strike of even a short duration may serve to illustrate to the members the seriousness of the company's position in bargaining and may lead to a reassessment of certain demands. An astute union leader can use the strike in such a way that the members see compromise in negotiations as "rational"; prior to the strike such a compromise may have been viewed as a "sellout."

Government Policy

The strike to change government policy is mostly used among public employees.[5] An early and successful example was the Postal strike of 1970. This strike forced the government to reconstitute the Postal Service as a quasi-private employer under the Postal Service Reorganization Act of 1970 and changed the status of postal workers from government employees to employees of a quasi-private enterprise covered by the National Labor Relations Act. The main effect of the strike was to give postal employees the right to negotiate over wages — a right they never enjoyed as federal government employees. The Professional Air

Traffic Controllers strike of 1981 can also be seen as an attempt (a failed one) to force the government to deal with air traffic controllers as a group not subject to the rules governing other federal employees. Many strikes of municipal employees are called to force a change in the nature of bargaining or a change in the rules governing the bargaining process. In addition, strikes such as these at the municipal level may be called to escalate the dispute to a level where the mayor, the city council, or even the governor become involved in the dispute.

Strike Strategy

The strike is a tactical weapon in collective bargaining; it is a method of imposing the costs of disagreement on management or on the union and thus is an instrument of bargaining power. Nonetheless, both labor and management need to exercise great caution in contemplating a strike. As discussed earlier, strikes can be very costly for everyone involved. Wages and revenue are lost, customers and jobs may be lost, morale may deteriorate, and bitterness between the parties may linger on for years following the strike. Strikes sometimes involve violence or property damage, and the long-term litigation that accompanies these issues may linger for years, adding to the costs of the strike. Considering all that is involved, some observers conclude that "no one wins a strike"; this may or may not be true, depending on the situation. What is true, however, is that careful consideration must be given to its costs and benefits before a strike begins.

Management

Anyone who has had much experience in the practice of collective bargaining knows that a strike is a possibility in almost any negotiation in the private sector. As the negotiations proceed through the stages of bargaining, expectations about the probability of the strike begin to form in the minds of negotiators on both sides of the bargaining table. Of course, the union has something of a tactical advantage concerning the strike issue because it is the union that makes the decision to strike — not management. It is unusual, however, that an experienced management negotiator is caught totally off guard by a strike.

One of the first issues that management has to consider involves the question of whether or not to try to operate the facility during the strike. Operations during the strike will produce some revenue for the organization and will enable the organization to supply some of its customers with the product or service. It will also demonstrate to the union the employer's determination to operate even in the face of the strike and may cause the union to reevaluate the costs of disagreement with the employer.

In any event, when a strike threat becomes a very real possibility the employer will have to take several immediate actions. First, the employer will have to notify customers that a strike is a possibility and advise them to purchase advance supplies of the product or to make alternative arrangements to purchase the product elsewhere. This will need to be done whether or not the employer tries to operate the facility during the strike. Of course, if the decision is made to continue operations, arrangements need to be made to bring in employees to work during the strike. Some organizations try to operate with managers and supervisors and perhaps members of the sales staff during the strike. Sometimes employees who work during a strike eat their meals at the workplace and sleep there at night rather than cross the picket line each day.

While the strike is in progress, and particularly if the employer is operating during the strike, there is a need for increased security around the workplace. The employer may consider making arrangements to hire more security personnel during the strike, perhaps even using the services of a security agency that specializes in this type of work. Sometimes movie or video cameras are used to document and record any instances of strike-related violence. This information may be of use in subsequent poststrike litigation. The employer wants to make sure that legal counsel is available at immediate notice to handle any legal issues that may arise during the strike. The employer wants also to keep in touch with the employees during the strike through mailed communications explaining to individual employees the employer's position in the dispute and explaining to employees their rights and possible losses during the strike as well.

In planning for the strike, the employer should pay careful attention to the firm's losses and gains as a result of the strike. In some cases the employer saves money during a strike. In a recent factfinding hearing conducted by the author in a small school district in Ohio, the school district negotiator dared the union to strike. "Go ahead, make my day," he taunted the union; the strike would mean that the school board would not have to pay the teachers' salaries, which averaged about $100 per day (the average teacher made about $18,000 for a 180-day school year). The school board had already made arrangements to replace all striking teachers (12 in the bargaining unit) with substitutes who were paid $35 per day and who received no benefits. The school district stood to save almost $4,000 a week in wage costs for every week the teachers were on strike. The negotiator remarked at the hearing, "A three-week strike will enable us to balance our budget — this is almost as good as passing a bond issue." Needless to say, the union did not go on strike in this district.

Few employers save money during a strike, however. Most lose money, sometimes a great deal of it. Before allowing the union to break off negotiations and take the employees out on strike the employer needs to ask himself or herself, How much revenue will be lost during the strike? How much will be saved by allowing the union to strike? For example, suppose that a union and an employer are 20¢ per hour apart in negotiating over wages, and the strike deadline is imminent. The bargaining unit consists of 100 production employees who produce a product that generates $80,000 worth of corporate earnings (in excess of costs) to the employer per week. The employer expects the strike to last two weeks and the union to capitulate and accept the employer's offer after that period, if the employer holds firm to the final offer made in negotiations. The calculation might go roughly like this.

Difference in wage demands	20¢ per hour
Number of working hours in a full year	2,080 hours
Number of employees	100
Net savings per year	$ 41,600
Life of the proposed contract	3 years
Savings over the life of the contract in wages	$124,800
Additional savings because of decreased social security and pension contributions (tied to annual savings)	10% of $124,800 =$ 12,480
Total savings in wages	$137,280
Total lost revenue due to a two-week strike	$160,000
Net return (or loss) from a two-week strike	($ 22,720)

In this case the employer would lose money from the strike. However, what if the employer was able to keep operating during the strike and to produce half of what would normally be produced during this period ($80,000 instead of $160,000)? Then the employer comes out ahead by $57,280. What if the strike drags on for four weeks instead of two and the employer was able to produce only 25 percent of normal production during the strike? Then the employer loses $102,720. What if the strike is four weeks long, the employer produces only 25 percent of normal production, and in the end the employer capitulates and agrees to the 20¢ per hour wage raise? Then the employer loses $240,000 that he or she would not have had to lose by agreeing with the union's wage demand in negotiations. The assumptions that are made and the gain and loss figures are all just guesses, but these are the kinds of calculation management must make in deciding on a strike strategy.

The Union

The union also has a strike strategy and must think about potential gains and losses before calling the members out on strike. For the union, the losses from the strike are the wages lost by the members, the dues money lost by the union (most unions do not collect dues money from strikers) and the strike benefits that may be paid to the members (maybe $40 or $50 per week). The loss to the union and its members is not quite so easy to calculate as is the loss to the employer. The union must consider its ability to actually shut down the employer's operations. In this example, if the union is not able to mount an effective picketing effort and the employer produces at 75 percent of the prestrike level, the employer's payoff from the strike would increase dramatically. Likewise, if the strike continues for very long the union knows that members will begin to defect and to cross the picket line, further increasing the revenue generated by the employer and further eroding the union's chances of winning the 20¢-per-hour wage raise. Alternatively, if the union's picket line is effective in keeping everyone out of the workplace and the employer is shut down entirely, the employer's losses will mount day by day and the union may achieve victory on this issue earlier than it had expected.

In short, the costs and benefits of striking and strike strategy to the union depend largely upon the union's ability to shut down the employer's operations in most situations. If the union leader knows that he or she has the support of the members, that the strike will inflict losses on the employer, and that the issue being negotiated is one that is within the employer's ability to pay, then the strike becomes a viable option. If, on the other hand, the prospects for success do not look as good and the prospects for failure are high, then the strike weapon should be reserved for a more propitious time.

Types of Strike and Forms of Industrial Conflict

Economic Strike

Under section 7 of the National Labor Relations Act (NLRA) employees are protected when they engage in concerted activities in support of collective bargaining. A strike was intended by Congress to be one of these types of concerted activities that was protected under the NLRA. The provisions of the NLRA, however, make it clear that not all strike activity is protected; there are some types of strike that are prohibited under the statutes. For example, strikes for the purpose of forcing an employer to recognize a union when another union already represents the employees are generally outlawed under section 8(b)(7) of the NLRA. Strikes among federal government employees were outlawed under section 305 of the Taft-Hartley Act.[6] Not only are certain strikes prohibited, but even legal strikes are regulated under the provisions of the NLRA. For example, before a labor organization can engage in a strike against an employer, it is required under the NLRA to give the employer 60 days' advance notice before the strike can begin. In addition, the union is required to give the Federal Mediation and Conciliation Service (FMCS) 30 days' notice before the strike begins. In the health care industry, the union must give a 90-day advance notice of a strike to the employer and a 60-day advance notice to the FMCS.

Even when the union has given its advance notice to the employer, however, it may not use its strike weapon for just any reason. According to section 8 of the NLRA, a strike is a protected act of employees only when it is used in connection with:

> any controversy concerning terms, tenure or conditions of employment, or concerning the association or representation of persons in negotiating, fixing, maintaining, changing, or seeking to arrange terms or conditions of employment, regardless of whether the disputants stand in the proximate relation of employer and employee.

This language limits the strike to issues involving bargaining issues usually categorized as the mandatory subjects of bargaining. When a labor dispute arises from these mandatory subjects of bargaining (wages, hours, and other terms and conditions of employment) and when a labor organization has given the requisite advance notice to the employer and the FMCS, then the strike becomes a protected activity under the NLRA. Strikers who enjoy such protections are called *economic strikers*.

Under the judicial interpretations of the NLRA, economic strikers are entitled to reinstatement by the employer once the strike has ended, even if it ended in defeat for the union. The employer has the right to replace economic strikers during the strike and even has the right to make these replacements permanent. If the economic striker has not been replaced, he or she has the right to apply for reemployment once the strike ends. The employer may not fire an employee or discriminate against the employee in subsequent employment simply because he or she has participated in an economic strike. In addition, no matter what the outcome of the strike, economic strikers retain the right to vote in any election supervised by the National Labor Relations Board (NLRB) at their former workplace within 12 months of the beginning of the strike.

The Unfair Labor Practice Strike

The Employer. It is possible that events that develop during the strike may change the nature of the strike. For example, suppose that after a legal economic strike began, the employer began engaging in unfair labor practices. The employer may have made threats to the strikers or may have taken other actions to discourage the union members' continued participation in the strike. The key point here is that the commission of unfair labor practices on the part of the employer transforms the economic strike into an employer unfair labor practice strike.[7] An employer unfair labor practice strike can also be called by the union to protest the commission of unfair labor practices by the employer during bargaining.

Workers who are involved in an employer unfair labor practice strike are entitled to reinstatement to their former jobs once an offer to return to work has been made to the employer. Furthermore, replacements hired to take the jobs of employer unfair labor practice strikers must be discharged to give the strikers back their old jobs. Importantly, employer unfair labor practice strikers are entitled to vote in all NLRB elections held at the worksite; replacements for these strikers are not so entitled.

The Union. In much the same way that a legal economic strike can be turned into an employer unfair labor practice strike by employer actions, an economic strike can be turned into a union unfair labor practice strike by the actions of a union, such as striking over nonmandatory items of bargaining or striking in advance of the 60-day notice to the employer.

Union unfair labor practice strikers lose almost all the protections given strikers under the NLRA. Union unfair labor practice strikers are not entitled to reinstatement once the strike is concluded or at any time during the course of the strike. In addition, union unfair labor practice strikers may lose their status as employees under the NLRA and may lose their right to vote in subsequent NLRB elections called at their former place of employment.

The Wildcat Strike. A wildcat strike is a strike called during the term of an existing labor agreement and is usually a strike unplanned by official union leaders. Wildcat strikes are almost always strikes called to protest some act of management or in support of worker grievances and are usually spontaneous work stoppages.[8] One industry that has had a large number of wildcat strikes in recent years is the coal mining industry.[9] Wildcat strikes are usually unprotected strikes under the NLRA and are usually violations of a collective bargaining agreement's no-strike clause as well.

When wildcat strikes violate the agreement the employer may legally discharge the strikers and if the local union participated in the strike or prolonged the strike the employer can sue the local union for damages incurred in the strike under section 301(a) of the NLRA. Of course, if the employer's actions that precipitated the strike were unfair labor practices, then it is possible that the strikers may be protected from discharge as employer unfair labor practice strikers.[10] Finally, the employer may reinstate wildcat strikers to their former jobs with a promise not to retaliate against anyone just to get the workers back on the job. There is no obligation or requirement that the employer discipline wildcat strikers.

The Sympathy Strike. A sympathy strike is a strike that is called by one union in support of a strike called by another union. A common form is a concerted refusal by one group of workers to cross the picket line set up by another group of workers. Generally speaking, workers have a right under section 7 of the NLRA to honor the picket line set up by workers in another union. If the parties have negotiated a clause in their labor agreement that prohibits employees from engaging in sympathetic strike action, however, this activity would not be protected.[11]

The employer may temporarily replace his or her employees who refuse to cross a picket line in order to carry on his or her own legitimate business interests.[12] A later NLRB ruling states that an employer may even have the right to permanently replace employees who engage in a sympathy strike.[13] The sympathy strike would be protected if the dispute that precipitated the sympathy strike in the first place was not subject to the grievance procedure, however.[14]

The Jurisdictional Dispute. A jurisdictional dispute is a dispute or a strike involving a disagreement between two unions as to whose members should do a particular type of work.[15] Jurisdictional disputes are most common in the construction industry and frequently involve a dispute over the issue of work assignment. Jurisdictional disputes can arise in a variety of ways. For example, if one local union has jurisdiction over work done on one side of a river and another local union has jurisdiction on the other side, who has the right to perform work on dams and bridges that cross the river? If carpenters have always done the work of building and taking down wooden forms for cement work, what might happen if the contractors began using metal forms that require the skills of an iron worker to build and tear down? Under section 8(b)(4)(D) of the NLRA jurisdictional strikes are generally illegal. The act defines a jurisdictional dispute as one whose object is:

> forcing or requiring any employer to assign particular work to employees in a particular labor organization or in a particular trade, craft, or class rather than to employees in another labor organization or in another trade, craft or class. . . .

Under section 10(k) of the NLRA, the NLRB has the power to resolve jurisdictional disputes that arise between two unions through an NLRB jurisdictional disputes hearing. The NLRB will also allow the parties to resolve the dispute themselves; a common method of voluntary adjustment in the construction industry prior to 1981 was for labor and management to submit their dispute to the Impartial Jurisdictional Disputes Board, maintained jointly by the AFL–CIO and the contractor associations. Dissatisfaction with the decisions of the Impartial Jurisdictional Disputes Board by both labor and management led to the board's demise in June of 1981. The NLRB will allow this method of resolution to solve the dispute if all three parties to the dispute (both unions and the employer) agree to be bound by the decision of the impartial board. If all parties do not agree to the impartial board's settlement of the dispute, then the NLRB will rule on the dispute. In any case, strikes over jurisdictional issues are unfair labor practices and are illegal; unions may be sued for damages for engaging in this type of strike.

The National Emergency Strike. A national emergency strike is one whose existence may have the effect of imperiling the safety or health of the citizens of the United States. The provision for dealing with national emergency strikes is found in sections 206–210 of the National Labor Relations Act (added by the Taft-Hartley Act of 1947). Under the national emergency strike procedure the president of the United States is empowered to appoint a board of inquiry to study the facts of the dispute and to make a report to the president. If in his or her opinion a strike has the potential to cause a national emergency, the president may then ask the attorney general of the United States to seek an injunction in federal court halting the dispute for 80 days. If the injunction is issued, the parties are then obligated to bargain for a 60-day period of time to resolve their dispute. If the parties are not successful in resolving their differences during this time, then the board of inquiry is required to summarize the final positions of the parties and to make a report to the president and the public.

The NLRB is required to conduct a poll among the striking employees asking them to accept or reject the employer's final offer at the close of the 60-day negotiating period. This poll takes no more than 15 days to conduct. Finally, the NLRB is given 5 days to count the ballots and to certify the results to the attorney general. If the employees accept the final offer of the employer in the poll, the strike is settled; if the employees reject the employer's final offer, the strike resumes.

The national emergency strike procedure has been used 35 times since the passage of the Taft-Hartley Act in 1947; at this writing it has not been used since 1978, when a federal judge refused to issue an injunction halting the coal strike of 1977–1978.

The topic of national emergency strikes and procedures to deal with them raises some controversy among experts in the field of labor–management relations. The consensus among those who have studied the problem in the greatest depth is that the national emergency strike procedure under the NLRA is open to some criticism, which may be very briefly summarized as follows.[16]

> The injunction used to stop strikes is a one-sided weapon. Forcing workers to return to work undermines the power of the strike and allows the employer to resume production for 60 days.

The injunction undermines the collective bargaining process because it relieves the employer and the union from the pressures
of the strike during the 60-day bargaining period.

The Taft-Hartley Act procedure does not stop strikes or solve the
problems that cause them. Once the 80-day cooling off period is
over, the parties are free to resume their strike or lockout.

The Taft-Hartley procedures are too predictable and too inflexible.
There is no possibility to alter the procedure to fit the needs of
the parties or the facts of a particular dispute.

The board of inquiry is given too passive a role in the dispute procedure. The board should have the power to recommend how to
solve the dispute.

Whatever the value of the national emergency disputes procedure under the NLRA, it is true that this process does not work very well to stop
strikes after they begin, or even to provide an alternative to them before
they begin. The national emergency strike procedure begins only after
a strike has started — a strike in a key, vital industry that arguably will
have the effect of threatening the safety and welfare of the citizens of
the United States. A later section of this chapter discusses some alternative approaches to dispute resolution that can be undertaken before
a strike begins or even as an alternative to a strike.

Measures of Strike Activity

Strike Frequency

There are a number of ways to measure strike activity, and one of the
keys to understanding the nature of strikes and industrial conflict lies
in understanding how strike activity is measured. In the United States
the Bureau of Labor Statistics (BLS, a division of the Department of
Labor) has been compiling strike statistics for almost 50 years. One index of strike activity used by the BLS involves counting the number of
strikes and is called the *frequency of strikes*. It can be seen from Table
12.1 and Figure 12.4 that the frequency of strike activity in the United
States has varied considerably over the past 50 years. For example, in
about half of the years since 1930, the number of strikes per year has
been at the level of 4,000 or higher. In some years, however, the level is
much lower (1930–1936). Contrastingly, in some years it has been much
higher than this level; in the period 1968–1977, for example, there were
over 5,000 strikes a year every year. The issues involved in strikes are
listed in Table 12.2.

Some care must be exercised in looking at the number of strikes every
year and interpreting this as a measure of overall strike activity. The
number of strikes every year seems to overstate the strike problem. Con-

TABLE 12-1 Work Stoppages Involving Six Workers or More, 1930–81[1] (workers and days idle in thousands)

Year	Stoppages Beginning in Year				Days Idle During Year		
	Number	Average Duration (calendar days)[2]	Workers Involved				
			Number (thousands)	Percentage of Total Employed[3]	Number (thousands)	Percentage of Estimated Total Working Time	Per Worker Involved
1930	637	22.3	183	0.8	3,320	([4])	18.1
1931	810	18.8	342	1.6	6,890	([4])	20.2
1932	841	19.6	324	1.8	10,500	([4])	32.4
1933	1,695	16.9	1,170	6.3	16,900	([4])	14.4
1934	1,856	19.5	1,470	7.2	19,600	([4])	13.4
1935	2,014	23.8	1,120	5.2	15,500	([4])	13.8
1936	2,172	23.3	789	3.1	13,900	([4])	17.6
1937	4,740	20.3	1,860	7.2	28,400	([4])	15.3
1938	2,772	23.6	688	2.8	9,150	([4])	13.3
1939	2,613	23.4	1,170	3.5	17,800	0.21	15.2
1940	2,508	20.9	577	1.7	6,700	.08	11.6
1941	4,288	18.3	2,360	6.1	23,000	.23	9.8
1942	2,968	11.7	840	2.0	4,180	.04	5.0
1943	3,752	5.0	1,980	4.6	13,500	.10	6.8
1944	4,956	5.6	2,120	4.8	8,720	.07	4.1
1945	4,750	9.9	3,470	8.2	38,000	.31	11.0
1946	4,985	24.2	4,600	10.5	116,000	1.04	25.2
1947	3,693	25.6	2,170	4.7	34,600	.30	15.9
1948	3,419	21.8	1,960	4.2	34,100	.28	17.4
1949	3,606	22.5	3,030	6.7	50,500	.44	16.7
1950	4,843	19.2	2,410	5.1	38,800	.33	16.1
1951	4,737	17.4	2,220	4.5	22,900	.18	10.3
1952	5,117	19.6	3,540	7.3	59,100	.48	16.7
1953	5,091	20.3	2,400	4.7	28,300	.22	11.8
1954	3,468	22.5	1,530	3.1	22,600	.18	14.7
1955	4,320	18.5	2,650	5.2	28,200	.22	10.7
1956	3,825	18.9	1,900	3.6	33,100	.24	17.4
1957	3,673	19.2	1,390	2.6	16,500	.12	11.4
1958	3,694	19.7	2,060	3.9	23,900	.18	11.6
1959	3,708	24.6	1,880	3.3	69,000	.50	36.7
1960	3,333	23.4	1,320	2.4	19,100	.14	14.5
1961	3,367	23.7	1,450	2.6	16,300	.11	11.2
1962	3,614	24.6	1,230	2.2	18,600	.13	15.0
1963	3,362	23.0	941	1.1	16,100	.11	17.1
1964	3,655	22.9	1,640	2.7	22,900	.15	14.0
1965	3,963	25.0	1,550	2.5	23,300	.15	15.1
1966	4,405	22.2	1,960	3.0	25,400	.15	12.9
1967	4,595	22.8	2,870	4.3	42,100	.25	14.7
1968	5,045	24.5	2,649	3.8	49,018	.28	18.5
1969	5,700	22.5	2,481	3.5	42,869	.24	17.3
1970	5,716	25.0	3,305	4.7	66,414	.37	20.1
1971	5,138	27.0	3,280	4.5	47,589	.26	14.5

(continued)

TABLE 12-1 *(continued)*

| | | | Stoppages Beginning in Year | | | Days Idle During Year | |
| | | | Workers Involved | | | | |
Year	Number	Average Duration (calendar days)[2]	Number (thousands)	Percentage of Total Employed[3]	Number (thousands)	Percentage of Estimated Total Working Time[3]	Per Worker Involved
1972	5,010	24.0	1,714	2.3	27,063	.15	15.8
1973	5,353	24.0	2,251	2.9	27,948	.14	12.4
1974	6,074	27.1	2,778	3.5	47,991	.24	17.3
1975	5,031	26.8	1,746	2.2	31,237	.16	17.9
1976	5,648	28.0	2,420	3.0	37,859	.19	15.6
1977	5,506	29.3	2,040	2.4	35,822	.17	17.6
1978	4,230	33.2	1,623	1.9	36,922	.17	22.8
1979	4,827	32.1	1,727	1.9	34,754	.15	20.1
1980	3,885	35.4	1,366	1.5	33,289	.14	24.4
1981	2,568	([4])	1,081	1.2	24,730	.11	22.9

[1]The number of stoppages and workers relate to those stoppages beginning in the year; average duration relates to stoppages ending in the year. Days of idleness includes all stoppages in effect. In these tables, workers are counted more than once if they were involved in more than 1 stoppage during the year.

[2]Figures are simple averages; each stoppage is given equal weight regardless of its size.

[3]Agricultural and government employees are included in the total employed and total working time, private household, forestry, and fishery employees are excluded. An explanation of the measurement of idleness as a percentage of the total employed labor force and of the total time worked found in "Total Economy Measure of Strike Idleness," *Monthly Labor Review,* October 1968.

[4]No information.

Source: Handbook of Labor Statistics, U.S. Department of Labor, Washington, DC, 1983, p. 380.

sider, for example, that there are approximately 190,000 labor agreements currently in effect in the United States, and that on average 63,000 or so of these agreements are renegotiated every year (most agreements are three years in duration). A frequency rate of 5,000 would mean that only about 8 percent of the agreements renegotiated each year resulted in strikes; a frequency rate of 4,000, only about 6 percent. Even these figures are overstated somewhat, because a certain number of disputes every year are not over issues relating to the renegotiation of an agreement but are rather over issues relating to interunion rivalry (jurisdictional disputes), or are strikes called during the term of the agreement to protest some action of the employer (wildcat strikes) or are in support of a strike called by another group of union employees (sympathy strikes). All things considered, probably no more than 5–6 percent of the labor agreements that are renegotiated every year involve the use of the strike. In the vast majority of cases (in excess of 90 percent) labor and management renegotiate the labor agreement without resorting to the strike.

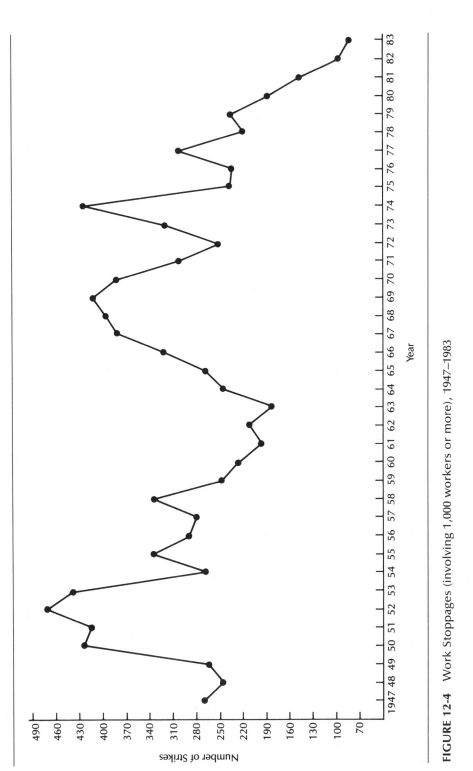

FIGURE 12-4   Work Stoppages (involving 1,000 workers or more), 1947–1983

TABLE 12-2   Percentage of Strikes (percentage of workers involved in strikes) by Major Issue, 1969–1981

Issue	1969	1970	1971	1972	1973	1974	1975	1976	1977	1978	1979	1980	1981
1. Wage changes	49.6	49.9	50.6	40.3	48.1	59.9	52.1	50.6	56.9	65.0	66.1	66.9	66.6
	(50.9)	(55.8)	(65.2)	(40.4)	(50.1)	(70.3)	(46.4)	(50.0)	(44.1)	(51.5)	(64.5)	(62.4)	(69.7)
2. Benefits	1.2	1.0	.8	1.8	1.5	1.2	1.1	.9	1.4	1.5	1.3	2.0	2.1
	(.6)	(1.9)	(2.4)	(2.3)	(1.9)	(1.4)	(1.3)	(.4)	(1.1)	(1.2)	(2.7)	(1.1)	(2.9)
3. Wage adjustments	5.1	3.8	3.1	5.0	3.4	2.4	2.5	2.5	2.6	3.0	2.1	1.3	1.3
	(5.8)	(7.2)	(2.9)	(3.7)	(3.7)	(2.4)	(2.2)	(2.1)	(3.2)	(3.7)	(2.0)	(3.1)	(.6)
4. Hours	.1	.1	.1	.1	.1	.1	.1	.1	.3	.4	.1	.2	.3
	—	—	—	—	—	(.3)	—	(.1)	(.1)	(.3)	(.1)	(.1)	(.1)
5. Other	1.5	1.9	2.3	1.9	1.7	1.6	1.5	2.5	5.0	4.7	5.8	5.3	4.7
	(.6)	(11.5)	(1.5)	(1.6)	(2.3)	(3.1)	(1.4)	(.8)	(3.5)	(2.5)	(3.2)	(2.6)	(2.0)
6. Union organization and security	10.4	10.3	9.4	10.2	8.3	5.7	5.3	5.8	4.6	6.4	5.2	5.3	6.6
	(10.1)	(3.2)	(5.4)	(5.7)	(5.2)	(1.7)	(5.3)	(5.2)	(2.0)	(2.4)	(2.8)	(2.6)	(2.9)
7. Job security	3.3	3.0	4.1	4.6	4.9	4.1	5.1	5.6	3.8	3.0	3.5	5.2	5.1
	(3.1)	(1.6)	(3.2)	(5.8)	(7.7)	(3.6)	(11.8)	(16.6)	(4.9)	(23.9)	(6.3)	(14.7)	(10.6)
8. Plant administration	15.5	16.1	17.6	23.3	22.7	18.4	22.7	22.8	18.2	12.0	12.8	9.9	10.8
	(20.7)	(12.1)	(15.8)	(31.7)	(23.8)	(13.5)	(24.7)	(20.2)	(34.2)	(10.6)	(15.4)	(10.4)	(9.4)
9. Other working conditions	4.0	3.1	3.0	4.3	2.7	1.5	2.7	3.3	2.5	1.3	1.2	1.4	1.1
	(4.0)	(1.8)	(1.2)	(3.6)	(1.7)	(1.0)	(2.3)	(2.1)	(3.1)	(1.9)	(.9)	(1.1)	(1.1)
10. Interunion matters	8.8	9.9	8.1	7.9	6.5	4.0	6.3	5.0	4.5	2.4	1.6	1.7	1.2
	(4.1)	(4.5)	(2.2)	(5.1)	(3.5)	(2.7)	(4.5)	(2.2)	(3.8)	(2.0)	(1.9)	(1.7)	(.8)
11. Not reported	.4	1.0	1.0	.6	1.2	1.1	.6	.8	.2	.3	.4	.8	.2
	(.1)	(.4)	(.1)	(.2)	(.3)	(.2)	(.1)	(.1)	—	(.1)	(.1)	(.2)	—

Source: Handbook of Labor Statistics, U.S. Department of Labor, Washington, DC, 1983, p. 385.

Number of Workers Involved

A second measure of strike activity is the number of workers involved in strikes. The number of workers involved in a strike is a measure of the impact of that strike on the union labor force. It is entirely possible that a small number of strikes can involve a large number of people and that only by knowing the amount of labor force involvement can one really measure the size of the strike. The data in Table 12.1 give a measure of the involvement of workers in strikes for the period 1930–1981; it can be seen that the number of workers involved in strikes varies widely, just as the number of strikes per year varies. In only 6 of the past 50 years have there been 3 million or more workers involved in strikes. In most years involvement was between 1,500,000 and 2,500,000 workers per year.

The data in Table 12.1 show that in most years less than 5 percent of the labor force is involved in strikes in any given year. Since 1978 the involvement figure has been quite low, ranging from 1.2 percent of the labor force in 1981 to 1.9 percent in 1978. Even if we were to look at involvement as a percentage of the union labor force only, we would find that in a year like 1980, for example, only about 6 percent of the union labor force was involved in strikes (1,366,000 strikers out of a labor force of 24 million union workers). This again indicates that the vast majority of workers (98 percent) in the economy as a whole was not affected by strikes and that the vast majority of even union workers was not affected by strikes (94 percent). The point remains that most people in the total labor force or even the union labor force are not affected by strikes each year.

Time Lost

A third way to look at strikes is to measure the amount of time lost because of strikes by those involved in them. This measure of strike activity involves multiplying the number of workers involved in strikes each year by the average duration of strikes in each particular year. This figure gives a measure of the idleness or days idle caused by strikes each year. Table 12.1 indicates that strikes involve a reasonably small amount of idleness in the U.S. economy. Only 5 times in the past 50 years have strikes resulted in more than 50 million days lost per year. Measured as a percentage of total working time in a given year, strikes usually result in less than one half of 1 percent of total working time lost. In only two years (1959 and 1946) was the idleness figure in excess of 0.5 percent and in only one year in modern times (1946) was the figure in excess of 1 percent. In very recent years the idleness figure has usually been less than 0.20 percent, meaning that less than one-fifth of 1 percent of working time was lost because of strikes in a particular year. Another way of looking at it is to say that 99.8 percent of working time was *not* lost because of strikes each year. Even if we were to confine our idleness to union workers, we would say that in 1980, for example, about 4 million workers (approximately one-sixth of the unionized labor force) lost 33,289,000 days because of strikes; this works out to about 0.6 percent of working time lost just for union members, leaving 99.4 percent of union members' time not lost because of strikes.*

Alternatives to the Strike

Mediation

Mediation is the most common method used in the United States to resolve conflicts between labor and management and to reduce the number of strikes (see Chapter 13). In the United States, most mediation services are provided by professional mediators who work either for the Federal Mediation and Conciliation Service (FMCS) or for one of the

---

*The 24 million union members in 1980 would work roughly 250 days per year each, or 5.6 billion days. The 33 million days lost to strikes represents about 0.6 percent of this 6.5 billion working-day year.

various labor relations agencies at the state level (such as the Wisconsin Employment Relations Commission). The employees of the FMCS and the state agencies are career civil servants and it is their mission to assist labor and management in resolving their disputes in bargaining. The mediator can fill a crucial role in negotiations by providing the parties with a mechanism to restore communications when the tensions of the negotiations have destroyed the possibility of free exchange of information between the parties. The mediator can fill an additional role in negotiations by making suggestions to the parties that may form an acceptable compromise to their positions.

The study of mediation is in its infancy and perhaps we will never have the rigorous scientific study of this process that will really help answer the question of how effective mediation is in resolving disputes. One study conducted by Kochan and Jick, however, concludes that mediation is most effective in dealing with disputes that are the result of a breakdown in communication or that are the product of interpersonal conflict between the negotiators.[17] This study found that mediation was least successful in resolving disputes involving differences over economic items. The result of this study led the authors to conclude that mediation can be effective in helping the parties to reach agreement where their bargaining ranges overlap. That is, where the goals in bargaining of the employer and the union are reasonably close and where there is the possibility that each party can achieve its goals without having to reformulate the limits of what each defines as an acceptable settlement, mediation has been found effective as a method of dispute resolution.

A recent study of mediation has found that there are dramatic differences between the styles of individual mediators. Two commonly observed types of mediator behavior were the "orchestrating" mediator and the "dealmaking" mediator.[18] These two styles of mediation reflect the differences in the philosophy of mediation held by persons who work in this field. The orchestrator mediator views his or her role in mediation as a passive role. The orchestrator does not attempt to move or pressure either party in the negotiation process to accept a particular position or to abandon a demand. The orchestrator is a facilitator — his or her only goal in the collective bargaining process is to keep the parties working at the process of negotiations until they are able to reach a mutually acceptable agreement. The orchestrator keeps the parties talking until an agreement is reached.

The dealmaker is a very active type of mediator. The dealmaker listens to the positions of each of the parties to the dispute, mentally arrives at what he or she feels to be the best method of resolving the dispute, and then uses the mediation procedure as an opportunity to move each of the parties to what the mediator feels to be the best solution to the problem.

In each instance, the mediator has no power to force or to compel the parties to reach agreement. One of the great weaknesses of mediation as a dispute resolution method is precisely this — the mediator has no power over the parties to make them do anything. About the only power the mediator has is to convene a meeting and to request that both of the parties attend. Failure to attend the meeting called by the mediator may be used as evidence of failing to meet the obligation of bargaining in good faith under sections 8(a)(5) or 8(b)(3) of the NLRA, but that is about all.

Relations by Objectives

The relations by objectives (RBO) program is sponsored by the FMCS and has as its purpose the goal of fundamentally changing the nature and quality of the labor–management relationship at the workplace. RBO programs are designed to work best where there is antagonism and distrust between the parties and where there exists a desire and a recognized need to change the relationship. In the RBO sessions labor and management talk about their differences and the reasons for the buildup of tension and antagonism in the relationship. Through discussion the parties develop and agree on strategies that will be used to improve the quality of the labor–management relationship.

Although it has been used only in a limited number of cases (Kochan reports 50 uses in the period 1973–1980)[19] the RBO program does represent an attempt, sponsored by the FMCS, to change relationships that have deteriorated and that have ceased to function effectively because of pent-up hostilities between the parties. The FMCS system offers the advantage of being quite low in cost and nonobstructionist to the relationship. Because the facilitator in the sessions is a FMCS employee with extensive experience in the field of labor–management relations, he or she is sensitive to the goals of each of the parties and perhaps is more attuned to the realities of modern bargaining practice than most outsiders or consultants might be.

Early Bird Bargaining

Early bird bargaining was an important part of the 1974, 1977, and 1980 Experimental Negotiating Agreements (ENA) between the United Steelworkers of America and the largest producers of basic steel in the United States. Under the early bird provisions of the ENA, the parties were to begin negotiating in February for the agreement that would expire in August. If the parties could not resolve their differences by April 15, then they would agree to submit their differences to arbitration.[20]

Under the ENA the union agreed to give up its right to strike in return for a guaranteed share of the cost savings associated with eliminating strikes in the industry. The producers were guaranteed a stable production horizon for at least three years and were promised a more cooperative relationship with the union. The ENA was not renewed in 1983 because of a change in union leadership and some misgivings on the part of rank and file members about the benefits of the program. Nevertheless, the ENA did serve for three bargaining rounds as one of the innovative and imaginative programs used to resolve labor–management conflict in a very conflict-laden industry. In 1985 the steelworkers called the first strike against a major steel producer in 25 years at Wheeling-Pittsburgh Steel. Although the company had filed for Chapter 11 bankruptcy protection against its creditors in April 1985 and predicted that the strike would mean a quick and certain death to the company, the union struck anyway. The demise of the ENA made the Wheeling-Pittsburgh strike possible and may signal the beginning of a new round of strikes in the steel industry. One interesting result of the ENA was the fact that because there were no strikes in the steel industry for many years, the union was able to accumulate a large strike fund, now estimated at over $200 million.[21]

Quality of Work Life Programs

The quality of work life (QWL) movement began as an outgrowth of the concern at the national level for improving job satisfaction and the general quality of the work experience for persons in the labor force. With the publication in 1973 of the Department of Health, Education, and Welfare's *Work in America*, people in all occupations became aware of the potential that job redesign, job enrichment, and worker participation in management could have for enhancing the quality of the working experience. Numerous experiments were begun that allowed work sharing, that promoted the development of autonomous work groups, and that encouraged employees to participate more fully in the governance of the workplace.

In many cases the QWL programs were instituted in nonunion work sites. In other cases, however, (the Rushton Mine Experiment[22] or the GM–UAW plan[23]) the QWL program was instituted as a cooperative effort on the part of both labor and management. In most cases the results seem to indicate an improvement in the quality of the labor–management relationship in addition to an improvement in the quality of the working experience of the employees.

Public Concern with Strikes

Given the figures produced above, one may be tempted to argue that strikes are of no consequence and that the public has no need to be alarmed about them. In a sense this position has some merit; a good case can be made for the fact that strikes are overpublicized and overdramatized, a disproportionate amount of the public's attention is devoted to the pathology of labor–management relations (conflict), and that not enough attention is devoted to the peaceful, normal day-to-day functioning of the bargaining process. At the same time that this argument is being made, however, the feeling lingers that strikes are indeed a problem and that public concern about them is justified. This position too has merit. There are a variety of reasons why strikes are of legitimate concern to the public.

Localized Effort

One of the reasons that strikes are of such concern to the public is that strikes in the United States generally have a localized effect. With the exception of the Steel strike of 1959, the Postal strike of 1970, the AT&T strike of 1978, the PATCO strike of 1981, and a few others, we really do not see strikes conducted on a national scale in the United States. Even strikes that affect a whole industry (such as the Rubber strike of 1976 or the Coal strike of 1977–1978) have mainly a local or at most a regional effect.

For most people in the United States the effects of the strike will be felt only after a long delay, and even then the effects are not likely to be great. To individuals living in a local community affected by a strike, however, the effects are felt immediately and are of great importance. If a large number of workers are idled because of a strike local merchants will notice an immediate drop in their business; banks will witness a decrease in deposits and an increase in withdrawals from savings; mortgage companies and landlords may witness defaults on loans and rental payments. If the employer attempts to operate the struck facility with supervisors or with nonunion replacements there may be violence; the community (and even families) may be split between those who support the strike and those who support the employer in the dispute. The strike may be a divisive force that affects the local community for years to come.[24]

Strike Losses

A second reason for public concern about strikes stems from the losses that are usually associated with strikes. The losses from strikes are borne most directly by the parties to the strike — labor and management. For management the strike means the cessation of most work activity at the struck facility. In some industries (e.g., oil refining, chemical production) this is not the case and supervisory personnel can keep the production facility operating almost as if nothing had happened; but in most industries the strike results in lost production for the employer. If the employer is heavily in debt this means that the employer will still have to pay the indebtedness on his or her physical facilities even though nothing, or next to nothing, is produced. If the employer tries to operate the facility with supervisors or with strike replacements the employer will have to pay for heat, light, and power to operate the facility and also for wages to the employees for a level of production that will almost certainly be less than what was achieved before the strike. If it is a long strike, the employer may lose the firm's best workers to competitors. In addition, if it is a long strike the employer may lose its best customers to competitors as well.

Losses are incurred on the employee side of the strike, too. While on strike, workers do not earn income. Many unions pay strikers some type of strike benefit, but this is usually a modest sum, in the neighborhood of $40 a week or so, and is hardly adequate to do much more than provide a meager food budget for strikers.* The figures on strike duration show that on average workers lose 20–30 days for the average strike (see Table 12.1). For some workers, however, strikes last much longer than the 20–30 day average. While most strikes are of short duration, there are a substantial number each year (usually 250–400) that involve a large amount of time lost. Suppose that you were involved in a 75-day strike. How much of a wage raise would you need over and above the employer's best and final offer at the conclusion of the bargaining to recoup your losses? A 75-day strike is 30 percent of a working year. For a worker earning $8.00 per hour a 75-day strike involves the loss of $4,800 in income — 30 percent of the employee's earnings. Will the employer be willing to grant the employees a 30 percent wage increase as a result of this strike? That is not likely. It may take the employees years to recover their losses from a strike. The same, of course, goes for the employer.

Destabilizing Effect

A third reason that strikes are of such concern to the public is because of their destabilizing effects. Because of their unpredictability and the losses they cause, strikes tend to destabilize expectations for the future for workers, employers, consumers, and investors. Strikes create an aura of uncertainty and introduce a random error term into the most elegantly crafted production forecasting models. Research has shown that the threat of a strike or the use of the strike depresses stock prices, sometimes for years into the future.[25] In addition, customers and clients of the struck firm may find that they are no longer able to purchase the product or consume the service produced by the employer. Workers who are employed at the struck firm may find that they can no longer make their mortgage payments or that they can no longer afford the tuition payments for children in college. At the extreme, workers on strike may find that they have lost their jobs to permanent replacements hired during the strike, or that the firm was forced to relocate or to close permanently because of losses incurred during the strike.

---

*In all states but New York and Rhode Island strikers are not eligible to receive unemployment insurance payments. In most states strikers are not eligible for public assistance such as food stamps.

Harm to Neutrals

Finally, the public is concerned about strikes because of the injury and harm suffered by neutrals to the strike or to those not directly involved in the dispute itself. Damage or harm or injury from strikes sometimes affects those who are not really involved in the strike at all. Workers in related industries may be idled from a strike in a vital industry. For example, a strike in the steel industry eventually affects all workers who supply products made of steel. Layoffs may result in the auto industry from shortages of steel. Workers may be idled in a variety of manufacturing, sales, transportation, and service jobs because of a shortage of just one vital commodity such as steel. Customers may be inconvenienced or at the extreme actually imperiled because of the absence of substitutes for the product or service produced by workers on strike. It does not take much imagination to visualize the possible effects to the public from a strike of firefighters of police. The same can be said for strikes involving health care workers (in some localities) or for employees of public utilities. The point here is that some workers supply products and services that cannot be easily replaced or duplicated, and an interruption in the production of these services or products can have an extremely high cost to the public.

Summary

This chapter has discussed the subject of strikes and industrial conflict. Three measures of strike activity were identified (frequency, worker involvement, and time lost) and the major trends in these measures for the U.S. economy were noted. Several legitimate concerns that the public may have regarding strikes were noted as well. Strikes may serve a variety of functions in negotiations; some of these functions are economic (remember the bargaining power model from Chapter 10) and some are for a more political purpose. In addition to serving a variety of purposes, strikes can take a variety of forms. Not all strikes are conducted during contract negotiations — some can occur while the collective agreement is in effect. Not all strikes are directed against the workers' employer; some strikes may be directed against other unions (jurisdictional strikes) or even against other employers (sympathy strikes).

There are many methods available to resolve labor–management disputes before the strike begins. Mediation is the most widely used and accepted method of dispute resolution. In some industries, experiments are being conducted to change labor–management relations to the point where strikes are unnecessary. Although these experiments have demonstrated some success, it is probably true that strikes will be an important aspect of the collective bargaining process for many years to come.

Discussion Questions

1. Based on your reading of the boxed material at the beginning of the chapter, how would you categorize the baseball strike of 1985? Who do you think won the strike? Why?

2. Why do you think the number of strikes has decreased during recent years? Can you name any strikes that have occurred in your area in the past year?

3. Some people feel that strikes are a serious threat to the economic system and that local judges should have the power to issue injunctions to stop strikes affecting the local economy. How would you feel about such a proposal?

4. Is real collective bargaining possible without the use of the strike threat? Explain your position.

5. What causes jurisdictional strikes? Why do you think employers are especially frustrated by this type of strike? Can you think of another way to resolve this type of dispute?

6. What personal qualities do you think would be important to the success of a mediator? If you were a mediator, would you be an orchestrator or a dealmaker? Which type do you think would be most effective in resolving disputes?

Notes

[1]See Thomas Kochan, *Collective Bargaining and Industrial Relations*, Homewood, IL: Irwin, 1980 pp. 240–241 for a more complete discussion of the Hicks model. The Hicks model itself is found in John R. Hicks, *The Theory of Wages*, New York: Macmillan, 1932, Chapter 2.

[2]John T. Dunlop, "The Function of the Strike." In John Dunlop and Neil Chamberlain, eds., *Frontiers of Collective Bargaining*, New York: Harper and Row, 1967, pp. 103–121.

[3]See William Serrin, "The Copper Miners May Be at the Point of No Return," *New York Times*, July 29, 1984: E3 for the details of such a strike at the Phelps Dodge Corporation in Morenci, Arizona.

[4]Dunlop, "The Function of the Strike," p. 108.

[5]Ibid., p. 109.

[6]See Charles Morris, *The Developing Labor Law*, Washington, DC: Bureau of National Affairs, 1983, p. 1004.

[7]Ibid., p. 1009.

[8]Alvin Gouldner, *Wildcat Strike*, Yellow Springs, OH: Antioch Press, 1954, p. 95.

[9]Jean Brett and Stephen Goldberg, "Wildcat Strikes in Bituminous Coal Mining," *Industrial and Labor Relations Review*, vol. 32, July 1979: 465–483.

[10]See *Arlans Department Store*, 133 NLRB 802 (1961).

[11]*Indianapolis Power and Light*, 273 NLRB No. 211 (1985).

[12]*Thurston Motor Lines Inc.*, 166 NLRB 862 (1967).

[13]*Butterworth-Manning-Ashmore Mortuary*, 270 NLRB No. 148 (1984).

[14]*Buffalo Forge* vs. *Steelworkers*, 428 US 397 (1976).

[15]Kenneth Strand, *Jurisdictional Disputes in Construction: The Causes, the Joint Board and the NLRB*, Pullman: Washington State University Press, 1961, p. 27.

[16]See Donald Cullen, *National Emergency Strikes*, Ithaca, NY: Cornell University Press, 1968, pp. 62–66.

[17]Thomas Kochan and Todd Jick, "The Public Sector Mediation Process: A Theory and Empirical Examination," *The Journal of Conflict Resolution*, 22, June 1978: 209–240.

[18]Deborah Kolb, *The Mediators*, Cambridge, MA: The MIT Press, 1983, p. 23–45.

[19]Kochan, *Collective Bargaining and Industrial Relations*, p. 434.

[20]Walter Baer, *Strikes*, New York: American Management Association, 1975, p. 192.

[21]Lindsey Gruson, "Union Prepares Strike at Wheeling-Pittsburgh," *New York Times*, July 21, 1985: 14.

[22]Ted Mills, "Alternating the Social Structure in Coal Mining: A Case Study," *Monthly Labor Review*, October 1976: 3–10.

[23]Stephen Fuller, "How Quality of Work Life Programs Work for G.M.," *Monthly Labor Review*, July 1980: 37–41.

[24]For a good discussion of this issue see Walter Uphoff, *Kohler on Strike*, Boston: Beacon Press, 1966, for an illustration of how this strike affected the community of Kohler, Wisconsin.

[25]George Neumann, "The Predictability of Strikes: Evidence from the Stock Market," *Industrial and Labor Relations Review*, vol. 33, July 1980: 525–535.

BRITISH NEWSCASTS STOPPED BY STRIKE

Broadcast Journalists Stage Walkout Over
BBC Banning of Ulster Documentary

By Jo Thomas

London, Thursday, Aug. 8 – Radio and television news broadcasts were blacked out for 24 hours Wednesday throughout Britain and Northern Ireland by journalists protesting a BBC decision to cancel a broadcast that featured a politician purported to be the chief of staff of the Irish Republican Army.

Shortly before the strike ended at midnight, the British Broadcasting System announced that it planned to broadcast the disputed documentary at a future date, but in altered form. . . .

Besides domestic newscasts, another victim of the 24-hour strike was the BBC's External Service, which goes out in English and 36 other languages to a worldwide audience of millions. It was silenced Wednesday for the first time in its 53-year history, and its scheduled programs were replaced by recorded music.

Radio listeners to the BBC World Service heard recorded music all day, from jazz to organ music. Four times an hour, the announcer read a statement explaining that he was sorry that the usual programs were not on the air.

Members of the BBC staff were on strike for 24 hours to protest a decision by the BBC's board of governors to withdraw a documentary about extremism in Northern Ireland after a request from the British Home Secretary.

"We wanted to highlight the whole program of press censorship and the climate in which journalists are being asked to work in this country," said Vincent Hanna, who represents BBC broadcast journalists at the National Union of Journalists.

At issue, journalists and some politicians said Wednesday, was the integrity of the BBC, which is state-owned but traditionally independent in its news coverage. Also at stake, they said, was how broadcast journalists, who come under state control to a far greater degree than print journalists, will be allowed to cover political violence in the future, especially in Northern Ireland. . . .

Britons who normally watch breakfast television awoke Wednesday to blank screens with explanatory notes from the BBC and from independent stations. Instead of news, current affairs and light-hearted chit chat, early-morning viewers on the BBC were told their day would start with "Pink Panther" cartoons at 9.

Mr. Milne, the BBC director general, said after meeting with Mr. Brittan on Wednesday that although he accepted the right of any citizen to comment on programs, when "such comment is further accompanied by a direct request to remove the program — no matter what its actual content and context — in this case by a minister of the crown, it will be assumed that government is seeking to dictate program policy."

"The BBC will firmly resist such pressure," he said.

All 2,000 members of the National Union of Journalists took part in the strike, and only 5 of Britain's 20 independent stations ran a news service, according to the union. Of the country's 48 independent radio stations, 45 were affected.

Chapter 13

Grievance Procedures and Grievance Arbitration

The work stoppage discussed in the box was a protest strike, a strike over a *grievance* — a management decision that affected the work group and a decision with which the work group did not agree. Protest or grievance strikes are relatively rare in the United States; in this country, when unionized employees do not agree with an action taken by the employer, they file written grievances protesting the decision. A grievance may be discussed at many different levels by representatives of labor and management in an attempt to resolve the problem. If no resolution is reached, an arbitrator may be called in to finally settle the problem. All the time the grievance is being considered, however, the employees stay on the job. The grievance is resolved through negotiation, not through the use of a strike. The resolution of workers' grievances necessitates that management and labor meet together regularly to discuss problems that may arise on a day-to-day basis.

The grievance procedure is a distinctive aspect of the labor relations system in the United States. In this country, the grievance negotiation process has supplanted the strike and the use of the courts in resolving issues arising while the collective bargaining agreement is in effect.

The Grievance Procedure

The historical antecedents to the modern grievance procedure can be traced back to the Anthracite Coal strike of 1902 (see Chapter 4). The presidential commission chartered to resolve the issues in this strike recommended that a permanent grievance procedure be established and further recommended that unresolved grievances be arbitrated.[1] Although the recommendations of the presidential commission were very slow in being accepted in anthracite coal mining, the idea of grievance processing was quick to develop in the clothing industry. The first formal procedure for the adjustment of workers' grievances was the procedure established at Hart, Shaffner and Marx Company in Chicago in 1910. An industry-wide grievance procedure and arbitration protocol was established in the ladies' garment industry the following year.[2] A procedure for resolving workers' grievances under collective agreements in the railroad industry was incorporated into the Railway Labor Act amendments of 1934. The National Railroad Adjustment Board is a federally funded grievance arbitration board that resolves workers' grievances in this industry.

It is interesting to note that the development of the grievance and arbitration system in the United States came largely outside the development of our statutory legal framework covering collective bargaining, with the sole exception of the railroad industry. There is nothing in the Wagner or the Taft-Hartley acts that specifically requires a particular type of grievance procedure or the arbitration of grievances. As a matter of fact, the word *arbitration* is never mentioned in the National Labor Relations Act (NLRA) or its amendments.

The prevalence of grievance procedures and grievance arbitration became widespread during and after World War II. The National War Labor Board regulated labor–management relations during World War II and is credited with instituting grievance and arbitration systems at many workplaces through its rulings.[3] The logic of negotiating over grievances rather than striking over them became apparent to most practitioners in the labor–management field; as a result, strikes over grievances were virtually eliminated during World War II. The tradition of negotiated grievance procedures was a lasting change in U.S. labor relations instituted during the war. Today more than 95 percent of all labor agreements provide for some type of grievance and arbitration procedure (see Chapter 11).

The grievance procedure serves three major purposes in the modern system of industrial relations: it functions as a method of contract interpretation and administration; it serves as a method of protecting individual rights under the collective bargaining agreement; and third, it serves to establish a permanent ongoing communication channel between labor and management and may serve to identify problem areas in the relationship.[4]

Administrative Function

The administrative function of the grievance procedure is the one that most people notice first. The grievance procedure serves to interpret the sometimes vague and imprecise language of the agreement into the real-world practice of labor relations. For example, consider the meaning of the following contract clause:

Hours of Work

> The normal work day shall consist of eight hours. Employees are expected to be at their work stations at 8:00 A.M. Employees are to receive a one-half hour lunch break at 12:00 noon. (In addition, employees are to receive a 15 minute paid break at 10:00 A.M., at 2:30 P.M., and every two hours thereafter.) The normal work day ends at 4:30 P.M.

The contract seems very clear. The portion in parentheses was new and had just been added in the most recently concluded contract negotiations. The union had bargained long and hard for the paid breaks and had made a sizable concession on wages to receive it. Prior to this agreement, workers were not paid for their breaks (although they were required to take them) and the normal quitting time for the eight-hour work day was 5:00 P.M.

One day not long after the contract went into effect, Bob Smith was asked to work one hour of overtime by his supervisor in the warehouse. At 4:30 when his normal shift ended, Bob Smith left his work station to go on a 15 minute break before beginning his overtime. His supervisor told Bob to get back to his work station — he had agreed to work one hour of overtime. Bob claimed that under the agreement he was entitled to a 15 minute break at 2:30 P.M. and "every two hours thereafter." Thus, he felt that he should have a break from 2:30 to 2:45 and from 4:30 to 4:45 if scheduled to work past the normal quitting time. For Bob, one hour of overtime really meant a 15 minute break and 45 minutes of work. The supervisor claimed that this was foolish and that no one needed a 15 minute break to prepare to work 45 more minutes. The supervisor offered to fill in for a couple of minutes if Bob needed to go to the restroom or wanted a drink of water, but he would not agree to a full 15 minute break. Besides, the supervisor pointed out, Bob was being paid 1½ times his hourly wage rate for the overtime hour; if he worked only 45 minutes for this "time and a half" he would effectively be receiving double time for the 45 minutes he was working (i.e., 1½ hours pay for 45 minutes of work). Finally, the supervisor pointed out that employees had never taken breaks prior to working short periods of overtime previously. The supervisor argued that the purpose of the paid breaks was to shorten the workday and that the company never intended to start a new tradition of paid breaks prior to short periods of overtime.

Bob reluctantly agreed to work a full 60 minutes but filed a grievance claiming that he was wrongfully denied his 15 minute break at 4:30. Bob asked that he be paid 1½ times his normal hourly rate for the 15 minute break he was denied. Bob's normal wage rate was $8.00 per hour; his grievance requested back pay of $3.00. Small potatoes — a minor matter. Who could care about a dispute involving $3.00?

Many other people could care. The company employed over 800 people and almost all of them were covered by the same contract. When employees in the production department heard about the Smith grievance they started filing grievances of their own, some of them amounting to close to $100. By the time all the "overtime break" grievances had been consolidated by the union, 118 workers were claiming that some additional compensation was due to them. The smallest claim was Smith's $3.00; the largest was for $210. The total consolidated bill came to $4,720 and was increasing every time someone worked past the 4:30 P.M. normal quitting time period and was not given a 15 minute break.

This is a classic contract interpretation grievance. The labor agreement was unclear and the words of the new agreement appeared to change long-established practice at the company. Labor and management differed in their interpretations of the new contract language. In this case the company and the union agreed in a memorandum of understanding that the 4:30 break would be a paid break only if workers were scheduled to work two hours of overtime or more at the end of their regular shifts. Workers who were scheduled to work less than two hours overtime would not receive a 15 minute paid break. The company agreed to pay all workers for their "lost breaks." The union agreed to the new interpretation of the hours-of-work clause in the agreement and also agreed not to file any more grievances of this type under this section of the contract. In this case the grievance procedure served as a mechanism whereby the unclear language of the agreement could be clarified. No strikes were called, no production time was lost, and the issue was resolved to everyone's satisfaction.

Jurisprudence

A second purpose the grievance procedure serves is to protect the rights of individual workers at the workplace from arbitrary and capricious acts of management. This is sometimes called the *jurisprudential* or the *adjudicatory* aspect of the grievance procedure.[5] This purpose of the grievance procedure may be illustrated by the following case.

At midnight on February 26 the company plant guard observed Mr. X (the grievant) in the management parking lot bobbing up and down behind a car. Upon close inspection the guard found the grievant crouching behind a car and also found a coffee cup half full of a bluish liquid hidden behind the right rear wheel of the car. The plant guard smelled the liquid and concluded that it was alcoholic. The grievant was taken to the plant office by the plant guard.

In explaining his actions, the grievant claimed that he went through the supervisor parking lot and into the employee parking lot to move his car while he was on break. He explained that he was crouched behind the car tying his shoe when the plant guard spotted him. He disclaimed any knowledge about the contents of the coffee cup. The grievant did not appear to be under the influence of alcohol when he was questioned in the company offices. The grievant had no prior history of rule infractions in his file. The substance in the coffee cup was never analyzed, although the plant supervisor smelled the liquid and agreed with the plant guard that it smelled like some kind of liquor. On the basis of the fact that the employee was observed crouching behind a car and that the employee was observed in close proximity to the contents of the coffee cup, he was fired. The charge was consumption and possession of alcoholic beverages on company premises, a violation of the company rules. The worker filed a grievance, claiming that he was unfairly discharged.[6]

This is a good example of an individual rights grievance. In a non-union plant in a case like this, the worker would have virtually no recourse to appeal his discharge. In a unionized plant with a grievance procedure the worker has a right to appeal the decision of the plant supervisor to higher levels of management and to a neutral outside arbitrator, if need be. In this case the worker was reinstated to his job by an arbitrator. The arbitrator heard the facts of the case and concluded that there was no reason to fire Mr. X just because he happened to be in the vicinity of a coffee cup full of a foul-smelling blue liquid during his break. The arbitrator pointed out that there was no evidence of liquor on Mr. X's breath as observed by either the plant guard or the plant supervisor. Furthermore, there was nothing to link the grievant to the cup — the plant guard never saw the grievant actually drink from the cup. Finally, there was no evidence that the cup contained an alcoholic beverage — the "blue liquid" was never analyzed for alcoholic content. It could have been brake fluid, antifreeze, transmission fluid, or any one of a variety of liquids consumed by cars, not humans, found in a parking lot.

The grievance procedure functioned in this case to protect Mr. X's job. This case is a small incident and it involves just one worker, Mr. X. The outcome of this grievance will not affect many people (probably just Mr. X and his family), not at all like the contract interpretation grievance discussed earlier. The outcome of this grievance is important, however, and the process used to produce this outcome is of vital importance to all employees in the plant. This grievance is important because it demonstrates that the employer under the collective agreement no longer has a unilateral right to discipline or discharge an employee. The grievance procedure ensures that when an employee is discharged or disciplined it must be for "just cause," and that the proper procedure has been followed in taking this action.

The arbitrator in his decision in this case stated that "discharge is the extreme industrial penalty and has been compared to capital punishment in criminal law."[7] One major purpose of the grievance procedure is to give workers an appeal process from discharge in the industrial setting much the same that they might have through the court system in criminal matters. The noted scholar Sumner Slichter described the judicial nature of the grievance procedure as "industrial jurisprudence" in the following words:

> Through the institution of the state, men devise schemes of positive law, construct administrative procedures for carrying them out, and complement both statute law and administrative rule with a system of judicial review. Similarly, laboring men, through unions, formulate policies to which they give expression in the form of shop rules and practices which are embodied in agreements with employers or are accorded less formal recognition and assent by management; shop committees, grievance procedures, and other means are evolved for applying these rules and policies; and rights and duties are claimed and recognized. When labor and management deal with labor relations analytically and systematically after such a fashion, it is proper to refer to the system as "industrial jurisprudence."[8]

Communication

A third function the grievance procedure may serve is to establish a line of communication between labor and management and to promote frequent interaction between the parties. One observer labels the grievance procedure "continuous collective bargaining" and points out that the presence of the grievance procedure in an agreement means that collective bargaining never really stops.[9] Labor and management are constantly meeting over grievances and discussing the meaning of the words in the agreement. Management can know immediately from reviewing its grievance files what sections of the contract are most subject to ambiguity and confusion and also which supervisors seem to have the most grievances in their departments. If the union is encountering problems in a certain department with a supervisor, it can make the employer aware of the situation immediately. The grievance procedure provides an excellent opportunity for both the union and the employer to "blow off some steam" and to confront the other party about problems. Many writers have observed that this cathartic release provided by the grievance procedure may be a key element in eliminating wildcat strikes at the workplace.[10]

Grievance Topics

Almost any item in the labor agreement can be a potential source of grievances. Grievances can occur when there is ambiguity in the language of the contract or where the parties have different opinions about what a particular clause is supposed to mean when it was negotiated. In addition, many types of grievances will arise from actions the employer may take involving individuals in the work group. Common subjects of grievances may include the following.

Discipline, Including Discharge

Discharge and discipline are probably the largest sources of grievances. Discipline and discharge can be meted out for violation of company rules such as absenteeism, insubordination, or incompetence. Discipline and discharge can also result from many types of employee misconduct such as dishonesty, fighting, gambling, intoxication, drug abuse, sleeping on the job, or improper dress and grooming. In filing grievances relating to discipline or discharge the employee may allege that the action taken by management was not justified because of the employee's innocence, because of the unreasonableness of the company rule, because of discriminatory treatment, or because the severity of the punishment did not fit the seriousness of the rule violation.[11]

Seniority

A second major subject matter of grievances arises from the seniority clause of the labor agreement. Seniority grievances can take a variety of forms. One common category of seniority grievances involves disputes about how seniority is to be measured. For example, what effect will temporary interruptions (such as jury duty, leaves of absence, military duty, or layoffs) have on seniority accumulation? What effect will temporary transfers out of the work unit or to a supervisory position have on seniority measurement? What effects do change of plant ownership or the merger of two work groups have on seniority? These are all issues that have been sources of workers' grievances. Seniority grievances may also arise out of issues involving the application of seniority. Seniority usually plays a major role in determining who will be laid off during a downturn in employment and who will be recalled when the economic picture brightens. In cases where employees feel that these procedures have been improperly applied, grievances will be filed.

Individual Personnel Actions

Grievances can arise out of worker dissatisfaction with certain types of personnel decisions made by the employer involving the transfer or promotion of employees. In many labor agreements there are certain procedures that the employer must follow in filling job vacancies; commonly the labor agreement will require that vacancies be posted and that employees be allowed to bid (or apply) for these vacancies. Grievances may result when the posting requirements are not met in filling job vacancies or individual workers may file grievances when their bids for vacancies are not accepted.

Seniority usually plays some role in promotion decisions but more commonly ability to do the job will be the key determining criterion in promotion decisions. Grievances are commonly filed over the definition of ability and the measurement of ability.

Management Rights

Grievances cannot be filed over matters specifically reserved in the labor agreement for the sole and exclusive decision of management. The effect of these decisions on the work group, however, can be the subject of grievances. If layoffs result from a management decision to halt the third shift in a production facility, for example, grievances may result from how the layoffs are administered, although the original decision to lay off the third shift probably would be left for the decision of management. In most cases a grievance cannot be filed to protest the decision to lay employees off because of lack of work. It is important to note, however, that grievances can result when management takes an action that it believes is under its sole and exclusive jurisdiction, but the union disagrees that the language of the agreement really gives management such discretion. For example, grievances may result from the introduction of new machinery or technology into a work site, or moving work from one location to another. Grievances may result when members of management perform work that is usually performed by members of the bargaining unit, or when the employer decides to subcontract out work to another company that previously was done by his or her own employees.

Finally, grievances may result from the imposition of work rules by the employer. Generally, employers have the right to promulgate reasonable rules to govern the workplace.[12] When the work group feels that the rules are unreasonable, however, or violate the letter or the spirit of the collective agreement, grievances will result.

Wages

As might be expected, the wage clause in the labor agreement is a major source of grievances. Grievances over wages and wage plans can come from a variety of sources. In workplaces that have wage incentive systems (such as piece-rate systems or time-saving systems) grievances commonly arise from procedures used to establish production quotas or time limits for completing a particular task. Grievances may be filed when workers feel that it was not possible for them to meet their production quota because of machine breakdowns or materials shortages. Workers may file grievances protesting the allocation of overtime work, or the rate of pay for overtime work or for holiday work. Finally, grievances may be filed where workers report for work and no work is available for them and the employees feel they should be compensated for reporting to work.

Grievances are almost always filed by the union (although the employer can conceivably file a grievance against the union) at the request of an individual member and are usually handled at the first few steps of the grievance procedure by the union steward. It is important to realize that in this process grievances can be caused by the action of the employer, the supervisor, the individual employee, or the union steward.[13] Furthermore, grievance filing can often be used as a tactic by the union to harass the employer or to fulfill the political ambitions of aggressive union officers.[14]

The Grievance Resolution Process

Number of Steps

Most grievance procedures have an established step-by-step process spelled out in the agreement that details what is to occur at each stage in the grievance resolution process. A typical grievance procedure in a labor agreement would have three or four steps and might be written into the labor agreement with the following type of language:

Grievance Procedure

Should any difference or grievance arise between the Company and the Union or any employee in the unit, as to the meaning and/or application of this Agreement, the procedure of settlement shall be in the following order and manner:

(1) Between the Chief Steward, Shop Steward and aggrieved employee and the Foreman and/or Supervisor of the department involved and/or his representative; failing an adjustment in this manner

(2) Between the International Representative or Representative and the Union Committee and the aggrieved and the Manager-Employee Relations and/or his representatives; failing an adjustment in this manner

(3) Between the Union Committee and a representative or representatives of the International Union and the Vice President of the Company and/or his designated representative or representatives.

It is the intention of both parties to expedite the handling and settlement of grievances. Neither party shall deliberately delay the settlement of grievances in any stage of the procedure.

No grievance shall be considered (1) unless the cause thereof shall have occurred within twenty (20) calendar days next preceding the date the grievance is submitted to the Foreman or (2) unless the cause thereof occurs during the aggrieved's absence due to vacation or sickness and the grievance is submitted within twenty (20) calendar days after his return to work.

The grievance shall be heard in the first step within a period of three (3) days from the time the grievance is called to the attention of the Foreman of the department involved. The Company shall give its first step answer within three (3) days of the hearing. The Union shall have three (3) days to appeal to Company's answer in the first step.

The grievance shall be heard in the second step within a period of ten (10) days from the time of the Union's appeal. The Company shall give its second step answer within three (3) days of the hearing. The Union shall have seven (7) days to appeal the Company's answer in the second step.

The grievance shall be heard in the third step within a period of thirty (30) days from the time of the Union's appeal. The Company shall give its third step answer within three (3) days of the hearing. The Union shall have thirty (30) days to appeal the Company's answer in the third step. Except by mutual agreement none of the foregoing steps in the grievance procedure shall be extended or by-passed. The grievance shall be reduced to writing by the aggrieved employee or Shop Steward before it is submitted and considered in the first step.

A grievance shall be settled on the basis of the Company's last answer unless, in the case of the first two steps, it is appealed by the Union to a subsequent step within the time limits above set forth after receiving the Company's answer and unless, in the case of the third step, it is appealed by the union to arbitration within thirty (30) days after receiving the Company's answer.

Arbitration

If a grievance shall not have been settled through the foregoing procedure, then either party may within thirty (30) days give the other party notice of its desire to submit the grievance to Arbitration. The parties shall select the arbitrator within ten (10) days of such notice but if the parties are unable to agree on a selection, the arbitrator shall be selected through the American Arbitration Association.

The Arbitrator shall fix a time, and a place for a hearing upon reasonable notice to each party. After such hearing the Arbitrator shall promptly render a decision which shall be binding upon both parties but the Arbitrator shall have no power to render a decision which adds to, subtracts from or modifies the Agreement; the decision shall be confined to the meaning of the contract provision which gave rise to the dispute.

The parties to the arbitration shall bear equally the expenses of the Arbitrator and the rental, if any, of the place of arbitration. All other expenses attendant to arbitration will be borne by the party incurring them, including the expenses of any witnesses called by such party.[15]

A typical grievance procedure such as that between Boise Cascade Company and the International Paperworkers Union has three main steps, as illustrated in Figure 13.1. In the first step the aggrieved employee is represented by one of two first-level union officials (chief steward, or shop steward), and his or her grievance is discussed with the foreman or supervisor of the department involved. In the second step the grievant is represented by a representative of the international union and by the plant-level grievance committee, and the employer is represented by the plant-level manager of employee relations. At the third step, if the grievance has still not been resolved, the union grievance committee and the representative of the international union meet with the corporate vice president in charge of labor and employee relations, or his or her representative, to discuss the grievance.

Time Limits

Specific time limits are written into the procedure. In the Boise Cascade–International Paperworkers contract, grievances must be submit-

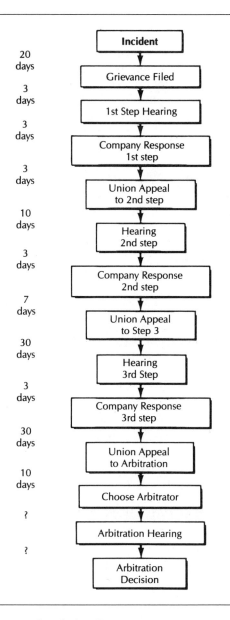

FIGURE 13-1   Grievance Resolution Process

ted within 20 days from the time that the alleged incident occurred, or 20 days after the employee's return to work if the incident caused a loss of work time. The grievance must be heard at step 1 within 3 days from the time the foreman is notified of the incident. The foreman must give his or her answer to the complaint within 3 days from the time the grievance is presented. If it disagrees with the foreman's answer to the complaint, the union must appeal to step 2 within 3 days. Within 10 days from this appeal the grievance must be heard at step 2. The company must provide the union with its response to the grievance within 3 days. If the union disagrees with the company's answer to the grievance at step 2, it has 7 days to appeal to step 3. The grievance must be heard at step 3 within 30 days from the time it is appealed. The company must provide an answer to the grievance within 3 days from the time the grievance is heard at step 3. If the union does not agree with the company's response to the grievance in step 3, it has 30 days to appeal to arbitration. The parties must then select an arbitrator to hear the case and resolve it once and for all within 10 days from the union's appeal.

If we were to total up all the time it would take to process the grievance through all the steps in the procedure, we would find that it would take 122 days to reach the point where the arbitrator is chosen. After that time it might well take 60 days before the arbitrator can hear the case and another 30 days (at least) for the arbitrator to render his or her decision. The whole process can very easily take 210 days, or even longer, to ultimately resolve the grievance. Not counting the incident itself, this grievance procedure actually is a 13-step procedure from start to finish. Note finally that the responsibility for moving the grievance from one step to the next is up to the union. As the contract states, a grievance shall be settled on the basis of the company's last answer unless it is appealed by the union to a subsequent step within the time limits specified.

It is important to point out that most grievances are settled at the first step or two of the procedure and that most grievances are resolved quickly. In cases involving the interpretation of important contract clauses, however, or in cases involving the discharge of an employee, the grievance may be processed through all the steps of the procedure up to and including arbitration.

It should be noted, however, that arbitration is not the only way to resolve disagreements between labor and management arising under an existing agreement. In some industries, notably coal mining, strikes during the term of the agreement are sometimes used to resolve grievances.[16] It has been a long tradition in the coal-mining industry to strike over any grievance related to safety issues. The miners claim that the grievance procedure is too slow and cumbersome to deal with issues of immediate concern, such as safety.

In some European countries, particularly France, West Germany,

Sweden, and Italy, workers' grievances are handled through the court system. In France, West Germany, and Sweden workers' grievances are handled by special labor courts. In Italy grievances are handled by the regular courts. In France the courts handle many thousands of cases per year; in West Germany the figure is even higher.[17] There have been several suggestions advanced through the years to substitute some type of labor court system for the system of private arbitration currently used in the United States.[18]

Arbitration of Grievances

The arbitration of grievances is the most common method of resolution when the parties cannot settle the matter themselves in the lower levels of the procedure. In the 1983 Bureau of National Affairs Survey, 97 percent of all labor agreements provided for arbitration as the final step in the grievance resolution process.[19]

The system of grievance arbitration in the United States as developed over the past 40 years or so has remained largely a private process and there are no current prospects for developing a labor court system in this country. It is possible to identify a number of advantages to maintaining a private, nonjudicial system of grievance arbitration over the alternative of a labor court system that would involve the litigation of grievances.

One of the most often cited advantages of arbitration over litigation is the saving of both time and expense by arbitration. In arbitration the parties do not have to be represented by legal counsel, and there is no need to pay court fees or to pay for the cost of a court reporter in most cases. In addition, the parties are free to schedule their arbitration case at their own convenience rather than wait for a spot on the crowded docket of the local court.[20]

Arbitration is also viewed as superior to regular court litigation in that in arbitration the parties can choose a neutral figure who has special knowledge and expertise in the labor relations field.[21] Rather than take the chance that the case might be heard by a judge with limited knowledge of the complexities of labor relations, in arbitration the parties are free to choose whomever they want to hear their case. Special rosters of qualified and experienced arbitrators are maintained by the Federal Mediation and Conciliation Service (FMCS) and by the American Arbitration Association (AAA). Both labor and management regularly use the services of the FMCS and the AAA when they need the services of an arbitrator. The most common method of choosing an arbitrator is for the parties to make a request to either the FMCS or the AAA for a list of seven qualified arbitrators. The parties then alternatively strike names from the list one at a time until the company has stricken three names and the union has stricken three names. The person remaining on the list will be chosen as the arbitrator. As might be expected, significant effort is expended on both parties' part to find just the right arbitrator. Research evidence exists that suggests that it is difficult to predict how an arbitrator will decide a case based on his or her background characteristics such as age, sex, prior work experience, education, or longevity as an arbitrator, however.[22]

A third advantage of arbitration over litigation is that arbitration procedures tend to be largely nonformal and nontechnical. One observer has commented:

> Arbitration proceedings are marked by a great degree of informality. There are no formal pleadings. In fact, most often there is no written statement of the issue except for a very poorly, often ungrammatically worded grievance in nonlegal form, prepared by the aggrieved employee or his union representative. Normally there are no attempts before the hearing to define the issues to be decided, as lawyers strive to do in litigation. Moreover, the hearing itself is often an amorphous, freewheeling affair, characterized by unorthodox arguments and presentations, in which the legal rules of evidence are usually ignored.[23]

It should be noted that this comment was meant to be a nonjudgmental description of the arbitration process. Arbitration cases are meant to be nontechnical because the real role of arbitration is to settle a dispute between labor and management that may be interfering with the production process. The parties need a realistic, workable, acceptable solution to their problem. Because it is quite possible that neither labor or management will be represented by legal counsel in the hearing and that a nonlawyer may be occupying the arbitrator's chair, it is not surprising to find a nonlegal, nontechnical procedure being followed in the procedure. It should be noted, however, that it is becoming more common to find legal counsel present in the arbitration process (most often representing management) and that the majority of arbitrators today have legal backgrounds. Nevertheless, it remains true that arbitration procedures are generally nonformal and nontechnical — especially when compared to the rigid legal standards of procedure found in criminal and civil court proceedings. Most arbitrators feel that there is an advantage in having a nontechnical hearing. Cases are not won or lost on technical details — evidence of all types and from all sources is admitted and given the consideration that the arbitrator feels it deserves.

A fourth advantage of arbitration over litigation is that the arbitration process is private and closed to the public. Testimony at the arbitration hearing is private and is usually not recorded on either a tape or a transcript. The proceedings are closed and the facts of the grievance never need be made public. If a worker has been discharged for drinking on the job or drug abuse, no one beyond the parties to the hearing need know the particulars of the case. Furthermore, the arbitrator's ruling in the case need not be made public and seldom appears in print. Arbitration can serve to protect the privacy of both workers and employers — privacy that would not be possible to preserve in a court case.

Finally, arbitration cases are decided on a case-by-case basis; there is no requirement to adhere to established precedent in arbitration as there is in court cases. Furthermore, arbitrators are given wide latitude to fashion what they feel are acceptable solutions to problems. Arbitrators are not bound to make a particular award or ruling even where they might find a party guilty of a rule infraction or contract violation. For example, an arbitrator may find in a discharge hearing that an employee was drinking on the job and that the company did have the right to fire him or her, but the arbitrator may reinstate the employee to his or her former position because of a long discipline-free prior work history or because the employee volunteers to seek alcoholism counseling. Such flexibility is not often available in court litigation, where the judge is bound by strict legal standards of precedent and where punishment is required in cases where wrongdoing is found. In arbitration the neutral figure is free to fashion a remedy to the problem that he or she feels is appropriate.

The Legal Status of the Grievance Procedure and Grievance Arbitration

As mentioned earlier, the National Labor Relations Act never specifically mentions arbitration as the final step in the process of grievance resolution. About the closest the NLRA comes to mentioning the grievance and arbitration process is in section 203(d) of the Taft-Hartley Act, where Congress declared that "the desirable method for settlement of grievance disputes arising over the application or interpretation of an existing collective bargaining agreement should be the method of dispute resolution agreed upon by the parties." In most labor agreements arbitration is the method.

The U.S. Supreme Court has had several opportunities to determine the legal standing of the grievance arbitration procedure, however. Several of these pioneering decisions follow.

Textile Workers of America *vs.* Lincoln Mills of Alabama *(353 U.S. 448) (1957)*

This case involved a number of grievances filed by members of the Textile Workers of America against their employer, Lincoln Mills of Alabama. The grievances, involving work loads and work assignments, were processed through all the stages of the grievance procedure up to the point of arbitration. When the union requested that the employer submit the grievances to arbitration as the contract required, the employer refused to do so.

At this point the union filed a suit against the employer in federal district court for violating the terms of the labor agreement. Remember that Congress amended the Taft-Hartley Act in 1947 to allow for suits by (and also for suits against) unions in section 301. Under section 301 the union filed suit against the employer seeking to compel it to submit the unresolved grievances to arbitration. The district court upheld the union's suit; the appeals court, however, did not. The appeals court ruled that while section 301 of the Taft-Hartley Act gives the union the right to sue the employer, there is nothing in section 301 that allows the court to order a particular remedy (such as forcing an employer to submit a grievance to arbitration) in these suits.[24]

The U.S. Supreme Court overruled the appeals court ruling and stated that section 301 did in fact allow the courts to make specific rulings in certain cases. The court ruled that where there was a no-strike pledge on the part of the union in the contract and an agreement by the employer to submit unresolved grievances to arbitration, these provisions of the contract can be enforced by legal action. In the words of the Supreme Court:

> Plainly the agreement to arbitrate grievances disputes is the *quid pro quo* for an agreement not to strike. Viewed in this light, the legislation does more than confer jurisdiction in the federal court over labor organizations. It expresses a federal policy that federal courts should enforce these agreements on behalf of or against labor organizations and that industrial peace can be best obtained only in that way.[25]

Note that the court used the term *quid pro quo* in discussing the relationship between the no-strike pledge on the part of the union and the agreement to arbitrate on the part of the employer. By using this terminology the court recognized that arbitration is a substitute for striking over grievances, and that by encouraging arbitration and enforcing arbitration clauses in labor agreements the court can best promote the interests of industrial peace. With this decision the court recognized the desirability of arbitration clauses in labor agreements and gave the federal court system the power to enforce these agreements to arbitrate.

The Steelworkers Trilogy (1960)

United Steelworkers of America vs. American Manufacturing Co. (363 U.S. 564) (1960).   This case is the first of three decisions all released on the same day in 1960 and all involving the Steelworkers Union (hence the name Steelworkers Trilogy). In this case an employee by the name of Sparks had suffered a work-related injury to his back in March 1957. The injury required surgery and Sparks was forced to quit his job because of the injury. Sparks was declared permanently partially disabled (25 percent) by the state workers' compensation bureau and he received in August 1957 a lump sum payment from the employer to compensate him for the disability. In September 1957 Mr. Sparks asked to be reinstated to his old position with the company. The company refused.

The union then filed a grievance against the employer under the labor agreement. When the grievance was not settled the union requested that the issue be submitted to arbitration as provided in the labor agreement. The employer refused to arbitrate the grievance, claiming that it was frivolous and baseless and that there was no obligation under the labor agreement to submit a nonmeritous grievance to arbitration. The district court and the appeals court both agreed with the employer's position in this case.

The U.S. Supreme Court, however, disagreed with this finding. In a very important ruling, the court ruled that the courts have no business weighing the merits of a grievance in a suit to compel arbitration. In this ruling the court declared that the interests of industrial justice are best served by letting the arbitrator determine the merits of a grievance — not the courts. In its decision the court stopped the parties from appealing to the court system before the grievance was ever arbitrated.

***United Steelworkers of America* vs. *Warrior and Gulf Navigation Co.* (363 U.S. 574) (1960).**   In this case the employer subcontracted out to another employer work that previously had been done by the aggrieved employees. The subcontracting arrangement resulted in the employer's laying off 19 employees, reducing the bargaining unit from 42 to 23. The employees filed a grievance maintaining that the subcontracting was a violation of the collective bargaining agreement. The grievance was not settled in the steps of the grievance procedure and the employees requested that the dispute be submitted to arbitration.

The employer refused to arbitrate the grievance, claiming that the decision to subcontract was solely a decision to be made by management and that the grievance was not arbitrable because of this. The district court and the federal appeals court both agreed with the employer.

The U.S. Supreme Court disagreed, ruling that issues may be expressly excluded from the grievance procedure only through clear and unambiguous language in the labor agreement to that effect. In this case the court found no such language excluding subcontracting issues from the grievance procedure. In the Supreme Court's own words:

> An order to arbitrate the particular grievance should not be denied unless it may be said with positive assurance that the arbitration clause is not susceptible to an interpretation that covers the asserted dispute. Doubts should be resolved in favor of coverage.[26]

In this ruling the U.S. Supreme Court says that all issues not specifically excluded from arbitration are subject to it. Thus, the scope of the grievance procedure and the arbitration process will encompass all issues arguably covered by the labor agreement and not expressly excluded from it.

***United Steelworkers of America* vs. *Enterprise Wheel and Car Corporation* (363 U.S. 593) (1960).**   This case has a slightly more complicated factual background than have the other two cases. In this case a group of employees walked off their jobs to protest the discharge of another employee. The local union officer told the men to return to work. When they did return to work they were told that they had been fired. The workers filed a grievance claiming that the discharge was unjustified. The employer disagreed. The grievance was processed but was not resolved after passing through the normal channels of the grievance procedure. The union requested that the dispute be submitted to arbitration. The employer refused and the union then went to district court and filed a suit seeking to compel the employer to arbitrate. The court ruled in the union's favor and the employer did submit the issue to arbitration. During this time the collective bargaining agreement expired and a new one was not renegotiated, although the union continued to represent the employees at Enterprise.

The arbitrator ruled that the employer's termination of the employees was too harsh, and he reduced the penalty for the walkout to a 10-day suspension without pay. The arbitrator ordered that the workers be reinstated back to their old jobs with full wages, benefits, and seniority minus the pay for the 10-day suspension. The employer refused to comply with the arbitrator's award. The union then went to district court again and the court ordered the employer to comply with the arbitrator's ruling. The employer appealed the district court ruling, and the appeals court held that the arbitrator's ruling was unenforceable both because the arbitrator's ruling was ambiguous in specifying the exact amount of back pay owed the grievants and because the collective bargaining agreement that gives the arbitrator his or her powers in the first place had expired. The union appealed the appeals court ruling to the U.S. Supreme Court.

The U.S. Supreme Court ruled in this case that it will not review arbitrators' awards, and that generally the arbitrator has no obligations to explain the logic he or she uses to arrive at the award to the courts. The court agreed that the arbitrator's ruling was ambiguous and that some clarification of the exact amount owed the grievants was necessary. The key issue in this case, however, concerned the court's refusal to review an arbitrator's award merely because the justices may have had a different opinion about the case than the arbitrator. In the words of Justice Douglas:

> The question of interpretation of the collective bargaining agreement is a question for the arbitrator. It is the arbitrator's construction which was bargained for; and so far as the arbitrator's decision concerns construction of the contract, the courts have no business overruling him because their interpretation of the contract is different from his.[27]

The Steelworkers Trilogy cases were of enormous importance in establishing the legal status of the arbitration procedure. In this series of rulings the court established that the arbitrator has the power to determine whether or not a grievance is arbitrable and that once his or her ruling is issued the courts generally will not review it.[28] In these rulings the justices of the U.S. Supreme Court recognized the importance of the grievance and arbitration system and the advantages that arbitration of grievances has over litigation. In the *Warrior and Gulf Navigation Co.* case, the Supreme Court justices summarized the High Court's view of the importance of the grievance procedure and the arbitration process in these words:

> The grievance machinery under a collective bargaining agreement is at the very heart of the system of industrial self government. Arbitration is the means of solving the unforeseeable by molding a system of private law for all the problems which may arise and to provide for their solution in a way which will generally accord with the variant needs and desires of the parties. The processing of disputes through the grievance machinery is actually a vehicle by which meaning and context are given to the collective bargaining agreement. . . . The grievance procedure is in other words a part of the continuous collective bargaining process.
>
> . . . the parties' objective in using the arbitration process is primarily to further their common goal of uninterrupted production under the agreement, to make the agreement fit their specialized needs. The ablest judge cannot be expected to bring the same experience and competence to bear upon the determination of a grievance, because he cannot be similarly informed.[29]

***Boy's Market Inc.* vs. *Retail Clerks Union Local 770* (398 U.S. 235) (1970).** The *Boy's Market* decision stems from a group of earlier U.S. Supreme Court decisions in 1962. These decisions had prohibited federal courts from issuing injunctions to halt illegal strikes but did allow employers to sue unions for damages resulting from illegal strikes[30] (such as strikes for grievances) and allowed employers to sue unions in either state or federal court for contract violations.[31]

In the *Boy's Market* case the central issue involved a work stoppage that resulted when a supervisor in a supermarket rearranged merchandise in a frozen food case. The union representative claimed that this was a violation of the collective bargaining agreement and demanded that the case be emptied and restocked by union personnel. The employer refused but offered to submit the issue to the grievance and arbitration procedure. The union refused to process the issue through the grievance procedure and called a strike to protest the employer's action instead.

The employer went immediately to district court to seek an injunction halting the strike and the picketing. The district court issued the injunction and ordered the union to cease its strike and to submit the issue to arbitration. The union appealed this ruling to the federal appeals court, and the appeals court lifted the injunction citing the 1962 *Sinclair* vs. *Atkinson*[32] ruling, which stated that the Norris-LaGuardia Act of 1932 prohibited federal courts from issuing injunctions to stop strikes.[33]

The U.S. Supreme Court in a dramatic decision overruled its earlier ruling in the *Sinclair* case and stated that henceforth federal courts may issue injunctions to stop strikes that are in violation of an existing labor agreement and that involve issues that could have been processed through the grievance procedure. The court in this decision gave even more prominence and status to the grievance procedure and arbitration by ruling that the remedy of arbitration to halt disputes between labor and management is preferable to a court suit even when the employer has the option of suing the union for contract violation. The court ruled that law suits, either during or after strikes, tend to aggravate labor relations problems rather than solve them.[34] The court in the *Boy's Market* ruling once again attaches great importance to the arbitration procedure as a method of resolving labor–management disputes.

National Labor Relations Board Cases Involving Arbitration: The Issue of Deferral

Paralleling the decisions of the U.S. Supreme Court regarding the legal status of grievance procedures and grievance arbitration were a series of decisions by the National Labor Relations Board (NLRB) regarding the relationship of arbitration to NLRA cases. The crucial issue the NLRB was forced to confront involved the relationship between the grievance procedure and the NLRB's own unfair labor practice litigation procedure when a violation of the labor agreement by the employer or the union was also a violation of the NLRA.

The conflict arises in cases where the employee or the employer feels that some action of the other party violates the labor agreement and also the NLRA. For example, a union activist claims that he or she was discharged without just cause (a violation of the labor agreement) and that the discharge was motivated by the employer's dislike of the union, which led him or her to systematically discriminate against union activists (a violation of sections 8a1 and 8a3 of the NLRA). What should the grievant do? Should he or she file an unfair labor practice complaint with the NLRB? Should he or she file a grievance? Should both be done at the same time? Or, finally, should he or she pursue one course of action first and then if dissatisfied pursue a different course (e.g., unfair labor practice complaint first, arbitration second)?

The NLRB faced this issue directly in 1971 and in a landmark case entitled *Collyer Insulated Wire* announced that it would defer unfair labor practice cases to arbitration where the unfair labor practice was also a violation of the labor agreement, when certain conditions were met: (1) where the parties had a stable bargaining relationship, (2) where the parties were willing to arbitrate the dispute, and (3) where the meaning of the labor agreement is the central issue in the dispute.[35] Presently the NLRB will automatically defer to arbitration cases arising out of sections 8(a)(1), 8(a)(3), 8(a)(5), and 8(b)(1), 8(b)(2), and 8(b)(3) of the NLRA unfair labor practices.[36] This type of deferral arbitration under the *Collyer* doctrine is called *prearbitral deferral*.

In cases where an arbitration ruling has already been rendered the board will generally not review the arbitrator's ruling. This principle is called *postarbitral deferral*. The leading NLRB case establishing this principle is *Spielberg Manufacturing Company*.[37] The Spielberg principle of postarbitral deferral means that the NLRB will generally refuse to review arbitration decisions over issues that are both contract violations and unfair labor practices. Under the *Spielberg* decision, however, this deferral to arbitration will occur only when certain standards are met (the Spielberg standards). When these standards are not met, then the board will review arbitration rulings. The Spielberg standards are as follows.

> The unfair labor practice issue must have been presented and addressed at the arbitration hearing.
>
> The proceedings at the hearing must be fair and impartial.
>
> All parties to the arbitration proceeding must have agreed to be bound by the decision.
>
> The decision of the arbitration must not be repugnant to the purposes of the NLRA.[38]

Of course, if any one of these standards is not met, then an arbitrator's ruling is not considered to have disposed of the issue and the grievant can present his or her case to the NLRB after arbitration. The combination of *Spielberg* and *Collyer* means that the board gives great deference to arbitrators' rulings and once again underscores the prominence that is accorded grievance arbitration in the U.S. system of labor law. To the greatest degree possible, the NLRB tries to stay out of the grievance arbitration procedure and encourages the parties to use the procedure to save their disputes.

Contemporary Issues in the Grievance Procedure and Grievance Arbitration

Time and Cost

One advantage of arbitration over litigation is the fact that arbitration is a faster and less expensive method of resolving disputes than is litigation. As the arbitration process has developed over time, however, this advantage has decreased somewhat. The "typical" grievance submitted to arbitration now regularly takes in excess of 200 days to resolve and will cost in excess of $900 just for the arbitrator's fee.[39] If the parties are represented by attorneys, or if a court reporter is present to keep a transcript of the proceeding, the costs will increase even more.

There are a variety of reasons why arbitration is becoming more expensive and the process is becoming more time-consuming. One of the factors responsible for the time delays is the shortage of skilled, experienced, acceptable arbitrators to handle cases. Although there are over 3,000 arbitrators listed on the FMCS and AAA rosters, no more than 300 to 400 of these can be considered mainline arbitrators.[40] The arbitrators that are considered mainline have all the cases they can handle, and more. It is not at all unusual to find highly accepted arbitrators who schedule 175 to 200 cases per year, of which approximately 75 percent will result in actual hearings. Sometimes the parties have to wait two or three months to get a spot on the arbitrator's calendar. Obviously, with a 60- to 90-day wait just to hear the case and another 30- to 45-day wait to receive the arbitrator's award, the process takes time. It should be noted, however, that the parties themselves are also guilty of expanding the length of time it takes to settle grievances before the case even gets to the arbitration step.[41]

A number of proposals have been advanced to deal with the problem of increasing cost and delay in the arbitration procedure. Some companies and unions have adopted expedited arbitration procedures that speed up the arbitration process. Notable successes have been recorded in using these expedited procedures, but they reduce time delays only in the last step of the grievance procedure (arbitration), not in the whole process.[42] Grievance mediation and joint factfinding have been tried as methods of dispute resolution short of arbitration. Here again some benefits are noted, mostly involving settling a large number of cases before they reach arbitration.[43] Finally, proposals have been advanced for training more arbitrators,[44] making larger number of expertly trained arbitrators available to hear cases and resulting in greater speed in arbitrator selection, lower fees, and a higher quality of decisions. Whether this new cadre of expertly trained neutrals would be chosen to hear cases, however, is an open question.[45]

The need to reform the present system of grievance arbitration to deal with the problems of time delay and expense is a real one and many feel that the present system is in some peril.[46] The movement to change the system will come from the parties themselves as a result of experimentation and cooperative problem solving in much the same way that the arbitration system in the United States developed in the first place. The development of methods of dispute resolution alternative to the traditional and formalized method of grievance arbitration, however, will likely be a major issue in labor–management relations in the future.

Fair Representation

Once it has been certified as a bargaining agent for a group of employees, a union is the exclusive representative for these employees — no other union may represent these employees for bargaining purposes — and it owes these employees the duty of representing them fairly, equally, and without discrimination. The union must represent all workers in a bargaining unit — even if they are not members of the union. The issue of fair representation is often raised in litigation involving the union's obligation to process workers' grievances and to arbitrate them if they are unresolved in the lower steps of the grievance procedure.

The concept of fair representation is not found in the statutes, but arises from a series of U.S. Supreme Court decisions beginning in 1944. The obligation of fair representation was first articulated by the Supreme Court in the famous case of *Steele* vs. *Louisville and Nashville Railroad* decided in 1944. In *Steele* the court outlined the broad obligation of the union to represent its members fairly and equally (the *Steele* case involved an issue of racial discrimination in representation). Additionally, in the *Steele* decision the court clearly stated that when a violation of the duty of fair representation occurs the affected employee may sue the union for damages.[47] In 1967 the Supreme Court made a very important ruling regarding the union's obligation to represent its members in grievance handling in the case of *Vaca* vs. *Sipes*.[48] In this case a worker by the name of Benjamin Owens had been discharged because of poor health. The union processed the grievance through the lower steps of the grievance procedure, but based on medical evidence decided not to submit the grievance to arbitration. The worker sued the union in municipal court for failing to represent him fairly. Because of the conflicting medical evidence, the jury felt that there was some reason to believe that the worker could perform his job and thus felt that the union should have pursued this grievance all the way through arbitration. The jury awarded monetary damages of $10,300 to the worker. The union appealed the decision, but the Missouri State Supreme Court affirmed the suit for damages. The original grievant, Owens, died while the appeal was pending and the administrator of his estate, Sipes, was named in subsequent litigation as the petitioner.

The union then appealed this ruling to the U.S. Supreme Court, which overturned the decisions of the lower courts in Missouri. The court ruled that the union breaches its duty to represent workers only when it acts in an arbitrary, discriminatory manner, or in bad faith. The U.S. Supreme Court found that the union did have a reason for making its decision not to process Owens' grievance to arbitration and that it did not act in an inconsistent or discriminatory manner toward the worker. Furthermore, the court ruled that the interests of effective and efficient labor relations can best be served by giving the union some discretion in deciding which grievances to arbitrate and which not to arbitrate. In the words of the court:

> Some have suggested that every individual employee should have the right to have his grievance taken to arbitration. Others have urged that the union be given substantial discretion (if the collective bargaining agreement so provided) to decide whether a grievance should be taken to

arbitration, subject only to the duty to refrain from patently wrongful conduct such as racial discrimination or personal hostility.

Though we accept the proposition that a union may not *arbitrarily ignore*
a meritorious grievance or process in a perfunctory fashion, we do not
agree that the individual employee has an absolute right to have his grievance taken to arbitration regardless of the provisions of the applicable
collective bargaining agreement.[49]

The U.S. Supreme Court has more recently ruled, however, that when
the union does act in a perfunctory or arbitrary manner in handling
workers' grievances or in presenting the case in arbitration that arbitration awards can be vacated[50] and that significant monetary damages
($30,000 in the *Bowen*[51] case) can be levied against the union for failing
to represent workers fairly. The issue of fair representation in arbitration presents a perplexing problem to union leaders, a problem that is
confounded by the time and expense involved in the arbitration procedure. If the union processes "marginal" grievances to arbitration it will
dissipate its time, efforts, energy, and resources in arbitrating cases that
it may have a high probability of losing. On the other hand, if the union
does not process meritorious grievances and then is found guilty of failing to represent its members fairly it can be subject to considerable
suits for damages from individual members. The union is involved in a
complex balancing process, weighing both the interests of the group as
a whole and the rights of individual members to fair representation. The
maintenance of this balance will likely be one of the major challenges
facing union leaders in the decades ahead.

Summary

Grievances can arise over a number of issues, some involving the actions of individual workers, others involving the interpretation of unclear contract language. The grievance procedure provides a forum for
labor and management to meet together and to peacefully resolve disputes arising from the workplace. The resolution of these grievances
requires almost continuous interaction between labor and management. Over 95 percent of all U.S. collective bargaining agreements include some method of grievance resolution.

If the parties cannot agree to the resolution of a grievance, an outside
arbitrator will be chosen to settle the problem. Arbitration has an important place in the grievance resolution process, a place that has been
recognized by several U.S. Supreme Court rulings. The NLRB has also
ruled on several occasions that it will defer unfair labor practice cases
that are also violations of the collective bargaining agreement to the
decisions of private arbitrators rather than rule on the cases itself. The
NLRB has further ruled that it will generally not review arbitrators'
decisions that have been rendered in these cases.

Grievance arbitration is so popular and so widespread in the U.S.

industrial relations system that there is some danger that the system is becoming overused. The shortage of skilled arbitrators, the increasing time and expense of the procedure, and the possibility of court suits initiated by workers who feel they have not been fairly represented are all seen as possible threats to the system that has worked so well for so long.

Discussion Questions

1. In this chapter we have described the grievance procedure as a peaceful alternative to strikes over grievances. Can you see any advantage to retaining the right to strike over grievances rather than processing them through the grievance procedure?
2. What would have been Bob Smith's remedy to his overtime grievance problem if he had been working in a nonunion workplace without a union contract?
3. How might the employer have handled the case of Mr. X differently and perhaps won the case involving the mysterious blue fluid?
4. It has been stated several times in this chapter that the grievance procedure is an example of continuous collective bargaining. How can this be seen as both an advantage and a disadvantage of the grievance procedure?
5. How would you feel about having the opportunity to submit disputes about the grading of your papers and exams to a grievance committee comprised of students and faculty? Do you see this as a way of strengthening or weakening the grading system as it now exists?
6. Why do you think the NLRB defers cases to arbitration rather than deciding them itself? Do you see this as giving too much power to the arbitrator?
7. What characteristics do you think it would take to be a good arbitrator? What do you see as the advantages and disadvantages of having an arbitrator with an extensive legal background hearing a case?

Notes

[1] Neil Chamberlain and James Kuhn, *Collective Bargaining*, 2nd ed., New York: McGraw-Hill, 1965, p. 145.

[2] Chamberlain and Kuhn, *Collective Bargaining*, p. 149, quoting Thomas Tongue, "The Development of Industrial Conciliation and Arbitration Under Trade Agreements," *Oregon Law Review* 17 (1938): 270.

[3] Chamberlain and Kuhn, *Collective Bargaining*, p. 147.

[4] See Bob Repas, *Contract Administration*, Washington, DC: Bureau of National Affairs, 1984, pp. 62–86 for an expansion of this list of purposes.

[5] See Kuhn, *Bargaining in the Grievance Settlement*, p. 22, or Chamberlain and Kuhn, *Collective Bargaining*, p. 146.

[6] The substantive facts of this case come from *Kast Metals Corp. Labor Arbitration Reports* 65 (1974): 783.

[7] Ibid., p. 784.

[8] Sumner Slichter, *Union Policies and Industrial Management*, Washington, DC: The Brookings Institute, 1941, p. 1.

[9] James W. Kuhn, *Bargaining in the Grievance Settlement*, New York: Columbia University Press, 1961, pp. 77–78.

[10] Repas, *Contract Administration*, p. 64.

[11]See *Grievance Guide*, 5th ed., Washington, DC: Bureau of National Affairs, 1978, p. 3.

[12]Ibid., p. 234.

[13]Dan Dalton and William Todor, "Manifest Needs of Stewards: Propensity to File a Grievance," *Journal of Applied Psychology*, December 1979: 754–769.

[14]Maurice Trotta, *Handling Grievances*, Washington, DC: Bureau of National Affairs, 1976, p. 42.

[15]Agreement between Boise Cascade Corporation and International Paperworkers Union, Rumford, Maine. Expired June 30, 1986. Reprinted by permission from *Collective Bargaining, Negotiations, and Contracts*, copyright 1984 by the Bureau of National Affairs, Inc., Washington, DC, pp. 51:401–402.

[16]Jeanne Brett and Stephen Goldberg, "Wildcat Strikes in Bituminous Coal Mining," *Industrial and Labor Relations Review*, July 1979: 463–483.

[17]Clyde Summers, "Labor Courts: Alternative to Arbitration," *Columbia Law Review* 72 (October 1972): 119–126.

[18]See for example Paul R. Hays, *Labor Arbitration: A Dissenting View*, New Haven: Yale University Press, 1966, or Florian Bartosic, "Labor Law Reform — the NLRB and A Labor Court," *Georgia Law Review* 4 (1970): 647–673.

[19]*Collective Bargaining Negotiation and Contracts*, p. 51: 5 (1983).

[20]Frank Elkouri and Edna Asper Elkouri, *How Arbitration Works*, Washington, DC: Bureau of National Affairs, 1973, p. 9.

[21]Ibid.

[22]H. G. Heneman III and Marcus H. Sandver, "Arbitrators' Backgrounds and Behavior" *Journal of Labor Research*, vol. 4., Spring 1983: 115–124.

[23]Joseph Brandschain, "Preparation and Trial of a Labor Arbitration Case." In Noel Levin, Gerald Asken, Jerome Rettig, and Joseph Wildebush, eds., *Arbitrating Labor Cases*, New York: Practising Law Institute, 1974, p. 132.

[24]*Lincoln Mills of Alabama* vs. *Textile Workers of America* 230 f. 2d. 81 (1956).

[25]*Textile Workers Union* vs. *Lincoln Mills of Alabama*, p. 456.

[26]Ibid., pp. 583–584.

[27]Ibid., p. 599.

[28]Russel A. Smith and Dallas Jones, "The Supreme Court and Labor Dispute Arbitration: The Emerging Federal Law," *Michigan Law Review*, March 1968: 361.

[29]*United Steelworkers* vs. *American Manufacturing*, pp. 581, 582.

[30]*Teamsters Local 174* vs. *Lucas Flour Co.*, 369 U.S. 95 (1962).

[31]*Charles Dowd Box Co.* vs. *Courtney*, 368 U.S. 502 (1962).

[32]*Sinclair Refining Co.* vs. *Atkinson*, 370 U.S. 195 (1962).

[33]*Boy's Market Inc.* vs. *Retail Clerks Local 770* 416 F. 2d. 368 (1969).

[34]*Boy's Market* vs. *Retail Clerks 770*, p. 249.

[35]*Collyer Insulated Wire Local Union 1098 International Brotherhood of Electrical Workers*, 192 NLRB 150, 77 LRRM 1931 (1971).

[36]*United Technologies Corporation*, 268 NLRB No. 83 (1984).

[37]*Spielberg Manufacturing Co.*, 112 NLRB 1080, 36 LRRM 1552 (1955).

[38]Charles Morris, *The Developing Labor Law*, Washington, DC: Bureau of National Affairs, 1983, p. 957. It should be noted that the Spielberg standards have been relaxed somewhat in the NLRB's recent *Olin Corporation* decision (268 NLRB No. 86) 1984.

[39]Marcus Sandver, Harry Blaine, and Mark Woyar, "Time and Cost Savings Through Expedited Arbitration Procedures," *Arbitration Journal* 36 (December 1981): 12.

[40]Anthony Sinicropi, "Arbitrator Development: Programs and Models," *Arbitration Journal* 32 (September 1982): 29.

[41]Peter Seitz, "Delay: The Asp in the Bosom of Arbitration," *Arbitration Journal* 36 (September 1981): 31.

[42]Sandver, Blaine and Woyar, "Time and Cost Savings through Expedited Arbitration Procedures," p. 13.

[43]John Kogel, Kathy Kelly, and Patrick Szymanski, "Labor Arbitration: Cutting Cost and Time Without Cutting Quality," *Arbitration Journal* 39 (September 1984): 36.

[44]Sinicropi, "Arbitrator Development," p. 30.

[45]Eric Lawson, "Arbitrator Acceptability: Factors Affecting Selection," *Arbitration Journal* 36 (December 1981): 22–29.

[46]Joseph Raffalle, "Lawyers in Labor Arbitration," *Arbitration Journal* 37 (September 1982): 11–23.

[47]323 U.S. 192, 207 (1944).

[48]386 U.S. 171 (1967). See also David Feller, "*Vaca* vs. *Sipes,* One Year Later," *New York University Conference on Labor,* 1969, p. 141.

[49]*Vaca* vs. *Sipes,* pp. 190–191.

[50]*Hines* vs. *Anchor Motor Freight,* 424 U.S. 554.

[51]*Charles V. Bowen* vs. *United States Postal Service* 103 S. Ct. 588 (1983).

CLAYTON TEACHERS VOTE NO

It was 11:00 P.M. on December 31 and Tom Olson should have been out celebrating. But he wasn't. Instead, Tom was watching the 11:00 news, waiting to hear the result of a vote — an important vote that would affect him and the rest of his family. Tom was waiting to hear the result of a strike vote taken by the local teachers' union just a few minutes before. The newscast began with the lead-in: "Clayton teachers vote no on contract proposal. Strike to begin January second." Tom's heart sank. "I knew this would happen," he complained bitterly.

Tom was a senior at Clayton High School, an affluent suburb north of Milwaukee, Wisconsin. The Clayton teachers had gone on strike once three years earlier during Tom's freshman year. The strike was a long one, 27 days. The lost school days were made up during spring break and during June and July. Tom remembered spending boring days at home during the freezing January weather watching situation comedy reruns on television. He also remembered sweating in the unairconditioned classrooms in July while his friends in the Milwaukee school district were swimming and enjoying summer vacation.

"Why can't they settle this and let us get back to school like we're supposed to?" Tom asked his father. "If the strike is a long one like last time I'll miss spring break. The one year I get to go to Florida and now it's going to be ruined by this strike. What if we have to go to school in June and July again? I'll never get a summer job if I can't start work until July! What about the summer vacation we planned to take after I graduate? What will we have to do now — cancel all our plans just because of this stupid teachers' strike? Don't the teachers and the administrators care about how this strike will affect us?"

"Son, the teachers and the administrators are in a tough situation," Tom's father George replied. George knew the situation well; a partner in his law firm was the chief negotiator for the Clayton school district's negotiating team. "The defeat of the school levy last November left the school district with very little money to run the school system," George explained. "The teachers are asking for an 8 percent initial raise and for 5 percent additional for each year after that. The school district just doesn't have that kind of money. It's as simple as that. The teachers claim they are underpaid compared to what teachers in Milwaukee make and that the benefits aren't as good, either," George continued. "The people in the community expect a Grade A educational system. That's the reason most of us have moved here from Milwaukee — because of the quality of the schools. Yet the community won't vote in a school levy that allows the district to maintain the standards that we've had in the past. The teachers want good salaries and benefits, yet the school district has to operate within its budget. As I said before, it's a tough situation. I'm sorry this had to happen, son, but it's a fact of life. Teachers' strikes are a sign of the times — part of the real world of the 1980s. About all we can do now is hope that the strike will be a short one."

Chapter 14

Labor Relations and Collective Bargaining in the Public Sector

Tom Olson was affected by a teachers' strike at his high school — not an uncommon event in modern times. Twenty years ago teachers' strikes, or strikes by any group of governmental or public employees, were unheard of. Today they occur with some frequency. The subject of public sector labor relations is important these days for a number of reasons. A large percentage of the labor force is employed in the governmental sector; recent figures indicate that about three million employees work for the federal government and about 13 million employees work for state and local governments.[1] This group of 16 million employees represents almost 20 percent of the labor force. Public employees are quite intensively unionized, and the unions in this sector are among the few unions that have showed growth over the past 20 years or so. In the federal government, about 50 percent of all employees belong to unions[2]; in state and local government the figure is about the same.[3] Both these figures have increased dramatically since 1965. Finally, public sector bargaining is interesting and important because public employees generally are not covered by the National Labor Relations Act but rather are covered by the Federal Civil Service Reform Act of 1978 (for federal employees) or by one of many different labor relations statutes for state and local employees. Forty states now have some type of statute regulating public sector labor relations, some states having several laws, each dealing with a different occupational group (e.g., fire-fighters, teachers, municipal employees).

Historical Background

Most of us tend to think of public sector collective bargaining as a recent development, and in a sense this is true. Most states did not legally sanction bargaining with their employees until the 1960s or 1970s; federal bargaining regulations date from 1962. Although it was not legally sanctioned, however, bargaining between unions and the federal government has a long history beginning in the naval shipyards in the 1830s. The result of this early experience in bargaining led to the establishment of the 10-hour day for government employees, signed into law by President Van Buren in 1840.[4]

In the Postal Service, local associations of workers began forming in the 1860s. The two major national unions in the industry began in 1888 with the postal clerks' union and in 1890 with the letter carriers' union. The division between postal clerks (mainly employees who work inside postal facilities) and letter carriers (employees who deliver the mail outside postal facilities) continues to the present day. The Knights of Labor provided organizational assistance to the postal workers in the 1860s, 1870s, and 1880s and chartered local unions of postal workers. The AFL chartered the first postal workers union in 1906.[5] Unions of other white collar federal civil service employees began in the first decade of the twentieth century as well.

At the state and local levels, unions among public employees date from the early formation of the National Education Association in the 1850s and the AFL-affiliated American Federation of Teachers in 1916. Firefighters and police had been organizing into local unions since the late 1800s and the AFL officially chartered the International Association of Firefighters in 1918. Other state, county, and municipal employees started their movement for unionization in 1932 with the Wisconsin State Employees Association, started in Madison, Wisconsin. In 1936 this organization changed its name to the American Federation of State, County, and Municipal Employees and became the first national union of nonteaching, nonuniformed state and local workers.

Major Organizations

The Postal Service

American Postal Workers Union and National Association of Letter Carriers. The larger of the two Postal Service unions is the American Postal Workers Union (APWU), formed in 1971 as the result of a merger of four unions: the United Federation of Postal Clerks, the National Association of Post Office and General Services Maintenance Employees, the National Federation of Post Office Motor Vehicle Operators, and the National Postal Unions.[6] The APWU is the largest union in the Postal Service, with a 1982 membership of 248,000 in 3,700 local unions throughout the United States.[7] The second major union in the Postal Service is the National Association of Letter Carriers (NALC), formed in 1899 in Milwaukee, Wisconsin, with 175,000 members in 4,300 local unions throughout the country in 1982.[8] Both the APWU and the NALC are affiliated with the AFL–CIO.

Federal Sector

American Federation of Government Employees.   The largest national union of federal employees is the American Federation of Government Employees (AFGE), with 210,000 members in 1982,[9] down from 300,000 in 1968 and 260,000 in 1976.[10] This union holds representation rights to a much larger number of workers than it enrolls as members; perhaps as many as 700,000 federal employees work in units covered by AFGE labor agreements.[11] This difference in numbers is because under federal regulations there can be no union or agency shop provisions in federal government labor agreements. Thus, even though a union may be certified as a bargaining agent for a group of federal employees and even though it may negotiate an agreement that covers all workers in that unit, there is no obligation that anyone covered by the agreement join the union.

The AFGE was started in 1932 after the existing union of federal employees in the AFL (the National Federation of Federal Employees) withdrew from the organization. The AFGE represents government employees all over the United States, although most of its membership is concentrated in Washington, D.C. and in the large military facilities in the southeastern United States. The AFGE's president, Kenneth Blaylock, is a relatively young (he was 41 years old when he became president in 1976), ambitious leader. Shortly after he was elected AFGE president, Blaylock began an aggressive campaign to organize uniformed military personnel into the union.[12] Action by Congress in 1977 prohibited uniformed military personnel from unionizing, however, and this effort on AFGE's part has been halted.

National Federation of Federal Employees.   The oldest continuously operating national union of nonpostal employees in the federal sector is the National Federation of Federal Employees (NFFE). NFFE was originally chartered as an AFL union in 1917, but withdrew from the AFL in 1931 in a dispute over the classification system for federal employees (the GS or general service schedule), which the NFFE leadership supported and which most AFL leaders opposed. The membership of NFFE is comprised of employees from many different branches of the federal service; NFFE and AFGE compete for members. In 1982 NFFE reported a membership of 52,000 members in 500 local unions around the country.[13] NFFE is not affiliated with the AFL–CIO.

National Association of Government Employees.   The National Association of Government Employees (NAGE) was founded in 1962 and was originally an association of veterans. The growth of NAGE over the past few years has been called "astonishing" by one author, and the organization has been successful in winning elections among civilian employees (both white and blue collar) in military installations, spacecraft launching facilities, and offices.[14] In 1983 the NAGE affiliated with the

Service Employees International Union and claimed 200,000 members, not all of whom are federal employees, however.[15]

National Treasury Employees Union.   The National Treasury Employees Union (NTEU) began in 1938 as the National Association of Collectors of Internal Revenue as an association of IRS field employees seeking civil service status.[16] The organization grew in size and scope and adopted the present name in 1973. Led by a young, aggressive leader named Robert Tobias (the former chief legal counsel of the NTEU), the NTEU is known as a militant, vigorous organization and has expanded its scope of membership beyond the IRS into other federal agencies such as the Federal Energy Administration. In 1982 the NTEU reported 55,000 members in 215 local unions.[17] The NTEU is not affiliated with the AFL–CIO.

State and Local Governments

It is difficult to identify all the major organizations representing employees in state and local government because of their diversity. Most states have some type of state employee association that represents state government employees within the state and that usually remains separate from any national labor organization. There are, however, a few large national organizations that do predominantly represent state and local employees.

National Education Association.   The largest group of employees at the state and local level are in education; the largest labor organization representing employees in education is the National Education Association (NEA), formed in 1857 as a professional mutual benefit association for teachers.[18] Originally the NEA had many administrators and superintendents as members and it functioned mostly as a professional association dedicated to the advancement of the teaching profession. Today the NEA is a large, powerful force in the field of public sector collective bargaining, claiming 1.6 million members in 1982 in 12,300 local organizations.[19] The NEA since 1976 has been officially classified as a labor union by the Bureau of Labor Statistics, although it has a considerable number of members who are not covered by a collective bargaining agreement or who are not part of any bargaining unit. Prior to 1961 the NEA did not actively promote collective negotiations for teachers; with the defection of its large New York City local union chapter to the American Federation of Teachers (AFT) in that year, however, the organization changed its policies and began advocating "professional negotiations" for teachers. The NEA is not now and never has been affiliated with the AFL–CIO.

American Federation of Teachers.   The main rival to the NEA is the American Federation of Teachers, founded in Chicago in 1916 as a national union of teachers affiliated with the AFL.[20] The AFT claimed 570,000 members in 1982 in 2,200 constituent local unions.[21] Many of AFT's members are in large urban areas such as New York, Chicago, Philadelphia, Detroit, Boston, Pittsburgh, Cleveland, Cincinnati, Minneapolis, Denver, and Baltimore.[22] The AFT has quite a decentralized bargaining structure and is extending its jurisdiction to include not just teachers but also bus drivers, maintenance and custodial employees, and food service employees in the educational industry. As with the NEA, many members of AFT are college faculty members; the AFT is credited with being the first union to negotiate a collective bargaining agreement for faculty members, in 1967 at the U.S. Merchant Marine Academy.[23]

American Federation of State, County, and Municipal Employees. The dominant union for noneducational, nonuniformed state and local public employees is the American Federation of State, County, and Municipal Employees (AFSCME), founded in Madison, Wisconsin in 1932 and given a national union charter by the AFL in 1936.[24] AFSCME is categorized as an industrial union of public employees and will admit to membership and organize virtually any group of public employees. While AFSCME has traditionally been regarded as a union mainly of city employees,[25] the union also has a considerable number of members who work for state and county governments. AFSCME has been one of the fastest growing unions in the entire labor movement. In 1960 it had 180,000 members; only 18 years later it had over one million members and for a brief period was the largest union in the AFL–CIO. (The Retail Clerks and Amalgamated Meatcutters merged in 1979 to form the United Food and Commercial Workers Union, which then became the largest AFL–CIO union.) AFSCME in 1982 claimed 950,000 members in 3,000 local unions.[26] Although AFSCME's membership has dropped slightly in very recent years because of layoffs in some municipalities, this union still maintains an aggressive and dynamic commitment to organizing and growth.

Firefighters and Police Unions. Firefighters are mainly organized into the International Association of Firefighters (IAFF), founded as an AFL affiliate in 1918 and remaining by far the dominant organization of firefighters. The IAFF claimed 163,000 members in 1,958 local unions in 1982.[27] In contrast to the firefighters, the police show no single unifying organization. Several organizations represent police officers, including AFSCME, the Teamsters, and the Service Employees International Union. Specialized unions representing only police are the International Conference of Police Associations, the Fraternal Order of Police (FOP), the International Brotherhood of Police Officers (an affiliate of the National Association of Government Employees, which in turn has affiliated with the Service Employees), the National Union of Police Officers, and the American Federation of Police. FOP, founded in 1915, is the union with the oldest heritage of representing police officers. It reported 160,000 members in 1,350 local unions (or lodges) around the country in 1982.[28]

State Employee Associations.   In addition to the national unions discussed in this section, there are also many state employee associations (SEA) operating independently of any national union. The trend for most large state employee associations has been to merge with one of the large national unions. For example, in 1978 the 250,000-member Civil Service Employees Association of New York merged with AFSCME, as did the 17,000-member Ohio Civil Service Employee Association in 1983. In 1984 the 60,000-member California State Employees Association merged with the Service Employees International Union. In many states, however, the state employee associations maintain independence from any national organization, for example, SEAs in Colorado, Maine, Montana, Nebraska, North Dakota, and Utah. In other states they are loosely confederated into the Assembly of Government Employees (AGE), an organization that allows the state employee associations a considerable amount of autonomy to run their own affairs. State employee associations affiliated with AGE include those of Alabama, Alaska, Idaho, Indiana, Maryland, North Carolina, Nevada, South Dakota, Vermont, Washington, and Wyoming.

Union Growth

It is important to remember that the widespread growth of labor relations in the public sector is a relatively recent development, most of this growth occurring in the years 1962–1978. The phenomenon of public sector union growth can in one sense be looked upon as an extension of the general union growth model introduced in Chapter 2: as a response to the tensions of work. In another sense, however, the public sector is sufficiently different and specialized from the private sector that a more detailed discussion of union growth in the public sector is warranted.

As discussed in Chapters 2 and 8, workers vote for unions in certification elections and join unions after certification for a variety of economic, sociological, and psychological reasons. Before even reaching the point of a certification election or bargaining, however, certain preconditions are necessary, such as a favorable legal environment, a cohesive work group, and the presence of certain tensions of work, before there will be a movement toward unionization at all. For public sector employees, one of the first of these work tensions was the low pay received by public sector workers compared to private sector workers.[29] The power of private sector unions and their aggressiveness made the disparity between private sector and public sector wages greater and greater in the post-World War II years. A second precondition that made the formation of public sector unions possible was weakness of individual bargaining in the public sector because of the absence of unique skills or specialized abilities by many public employees.[30] Finally, there was a sense of community among many public employees, evident among groups like public school teachers and some civil service groups that had been organized into professional associations for many years.

Rapid Growth in the 1960s

Beginning sometime in the late 1950s and the very early 1960s, events changed just enough to precipitate a growth in unionism that up to that point had been only a possibility — not a fact. Economic conditions changed just enough, for example, to make the movement toward unionization imperative for some workers. As inflation increased in the early 1960s and as the labor market tightened (unemployment decreased), the potential bargaining power of public employees increased.[31] Coupled with the squeeze of inflation on workers' wages was the growth in total employment in the government sector, especially at the state and local government levels. During the 1950s total employment in state and local government grew almost 50 percent, from 4 million in 1950 to over 6 million in 1960 (Table 14.1).[32] Furthermore, this growth accelerated in the years 1957–1962, making public organizations larger, more impersonal, and more bureaucratic; increasing the tensions of work; and making unionization more of a possibility. Finally, many public employers did nothing to ameliorate or to neutralize the increase in the tensions experienced by their employees. It has been pointed out by several authors that the professionalization of the personnel field was not well advanced in the public sector at this time, and that even the rudiments of the "human relations" school of management was foreign to most public employers.[33]

Finally events changed enough that by 1962 or 1963 the movement toward unionization for public employees became inevitable. During the 1960s and 1970s, forces served to accelerate the union movement that had already begun. The growth of government employment at the state and local levels continued all during this period. Inflation continued and spiraled upward into the double digits by 1970. Public attitudes and worker attitudes toward unionization and toward militant action became more liberalized. The civil rights demonstrations and the student riots of the 1960s demonstrated to public workers the effectiveness of civil disobedience in achieving change. In some cases civil rights issues became public sector workers' issues. Who can forget that Martin Luther King, Jr. was assassinated while in Memphis to support a municipal workers' strike in 1968?

As the number of public sector workers joining unions increased, the unions themselves increased their zeal and their organizing activity. Unions are able to pool more dues monies into organizing when the organizations are growing. In addition, collective bargaining gains at-

TABLE 14-1   Total and Governmental Employment in the United States, 1951–1980 (in thousands)

Year	Total	Government Total	Federal	State and Local
1951	47,819	6,389	2,302	4,087
1952	48,793	6,609	2,420	4,188
1953	50,202	6,645	2,305	4,340
1954	48,990	6,751	2,188	4,563
1955	50,641	6,914	2,187	4,727
1956	52,369	7,278	2,209	5,069
1957	52,853	7,616	2,217	5,399
1958	51,624	7,839	2,191	5,648
1959	53,268	8,083	2,233	5,850
1960	54,189	8,353	2,270	6,083
1961	53,999	8,594	2,279	6,315
1962	55,549	8,890	2,340	6,550
1963	56,653	9,225	2,358	6,868
1964	58,283	9,596	2,348	7,248
1965	60,765	10,074	2,378	7,696
1966	63,901	10,784	2,564	8,220
1967	65,803	11,391	2,719	8,672
1968	67,897	11,839	2,737	9,120
1969	70,384	12,195	2,758	9,437
1970	70,880	12,554	2,731	9,823
1971	71,214	12,881	2,696	10,185
1972	73,675	13,334	2,684	10,649
1973	76,790	13,732	2,663	11,068
1974	78,265	14,170	2,724	11,446
1975	78,945	14,686	2,748	11,937
1976	79,382	14,871	2,733	12,138
1977	82,471	15,127	2,727	12,399
1978	86,697	15,672	2,753	12,919
1979	89,823	15,947	2,773	13,147
1980	90,564	16,249	2,866	13,383

Source: Richard C. Kearney, *Labor Relations in the Public Sector,* Marcel Dekker, Inc., N.Y., 1984. Reprinted from *Labor Relations in the Public Sector,* by courtesy of Marcel Dekker, Inc.

tracted many workers voluntarily. Some interunion rivalries such as those between AFT and NEA and between AFSCME and independent state employee associations made the organizing campaigns seem more intense and increased worker involvement in them.[34] Contrasted with this verve, excitement, and activity on the part of union organizers was a lack of resistance and the absence of a sophisticated response to organizing on the part of many public employers.[35] Large-scale public opinion shifts against public workers probably did not begin until well into the 1970s, when fears about the financial health of major cities such as New York and Cleveland began to be partially blamed on excessive wages and benefits negotiated by public workers' unions.

A final major factor accounting for the growth of public sector unions in the 1960s and 1970s is the change in the legal environment controlling public sector collective bargaining. One major reason for this change was the U.S. Supreme Court ruling in *Baker* vs. *Carr*,[36] which required a reorganization of the U.S. House of Representatives along the "one person, one vote" principle and the subsequent Supreme Court ruling in 1964 (*Reynolds* vs. *Simms*[37]) that required state legislatures to be organized in the same manner. This reorganization at the state level in particular gave urban areas more representation in state government and made state legislatures more sensitive to the needs of constituents in big cities, constituents who were more likely to be prounion or at least less likely to be antiunion than those from rural areas.[38]

One result of this reorganization was the passage of state level legislation that for the first time in many states protected the rights of public workers to join unions and encouraged the process of collective bargaining. In many states these laws passed in the 1960s and 1970s became the equivalent of "little Wagner Acts" for public employees. At the federal level the major change in the legal environment for public employee bargaining came with the election to the U.S. presidency of John F. Kennedy in 1960 and Kennedy's subsequent signing of Executive Order 10988 in 1962 allowing federal employees the right to join unions and to engage in limited bargaining with federal employers. Although there is some academic debate about whether changes in public policy caused the growth of public employee unions during the 1960s or whether the growth of public employee unions caused the change in public policy, there is no debating that the changes that did occur in the legal environment made the future of public employee bargaining more secure and gave public employee bargaining the institutional permanence it enjoys today.

The Legal Environment

As discussed in Chapters 7 and 8, the legal system has a profound effect on the conduct of labor–management relations. Understanding the statutes and regulations that control public sector labor relations will contribute substantially to the understanding of labor relations in the public sector.

The Postal Service

Labor relations in the Postal Service is controlled by the Postal Reorganization Act passed in 1970. The Postal Service represents a unique entity within the general framework of public sector labor–management relations. It is an agency of government that supplies a unique and virtually monopolistic service to virtually every household in the country every day. It is truly a national service with offices in even the smallest of towns stretching from the Aleutian Islands to the Florida

Keys and from the northernmost tip of Maine to the southernmost Hawaiian island. The products manufactured and services provided by the Postal Service are sold for a fee to the consumers. Unlike many other agencies of the government, the Postal Service has a steady source of revenue from its customers and can conceivably operate without any subsidy on the part of taxpayers. Finally, the Postal Service has had a long tradition of unionization among its employees and has for a long time been the most intensively unionized segment of government. In addition, the massive size of the Postal Service makes it one of the largest employers in the country.

Postal Bargaining Under Executive Order 10988. With the signing of Executive Order 10988 by President Kennedy in 1962, collective bargaining was formally allowed for federal employees. The postal unions were one of the first to take advantage of this liberalization of federal policy and negotiated a national postal agreement in March 1963. This agreement was negotiated by the six national unions in the Postal Service at the time and covered over 620,000 employees (87 percent of total Postal Service employment at the time).[39] This initial agreement was followed by contracts negotiated in 1964, 1966, and 1968. With each round of negotiations the parties learned more and more about the process of collective bargaining, and concessions on each side were not as freely exchanged as they had been in 1963. Pressures began to build among workers to change inequities in the wage system (an item that could not be negotiated); pressures were building on management to protect and expand management rights. The 1969 negotiations were arduous and contentious, but after long months of bargaining an agreement was reached. The negotiations in 1970 were not so successful. In March 1970 the United States witnessed its first nationwide federal employee strike in the Postal Service.

A movement to reorganize the Postal Service had been started as early as 1967 by President Lyndon Johnson. A presidential task force in 1968 recommended that the post office department be abolished and reconstituted as an independent government corporation operating on a self-supporting basis. The task force recommendation did not receive congressional support in 1968, however. The movement for postal reform strengthened with the election of Richard Nixon to the presidency in 1968. Congress debated various versions of reform legislation in 1969 and early 1970, but no consensus on any particular bill seemed to emerge. With the postal strike in March 1970, however, attention was given to the issue of postal reform, especially reform of the practice of labor relations.

The Postal Reorganization Act of 1970. The settlement of the Postal strike was the result of negotiations between Secretary of Labor George Shultz, Postmaster General Winton M. Blount, AFL–CIO President

George Meany, and postal union leaders.[40] These negotiations produced not only a settlement to the strike, but also a new proposal for reorganizing the Postal Service. President Nixon endorsed the negotiated settlement in April 1970; Congress passed the statute codifying the negotiated settlement in August and titled it the Postal Reorganization Act of 1970. The immediate effect of the settlement was a 14 percent pay raise for postal workers in 1970.[41]

The Postal Reorganization Act created the U.S. Postal Service and chartered it as an independent corporation within the executive branch of the U.S. government. The act created an independent 11-person Board of Governors to oversee the Postal Service and to choose its director. In addition, a separate 5-person Postal Rate Commission was established by the statute to set postal rates and to guarantee a level of revenue to the USPS such that it could eventually operate without the need for government subsidy. The labor relations provisions of the Postal Reorganization Act were equally broad-sweeping and were the real reason for its passage in the first place. Beginning immediately, labor relations in the Postal Service were to be governed by the provisions of the National Labor Relations Act — not by the Federal Executive Orders covering other federal employees. Surely this was a radical transformation for labor relations in the government; at that time the Postal Service was the largest federal agency, having twice as many civilian employees as the next largest agency, the Defense Department.

The Postal Reorganization Act allowed for negotiation of wages and benefits, something not allowed in any other statute regulating federal employees either before or since. The National Labor Relations Board (NLRB) was given the power to interpret and enforce the new statute, to investigate unfair labor practices, and to conduct representation elections. The only real difference that remained between labor relations in the Postal Service and all private industry was that under the Reorganization Act strikes were prohibited; factfinding and arbitration were to be used to resolve any issues over which the parties were unable to agree within 180 days from the beginning of negotiations. The statute appears to be working well and no strikes have occurred in the Postal Service in the past 15 years. In February 1985 the unresolved issues from the 1984 round of negotiations were resolved by an arbitration panel — the first time this provision of the Postal Reorganization Act has been used. The labor agreement in the Postal Service maintains its distinction as the largest single agreement covering the greatest number of workers in the country.

The Federal Government

Labor relations for most employees of the federal government are controlled by the provisions of the Civil Service Reform Act (CSRA) of 1978. The CSRA is the last in a long line of laws regulating the employment relationship between the federal government and its employees. In 1883

Congress passed the Pendleton Act, requiring that federal employees be employed on the merit principle and that Congress be given the sole and exclusive right to regulate wages, hours, fringe benefits, and working conditions for federal workers. In 1912 the Lloyd-LaFollette Act was passed, giving federal employees the right to join labor organizations and to petition Congress for changes in wages and working conditions. The Wagner Act, the Taft-Hartley Act, and the Landrum-Griffin Act (see Chapter 7) all generally ignored the issue of labor–management relations in the federal sector with the exception that section 305 of the Taft-Hartley Act outlaws strikes by federal employees.

With Kennedy's election to the presidency in 1960, however, the subject of federal sector labor relations received renewed attention. Kennedy had been elected with the help of active support from organized labor and with considerable support from the postal workers' unions. Soon after his election Kennedy chartered a blue-ribbon task force to investigate the state of labor–management relations in the federal service. The task force's recommendations were issued in 1961 and Kennedy incorporated most of these into his Executive Order 10988, which he signed in 1962.

Executive Order 10988.   Executive Order 10988 for the first time in U.S. history allowed for collective bargaining by federal government employees. The order established a procedure for union recognition and for exclusive union representation when the union was chosen by the majority of employees in a bargaining unit. The exclusive recognition provision allowed unions to meet and confer with management over issues such as personnel policies and working conditions. Congress still retained the right to set employee wages and benefits — a right it has never relinquished. The executive order spelled out the criteria for the determination of the bargaining units, much the same as that found in section 9 of the NLRA. A Code of Fair Labor Practices was written into Executive Order 10988 containing many of the provisions of sections 8(a) and 8(b) of the NLRA. Finally, the executive order enunciated a statement of management rights and reserved certain issues for the sole and exclusive decisionmaking of management. These rights were not negotiable and included rights such as:

(a) to direct employees of the agency,

(b) to hire, promote, transfer, assign, and retain employees in positions with the agency, and to suspend, demote, discharge, or take disciplinary action . . . ,

(c) to relieve employees from duties because of lack of work or for other legitimate reasons,

(d) to maintain the efficiency of government operations entrusted to them,

(e) to determine the methods, means and personnel by which such operations are to be conducted; and

(f) to take whatever actions may be necessary to carry out the mission of the agency in situations of emergency.[42]

Subsequent Executive Orders. Executive Order 10988 was significantly amended in 1969 with President Nixon's Executive Order 11491. The provisions of this executive order provided for a special federal agency to administer federal labor–management relations laws: the Federal Labor Relations Council. In addition, Executive Order 11491 allowed for the first time the final and binding arbitration of federal workers' grievances. A panel for dealing with bargaining impasses between labor and management was established (the Federal Services Impasse Panel) and was given the power to resolve federal sector labor–management disputes. Further changes in federal sector labor–management relations were introduced with Nixon's 1971 Executive Order 11616 and with President Ford's Executive Order 11838 signed in 1975. The major effect of these orders was to strengthen the grievance procedure (11616) and to broaden the scope of bargaining to include working conditions (11838).

The Civil Service Reform Act of 1978. The big change in federal sector labor–management relations came in 1978 with the passage by Congress of the Civil Service Reform Act during the Carter administration. The CSRA differs fundamentally in structure from the executive orders in that only a subsequent act of Congress can modify or eliminate a congressional statute; an executive order, by contrast, can be changed or modified by presidential initiative that does not have to be subjected to the rigors of congressional debate. Thus, the CSRA gave permanence and stability to federal labor–management relations that only an act of Congress can provide.

The CSRA is a very broad piece of legislation that makes many changes in the federal civil service system. The labor–relations provisions of the CSRA are found in section 7 of the act. In many respects the CSRA merely codifies and restates provisions found in the executive orders passed earlier. In other respects, however, the CSRA adds a new dimension to the regulation of federal labor–management relations by making explicit employee rights that had been implicit in the executive orders. For example, the CSRA clearly states that employees have "the right to join, form, and assist any labor organization, or to refrain from any such activity, freely and without fear of reprisal, and each employee shall be protected in the exercise of such rights." Furthermore, employees are given the right to engage in collective bargaining with respect to conditions of employment (defined as personnel policies, practices and matters, whether established by rule, regulation, or otherwise affecting working conditions). Wages and benefits are excluded from the scope of bargaining as they were under the executive orders.[43]

In addition, the act established a new administrative agency, the Federal Labor Relations Authority (FLRA) a three-person board to administer the law. The duties of the FLRA involve conducting representation elections, investigating allegations of unfair labor practices, resolving unit determination issues, to oversee the continued operation of the Federal Services Impasse Panel and to provide for Federal Mediation and Conciliation Service (FMCS) mediation of disputes. In addition, the FLSA was given expanded enforcement powers such as the right to issue cease and desist orders and the right to subpoena witnesses.

A final major change in federal sector labor relations brought about by the CSRA concerns the expansion of the grievance procedure. Under the CSRA all federal sector labor agreements must include a negotiated grievance procedure with binding arbitration as the final step.[44] Under the executive orders grievance procedures were not required in labor agreements.

The passage of the Civil Service Reform Act marks the beginning of the "statutory era" of labor relations law in the federal sector. Although the CSRA did not fundamentally or radically alter labor relations in the federal sector, it did provide for more stability and more predictability in the dealings between the parties. It is notable that federal employees still do not have the right to negotiate about wages or benefits even after the passage of the CSRA. The narrowness of the scope of bargaining distinguishes federal employee labor legislation from many other public sector bargaining laws.

State and Local Governments

After reading about the evolution of collective bargaining law in the federal sector, the casual observer may confess to some confusion with the changes from one executive order to the next and with the differences between employee bargaining rights in the postal sector compared to those in the rest of the federal government. By comparison to the tangled welter of laws at the state and local government levels, however, the statutes governing federal employees appear simple. One recent survey estimates that there are more than 100 separate state statutes governing labor relations at the state and local levels, and more are being passed all the time.[45] Indeed, the differences among the various state statutes are so great that almost any general statement summarizing the nature of the legal regulations of labor relations at the state and local levels would be incomplete. Some state and local ordinances actually outlaw collective bargaining by public employers; some embrace the collective bargaining concept in total and even protect the rights of public employees to go on strike. A summary of the statutes of state public employee bargaining laws is given in Table 14.2.

As of 1985 there were no northern or major industrial states without

TABLE 14-2　State Public Employee Bargaining Laws in Effect in 1985

State	State	Local	Police	Firefighters	Teachers
Alabama	−	−	−	*	−
Alaska	+	+	+	+	+
Arizona	−	−	−	−	−
Arkansas	−	−	−	−	−
California	+	+	+	+	+
Colorado	−	−	−	−	−
Connecticut	+	+	+	+	+
Delaware	+	+	+	+	+
Florida	+	+	+	+	+
Georgia	−	−	−	+	−
Hawaii	+	+	+	+	+
Idaho	−	−	−	+	+
Illinois	+	+	+	+	+
Indiana	− a	− a	−	−	+
Iowa	+	+	+	+	+
Kansas	*	*	*	*	+
Kentucky	−	−	+	+	−
Louisiana	−	−	−	−	−
Maine	+	+	+	+	+
Maryland	−	−	−	−	+
Massachusetts	+	+	+	+	+
Michigan	+	+	+	+	+
Minnesota	+	+	+	+	+
Mississippi	−	−	−	−	−
Missouri	*	*	−	*	−
Montana	+	+	+	+	+
Nebraska	+	+	+	+	+
Nevada	−	+	+	+	+
New Hampshire	+	+	+	+	+
New Jersey	+	+	+	+	+
New Mexico	+	−	−	−	−
New York	+	+	+	+	+
North Carolina	x	x	x	x	x
North Dakota	−	−	−	−	*
Ohio	+	+	+	+	+
Oklahoma	−	−	*	*	+
Oregon	+	+	+	+	+
Pennsylvania	+	+	+	+	+
Rhode Island	+	+	+	+	+
South Carolina	−	−	−	−	−
South Dakota	+	+	+	+	+
Tennessee	−	−	−	−	+
Texas	−	−	+	+	−
Utah	−	−	−	− b	−
Vermont	+	+	+	+	+
Virginia	−	−	−	−	−
Washington	+	+	+	+	+
West Virginia	−	−	−	−	−

(continued)

TABLE 14-2   *(continued)*

State	State	Local	Police	Firefighters	Teachers
Wisconsin	+	+	+	+	+
Wyoming	−	−	−	+	−

Summary: Full collective bargaining for all   25
           Full or limited collective bargaining for at least one group   15
           No statute or bargaining prohibited   10

Legend: + = full collective bargaining rights; * = limited bargaining rights;
x = bargaining prohibited by statute; − = no statute.
ªLaw repealed in 1982.
ᵇLaw declared unconstitutional in 1977.

Source: Reprinted by permission from *Government Employee Relations Report Reference File,* copyright 1985 by the Bureau of National Affairs, Inc., Washington, DC.

public employee bargaining laws. The 10 states with no bargaining laws form three regional clusters of states with contiguous boundaries: the Southwest-Mountain state group of Utah, Arizona, and Colorado; the Deep South group of Arkansas, Louisiana, and Mississippi; and the Middle Atlantic-Appalachian group of West Virginia, Virginia, North Carolina, and South Carolina. If Alabama and Georgia are added (each has a statute that applies only to firefighters), the Southwest and the Middle Atlantic groups would combine to form a contiguous group of states with no public employee bargaining laws running from Virginia through Louisiana. It is interesting to note that most of the states without public employee bargaining laws are right-to-work states. The only states without public employee bargaining laws that are not right-to-work states are Colorado and West Virginia. Only 4 of the 21 right-to-work states have comprehensive public employee statutes (Florida, Iowa, Nebraska, and South Dakota).

Most of the public employee bargaining legislation listed in Table 14.2 was passed in the 1960s and 1970s. Eighteen states passed some type of law before 1970, 18 passed legislation during the 1970s, and 4 were passed in the 1980s. Once a statute is passed, the legislative process is not ended; the laws will be updated and amended as needed.

Basic Issues Covered in State Legislation.   Although there are wide differences in the design and operation of state public employee bargaining statutes, all laws covering the labor relations function eventually have to deal with seven very basic topics.

> Whom does the statute cover? What employee groups are included and excluded?
>
> What are the basic rights of employees and employers under the statute?

What procedure is to be followed in certifying the union as bargaining agent and what criteria will be used to determine appropriate bargaining units?

What practices of employers and unions are outlawed by the statute?

What are the permissible subjects of bargaining? Are there any subjects that the parties are not permitted to negotiate about?

How will impasses in negotiations be handled? Will strikes be permitted or prohibited?

How will the act be administered? What will be the powers of the administrative agency?

Coverage.   Most of the state statutes listed in Table 14.2 have comprehensive coverage for all public employees in the state. Many state laws, however, cover one group of employees but not another. Some states have public employee bargaining laws that cover only teachers (Indiana, Maryland, North Dakota, and Tennessee); others have comprehensive bargaining provisions for teachers but not for some other groups of public employees (Idaho, Indiana, Kansas, Nevada, Oklahoma, and Tennessee). Of the 40 states that have any type of statute, 33 cover teachers. Moreover, only one of these statutes (North Dakota) provides for less than full collective bargaining.

Firefighters are covered by some type of statute in 35 states, but in only 31 of these does the statute provide for a complete bargaining relationship. In three states (Alabama, Georgia, and Wyoming), firefighters are the only public employee group covered by a public employee bargaining statute. The Utah statute passed in 1975 covered only firefighters but it was declared unconstitutional by an act of the state supreme court in 1977. In the others (Alabama, Kansas, Missouri, and Oklahoma) the law provides for a "meet and confer" type of relationship between labor and management that gives the public employer more power to make the final decision about the determination of wages and hours than does a full bargaining relationship. In all states with public employee bargaining laws, firefighters are prohibited from striking.

Police are covered by some type of labor relations statute in 30 states, in 28 of which the police have full bargaining rights. No state statute covers only police, although two state statutes (Kentucky and Texas) cover only police and firefighters and exclude all other employees. The statute in Kentucky covers only police and firefighters in cities of over 300,000 population (only Louisville meets this limit). In Texas, cities are allowed to bargain with police and firefighters, but such action must be approved by popular referendum of the voters before it can begin. As with firefighters, police are prohibited from striking in all state statutes.

Municipal employees are allowed full collective bargaining rights with their employers in 26 states, and 28 states provide for some type of statute governing labor relations at the local level. There are no states having laws that cover only municipal employees. In many cities, however, employees bargain under local ordinances or under local memorandums of understanding with city governments even where no statute exists. This was common in many Ohio cities, for example, prior to the passage of the state public employee bargaining act in 1983.

State workers are covered by 28 state laws, 26 of which provide for full collective bargaining. In Nevada state employees are the only ones excluded from the state's public employee bargaining law; in New Mexico, however, they are the only employee group covered by statute.

Basic Rights of Employees and Employers.   Most state statutes provide for basic worker rights patterned after the section 7 rights of the NLRA: the rights to join, form, and assist labor organizations; to bargain collectively through elected representatives; to engage in concerted activity for mutual aid or protection in support of bargaining; and to refrain from union activity. In some statutes the act may add that employees have the right to full and equal representation by the union, free from discrimination.

Employer rights are usually mentioned in the statutes as well, including such items as the rights to determine managerial policy and the direction of the agency; to supervise employees; to evaluate employee performance; and to hire, promote, and transfer employees. To some extent the statement of employer rights in the statute limits the scope of bargaining (items relating to employer rights are excluded) and limits the types of issues that are subject to the grievance procedure as well.

Recognition and Unit Determination.   The procedure for union recognition in the public sector is usually through a secret ballot election, much the same as provided in section 9 of the NLRA. In many instances, however, public employee bargaining statutes are passed after labor and management have already been negotiating, sometimes for several years. In those cases, existing bargaining units are allowed to be "grandfathered" in, meaning that existing units will automatically be certified as bargaining representatives based on past practice or on some evidence (usually through membership rosters) that the union represents a majority. Most statutes provide for the principle of exclusive representation, under which there can be only one union representing one unit of employees. Most statutes also have a procedure for decertifying the union if the employees no longer wish to be represented for bargaining purposes or if they wish to be represented by another labor organization.

The issue of unit determination is a complex one usually handled on a case-by-case basis by the agency administering the act, much the same way that the NLRB handles unit issues in the private sector. In some statutes, however, bargaining units are predetermined and are written into the law. In the Hawaii bargaining law, for example, there are statewide units of teachers, state workers, firefighters, and police. In other states, like New York, the units are on a occupation-by-occupation and agency-by-agency basis. For example, clerical employees of the state Department of Education might be in one unit while clerical employees of the Department of Transportation would be in another. In some cases separate firefighters' statutes or separate teachers' statutes predetermine the unit.

Unfair Labor Practices.   The states commonly borrow from section 8 of the NLRA in listing unfair labor practices, although some go beyond the listing in 8(a) and 8(b) to deal with special problems unique to public employment. A common list of employer unfair labor practices may be as follows:

> To interfere with or coerce employees from exercising their basic rights under the law.
>
> To interfere with the formation or operation of a public employee labor organization.
>
> To discriminate against employees in the employment relationship because of their union activity.
>
> To retaliate against employees who give testimony or file charges under the act.
>
> To refuse to bargain collectively with the elected representatives of the work group.
>
> To fail to process grievances in a timely fashion.
>
> To lock out employees for the purpose of bringing pressure to bear on them during negotiations.
>
> To cause an employee organization to fail in its duty to represent its members fairly.

A list of union unfair labor practices may include the following:

> To restrain employers from exercising their basic rights under the statute.
>
> To cause an employer to fail to discharge his or her responsibilities under the act.
>
> To refuse to bargain in good faith with the employer.
>
> To strike or picket an employer because of a jurisdictional dispute with another union.
>
> To strike in violation of the statute.
>
> To fail to fairly and equally represent all employees in an exclusive bargaining unit.
>
> To picket the private residence of a public employer.

To slow down or to interfere with the efficient operation of the unit.

In most state statutes, unfair labor practices are investigated by the agency empowered to administer the act, which is given the power to issue cease and desist orders when it finds that an unfair labor practice has been committed by either labor or management.

Scope of Bargaining.   Under most public employee bargaining laws the scope of bargaining is quite broad and includes wages, hours, and other terms and conditions of employment — the definition of the scope of bargaining found in section 8(d) of the NLRA. However, there are differences between the scope of bargaining usually found in the private sector and in the public sector. In the private sector, for example, there are no exclusory management rights named in the statute; in the public sector some items are usually statutorily excluded from negotiations. In some states items covered by civil service regulations or teacher tenure laws are excluded from negotiations.

One issue that definitely is different in the scope of bargaining between the public sector and the private sector is the issue of union security. In the private sector the union may negotiate the union shop in the labor agreement except in the 21 right-to-work states where the union shop is outlawed. In the public sector, however, the union shop is allowed in the state statutes only in Alaska, Maine, Kentucky, Vermont, and Washington. In a number of other states, the maximum amount of union security that may be negotiated is the agency shop (Connecticut, Michigan, Montana, Ohio, Oregon, Rhode Island, Vermont, and Wisconsin). The U.S. Supreme Court ruled in 1977 that agency shop provisions in public employee bargaining are not unconstitutional.[46] In many states, however, union security of any type is outside the scope of bargaining in public employee negotiations.

Impasse Resolution.   Another area in which there is a significant difference between private sector and public sector collective bargaining is in the area of impasse and dispute resolution. In the private sector there is a provision in section 8(d) of the NLRA providing for 30-day notice to the FMCS before contract expiration and for mediation of unresolved contract items, but that is the extent of the NLRA's provision dealing with dispute resolution (with the exception of national emergency strike procedures). In the private sector collective bargaining impasses may result in a strike and the issue is resolved between the parties based on their bargaining power.

Contrastingly, considerable attention is paid in the public sector to resolving and avoiding disputes and resolving collective bargaining impasses. In most public sector collective bargaining statutes the strike is prohibited, and some type of alternative dispute settlement mechanism is substituted. The only states that permit public employees to strike are Vermont, Montana, Pennsylvania, Hawaii, Alaska, Minnesota, Oregon, Illinois, and Ohio. In no state do police and firefighters have the right to strike.

However, there is always some substitute for the strike or some alternative dispute resolution mechanism outlined in the public employee bargaining statute. In most state laws there is a stepwise dispute resolution procedure which begins with mediation (discussed in Chapter 13). If mediation is not successful in resolving the dispute, factfinding may then be used to try to settle the matter. If factfinding is not successful, interest arbitration may be used as the final stage in the dispute resolution process. Factfinding and interest arbitration are discussed in the next section of this chapter.

Administrative Agencies.   In most states an independent governmental agency is established solely to administer the state public employee bargaining law. The agency is usually chartered by the legislature and is called the Public Employee Relations Board (PERB) or the State Employment Relations Board (SERB). In most states this agency has powers much like the NLRB; that is, the agency has the power to conduct representation elections, to investigate unfair labor practices, to issue cease and desist orders to enforce the law, and to seek enforcement of its orders in state court. In most states the PERB or SERB is a three- or five-person panel appointed by the governor. In all states there is recognized a need to keep the administrative agency apolitical, or at least bipartisan.

Conflict Resolution

If mediation does not settle a public sector labor dispute, factfinding and interest arbitration replace the forbidden strike for that purpose.

Factfinding

The theory behind factfinding is that disputes are caused by irrational and undefensible positions of the parties and that by bringing a neutral expert into the dispute to study the facts of the case a rational solution to the dispute may be found. Factfinding is most often used in resolving public employee disputes and is rarely used in the private sector. Factfinding may be distinguished from mediation in two important respects. First, the factfinder is usually someone who is an expert in labor relations but who is usually not someone who resolves disputes on a full-time basis and is usually not a career civil servant. Second, the factfinder attempts to find a solution to the dispute between the parties and after studying the facts of the case will usually make a recommendation as to how to solve the dispute. The factfinder not only studies the case and tries to illuminate the true facts surrounding the dispute, but he or she also writes up a decision that will resolve the dispute in what the factfinder views as the best way possible.

Although the parties do not have to follow the factfinder's recommendation, it is generally believed that the rule of reason (and perhaps the pressure of public opinion) will carry sufficient weight to move the parties to adopt the factfinder's recommendations once these recommendations become public. After all, who could refuse to abide by a report made by a scholarly and sage factfinder after hours of exhaustive study and reflection? The record indicates that many people do. In fact, if anything the popularity of factfinding is declining rather than increasing as a method of dispute resolution.[47]

There are a number of reasons for this decline in popularity in factfinding. The expense incurred and the time involved in the exercise perhaps should result in more than just a recommendation for a settlement. Furthermore, factfinding does nothing to move the parties closer together or to strengthen the bargaining process. The emphasis is not on persuasion of one's opponent, but on an appeal to a neutral, to a disinterested outsider. The behavior of the parties in factfinding is designed to emphasize the reasonableness of conflicting positions, not to find a common ground in a compromise solution.

Interest Arbitration

Like factfinding, interest arbitration is used almost exclusively to solve public sector disputes. Interest arbitration is the process through which a neutral third party makes the decision that resolves the issues causing the dispute. In interest arbitration (sometimes called *contract arbitration*) a neutral party comes into the dispute, hears the position of each party, and then renders a decision resolving the issues in dispute. Interest arbitration differs from grievance arbitration (sometimes called *rights arbitration*) in that the interest arbitrator resolves issues involving the negotiation of a new contract while the grievance arbitrator resolves issues arising under an existing contract.

The major difference between arbitration and factfinding is that the arbitrator's decision is final and binding on the parties — in factfinding the neutral third party makes formal recommendations on how to resolve the dispute but neither side is compelled to accept the factfinder's recommendations. Factfinding and arbitration have a number of similarities, as well. For instance, in both factfinding and arbitration the neutral is chosen by the parties from a panel of qualified neutrals maintained by either the American Arbitration Association (AAA), the Federal Mediation and Conciliation Service (FMCS), or an agency of the state government (Ohio's State Employment Relations Board, for example). In both factfinding and arbitration the neutral works in an ad hoc capacity and the fees charged by the neutral (varying from $300 to $600 per day) are paid by both parties receiving the services. In both factfinding and arbitration a hearing is conducted, presided over by the neutral, and the parties present their positions in an established, formal procedure. In both factfindng and arbitration, the neutral listens to the positions of the parties, weighs the evidence carefully, and drafts a decision that he or she feels is fair to both parties involved.

Advantages of Arbitration

The resolution of issues in dispute through the use of a third party presents a number of advantages to both labor and management and also to the public. One advantage is that the resolution of disputes by a third party provides a sense of finality to the bargaining process. In the public sector, where strikes for most employees in most states are prohibited, arbitration is the last step in the negotiation process. Although in most jurisdictions the parties cannot legally strike, at least the presence of arbitration guarantees that the issues will be resolved. In some states quite rigid timetables are imposed on the parties, with arbitration beginning automatically if the parties cannot reach some agreement at a specified time (30 days before the current agreement expires, for example). The presence of a dispute resolution procedure that must be used to resolve disagreements between the parties may force the parties to be more serious in bargaining as the deadline approaches than they would be if they knew that nothing was going to happen if they did not reach agreement by a certain date.[48]

A second advantage of arbitration is that some method is provided to actually resolve the issues in dispute. Without the use of the strike not only could negotiations drag on forever, but also nothing would ever get resolved in bargaining. With arbitration, the arbitrator hears the case, considers the evidence, and renders a decision. The issue is resolved and the dispute is ended.

Arbitration also makes the public aware of the dispute and the positions of each party to the dispute. Furthermore, if the factfinder's recommendations are made public (which they usually are) or if the arbitrator's award is published (which it usually is), the public can have a good look at how, in the arbitrator's eyes, the issue should be resolved. The public thus becomes more informed about labor relations matters and more aware of the nature of the disagreements between labor and management in negotiations, and of how these disagreements are resolved.

The arbitration process is judicial and to some extent substitutes the rule of law and reason for the rule of power and might in bargaining. In most negotiations the most powerful party wins in bargaining; in arbitration the party with the best case wins. Thus, the strike and all its attendant inconveniences and perils is eliminated and in its place is substituted a reasonable, rational and civilized procedure to resolve differences. The parties no longer need to rely on power to achieve their goals in bargaining in the presence of arbitration.

Disadvantages of Arbitration

Of course it can be pointed out that arbitration has numerous weaknesses as well as strengths. There have been many instances in factfinding, for example, where both parties reject the factfinder's recommendations and the dispute is not solved at all. Even in interest arbitration there are instances where one party or the other rejects the arbitrator's ruling and in some cases resorts to the use of the strike. In many states the arbitrator's ruling is reviewable in the court system and it may be overturned by judicial review. The presence of judicial review weakens the sense of finality and resolution that arbitration is supposed to give to the negotiations process.

Arbitration does not always eliminate strikes. There are numerous examples of strikes in opposition to arbitrators' awards (Montreal Police, 1970), of strikes to pressure the other party to accept a factfinder's award, or strikes before the arbitration procedure even begins. While research evidence may demonstrate that arbitration reduces the number of strikes, it is doubtful if strikes can ever be eliminated entirely.[49]

Another disadvantage of arbitration is the fact that the parties have given up their own power to make a determination of issues in dispute and have delegated this power to a third party. For the management official this means that a little of the power and authority given to him or her by the voters to make decisions about running the organization must now be transferred to the arbitrator. For the union leader, the power to accept or reject certain provisions in the agreement is now curtailed and the arbitrator retains final authority to make decisions that affect the wages and working conditions of the union members. In the presence of arbitration the power to make final decisions affecting the constituents on both sides of the bargaining table is taken from the advocates and given to the neutral.

In addition, arbitration serves to undermine the bargaining process. In particular, evidence is available suggesting that arbitration (and to a lesser extent, factfinding) also produce what are called a narcotic effect and a chilling effect on negotiations. The narcotic effect refers to the tendency of the parties to use factfinding and arbitration over and over again once they have tried it the first time. Evidence exists supporting the contention that once the parties use some type of dispute resolution procedure in year 1, the probability that this method of dispute resolution will be used again in years 2, 3, 4, 5 and so on increases.[50] Furthermore, research evidence also exists showing that the presence of arbitration in bargaining produces a chilling effect, which means that the parties will resolve fewer issues in bargaining than before and will increasingly rely on letting the neutral resolve their disputes rather than doing it through bargaining. As times goes on, the parties will have a larger and larger number of issues in dispute when bargaining reaches its final stage in the presence of arbitration than they would have had otherwise.[51]

A final criticism of arbitration is the evidence based on research that seems to demonstrate that wages are higher in settlements written by arbitrators than in those negotiated by the parties themselves. Although the evidence is not conclusive and there is not universal agreement on the size of the effects, most studies have found that arbitration raises wages anywhere from 0–5 percent to 11–12 percent above the level that wages would have been in the absence of arbitration.[52]

Final Offer Arbitration

In an attempt to deal with some of the criticisms of conventional arbitration some states (most notably Wisconsin, Michigan, Iowa, Massachusetts, and Ohio) are using what is called a final offer arbitration procedure to resolve public sector disputes. Final offer arbitration may be distinguished from conventional arbitration on one major procedural difference. In conventional arbitration the arbitrator is free to fashion any solution to the dispute that he or she may feel is appropriate. For example, if the union comes to the arbitration hearing asking for a wage increase of 50 cents per hour and the management group comes to the hearing offering a wage increase of 10 cents per hour, the arbitrator can resolve the dispute by splitting the difference and giving the union a wage increase of 30 cents per hour. In such a setting, it does not take too much imagination to conceive of a method whereby each party may try to manipulate the system to its own advantage. The union, knowing that the arbitrator will split the difference between the parties, will be motivated to come into the hearing with a large demand — maybe 60, 70, or 80 cents per hour rather than 50 cents in an effort to move the wage figure to a more generous amount. The employer too will play the same game and rather than even offering 10 cents, may offer nothing or maybe even ask for concessions of − 10 or − 20 cents per hour. The feeling among both practitioners and theoreticians is that conventional arbitration may serve to inhibit the bargaining process and may motivate the parties to stay far apart in their wage demands during negotiations rather than to move closer in their positions as the process continues.

Final offer arbitration is an attempt to supply more motivation to the parties to move to compromise during the negotiations process. In final offer arbitration the arbitrator is bound to accept either one or the other of the parties' final offers submitted at the arbitration hearing. Sometimes the final offers are submitted secretly in sealed envelopes without consultation with the other party; this creates a great deal of uncertainty about what each representative will put in his or her envelope. Take, for example, the illustration above. Suppose that the real goal of the union leader is to achieve a wage raise of 35 cents per hour for his or her members; the union was "demanding" 50 cents only because it knew that the arbitrator was not going to give the union everything it asked for. Suppose further that the management group really would have been willing to pay 30 cents per hour but was afraid to offer 30 cents for fear that the arbitrator would take this as a starting point and would compromise this position upward somewhat to accommodate the union. If two negotiating parties are forced to submit a secret final offer and if their arbitrator is bound to choose the most reasonable or best final offer, how might the parties change their behavior in bargaining from that of conventional arbitration?

The parties would thus become extremely interested in knowing just what the bargaining goal of the opponent actually is. If the union leader knows that the management goal is 30 cents per hour and if he or she feels this a reasonable offer, the union official might submit a final offer figure of 32 or 33 cents in an attempt to get a little more than what the management offer was, but not enough to push so high (35 cents) so that the union offer would be judged unacceptable. Likewise, management also would like to know what the union is going to offer. If management knows that the union is going to demand 35 cents per hour and if it felt this a fair and reasonable offer, the management might put 32 or 33 cents per hour in its final offer in a hope that the arbitrator might find this more reasonable than the 30 cents the management group was going to offer. Theoretically, it is possible under final offer arbitration that the arbitrator will open up both envelopes to find that both contain the same wage offer or demand, say 32 or 33 cents per hour. The motivation in final offer arbitration is to find out as much as possible about the real bargaining position of your opponent. The more you know about the real goals of your opponent, the more confident you can be about the demand or offer that is going to be put in the final offer envelope. The way that you discover the goal of your opponent is through exhaustive negotiations, and the way that you get your opponent to reveal his or her true goal in bargaining is through revealing more and more of your own goals in negotiations. In theory, final offer arbitration should encourage more, not less, interaction and interchange in bargaining and should therefore promote negotiated settlements, not arbitrated ones.

The research evidence supporting the theory of final offer arbitration is sketchy, but there does seem to be some support from laboratory research for the position that final offer arbitration does reduce the chilling effect on negotiation by encouraging the parties to settle their differences through bargaining, not through arbitration.[53] Not all field studies of final offer arbitration, however, support the contention that final offer strengthens the bargaining process, although some do.[54] New research results appear every year on this topic, however, and the answer to the question, How do we improve dispute resolution procedures? will be resolved through research and experimentation.

The Impact of Unionization

There are a number of research studies that have investigated the effect of collective bargaining on the budgetary process and on the practice of personnel management in the public sector. This section measures and assesses the effects that unions have had on the operation of public management and points out similarities and differences between the union's effects in the public and private sectors (see also Chapter 11).

The Budget Process

In general, the budget process is probably lengthened because of the presence of unions and collective bargaining in municipal government.[55] In addition, research shows that unionization may cause a reduction in the level of municipal services provided in large cities and an increase in expenditures for services in smaller cities.[56] In a study in 1979, Kearney found that cities with unionized police forces had between 3.6 and 7.1 percent higher personnel expenditures than cities with nonunionized police departments.[57] These results seem to indicate that the presence of a union does have some effect of increasing expenditures in municipal government and of reallocating resources in favor of the labor input.

Wages

The effects of unions on public employee wage levels has been the topic of extensive research in the past 10 to 15 years. The studies are numerous and the results are sometimes conflicting, indicating the complexity of the issue and the variability in the impact that public sector unions have had on wages. For public school teachers the impact of unions on wages has been estimated to vary between 2 and 28 percent, with an average impact of 5 percent annually.[58] Other studies have found virtually no effect of teachers' unions on the salaries of school teachers at the local level.[59]

For other work groups wage effects of public sector unions have generally been found to be small. In studies of police wages,[60] of sanitation workers' wages,[61] and of clerical workers' wages[62] in municipal government, the union effect on wages was usually found to be 15 percent or less. Similar results have been found in empirical results for firefighters' unions, which show a union wage effect averaging 12 percent.[63] The "small" union wage effect in the public sector is contrasted with the larger wage effect for unions in the private sector, which is usually estimated at 15–20 percent. Needless to say, more work needs to be done to strengthen research findings on this issue. Nevertheless, it is safe to conclude that unions do have a significant effect on the wages of public employees, although the magnitude of this effect may be somewhat smaller overall than it is for private sector workers.

Personnel Management

Although this is a difficult subject to research because of the difficulty in quantifying the data, research results show that unionism and collective bargaining tend to centralize and concentrate decisionmaking about personnel matters in the hands of a specialized personnel function, usually in the executive branch of government.[64] If anything, collective bargaining strengthens the power and prominence of individuals in the personnel function and weakens the role of the civil service system in administering the work group. Furthermore, as bargaining develops, all manner of items previously reserved for the sole and exclusive decisionmaking of management now become negotiable. It is almost axiomatic that as the bargaining relationship develops subjects such as hiring standards, promotion policy, layoff policy, training policy, discipline policy, position classification, and workload and staffing policy will all eventually find their way into negotiations. The democratization of the workplace through collective bargaining inevitably results in the employees having some voice over almost all items affecting the use of personnel at the workplace.

Summary

Much of what has been learned about labor relations in the private sector applies to the public sector, but there are some differences. Most public employee labor organizations have had a long history, but have not had the tradition of violence and employer opposition that most private sector unions have had. Union growth has been relatively recent and quite rapid among public sector labor organizations. The process of collective bargaining over wages and benefits and striking among public employees is a relatively recent development as well.

One of the greatest differences between collective bargaining in the private and public sectors is the differences in the legal controls on bargaining. In the federal sector, bargaining is now regulated by either the Postal Reorganization Act of 1970 (for postal employees) or the Civil Service Reform Act of 1978 (for most other federal employees, excluding those in military service). While the Postal Reorganization Act gives postal workers very broad bargaining rights under the NLRA, the Civil Service Reform Act continues to restrict federal employees to negotiating only over nonwage and nonbenefits items. At the state and local levels, an array of over 100 separate statutes regulates labor relations for these public employees. Rights under the state statutes vary from broad comprehensive laws approximating employee rights to bargain and join unions found in the NLRA to statutes actually prohibiting bargaining for public employees.

Discussion Questions

1. What would you do if you were in Tom Olson's situation? Is there any legitimate role that students can play in the negotiations process between teachers and administrators?
2. Why do you think federal employees are not allowed to negotiate wages and

benefits? What effect would changing this provision of the CSRA have on the federal budgeting process?

3. What factors do you see as most important in explaining the growth of public employee unions in the 1960s and 1970s? How have these conditions changed in the 1980s?

4. Is there a public employee collective bargaining statute in effect in your state? When was it passed? How does it compare to other public employee bargaining statutes discussed in this chapter?

5. Should public employees have the right to strike? Why or why not?

6. At the present time, members of the military forces are prohibited from joining unions and bargaining. How do you think the unionization of military personnel would affect the operation of the military services?

7. How does the effect of unions on wages compare between the private and the public sectors? Why is there a difference in the wage effects of unions for these groups of employees?

Notes

[1]*Monthly Labor Review* 106 (December 1983): 71.

[2]Richard C. Kearney, *Labor Relations in the Public Sector,* New York: Marcel Dekker, 1984, p. 17.

[3]U.S. Bureau of the Census, *Labor Management Relations in State and Local Governments: 1980,* Washington, DC: U.S. Government Printing Office, 1981, p. 9.

[4]Murray B. Nesbitt, *Labor Relations in the Federal Government Service,* Washington, DC: Bureau of National Affairs, 1976, p. 22.

[5]Ibid., p. 40.

[6]Ibid., p. 51.

[7]Courtney D. Gifford, *Direction of U.S. Labor Organizations, 1984–85,* Washington, DC: Bureau of National Affairs, 1984, p. 31.

[8]Ibid., p. 24.

[9]Ibid., p. 22.

[10]James L. Stern, "Unionism in the Public Sector," in Benjamin Aaron, Joseph Grodin, and James L. Stern, eds., *Public Sector Bargaining,* Madison, WI: Industrial Relations Research Association, 1979, p. 56.

[11]Kearney, *Labor Relations in the Public Sector,* p. 16.

[12]Stern, "Unionism in the Public Sector," p. 57.

[13]Gifford, *Direction of U.S. Labor Organizations, 1984–85,* p. 20.

[14]Nesbitt, *Labor Relations in the Federal Government Service,* p. 34. The Professional Air Traffic Controllers Organization (PATCO) was originally part of NAGE, but formed a separate organization in the early 1970s.

[15]Gifford, *Direction of U.S. Labor Organizations, 1984–85,* p. 22.

[16]Stern, "Unionism in the Public Sector," p. 67.

[17]Gifford, *Direction of U.S. Labor Organizations, 1984–85,* p. 36.

[18]Stern, "Unionism in the Public Sector," p. 63.

[19]Gifford, *Direction of U.S. Labor Organizations, 1984–85,* p. 19.

[20]Stern, "Unionism in the Public Sector," p. 66.

[21]Gifford, *Direction of U.S. Labor Organizations, 1984–85,* p. 34.

[22]Stern, "Unionism in the Public Sector," p. 66.

[23]Kearney, *Labor Relations in the Public Sector,* p. 31.

[24]Stern, "Unionism in the Public Sector," p. 74.

[25]Jack Steiber, "Collective Bargaining in the Public Sector," in Lloyd Ulman, ed., *Challenges to Collective Bargaining,* Englewood Cliffs, NJ: Prentice-Hall, 1967, p. 2.

[26]Gifford, *Direction of U.S. Labor Organizations, 1984–85,* p. 33.

[27]Ibid., p. 20.

[28]Ibid., p. 30.

[29]Stieber, "Collective Bargaining in the Public Sector," p. 69.

[30]E. Wight Bakke, "Reflections on the Future of Bargaining in the Public Sector," *Monthly Labor Review* 83 (July 1970): 21–25.

[31]Harry Cohany and Lucretia Dewey, "Union Membership among Government Employees," *Monthly Labor Review* 93 (July 1970): 19.

[32]Kearney, *Labor Relations in the Public Sector*, p. 12.

[33]See Cohany and Dewey, "Union Membership among Government Employees," see also Steiber, "Collective Bargaining in the Public Sector," p. 69.

[34]John Burton, Jr., "The Extent of Collective Bargaining in the Public Sector," in Aaron, Grodin, and Stern, eds., *Public Sector Bargaining*, p. 12.

[35]Arnold Weber, "Prospects for the Future," in Andria Knapp, ed., *Labor Relations Law in the Public Sector*, Chicago: American Bar Association, 1977, p. 5.

[36]*Baker* vs. *Carr*, 369 U.S. 186 (1962).

[37]*Reynolds* vs. *Simms*, 84 S. CT. 1362.

[38]Kearney, *Labor Relations in the Public Sector*, p. 14; see also Steiber, "Collective Bargaining in the Public Sector," p. 68.

[39]Nesbitt, *Labor Relations in the Federal Government Service*, p. 318.

[40]Ibid., p. 339.

[41]Ibid., p. 329.

[42]Kearney, *Labor Relations in the Public Sector*, p. 44.

[43]Ibid., p. 47.

[44]Ibid., p. 48.

[45]Ibid., p. 53.

[46]*Abood* vs. *Detroit Board of Education*, 430 U.S. 209 (1977).

[47]Thomas Kochan, *Collective Bargaining and Industrial Relations*, Homewood, IL: Irwin, 1980, p. 293.

[48]Arnold Zack, *Understanding Fact Finding and Arbitration in the Public Sector*, 3rd ed., Washington, DC: GPO, 1980, p. 8.

[49]Kochan, *Collective Bargaining and Industrial Relations*, p. 295.

[50]Ibid., p. 296.

[51]Thomas Kochan, "The Dynamics of Dispute Resolution in the Public Sector," in Benjamin Aaron, Joseph Grodin, and James L. Stern, eds., *Collective Bargaining in Public Employment*, Washington, DC: Bureau of National Affairs, 1979, p. 176.

[52]See Thomas A. Kochan, Mordechai Mironi, Ronald Ehrenberg, Jean Baderschneider, and Todd Jick, *Dispute Resolution under Fact Finding and Arbitration*, New York: American Arbitration Association, 1979; and also Craig Olson, "The Impact of Arbitration on the Wages of Firefighters," *Industrial Relations*, Fall 1980: 325–339.

[53]William Notz and Federick A. Starke, "Final Offer Versus Conventional Arbitration as a Means of Conflict Management," *Administrative Science Quarterly*, 23 (June 1978): 189–203.

[54]See James L. Stern, Charles M. Rehms, J. Joseph Loewenberg, Hirshel Kasper, and Barbara Dennis, *Final Offer Arbitration*, Lexington, MA: Lexington Books, 1975; and Gary Long and Peter Feuille, "Final Offer Arbitration: Sudden Death in Eugene," *Industrial and Labor Relations Review*, January 1974: 186–203.

[55]Richard Kearney, "Municipal Budgetary and Collective Bargaining: The Case of Iowa," *Public Personnel Management* 9 (2) (1980): 108–115.

[56]Stanley Benecki, "Municipal Expenditure Levels and Collective Bargaining," *Industrial Relations* 17 (May 1978): 216–230.

[57]Richard C. Kearney, "The Impact of Police Unionization on Municipal Budgetary Outcomes," *International Journal of Public Administration* 1 (4) (1979): 361–379.

[58]Kearney, *Labor Relations In the Public Sector*, p. 143.

[59]Daniel J. B. Mitchell, "The Impact of Collective Bargaining on Compensation in the Public Sector," in Aaron et al., *Collective Bargaining in Public Employment*, p. 134.

[60]Ronald Ehhrenberg and G. S. Goldstein, "A Model of Public Sector Wage Determination," *Journal of Urban Economics* 2 (July 1975): 223–245.

[61]Linda Edwards and Franklin Edwards, "Wellington-Winter Revisited: The Case of Municipal Sanitation Workers," *Industrial and Labor Relations Review* 35 (April 1982): 307–318.

[62]Ehrenberg and Goldstein, "A Model of Public Sector Wage Determination," pp. 243–244.

[63]Russel Smith and William Lyons, "The Impact of Fire Fighter Unionization on Wages and Working Conditions in American Cities," *Public Administration Review* 40 (December 1980): 568–574.

[64]John F. Burton, "Local Government Bargaining and Management Structure," *Industrial Relations* 11 (May 1972): 123–139.

Appendix A

Collective Bargaining Simulations

Midwest Steel: A Case Study in Collective Negotiations

Background: Midwest Steel

Railroading was the growth industry in turn-of-the-century America. In less than 50 years, the railroad industry had transformed the United States from a rural, largely pioneer society into an urban industrial giant. But, while the railroads were rapidly bringing industrialization into the heartland of America — in preparation for the sophistication of the twentieth century — the old link-and-pin-style car coupler system continued to haunt passengers, shippers, and workers alike. It was inefficient, unreliable, and extremely hazardous to railroad workers.

By the mid-1880s, management of the young and struggling Midwest Malleable Iron Company made the decision to create its own niche in the marketplace. Working with railroad pattern maker James A. Timms, the company devoted many years to expensive research and development, which paid off with the creation of a safe, efficient, and reliable automatic coupler.

At the turn of the century, larger locomotives and longer trains demonstrated that malleable iron was not strong enough to haul the products of American industry. Once again, Midwest management anticipated a need and responded. In 1902, Midwest Malleable converted from malleable iron to steel castings in a modern plant in Columbus, Ohio, launching another era of growth and change. A name change to Midwest Steel followed. The expansion permitted Midwest's research and development engineers to probe for new markets.

The company's industrial innovation and growth potential did not go unnoticed. By 1905, the company had attracted not just the attention but the investment capital and personal interest of the most powerful and influential capitalists in America.

During the early part of the twentieth century, Midwest diversified into the manufacture of virtually every cast part required on a railroad freight car and established the Steel Castings Division. Today, more than 90 years after its founding, the division is the largest steel foundry at one location in the United States, supplying couplers, four- and six-wheel side frames, bolsters, car frames, and underbodies to virtually every railroad in the country.

The railroad market, with its characteristic cyclical peaks and valleys, was the sole business served by Midwest Steel Castings for more than half a century, except for those periods during World Wars I and II when it produced armaments. By the 1960s, Midwest management recognized that the spread of the interstate highway system would have a profound effect upon the railroads. Industry would become increasingly dependent upon long-haul trucks for freight handling, and the public would become more dependent upon the automobile for intercity transportation. Management embarked upon a cautious but determined search for new, untapped markets.

By the mid-1960s, management had made one of its most important decisions — to enter the growing plastic molding industry. The automotive and appliance industries were committed to conversion of many metal, wood, and leather parts to plastic, and there did not yet appear to be leaders in the custom plastic molding industry. Before the auto makers would commit to significant conversion to plastic parts from outside suppliers, they required assurance that there would be ample plant capacity for their growing needs, recognition of rigid quality and production requirements, and sophisticated management skills. Midwest Steel filled the void, much as it did 75 years earlier for the railroad industry. With this change, Midwest Steel Castings became Midwest International, Inc.

In 1986, the company's plastic operations accounted for more than $50 million in sales, or over three-and-one-half times the combined sales of the plastic companies at the time of their acquisition. Midwest Steel, meanwhile, likewise expanded its market to provide steel castings ranging in size from 200 pounds to 30 tons each. In the process, the company diversified into mass transit, armaments, and many industrial markets, making castings for mining, oil exploration, and heavy construction. Extensive machining and welding operations were added. Nonrailroad volume now accounts for 40 percent of Midwest Steel's sales. A $20 million expansion program that will increase Midwest Steel's production capacity by 65 percent by 1990 was started in 1983 and is still underway today.

Beginning in the spring of 1980, Midwest Steel began to feel the effects of the recession which had begun earlier in the year in the auto industry. By the summer of 1980, the company was forced to lay off 200 workers from its production force of 2,000 employees; in October, Midwest Steel laid off 200 more production employees and 75 office and clerical workers from an office staff of about 450 employees. In January of 1981, the company laid off 350 more production employees.

In February of 1981, Midwest management and the union (the United Steelworkers of America, Local 2342) began negotiations on a new labor agreement. Due to the depressed nature of the industry, Midwest Steel demanded wage and benefit concessions of about $2.50 per hour from the union. The union stubbornly refused to grant concessions. A two-month strike in May and June of 1981 followed; the third strike at Midwest Steel in the past 20 years.

In July of 1981, the parties signed a new agreement which provided for wage concessions of $1.50 per hour and some reduction in benefits upon the effective date of the contract (July 1, 1981). It also provided for a 50-cent-per-hour wage raise on July 1, 1982, and a 50-cent-per-hour wage raise on July 1, 1983. By July 1, 1984, the employees were still paid 50 cents per hour less than they were on June 30, 1981. Negotiations began on the new contract on May 1, 1984.

As the parties prepared for negotiations, the economic picture looked a little brighter than it did in 1981. Sales were up over the 1981 level, although sales in the previous two years (1982 and 1983) did not grow very rapidly. Sales forecasts for 1984 were expected to be about the same as for 1983. The modernization program (largely made possible from labor cost savings resulting from the wage concessions) drew cash from the company, but was the only hope for the future if the company were to continue competing in the steel castings industry.

Background: Steelworkers Local 2342

Since 1942, the employees at Midwest Steel have been represented by Local 2342 of the United Steelworkers of America. Prior to 1942, during the 1920s and 1930s, the employees at Midwest Steel were enrolled in a company union. A ruling by the NLRB in 1942 established the United Steelworkers of America as the exclusive representative for the employees at Midwest Steel.

Although labor relations at Midwest Steel during the 1940s and 1950s were sometimes tumultuous, the climate of labor-management relations during the early 1970s was generally peaceful and mature. In the ten years preceding negotiations, the labor relations climate of Midwest Steel worsened. The company and the union had a six-week strike over wages during contract negotiations in 1978, and an eight-week strike in 1981. The local union at Midwest Steel in 1984 had about 1,000 working members, with 650 members on layoff subject to recall.

The leaders of Steelworkers 2342 prided themselves on their responsiveness to their members' wishes and on the firm and aggressive stance they took in dealing with management. The president, secretary-treasurer, and first vice-president of Steelworkers 2342 all had been in office over six years; all were on the bargaining committee which negotiated the contract in 1981, and all were on the 1984 bargaining committee.

The membership of Steelworkers Local 2342 was predominantly comprised of unskilled and semiskilled production workers. Only 150 of the currently employed workforce occupied skilled labor positions and 35 of these persons were in a separate bargaining unit represented by the Patternmakers League of North America. The vast majority of the members of Local 2342 were male (90 percent) and a large proportion of the labor force was black (65 percent). The president and the secretary-treasurer of the local union and the International Representative of the Steelworkers Union (the fourth member and spokesman for the union's bargaining team) were all black and each had at least 15 years of shop floor working experience at Midwest Steel. The union leaders were tough, experienced, and not afraid to confront management on important issues.

Union's Initial Demands

When bargaining began on May 1, 1984, the union presented the company with the following list of initial demands:

1. An increase in the shift differential to 35 cents per hour for second shift and 40 cents per hour for the third shift.
2. Change in the cost-of-living formula to provide a 1-cent-per-hour wage increase for every .3 percentage change in the C.P.I.
3. A general across-the-board wage increase for all job grades listed in Appendix II of the labor agreement:

   75 cents for the first year
   40 cents for the second year
   40 cents for the third year

   in addition to the cost-of-living allowances.
4. Bereavement pay of $200 upon the death of an immediate family member.
5. Restoration of vacation schedule to 1981 levels by adding one week for each length of service category.
6. Addition of one new paid holiday:

   January 15 — Martin Luther King's Birthday
7. An increase in life insurance to:

   $11,500 the first year
   $13,500 the second year
   $15,000 the third year

8. An increase in sickness and accident benefits to:

   $200 per week the first year
   $225 per week the second year
   $235 per week the third year

9. An increase in the duration of sickness and accident benefits to 50 weeks.
10. Increase of the pension multiplier to $15.50 per year of service.
11. Addition of a new section of the contract with the following language:

   #### SUBCONTRACTING

   a. Production, service, maintenance, repair, and installation work performed by members of the bargaining unit shall not be contracted out by the company unless agreed to in advance by a contracting-out committee.
   b. Production, service, maintenance, repair, and installation work shall never be contracted out when employees in occupations appropriate to perform such work are on layoff status.
   c. A committee consisting of four persons, two designated by the union and two designated by the company, shall attempt to resolve all questions in connection with the contracting out of work.
   d. Should the committee be unable to resolve any questions arising out of a subcontracting issue, the matter may be submitted to the grievance procedure up to and including arbitration.

12. Submittal of any grievance arising out of company actions dealing with discharge and discipline to an expedited arbitration procedure. Under the rules of this expedited procedure the arbitrator must render an award within 48 hours after the close of the hearing and the arbitrator's fee is limited to $250. The expedited arbitration procedure is to conform with the "Rules of Procedure for Expedited Arbitration" as established by the American Arbitration Association.

Company Demands

In its initial demands, the company sought three main goals:

1. Increased flexibility in utilizing the labor force currently employed.
2. Moderation of across-the-board wage increases.
3. A limit to the amount of money going to pay for cost-of-living adjustment (COLA) increases.

In particular, the company asked the union to:

1. Cap the COLA escalator to a maximum of 15 cents per year.
2. Surrender super seniority for union stewards.

3. Agree that ability to perform the work shall be the major determining criterion in promotions, filling job vacancies, layoff, and recall.
4. Agree that employees can be worked up to 10 hours per week by mandatory overtime.
5. Agree that limitations on Saturday and Sunday overtime be eliminated from the contract.
6. Agree to a 10-cent-per-hour per-year across-the-board wage increase.
7. Agree to no change in present insurance and hospitalization.
8. Agree to no change in present pension benefits.

The company realized that it would not be able to get everything it wanted in the negotiations, but Midwest Steel felt increasing pressure from competition and realized that it needed *changes* in the labor agreement if it were going to remain in business.

CURRENT COLLECTIVE BARGAINING AGREEMENT

This Agreement, dated July 1, 1981, is entered into between Midwest Steel Castings Company, Columbus, Ohio (hereinafter called the "Company"), and the United Steelworkers of America (hereinafter called the "Union").

SECTION I — INTENT AND PURPOSE

1. It is the intent and purpose of the parties hereto that the Agreement will promote and improve industrial and economic relationships between those employees who are in the Bargaining Unit and the Company, and to set forth herein the basic Agreement covering rates of pay, hours of work, and other conditions of employment to be observed by the parties hereto.

2. The term "employee," as used in the Agreement, shall include all production, maintenance, and hourly rated shop clerical employees of the Company, excluding foremen, plant guards, watchmen, pattern makers and pattern maker apprentices, and all office clerical and salaried employees.

3. The Company agrees not to negotiate working conditions, wages, rates, hours of employment, or grievances, except through a committee appointed or elected by the Union. This Section shall not be construed to deprive any employee of his rights under federal or state laws.

SECTION II — RECOGNITION

1. The Company recognizes the Union as the exclusive bargaining agency for all employees of the Company as defined in Section I.

2. The Company recognizes and will not interfere with the rights of its employees to become members of the Union. The Union and the Company agree that neither it, nor any of its officers or members, will engage in any Union activity while such employees are on Company time, and the Company may discipline any employee who shall be proved guilty of violating this provision. Any dispute as to the facts shall be adjusted in accordance with the provisions of Section VII — Adjustment of Grievances.

3. Any employee who is a member of the Union in good standing on the effective date of this Agreement shall, as a condition of employment, maintain his membership in the Union to the extent of paying membership dues and assessments uniformly levied against all Union members.

a. Any employees hired on or after the effective date of this Agreement shall become a member of the Union after the completion of two (2) calendar months of employment. Such employee shall thereafter maintain his membership in the Union to the extent as provided in Paragraph 3(b).

b. Initiation fees for membership in the Union shall not exceed the minimum prescribed by the Constitution of the International Union at the time the employee becomes a member.

4. During the term of this agreement, the Company will deduct Union initiation fees, monthly membership dues, and any assessments permitted by law as designated and directed by the International Treasurer of the Union and as authorized by individually signed checkoff authorization cards submitted to the Company.

SECTION III — WAGES

1. Job classifications, labor grades, and occupational hourly wage rates for production, maintenance, and shop clerical employees in the bargaining unit, effective July 1, 1981, July 1, 1982, and July 1, 1983, are set forth in Appendices I and II.

2. The Company shall establish production standards for incentive work where applicable and shall use recognized time-study principles and methods.

3. The Company will pay a premium of 20 cents per hour for hours worked on second shift and 25 cents per hour for hours worked on third shift, effective July 1, 1981.

4. Effective each adjustment date, a Cost-of-Living Adjustment equal to 1 cent per hour for each full .4 of a point change in the Consumer Price Index shall become payable for all hours.

5. Cost-of-Living Adjustments will be an add-on during the contract period July 1, 1981–July 1, 1984.

6. There will be no cap on the Cost-of-Living Adjustment during the life of the contract.

7. Wages will be decreased $1.50 per hour across the board on July 1, 1981. The new wage rates for all jobs at Midwest Steel are listed in Appendix A. Wages will increase during the term of this contract in the following manner:

July 1, 1982 - 50 cents per hour
July 1, 1983 - 50 cents per hour

SECTION IV — HOURS OF WORK AND OVERTIME

1. This Section is intended to provide a basis of calculating overtime and shall not be construed as a guarantee of hours per workday or workweek.

2. Time and one-half shall be paid for all hours worked in excess of eight (8) hours in a workday and for all hours worked in excess of forty (40) hours in a workweek.

3. Time and one-half shall be paid for Saturday work and double time shall be paid for Sunday work and holiday work. All time worked between 7:00 a.m. Sunday and 7:00 a.m. Monday is to be paid at double time rate.

4. There shall be no duplication or pyramiding of overtime payments.

If more than eight (8) hours are worked on Saturday or Sunday shifts, only the overtime rate provided for such shifts shall be paid for such excess hours.

5. Any employee called or scheduled back to work after finishing his regular turn and before sixteen (16) hours rest is guaranteed four (4) hours at the overtime rate or until the start of employee's regular shift, whichever comes first.

6. The Company will distribute regularly scheduled overtime equitably among qualified experienced employees in the same job occupation. No employee shall be scheduled for such overtime for more than two (2) weeks, as against other employees qualified and experienced in the work to be performed.

No employee will be required to work more than two (2) consecutive weekends, nor be required to work in excess of a total of eight (8) hours a day on Saturday or Sunday.

SECTION V — VACATIONS

1. Each employee with continuous service as defined in Section VIII of this Agreement, as of July 1, 1981, and each subsequent July 1 thereafter, during the term of this Agreement shall be entitled to vacation and/or vacation allowance as follows:

Years of Continuous Service	Number Weeks Vacation
6 months but less than 1	0
1 year but less than 3	1½
3 years but less than 5	2
5 years but less than 10	3
10 years but less than 15	4
15 years but less than 20	4½
20 years but less than 25	5
25 years and over	6

SECTION VI — SENIORITY

1. The parties recognize that promotional opportunity and job security, in the event of promotions, decreases of forces, and rehirings after layoffs, should increase in proportion to length of continuous service and that in the administration of this Section the intent will be that full consideration shall be given continuous service in such cases. Further, it is the intent in the administration of this Section that there shall be no discrimination because of sex, race, creed, or national origin. In recognition, however, of the responsibility of the Company for the efficient operation of the plant, it is understood and agreed that in all cases of:

a. Promotions (except promotions to positions excluded under the definition of "Employee" herein above): the following factors as listed below shall be considered; however, only when factors (2) and (3) are relatively equal, length of continuous service (factor 1) shall govern.
   (1) Continuous service
   (2) Ability to perform the work
   (3) Physical fitness

2. All job vacancies will be posted plantwide. Promotions to job vacancies will follow the provisions set forth above.

3. Job vacancies will be posted for three (3) working days, and include the following information:

    a. Shift/department, job title, and rate

    b. Location of job

    c. Incentive/nonincentive

    d. Job description available in Personnel Department at time of bid

4. The parties recognize that job security, in the event of decrease in forces and recall after layoff, should be in relation to length of continuous service. The following factors shall be considered; however, only where factors (b) and (c) are relatively equal, length of service (a) shall govern.

    a. Continuous service

    b. Ability to perform the work

    c. Physical fitness

5. It is agreed that all elected officers and grievance committee personnel shall hold super seniority for layoff purposes only in the department in which each holds seniority.

SECTION VII — ADJUSTMENT OF GRIEVANCES

1. The Grievance Committee for the plant shall consist of not less than three (3) employees of the plant and not more than twelve (12) such employees designated by the Union, who will be afforded such time off without pay as may be required:

    a. To attend regularly scheduled Committee meetings;

    b. To attend meetings pertaining to discharge or other matters which reasonably cannot be delayed until the time of the next scheduled meeting; and

    c. To visit departments other than their own at all reasonable times, only for the purpose of handling grievances, after notice to the head of the department to be visited and permission from their own departmental superintendent or the superintendent's designated representative.

    d. The Company will pay the committee for six (6) hours per month for grievance hearings.

2. Should there arise between the Company and the Union any differences which involve the interpretation of or application of or compliance with the provisions of the Agreement, there shall be no suspensions of work on account of such differences, and an earnest effort shall be made to settle such differences promptly in the manner outlined:

Step 1.   Any employee or group of employees having a complaint in connection with his or their work shall first see his immediate foreman and, at the option of the employee or group, may be with or without a Union Representative. The foreman cannot refuse the request of the employee or group for Union Representation. Such meeting shall be held within a seventy-two (72)-hour period from the time the incident causing the complaint occurred (two weeks, if involving a pay/incentive problem) or such complaint shall be considered void and not subject to the grievance procedure. The employee shall request the presence of his Union Representative at the meeting. The foreman shall verbally give his answer to the complaint promptly but not later than forty-eight (48) hours from the time of discussion.

Step 2. If the complaint is not settled in Step 1, it may be appealed to the next higher step of this procedure. It shall then be reduced to writing on the form provided and submitted not later than at the end of the third working day after the day of the disposition by the foreman and presented to the general foreman and/or superintendent of the department. If the general foreman and/or superintendent and the Union departmental representative feel the need for aid in arriving at a decision, they may, by agreement, invite such additional Company and Union representatives as may be necessary or available to participate in the discussion and investigation. However, such additional participants shall not relieve the general foreman and superintendent or the Union departmental representative from responsibility for resolving the problem. Such appeal will be heard not later than the end of the third working day following the date of the appeal, but not during the hours of the employee's shift.

Step 3. If the grievance is not settled at Step 2, it may be appealed to the next higher step of this procedure. Such an appeal shall be so indicated on the forms provided, and not later than the end of the third working day after the day of the disposition stated in Step 2. The Company agrees to provide for a meeting at the Company offices between the members of the Grievance Committee, a representative of the International Union and representatives of the Company, if requested, within five (5) days from the date of the request for the purpose of discussing grievances not settled in the preceding steps. Not later than two (2) working days immediately preceding the date set for such meetings, the International Representative shall submit to the Industrial Relations Director of the Company a list of grievances to be discusssed at the next scheduled meeting. It is agreed that only those grievances so listed will be discussed unless otherwise mutually agreed to by the parties. If requested, two (2) copies of accurate minutes of such meetings will be prepared and submitted to the International Representative. The representative of the Company shall answer the grievance not later than the end of the fifth working day following such meeting unless mutually agreed to by the parties to extend.

Step 4. Grievances involving the interpretation, application, or violation of specific terms of this Agreement shall, upon the request of either party within fifteen (15) days from the date of the decision made in Step 3, be submitted to an impartial arbitrator, who shall be selected by the parties within ten (10) days from the date of the request to arbitrate.

Step 5. The award of the arbitrator shall be final and binding upon the parties except as otherwise provided by law. The expense of any arbitration proceeding shall be shared equally by the Company and the Union. The arbitrator shall not have the authority to add to, detract from, or in any way alter the terms of this Agreement. Grievances which are not appealed in the manner and within the time aforesaid shall be considered settled on the basis of the decision last made and shall not be eligible for further appeal.

SECTION VIII — MANAGEMENT

The Management of the plant and the direction of the working forces including the right to hire, promote, suspend, demote, discharge for cause, transfer, or change processes, and the right to relieve employees from duties because of lack of work or other reason which may arise, is vested exclusively in the Company. The Company will not, however, use the provisions of this Section for the purpose of discrimination against any member of the Union because of such membership or Union activity.

SECTION IX — HOLIDAYS

The following days shall be considered holidays:

New Year's Day	Labor Day
President's Day	Thanksgiving Day
Good Friday	Day after Thanksgiving
Memorial Day	Day before Christmas
July Fourth	December 31

1. All employees, other than probationary employees, shall be paid for holidays not worked on the basis of employee's hourly straight time earnings from week preceding holiday times eight (8). The cost-of-living adjustment will be included in the computation of holiday pay.

SECTION X — INSURANCE AND HOSPITALIZATION

1. The following insurance, hospital, and surgical benefits for employees will be provided effective July 1, 1981.

Effective July 1, 1981

$8,500.00	Group Life Insurance
$8,500.00	Accidental Death
$8,500.00	Accidental Dismemberment
125.00	Weekly Sick Benefit and Weekly Nonoccupational Accident Benefit (such benefits payable beginning eighth day of sickness or after nonoccupational accident and to continue for maximum of 26 weeks).

Effective July 1, 1982

$9,000.00	Group Life Insurance
$9,000.00	Accidental Death
$9,000.00	Accidental Dismemberment
130.00	Weekly Sick Benefit and Weekly Nonoccupational Accident Benefit

Effective July 1, 1983

$10,000.00	Group Life Insurance
$10,000.00	Accidental Death
$10,000.00	Accidental Dismemberment
135.00	Weekly Sick Benefit and Weekly Nonoccupational Accident Benefit

2. The Hospitalization, Major Medical, Dental Program, and Drug Plan will continue in force for the duration of the Agreement.

SECTION XI — TERMINATION

This Agreement shall remain in effect until midnight June 30, 1984. Either party may, on or before April 30, 1984, give notice to the other party by registered mail of the desire of the party giving such notice to negotiate with respect to all of the terms of this Agreement.

If such notice is given, the parties shall meet within thirty (30) days after April 30, 1984, and, if the parties fail to agree with respect to such terms, either party may resort to strike or lockout, as the case may be, in support of its position.

PENSION AGREEMENT

Exhibit 1

This Pension Agreement dated the first day of July, 1981, is between Midwest Steel Castings (hereinafter referred to as the "Company") and the United Steelworkers of America, AFL-CIO (hereinafter referred to as the "Union").

The parties hereto having reached an agreement on the subject of a revised Pension Plan to become effective July 1, 1981, it is, therefore, agreed between the parties as follows:

SECTION I — ELIGIBILITY

A. Eligibility for Employees Retiring on or after July 1, 1981

1. Any employee in the Bargaining Unit who retires from the service of the Company on or after July 1, 1981, and:
   a. Has attained the age of sixty-two (62), and
   b. Has had no less than ten (10) years of continuous service as defined in Section III herein shall be entitled to receive a pension benefit upon retirement in the amount specified in Section II, Paragraph A-1.

2. Any employee in the Bargaining Unit who completes thirty (30) years of continuous service as defined in Section III herein, shall be entitled to receive a benefit upon retirement in the amount specified in Section II, Paragraph A-1 regardless of his physical age.

3. Any employee in the Bargaining Unit who shall become permanently and total disabled, and who shall have no less than ten (10) years of continuous service, as defined in Section III, herein, prior to becoming permanently and totally disabled, shall be eligible to receive a pension on the conditions specified in this agreement and in the amount specified in Section II, Paragraph B-1.

SECTION II — AMOUNT OF PENSION

A. Normal Retirement

1. An employee who retires on or after July 1, 1981, and who meets the eligibility requirements of Section I, Paragraphs A-1 and 2 shall receive a monthly benefit based upon his years of continuous service equal to ten dollars ($10) multiplied by such years of continuous service, subject to all the deductions provided for in other provisions of the Agreement.

APPENDIX I   Job Occupations

Job Title	Evaluated Job Class
Molding departments	
Tool Room Attendant	6
Steel Pouring	15
Supervisor–Molding Gangs	15
Inspector–Pouring Floor	10
General Labor	2
Operating Forklift Truck	6
Core Carrier–West Molding	4
Machine Men–Moldmaster	5
Core departments	
Making Class I Cores	11
Core Maker Helper	3
Labor–General	2
Oven Tender	10
Oven Tender–Industrial Cores	6
Finishing departments	
Chairman (Coupler)	6
Craneman (Coupler)	8
Stationary Grinder	7
Welder 9	
Operator–Cold Press	10
Tool Room Blacksmith	9
Production machining	
Operator–Turret Lathe	12
Operator–Surface Grinder	8
Operator–Radial Drill Press	8
Machinist–All Around	19
Group Leader–Machinists	21
Tool Grinder/Utility Man	15
Mechanical department	
Tool Room Attendant	14
Tool Room Helper	9
Electrician	19
Maintenance Man	11
Mechanic	16
Yard department	
Locomotive Crane Helper	6
Locomotive Crane Operator	12
Pattern department	
Aluminum Molder	13
Maintenance of Molding Equipment and Patterns	10
Power department	
Stationary Engineer	17
Quality control departments	
Inspector–Finishing Departments	10
Quality Control Inspector–Finishing Departments	14
Quality Control Precision Layout Finishing Departments	17

APPENDIX II   Changes in Rates of Pay — Nonincentive Work

Class Number	Rate Effective July 1, 1981*	Rate Effective July 1, 1982*	Rate Effective July 1, 1983
1	5.73	6.23	6.73
2	5.73	6.23	6.73
3	5.79	6.29	6.79
4	5.85	6.35	6.85
5	5.91	6.41	6.91
6	5.97	6.47	6.97
7	6.03	6.53	7.03
8	6.09	6.59	7.09
9	6.15	6.65	7.15
10	6.21	6.71	7.21
11	6.27	6.77	7.27
12	6.33	6.83	7.33
13	6.39	6.89	7.39
14	6.45	6.95	7.45
15	6.51	7.01	7.51
16	6.57	7.07	7.57
17	6.63	7.13	7.63
18	6.69	7.19	7.69
19	6.75	7.25	7.75
20	6.81	7.31	7.81
21	6.87	7.37	7.87

*Plus Quarterly Cost-of-Living Adjustments beginning April 1, 1981, through April 1, 1984.

Midwest Steel Financial Data

	1983	1982	1981
Financial results, year ended May 31			
Net Sales and Revenues	$71,604.25	$69,538.50	$47,875.25
Cost of Goods Sold	57,512.50	56,432.00	39,016.25
Gross Margin	14,091.75	13,106.50	8,859.00
Operating Expenses			
Selling, General and			
Administrative	5,441.00	4,497.00	2,880.25
Interest	1,082.50	763.75	500.00
Total	6,523.50	5,260.75	3,380.25
Earnings Before Taxes	7,568.25	7,845.75	5,478.75
Income Taxes	3,647.75	3,809.00	2,706.25
Net Earnings	3,920.50	4,036.75	2,772.50
Per Share	.40	.368	.255
Depreciation	866.50	673.25	482.25
Funds from Operations	5,532.25	5,102.00	3,495.75
Cash Dividends	1,359.50	989.00	607.00
Per Share	.120	.090	.056
Capital Expenditures — Net	2,902.25	940.50	922.00
Average Shares Outstanding	2,761.25	2,746.75	2,724.25

(continued)

	1983	1982	1981
Financial position, at May 31			
Current Assets	$29,516.25	$20,649.50	$15,723.75
Current Liabilities	16,258.00	9,328.25	8,472.25
Working Capital	13,258.25	11,321.25	7,251.50
Fixed Assets	25,283.25	9,441.75	9,370.00
Total Assets	55,970.75	30,696.50	25,601.75
Long-Term Debt	16,402.00	7,640.75	6,622.00
Shareholders' Equity	21,203.00	12,827.75	9,791.50
Per Share	1.715	1.168	.890
Total Capitalization	37,605.00	20,468.50	16,413.50
Shares Outstanding	3,090.75	2,746.75	2,747.50

Note: Dollars in thousands, except per share amounts.

Plain County Sheriffs

Background

Plain City is the largest city (pop. 19,000) and county seat of Plain County, Ohio. Plain County is a rural county with a population of about 35,000 (1985) and 429 square miles of land area, most of it farmland. There is little industrial development. Most of the elected officials of Plain County are Republicans.

In July of 1984, a secret ballot election was conducted by the State Employment Relations Board among employees of the Plain County Sheriff's Department to determine their interest in union representation. Seventeen of the eighteen nonmanagerial employees of the department voted in the election. The vote was 14 in favor of the union and 3 against. The union that was chosen to represent the Sheriff's Department employees was the Teamsters Union. The bargaining unit is comprised of nine patrol officers and nine correction officers. The patrol officers work mostly in cars on road patrol and the corrections officers are guards and officers in the county jail.

Negotiations began in August of 1984. The employer was represented by Alan Smith, president of Smith, Foster and Associates, a large, well-known, reputable management consulting firm from Cleveland. Mr. Smith is a former steelworker and local union president who formed the consulting firm when the steel mill he was working in closed in 1977. In eight years, Mr. Smith saw his firm grow to become one of the largest and best known public management consulting firms in the Midwest. He has a reputation for being very tough in negotiations and for having a mind for details. Also sitting at the bargaining table was one of Mr. Smith's assistants (an attorney) and both of the Sheriff's Department supervisors. Occasionally, the sheriff (an elected official) visited the negotiation sessions himself.

The employees were represented by David Westerman, an attorney and senior partner with Westerman and Shoup, a law firm from Cincinnati, Ohio, that represents only unions as clients. Westerman and Shoup is the second largest law firm in Ohio that represents solely labor clients. The Ohio Conference of Teamsters is Westerman and Shoup's main client. Mr. Westerman is the former chairman of the Labor Law Section of the Ohio Bar Association. He is on the Board of Directors of *Labor Law Journal*, a nationally known publication. He is known and respected as a man of reason and rationality. Mr. Westerman is also known as a tough and competitive negotiator who knows every negotiating trick in the book. He was assisted in the negotiations by a junior associate from his firm. Also sitting at the bargaining table were the president of the local Deputy Sheriff's Union and an international representative of the Teamsters Union from Cleveland.

Background of Negotiations

This is the first agreement to be negotiated between the union and the Sheriff's Department. The main reason that the employees voted for the union to represent them was to achieve a higher level of pay and benefits.

Negotiations began in August of 1984. The union at that time submitted a list of 21 initial proposals for negotiations; these included:

*1. Union Recognition
 2. Union Security
*3. Union Rights of Representation
*4. Nondiscrimination
*5. Grievance and Arbitration Procedure
*6. Discipline
*7. Safety and Health
 8. Wages
 9. Holidays
 10. Sick Leave
*11. Leaves and Leave of Absence
 12. Health Insurance
*13. Life Insurance
*14. Bidding on Job Vacancies
*15. Layoff and Recall
 16. Uniforms
 17. Probationary Periods
*18. Overtime and Hours of Work
*19. Management Rights
 20. No Strike
 21. Duration

Negotiations were conducted on August 8, 1984, for four hours, and the parties did little more than talk out the union's initial demands. No issues were resolved at this meeting.

The parties met again on August 27, 1984, for three hours to talk about the employer's responses to each of the union's demands. Again, no agreement was reached on an issue. The parties were scheduled to meet again on September 5, 1984, but this meeting was cancelled by the union. The parties agreed to meet on September 12, 1984, but this meeting was cancelled by the employer.

*Indicates an agreed-upon item.

The parties did not meet again until October 3, 1984. At that meeting, the employer provided the union with some data on the earnings of the members of the Sheriff's Department and on the budget of the department. No issues were resolved at this meeting. The next meeting was scheduled for October 15, 1984, but this meeting was cancelled by the employer due to a conflict in Mr. Smith's schedule. The next scheduled meeting — set for November 5 — was also cancelled by the employer. On November 6, 1984, the union filed unfair labor practice charges against the county for failing to negotiate in good faith.

The county and the union next met on November 7, 1984. New proposals relating to Items 1, 3, 4, 5, 6, 7, 11, 13, 14, 15, 18, 19, and 20 on the bargaining agenda were then given to the union by the County Sheriff's Department. (The union withdrew the unfair labor practice charge on November 12.) Negotiations on these issues continued on November 12, 14, and 20, 1984, and by November 21, all of these issues had been resolved and the parties had reached tentative agreement.

On December 7, the parties met again to address the unresolved issues. The union submitted to the county a modified set of demands. At a meeting between the parties on December 14, management responded to these modified demands with a restatement of its original position, first given to the union on August 27. A meeting was scheduled for December 20, but it was cancelled because of inclement weather. Due to the holidays, no new meetings were scheduled until January 3, 1985.

At the January 3, 1985 meeting, the union resubmitted to the county the same list of modified demands it had given the county on December 7, 1984. The parties met again on January 11, 1985, and the country had no new position on any of the unresolved issues. A meeting scheduled for January 18, 1985, was cancelled by the employer. On January 21, 1985, the union again filed unfair labor practice charges against the employer for refusing to bargain in good faith. No further negotiations were held, pending the outcome of the unfair labor practice charges.

On March 1, 1985, a hearing was conducted before the Ohio SERB regarding the alleged unfair labor practices by the County Sheriff's Department. On March 15, 1985, the hearing officer ruled that no unfair labor practice charges could be sustained against the employer. He did rule, however, that the parties were at the point of impasse in negotiations. Under Ohio law, once the parties have reached an impasse in initial negotiations, they must begin a procedure to resolve their dispute. This includes mediation, factfinding, and final offer arbitration. This procedure must begin no later than 14 days from the date that the impasse ruling was certified (that is, March 29, 1985).

Neither of the parties to the negotiations wanted to go through the dispute resolution procedure; they saw it as expensive and time-consuming. The union members were already unhappy with the time it had taken to resolve the small number of items already negotiated. The County Board of Commissioners was unhappy over the mounting cost of negotiations, at this point well over $30,000 in consultants' billings. Pressure was on both parties to resolve the outstanding issues before March 29, 1985, when the state-mandated dispute resolution procedure was to begin.

The Issues and Positions of the Parties

The parties disagreed on eight issues:

Union Security.   In its demand on this issue, the union requested that the agency shop and a dues checkoff be included in the contract. Under the agency shop arrangement, members of the bargaining unit need not join the union, but all nonunion employees in the bargaining unit would have to pay a monthly "fair share" to the union. Assessments would be approximately equal to the dues paid by members. Under the dues check-off, a process would be established whereby all members of the bargaining unit would have their dues or fair share fee deducted from their paychecks and sent directly to the union. The union argued that it needed the agency shop provision to pay the expenses associated with providing services to the bargaining unit. The dues checkoff would elim-inate the problems associated with collecting dues in cash at the workplace.

The employer's position on the union security issue was that the agency shop and checkoff serve only to enhance the union's power and performance at the workplace, with no benefit to the employer. For many of the county commissioners, the agency shop was an emotional issue. They saw the checkoff as a way of extracting money from the Sheriff's Department employees that should be paid voluntarily, if at all.

Wages.   The union position on this issue was simple — compared to sheriffs in other counties, the sheriffs in Plain County were underpaid. In support of this position, the union provided data from a survey of 20 other counties throughout Ohio, all roughly the same size as Plain County. In its initial demands, the union had requested a 10 percent increase in starting salaries for the two categories of Sheriff's Depart-ment employees in the first year of the agreement, and a 10 percent increase in the second year. In the modified demands, the union asked for a 12 percent raise in the first year and a 5 percent raise in the second year.

The employer, citing financial exigency as the reason, offered a 3 per-cent pay raise each year of the contract for three years. The employer did not dispute the data used by the union in making its demands, but claimed inability to pay a wage raise of 17 percent over two years. The employer further emphasized that if wage raises of 17 percent were given to the Sheriff's Department employees, very shortly all other county employees would be clamoring for similar increases. An increase of this magnitude would bankrupt the county. (See wage comparison data on page 434.)

Holidays.   The union requested that the employer grant three additional paid holidays. At the time of negotiations, there were nine paid holidays:

1. New Year's Day
2. Presidents' Day
3. Memorial Day
4. Independence Day
5. Labor Day
6. Columbus Day
7. Veterans Day
8. Thanksgiving Day
9. Christmas Day

The union requested:

1. Martin Luther King Day
2. Good Friday
3. Christmas Eve

The employer refused to respond to the union's demands other than to plead that it could not afford the additional holiday pay. Because the Sheriff's Department always had a minimum of one officer on patrol duty and one on duty at the county jail 24 hours a day, 365 days a year, and because those who worked on a holiday received double time (two times normal pay), increasing the number of holidays would increase labor costs.

Sick Leave.   The union proposal was that employees should accumulate one day of sick leave a month. The union further demanded that employees be able to "bank" unused sick leave and to collect the dollar value of unused sick leave at the employee's existing wage rate at any time he or she wishes after one year of employment. Thus, if an employee were to have accumulated 100 days of unused sick leave at retirement, he or she would be paid for 100 days of additional work.

The employer proposed that sick leave should accumulate at the existing rate (6 days per year; one-half day per month) and that no more than 25 percent of unused sick leave could be "cashed back" — and then only at retirement. An employee with 100 days of unused sick leave at retirement would collect only for 25 additional days.

Health Insurance.   At the time of negotiations, the county provided health insurance only for its employees, not for members of the employees' families. The policy was followed for all county employees. The union demanded that the Sheriff's Department employees receive full family-plan health insurance coverage.

The county refused to provide family coverage. The main reason given was cost. Single coverage cost about $95 per month per employee. Family coverage would have cost $266 per month per employee. Thirteen of the eighteen employees had families. The employer offered, however, to purchase family coverage for employees with families and then to deduct the additional cost ($171 per month) from employees' paychecks.

Uniforms. Police uniforms are expensive — between $60 and $110, depending on fabric weight and ornamentation — and need to be properly cleaned and maintained. The union requested that officers be issued four new uniforms (two winter and two summer) when they are hired and that the uniforms be cleaned at the county's expense once a week. Furthermore, the union requested a $20-a-month uniform allowance to be used at the employee's discretion.

The county wanted to maintain the existing policy on uniforms: employees purchase their own uniforms, pay for their own cleaning, and the county provides a $10 per month uniform allowance. The county feels no obligation to provide their employees with work clothes.

Probationary Periods. The union requested that the six-month probationary period for newly hired employees be reduced to 30 days. While an employee is on probation, he or she is not covered by the portions of the agreement that govern discharge. For example, the employee may be discharged without recourse to the grievance procedure. The union felt that this gives the sheriff and his or her supervisors too much control over newly hired employees.

The employer claimed that a long probationary period is necessary in case an error was made in hiring the new officer. If the new person isn't going to "work out" in police work, the sheriff and supervisors wanted to have the flexibility to discharge that person immediately without interference from the union.

Duration. The union asked for a two-year agreement with a 12 percent raise in the first year and a 5 percent raise in the second. The employer asked for a three-year contract with a 3 percent raise each year.

Financial Data

Historical

	Total County Appropriations	Sheriff's Budget	Countywide Surplus
1985	$4,832,674	$515,421	$0 (projected)
1984	4,886,755	515,064	82,726
1983	4,702,908	508,667	101,933
1982	4,914,829	422,772	339,184
1981	4,359,954	379,692	165,510
1980	3,674,204	345,410	239,099

1985 Sheriff's Budget

1. *Salaries:*
Sheriff	$ 23,625
Employees	326,131
Retirement for employees	65,322
Workers Compensation insurance	5,361
2. Supplies — 35,080
3. Equipment and uniforms — 7,918
4. Building maintenance — 7,015
5. Training budget — 1,191
6. Travel — 2,756
7. Advertising — 24
8. Vehicle operation and repair — 40,308
9. Vehicle cleaning — 690

$515,421

Wage Comparison Data

County	1985 Budget	Patrol Officer Salary (1985)	Jailers' Salary (1985)
Allen	$ 808,618	$14,000	$14,000
Barrett	880,347	16,096	16,096
Collins	556,390	17,434	17,434
Daniels	476,000	14,000	11,500
Essex	1,070,950	19,938	15,784
Fulmer	646,118	15,800	11,000
Green	492,587	12,000	10,504
Helton	638,837	16,765	10,440
Isaly	571,272	12,209	10,233
Jefferson	763,240	13,800	13,800
Kirk	522,640	15,000	13,374
Lincoln	922,202	13,374	13,374
Madison	703,974	15,163	11,315
Ordin	763,894	13,000	13,000
Putnam	604,000	14,000	13,000
Quartes	844,707	13,000	13,000
Richards	1,000,000	15,600	11,440
Simons	571,201	14,500	13,500
Plain Co.	515,421	12,700	10,660

Appendix B

Grievance Cases

Case 1: Seniority or Ability?

Background

This case involves a large automobile parts manufacturer, Raydon Manufacturing Corporation, and the Allied Industrial Workers, an industrial union headquartered in Milwaukee, Wisconsin. The grievance was filed by Calvin Keller, a skilled machinist who operates a turret lathe at the Raydon facility. Mr. Keller had been employed at Raydon since March 21, 1975. In June of 1983, Raydon found it necessary to lay off a number of employees in the machine shop due to a drop in the demand for Raydon products. The layoff was expected to be temporary (60 days or so), but no one was exactly sure how long it would last. The employees who would be affected were all skilled machinists who operated lathes or milling machines. Due to the company's location in an eastern suburb of Detroit, and due to the high unemployment rate in manufacturing at the time, the prospects of obtaining comparable employment during the layoff period were not bright. The employees in the machine shop at Raydon averaged about $13.00 per hour in wages. Average weekly take-home pay was close to $400, including some overtime. Unemployment benefits would pay the average employee about $210 per week.

On June 12, 1983, the plant superintendent, Sheldon Smith, submitted a list to the union steward for the machine shop, Allen Fry, of the persons in the machine shop who were to be laid off. The layoff was based on certain machines which were to be closed down for the layoff period. Generally, it was the older, less efficient machines that were to be shut down; two of the employees who ran these machines were long-time employees. Mr. Keller was not on this list.

Mr. Fry, the union steward, protested this method of arriving at the layoff decision. Mr. Fry pointed out that the labor agreement required that layoff be made on the basis of seniority unless there was a marked difference in ability among the employees.

On June 20, 1983, Sheldon Smith submitted a new list to the union. The new layoff list targeted four of the twelve machine shop employees for layoff. As before, there were some employees with considerable service that were to be laid off, but this time the company asserted that the layoffs were based on efficiency ratings maintained by the production department. The least efficient employees were to be laid off. Mr. Keller was now on the list. In discussions among the group, it was learned that the two junior employees on the original layoff list had approached Mr. Smith and suggested that efficiency ratings be used as the basis for layoff. The layoffs were to be effective June 27, 1983.

Three of the four employees who were targeted for layoff chose to exercise their right to bump. Through the bumping process, the machinists would displace less skilled production workers on the assembly line who had less seniority. Bumping to a lower-rated position meant a cut in pay (from $13.00 per hour to about $9.00 per hour) and a switch to a much less desirable job. In the machine room, the work was skilled, challenging, self-paced, and had variety. On the assembly line, the work was repetitive, machine-paced, and quite physically demanding. The pay for assembly-line jobs, however, was better than what one would receive from unemployment insurance.

Mr. Keller did not exercise his right to bump. He did not want to work on the assembly line; he wanted to stay in the machine shop at his old job. Mr. Keller accepted the layoff, and then immediately filed a grievance claiming that his rights under the collective agreement had been violated. In his grievance, Mr. Keller asked for reinstatement to his old job and for back wages equal to the difference between what he received in unemployment insurance benefits and the income he would have received had he continued as a lathe operator. The grievance was filed on June 29, 1983. Mr. Keller was laid off on June 27, 1983; he was recalled from layoff on November 14, 1983, and continues to work in the machine shop to this day.

The grievance was processed through the three stages of the grievance procedure in accordance with the labor agreement. The representatives of the union and the company disagreed over the grievance at every stage of the procedure. The case was heard by the arbitrator on February 18, 1984.

The Labor Agreement

The parties to this case were signatories to a June 1, 1982, labor agreement, which was due to expire on May 30, 1985. Relevant portions of this agreement follow:

ARTICLE I — PREAMBLE

The intent and purpose of the parties hereto is that this agreement will promote, improve, and maintain industrial, economic, and harmonious relations between the Union and the Company, and to set forth herein the basic agreement covering the rates of pay, hours of work, and conditions of employment to be observed by the Union and the Company.

The Union agrees to cooperate with the Company to increase productivity. The Union will urge its members to produce more and will work with the Company to eliminate causes of inefficiency.

ARTICLE 18 — MANAGEMENT'S RIGHTS

The Management of the plant and of the work and direction and classification of the working forces, including the right to hire, suspend, or discharge for proper cause, or transfer, and the right to relieve employees from duty because of lack of work or for any other legitimate reason shall be vested in the Company subject to the rules of this agreement. This authority will not and cannot be used for the purpose of discrimination.

The Company reserves the right to adopt, establish, submit, revise, and enforce reasonable factory and safety rules. Such rules shall not be used for the purpose of unlawful discrimination or to violate the express provisions of this agreement.

ARTICLE 21 — SENIORITY

Section 1. In promotion, demotion, layoff, and restoration to service, plant seniority shall prevail unless there is a marked difference in ability. In this connection Management and the Shop Committee shall confer prior to promotion, layoff, or restoration of service, and in the event Management and the Shop Committee are unable to agree, Management shall have the right to make the determination, subject to the grievance procedure provided in the contract.

Positions of the Parties

Company Position

The company claimed that Articles 1, 18, and 21 allowed it to take the steps it did in making the layoffs in June of 1983. In Article 1, the union pledges to help the company increase productivity. Only through retaining the most productive employees in the machine shop during the layoff period would productivity be enhanced, the company maintained. In Article 18, the company is given the right to "relieve employees from work because of lack of work." In Article 21, the agreement states that in making layoff decisions, seniority shall prevail unless there is a marked difference in ability; the company claimed that there were marked differences in ability between the grievant, Mr. Keller, and the other employees who were retained.

As evidence of the ability differences between the employees in the machine shop, the company submitted to the arbitrator the efficiency ratings of the twelve employees in the machine shop for the last quarter of 1982 and the first quarter of 1983 (see Tables 1 and 2).

The efficiency ratings were a relatively new feature in the machine shop at Raydon. In the spring of 1982, the company had hired a mechanical engineering consulting firm to establish production guidelines for the various machines in the machine shop. Because each machine was slightly different, separate production standards were established

TABLE 1   Relative Efficiency of Machine Shop Employees — Last Quarter 1982

Name	Seniority Date	Efficiency Rating
1. Jackson	2/14/73	118
2. Fletcher	8/29/74	117
3. Madison	8/1/79	117
4. Kelley	7/8/76	116
5. Keys	3/20/61	114
6. Alexander	3/3/65	113
7. Burdetsky	9/10/79	110
8. Keller	3/21/75	108
9. Fisher	8/13/70	103
10. Fleishman	4/7/82	100
11. Roth	6/20/81	95
12. Suoboda	11/29/78	90

for each machine. Time standards were established for Category I work, the type of work that was most commonly done on a particular machine. Not all work on every machine was Category I work; it varied from machine to machine and from operator to operator. Sometimes a rush job would come in and the machine operator would have to take the material he or she was machining out of the lathe or milling machine and work on the priority item for a time before he or she could finish work on the original material. Sometimes the operator worked on material for which a standard had not been established. Category I work accounted for about 50 percent of most employees' work load in the machine shop. Nevertheless, the efficiency standards were established by a reputable company using a methodology of time and motion

TABLE 2   Relative Efficiency of Machine Shop Employees — First Quarter 1983

Name	Seniority Date	Efficiency Rating
1. Madison	8/1/79	127
2. Fletcher	8/29/74	124
3. Jackson	2/14/73	120
4. Alexander	3/3/65	118
5. Burdetsky	9/10/79	118
6. Fisher	8/13/70	116
7. Kelley	7/8/76	110
8. Suoboda	11/29/78	109
9. Keller	3/21/75	104
10. Keys	3/20/61	101
11. Roth	6/20/81	92
12. Fleishman	4/7/82	90

study that had been accepted in industry for 20 years. If an operator operates at an efficiency rating of 100, he or she is working at the production rate established by the consultants. A rating of above 100 indicates above-standard production; a rating of below 100 indicates a production rate below the established standard. The company maintained that the efficiency ratings showed marked differences in the abilities of the employees in the machine shop.

The company further argued in its presentation that similar production standards had been established in the Tool and Die Department in 1980 by the same consulting firm. Furthermore, layoffs in the Tool and Die Department had been based on these standards three times in the past, and the union had not objected. The company argued that the use of production standards to rank employees for layoff was established past practice of the company and accepted by the union since it had not protested layoffs made on this basis previously.

Union Position

In its presentation, the union made two main arguments. First, the union argued that the efficiency ratings violated established past practice in the machine shop. The union introduced into the record the fact that since 1956, when the company and the union began negotiating, no employee of Raydon Corporation has ever been laid off because of his or her efficiency ratings. The union admitted that employees were targeted for layoff in the Tool and Die Department based on their efficiency ratings, but it emphasized that these employees were not laid off, but rather bumped into lower-rated classifications. These job changes were technically "transfers."

Second, the union questioned the validity of the efficiency ratings that had been established. The union pointed out that efficiency ratings change over time and that, in any case, Keller's production always met or exceeded the standards established by the consultants. Additionally, the union claimed that interpersonal comparisons such as the company was making were meaningless because every machine was different and every employee did a different amount of Category I work, depending on which machine he or she worked on.

In the conclusion of its case, the union asked the arbitrator to make Mr. Keller "whole" by ordering the company to pay him the difference between his unemployment insurance earnings and the amount he would have earned had he remained employed in the machine shop the whole time. Furthermore, the union asked that the arbitrator order the company to cease and desist from making personnel decisions based on efficiency ratings until the union and the company could bargain over this issue and include specific language to deal with it in the collective agreement. Until then, the union asked that past practice continue and that all layoffs be made on the basis of seniority.

Case 2: Ban the Radios!*

Background

American Pottery and Ceramics Corporation is a large ceramic products firm with plants in five states in the Midwest and in the Southeast. In 1951 the Spoondale Division was purchased by APC from the Donnely family. The firm had been run by John T. Donnely with a strong paternalistic hand from the time of its formation in 1926 until his death in 1943. Following the death of the elder Donnely, the firm began a decline under the management of his sons. It was on the verge of bankruptcy in 1951 when APC bought it. Since its purchase, the Spoondale operation has almost doubled in size.

The company recently began to produce certain plastic products to replace or supplement ceramic products used in the manufacture of electrical transmission equipment. This development, plus increased demand for products already manufactured by the company, created a need for additional space. A north wing was recently added to the existing plant and a second structure that includes warehousing space is being constructed adjacent to the existing structure.

The profit picture of the firm has improved steadily since the introduction of a modernization program in 1952. Although net profit was off slightly in 1986 from an all-time high in 1978, sales and earnings were up from the previous year. The picture for 1987 looks even brighter as the addition of new products has brought a windfall of industrial contracts to replace the government contracts that have been drying up over the last several years.

Location of Plant

The Spoondale plant is located in the town of Spoondale, Ohio. Spoondale has a population of 6,200 according to the 1980 census and lies in a farming area northwest of Dayton, Ohio, and southwest of Toledo. The community is a relatively conservative one, economically based on a mixture of agriculture and manufacturing. Other manufacturers in Spoondale include: the Beaver Valley Packing Company, a small meat packing operation; Mercer Camper Company, a manufacturer of camper trailers; Buckeye Milling Corporation, a producer of animal feeds; and Spoondale Elevators, a grain storage operation.

Spoondale has a largely captive labor market due to the absence of any industry within a 25-mile radius of the town. Consequently, the Spoondale plant of APC draws its working force not only from the town

*This case was prepared by R. Michael Montgomery of The Ohio State University Labor Education and Research Service and was edited by Marcus Sandver for this text.

but from a large rural area surrounding the town, including the smaller towns of Douglas, Crawfordsville, Carthage, Hobart, Williams Grove, and New Harmony.

Union and Labor Relations

The Spoondale plant was organized by the then-international Union of Operative Potters shortly after it was purchased from the Donnely family. At that time the Potters had already organized the other three plants then operated by APC. After a bitter struggle for recognition, which culminated in a 12-week strike, the company and union began bargaining, but the first contract was not signed until 1952. A rather cool relationship resulted, and strikes occurred before the settlement of contracts in 1954, 1956, 1962, and 1964. The leadership of the local union and the management of the Spoondale plant have both changed over the years, however, and there has not been a strike at Spoondale in over 20 years. Since the 1964 strike, the attitude of both parties in negotiations has been aggressive but not hostile, and little of the outright mistrust of the old days remains. Emphasis in contract negotiations has been largely on wage issues in recent years. The union leaders are in general agreement with management on the use of problem-solving approaches and many grievances are settled at the first step. Seldom in the last decade has a grievance gone to arbitration. Union leaders have had the strong support of the membership on matters of contract negotiations and grievance handling, however. Hence, they will not hesitate to seek arbitration when a satisfactory settlement cannot be reached with the company.

The Grievance

History

The company issued a memorandum on August 24, 1984, which was posted on all company bulletin boards (see Figure 1). A portion of that memorandum stated that: "All transistor radios . . . are outlawed in the plant."

The union grievance committee subsequently met with company representative and verbally challenged the company's right to ban radios in the plant. In response, the plant manager contended that the ban was a clarification of existing company rules relating to inefficiency and safety on the job. He argued that production declines had been traced to the general use of transistor radios by members of the workforce, and that the company feared that the inattentiveness that caused the production losses might also result in injuries. The union committee refused to accept the company arguments, but declined to file a grievance at that point, stating that the union would reserve the right to challenge the validity of the rule at such time as a member of the bargaining unit might be punished under the new rule.

TO: All Employees of APC

FROM: Robert Olin, President

DATE: August 24, 1984

1. I regret to note that our production of item
   #4374 is down about 15% this month, and the
   problem appears to be related in part to
   employees in the production and maintenance
   departments returning late from coffee breaks
   and lining up early at the time clocks. This has
   the effect of upsetting coordination of
   production greatly. Please observe time rules in
   the future.

2. This morning, I noticed a transistor radio in
   the plant and I asked the employee to remove it.

   This is to advise all concerned that transistor
   radios will not be permitted in the plant.

   An employee listening to a transistor radio
   could not have his full attention on his job,
   and there is a safety hazard in the event he
   might not hear someone speak to him. All
   transistor radios, therefore, are outlawed in
   the plant.

   Your cooperation on these two points will be
   appreciated.

FIGURE 1 APC Memorandum

A month later the rule was verbally amended by the company to allow the use of radios in the plant with the permission of supervisors
when events of special interest were to be broadcast. This amendment
was made as a result of requests by union stewards that the employees
be allowed to bring radios into the plant for the upcoming 1984 World
Series.

Several oral reprimands, none of which resulted in the filing of grievances, were issued regarding the use of radios during the latter part
1984. In January, 1985, three written reprimands were issued which re-

sulted in grievances. Two of the reprimands over which these grievances were filed were withdrawn by the company in second-step arbitration with the answer that the employees involved were new hires and the company felt that they had been honestly confused about the rule. The third grievance was denied with the answer that the rule itself was proper and that it had been properly applied in this case. Bargaining for a new contract was then in progress between the parties and, although the union did not appeal the grievance from the third step, it was brought up at the bargaining table. The new contract was settled without agreement being reached on this grievance, which had become known as the Hildebrandt Grievance.

Enforcement of the radio rule became more lax after the new contract was signed, however, and radios were in general use throughout the plant during the 1985 World Series without any specific permission for their use being granted.

Then, in November of 1985, the company began to issue oral warnings about radios. The union protested but no grievances were filed.

After an inspection by OSHA in November, 1985, the company began to enforce the radio rule with even more vigor. A new memorandum was posted on all company bulletin boards on November 21, 1985, restating the ban on transistor radios (see Figure 2). In a meeting with the union grievance committee, the company argued that damage to products resulting from inattentiveness to the job and safety considerations dictated that the radio rule would have to be strictly enforced in the future. The union protested the rule once again; however, the company contended that the rule was proper and that the union had recognized that fact when they chose to drop the Hildebrandt Grievance. Furthermore, they argued, the work force was properly warned by the posting of November 21 that any further violations of the rule would result in disciplinary action more severe than oral warnings.

The Situation

A joint safety committee had been set up by the union and the company under provisions of the 1985 collective bargaining agreement. In February, 1986, this committee agreed to make monthly walk-around inspections of the workplace to spot any health or safety problems that might require correction. The first inspection by this committee was conducted on March 3, 1986. During the course of the inspection, R. A. Dickey, the company personnel manager and chairman of the safety committee, and Marvin Otte, the union grievance committee chairman and a union member of the safety committee, engaged in several arguments about conditions in the plant that Otte considered to be dangerous to the safety of workers. One argument over what Otte considered to be excessively high noise levels in a plastic stamping operation was especially heated. Late in the afternoon of March 3, the committee en-

---

TO: All employees of APC

FROM: R. B. Martin, Plant Manager

DATE: November 21, 1985

SUBJECT: Transistor Radios in the Plant

A plant notice was posted in 1984 banning the use
of transistor radios in the plant. This was later
changed by verbal notification to the union
committees to the effect that when there was to be
a broadcast of widespread interest, and with the
approval of the foreman, radios could be brought
in. This qualification on the use of radios is not
unreasonable and is in line with the practices at
our other plants, including the Riverside unit.

The quality requirements of our customers and the
quality consciousness of our competition require
that we devote all of our available attention to
maintaining and improving our present quality
level, and I feel that the uncontrolled use of
radios is not consistent with this goal.

Another consideration is that of safety and the
potential hazards that could result because an
individual's attention was not on what he, or
someone else, was doing.

Therefore, radios are not to be brought into the
plant except when there is to be a broadcast of
widespread interest and with prior approval of the
foreman.

FIGURE 2   APC Memorandum

tered the shipping and receiving department. Upon spotting three employees with transistor radios in the area, Dickey pointed them out to
Otte, stating that the only real safety problems in the plant were the
employees themselves. Dickey approached the employees and repri-
manded them for using the radios, citing them as a safety hazard. Otte
then approached Dickey and accused him of harassing union members.
The two then engaged in another heated argument.

The next day Dickey issued written reprimands to the three employ-

TO: Shipping and Receiving Dept. employees
        Sharon Kobziak, Lloyd Mitchell, and Merle
        Martin.

FROM: R. A. Dickey, Personnel Manager

DATE: March 4, 1986

This is to inform you that an official reprimand is
being placed in your personnel folder for
disobeying instructions and playing a radio on
company premises in violation of written
instructions to the contrary.

Another such activity on your part will result in
stronger action, up to and including the
possibility of suspension from work, by management
of this company. For the sake of yourselves and
other employees, you are urged to refrain from such
activities and obey all plant rules in the future.

Transistor radios have been outlawed in the plant
since August 24, 1984, except for public events of
importance, when the foreman in charge has given
permission in advance of such event.

FIGURE 3 APC Memorandum

ees in the shipping and receiving department (see Figure 3). On Monday morning, March 10, 1986, a grievance was filed by the affected employees.

Since Dickey had issued the reprimands, the first step of the grievance procedure was skipped. A second-step meeting was held on Tuesday, March 11, with Dickey; Otte; Bob Ganlette, the shipping and receiving department steward; Frank Lyons, the shipping and receiving department superintendent; and the grievants. The meeting deteriorated into a shouting match between Otte and Dickey, and Dickey wrote out an answer denying the grievance, handed it to Otte, and adjourned the meeting.

The regular meeting between the union grievance committee and the company labor relations committee was held on Monday, March 24. The Radio Grievance, as it had become known, was taken up during the course of that meeting. John Galeski, the president of Local 500, argued the union's position, challenging the company's right to issue the radio rule to begin with and further arguing that the rule had not been uniformly enforced since its issuance. In any case, he claimed, the employees involved had not been properly disciplined since there was no evidence that they had ever been orally warned about radios before they were issued the written warnings. R. B. Martin, the plant manager, represented the company at the meeting. He contended that the rule had been properly issued and properly applied in the case, citing the company's concern for safety. A week after the March 24 meeting, Martin formally answered the grievance in writing, again denying it.

On April 15, 1986, a fourth-step meeting was held between International Vice-President Stanley McGraw and Spoondale Division President Robert Olin. Olin offered to withdraw the reprimands if the union would admit that the radio rule had been properly issued and that the company had sole discretion in matters of health and safety in the plant. McGraw rejected the offer and demanded arbitration of the case.

A formal written denial of the grievance was delivered to the union on May 2, 1986. An arbitrator was selected and a hearing on the grievance subsequently set up for June 27, 1986, at the offices of the company in Spoondale.

Portions of the Collective Bargaining Agreement

PREAMBLE

This Agreement, dated February 4, 1985, is entered into by AMERICAN POTTERY AND CERAMICS CORPORATION, hereinafter referred to as the "Company" and the INTERNATIONAL BROTHERHOOD OF POTTERY AND ALLIED WORKERS, Local 500, hereinafter referred to as the "Union."

ARTICLE 1 — PURPOSE

The purpose of the Company and the Union in entering into this Labor Agreement is to promote harmony and efficiency in the plants of the Company; to set forth their agreement on rates of pay, wages, hours of employment and other conditions of employment; to provide for the peaceful adjustment of differences which may arise; and to achieve uninterrupted operations in the plants.

ARTICLE 2 — MANAGEMENT

(a) Subject to the provisions of this agreement, the management of the plant and the direction of the working forces, including the right to plan, direct, and control plant operations; to hire and instruct; to obtain maximum operating efficiency; to introduce new, improved, or altered production methods or facilities; to promote, demote, transfer, lay off, discipline, and to suspend or discharge for proper cause, is vested exclusively in the Company.

(b) The rights herein set forth will not be exercised for the purpose of interfering with the right of employees to become members of the Union, against employees because of membership in or activity in behalf of the Union, or for discriminating against employees for any other cause.

ARTICLE 3 — RECOGNITION AND UNION SECURITY

Section 1. Collective Bargaining Representation. The Company recognizes the Union as the sole and exclusive collective bargaining representative, during the life of this agreement, for all of the employees at the Spoondale, Ohio, plant of the Company and, as defined in Section 2 of this Article, in the matter of wages, rates of pay, hours of employment, or other conditions of employment.

Section 2. Collective Bargaining Unit. The term "employee" as used in this Agreement applies to all employees in the Spoondale plant of the Company listed in this Agreement, except and excluding the following groups:

All supervisory, technical, clerical, and plant protection employees.

Section 3. Union Security.

(a) All employees are covered by this Agreement who are now members of the Union in good standing during the term of this Agreement, to the extent of paying membership dues as certified by the Secretary-Treasurer of the Union.

(b) All new employees and those rehired after a break in continuity of service, as defined in Article 13, who are covered by this Agreement, after 30 calendar days must become and remain members of the Union in good standing to the extent of paying membership dues as certified by the Secretary-Treasurer of the Union.

(c) This shall not apply to any employee who is in the employ of the Company on the effective date of this Agreement and who is not a member of the Union in good standing on such date. However, if he voluntarily joins the Union subsequent to such date, he shall maintain his membership as above provided.

ARTICLE 11 — SETTLEMENT OF GRIEVANCES

Section 1. Any grievance involving:

(a) Application of interpretation of this agreement, on

(b) Matters of wages or job content, which an employee of the Union may desire to discuss and adjust with the Company may be handled as follows:

1. Between the aggrieved employee and his foreman, provided that the employee shall be accompanied by or represented by his Steward.

2. The Department Grievance Committee Man and the Personnel Manager, together with the aggrieved employee and/or his Steward and the Department Superintendent, shall investigate the grievance. The grievance shall be reduced to writing at this stage. A written answer shall be made to the grievance by the Personnel Manager within five (5) working days after the second-step meeting to investigate the grievance.

3. The Union Grievance Committee and the Company Labor Relations Committee shall place the grievance on the agenda for the next meeting of the Committee. The Grievance Committee shall meet with the Company's Labor Relations Committee once each month to consider those written grievances on the agenda. The Chairman of the Labor Relations Committee shall give a written answer to the grievance within seven (7) days of this meeting.

4. The Union President and/or Union International Representative and

the General Management of the Company shall meet within thirty (30) days after the answer is given under the third step and shall attempt to settle the dispute. The General Management of the Company shall give a written answer to the grievance within fourteen (14) days after this meeting.

5. Provided the grievance has not been settled in Step 4, it may be referred to arbitration by the unsatisfied party as provided in Section 2, below.

Section 2. In view of the foregoing, if a grievance is not adjusted through the first four steps of the grievance procedure, either party may submit the grievance for binding decision by an arbitrator under the rules and in the manner set out below:

(a) Within thirty (30) days after the answer is given in Step 4, the party desiring arbitration shall address a request to the American Arbitration Association for a list of arbitrators.

(b) The Union Grievance Committee and the Company Labor Relations Committee shall then meet and select an arbitrator from the list provided.

(c) The sole function of said arbitrator shall be to interpret the meaning of the articles of this contract and shall not have the power to add to, subtract from, or modify in any way the terms of the agreement.

(d) Each party shall bear its own expenses in connection with the proceedings, but shall share equally in any expense jointly incurred.

(e) Unless jointly stipulated otherwise, the decision in such proceedings shall be rendered within thirty (30) days of the conclusion of the hearing and shall be final and binding on both parties.

ARTICLE 17 — GENERAL

Section 1. The Company will formulate rules to govern working conditions in the plant for the regulation of conduct of all employees. Any question as to the penalty imposed for the violation of these rules shall be subject to the grievance procedure.

COMPANY RULES

1. Any employee who refuses to obey the orders and instructions of his foreman or interferes with other employees doing their jobs will receive an oral warning the first time, a written warning the second time, and will be subject to discharge for the third offense.

2. Any employee committing acts of negligence that would cause damage to property or that would endanger the life or health of fellow employees will be subject to discharge.

3. Any employee under the influence of alcohol while on the job will be subject to discharge.

4. All employees are required to report to work on time. Failure to do so will not be excused except when the delay is unavoidable.

5. All employees are required to do their work promptly and efficiently in a workmanlike manner. Any employee failing to do so will receive an oral warning the first time, a written warning the second, and will be subject to discharge for the third offense.

6. Your company will continue, until further notice, its policy of accepting reasonable requests by an employee for layoff. An employee must give his foreman at least two hours' notice before any expected layoff. Failure to give this notice will result in the following:

For the first offense:	Oral warning
For the second offense:	Written warning
For the third offense:	Five-day layoff
For the fourth offense:	Ten-day layoff
For the fifth offense:	Discharge

Case 3: Absenteeism or Injury?*

Background

Central Power Corporation is an electric power utility serving three midwestern states. It is a partially owned subsidiary of a larger corporation which has holdings in the utility industry and utility-related industries in the eastern, southwestern, and midwestern United States.

One of Central's generating plants is located near the town of Daysville, Wisconsin (population 19,600 according to the 1980 census). Daysville lies in a farming area northwest of Madison. The community is a politically conservative one, economically based on a mixture of agriculture and manufacturing.

The Daysville plant was organized by IBEW (International Brotherhood of Electrical Workers) shortly after it was put on line by Central in 1951. At that time, IBEW had already organized the other facilities operated by Central. There was little animosity between labor and management at the Daysville facility for the first 17 years after the union organized the work group. The leadership of the local union changed in 1968 and a new, more aggressive person was elected local union president. The first strike ever at Daysville occurred during the 1968 negotiations. For several years after the 1968 strike, the attitude of both parties in negotiations was aggressive and hostile. Emphasis in contract negotiations was largely on wage issues during these years. Few grievances were settled at the first step and many went to arbitration. The relationship between labor and management improved markedly in 1977, however, with the hiring of Art Evans as personnel manager. In 1981 Evans was transferred to the Central corporate staff, and he was replaced by Al Wasserman.

Within months of Wasserman's arrival at the Daysville facility, distrust crept back into the relationship. The company instituted some unpopular policies which have resulted in a greater number of grievances being filed recently than had been experienced in a number of years, and, at the same time, both parties have been less willing to settle at the first step. One policy that has been especially unpopular has been the attendance program established in March, 1982, shortly after the current three-year contract between the parties went into effect.

There have been a number of grievances regarding disciplinary actions taken under the attendance program. Three of these have involved

*This case was prepared by R. Michael Montgomery of The Ohio State University Labor Education and Research Service and was edited by Marcus Sandver for this text.

discharges. No attendance program grievance had been arbitrated prior to the current one, however.

The Grievance

The Situation

Frank Walters is fifty-four years old and has a record of twenty-seven years' service with Central Power. According to the provisions of the present agreement between the company and union, Frank is entitled to retire in three years with full pension. Frank was employed as a first class lineman in March, 1984, when he was terminated by the company.

Some five years earlier, Frank had been involved in an automobile collision that left him with back injuries and a broken shoulder. He was hospitalized for several weeks as a result of his injuries, but returned to work on light duties after about a month, and the company health plan paid his medical expenses. He did not complain of back problems until three years later, when he missed several days of work over a three-month period during the spring and summer of 1982. He was issued first a verbal warning and then a written warning about these absences. A grievance was filed in August, 1982, regarding the written warning but was dropped after the second step. Frank contended that his back injury had flared up during this period, causing him to miss work.

During the next 12 months, Frank missed six days of work, complaining of his back in each instance. In the fall of 1983, he missed three days in a row — September 26, 27, and 28. He reported each day before his shift that he would not be in because of back pains. The following week, Frank was absent on October 6 and 7, again notifying the company in advance of his shift each day. Again, Frank blamed his back condition for his absences. When Frank returned to work on October 10, his foreman told him that he had had seven absences since April 1, 1983 (including absences on May 31 and June 27, 1983) and advised him that any further absences would result in a verbal warning being entered in his record. Frank was again absent on October 14, but brought a doctor's note in with him when he returned to work on October 17. The note indicated that the doctor had seen him for back problems on October 14. Frank received a verbal warning from his foreman, despite the note. Later that day, he received a copy of a notice of verbal warning with a note referring to the company attendance policy defining an unexcused absence as including short-term illnesses. Frank asked to see his steward and together they protested the warning, contending that the doctor's note established that his absence was justified. His foreman rejected the protest, pointing out the attendance policy definition of an unexcused absence. No written grievance was filed.

Frank worked without incident until November 25. After reporting to work following the Thanksgiving holiday, Frank complained of back pains. The foreman excused him from work after six hours on the job when Frank told him that he couldn't stand the pain any longer. Frank missed work again the following Monday. When he returned to work on November 29, he was told to see Mr. Wasserman, the company personnel manager. Wasserman told Frank that he was issuing him a written warning for nine days of absenteeism. Furthermore, he was told that he would not be paid for the Thanksgiving holiday since he left work early on his next scheduled day following the holiday, and the contract required that the last scheduled day before and next scheduled day after a holiday be worked in order to receive holiday pay. Frank again demanded to see a steward. Frank and his steward protested the warning, contending that the doctor's letter presented on October 17 established that Frank's back problems were valid and thus should have been excused. They also contended that Frank's foreman had in fact excused him on November 25, thus making his absence on the following Monday, November 28, an excused absence. The holiday pay issue was also protested. Wasserman refused to alter his decision on either of the issues, however. Subsequently, the holiday pay issue was grieved and eventually settled in the fourth step, with the company paying Frank for the holiday. The written warning for absenteeism was not further grieved.

On December 12 and 13, Frank was again absent. He called in to report off (that is, to say he would not be coming to work) before the beginning of his shift on each day saying that he had strained his back shoveling snow after a heavy snowfall on December 10. (He was not scheduled to work on December 10.) When he returned to work on December 14, he received a note saying that he was receiving a three-day administrative discipline suspension for the absence of December 13. He did not protest the discipline suspension.

A month later, on January 16, Frank called in to report off complaining of a severe cold. Eventually he was diagnosed as having bronchial pneumonia and he stayed out of work for nearly a month before his doctor released him to return. The company health plan paid for medical expenses resulting from the illness, and all Frank's absences from January 16 until he was released by his doctor were excused.

Frank returned to work on February 13 but was again absent on February 16, 17, 18, and 19. He called in each day to report off, complaining of a relapse of pneumonia, and presented a note from his doctor when he returned to work on February 20. The note indicated that he had been treated on February 16 for bronchitis and advised to remain home and rest for the remainder of the week.

On February 24, he was again absent. He did not call in, but he brought a note from his doctor when he returned to work on the February 27. The note specified that the doctor had seen him on February 24. Frank claimed that he had suffered another relapse of pneumonia, but the doctor's note made no reference to the reason for treatment.

The next day, February 29, he received a notice of a 30-day administrative discipline for excessive absenteeism. Frank saw his steward and went with him to Mr. Wasserman's office to protest the warning. Wasserman refused to withdraw the warning despite Frank's protest that the absence was a continuation of his bout with pneumonia and that the company had excused all absences related to the pneumonia.

On March 1, a written grievance was filed on the warning. This was also denied by Mr. Wasserman, and a third-step meeting was scheduled for March 12. Later the same day, Frank complained to his foreman of back pains. Two hours later, after Frank had worked seven hours of his shift, the foreman excused him from work.

Frank came into work on March 2, but complained of back pains again and was excused by his foreman after working six hours. On Monday, March 5, Frank was late arriving at work. He reported five minutes late, complaining to his foreman that he almost didn't come to work because of back pains. However, he worked out the day. He reported on time the following day but complained again about back pains and, after working six hours, asked to be excused for the rest of the day. His foreman excused him, but when Frank came in the following morning, he was told to see Wasserman. Wasserman told him that he was discharged for excessive absenteeism.

Subsequently, the following events took place:

Wednesday, March 7: Wasserman wrote the discharge letter terminating Frank. Copies were sent by registered mail to Frank and to the union president.

Monday, March 12: Upon receiving notice of Frank's termination, the union president, John Adams, went to Frank's home where he wrote up a grievance and had Frank sign it.

Tuesday, March 13: The union filed the grievance, setting a second-step meeting with Wasserman for the next morning.

Wednesday, March 14: The second-step meeting was held. Frank attended. Wasserman answered the grievance later the same day, denying it. A third-step meeting was scheduled for the monthly labor relations–grievance committee session on April 9.

Monday, April 9: The grievance was taken up for its third-step hearing with the company labor relations committee.

Wednesday, April 11: The labor relations committee report was issued, including a denial of the grievance.

Thursday, April 12: A fourth-step meeting was arranged for April 24, but subsequently this meeting was postponed until May 1.

Tuesday, May 1: The fourth-step meeting was held.

Friday, May 11: The company sent its written answer to the union. It pointed out that Frank had 12 full days of absences, and, in addition, had .250 days charged for November 25, 1983; .250 days for March 1; .250 days for March 2; .125 days for March 5;

and .250 days for March 6. Since this accumulated to a total of 13.125 days of absence, Frank was justifiably discharged for excessive absences according to the terms of the attendance program as of March 7, 1984.

Monday, May 21: The union appealed to arbitration.

Monday, July 1: The arbitration hearing was set for Wednesday, August 1, 1984, at the offices of the company at Daysville, Wisconsin.

Grievance Setting and Positions of the Parties

Several grievances regarding the application of the attendance program had been filed by the union during the two years preceding this case, but the company's right to establish the policy had never been challenged. Most of these grievances involved verbal warnings or written warnings and, in most cases, the union failed to appeal further after a denial at the first or second step. All other grievances were withdrawn by written notice to the company after the fourth step. In most cases, they were withdrawn without prejudice after the grievant had earned credit days to extend the number of days of absences required before discharge, or because a discipline step was removed from the grievant's file at the end of the program year on April 1, 1983 or April 1, 1984. (Credit days erase absences and are given when employees agree to work a specified amount of overtime in a pay period.) Several grievances, including the three discharge cases, were withdrawn without prejudice by written notice after the fourth step upon request of the grievant.

These aspects of the application of the policy that have been challenged by the union include:

1. *Definition of an unexcused absence.* The union has argued that an unexcused absence is one for which an employee does not have a legitimate reason. Illnesses for which employees can produce doctor's notes or absences due to weather conditions should be considered excused absences, for instance. The company has argued that only those absences listed in the policy statement as excluded from being counted as unexcused should be considered as excused.

2. *Administrative discipline.* The union has argued that a suspension must always be given by the company where called for in the progression of disciplinary steps unless it is impractical because of work schedules. Management has argued that they may apply suspension or administrative discipline at their option as they deem necessary for efficient operation or as appropriate to correct a particular employee's conduct.

3. *Timing of discipline.* The union has argued that a disciplinary step may not be applied until the employee is aware of the application of a previous step. Several grievances have involved the co-issuance of

verbal and written warnings where the eighth and ninth day of absenteeism were successive. There have also been instances of the co-issuance of disciplinary action where the ninth and tenth, or tenth and eleventh, days have been successive. The company has argued that all employees are counselled before any disciplinary action is taken and are made aware of the consequences of their actions. Furthermore, the company has contended, the program provides for a sufficient number of disciplinary steps to afford any employee reasonable opportunity to correct his or her conduct.

The current grievance has raised several issues not addressed in previous grievances. These questions are:

1. *Three successive administrative disciplines.* All three employees previously discharged actually served the three-, ten-, and thirty-day suspensions and no employee other than Frank had ever been issued a thirty-day administrative discipline.
2. *Legitimate illnesses.* None of the three employees previously discharged had been able to show that any of their absences were for legitimate illnesses.
3. *Partial absenteeism.* While some grievances involved discipline for accumulated partial absenteeism, no discipline beyond three-day suspensions had ever been issued where a full day was accumulated through partial absences.
4. *Excused from completion of shift by foreman.* Most partial absenteeism was accumulated through tardiness or leaving work without permission. Other employees had been excused from work early due to family or personal emergencies, occupational injuries, illnesses that subsequently involved a long-term disability, and, on some occasions, to keep doctors' appointments, without partial absences being assessed against them. In all instances where employees were allowed to leave work early for any other reason, partial absences were assessed, but because none of those other instances ever resulted in disciplinary action, the question had never been raised in any previous grievance.

Position of the Union Prior to Arbitration

The grievant was unjustly discharged. Discharge was improper for the following reasons:

1. All of the grievant's absences were for valid medical reasons and should have been excused.
2. The grievant had doctor's notes for the absences of November 14, December 12, and February 24. These absences, at least, should be excused for that reason.
3. All instances of partial absenteeism should be excused when the grievant left work early since his foreman excused him from work in those instances. The grievant was led to believe that being excused

by his foreman constituted an excused absence under the attendance program, which should not be counted against him. The first he knew that those absences would be counted was when he was discharged for them.

4. The grievant was improperly issued a ten-day administrative discipline, since this was co-issued with a three-day administrative discipline. The ten-day discipline should not have been issued on December 15 since he had not had an opportunity to correct his conduct after the three-day discipline, which was also issued on December 15. The ten-day discipline should have been issued, if proper, on February 29 and the thirty-day discipline, if proper, on March 7, leaving the grievant one step short of discharge when all discipline was rolled back one step on April 1.

5. It was improper for the company to issue three successive administrative disciplines, in any case. The company did not show nor even argue that its scheduling prohibited actual suspensions being applied. No one else had ever been subjected to three administrative disciplines in a row, and no one had ever been subjected to a 30-day administrative discipline. Failure to apply actual suspensions resulted in the grievant not being given sufficient opportunity to correct his conduct. Moreover, if the grievant had actually been suspended for 30 days on February 29, the program year would have lapsed. He could not have accumulated any further absences during the program year and thus could not have been discharged and, in addition, the 30-day suspension would have been removed from his record on April 1, leaving him one step short of discharge again.

6. The company acted in bad faith. The grievant was purposely not suspended on February 29 to give the company an opportunity to trap him before the program year lapsed. His foreman then excused him without warning him that the part-days for which he was being excused would be counted against him.

The grievant should be reinstated.

Position of the Company Prior to Arbitration

The grievant was justly discharged for excessive absenteeism. Discharge was proper for the following reasons:

1. None of the grievant's absences were excused under the definition of unexcused absences in the attendance program policy statement.

2. The grievant did, in fact, accumulate 13.125 days of unexcused absences between April 1, 1983, and March 6, 1984. The attendance program provides for termination after 13 days of unexcused absences in a program year.

3. The grievant was aware as early as December 2, 1983, that partial days of absence count toward full days even when an employee is permitted by his foreman to go home early, as occurred with the

grievant on November 25. His cumulative days of absenteeism appeared on each of his paychecks, and all paychecks, beginning with that of December 2, included the .250 days assessed for that absence.

4. No disciplinary action issued prior to January 29 is in issue here since only one was grieved and that one was settled to the grievant's satisfaction without withdrawal of the warning involved.

5. Nothing prevents the company from administering discipline as it sees fit or in directing the workforce as it sees fit. The grievant was a first class lineman. The company could not afford to do without his services while he served suspensions. His absenteeism was especially injurious to the company for the same reason. In light of the fact that the grievant was given the benefit of the doubt on his absences of February 16 and 17, and the fact that his attendance record had been deteriorating rapidly, and that he failed to call in expected absences, the decision was made that suspension would be inappropriate in this case.

6. The grievant had been warned on February 28 that further unexcused absences might result in discharge. He was aware at that time he had 12.250 unexcused absences and that leaving work would result in more partial absences being accumulated. The grievant was properly discharged under the terms of the attendance program when his partial absences accumulated beyond 13 full days.

Grievance should be denied.

Portions of the Collective Bargaining Agreement

PREAMBLE

This Agreement, made and entered into by and between **CENTRAL POWER CORPORATION**, hereinafter referred to as the "Company," and Local 2700, **INTERNATIONAL BROTHERHOOD OF ELECTRICAL WORKERS**, hereinafter referred to as the "Union," shall be in full force and effect for a period of three (3) years from and after February 4, 1982.

ARTICLE 1 — PURPOSE

The purpose of the Company and the Union in entering into this Labor Agreement is to promote harmony and efficiency in the plants of the Company; to set forth their agreement on rates of pay, wages, hours of employment, and other conditions of employment; to provide for the peaceful adjustment of differences which may arise; and to achieve uninterrupted operations in the plants.

ARTICLE 2 — MANAGEMENT

Subject to the provisions of this agreement, the management of the plant and the direction of the working forces, including the right to plan, direct, and control plant operations; to hire and instruct; to obtain maximum operating efficiency; to introduce new, improved, or altered production methods or facilities; to promote, demote, transfer, lay off, discipline, and to suspend or discharge for proper cause, is vested exclusively in the Company.

ARTICLE 11 — SETTLEMENT OF GRIEVANCES

Section 1. Any grievance involving:

(a) Application of interpretation of this agreement, on

(b) Matters of wages or job content, which an employee of the Union may desire to desire to discuss and adjust with the Company may be handled as follows:

1. Between the aggrieved employee and his foreman, provided that the employee shall be accompanied by or represented by his Steward.

2. The Department Grievance Committee Man and the Personnel Manager, together with the aggrieved employee and/or his Steward and the Department Superintendent, shall investigate the grievance. The grievance shall be reduced to writing at this stage. A written answer shall be made to the grievance by the Personnel Manager within five (5) working days after the second-step meeting to investigate the grievance.

3. The Union Grievance Committee and the Company Labor Relations Committee shall place the grievance on the agenda for the next meeting of the Committee. The Grievance Committee shall meet with the Company's Labor Relations Committee once each month to consider those written grievances on the agenda. The Chairman of the Labor Relations Committee shall give a written answer to the grievance within seven (7) days of this meeting.

4. The Union President and/or Union International Representative and the General Management of the Company shall meet within thirty (30) days after the answer is given under the third step and shall attempt to settle the dispute. The General Management of the Company shall give a written answer to the grievance within fourteen (14) days after this meeting.

5. Provided the grievance has not been settled in Step 4, it may be referred to arbitration by the unsatisfied party as provided in Section 2, below.

Section 2. In view of the foregoing, if a grievance is not adjusted through the first four steps of the grievance procedure, either party may submit the grievance for binding decision by an arbitrator under the rules and in the manner set out below:

(a) Within thirty (30) days after the answer is given in Step 4, the party desiring arbitration shall address a request to the other party requesting arbitration and they shall jointly apply to the American Arbitration Association for a list of arbitrators.

(b) The Union Grievance Committee and the Company Labor Relations Committee shall then meet and select an arbitrator from the list provided.

(c) The sole function of said arbitrator shall be to interpret the meaning of the articles of this contract and shall not have the power to add to, subtract from, or modify in any way the terms of the agreement.

(d) Each party shall bear its own expenses in connection with the proceedings, but shall share equally in any expense jointly incurred.

(e) Unless jointly stipulated otherwise, the decision in such proceedings shall be rendered within thirty (30) days of the conclusion of the hearing and shall be final and binding on both parties.

ARTICLE 17 — GENERAL

Section 1. The Company will formulate rules to govern working conditions in the plant for the regulation of conduct of all employees. Any question as to the penalty imposed for the violation of these rules shall be subject to the grievance procedure.

Central Power Corporation's Hourly Attendance Program

POSITIVE INCENTIVES FOR WORK ATTENDANCE

1. In the spirit of this new, more positive approach to employee attendance, the company will clear all days of absenteeism from all active employee's records effective April 1, 1982. The company will again clear all days of absenteeism from employee records on each succeeding April 1. One documented step of attendance-related discipline will be removed from the employee's records effective each April 1.

2. An hourly employee who achieves perfect attendance for any six consecutive months after March 31, 1982, and while continuously actively at work, will be given, at his/her option, a day's pay (eight hours straight time) or a day off with eight hours straight time pay. Additionally, the employees will receive a one-day credit to be applied toward future absences. The maximum number of credit days that can be accumulated will be five. If an employee has earned five credit days, then he/she would not be terminated until the eighteenth day of absence in one Program Year. This banked credit day doesn't apply toward perfect attendance.

> For every eight hours of accumulated overtime worked at time and one-half, an employee will receive a one-half hour credit toward any unexcused absence for the effective Program Year. Additionally, when double time is paid for time worked by an employee on the seventh consecutive day worked in his regularly scheduled work week, that employee will receive a one-hour credit for every eight hours of accumulated hours worked on said day. The credit will apply towards any unexcused absence for the effective Program Year.

> Employee is to notify department scheduler when qualified for this award.

> If a day off is chosen, it must be taken within a year from the date of eligibility and on a date mutually agreeable between employee and supervisor.

> If a day off is chosen, it will be considered a day worked for purposes of computing consecutive days worked. For overtime accumulation purposes, the day off will not be considered a missed overtime opportunity.

> Next award is available six months after last qualifying date if consecutive perfect attendance is maintained and employee continues to be actively at work.

> Perfect attendance is an ongoing accumulation of continuous attendance beginning with the employee's last day of absenteeism.

3. The Company will continue to investigate potential voluntary programs to confidentially counsel and treat employees involved in alcohol or drug abuse.

DISCIPLINARY INCENTIVES FOR IMPROVING WORK ATTENDANCE

1. In this new program, absenteeism that exceeds six days in the 12-month Program Year is considered excessive. It is above national average. Employees whose absenteeism reaches six days in the Program Year will be counselled about their absenteeism by their supervisor. (Supervisors are encouraged to counsel employees after any incidence of absenteeism.)

2. Employees who are absent more than seven days in any Program Year will normally be given progressive discipline as follows:

Days Absent	Discipline
8	Verbal Warning
9	Written Warning
10	Three Days Administrative Discipline (or suspension)
11	10 Days Administrative Discipline (or suspension)
12	30 Days Administrative Discipline (or suspension)
13	Termination

3. Absenteeism is counted by full days of unexcused absence and also by accumulating any partial absenteeism as follows:

Type of Partial Absenteeism	Days Absent to Be Counted	Example 8-Hour Shift
Late by 0.1 hours or less (except for the above. . .)	.125	Worked 7.9 to 8.0 hours
Worked 75% shift or more	.250	Worked 6.0 to 7.8 hours
Worked 50% to 74% of shift	.500	Worked 4.0 to 5.9 hours
Worked 25% to 49% of shift	.750	Worked 2.0 to 3.9 hours
Worked 0% to 25% of shift	1.000	Worked 0 to 1.9 hours

4. The company will continue providing each active employee with a record of his or her cumulative days of full or partial absenteeism and days of sick leave for the current Program Year on their paychecks once each month. It will show net days of absenteeism, including any days cleared from their record.

SICK LEAVE

Sickness and Accident (S&A) Benefits are available for those individuals who encounter legitimate health problems that make it medically unwise for them to come to work. These are necessary benefits. There are, however, a *few* employees who abuse sick leave by staying out longer than really necessary or by exaggerating the seriousness of a health condition to their physicians. In such cases, the company may pay out wasteful and unnecessary S&A payments and fellow workers have to fill in on the job longer than is necessary. The company understands and is sympathetic to legitimate illness. On the other hand, the company intends to make more thorough reviews of S&A cases to ensure that no employees abuse the benefit to the detriment of the company *and* their fellow workers.

DURATION OF PROGRAM

This program is a *positive* attempt to reduce absenteeism and encourage greater attendance to the mutual benefit of the company and you, the employee. The program may be modified or discontinued by the company at any time. In addition, prior to the end of each Program Year, results will be reviewed and the program will be continued, expanded, modified, or discontinued based on the prior year's attendance results. This document does not constitute an agreement under any term(s) of the labor agreement.

ATTENDANCE PROGRAM OBJECTIVES

We believe that Central Power Corporation employees have a responsibility to be at work on a regular basis. Dependable employees are critical to the company's ability to operate. We also believe that employees deserve holiday and vacation time to rest and relax and that there will be occasional legitimate reasons to be absent from work for other urgent matters of health or critical personal need. We believe the company should provide reasonable accommodation to these important employee needs. We believe employees, in turn, should make every effort to report to work regularly and on time as part of their obligation to the company and to their fellow workers who have to do the absentee's work.

The objectives of the Central Power Corporation's Hourly Attendance Program are:

To provide special recognition to employees whose attendance record is clearly outstanding.

To provide a way in which employees' legitimate and urgent needs can be accommodated to a reasonable degree.

To seek to improve the Central work environment and general employee motivation.

To improve the discipline system and increase its effectiveness for absenteeism control.

To substantially reduce absenteeism and to maintain a percentage of absenteeism well below the national average of 1.9%.

DEFINITIONS OF TERMS USED IN CENTRAL POWER CORPORATION'S
HOURLY EMPLOYEE ATTENDANCE PROGRAM

Absenteeism: Unexcused absence of one or more days due to short-term illness or other personal reasons. *Excludes* absence due to authorized sick leave, vacation, company holidays if not scheduled to work, jury or witness duty, death in family, military leave, situations of personal extreme emergencies.

Partial Absenteeism: Any incident of working less than a full schedule shift, initiated by the employee. Commonly known as tardiness or as partial days worked.

Sick Leave: Absence under sickness and accident benefit coverage provided for a nonoccupational illness while under the care of a physician for a disability which continues for eight or more consecutive days.

Perfect Attendance: No absenteeism, and no partial absenteeism (that cumulatively totals to a day or more), and no sick leave.

Counselling: Verbal conversation between a supervisor and an employee for the purpose of counselling the employee about his or her performance. A nondisciplinary conversation to assist the employee in achieving better performance and avoidance of discipline.

Administrative Discipline: Disciplinary layoff served at work with pay in lieu of time off without pay. Administrative discipline days are noted on employee's record and are counted in determining progressive discipline.

Attendance Program Year: A program year in the context of this program is defined as a 12-month consecutive period beginning each April 1 and ending the following March 31.

Sample Attendance Record

Frank Walters, 1983 Program Year

Date	Status	Hrs	Date	Status	Hrs	Date	Status	Hrs
4/1	Holiday		5/8	Off		6/14		8
4/2	Off		5/9		8	6/15		8
			5/10		8	6/16		8
4/3	Off		5/11		8	6/17		8
4/4	Absent	*	5/12		8	6/18	Off	
4/5		8	5/13		8			
4/6		8	5/14		8	6/19		6
4/7		8				6/20		8
4/8		8	5/15		8	6/21		8
4/9		8	5/16		8	6/22		8
			5/17		8	6/23		8
4/10		8	5/18		8	6/24		8
4/11		8	5/19		8	6/25	Off	
4/12		8	5/20	Off				
4/13		8	5/21	Off		6/26	Off	
4/14		8				6/27	Absent	
4/15		8	5/22	Off		6/28		8
4/16	Off		5/23	Absent	*	6/29		8
			5/24		8	6/30		8
4/17	Off		5/25		8	7/1		8
4/18		8	5/26		8	7/2		8
4/19		8	5/27		8			
4/20		8	5/28	Off		7/3		8
4/21		8				7/4	Holiday	8
4/22		8	5/29	Off		7/5		8
4/23	Off		5/30	Holiday		7/6		8
			5/31	Absent		7/7		8
4/24			6/1		8	7/8		8
4/25		8	6/2		8	7/9		8
4/26		8	6/3		8			
4/27		8	6/4		8	7/10		8
4/28		8				7/11		8
4/29		8	6/5	Off		7/12		8
4/30	Off		6/6		8	7/13		8
			6/7		8	7/14		8
5/1	Off		6/8		8	7/15		8
5/2		8	6/9		8	7/16		4
5/3		8	6/10		8			
5/4		8	6/11	Off		7/17		2
5/5		8				7/18		8
5/6		8	6/12	Off		7/19		8
5/7	Off		6/13		8	7/20		8
						7/21		8

*Absence cleared from absentee record by accumulated overtime credit.

(continued)

Frank Walters, 1983 Program Year (continued)

7/22		8	8/80	Vacation		10/9	Off	
7/23	Off		8/31	Vacation		10/10		8
			9/1	Vacation		10/11		8
7/24	Off		9/2	Vacation		10/12		8
7/25		8	9/3	Off		10/13		8
7/26		8				10/14	Absent	
7/27		8	9/4	Off		10/15		8
7/28		8	9/5	Holiday				
7/29		8	9/6		8	10/16	Off	
7/30		4	9/7		8	10/17		8
			9/8		8	10/18		8
7/31		12	9/9		8	10/19		8
8/1		12	9/10	Off		10/20		8
8/2		12				10/21		8
8/3		12	9/11	Off		10/22		4
8/4		10	9/12		8			
8/5		8	9/13		8	10/23		4
8/6		8	9/14		8	10/24		8
			9/15		8	10/25		8
8/7		8	9/16		8	10/26		8
8/8		8	9/17	Off		10/27		8
8/9		8				10/28		8
8/10		8	9/18	Off		10/29	Off	
8/11		8	9/19		8			
8/12		8	9/20		8	10/30	Off	
8/13	Off		9/21		8	10/31		8
			9/22		8	11/1		8
8/14	Off		9/23		8	11/2		8
8/15	Vacation		9/24	Off		11/3		8
8/16	Vacation					11/4		12
8/17	Vacation		9/25	Off		11/5		12
8/18	Vacation		9/26	Absent				
8/19	Vacation		9/27	Absent		11/6		10
8/20	Off		9/28	Absent		11/7		8
			9/29		8	11/8		8
8/21	Off		9/30		8	11/9		8
8/22	Vacation		10/1	Off		11/10		8
8/23	Vacation					11/11	Holiday	
8/24	Vacation		10/2	Off		11/12	Off	
8/25	Vacation		10/3		8			
8/26	Vacation		10/4		8	11/13	Off	
8/27	Off		10/5		8	11/14		8
			10/6	Absent		11/15		8
8/28	Off		10/7	Absent		11/16		8
8/29	Vacation		10/8	Off		11/17		8

Frank Walters, 1983 Program Year (continued)

Date		Hours	Date		Hours	Date		Hours
11/18		8	12/25	Off		1/31	Sick Leave	
11/19	Off		12/26	Holiday		2/1	Sick Leave	
			12/27	Vacation		2/2	Sick Leave	
11/20	Off		12/28	Vacation		2/3	Sick Leave	
11/21		8	12/29	Vacation		2/4	Sick Leave	
11/22		8	12/30	Holiday				
11/23		8	12/31	Off		2/5	Sick Leave	
11/24	Holiday					2/6	Sick Leave	
11/25		6	1/1	Off		2/7	Sick Leave	
11/26	Off		1/2	Holiday		2/8	Sick Leave	
		1984	1/3	Vacation		2/9	Sick Leave	
11/27	Off		1/4	Vacation		2/10	Sick Leave	
11/28	Absent		1/5	Vacation		2/11	Sick Leave	
11/29		8	1/6	Credit				
11/30		8		day†		2/12	Sick Leave	
12/1		8	1/7	Off		2/13		8
12/2		12				2/14		8
12/3		12	1/8	Off	8	2/25		8
			1/9		8	2/16	Sick Leave	
12/4		12	1/10		8	2/17	Sick Leave	
12/5		12	1/11		8	2/18	Sick Leave	
12/6		8	1/12		8			
12/7		8	1/13		8	2/19	Sick Leave	
12/8		8	1/14	Off		2/20		8
12/9		8				2/21		8
12/10	Off		1/15	Off		2/22		8
			1/16	Sick Leave		2/23		8
12/11	Off		1/17	Sick Leave		2/24	Absent	
12/12	Absent		1/18	Sick Leave		2/25	Off	
12/13	Absent		1/19	Sick Leave				
12/14	3 day sus.	8	1/20	Sick Leave		2/26	Off	
12/15	Adm.	8	1/21	Sick Leave		2/27		8
12/16		8				2/28 2/29	Admin	8
12/17	Off		1/22	Sick Leave		3/1	Sus.	7
			1/23	Sick Leave		3/2		6
12/18	Off		1/24	Sick Leave		3/3	Off	
12/19	Vacation		1/25	Sick Leave				
12/20	Vacation		1/26	Sick Leave		3/4	Off	
12/21	Vacation		1/27	Sick Leave		3/5		7.9
12/22	Vacation		1/28	Sick Leave		3/6		6.4
12/23	Holiday					3/7	Terminated	
12/24	Off		1/29	Sick Leave				
			1/30	Sick Leave				

†Credit Day for accumulated overtime credit.

Frank Walters's Summary of Attendance, 1983 Attendance Year

Month	*Hours Regularly Scheduled to Work*	*Hours Worked (Includes Overtime)*	*Hours Absent*	*% Absent*
April '83	160	168	8	5
May	168	160	16	10
June	176	182	8	5
July	160	222	0	0
August	80	110	0	0
September	152	128	24	16
October	168	168	16	10
November	160	176	10	6
December	96	112	16	17
January '84	40	40	0	0
February	88	80	8	9
March (through 3/6)	32	27.3	4.7	15
YEAR TOTAL (4/1/83 through 3/6/84)	1,480	1,573.3	110.7	7.5%

Case 4: Flight or Fright?

Background

The Kelso-Tilden Corporation is a large manufacturer of component parts for automobiles and trucks and serves as a supplier for all three of the major U.S. automakers (GM, Ford, and Chrysler). Kelso-Tilden has 14 manufacturing plants located in Ohio, Michigan, Indiana, and Illinois. The Kelso-Tilden Plant No. 1, which was built in 1911, is the oldest and largest facility operated by the corporation. Today 1,800 people work at this facility. It is located in a medium-sized city 45 miles northwest of Detroit. The factory is a looming red brick structure covered with a black patina of soot, dirt, and smoke accumulated over the past 75 years from emissions of the foundry attached to the manufacturing facility. Inside the huge building are monstrous hydraulic presses (capacity of the largest is 40 tons), stamping machines, drop forge hammers, and overhead cranes hauling material from one end of the factory to another. In addition to the foundry and stamping operation, there is also an assembly operation at the rear of the facility. The major products produced at the Kelso-Tilden Plant No. 1 are brakes, axles, drive lines, and transmission housings for earthmoving equipment and heavy duty trucks. The work at Kelso-Tilden No. 1 is dirty, heavy, and dangerous. The workforce is represented by the Allied Industrial Workers of America; the Kelso-Tilden Plant No. 1 has been unionized since 1947. In the 1940s and 1950s, labor–management relations at K-T Plant No. 1 were characterized by hostility and bitterness. There were strikes during the contract negotiations in 1947, 1950, 1956, and 1959. The strike in 1959 was extended (68 days) and violent. When the company attempted to move strikebreakers through the picket line after the strike had been in duration for 60 days, the picketers reacted by stoning the plant and smashing the windows of the strikebreakers' cars. The police intervened and did their best to stop the property damage, but sporadic acts of damage to company property continued until the strike was settled. Subsequent strikes in 1968 and 1979 were of short duration and peaceful. Nevertheless, the labor relations climate at K-T Plant No. 1 is confrontational; the parties regard each other as adversaries.

The Issue

At 12:18 A.M. on Friday, March 13, 1986, Officer John Galesworthy observed the grievant, Fred Jackson, climbing over the 7-foot-high cyclone chain-link fence at the rear of the K-T Plant No. 1. The grievant was carrying a brown mesh bag in his left hand when first observed by the officer. A light blue 1972 Ford F-100 pickup truck was parked on the street close to where the grievant was first spotted. Subsequent checks revealed that the pickup belonged to the grievant. A 10-foot piece of galvanized conduit pipe was seen propped against the fence.

Upon spotting the grievant, Officer Galesworthy stopped his marked police car, got out of his car, and shone a spotlight on the grievant. The grievant then dropped his bag and began to flee on foot across the street and into a vacant lot at the rear of the K-T facility. Officer Galesworthy gave chase on foot, ordering the grievant to stop. He did not immediately do so. After a short chase, however, the grievant stopped running, was apprehended and handcuffed. The grievant was then arrested, booked on charges, and released on bond.

Upon inspecting the materials in the brown mesh bag, the officer noticed that the bag contained electrical couplers, switches, relays, and circuit breakers. The bag itself was a brown burlap bag which at one time contained rolls of copper wire. On the outside, the bag bore a stenciled address label from the manufacturer to K-T Plant No. 1. Officer Galesworthy took the bag and its contents back to the plant for identification. The supervisor of the electrical shop at the plant confirmed that the bag was of the type in which K-T received electrical parts from the manufacturer. Further, the supervisor identified the electrical parts and the conduit pipe found in the bag as the types of parts that could be found in the K-T electrical parts storeroom. The grievant was employed at K-T as a clerk in the storeroom in which electrical parts, plumbing parts, and paint were stored. Interviews with the two plant electricians who worked on second shift confirmed that the grievant had asked them questions recently about how different types of relays and couplers fitted together and they stated that they had shown the grievant how to assemble relays of the type found in the bag. The value of the electrical equipment was estimated to be $250. Because of the casual inventorying of electrical parts, it was not possible to ascertain if there were parts missing from the storeroom. If an electrician needed a coupler, the stock clerk would provide it and he would order more when the stock became depleted. The use of individual items such as these was not recorded on a part-by-part basis.

On Monday, March 16, 1986, the grievant punched his timecard at 2:52 P.M. and reported to his station in the stockroom at 2:55. There he was met by his department foreman, Dan Wash, and the plant superintendent, Mike Freebis. The grievant was then told that the company was filing charges of theft against him and that his employment was terminated due to the theft of company property. That afternoon the grievant filed a grievance against the company for unjust discharge and asked that he be restored to his position in the stockroom with all back pay and benefits returned to him.

Relevant Portions of the Labor Agreement

ARTICLE 6 — SHOP RULES AND REGULATIONS

The purpose of these rules and regulations, which are not necessarily all-inclusive, is not to restrict the rights of any employee but to define acceptable rules of conduct and protect the rights of all employees and ensure cooperation.

Committing one of the following violations will be sufficient grounds for disciplinary action, ranging from reprimand to immediate discharge depending on the seriousness of the offense in the judgment of management.

1. Falsification of personnel records
2. Absence without reasonable cause
3. Excessive absenteeism
4. Leaving the plant during working hours without permission
5. Fighting
6. Possession of weapons
7. Theft of company property
8. Insubordination
9. Sabotage
10. Gambling
11. Disregarding safety rules
12. Possession of, drinking of, any alcoholic beverage on company property at any time. Reporting to work under the influence of alcohol.
13. Possession of, use of, narcotics on company property at any time. Reporting to work under the influence of narcotics.

ARTICLE 13 — GRIEVANCE PROCEDURE

Any employee who has been disciplined or discharged may request the presence of the chief steward of his department to discuss the case with him in an office provided by the company on company property. If the disciplined employee so desires, he will be granted a hearing. Such hearing will be scheduled before noon on the next regularly scheduled working day and will be attended by the grievant, the chief steward, and a representative of management. If the grievance is not resolved at this step, another meeting will be scheduled no later than ten working days later to consider the grievance. At this second-step meeting the union must have the details of the grievance and its position on the issues in writing and presented in both written and verbal form to management. Management must respond in writing to the written grievance no later than ten working days after the second-step meeting. If the grievance is still not resolved, the union must petition management to submit the case to arbitration no later than ten days after receiving management's second-step answer to the grievance.

Positions of the Parties

Company Position

The company maintains that the grievant, Fred Jackson, was stealing company property from the electrical equipment storeroom on March 13. As evidence, the company cites the fact that Jackson was seen in possession of a bag full of electrical parts of the type used at K-T Plant No. 1 at the time he was apprehended. Further, the company cites the fact that Jackson had punched his timecard at 12:05, but was observed back on company property at 12:15, climbing over the fence at the rear of the facility. Mr. Jackson had consulted with the plant electricians earlier in the evening about how to assemble parts of the type he was found in possession of. Finally, the company cited the fact that Mr. Jackson fled from the police prior to his apprehension. Further, the company brought out the fact that Mr. Jackson had been tried and acquitted on robbery charges eight years earlier.

Union Position

The grievant claims that the company has no just cause for discharging him. The grievant's and the union's position is that Mr. Jackson bought the electrical parts at a local hardware store and that he brought them back into the plant to ask the electricians, on their lunch hour, how to assemble them. The grievant states that he bought the same type of parts at the hardware store as K-T stocked in their storeroom because the electricians had told him that these were the best parts available. In addition, the grievant states that he knew that he would need help assembling the electrical parts and he wanted to purchase parts with which his associates were familiar so they could help him. The grievant was building a new house, himself, and was able to produce credit card receipts from a local hardware store for "electrical parts" in excess of $300.

The grievant stated that he was using the rear approach to the plant because it was easier to haul the parts from his pickup into the plant if it was parked at the rear of the facility rather than at the front. Further, the grievant stated that he had just finished threading the end of the conduit using the company's mechanical tap and die equipment and he was returning the conduit to his truck.

In reply to the charge that he was fleeing to avoid arrest, the grievant admitted that he had at first run from Officer Galesworthy. The grievant stated that he ran due to an unreasoning fear of police officers. The grievant pointed out that after coming to his senses and controlling his fear, he stopped and surrendered to the police officer when he realized that he had done no wrong and that he had nothing to fear.

Case 5: Insubordination or Concern for Safety?

Background

Ottoman-Edison Corporation is a specialty steel manufacturer located in north central Ohio, about midway between Cleveland and Columbus. The corporation has been manufacturing specialty steel material (mostly stainless steel) since 1927 at this single facility. The manufacturing facility is housed in long, low sheds interconnected by a rail line. Raw materials (limestone, iron ore, and mineral additives) are brought in by rail to the furnace room where they are stockpiled to be used as needed. When steel is to be made, raw materials are placed in a large kettle-like cauldron or crucible. Carbon ore rods are then inserted into the crucible, an electrical charge is passed between them for some minutes, and the material in the crucible heats under extreme temperature to become molten steel. The molten steel is then poured into molds to cool. Once cooled, the ingots are run through a rolling mill process to produce long sheets of steel plate of any desired thickness. At the end of the process the coils of steel plate are loaded onto trucks for transport to customers.

Although most of the material is handled by overhead cranes or by rail-mounted mobile cranes, there is occasionally a need to use a truck-mounted mobile crane to handle some jobs. On February 17, 1985, such a need arose. Due to truck driver error, four large rolls of stainless steel plate rolled off the rear of a semi-truck as it was leaving the Ottoman-Edison facility. Each coil weighed approximately 10,000 pounds. In addition, three of the coils had rolled off the paved road leading out of the manufacturing facility onto a frozen, muddy field adjacent to the road. The steel coils needed to be taken immediately back into the warehouse out of the weather. Failure to do so may have caused irreparable damage to the coils due to rust.

The Issue

The regular operator of the truck-mounted mobile crane was Otis Anderson. Mr. Anderson was on vacation when the incident occurred. The production supervisor, Mr. Foxboro, when informed of the incident and of Mr. Anderson's absence, requested Jerry Hall, an operator of a track-mounted overhead crane in the furnace room, to operate the truck-mounted mobile crane to move the four coils of steel. Jerry Hall refused, claiming that based on an experience one-and-a-half years ago, he believed the truck-mounted crane was unsafe and not properly outfitted to lift material as heavy as the steel coils in an unpaved area such as the field. Mr. Foxboro then *ordered* Mr. Hall to operate the truck-mounted crane or face suspension. Mr. Hall refused, citing safety concerns. He was then suspended without pay from work for five days and sent home.

Next, Mr. Foxboro approached Alex Geraldson, the operator of the rail-mounted mobile crane and requested that he move the steel coils, using the truck-mounted mobile crane. Mr. Geraldson refused to operate the truck-mounted crane, citing safety as the main concern. Mr. Geraldson noted that the truck-mounted crane was a 1953 model and that it had not been overhauled in a long time. Mr. Geraldson further stated that he had operated the truck-mounted crane once within the past year and that he noticed that the cable brake slipped when lifting large loads. Mr. Foxboro then ordered Mr. Geraldson to operate the truck-mounted crane or face suspension similar to that received by Mr. Hall. Mr. Geraldson refused the order and he was also suspended without pay for five days and sent home.

Mr. Foxboro then contacted Alvin Tumer, who was the second-shift rail-mounted crane operator, and asked him to come to work immediately and load the steel coils using the truck-mounted crane. Mr. Tumer, who had never operated the truck-mounted crane previously, complied with the request. While lifting the first coil of steel the cable brake slipped and the coil crashed to the ground. A maintenance mechanic was called to tighten the cable brake. Upon inspection, it was found that the cable brake pads were worn and that the idler gears were stripped. In a matter of hours, these were replaced and the steel coils were loaded without further incident.

Relevant Contract Provisions

ARTICLE 11 — SAFETY RULES

The Company agrees to make reasonable provisions for the safety and health of the employees during the hours of their employment. The Company will provide the necessary protective devices to protect employees from injury and sickness and the employees shall be required to use all such equipment and safety devices as directed of the company.

Employees are not to start on any job until they have been instructed by the foreman as to how to do the job safely. In no case are employees to operate any piece of equipment or do any class of work other than that assigned, unless they are specifically told to do so by a foreman or representative of management.

ARTICLE 18 — WORK RULES

Committing any of the following violations will be sufficient grounds for disciplinary action ranging from reprimand to immediate discharge, depending upon the seriousness of the offense in the judgment of management.

. . .

e. Refusal to obey orders of foremen or other supervision.
f. Refusal or failure to do job assignment (do the work assigned to you and follow instructions; any complaint may be taken up later through the regular channels).

. . .

m. Disregard of safety rules or common safety practices.

ARTICLE 1 — MANAGEMENT RIGHTS

The right to hire, promote, assign, discharge, or discipline for cause and to maintain discipline and efficiency of employees is the sole responsibility of the company, subject to the seniority rules, grievance procedure, and other provisions of this agreement. In addition, the products to be manufactured, the location of plants, the schedules of production, the methods, processes, and means of manufacturing are solely and exclusively the right of the company.

Positions of the Parties

Company

The Company feels it was justified in suspending Hall and Geraldson. They were both experienced crane operators who had previous experience on the truck-mounted crane. They both refused a direct order from Mr. Foxboro in violation of Article 18 (e) and (f) of the labor agreement. The fact that another employee was called in to do the work, and did it safely, justifies the company position that the crane was safe to operate. The employer needs a disciplined and productive workforce that will carry out the orders of management. Failure to follow these orders should rightfully lead to discipline.

Union Position

The union maintains that Hall and Geraldson were within their rights under the agreement in refusing to work on the truck-mounted mobile crane. The union points out that both men had prior experience on the crane and both knew its limitations. The union maintains that the company violated Article 11 of the agreement in that it did not make reasonable provisions for the safety of the crane operator nor were Hall and Geraldson properly instructed in the safe operation of the mobile crane by Mr. Foxboro, who had never operated a mobile crane. Further, the union points to the slippage of the cable brake and the dropping of the first steel coil as evidence of the unsafe nature of the mobile crane. The operator of the crane could have been killed or seriously injured had the cable brake slipped while the steel coil was being hoisted over the cab of the crane. The operators Hall and Geraldson were justified by a concern for their own safety to refuse to operate the crane. The company violated Article 11 of the agreement by not making proper allowances for the safe operation of the crane. Therefore, Hall and Geraldson should have the suspension removed from their records and should be paid five days' pay to make up for the time they were unfairly suspended from employment.

Case 6: Supervisors Performing Bargaining Unit Work — Emergency or Snow Job?

Background

Urbantown is a medium-sized city with a population of 240,000, according to the 1980 census. It is located in western Ohio. Urbantown is a manufacturing city, and its labor force generally is heavily unionized. The municipal employees of Urbantown, with the exception of police and firefighters, are represented by the American Federation of State, County, and Municipal Employees. The bargaining unit is composed of about 750 people who work in the street and road maintenance department, the water and sewers department, the building inspection department, and the municipal utilities department. The city maintains a municipal garage facility, two water treatment facilities, two sewage processing plants and a small city electric power plant which produces electricity for street lighting and for some small commercial customers.

Labor relations between the union and Urbantown city government have always been good. There have been no strikes among Urbantown city employees in the 24 years that the union and city government have been negotiating. About 80 percent of the members of the bargaining unit are members of AFSCME, although there is no union or agency shop clause in the labor agreement.

The Issue

On December 14, 1985, at about 9:00 P.M., a surprise snowstorm of considerable magnitude descended on Urbantown and the surrounding area. Within minutes of its beginning, snow began accumulating. Rather than stopping after depositing an inch or two (as predicted by the weather forecasters), the storm intensified: the wind increased, and the snow began falling more heavily. Tom Scanlon, the second shift foreman at the garage, knew that he needed to get the salt trucks and snowplows on the road as soon as possible. He immediately began calling employees who usually work on the first shift to come back to work to begin operating the plows. He immediately dispatched the nine people he had on hand and ordered them to begin clearing the streets. By 10:00 P.M., Tom had contacted five more day shift drivers, but needed one more driver to operate the full complement of snow-removal equipment. The snow was falling heavily, and the one remaining truck sat idly as the snow piled up. Tom tried calling all the three remaining drivers on his list one more time, with no response from them. In frustration and desperation, Tom jumped in the truck himself and began plowing snow. When he came back at about 12:30 A.M. to refill the sand and salt supply on his truck, one of the men from first shift whom he had been trying to call earlier, Fred Sims, was waiting in the dispatch office. Tom turned the truck over to Fred, who operated the vehicle throughout the rest of the night. By 6:00 A.M., the snow had tapered off to flurries. In all, 18 inches of snow fell during the night, making the storm of December 14 one of the biggest in Urbantown in five years. Due to the speed with which Tom Scanlon was able to dispatch the salt trucks and snow plows during the night, the streets were reasonably clear for the morning rush hour. A potential traffic disruption of major proportion was averted by Tom's actions.

On December 15, three employees in the street and road department filed grievances. All claimed that some back wages were due them because of overtime work they lost due to Tom's handling of the staffing shortage. The two employees who had never been contacted (Tony Campino and Bob Milstead) both claimed they were denied eight hours of overtime by Tom Scanlon's actions. Both Campino and Milstead claimed that if Tom Scanlon had stayed in the dispatch office and continued to call that he would have reached one of them eventually (both returned home before 10:30 P.M.). The truck driver, Fred Sims, who did work that evening, requested two hours of additional overtime pay because he had to wait until 12:30 A.M. to begin work when Scanlon returned with the truck. Sims's wife gave him the message that Scanlon called at 10:00 when he returned home at 10:35. He called Scanlon back at 10:40 but there was no answer. He waited for Scanlon at the city garage from 10:45 until Scanlon arrived back with the truck at about 12:30 or 12:45 A.M.

Relevant Portions of the Labor Agreement

ARTICLE 17

No representative of management will perform any work normally performed by members of the Bargaining Unit, or which would deprive any employee of his normal duties. This does not prevent foremen and supervisors from performing necessary functions of instrumentation, emergency relief duty, or experimental work.

Positions of the Parties

Management

City management maintained that Tom Scanlon was performing emergency relief duty by driving one of the snow plows when he could not contact an employee to drive the last truck. Management felt that the sheer magnitude of the snow and the ferocity of the storm made this an emergency situation. Thus, Scanlon's action was justified under the agreement, and the city management asserted that the overtime claims of Campino and Milstead should be denied. Further, the city management took the stand that Sims's claim for additional overtime should be denied because, although he was available for work, he didn't actually work the two hours.

Union Position

The union felt that this grievance was to some extent a policy grievance. The union does not want to have supervisors and foremen routinely taking over the work that is normally performed by members of the bargaining unit. In the union's opinion, there was no emergency on the night of December 14. Fourteen of the fifteen salt trucks and plows were operating when Scanlon took off in the one remaining truck. If Scanlon had waited just 30 minutes more, one of the bargaining unit members could have performed the work. Scanlon was not justified in his actions of leaving the dispatch room; because of his impetuousness, he cheated Sims out of two hours of overtime work and, possibly, Campino or Milstead out of eight hours of work. The three employees should be compensated for these hours.

Appendix C

Labor Management Relations Act, 1947

Text of Labor Management Relations Act, 1947, as Amended by Public Law 86–257, 1959*

[Public Law 101 — 80th Congress]

AN ACT

To amend the National Labor Relations Act, to provide additional facilities for the mediation of labor disputes affecting commerce, to equalize legal responsibilities of labor organizations and employers, and for other purposes.

Be it enacted by the Senate and House of Representatives of the United States of America in Congress assembled.

SHORT TITLE AND DECLARATION OF POLICY

SECTION 1.　(a) This Act may be cited as the "Labor Management Relations Act, 1947."

Reprinted from U.S. Government Printing Office: 1956 0—792-030, Washington, D.C., 20402.

*Section 201(d) and (e) of the Labor-Management Reporting and Disclosure Act of 1959 which repealed Section 9(f), (g), and (h) of the Labor Management Relations Act, 1947, and Section 505 amending Section 302(a), (b), and (c) of the Labor Management Relations Act, 1947, took effect upon enactment of Public Law 86-257, September 14, 1959. As to the other amendments of the Labor Management Relations Act, 1947, Sections 707 of the Labor-Management Reporting and Disclosure Act provides:

The amendments made by this title shall take effect sixty days after the date of the enactment of this Act and no provision of this title shall be deemed to make an unfair labor practice, any act which is performed prior to such effective date which did not constitute an unfair labor practice prior thereto.

(b) Industrial strife which interferes with the normal flow of commerce and with the full production of articles and commodities for commerce, can be avoided or substantially minimized if employers, employees, and labor organizations each recognize under law one another's legitimate rights in their relations with each other, and above all recognize under law that neither party has any right in its relations with any other to engage in acts or practices which jeopardize the public health, safety, or interest.

It is the purpose and policy of this Act, in order to promote the full flow of commerce, to prescribe the legitimate rights of both employees and employers in their relations affecting commerce, to provide orderly and peaceful procedures for preventing the interference by either with the legitimate rights of the other, to protect the rights of individual employees in their relations with labor organizations whose activities affect commerce, to define and proscribe practices on the part of labor and management which affect commerce and are inimical to the general welfare, and to protect the rights of the public in connection with labor disputes affecting commerce.

TITLE I — AMENDMENT OF NATIONAL LABOR RELATIONS ACT

SEC. 101.   The National Labor Relations Act is hereby amended to read as follows:

FINDINGS AND POLICIES

SECTION 1.   The denial by some employers of the right of employees to organize and the refusal by some employers to accept the procedure of collective bargaining lead to strikes and other forms of industrial strife or unrest, which have the intent or the necessary effect of burdening or obstructing commerce by (a) impairing the efficiency, safety, or operation of the instrumentalities of commerce; (b) occurring in the current of commerce; (c) materially affecting, restraining, or controlling the flow of raw materials or manufactured or processed goods from or into the channels of commerce, or the prices of such materials or goods in commerce; or (d) causing diminution of employment and wages in such volume as substantially to impair or disrupt the market for goods flowing from or into the channels of commerce.

The inequality of bargaining power between employees who do not possess full freedom of association or actual liberty of contract, and employers who are organized in the corporate or other forms of ownership association substantially burdens and affects the flow of commerce, and tends to aggravate recurrent business depressions, by depressing wage rates and the purchasing power of wage earners in industry and by preventing the stabilization of competitive wage rates and working conditions within and between industries.

Experience has proved that protection by law of the right of employees to organize and bargain collectively safeguards commerce from injury, impairment, or interruption, and promotes the flow of commerce by removing certain recognized sources of industrial strife and unrest, by encouraging practices fundamental to the friendly adjustment of industrial disputes arising out of differences as to wages, hours, or other working conditions, and by restoring equality of bargaining power between employers and employees.

Experience has further demonstrated that certain practices by some labor organizations, their officers, and members have the intent or the necessary effect of burdening or obstructing commerce by preventing the free flow of goods in such commerce through strikes and other forms of industrial unrest or through concerted activities which impair the interest of the public in the free flow of such commerce. The elimination of such practices is a necessary condition to the assurance of the rights herein guaranteed.

It is hereby declared to be the policy of the United States to eliminate the causes of certain substantial obstructions to the free flow of commerce and to mitigate and eliminate these obstructions when they have occurred by encouraging the practice and procedure of collective bargaining and by protecting the exercise by workers of full freedom of association, self-organization, and designation of representatives of their own choosing, for the purpose of negotiating the terms and conditions of their employment or other mutual aid or protection.

DEFINITIONS

Sec. 2 When used in this Act —

(1) The term "person" includes one or more individuals, labor organizations, partnerships, associations, corporations, legal representatives, trustees, trustees in bankruptcy, or receivers.

(2) The term "employer" includes any person acting as an agent of an employer, directly or indirectly, but shall not include the United States or any wholly owned Government corporation, or any Federal Reserve Bank, or any State or political subdivision thereof, or any corporation or association operating a hospital, if no part of the net earnings inures to the benefit of any private shareholder or individual, or any person subject to the Railway Labor Act, as amended from time to time, or any labor organization (other than when acting as an employer), or anyone acting in the capacity of officer or agent of such labor organization.

(3) The term "employee" shall include any employee, and shall not be limited to the employees of a particular employer, unless the Act explicitly states otherwise, and shall include any individual whose work has ceased as a consequence of, or in connection with, any current labor dispute or because of any unfair labor practice, and who has not obtained any other regular and substantially equivalent employment, or in the domestic service of any family or person at his home, or any individual employed by his parent or spouse, or any individual having the status of an independent contractor, or any individual employed as a supervisor, or any individual employed by an employer subject to the Railway Labor Act, as amended from time to time, or by any other person who is not an employer as herein defined.

(4) The term "representatives" includes any individual or labor organization.

(5) The term "labor organization" means any organization of any kind, or any agency or employee representation committee or plan, in which employees participate and which exists for the purpose, in whole or in part, of dealing with employers concerning grievances, labor disputes, wages, rates of pay, hours of employment, or conditions of work.

(6) The term "commerce" means trade, traffic, commerce, transportation, or communication among the several States, or between the District of Columbia or any Territory of the United States and any State or other Territory, or between any foreign country and any State, Territory, or the District of Columbia, or within the District of Columbia or any Territory, or between points in the same State but through any other State or any Territory or the District of Columbia or any foreign country.

(7) The term "affecting commerce" means in commerce, or burdening or obstructing commerce or the free flow of commerce, or having led or tending to lead to a labor dispute burdening or obstructing commerce or the free flow of commerce.

(8) The term "unfair labor practice" means any unfair labor practice listed in section 8.

(9) The term "labor dispute" includes any controversy concerning terms, tenure or conditions of employment, or concerning the association or representation of persons in negotiating, fixing, maintaining, changing, or seeking to arrange terms or conditions of employment, regardless of whether the disputants stand in the proximate relation of employer and employee.

(10) The term "National Labor Relations Board" means the National Labor Relations Board provided for in section 3 of this Act.

(11) The term "supervisor" means any individual having authority, in the interest of the employer, to hire, transfer, suspend, lay off, recall, promote, discharge, assign, reward, or discipline other employees, or responsibly to direct them, or to adjust their grievances, or effectively to recommend such action, if in connection with the foregoing the exercise of such authority is not of a merely routine or clerical nature, but requires the use of independent judgment.

(12) The term "professional employee" means —

(a) any employee engaged in work (i) predominantly intellectual and varied in character as opposed to routine mental, manual, mechanical, or physical work; (ii) involving the consistent exercise of discretion and judgment in its performance; (iii) of such a character that the output produced or the result accomplished cannot be standardized in relation to a given period of time; (iv) requiring knowledge of an advanced type in a field of science or learning customarily acquired by a prolonged course of specialized intellectual instruction and study in an institution of higher learning or a hospital, as distinguished from a general academic education or from an apprenticeship or from training in the performance of routine mental, manual, or physical processes; or

(b) any employee, who (i) has completed the courses of specialized intellectual instruction and study described in clause (iv) of paragraph (a), and (ii) is performing related work under the supervision of a professional person to qualify himself to become a professional employee as defined in paragraph (a).

(13) In determining whether any person is acting as an "agent" of another person so as to make such other person responsible for his acts, the question of whether the specific acts performed were actually authorized or subsequently ratified shall not be controlling.

NATIONAL LABOR RELATIONS BOARD

SEC. 3. (a) The National Labor Relations Board (hereinafter called the "Board") created by this Act prior to its amendment by the Labor Management Relations Act, 1947, is hereby continued as an agency of the United States, except that the Board shall consist of five instead of three members, appointed by the President by and with the advice and consent of the Senate. Of the two additional members so provided for, one shall be appointed for a term of five years and the other for a term of two years. Their successors, and the successors of the other members, shall be appointed for terms of five years each, excepting that any individual chosen to fill a vacancy shall be appointed only for the unexpired term of the member whom he shall succeed. The President shall designate one member to serve as Chairman of the Board. Any member of the Board may be removed by the President, upon notice and hearing, for neglect of duty or malfeasance in office, but for no other cause.

(b) The Board is authorized to delegate to any group of three of more members any or all of the powers which it may itself exercise. The Board is also authorized to delegate to its regional directors its powers under section 9 to determine the unit appropriate for the purpose of collective bargaining, to investigate and provide for hearings, and determine whether a question of representation exists, and to direct an election or take a secret ballot under subsection (c) or (e) of section 9 and certify the results thereof, except that upon the filing of a request therefor with the Board by any interested person, the Board may review any action of a regional director delegated to him under this paragraph, but such a review shall not, unless specifically ordered by the Board, operate as a stay of any action taken by the regional director. A vacancy in the Board shall not impair the right of the remaining members to exercise all of the powers of the Board, except that two members shall constitute a quorum of any group designated pursuant to the first sentence hereof. The Board shall have an official seal which shall be judicially noticed.

(c) The Board shall at the close of each fiscal year make a report in writing to Congress and to the President stating in detail the cases it has heard, the decisions it has rendered, the names, salaries, and duties of all employees and officers in the employ or under the supervision of the Board, and an account of all moneys it has disbursed.

(d) There shall be a General Counsel of the Board who shall be appointed by the President, by and with the advice and consent of the Senate, for a term of four years. The General Counsel of the Board shall exercise general supervision over all attorneys employed by the Board (other than trial examiners and legal assistants to Board members) and over the officers and employees in the regional offices. He shall have final authority, on behalf of the Board, in respect of the investigation of charges and issuance of complaints under section 10, and in respect of the prosecution of such complaints before the Board, and shall have such other duties as the Board may prescribe or as may be provided by law. In case of a vacancy in the office of the General Counsel the President is authorized to designate the officer or employee who shall act as General Counsel during such vacancy, but no person or persons so designated shall so act (1) for more than forty days when the Congress is in session unless a nomination to fill such vacancy shall have been submitted to the Senate, or (2) after the adjournment *sine die* of the session of the Senate in which such nomination was submitted.

SEC. 4. (a) Each member of the Board and the General Counsel of the Board shall receive a salary of $12,000* a year, shall be eligible for reappointment, and shall not engage in any other business, vocation, or employment. The Board shall appoint an executive secretary, and such attorneys, examiners, and regional directors, and such other employees as it may from time to time find

*Pursuant to Public Law 88-426, 88th Congress, 2d Session, Title III, approved August 14, 1964, the salary of the Chairman of the Board shall be $28,500 per year and the salaries of the General Counsel and each Board member shall be $27,000 per year.

necessary for the proper performance of its duties. The Board may not employ any attorneys for the purpose of reviewing transcripts of hearings or preparing drafts of opinions except that any attorney employed for assignment as a legal assistant to any Board member may for such Board member review such transcripts and prepare such drafts. No trial examiner's report shall be reviewed, either before or after its publication, by any person other than a member of the Board or his legal assistant, and no trial examiner shall advise or consult with the Board with respect to exceptions taken to his findings, rulings, or recommendations. The Board may establish or utilize such regional, local, or other agencies, and utilize such voluntary and uncompensated services, as may from time to time be needed. Attorneys appointed under this section may, at the direction of the Board, appear for and represent the Board in any case in court. Nothing in this Act shall be construed to authorize the Board to appoint individuals for the purpose of conciliation or mediation, or for economic analysis.

(b) All of the expenses of the Board, including all necessary traveling and subsistence expenses outside the District of Columbia incurred by the members or employees of the Board under its orders, shall be allowed and paid on the presentation of itemized vouchers therefor approved by the Board or by any individual it designates for that purpose.

Sec. 5.   The principal office of the Board shall be in the District of Columbia, but it may meet and exercise any or all of its powers at any other place. The Board may, by one or more of its members or by such agents or agencies as it may designate, prosecute any inquiry necessary to its functions in any part of the United States. A member who participates in such an inquiry shall not be disqualified from subsequently participating in a decision of the Board in the same case.

Sec. 6.   The Board shall have authority from time to time to make, amend, and rescind, in the manner prescribed by the Administrative Procedure Act, such rules and regulations as may be necessary to carry out the provisions of this Act.

RIGHTS OF EMPLOYEES

Sec. 7.   Employees shall have the right to self-organization, to form, join, or assist labor organizations, to bargain collectively through representatives of their own choosing, and to engage in other concerted activities for the purpose of collective bargaining or other mutual aid or protection, and shall also have the right to refrain from any or all of such activities except to the extent that such right may be affected by an agreement requiring membership in a labor organization as a condition of employment as authorized in section 8(a)(3).

UNFAIR LABOR PRACTICES

Sec. 8.   (a) It shall be an unfair labor practice for an employer —
(1) to interfere with, restrain, or coerce employees in the exercise of the rights guaranteed in section 7;
(2) to dominate or interfere with the formation or administration of any labor organization or contribute financial or other support to it: *Provided*, That subject to rules and regulations made and published by the Board pursuant to section 6, an employer shall not be prohibited from permitting employees to confer with him during working hours without loss of time or pay;

outlaws Company Unions

(3) by discrimination in regard to hire or tenure of employment or any term or condition of employment to encourage or discourage membership in any labor organization: *Provided*, That nothing in this Act, or in any other statute of the United States, shall preclude an employer from making an agreement with a labor organization (not established, maintained, or assisted by any action defined in section 8(a) of this Act as an unfair labor practice) to require as a condition of employment membership therein on or after the thirtieth day following the beginning of such employment or the effective date of such agreement, whichever is the later, (i) if such labor organization is the representative of the employees as provided in section 9(a), in the appropriate collective-bargaining unit covered by such agreement when made, and (ii) unless following an election held as provided in section 9(e) within one year preceding the effective date of such agreement, the Board shall have certified that at least a majority of the employees eligible to vote in such election have voted to rescind the authority of such labor organization to make such an agreement: *Provided further*, That no employer shall justify any discrimination against an employee for nonmembership in a labor organization (A) if he has reasonable grounds for believing that such membership was not available to the employee on the same terms and conditions generally applicable to other members, or (B) if he has reasonable grounds for believing that membership was denied or terminated for reasons other than the failure of the employee to tender the periodic dues and the initiation fees uniformly required as a condition of acquiring or retaining membership;

(4) to discharge or otherwise discriminate against an employee because he has filed charges or given testimony under this Act; NLRB Activity

(5) to refuse to bargain collectively with the representatives of his employees, subject to the provisions of section 9(a). in good faith

(b) It shall be unfair labor practice for a labor organization or its agents —

(1) to restrain or coerce (A) employees in the exercise of the rights guaranteed in section 7: *Provided*, That this paragraph shall not impair the right of a labor organization to prescribe its own rules with respect to the acquisition or retention of membership therein; or (B) an employer in the selection of his representatives for the purposes of collective bargaining or the adjustment of grievances;

(2) to cause or attempt to cause an employer to discriminate against an employee in violation of subsection (a)(3) or to discriminate against an employee with respect to whom membership in such organization has been denied or terminated on some ground other than his failure to tender the periodic dues and the initiation fees uniformly required as a condition of acquiring or retaining membership;

(3) to refuse to bargain collectively with an employer, provided it is the representative of his employees subject to the provisions of section 9(a); in good faith

(4) (i) to engage in, or to induce or encourage any individual employed by any person engaged in commerce or in an industry affecting commerce to engage in, a strike or a refusal in the course of his employment to use, manufacture, process, transport, or otherwise handle or work on any goods, articles, materials, or commodities or to perform any services; or (ii) to threaten, coerce, or restrain any person engaged in commerce or in an industry affecting commerce, where in either case an object thereof is:

(A) forcing or requiring any employer or self-employed person to join any labor or employer organization or to enter into any agreement which is prohibited by section 8(e);

(B) forcing or requiring any person to cease using, selling, handling, transporting, or otherwise dealing in the products of any other producer, processor, or manufacturer, or to cease doing business with any other person, or forcing or requiring any other employer to recognize or bargain with a labor organization as the representative of his employees unless such labor organization has been certified as the representative of such employees under the provisions of section 9: *Provided*, That nothing contained in this clause (B) shall be construed to make unlawful, where not otherwise unlawful, any primary strike or primary picketing;

(C) forcing or requiring any employer to recognize or bargain with a particular labor organization as the representative of his employees if another labor organization has been certified as the representative of such employees under the provisions of section 9;

(D) forcing or requiring any employer to assign particular work to employees in a particular labor organization or in a particular trade, craft, or class rather than to employees in another labor organization or in another trade, craft, or class, unless such employer is failing to conform to an order or certification of the Board determining the bargaining representative for employees performing such work:

Provided, That nothing contained in this subsection (b) shall be construed to make unlawful a refusal by any person to enter upon the premises of any employer (other than his own employer), if the employees of such employer are engaged in a strike ratified or approved by a representative of such employees whom such employer is required to recognize under this Act: *Provided further*, That for the purposes of this paragraph (4) only, nothing contained in such paragraph shall be construed to prohibit publicity, other than picketing, for the purpose of truthfully advising the public, including consumers and members of a labor organization, that a product or products are produced by an employer with whom the labor organization has a primary dispute and are distributed by another employer, as long as such publicity does not have an effect of inducing any individual employed by any person other than the primary employer in the course of his employment to refuse to pick up, deliver, or transport any goods, or not to perform any services, at the establishment of the employer engaged in such distribution;

(5) to require of employees covered by an agreement authorized under subsection (a)(3) the payment, as a condition precedent to becoming a member of such organization, of a fee in an amount which the Board finds excessive or discriminatory under all the circumstances. In making such a finding, the Board shall consider, among other relevant factors, the practices and customs of labor organizations in the particular industry, and the wages currently paid to the employees affected;

(6) to cause or attempt to cause an employer to pay or deliver or agree to pay or deliver any money or other thing of value, in the nature of an exaction, for services which are not performed or not to be performed; and feather bedding

(7) to picket or cause to be picketed, or threaten to picket or cause to be picketed, any employer where an object thereof is forcing or requiring an employer to recognize or bargain with a labor organization as the representative

of his employees, or forcing or requiring the employees of an employer to accept or select such labor organization as their collective bargaining representative, unless such labor organization is currently certified as the representative of such employees: picketing by non- certified union

(A) where the employer has lawfully recognized in accordance with this Act any other labor organization and a question concerning representation may not appropriately be raised under section 9(c) of this Act.

(B) where within the preceding twelve months a valid election under section 9(c) of this Act has been conducted, or

(C) where such picketing has been conducted without a petition under section 9(c) being filed within a reasonable period of time not to exceed thirty days from the commencement of such picketing: *Provided*, That when such a petition has been filed the Board shall forthwith, without regard to the provisions of section 9(c)(1) or the absence of a showing of a substantial interest on the part of the labor organization, direct an election in such unit as the Board finds to be appropriate and shall certify the results thereof: *Provided further*, That nothing in this subparagraph (C) shall be construed to prohibit any picketing or other publicity for the purpose of truthfully advising the public (including consumers) that an employer does not employ members of, or have a contract with, a labor organization, unless an effect of such picketing is to induce any individual employed by any other person in the course of his employment, not to pick up, deliver or transport any goods or not to perform any services.

Nothing in this paragraph (7) shall be construed to permit any act which would otherwise be an unfair labor practice under this section 8(b).

(c) The expressing of any views, argument, or opinion, or the dissemination thereof, whether in written, printed, graphic, or visual form, shall not constitute or be evidence of an unfair labor practice under any of the provisions of this Act, if such expressions contains no threat of reprisal or force or promise of benefit.

(d) For the purposes of this section, to bargain collectively is the performance of the mutual obligation of the employer and the representative of the employees to meet at reasonable times and confer in good faith with respect to wages, hours, and other terms and conditions of employment, or the negotiation of an agreement, or any question arising thereunder, and the execution of a written contract incorporating any agreement reached if requested by either party, but such obligation does not compel either party to agree to a proposal or require the making of a concession: *Provided*, That where there is in effect a collective-bargaining contract covering employees in an industry affecting commerce, the duty to bargain collectively shall also mean that no party to such contract shall terminate or modify such contract, unless the party desiring such termination or modification —

(1) serves a written notice upon the other party to the contract of the proposed termination or modification sixty days prior to the expiration date thereof, or in the event such contract contains no expiration date, sixty days prior to the time it is proposed to make such termination or modification;

(2) offers to meet and confer with the other party for the purpose of negotiating a new contract or a contract containing the proposed modifications;

(3) notifies the Federal Mediation and Conciliation Service within thirty days after such notice of the existence of a dispute, and simultaneously therewith notifies any State or Territorial agency established to mediate and conciliate disputes within the State or Territory where the dispute occurred, provided no agreement has been reached by that time; and

(4) continues in full force and effect, without resorting to strike or lockout, all the terms and conditions of the existing contract for a period of sixty days after such notice is given or until the expiration date of such contract, whichever occurs later:

The duties imposed upon employers, employees, and labor organizations by paragraphs (2), (3), and (4) shall become inapplicable upon an intervening certification of the Board, under which the labor organization or individual, which is a party to the contract, has been superseded as or ceased to be the representative of the employees subject to the provisions of section 9(a), and the duties so imposed shall not be construed as requiring either party to discuss or agree to any modification of the terms and conditions contained in a contract for a fixed period, if such modification is to become effective before such terms and conditions can be reopened under the provisions of the contract. Any employee who engages in a strike within the sixty-day period specified in this subsection shall lose his status as an employee of the employer engaged in the particular labor dispute, for the purposes of sections 8, 9, and 10 of this Act, as amended, but such loss of status for such employee shall terminate if and when he is reemployed by such employer.

(e) It shall be an unfair labor practice for any labor organization and any employer to enter into any contract or agreement, express or implied, whereby such employer ceases or refrains or agrees to cease or refrain from handling, using, selling, transporting or otherwise dealing in any of the products of any other employer, or to cease doing business with any other person, and any contract or agreement entered into heretofore or hereafter containing such an agreement shall be to such extent unenforceable and void: *Provided,* That nothing in this subsection (e) shall apply to an agreement between a labor organization and an employer in the construction industry relating to the contracting or subcontracting of work to be done at the site of the construction, alteration, painting, or repair of a building, structure, or other work: *Provided further,* That for the purposes of this subsection (e) and section 8(b)(4)(B) the terms "any employer", "any person engaged in commerce or in industry affecting commerce", and "any person" when used in relation to the terms "any other producer, processor, or manufacturer", "any other employer", or "any other person" shall not include persons in the relation of a jobber, manufacturer, contractor, or subcontractor working on the goods or premises of the jobber or manufacturer or performing parts of an integrated process of production in the apparel and clothing industry: *Provided further,* That nothing in this Act shall prohibit the enforcement of any agreement which is within the foregoing exception.

(f) It shall not be an unfair labor practice under subsections (a) and (b) of this section for an employer engaged primarily in the building and construction industry to make an agreement covering employees engaged (or who, upon their employment, will be engaged) in the building and construction industry with a labor organization of which building and construction employees are members (not established, maintained, or assisted by any action defined in section 8(a) of this Act as an unfair labor practice) because (1) the majority status of such labor organization has not been established under the provisions of section 9 of this Act prior to the making of such agreement, or (2) such agreement requires as a condition of employment, membership in such labor organization after the seventh day following the beginning of such employment or the effective date of the agreement, whichever is later, or (3) such agreement requires the employer to notify such labor organization of opportunities for employment with such employer, or gives such labor organization an opportunity to refer qualified applicants for such employment, or (4) such agreement specifies minimum training or experience qualifications for employment or provides for priority in opportunities for employment based upon length of service with such employer, in the industry or in the particular geographical area: *Provided,* That nothing in this subsection shall set aside the final proviso to section 8(a)(3) of this act: *Provided further,* That any agreement which would be invalid, but for clause (1) of this subsection, shall not be a bar to a petition filed pursuant to section 9(c) or 9(e).*

REPRESENTATIVES AND ELECTIONS

SEC. 9. (a) Representatives designated or selected for the purposes of collective bargaining by the majority of the employees in a unit appropriate for such purposes, shall be the exclusive representatives of all the employees in such unit for the purposes of collective bargaining in respect to rates of pay, wages, hours of employment, or other conditions of employment: *Provided,* That any individual employee or a group of employees shall have the right at any time to present grievances to their employer and to have such grievances adjusted, without the intervention of the bargaining representative, as long as the adjustment is not inconsistent with the terms of a collective-bargaining contract or agreement then in effect: *Provided further,* That the bargaining representative has been given opportunity to be present at such adjustment.

[handwritten margin note: unique to U.S. labor law.]

(b) The Board shall decide in each case whether, in order to assure to employees the fullest freedom in exercising the rights guaranteed by this Act, the unit appropriate for the purposes of collective bargaining shall be the employer unit, craft unit, plant unit, or subdivision thereof: *Provided,* That the Board shall not (1) decide that any unit is appropriate for such purposes if such unit includes both professional employees and employees who are not professional employees unless a majority of such professional employees vote for inclusion in such unit; or (2) decide that any craft unit is inappropriate for such purposes on the ground that a different unit has been established by a prior Board determination, unless a majority of the employees in the proposed craft unit vote against separate representation or (3) decide that any unit is appropriate for such purposes if it includes, together with other employees, any individual employed as a guard to enforce against employees and other persons rules to pro-

---

*Section 8(f) is inserted in the Act by subsection (a) of Section 705 of Public Law 86-257. Section 705(b) provides:

Nothing contained in the amendment made by subsection (a) shall be construed as authorizing the execution or application of agreements requiring membership in a labor organization as a condition of employment in any State or Territory in which such execution or application is prohibited by State or Territorial law.

tect property of the employer or to protect the safety of persons on the employer's premises; but no labor organization shall be certified as the representataive of employees in a bargaining unit of guards if such organization admits to membership, or is affiliated directly or indirectly with an organization which admits to membership, employees other than guards.

(c) (1) Wherever a petition shall have been filed, in accordance with such regulations as may be prescribed by the Board —

(A) by an employee or group of employees or any individual or labor organization acting in their behalf alleging that a substantial number of employees (i) wish to be represented for collective bargaining and that their employer declines to recognize their representative as the representative defined in section 9(a), or (ii) assert that the individual or labor organization, which has been certified or is being currently recognized by their employer as the bargaining representative, is no longer a representataive as defined in section 9(a); or

(B) by an employer, alleging that one or more individuals or labor organizations have presented to him a claim to be recognized as the representative defined in section 9(a);

the Board shall investigate such petition and if it has reasonable cause to believe that a question of representation affecting commerce exists shall provide for an appropriate hearing upon due notice. Such hearing may be conducted by an officer or employee of the regional office, who shall not make any recommendations with respect thereto. If the Board finds upon the record of such hearing that such a question of representation exists, it shall direct an election by secret ballot and shall certify the results thereof.

(2) In determining whether or not a question of representation affecting commerce exists, the same regulations and rules of decision shall apply irrespective of the identity of the persons filing the petition or the kind of relief sought and in no case shall the Board deny a labor organization a place on the ballot by reason of an order with respect to such labor organization or its predecessor not issued in conformity with section 10(c).

(3) No election shall be directed in any bargaining unit or any subdivision within which, in the preceding twelve-month period, a valid election shall have been held. Employees engaged in an economic strike who are not entitled to reinstatement shall be eligible to vote under such regulations as the Board shall find are consistent with the purposes and provisions of this Act in any election conducted within twelve months after the commencement of the strike. In any election where none of the choices on the ballot receives a majority, a run-off shall be conducted, the ballot providing for a selection between the two choices receiving the largest and second largest number of valid votes cast in the election.

(4) Nothing in this section shall be construed to prohibit the waiving of hearings by stipulation for the purpose of a consent election in conformity with regulations and rules of decision of the Board.

(5) In determining whether a unit is appropriate for the purposes specified in subsection (b) the extent to which the employees have organized shall not be controlling.

(d) Whenever an order of the Board made pursuant to section 10(c) is based in whole or in part upon facts certified following an investigation pursuant to subsection (c) of this section and there is a petition for the enforcement or review of such order, such certification and the record of such investigation shall be included in the transcript of the entire record required to be filed under section 10(e) or 10(f), and thereupon the decree of the court enforcing, modifying, or setting aside in whole or in part the order of the Board shall be made and entered upon the pleadings, testimony, and proceedings set forth in such transcript.

(e)(1) Upon the filing with the Board, by 30 per centum or more of the employees in a bargaining unit covered by an agreement between their employer and a labor organization made pursuant to section 8(a)(e), of a petition alleging they desire that such authority be rescinded, the Board shall take a secret ballot of the employees in such unit and certify the results thereof to such labor organization and to the employer.

(2) No election shall be conducted pursuant to this subsection in any bargaining unit or any subdivision within which, in the preceding twelve-month period, a valid election shall have been held.

PREVENTION OF UNFAIR LABOR PRACTICES

Sec. 10. (a) The Board is empowered, as hereinafter provided, to prevent any person from engaging in any unfair labor practice (listed in section 8) affecting commerce. This power shall not be affected by any other means of adjustment or prevention that has been or may be established by agreement, law, or otherwise: *Provided*, That the Board is empowered by agreement with any agency of any State or Territory to cede to such agency jurisdiction over any cases in any industry (other than mining, manufacturing, communications, and transportation except where predominantly local in character) even though such cases may involve labor disputes affecting commerce, unless the provision of the State or Territorial statute applicable to the determination of such cases by such agency is inconsistent with the corresponding provision of this Act or has received a construction inconsistent therewith.

(b) Whenever it is charged that any person has engaged in or is engaging in any such unfair labor practice, the Board, or any agent or agency designated by the Board for such purposes, shall have power to issue and cause to be served upon such person a complaint stating the charges in that respect, and containing a notice of hearing before the Board or a member thereof, or before a designated agent or agency, at a place therein fixed, not less than five days after the serving of said complaint: *Provided*, That no complaint shall issue based upon any unfair labor practice occurring more than six months prior to the filing of the charge with the Board and the service of a copy thereof upon the person against whom such charge is made, unless the person aggrieved thereby was prevented from filing such charge by reason of service in the armed forces, in which event the six-month period shall be computed from the day of his discharge. Any such complaint may be amended by the member, agent, or agency conducting the hearing or the Board in its discretion at any time prior to the issuance of an order based thereon. The person so complained of shall have the right to file an answer to the original or amended complaint and to appear in person or otherwise and give testimony at the place and time fixed in the complaint. In the discretion of the member, agent, or agency conducting the hearing or the Board, any other person may be allowed to intervene in the said proceeding and to present testimony. Any such proceeding shall, so far as practicable, be conducted in accordance with the rules of evidence applicable in the district courts of the United States under the rules of civil procedure for the district courts of the United States, adopted by the Supreme Court of the United States pursuant to the Act of June 19, 1934 (U.S.C., title 28, secs. 723-B, 723-C).

(c) The testimony taken by such member, agent, or agency or the Board shall be reduced to writing and filed with the Board. Thereafter, in its discretion, the Board upon notice may take further testimony or hear argument. If upon the preponderance of the testimony taken the Board shall be of the opinion that any person named in the complaint has engaged in or is engaging in any such unfair labor practice, then the Board shall state its findings of fact and shall issue and cause to be served on such person an order requiring such person to cease and desist from such unfair labor practice, and to take such affirmative action including reinstatement of employees with or without back pay, as will effectuate the policies of this Act: *Provided,* That where an order directs reinstatement of an employee, back pay may be required of the employer or labor organization, as the case may be, responsible for the discrimination suffered by him: *And provided further,* That in determining whether a complaint shall issue alleging a violation of section 8(a)(1) or section 8(a)(2), and in deciding such cases, the same regulations and rules of decision shall apply irrespective of whether or not the labor organization affected is affiliated with a labor organization national or international in scope. Such order may further require such person to make reports from time to time showing the extent to which it has complied with the order. If upon the preponderance of the testimony taken the Board shall not be of the opinion that the person named in the complaint has engaged in or is engaging in any such unfair labor practice, then the Board shall state its findings of fact and shall issue an order dismissing the said complaint. No order of the Board shall require the reinstatement of an individual as an employee who has been suspended or discharged, or the payment to him of any back pay, if such individual was suspended or discharged for cause. In case the evidence is presented before a member of the Board, or before an examiner or examiners thereof, such member, or such examiner or examiners, as the case may be, shall issue and cause to be served on the parties to the proceeding a proposed report, together with a recommended order, which shall be filed with the Board, and if no exceptions are filed within twenty days after service thereof upon such parties, or within such further period as the Board may authorize, such recommended order shall become the order of the Board and become effective as therein prescribed.

(d) Until the record in a case shall have been filed in a court, as hereinafter provided, the Board may at any time, upon reasonable notice and in such manner as it shall deem proper, modify or set aside, in whole or in part, any finding or order made or issued by it.

(e) The Board shall have power to petition any court of appeals of the United States, or if all the courts of appeals to which application may be made are in vacation, any district court of the United States, within any circuit or district, respectively, wherein the unfair labor practice in question occurred or wherein such person resides or transacts business, for the enforcement of such order and for appropriate temporary relief or restraining order, and shall file in the court the record in the proceedings, as provided in section 2112 of title 28, United States Code. Upon the filing of such petition, the court shall cause notice thereof to be served upon such person, and thereupon shall have jurisdiction of the proceeding and of the question determined therein, and shall have power to grant such temporary relief or restraining order as it deems just and proper, and to make and enter a decree enforcing, modifying, and enforcing as so modified, or setting aside in whole or in part the order of the Board. No objection that has not been urged before the Board, its member, agent, or agency, shall be considered by the court, unless the failure or neglect to urge such objection shall be excused because of extraordinary circumstances. The findings of the Board with respect to questions of fact if supported by substantial evidence on the record considered as a whole shall be conclusive. If either party shall apply to the court for leave to adduce additional evidence and shall show to the satisfaction of the court that such additional evidence is material and that there were reasonable grounds for the failure to adduce such evidence in the hearing before the Board, its member, agent, or agency, the court may order such additional evidence to be taken before the Board, its member, agent, or agency, and to be made a part of the record. The Board may modify its findings as to the facts, or make new findings, by reason of additional evidence so taken and filed, and it shall file such modified or new findings, which findings with respect to questions of fact if supported by substantial evidence on the record considered as a whole shall be conclusive, and shall file its recommendations, if any, for the modification or setting aside of its original order. Upon the filing of the record with it the jurisdiction of the court shall be exclusive and its judgment and decree shall be final, except that the same shall be subject to review by the appropriate United States court of appeals if application was made to the district court as hereinabove provided, and by the Supreme Court of the United States upon writ of certiorari or certification as provided in section 1254 of title 28.

(f) Any person aggrieved by a final order of the Board granting or denying in whole or in part the relief sought may obtain a review of such order in any circuit court of appeals of the United States in the circuit wherein the unfair labor practice in question was alleged to have been engaged in or wherein such person resides or transacts business, or in the United States Court of Appeals for the District of Columbia, by filing in such court a written petition praying that the order of the Board be modified or set aside. A copy of such petition shall be forthwith transmitted by the clerk of the court to the Board, and thereupon the aggrieved party shall file in the court the record in the proceeding, certified by the Board, as provided in section 2112 of title 28, United States Code. Upon the filing of such petition, the court shall proceed in the same manner as in the case of an application by the Board under subsection (e) of this section, and shall have the same jurisdiction to grant to the Board such temporary relief or restraining order as it deems just and proper, and in like manner to make and enter a decree enforcing, modifying, and enforcing as so modified, or setting aside in whole or in part the order of the Board; the findings of the Board with respect to questions of fact if supported by substantial evidence on the record considered as a whole shall in like manner be conclusive.

(g) The commencement of proceedings under subsection (e) or (f) of this section shall not, unless specifically ordered by the court, operate as a stay of the Board's order.

(h) When granting appropriate temporary relief or a restraining order, or making and entering a decree enforcing, modifying, and enforcing as so modified, or setting aside in whole or in part an order of the Board, as provided in this section, the jurisdiction of courts sitting in equity shall not be limited by the Act entitled "An Act to amend the Judicial Code and to define and limit the jurisdiction of courts sitting in equity, and for other purposes," approved March 23, 1932 (U.S.C., Supp. VII, title 29, secs. 101-115).

(i) Petitions filed under this Act shall be heard expeditiously, and if possible within ten days after they have been docketed.

(j) The Board shall have power, upon issuance of a complaint as provided in subsection (b) charging that any person has engaged in or is engaging in an unfair labor practice, to petition any district court of the United States (including the District Court of the United States for the District of Columbia), within any district wherein the unfair labor practice in question is alleged to have occurred or wherein such person resides or transacts business, for appropriate temporary relief or restraining order. Upon the filing of any such petition the court shall cause notice thereof to be served upon such person, and thereupon shall have jurisdiction to grant to the Board such temporary relief or restraining order as it deems just and proper.

(k) Whenever it is charged that any person has engaged in an unfair labor practice within the meaning of paragraph (4)(D) of section 8(b), the Board is empowered and directed to hear and determine the dispute out of which such unfair labor practice shall have arisen, unless, within ten days after notice that such charge has been filed, the parties to such dispute submit to the Board satisfactory evidence that they have adjusted, or agreed upon methods for the voluntary adjustment of, the dispute. Upon compliance by the parties to the dispute with the decision of the Board or upon such voluntary adjustment of the dispute, such charge shall be dismissed.

(l) Whenever it is charged that any person has engaged in an unfair labor practice within the meaning of paragraph (4) (A), (B), or (C) of section 8(b), or section 8(e) or section 8(b)(7), the preliminary investigation of such charge shall be made forthwith and given priority over all other cases except cases of like character in the office where it is filed or to which it is referred. If, after such investigation, the officer or regional attorney to whom the matter may be referred has reasonable cause to believe such charge is true and that a complaint should issue, he shall, on behalf of the Board, petition any district court of the United States (including the District Court of the United States for the District of Columbia) within any district where the unfair labor practice in question has occurred, is alleged to have occurred, or wherein such person resides or transacts business, for appropriate injunctive relief pending the final adjudication of the Board with respect to such matter. Upon the filing of any such petition the district court shall have jurisdiction to grant such injunctive relief or temporary restraining order as it deems just and proper, notwithstanding any other provision of law: *Provided further,* That no temporary restraining order shall be issued without notice unless a petition alleges that substantial and irreparable injury to the charging party will be unavoidable and such temporary restraining order shall be effective for no longer than five days and will become void at the expiration of such period: *Provided further,* That such officer or regional attorney shall not apply for any restraining order under section 8(b)(7) if a charge against the employer under section 8(a)(2) has been filed and after the preliminary investigation, he has reasonable cause to believe that such charge is true and that a complaint should issue. Upon filing of any such petition the courts shall cause notice thereof to be served upon any person involved in the charge and such person, including the charging party, shall be given an opportunity to appear by counsel and present any relevant testimony: *Provided further,* That for the purposes of this subsection district courts shall be deemed to have jurisdiction of a labor organization (1) in the district in which such organization maintains its principal office, or (2) in any district in which its duly authorized officers or agents are engaged in promoting or protecting the interests of employee members. The service of legal process upon such officer or agent shall constitute service upon the labor organization and make such organizations a party to the suit. In situations where such relief is appropriate the procedure specified herein shall apply to charges with respect to section 8(b)(4)(D).

(m) Whenever it is charged that any person has engaged in an unfair labor practice within the meaning of subsection (a)(3) or (b)(2) of section 8, such charge shall be given priority over all other cases except cases of like character in the office where it is filed or to which it is referred and cases given priority under subsection (l).

INVESTIGATORY POWERS

SEC. 11.   For the purpose of all hearings and investigations, which, in the opinion of the Board, are necessary and proper for the exercise of the powers vested in it by section 9 and section 10 —

(1) The Board, or its duly authorized agents or agencies, shall at all reasonable times have access to, for the purpose of examination, and the right to copy any evidence of any person being investigated or proceeded against that relates to any matter under investigation or in question. The Board, or any member thereof, shall upon application of any party to such proceedings, forthwith issue to such party subpoenas requiring the attendance and testimony of witnesses or the production of any evidence in such proceeding or investigation requested in such application. Within five days after the service of a subpoena on any person requiring the production of any evidence in his possession or under his control, such person may petition the Board to revoke, and the Board shall revoke, such subpoena if in its opinion the evidence whose production is required does not relate to any matter under investigation, or any matter in question in such proceedings, or if in its opinion such subpoena does not describe with sufficient particularity the evidence whose production is required. Any member of the Board, or any agent or agency designated by the Board for such purposes, may administer oaths and affirmations, examine witnesses, and receive evidence. Such attendance of witnesses and the production of such evidence may be required from any place in the United States or any Territory or possession thereof, at any designated place of hearing.

(2) In case of contumacy or refusal to obey a subpoena issued to any person, any district court of the United States or the United States courts of any Territory or possession, or the District Court of the United States for the District of Columbia, within the jurisdiction of which the inquiry is carried on or within the jurisdiction of which said person guilty of contumacy or refusal to obey is found or resides or transacts business, upon application by the Board shall have jurisdiction to issue to such person an order requiring such person to appear before the Board, its member, agent, or agency, there to produce evidence if so ordered, or there to give testimony touching the matter under investigation or

in question; and any failure to obey such order of the court may be punished by said court as a contempt thereof.

(3) No person shall be excused from attending and testifying or from producing books, records, correspondence, documents, or other evidence in obedience to the subpoena of the Board, on the ground that the testimony or evidence required of him may tend to incriminate him or subject him to a penalty or forfeiture; but no individual shall be prosecuted or subjected to any penalty or forfeiture for or on account of any transaction, matter, or thing concerning which he is compelled, after having claimed his privilege against self-incrimination, to testify or produce evidence, except that such individual so testifying shall not be exempt from prosecution and punishment for perjury committed in so testifying.

(4) Complaints, orders, and other process and papers of the Board, its member, agent, or agency, may be served either personally or by registered mail or by telegraph or by leaving a copy thereof at the principal office or place of business of the person required to be served. The verified return by the individual so serving the same setting forth the manner of such service shall be proof of the same, and the return post office receipt or telegraph receipt therefor when registered and mailed or telegraphed as aforesaid shall be proof of service of the same. Witnesses summoned before the Board, its member, agent, or agency, shall be paid the same fees and mileage that are paid witnesses in the courts of the United States, and witnesses whose depositions are taken and the persons taking the same shall severally be entitled to the same fees as are paid for like services in the courts of the United States.

(5) All process of any court to which application may be made under this Act may be served in the judicial district wherein the defendant or other person required to be served resides or may be found.

(6) The several departments and agencies of the Government, when directed by the President, shall furnish the Board, upon its request, all records, papers, and information in their possession relating to any matter before the Board.

SEC. 12.   Any person who shall willfully resist, prevent, impede, or interfere with any member of the Board or any of its agents or agencies in the performance of duties pursuant to this Act shall be punished by a fine of not more than $5,000 or by imprisonment for not more than one year, or both.

LIMITATIONS

SEC. 13.   Nothing in this Act, except as specifically provided for herein, shall be construed so as either to interfere with or impede or diminish in any way the right to strike, or to affect the limitations or qualifications on that right.

SEC. 14.   (a) Nothing herein shall prohibit any individual employed as a supervisor from becoming or remaining a member of a labor organization, but no employer subject to this Act shall be compelled to deem individuals defined herein as supervisors as employees for the purpose of any law, either national or local, relating to collective bargaining.

(b) Nothing in this Act shall be construed as authorizing the execution or application of agreements requiring membership in a labor organization as a condition of employment in any State or Territory in which such execution or application is prohibited by State or Territorial law.

(c)(1) The Board, in its discretion, may, by rule of decision or by published rules adopted pursuant to the Administrative Procedure Act, decline to assert jurisdiction over any labor dispute involving any class or category of employers, where, in the opinion of the Board, the effect of such labor dispute on commerce is not sufficiently substantial to warrant the exercise of its jurisdiction: *Provided*, That the Board shall not decline to assert jurisdiction over any labor dispute over which it would assert jurisdiction under the standards prevailing upon August 1, 1959.

(2) Nothing in this Act shall be deemed to prevent or bar any agency or the courts of any State or Territory (including the Commonwealth of Puerto Rico, Guam, and the Virgin Islands), from assuming and asserting jurisdiction over labor disputes over which the Board declines, pursuant to paragraph (1) of this subsection, to assert jurisdiction.

SEC. 15.   Wherever the application of the provisions of section 272 of chapter 10 of the Act entitled "An Act to establish a uniform system of bankruptcy throughout the United States," approved July 1, 1898, and Acts amendatory thereof and supplementary thereto (U.S.C., title 11, sec. 672), conflicts with the application of the provisions of this Act, this Act shall prevail: *Provided*, That in any situation where the provisions of this Act cannot be validly enforced, the provisions of such other Acts shall remain in full force and effect.

SEC. 16.   If any provision of this Act, or the application of such provision to any person or circumstances, shall be held invalid, the remainder of this Act, or the application of such provision to persons or circumstances other than those as to which it is held invalid, shall not be affected thereby.

SEC. 17.   This Act may be cited as the "National Labor Relations Act."

SEC. 18.   No petition entertained, no investigation made, no election held, and no certification issued by the National Labor Relations Board, under any of the provisions of section 9 of the National Labor Relations Act, as amended, shall be invalid by reason of the failure of the Congress of Industrial Organizations to have complied with the requirements of section 9(f), (g), or (h) of the aforesaid Act prior to December 22, 1949, or by reason of the failure of the American Federation of Labor to have complied with the provisions of section 9(f), (g), or (h) of the aforesaid Act prior to November 7, 1947: *Provided*, That no liability shall be imposed under any provision of this Act upon any person for failure to honor any election or certificate referred to above, prior to the effective date of this amendment: *Provided, however*, That this proviso shall not have the effect of setting aside or in any way affecting judgments or decrees heretofore entered under section 10(e) or (f) and which have become final.

EFFECTIVE DATE OF CERTAIN CHANGES[*]

SEC. 102.   No provision of this title shall be deemed to make an unfair labor practice any act which was performed prior to the date of the enactment of this Act which did not constitute an unfair labor practice prior thereto, and the provisions of section 8(a)(3) and section 8(b)(2) of the National Labor Relations Act as amended by this title shall not make an unfair labor practice the performance of any obligation under a collective-bargaining agreement entered into prior to the date of the enactment of this Act, or (in the case of an agreement

*The effective date referred to in Sections 102, 103, and 104 is August 22, 1947. For effective dates of 1959 amendments, see footnote on first page of this text.

for a period of not more than one year) entered into on or after such date of enactment, but prior to the effective date of this title, if the performance of such obligation would not have constituted an unfair labor practice under section 8(3) of the National Labor Relations Act prior to the effective date of this title, unless such agreement was renewed or extended subsequent thereto.

SEC. 103.   No provisions of this title shall affect any certification of representatives or any determination as to the appropriate collective-bargaining unit, which was made under section 9 of the National Labor Relations Act prior to the effective date of this title until one year after the date of such certification or if, in respect of any such certification, a collective-bargaining contract was entered into prior to the effective date of this title, until the end of the contract period or until one year after such date, whichever first occurs.

SEC. 104.   The amendments made by this title shall take effect sixty days after the date of the enactment of this Act, except that the authority of the President to appoint certain officers conferred upon him by section 3 of the National Labor Relations Act as amended by this title may be exercised forthwith.

TITLE II — CONCILIATION OF LABOR DISPUTES IN INDUSTRIES AFFECTING COMMERCE; NATIONAL EMERGENCIES

SEC. 201.   That it is the policy of the United States that —

(a) sound and stable industrial peace and the advancement of the general welfare, health, and safety of the Nation and of the best interest of employers and employees can most satisfactorily be secured by the settlement of issues between employers and employees through the processes of conference and collective bargaining between employers and the representatives of their employees;

(b) the settlement of issues between employers and employees through collective bargaining may be advanced by making available full and adequate governmental facilities for conciliation, mediation, and voluntary arbitration to aid and encourage employers and the representatives of their employees to reach and maintain agreements concerning rates of pay, hours, and working conditions, and to make all reasonable efforts to settle their differences by mutual agreement reached through conferences and collective bargaining or by such methods as may be provided for in any applicable agreement for the settlement of disputes; and

(c) certain controversies which arise between parties to collective-bargaining agreements may be avoided or minimized by making available full and adequate governmental facilities for furnishing assistance to employers and the representatives of their employees in formulating for inclusion within such agreements provision for adequate notice of any proposed changes in the terms of such agreements, for the final adjustment of grievances or questions regarding the application or interpretation of such agreements, and other provisions designed to prevent the subsequent arising of such controversies.

SEC. 202.   (a) There is hereby created an independent agency to be known as the Federal Mediation and Conciliation Service (herein referred to as the "Service," except that for sixty days after the date of the enactment of this Act such term shall refer to the Conciliation Service of the Department of Labor). The Service shall be under the direction of a Federal Mediation and Conciliation

Director (hereinafter referred to as the "Director"), who shall be appointed by the President by and with the advice and consent of the Senate. The Director shall receive compensation at the rate of $12,000* per annum. The Director shall not engage in any other business, vocation, or employment.

(b) The Director is authorized, subject to the civil-service laws, to appoint such clerical and other personnel as may be necessary for the execution of the functions of the Service, and shall fix their compensation in accordance with the Classification Act of 1923, as amended, and may, without regard to the provisions of the civil-service laws and the Classification Act of 1923, as amended, appoint and fix the compensation of such conciliators and mediators as may be necessary to carry out the functions of the Service. The Director is authorized to make such expenditures for supplies, facilities, and services as he deems necessary. Such expenditures shall be allowed and paid upon presentation of itemized vouchers therefor approved by the Director or by any employee designated by him for that purpose.

(c) The principal office of the Service shall be in the District of Columbia, but the Director may establish regional offices convenient to localities in which labor controversies are likely to arise. The Director may by order, subject to revocation at any time, delegate any authority and discretion conferred upon him by this Act to any regional director, or other officer or employee of the Service. The Director may establish suitable procedures for cooperation with State and local mediation agencies. The Director shall make an annual report in writing to Congress at the end of the fiscal year.

(d) All mediation and conciliation functions of the Secretary of Labor or the United States Conciliation Service under section 8 of the Act entitled "An Act to create a Department of Labor," approved March 4, 1913 (U.S.C., title 29, sec. 51), and all functions of the United States Conciliation Service under any other law are hereby transferred to the Federal Mediation and Conciliation Service, together with the personnel and records of the United States Conciliation Service. Such transfer shall take effect upon the sixtieth day after the date of enactment of this Act. Such transfer shall not affect any proceedings pending before the United States Conciliation Service or any certification, order, rule, or regulation theretofore made by it or by the Secretary of Labor. The Director and the Service shall not be subject in any way to the jurisdiction or authority of the Secretary of labor or any official or division of the Department of Labor.

FUNCTIONS OF THE SERVICE

SEC. 203.   (a) It shall be the duty of the Service, in order to prevent or minimize interruptions of the free flow of commerce growing out of labor disputes, to assist parties to labor disputes in industries affecting commerce to settle such disputes through conciliation and mediation.

(b) The Service may proffer its services in any labor dispute in any industry affecting commerce, either upon its own motion or upon the request of one or more of the parties to the dispute, whenever in its judgment such dispute threatens to cause a substantial interruption of commerce. The Director and the Service are directed to avoid attempting to mediate disputes which would have

*Pursuant to Public Law 88-426, 88th Congress, 2d Session. Title III, approved August 14, 1964, the salary of the Director shall be $27,000 per year.

only a minor effect on interstate commerce if State or other conciliation services are available to the parties. Whenever the Service does proffer its services in any dispute, it shall be the duty of the Service promptly to put itself in communication with the parties and to use its best efforts, by mediation and conciliation, to bring them to agreement.

(c) If the Director is not able to bring the parties to agreement by conciliation within a reasonable time, he shall seek to induce the parties voluntarily to seek other means of settling the dispute without resort to strike, lock-out, or other coercion, including submission to the employees in the bargaining unit of the employer's last offer of settlement for approval or rejection in a secret ballot. The failure or refusal of either party to agree to any procedure suggested by the Director shall not be deemed a violation of any duty or obligation imposed by this Act.

(d) Final adjustment by a method agreed upon by the parties is hereby declared to be the desirable method for settlement of grievance disputes arising over the application or interpretation of an existing collective-bargaining agreement. The Service is directed to make its conciliation and mediation services available in the settlement of such grievance disputes only as a last resort and in exceptional cases.

SEC. 204. (a) In order to prevent or minimize interruptions of the free flow of commerce growing out of labor disputes, employers and employees and their representatives, in any industry affecting commerce, shall —

(1) exert every reasonable effort to make and maintain agreements concerning rates of pay, hours, and working conditions, including provision for adequate notice of any proposed change in the terms of such agreements;

(2) whenever a dispute arises over the terms or application of a collective-bargaining agreement and a conference is requested by a party or prospective party thereto, arrange promptly for such a conference to be held and endeavor in such conference to settle such dispute expeditiously; and

(3) in case such dispute is not settled by conference, participate fully and promptly in such meetings as may be undertaken by the Service under this Act for the purpose of aiding in a settlement of the dispute.

SEC. 205. (a) There is hereby created a National Labor-Management Panel which shall be composed of twelve members appointed by the President, six of whom shall be selected from among persons outstanding in the field of management and six of whom shall be selected from among persons outstanding in the field of labor. Each member shall hold office for a term of three years, except that any member appointed to fill a vacancy occurring prior to the expiration of the term for which his predecessor was appointed shall be appointed for the remainder of such term, and the terms of office of the members first taking office shall expire, as designated by the President at the time of appointment, four at the end of the first year, four at the end of the second year, and four at the end of the third year after the date of appointment. Members of the panel, when serving on business of the panel, shall be paid compensation at the rate of $25 per day, and shall also be entitled to receive an allowance for actual and necessary travel and subsistence expenses while so serving away from their places of residence.

(b) It shall be the duty of the panel, at the request of the Director, to advise in the avoidance of industrial controversies and the manner in which mediation and voluntary adjustment shall be administered, particularly with reference to controversies affecting the general welfare of the country.

NATIONAL EMERGENCIES

SEC. 206.   Whenever in the opinion of the President of the United States, a threatened or actual strike or lock-out affecting an entire industry or a substantial part thereof engaged in trade, commerce, transportation, transmission, or communication among the several States or with foreign nations, or engaged in the production of goods for commerce, will, if permitted to occur or to continue, imperil the national health or safety, he may appoint a board of inquiry to inquire into the issues involved in the dispute and to make a written report to him within such time as he shall prescribe. Such report shall include a statement of the facts with respect to the dispute, including each party's statement of its position but shall not contain any recommendations. The President shall file a copy of such report with the Service and shall make its contents available to the public.

SEC. 207.   (a) A board of inquiry shall be composed of a chairman and such other members as the President shall determine, and shall have power to sit and act in any place within the United States and to conduct such hearings either in public or in private, as it may deem necessary or proper, to ascertain the facts with respect to the causes and circumstances of the dispute.

(b) Members of a board of inquiry shall receive compensation at the rate of $50 for each day actually spent by them in the work of the board, together with necessary travel and subsistence expenses.

(c) For the purpose of any hearing or inquiry conducted by any board appointed under this title, the provisions of sections 9 and 10 (relating to the attendance of witnesses and the production of books, papers, and documents) of the Federal Trade Commission Act of September 16, 1914, as amended (U.S.C. 19, title 15, secs. 49 and 50, as amended), are hereby made applicable to the powers and duties of such board.

SEC. 208.   (a) Upon receiving a report from a board of inquiry the President may direct the Attorney General to petition any district court of the United States having jurisdiction of the parties to enjoin such strike or lock-out or the continuing thereof, and if the court finds that such threatened or actual strike or lock-out —

(i) affects an entire industry or a substantial part thereof engaged in trade, commerce, transportation, transmission, or communication among the several States or with foreign nations, or engaged in the production of goods for commerce; and

(ii) if permitted to occur or to continue, will imperil the national health or safety, it shall have jurisdiction to enjoin any such strike or lock-out, or the continuing thereof, and to make such other orders as may be appropriate.

(b) In any case, the provisions of the Act of March 23, 1932, entitled "An Act to amend the Judicial Code and to define and limit the jurisdiction of courts sitting in equity, and for other purposes," shall not be applicable.

(c) The order or orders of the court shall be subject to review by the appropriate circuit court of appeals and by the Supreme Court upon writ of certiorari or certification as provided in sections 239 and 240 of the Judicial Code, as amended (U.S.C., title 29, secs. 346 and 347).

SEC. 209.   (a) Whenever a district court has issued an order under section 208 enjoining acts or practices which imperil or threaten to imperil the national health or safety, it shall be the duty of the parties to the labor dispute giving rise to such order to make every effort to adjust and settle their differences, with the assistance of the Service created by this Act. Neither party shall be under any duty to accept, in whole or in part, any proposal of settlement made by the Service.

(b) Upon the issuance of such order, the President shall reconvene the board of inquiry which has previously reported with respect to the dispute. At the end of a sixty-day period (unless the dispute has been settled by that time), the board of inquiry shall report to the President the current position of the parties and the efforts which has been made for settlement, and shall include a statement by each party of its position and a statement of the employer's last offer of settlement. The President shall make such report available to the public. The National Labor Relations Board, within the succeeding fifteen days, shall take a secret ballot of the employees of each employer involved in the dispute on the question of whether they wish to accept the final offer of settlement made by their employer as stated by him and shall certify the results thereof to the Attorney General within five days thereafter.

SEC. 210.   Upon the certification of the results of such ballot or upon a settlement being reached, whichever happens sooner, the Attorney General shall move the court to discharge the injunction, which motion shall then be granted and the injunction discharged. When such motion is granted, the President shall submit to the Congress a full and comprehensive report of the proceedings, including the findings of the board of inquiry and the ballot taken by the National Labor Relations Board, together with such recommendations as he may see fit to make for consideration and appropriate action.

COMPILATION OF COLLECTIVE-BARGAINING AGREEMENTS, ETC.

SEC. 211.   (a) For the guidance and information of interested representatives of employers, employees, and the general public, the Bureau of Labor Statistics of the Department of Labor shall maintain a file of copies of all available collective-bargaining agreements and other available agreements and actions thereunder settling or adjusting labor disputes. Such file shall be open to inspection under appropriate conditions prescribed by the Secretary of Labor, except that no specific information submitted in confidence shall be disclosed.

(b) The Bureau of Labor Statistics in the Department of Labor is authorized to furnish upon request of the Service, or employers, employees, or their representatives, all available data and factual information which may aid in the settlement of any labor dispute, except that no specific information submitted in confidence shall be disclosed.

EXEMPTION OF RAILWAY LABOR ACT

SEC. 212.   The provisions of this title shall not be applicable with respect to any matter which is subject to the provisions of the Railway Labor Act, as amended from time to time.

TITLE III

SUITS BY AND AGAINST LABOR ORGANIZATIONS

SEC. 301. (a) Suits for violation of contracts between an employer and a labor organization representing employees in an industry affecting commerce as defined in this Act, or between any such labor organizations, may be brought in any district court of the United States having jurisdiction of the parties, without respect to the amount in controversy or without regard to the citizenship of the parties.

(b) Any labor organization which represents employees in an industry affecting commerce as defined in this Act and any employer whose activities affect commerce as defined in this Act shall be bound by the acts of its agents. Any such labor organization may sue or be sued as an entity and in behalf of the employees whom it represents in the courts of the United States. Any money judgment against a labor organization in a district court of the United States shall be enforceable only against the organization as an entity and against its assets, and shall not be enforceable against any individual member or his assets.

(c) For the purposes of actions and proceedings by or against labor organizations in the district courts of the United States, district courts shall be deemed to have jurisdiction of a labor organization (1) in the district in which such organization maintains its principal offices, or (2) in any district in which its duly authorized officers or agents are engaged in representing or acting for employee members.

(d) The service of summons, subpoena, or other legal process of any court of the United States upon an officer or agent of a labor organization, in his capacity as such, shall constitute service upon the labor organization.

(e) For the purposes of this section, in determining whether any person is acting as an "agent" of another person so as to make such other person responsible for his acts, the question of whether the specific acts performed were actually authorized or subsequently ratified shall not be controlling.

RESTRICTIONS ON PAYMENTS TO EMPLOYEE REPRESENTATIVES

SEC. 302. (a) It shall be unlawful for any employer or association of employers or any person who acts as a labor relations expert, adviser, or consultant to an employer or who acts in the interest of an employer to pay, lend, or deliver, or agree to pay, lend, or deliver, any money or other thing of value —

(1) to any representative of any of his employees who are employed in an industry affecting commerce; or

(2) to any labor organization, or any officer or employee thereof, which represents, seeks to represent, or would admit to membership, any of the employees of such employer who are employed in an industry affecting commerce; or

(3) to any employee or group or committee of employees of such employer employed in an industry affecting commerce in excess of their normal compensation for the purpose of causing such employee or group or committee directly or indirectly to influence any other employees in the exercise of the right to organize and bargain collectively through representatives of their own choosing; or

(4) to any officer or employee of a labor organization engaged in an industry affecting commerce with intent to influence him in respect to any of his actions, decisions, or duties as a representative of employees or as such officer or employee of such labor organization.

(b)(1) It shall be unlawful for any person to request, demand, receive, or accept, or agree to receive or accept, any payment, loan, or delivery of any money or other thing of value prohibited by subsection (a).

(2) It shall be unlawful for any labor organization, or for any person acting as an officer, agent, representative, or employee of such labor organization, to demand or accept from the operator of any motor vehicle (as defined in part II of the Interstate Commerce Act) employed in the transportation of property in commerce, or the employer of any such operator, any money or other thing of value payable to such organization or to an officer, agent, representative or employee thereof as a fee or charge for the unloading, or the connection with the unloading, of the cargo of such vehicle: *Provided,* That nothing in this paragraph shall be construed to make unlawful any payment by an employer to any of his employees as compensation for their services as employees.

(c) The provisions of this section shall not be applicable (1) in respect to any money or other thing of value payable by an employer to any of his employees whose established duties include acting openly for such employer in matters of labor relations or personnel administration or to any representative of his employees, or to any officer or employee of a labor organization, who is also an employee or former employee of such employer, as compensation for, or by reason of, his service as an employee of such employer; (2) with respect to the payment or delivery of any money or other thing of value in satisfaction of a judgment of any court or a decision or award of an arbitrator or impartial chairman or in compromise, adjustment, settlement, or release of any claim, complaint, grievance, or dispute in the absence of fraud or duress; (3) with respect to the sale or purchase of an article or commodity at the prevailing market price in the regular course of business; (4) with respect to money deducted from the wages of employees in payment of membership dues in a labor organization: *Provided,* That the employer has received from each employee, on whose account such deductions are made, a written assignment which shall not be irrevocable for a period of more than one year, or beyond the termination date of the applicable collective agreement, whichever occurs sooner; (5) with respect to money or other thing of value paid to a trust fund established by such representative, for the sole and exclusive benefit of the employees of such employer, and their families and dependents (or of such employees, families, and dependents jointly with the employees of other employers making similar payments, and their families and dependents): *Provided,* That (A) such payments are held in trust for the purpose of paying, either from principal or income or both, for the benefit of employees, their families and dependents, for medical or hospital care, pensions on retirement or death of employees, compensation for injuries or illness resulting from occupational activity or insurance to provide any of the foregoing, or unemployment benefits or life insurance, disability and sickness insurance, or accident insurance; (B) the detailed basis on which such payments are to be made is specified in a written agreement with the employer, and employees and employers are equally represented in the administration of such fund, together with such neutral persons as the representatives of the employers and the representatives of employees may agree upon and in the event the employer and employee groups deadlock on the administration of such fund and there are no neutral persons empowered to break such deadlock, such agreement provides that the two groups shall agree on an impartial umpire to decide such dispute, or in event of their failure to agree within a reasonable length of time, an impartial umpire to decide such dispute shall, on petition of either group, be appointed by the district court of the United States for the district where the trust fund has its principal office, and shall also contain provisions for an annual audit of the trust fund, a statement of the results of which shall be available for inspection by interested persons at the principal office of the trust fund and at such other places as may be designated in such written agreement; and (C) such payments as are intended to be used for the purpose of providing pensions or annuities for employees are made to a separate trust which provides that the funds held therein cannot be used for any purpose other than paying such pensions or annuities; or (6) with respect to money or other thing of value paid by any employer to a trust fund established by such representative for the purpose of pooled vacation, holiday, severance or similar benefits, or defraying costs of apprenticeship or other training program: *Provided,* That the requirements of clause (B) of the proviso to clause (5) of this subsection shall apply to such trust funds.

(d) Any person who willfully violates any of the provisions of this section shall, upon conviction thereof, be guilty of a misdemeanor and be subject to a fine of not more than $10,000 or to imprisonment for not more than one year, or both.

(e) The district courts of the United States and the United States courts of the Territories and possessions shall have jurisdiction, for cause shown, and subject to the provisions of section 17 (relating to notice to opposite party) of the Act entitled "An Act to supplement existing laws against unlawful restraints and monopolies, and for other purposes," approved October 15, 1914, as amended (U.S.C., title 28, sec. 381), to restrain violations of this section, without regard to the provisions of sections 6 and 20 of such Act of October 15, 1914, as amended (U.S.C., title 15, sec. 17, and title 29, sec. 52), and the provisions of the Act entitled "An Act to amend the Judicial Code and to define and limit the jurisdiction of courts sitting in equity, and for other purposes," approved March 23, 1932 (U.S.C., title 29, secs. 101–115).

(f) This section shall not apply to any contract in force on the date of enactment of this Act, until the expiration of such contract, or until July 1, 1948, whichever first occurs.

(g) Compliance with the restrictions contained in subsection (c)(5)(B) upon contributions to trust funds, otherwise lawful, shall not be applicable to contributions to such trust funds established by collective agreement prior to January 1, 1946, nor shall subsection (c)(5)(A) be construed as prohibiting contributions to such trust funds if prior to January 1, 1947, such funds contained provisions for pooled vacation benefits.

BOYCOTTS AND OTHER UNLAWFUL COMBINATIONS

SEC. 303. (a) It shall be unlawful, for the purpose of this section only, in an industry or activity affecting commerce, for any labor organization to engage in any activity or conduct defined as an unfair labor practice in section 8(b)(4) of the National Labor Relations Act, as amended.

(b) Whoever shall be injured in his business or property by reason of any violation of subsection (a) may sue therefore in any district court of the United States subject to the limitations and provisions of section 301 hereof without respect to the amount in controversy, or in any other court having jurisdiction of the parties, and shall recover the damages by him sustained and the cost of the suit.

RESTRICTION ON POLITICAL CONTRIBUTIONS

SEC. 304.   Section 313 of the Federal Corrupt Practices Act, 1925 (U.S.C., 1940 edition, title 2, sec. 251; Supp. V, title 50, App., sec. 1509), as amended, is amended to read as follows:

SEC. 313.   It is unlawful for any national bank, or any corporation organized by authority of any law of Congress to make a contribution or expenditure in connection with any election to any political office, or in connection with any primary election or political convention or caucus held to select candidates for any political office, or for any corporation whatever, or any labor organization to make a contribution or expenditure in connection with any election at which Presidential and Vice Presidential electors or a Senator or Representative in, or a Delegate or Resident Commissioner to Congress are to be voted for, or in connection with any primary election or political convention or caucus held to select candidates for any of the foregoing offices, or for any candidate, political committee, or other person to accept or receive any contribution prohibited by this section. Every corporation or labor organization which makes any contribution or expenditure in violation of this section shall be fined not more than $5,000; and every officer or director of any corporation, or officer of any labor organization, who consents to any contribution or expenditure by the corporation or labor organization, as the case may be, in violation of this section shall be fined no more than $1,000 or imprisoned for not more than one year, or both. For the purposes of this section "labor organization" means any organization of any kind, or any agency or employee representation committee or plan, in which employees participate and which exists for the purpose, in whole or in part, of dealing with employers concerning grievances, labor disputes, wages, rates of pay, hours of employment, or conditions of work.

TITLE IV

CREATION OF JOINT COMMITTEE TO STUDY AND REPORT ON BASIC PROBLEMS AFFECTING FRIENDLY LABOR RELATIONS AND PRODUCTIVITY

*   *

TITLE V

DEFINITIONS

SEC. 501.   When used in this Act —

(1) The term "industry affecting commerce" means any industry or activity in commerce or in which a labor dispute would burden or obstruct commerce or tend to burden or obstruct commerce or the free flow of commerce.

(2) The term "strike" includes any strike or other concerted stoppage of work by employees (including a stoppage by reason of the expiration of a collective-

bargaining agreement) and any concerted slow-down or other concerted interruption of operations by employees.

(3) The terms "commerce," "labor disputes," "employer," "employee," "labor organization," "representative," "person," and "supervisor" shall have the same meaning as when used in the National Labor Relations Act as amended by this Act.

SAVING PROVISION

SEC. 502.   Nothing in this Act shall be construed to require an individual employee to render labor or service without his consent, nor shall anything in this Act be construed to make the quitting of his labor by an individual employee an illegal act; nor shall any court issue any process to compel the performance by an individual employee of such labor or service, without his consent; nor shall the quitting of labor by an employee or employees in good faith because of abnormally dangerous conditions for work at the place of employment of such employee or employees be deemed a strike under this Act.

SEPARABILITY

SEC. 503.   If any provision of this Act, or the application of such provision to any person or circumstance, shall be held invalid, the remainder of this Act, or the application of such provision to persons or circumstances other than those as to which it is held invalid, shall not be affected thereby.

Index